DEFENSE FOR MARX

A NEW INTERPRETATION OF MARXIST PHILOSOPHY

DEFENSE FOR MARX

A NEW INTERPRETATION OF MARXIST PHILOSOPHY

By Yang Geng

Translated by Cheng Zhou and Li Ling
English Edition edited by Walterio Barra Cabello

CANUT INTERNATIONAL PUBLISHERS
Istanbul ▪ Berlin ▪ London ▪ Santiago

Originally published as *Defense For Marx. A New Interpretation of Marxist Philosophy* in 2010 as Third Edition by China Renmin University Press.

Original Chinese Third Edition Copyright © 2010 by Yang Geng
ISBN: 978-7-300-12195-6

Canut International Publishers
Published by Canut International Publishers
Canut Int. Turkey, Balipaşa Cad. 155a, Tel : 0-212-5124356, İstanbul, Turkey
Canut Int. Germany, Yorckstr. 66, D-10965, Berlin, Germany
Canut Int. UK, 12a Guernsay Road, London E11 4BJ, England
Web: http://www.leftreader.com
E-Mail: canut@leftreader.com

First Published by Heilongjiang People's Press 2002
Published by Beijing Normal University Publishing House 2004
Published by China Renmin University Press 2010
1 2 3 4 5 6 7 8 - 16 15 14 13 12 11 10 09

English Print Edition: Defense For Marx.
A New Interpretation of Marxist Philosophy
ISBN: 978-605-86254-6-4

English Digital Edition
ISBN: 978-605-86254-7-1

Printed in England
Lightning Source UK Ltd.
Chapter House
Pitfield
Kiln Farm
Milton Keynes
MK11 3LW
United Kingdom

CONTENTS

PART II

AUTHOR'S NOTES FOR THE THIRD EDITION

In 2002, the first edition of my academic monograph *Defense for Marx* was published by Heilongjiang People's Press. During the ten months from January to October in 2002, "the first edition" was successively printed for three times; in 2004, the second edition of *Defense for Marx* was published by Beijing Normal University Publishing House, and unexpectedly, "the second edition" was also printed for three times in succession. For a philosophical monograph, it is really not easy to be printed for six times successively and sold by more than 20 thousand copies. I am deeply touched by the great kindness of readers. As the year of 2010 just arrives, China Renmin University Press is planning to publish the third edition of *Defense for Marx*, thus I cannot help thinking of my years in China Renmin University.

I was introduced by Professor Wang Yongxiang into China Renmin University to study for my master's degree in 1986, and then, I really entered "the gate of philosophy" under the academic guidance of Professor Wang; in 1988, I graduated in advance and stayed at the university for teaching, and at the same time, I studied for my doctor's degree under the instruction of Professor Chen Xianda, and then, I went deep into philosophy under the thinking guidance of him; besides, the ability of "grand narrative" of my best friend Professor Chen Zhiliang guided me to the large stage of philosophical research. I deeply appreciate my two tutors – Professor Wang Yongxiang and Professor Chen Xianda – and my best friend Professor Chen Zhiliang. From them, I not only appreciate the literary talent of philosophers but also their elegant demeanor, not only learn the literary quality of philosophers but also their moral quality, and have learnt not only how to "write" but also how to "behave". Thus, I think of a praise said by Candide to the erudite old man Pangloss in Voltaire's *Candide*, "Without you, here means nothing to me."

I entered China Renmin University reading and learning the textbooks published by China Renmin University Press, and then became an author and the chief editor of the press. In was in China Renmin University that I naturally finished my transition from "being independent at thirty" to "beginning to be immune from perplexities at forty" and grew up into a mature person; it was also in China Renmin University that my "identity" changed dramatically: exceptionally being recommended to study for a doctor's degree in advance without examination, exceptionally being rated as associate professor, professor, doctoral tutor ... China Renmin University teached me how to learn, how to think, how to work, and even how to live. So, I am very grateful to China Renmin University Press for publishing the third edition of *Defense for Marx* when I "know the Decree of Heaven" and step into my life stage when "sunset is magnificent, but it is almost dusk". China Renmin University, the place where I never want to leave, is and will be always on my mind.

Compared with "the second edition", "the third edition" changes a lot: nine chapters, namely "The Historical Morphologies of Materialism and the Theoretical Space of Historical Materialism", "The Relationship between Society and Nature: A New Interpretation", "Essence of Society and Particularity of its Development Process: A New Interpretation", "Marx's Method of Social Organism", "Marx's 'Method of Thinking Post Festum': Principle, Content and Significance", "Marx's Scientific Abstract Method: A New Interpretation", "Historical Process and Thinking Logic of Marx in Founding Historical Materialism", "Modern Turn of Western Philosophy of History and the Enlightenment thereof", and "Generation, Paradigm and Historical Transformation of the Methods of Social Science – Features and Modernity of Marx's Methods for Social Research", and appendix "'Integration' of Dialectical Materialism and Historical Materialism: Connotation, Foundation and Problems" are deleted; five chapters are added, namely "The Significance of World Outlook of Practice: A New Interpretation of Marxist World Outlook", "Dialectical Negation and Negative Dialectics: A New Interpretation of Marxist Dialectics", "Genesis, Essence and Process: A New Interpretation of Marxist Epistemology (I)", "The Realm of Necessity and The Realm of Freedom: A New Interpretation", and "Post-Marxism: Historical Context and Multiple Logics — From Marx's Point of View". Besides, the chapter "Natural, Derivative and Transcending Formations in Social Development" is condensed and merged with "'Natural Historical Process' of Social Development: A New Interpretation" into one chapter.

The purpose of such an adjustment is still for striving to expound the basic opinions of Marxist philosophy, which have become "common sense", by virtue of new research achievements of science and philosophy, reveal the basic opinions of Marxist philosophy that are ignored or forgotten by the classical textbook of Marxist philosophy, and probe deep into and systematically demonstrate the opinions that Marx has ever expounded but not sufficiently developed and meanwhile coincide with major contemporary issues in order to upgrade them into the basic opinions of Marxist philosophy and thereby highlight the modernity and contemporary significance of Marxist philosophy.

After the publication of the second edition of *Defense for Marx*, my thoughts and opinions were also changing greatly, but I do not want to alter the general logic and basic opinions of *Defense for Marx*. As a result, I select an academic self-account, an interview, and four articles as the appendices of the book, so that readers can know the changes in my thoughts and opinions during 2005 – 2009. With them, readers can "know by a handful the whole sack".

Professor He Yaomin, President of China Renmin University Press, chief editor Professor Zhou Weihua, and Li Yanhui, Director of Academic Publishing Center list the book, despite of its deficiencies, into the "Major Humanistic System of Contemporary China"; Ma Xiaowei of Beijing Normal University Publishing House and Yang Zongyuan of China Renmin University Press have made pain efforts respectively in proofreading and editing the manuscript. Here, I want to express my sincere and deep thanks to all of them.

I remember Wittgenstein had said that "a man dealing with philosophy is eager for the peace in thought". After the publication of the third edition of *Defense for Marx*, I look forward to "the peace in thought".

Yang Geng

Jan. 24, 2010

Shiyu Garden, Century Town, Beijing

AUTHOR'S NOTES FOR THE SECOND EDITION

The book in front of readers is the second edition of my book *Defense for Marx* published by Heilongjiang People's Press in 2001.

I published my first paper collection – *Collected Works of Yang Geng* – in 1998 under the encouragement my upperclassman Professor Yu Wujin; and in 2002, four years later, I published my second paper collection – *Defense for Marx*, under the promotion of my student Doctor Li Yili. Unexpectedly, during the ten months from January to October in 2002, *Defense for Marx* was printed for three times. Maybe that was because my persistence touched the readers, but more importantly, I am deeply touched by the great kindness of readers. So on the occasion that the second edition of *Defense for Marx* is going to be published, I cannot help thinking of my teachers, friends and my family members, because I could not grow up without their family affection and friendship; at the same time, I also think of those people who have ever misunderstood, prejudiced against and even been "hostile" to me, because I could not become mature without their misunderstandings and censures. As soon as man "learns to walk, he learns also to fall, and only by falling does he learn to walk" (Marx) As to me, family affection and friendship, as well as grievance and hardship, are all a fortune, a fortune that is indispensable.

My research area is Marxist philosophy. I notice that the "image" of Marx is constantly changing after his death, and the longer he leaves us, the more the cognitions on him are diverged, just as the farther a man goes away, the more vague his image is. The drastic changes in Soviet Union and East Europe made Marx the "defendant" rather than the "plaintiff" in the debates of ideology and culture at the turn of the century, and his "image" was smeared by the "plaintiff" at will. As a Marxist, I must defend "absent" Marx; I am a researcher of Marxist philosophy, so all my works is the result of my rereading of Marx, or a new interpretation of Marxist philosophy. So I name the second edition as *Defense for Marx – A New Interpretation of Marxist Philosophy*.

Compared with the first edition, the second edition changes a lot: first, the preface "The Road of Glory is Narrow" is changed into "Marxist Philosophy: The Truth and Conscience of Our Times"; second, the four volumes are changed into Part One and Part Two, and the original

Volume IV is completely omitted; third, the article structure is adjusted, and besides Volume IV, eight chapters are deleted, namely "The Meeting of Marxist Philosophy and Postmodernism in Contemporary Era", "Theoretical Defense for Marx", "Material, Practice, World: Rethinking of the Three Basic Categories of Marxist Philosophy", "Subject Design, Material Analysis and Model Interpretation: Basic Links in Social Scientific Research", "Marxist Philosophy and Textbook of Marxist Philosophy", "Study on Historical Materialism: Problems, Opinions and Train of Thought", "Historical Meditation on the Theoretical Basis of Historical Materialism", and "Rethinking of the Theoretical Source of Historical Materialism", and ten chapters are added, namely "Postmodern Connotation of Marxist Philosophy", "Marxist Practical Ontology: A New Interpretation", "The Relationship between Society and Nature: A New Interpretation", "'Natural Historical Process' of Social Development: A New Interpretation", "Marx's View of Historical Necessity: A New Interpretation", "Marx's Theory of Practical Reflection: Connotation, Features and Significance", "The Ontology Thoughts of Stalin and Lukacs: A Comparative Study", "Husserl: Turning from Transcendental Ego to Life-world", "Postmodernism: Background, Essence and Significance", and "Postcolonialism: Essence, Features and Limitations".

The second edition is apparently a collection of papers, but in fact it is an academic monograph edited revolving around Marxist philosophy and its contemporary significance; there are internal connections between the papers in each part, and all of the papers constitute a theoretical whole. In the book, Part One, focusing on the studies of the basic features and opinions of Marxist philosophy, puts Marxist philosophy into the grand theoretical backgrounds of history of western philosophy and modern western philosophy, including postmodernism, to explore anew its theme, system features and contemporary significance, and strives to expound the basic opinions of Marxist philosophy, which have become "common sense", by virtue of new research achievements of science and philosophy, reveal the basic opinions of Marxist philosophy that are ignored or forgotten by the classic textbook of Marxist philosophy, and probe deep into and systematically demonstrate the opinions that Marx has ever expounded but not sufficiently developed and meanwhile coincide with major contemporary issues in order to upgrade them into the basic opinions of Marxist philosophy. With emphasis laid on the studies of the history of Marxist philosophy, history of western philosophy, and modern western philosophy, Part Two reinvestigates the historical process and thinking logic of Marx in founding historical materialism, explores the evolution of the ontology of Marxist philosophy after Marx, and analyzes, from Marx's point of view, the western philosophy of history, methods of western social science, postmodernism, post-colonialism, and the thought changes of Husserl and Derrida, with a view to highlighting the contemporary significance of Marxist philosophy.

I try hard to rebuild the "image" of Marx in such a way and show the realistic concern and ultimate concern of Marxist philosophy about the existence and value of man and the unity between the two concerns, thereby defending Marx on this ground. Meanwhile, I know very well that Marxist philosophy is both broad and profound, and this book is just "the tip of the iceberg" with respect to the interpretation of it. For me, my thinking should advance continuously towards the deep of the theoretical treasury of Marxist philosophy. "People often have a chance to give a great lesson, namely admitting their deficiencies." (Diderot) I do not deny my deficiencies in life experience, intellectual structure and thinking mode, and I am also aware of all the defects in this book. In the words of Wittgenstein, this book "is just a mirror, with which a reader can see all defects in his thought and thereby correct his train of thought by this way".

The papers included in this book span a time period of twenty years, i.e. from 1984 – 2004. During that period, my thoughts and opinions were changing fiercely; therefore the opinions herein are not consistent. But I do not want to make any modification to uniform the opinions in the book, because these papers reflect different issues I focused on in different stages, record my mental journey of rereading Marx, and embody my past and present philosophical studies and corresponding levels. "Only being fully aware of the past can we see the present clearly; only by deeply meditating the significance of the past can we find the significance of the future." (Herzen)

Yang Geng

July 31, 2004

Beijing Normal University

AUTHOR'S PREFACE FOR THE THIRD EDITION

MARXIST PHILOSOPHY: THE TRUTH AND CONSCIENCE OF OUR TIMES

This is a record of the interview of journalist Xin Wen from *Academic Monthly* with me, and it reflects my academic viewpoints in a relatively accurate way, therefore I use it as the preface of the book. The original of this interview record was carried in *Academic Monthly*, 2005 (First Issue).

Xin Wen (hereinafter referred to as "Xin"): Professor Yang, you are a famous Marxist philosopher and theorist in China. I notice that an article in *Theory Front*, Issue 1, 2000 mentions that your interpretation paradigm of Marxist philosophy "provides a new way for comprehending Marxist philosophy, breaks through the traditional theoretical framework of Marxist philosophy, builds a new Marxist philosophy system, and has a groundbreaking significance for the reform and construction of Chinese philosophy system".

Yang Geng (hereinafter referred to as "Yang"): I think I am overrated, and I really do not deserve this, but I do have my own opinions on Marxist philosophy. From my point of view, Marxist philosophy has an epoch-making significance in the history of philosophy in that it realizes the fundamental theme transformation of philosophy – from the universe to human world, and pays attention to human living condition and the elimination of alienation, as well as the proletariat and the emancipation of mankind. When Marx turned his eyes to human world, he started to seek the basis for comprehending and interpreting such a world, and finally he found it, that is, the practical activity of mankind. Practice, as the real noumenon of human world, is the foundation for the existence and development of human world, and this is a dynamic noumenon in continuous evolution and generation; the human world is therefore made an open system with larger and larger scale and more and more tiers.

Xin: First of all, I would like to request you to briefly summarize your interpretation paradigm of Marxist philosophy. How do you understand Marxist philosophy?

Yang: Marx reveals that men maintain their survival in the process of actively transforming nature by utilizing instruments, and practice is the foundation for their living, and constitutes the special life form of mankind, namely the mode of being and living noumenon of man. The existence of human beings, including the alienation of their living condition and its sublation, happens and finishes in the process of practical activity. When confirming practice is the noumenon of human world, Marx also confirms that practice is the base for the sensuous existence of man, and human beings create their existence through practice, so practice is the noumenon of the existence of man. In this sense, Marxist philosophy is the ontology of existentialism, i.e. practical ontology.

Xin: That's right. The drawback of traditional ontology is that the universe noumenon it pursues is an "unmoved mover" – the so-called "ultimate being" behind all the real things. Actually no matter whether such noumenon is "abstract spirit" or "abstract substance", it is an abstract noumenon disconnected with the real society, real mankind and their activities. It is impossible to perceive reality based on such abstract being or noumenon. So, what do you think features the practical ontology of Marx?

Yang: The practical ontology of Marx sets the existence of man as the goal embraced by philosophy. What is pursued by such ontology is not the so-called "ultimate being", but what makes the existence of "thing, reality and sensuousness" what it is, namely the significance of their existence. The significance lies in the living practice of mankind; in other words, "thing, reality and sensuousness" are linked with human beings and their living practice, and the ontology is closely related to the living practice of mankind. That's why Marx believed that "thing, reality and sensuousness" should not be conceived only in the form of object, but "as practice, the human sensuous activity" "subjectively", and expressly pointed out that "for the practical materialist, i.e. the communist, it is a question of revolutionizing the existing world, of practically attacking and changing existing things." In this way, Marxist practical ontology opens up a path of conceiving the reality through ontology.

Xin: Your interpretation paradigm provides a new approach to conceiving Marxist philosophy, and breaks through the traditional theoretical framework of Marxist philosophy.

Yang: The traditional theoretical framework of Marxist philosophy is the textbook system of Marxist philosophy. In the aspect of mode, such textbook system was formed in the Second Section "Dialectical and Historical Materialism", Chapter Four of *Soviet Union Communist Party (Bolshevik) Party Concise Guide*. Dialectical materialism in this textbook system is a kind of method and theory which studies and interprets nature respectively, and historical materialism is just the extension and application of dialectical materialism – a kind of view of nature – to the domain of social history. In such dialectical materialism, nature is separated from real mankind and their activity and abstracted from history. After such separation and abstraction, "abstract substance" becomes the cornerstone of traditional Marxist textbook system, and the ontology based on nature is formed. This is the fundamental defect; it actually interprets the new materialism of Marx with the logic of early modern materialism, and ignores to a quite large extent the epoch-making contribution of Marxist philosophy. The critique and finalization of metaphysics by Marx, basically speaking, is initiated and carried out at the level of ontology, and the essential feature is that Marx does not conceive and grasp the issue of beings in an abstract sur-real manner, but comprehends and grasps the existence of human beings from the starting point of practice, interprets the significance of beings based on the existence of human beings, and also highlights the fundamental feature of beings – historicity. So, confirming Marxist philosophy as practical ontology breaks through the traditional textbook system of Marxist philosophy radically, and lays theoretical foundation for rebuilding Marxist philosophy.

Xin: Ontology is closely related to "metaphysics". I remember you pointed out in an article published in *Guangming Daily* in 1989 that "rejecting metaphysics is the basic principle of Marxist philosophy", which had caused lots of disputes. More than a decade has passed. Have you abandoned or still insist on this point of view?

Yang: I still insist on this point of view, and even have more profound cognition of it. In my opinion, seen from the angle of history, "metaphysics" had established a strict logical rule for exploring the essence of beings and the ultimate being of the world, that is, starting from axiom and theorem to reach an inevitable conclusion following the inference rule. That undeniably was of positive significance, marking the formation of philosophy as a theoretical form. However, the beings in "metaphysics" were gradually deviated by the philosophers after Aristotle into the beings separated from the real things and beyond mankind, i.e. into a completely abstract "thing-in-itself". Hence, till the mid-nineteenth century, when natural sciences "marked out their independent fields", and the development of society made "real beings and earthly things the center of all interest", the western philosophy started a new tide of opposing metaphysics again. Comte and Marx raised the banner of "rejecting metaphysics" at the same era. The former criticized metaphysics in the principle of verification of natural sciences, while the latter's critique was from the point of practical activity – the mode of being of man. Though Marx's rejection of metaphysics overlaps with that of Comte with respect to the times – both are the critique by modern spirit on early modern and ancient spirits, the two are essentially different in the aspect of directionality: Comte thought that through rejection of metaphysics, philosophy should tend to natural science, be limited within the scope of phenomenon, knowledge and verifiability, and pursue to transform and transcend traditional philosophy with the spirit of positive science; Marx, however, brought forward another train of thought – after "the rejection of metaphysics", philosophy should scrutinize the existence of human beings, deeply criticize the alienated living condition of man, and pay close attention to the value, emancipation and all-around development of man. In the eyes of Marx, from then on, metaphysics would be defeated forever by materialism, which has now been perfected by the work of speculation itself and coincides with humanism.

Xin: You have also mentioned the concept of materialism. It is generally thought that naive materialism, metaphysical materialism and dialectical materialism are three historical morphologies of materialism, which seems to have become a final conclusion. However, you put forward in the article *A New Look at the Historical Morphologies of Materialism and the Theoretical Space of Historical Materialism* published in *Academic Research*, Issue 1, 2001 that the three historical morphologies of materialism are natural materialism, humanistic materialism and historical materialism. Such a classification is quite novel. What is your basis and meaning for the classification?

Yang: Classifying the basic morphologies of materialism into naive materialism, metaphysical materialism and dialectical materialism has its reasonable factors, but the reasonable factors are dissolved into unreasonable understanding. According to this classification, the theoretical themes of the three morphologies of materialism, namely naive materialism, metaphysical materialism and dialectical materialism, do not take fundamental change – the three all take "the whole world" as study object, and the only difference is that naive materialism regards the world as a chaotic whole, metaphysical materialism conceives the world as a static and isolated thing, and dialectical materialism understands the world as a system of substances with universal connections and in eternal development and defines historical materialism as the extension and application of dialectical materialism to the domain of social history. The gravest drawback of this classification rests with its ignorance of such an essential issue as the transformation of theoretical theme in the development course of materialism, and its obliteration of the epoch-making contribution of historical materialism to a quite large extent. Evaluated on the essential issue of theoretical theme's historical transformation, the development of materialism goes through three historical stages, forming three historical morphologies, i.e. natural materialism, humanistic materialism and historical materialism. With its origin traced back to ancient Greek philosophy, natural materialism becomes systematic in the theory of Hobbes, and extends to the mechanical materialism in French materialism. In general, it restores the whole world to a natural substance with the principle of "time priority", and conceives man as a manifestation of natural substances and substance as the subject of all changes. Humanistic materialism originated from the other school of French materialism, namely "real humanism", and obtained its typical form from Feuerbach. Feuerbach pursued to comprehend the world and construct a philosophical system in the basic principle of "real man", but he ignored that practice is the mode of being of man, the essence of social life, and the noumenon of sensuous world. For this reason, he finally ended up with abstract man, while ignoring the initiative and historicity of man. In humanistic materialism, nature and history are in antithetical position, thus materialism and history are diverged from each other completely. Transcendence over humanistic materialism and establishment of materialism amalgamated with history, namely historical materialism, were the dual requirement of both theory and history. In other words, historical materialism was the third historical morphology of materialism.

Xin: But it is usually believed that historical materialism is rather a kind of conception or philosophy of history than a complete philosophical morphology. You also hold the point of view that historical materialism is the philosophy of history unifying historical ontology and historical epistemology. But you mentioned in the article A New Look at the

Historical Morphologies of Materialism and the Theoretical Space of Historical Materialism published in Academic Research that historical materialism is a complete morphology of Marxist philosophy, and Marxist philosophy belongs to historical materialism. And you have restated and further elaborated this opinion in the article Historical Materialism: A Re-thinking published in Hebei Journal, Issue 6, 2003.

Yang: I had been puzzled by two problems while studying Marxist philosophy: one was the relationship between historical materialism and dialectical materialism, and the other was the relationship between historical materialism and practical materialism. According to the article *Principle of Constructing the Modern Morphology of Historical Materialism* I published in your journal in 1990, historical materialism was the unification of historical ontology with historical epistemology; that conclusion was based on an unconscious theoretical precondition – dialectical materialism was the theoretical foundation of historical materialism. In my article *Practical Materialism: the Banner of Philosophy in Our Times* published in *Jianghai Academic Journal* in 1989, I put forward that Marxist philosophy fell under practical materialism, as well as practical ontology, but I intentionally avoided mentioning the relationship between practical materialism and historical materialism. It seemed that the "integration" of Marxist philosophy was impossible to be completely realized as long as the two problems were not resolved. Hence, I started to review the theoretical space of historical materialism again.

Along with the deepening of research, I gradually realized that seen from the angle of form, historical materialism merely studies human society or human history, seemingly unrelated with nature, but the problem is that society is formed and developed in the process of material exchange between man and nature, and for the purpose of the material exchange between man and nature, men must exchange their activities with each other. In order words, the living practical activity and actual daily life of man always involve, and are embodied by, the relationships or contradictions respectively between man and nature and between man and man. The basic issue focused on and to be solved by historical materialism is such relationship. Social life is essentially practical, and history is just the development of practical activity of man in time. History, in Marx's words, is nothing but the activity of man who is pursuing his own objectives. As a result, "history" in the concept of historical materialism refers to the sphere where human activity and inner contradictions thereof, namely the contradictions between man and nature and between man and man, are developed. A new theoretical space, i.e. a self-contained and complete, materialistic and dialectical picture of world, is shown by historical materialism by discussing the relationships between man and nature and between man and man, with real man and their development as thinking coordinates and practice as starting point and constructing principle. This means that historical materialism is not only a conception of history, but more importantly, a materialistic world outlook. Because historical materialism connotes "negative dialectics", it is called by Marx "actually a critical view of the world".

As far as I'm concerned, Marxist philosophy belongs to historical materialism, and dialectical materialism is just the pronoun of historical materialism. Practice is the essence of all social life, and practical activity itself is a kind of "negative dialectics". For this reason, historical materialism itself, as the philosophical reflection of all social life, implies "negative dialectics", and therefore is the unification of materialism with dialectics. Dialectics is critical and revolutionary essentially. Regarding it as the pronoun of historical materialism is for the purpose of highlighting the dimension of dialectics implied by historical materialism and its critical and revolutionary properties, while deeming practical materialism as another pronoun of historical materialism is for highlighting its dimension of practice and its primacy and fundamentality.

Xin: So, in Marxist philosophy, there is not an independent dialectical materialism as theoretical foundation, or an independent historical materialism with the nature of application. Your opinion mentioned above basically resolves the issue of "integration" of Marxist philosophy, and highlights and deepens the understanding on the viewpoint that "historical materialism is the first great discovery of Marx".

Yang: I should say that I haven't resolved the issue of "integration" of Marxist philosophy in a fundamental manner, and I just provide a new train of thought for resolving the issue concerning the relationships between the "integration" of Marxist philosophy and dialectical materialism, historical materialism and practical materialism.

Xin: As far as I know, you explicitly proposed to "reread Marx" in *Chinese Reader's Weekly* in 1995, and thought that all of your theoretical researches could be summarized in that way. I'm really curious about what reasons have propelled you to reread Marx.

Yang: In the history of thoughts, "rereading" is a common phenomenon. Hegel reread Plato, Peirce reread Kant, and Goethe reread Raphael ... The history of thoughts is, to a certain extent, the history during which the descendants unceasingly "reread" the predecessors, so the history of thoughts and the history of philosophy are "rewritten" or changed constantly. Masters have been "rereading" one after another, so should I, such an unknown. Rereading Marx is by no means "groaning without pain" or "making trouble out of nothing", but is the need of developments of contemporary practice, science and philosophy itself. There is an interesting phenomenon frequently happening in history – a viewpoint, theory or even the whole doctrine of a great ideologist always tends to show its real spirit and intrinsic value and catch the attention of people again after the ideologist's death and a relatively long historical movement, so is the historical destiny of Marxist philosophy. The historical movements in the twentieth century and the development predicament of contemporary philosophy make some important viewpoints in Marxist philosophy and the intrinsic value of his theories highlighted, such as theory of world history, theory of social interaction, theory of reflection on practice, etc., thereby revealing the real spirit and contemporary significance of Marxist philosophy. As a result, rereading and reevaluating Marxist philosophy becomes an inevitable trend. On a personal note, it is the painful tragedy of Chinese nation caused by "the Great Cultural Revolution" and the reform and opening-up of contemporary China, especially the practice of socialist market-oriented economy, that propel me to reread Marx. Marxist philosophy itself is generated against the background of market-oriented economy. Along with establishment of the system of socialist market-oriented economy, Marx is walking towards us, closer and closer to us, rather than farther and farther. In a word, Marxist philosophy still has a "shocking sense of space".

Xin: Please briefly introduce how you reread Marx.

Yang: During "rereading", I have gone through an exploring process from Marxist philosophy to the history respectively of Marxist philosophy and western philosophy, to modern western philosophy and contemporary social development theory, and then back to Marxist philosophy, aiming at studying Marxist philosophy against a broad historical background and theoretical space. In my opinion, the study on Marxist philosophy cannot be separated from the study on the history of Marxist philosophy, and only when grasping the mental journey of Marx and the evolution course of Marxist philosophy after Marx can one really understand the true essence of Marxist philosophy, and when and to what extent it had been misread; only by placing Marxist philosophy into the historical evolvement of western philosophy for study can one really grasp the substantial significance of Marxist philosophy on the transformation of old philosophy, and really realize its epoch-making contribution; only by comparing Marxist philosophy with modern western philosophy and contemporary social development theory for study can one really know the limitation of Marxist philosophy, and meanwhile further understand the greatness of Marxist philosophy, and why it is "the untranscendable semantic horizon" of our times.

In such a process of rereading Marx, a huge statue of heroes appeared in front of my eyes. I deeply feel the solemn beauty of ideologists pursuing truth and faith, and realize that Marxist philosophy is still the truth and conscience of our times. Philosophy is both my job and career, so I specially paid attention to studying the philosophy of Marx while rereading him, but I also "made up my lessons" of scientific socialism and theoretical economics. Marxist philosophy does not belong to "academism", and its basic principle is generated in the process of expounding scientific socialism, whose basic principle is embodied in Marxist philosophy in turn; therefore the two are closely associated with each other, and even fuse with each other. Marxist philosophy was generated from the critiques both on classical German philosophy and classical British economics. The economics of Marx is not only a theory about capital, but the theoretical critique or critical theory related to capital; the social attribute of man covered by the natural attribute of material and the interpersonal relationship covered by the relationship between materials revealed by Marx's economics are of great philosophical significance. Spiritual production is different from material production of flesh, since race continuation based on gene as genetic material is congeneric, whereas philosophical thinking can, and should, lead to new philosophical form through absorbing, digesting and recreating the fruits of different disciplines. Just as related breeding is prejudicial to species development, the research on philosophy should also break through the limitation from one to another.

Xin: Seen from the papers you have published, another outstanding feature of your study on philosophy is the combination of theory with reality. I would like to ask you to talk about your opinions in respect of this.

Yang: First of all, this involves the function of philosophy. What is it? Or what should philosophy do? This is the question mostly concerning philosophers. Different philosophers from different countries in different times have different opinions on it. It is demonstrated by the human history of thoughts that in the development course of any discipline, besides new issues concerned, such issues as its object, properties and function that belong to the directional and fundamental theoretical problems for the development of discipline often need re-discussing, so it is for philosophy. Fundamentally speaking, we should judge the position and function of philosophy based on the demand of times, knowledge level of human beings, and knowledge structure formed on that basis. Philosophy should, anyway, provide a critical spirit and a reflection method for men to cognize and transform the real world, and mould and lead to new spirits of times by virtue of its attributes of reflection, critique and ideality.

As far as I'm concerned, the unity of philosophy and times is realized by its real political effect. Only with philosophical consciousness and keen political vision can a philosopher understand and grasp the demand of times. This actually involves the relationship between philosophy and reality. On the one hand, philosophy cannot be separated from reality, and it must face realistic issues directly when resolving the subject of times, otherwise it will become rootless duckweed; on the other hand, philosophy has to enter the field of abstract conception movement, and reflects the movement of reality with conception movement, otherwise it can hardly be called philosophy. Philosophy must be linked with reality in a philosophical way to solve the subject of times. I always believe that the research on philosophy should not become the "conversation" between philosophers or the "soliloquy" of an individual philosopher, and instead, philosophy must "have conversation with" reality.

As far as I'm concerned, philosophy should not only go deep into but also surpass reality. It is impossible for a philosophy that only adapts to reality to look far ahead. The most essential reality of China at present is reform and opening-up and modernization. The most prominent feature and most significant meaning of such a social practice is that it concentrates three major social transformations, namely modernization, marketization and socialist reform, into the same era and space, forming an extremely special, complex, difficult, magnificent and great social transition. It will inevitably give rise to a series of significant and profound philosophical problems, and provide an extensive social space for the philosophical thinking of men. It is the obligatory mission of contemporary Chinese philosophy to focus on such reality, discuss and grasp its regularities, and set up contemporary spiritual pillar for the Chinese nation. It is the conscience and mission that contemporary Chinese philosophers should assume to, by generally grasping the reform and opening-up and modernization of contemporary China, arouse philosophical thinking on the nation's modes of thinking, living and working, as well as social development, and in turn to guide the movement of reality with philosophical concepts oriented to the 21st century.

Xin: What are the theoretical goal and state you are pursuing in the research on philosophy?

Yang: The theoretical goal I'm pursuing is the unity of innovation seeking and truth seeking; as for theoretical form what I'm pursing is poetic language and rigorous logic; as for the theoretical state what I'm pursuing is constructing the space of philosophy, and molding the individuality of thinking. I really hope that my research on philosophy is ploughing and weeding "in the fields of hope", and sincerely expect that my research can make contribution to the rise of Chinese nation again; however, I know well that I am "more than willing but lacking the power" to realize this, so, hard work is my sole choice.

Yang Geng

Jan. 24, 2010

Shiyu Garden, Century Town, Beijing

PUBLISHER'S NOTE

A New Interpretation of Marxist Philosophy (third edition) is another meticulous work by Yang Geng. The third Chinese edition of this thought provoking work was published by Renmin University Press in 2011, he also made some revision for the English edition.

I can easily say this book brings a brand new interpretation of Marxist philosophy. His work is part of recent ontology debates and researches in China, which underlines the significance of practice view in Marx's philosophy. According to Yang, when Marx turned his eyes to human world, he started to seek the basis for comprehending and interpreting such a world, and finally he found it, that is, the practical activity of mankind. Practice, as the real noumenon of human world, is the foundation for the existence and development of human world, and this is a dynamic noumenon which is in continuous evolution and generation; thus human world constitutes an open system with larger and larger in scale and more and more tiers.

Marx reveals that men maintain their survival in the process of actively transforming nature by utilizing instruments, and practice is the foundation for their living, and constitutes the special life form of mankind, namely the mode of being and living noumenon of man. The existence of human beings, including the alienation of their living condition and its sublation, happens and finishes in the process of practical activity. Yang, believes that Marx clearly affirms practice is the noumenon of human world, and also confirms that practice is the base for the sensuous existence of man, and human beings create their existence through practice, so practice is the noumenon of the existence of man. In this sense, Marxist philosophy is the ontology of existentialism, i.e. practical ontology.

Marx's practice view is for long being debated among philosophical researches, and some researchers and schools have been calling themselves praxis philosophers in the West and East. It is not surprising that this debate has also reached China, to this land which is one of the main cradles of practical philosophy. Therefore readers who search the true status of practice in Marx's philosophy, and explore its relation with Marx's materialist dialectics and historical materialism may have an exciting philosophical journey throughout Yang's book. I am sure this book will be a new bridge among Marxist philosophical researchers and readers in China and other parts of the world.

Yang carefully expounds the basic opinions of Marxist philosophy that are ignored or forgotten by the current textbook version, and probes deeply into those opinions that Marx has ever discussed but not sufficiently developed. He chooses such issues of Marxist philosophy which coincide with major contemporary issues and tries to upgrade them into the basic opinions of Marxist philosophy. Thus the book demonstrates the vitality the modernity and the contemporary significance of Marxist philosophy.

The book consists of two parts and the second part studies, the schools of French materialism, social philosophy of French socialism, the relation between Hegel, Feuerbach and Marx, ontology thoughts of Soviet school and Lukacs, philosophical turn of Husserl forward life-world idea, significance of Derrida's *Specters of Marx*, the relations between postmodern philosophy and Marxist philosophy. In the last two chapters, Yang studies post-colonialist thought and Post-Marxism thoughts and their theoretical logics.

For several reasons Derrida's works have drawn great attention and debate in China. In this second part, Yang, evaluates the enduring work of Derrida, *Specters of Marx*. Yang points out that Derrida is not the first person who regards methodology as the essence of Marxism. Lukacs also thinks that the essence of Marxism is its methodology, and even if all the conclusions of Marxism were wrong, as long as its method is right, Marxism would still be insurmountable. At this point, Derrida and Lukacs happen to have the same view. In *Specters of Marx*, Derrida on the one side stresses that essence and critical spirit are the essence of Marxism, and that this heritage that must be inherited. On the other side he emphasizes that this critical spirit should be differentiated from other Marxist spirits and the latter should be discarded: The latter which is fixed in those basic concepts related to labor, the mode of production, social class, the history of state apparatus, etc.

I am proud of presenting this book of Canut from an innovative philosopher in mainland China, who "rereads Marx" tries to provide a new train of thought to "integrate" Marxist philosophy with practical materialism, dialectical materialism and historical materialism.

Finally, I would like to thank Renmin University Press and her editors, for their efforts in realizing this book. I also thank Cheng Zhuo and Li Ling for their tireless translation work.

Walterio Barra Cabello

Viña del Mar- Chile

July 2013

PART ONE

CHAPTER I

THE THEME AND SYSTEM OF MARXIST PHILOSOPHY: A NEW INTERPRETATION

The foundation of Marxist philosophy is like a splendid sunrise in the human history of thoughts, fundamentally transforming the theme, function and thinking mode of philosophy; however, it has also been facing distortions, criticisms and challenges from different aspects. It is demonstrated by the human history of thoughts that in the development course of any science, besides new issues concerned, such issues as its theme and function that belong to the directional and fundamental theoretical problems for the development of discipline often need re-discussing, so it is for philosophy and Marxist philosophy. "Well knowing does not mean truly knowing", therefore accurately and comprehensively understanding Marxist philosophy is still a major theoretical subject.

1 PHILOSOPHICAL INTERPRETATION OF THE SUBJECT OF TIMES

A philosophical system is always named after a philosopher, but it is never exclusive to any individual philosopher. As Hegel ever said, philosophy is "the times concentratedly expressed by thoughts". Marx took this point of view a further step – "a real philosophy is the essence of the spirit of its own times". Despite the abstract extent of mode or the "individuality", the philosophical systems created by philosophers are all associated closely with the times of philosophers. Leaving their own times, the straightforward and fiery character of French enlightenment philosophy and the intricate and obscure feature of classical German philosophy are both incomprehensible.

The occurrence of any philosophical system, fundamentally, is related to the times that it is in, and it is the product of a certain times. The generation of Marxist philosophy was exactly the inevitable outcome of social development in the mid-nineteenth century. The British Industrial Revolution and its consequence, the French political revolution and its consequence, and the formation of world history and its significance were three main fruits of the historic creative activities by the bourgeoisie, and these fruits and the social contradictions of great scale and modern form resulting from them were the primary cause promoting Marx to create the "new materialism", and it was them that constituted the times background against which Marxist philosophy was generated.

The British Industrial Revolution initiated in the 1760s had won its decisive victory till the 1840s, when the production had been mechanized and socialized. The French Revolution started in 1789 also obtained historic victory after overthrowing the restoration dynasty in 1830, establishing and consolidating the capitalist system. The victory of the British Industrial Revolution and the French Revolution marked the human history had developed from the feudal era into the era of capitalism, meanwhile from the times when "natural connection is dominant" into the times when "factors created by society and history predominate over others", and from the times of "personal dependence" into the times of "personal independence founded on objective dependence"[1]. While winning great victory, the bourgeoisie also brought a huge social

---

1   *Karl Marx and Friedrich Engels.* Beijing: People's Publishing House, 1979: 1st Chinese Ed., Vol. 46 (I), pp. 45 and 104.

problem for themselves – the irreconcilable contradiction between production socialization and private ownership of the means of production, resulting in alienations of man and the human world. In other words, the living condition of men is alienated in capitalist society, and under such an alienated condition, the individuality of man is dissolved, and people become "one-dimensional men".

The characteristics and inner contradictions of times will be reflected in theories inevitably.

The classical political economics of England reflects the victory of the bourgeoisie in the economic field. Adam Smith et al. turned the source of social wealth to the "activity of subject" from object, and formed the concept of "labor in general" and created the labor theory of value based on abstraction. The formation of the concept of "labor in general" marked human beings entered "modern society", because only in modern society, labor "is not a rule associated with individuals on the basis of a particularity any longer", and "an individual is prone to shift from one labor type to another, and certain labor types are occasional for them, thus being indistinctive"[2].

The historiography during the French Restoration period was formed based upon the summary of the French Revolution and its historical course. According to Thierry et al., history is being created by the masses of people; European history since the Middle Ages is actually the history of class struggle, and the class struggle based on different interests forms the power driving historical development; property relationship constitutes the foundation of political system. Engels rated these views highly, and believed that the historiography during the French Restoration period shook "the whole conception of history up to the present"[3] and strove to discover the materialistic conception of history.

The "critical-utopian socialism" of England and France reflects the inner contradictions in capitalist society. Among the critiques of capitalist system, Saint-Simon et al. found that ownership was the "cornerstone for the edifice of society", and thought that historical movement had its inherent laws, that was to say, capitalism would be doomed inevitably like those social systems in the past, and give place to new type of

---

2   Ibid., p. 42.
3   *Selected Works of Karl Marx and Friedrich Engels.* Beijing: People's Publishing House, 1995: 2nd Ed., Vol. 4, p. 733.

society in which everyone was entitled to free and all-around development. Although the critical-utopian socialism belongs to non-scientific form on the whole, it differs from previous utopianism qualitatively – it, generated in new times, reflects the inner contradictions of such times. Despite its failure to solve the problem, the critical-utopian socialism put forward a question, i.e. where the human history should go, which became the subject of times in the mid-nineteenth century. New era was calling for new theory.

Marxist philosophy does not belong to "academism", nor it is the product extended from the themes of philosophies before. The foundation of Marxist philosophy was closely associated and integrated with the resolution to the subject of times. At the same time, while solving the subject of times and founding the new materialism, Marx critically studied and philosophically reviewed the classical British political economics, the historiography during the French Restoration period and the critical-utopian socialism of England and France, which, together with the classical German philosophy, constituted the theoretical source of Marxist philosophy. Spiritual production is different from material production of flesh, since human race continuation based on physical heredity is congeneric, whereas philosophical thinking can lead to new philosophical form through absorbing, digesting and recreating the fruits of different disciplines. The new materialism of Marx doubtlessly belongs to philosophy, but its theoretical source was not limited to philosophy. Just like related breeding is prejudicial to species development, a creative philosophical theory will certainly break through the limitation from one philosophy to another.

Marx also attached great importance to philosophical thinking, and critique of philosophy run through his resolution to the subject of times. "Germany is a philosophical nation", where any social change will be firstly shown by theoretical and philosophical activities. "Even historically, theoretical emancipation has specific practical significance for Germany. For Germany's revolutionary past is theoretical, it is the Reformation. As the revolution then began in the brain of the monk, so now it begins in the brain of the philosopher."[4] The way Marx had taken was a typical way of German.

---

4 *Selected Works of Karl Marx and Friedrich Engels*. Beijing: People's Publishing House, 1995: 2nd Ed., Vol. 1, p. 10.

I learn through profoundly rethinking the history of Marxism that Marx solved the subject of times not directly starting out from reality, but through critique and transformation of philosophy before returning to reality. Every step forward by Marx, as to speak, was achieved through critiques on philosophy – "critique on Hegel's philosophy of right", "critique on Hegel's dialectics and entire philosophy", "critique on critical criticism", "critique on French materialism", "critique on philosophical forms after Hegel", etc. This series of critiques strictly armed Marx theoretically, and enabled him to understand modern philosophy, philosophy itself and other various theories more thoroughly and cognize the realistic social contradictions more deeply, thereby creating his new materialism. The creation of new materialism, in turn, made Marx think at a higher position and in a more incisive manner than his contemporaries, and gave him forward-looking profound wisdom to scientifically resolve the subject of times.

Prior to the generation of Marxist philosophy, philosophy was mainly featured by nationality. The philosophies of Confucius, Lao-tse, Kant and Hegel had exerted influence on other nations, but the influence was still confined to cultural exchange and communication, and did not change the nationality of philosophy – the Lao-Zhuang philosophy was still Chinese philosophy, Hegelian philosophy belonged to German philosophy, and so forth. Marxist philosophy is different for it is a world theory. Though Germany is the hometown of Marx, Marxist philosophy is a "world philosophy" instead of being exclusive to Germany. Marx had ever foreseen that such an era would come inevitably: "philosophy then ceases to be a particular system in relation to other particular systems; it becomes philosophy in general in relation to the world, i.e. the philosophy of the contemporary world."[5] Marxist philosophy itself is such a world philosophy, the product of world history.

The world history mentioned here is not in the ordinary sense of historiography, namely the whole human history, but refers to the history since world "integration" resulting from mutual influence, restriction and penetration of various nations and countries in a comprehensive way. As an experienced fact today, the world history took its form in the nineteenth century. Marx noticed this historical trend depending on his extraordinary insight, and represented such a trend with the

5 *Karl Marx and Friedrich Engels*. Beijing: People's Publishing House, 1956: 1st Chinese Ed., Vol. 1, p. 121.

proposition of "transformation of history into world history"; besides, he also pointed out clearly that the bourgeoisie "produced world history for the first time, insofar as it made all civilized nations and every individual member of them dependent for the satisfaction of their wants on the whole world, thus destroying the former natural exclusiveness of separate nations."[6]

As a result of the formation of world history, the previous state of exclusiveness and self-sufficiency is replaced by the interaction and interdependence between various nations in all aspects, continuously eliminating national one-sidedness and limitation. It is true with regard to both material and spiritual productions. There is not only world market but "a kind of world literature", i.e. a spiritual product of world. Marxist philosophy is such a spiritual product of world, as well as a world philosophy generated against the grand times background of world history. It is because Marxist philosophy is a world philosophy that it "has found representatives far beyond the boundaries of Germany and Europe and in all the literary languages of the world"[7], thereby being able to take root, grow and bear fruit in different nations and become a part of various national cultures.

2 FUNDAMENTAL TRANSFORMATION OF THE THEME OF PHILOSOPHY

It is undoubted that Marxist philosophy is a kind of materialistic philosophy, but the theme of materialistic philosophy changes along with the development of times. Marxist philosophy, as new materialism, is by no means the extension and solution to the original theme of the old materialism and even the whole traditional philosophy. Contrarily, it realized the theme transformation and object change of philosophy, and constructed a new philosophical field based on that. Engels even described the characteristics of new materialism in such a way, "It is no longer a philosophy at all, but simply a world outlook."[8] This, of course, does not mean that the new materialism does not belong to philosophy, but that it is not the philosophy in traditional sense. Fundamentally speaking, Marxist philosophy falls under in the category of modern philosophy and belongs to modern materialism.

---

6 *Selected Works of Karl Marx and Friedrich Engels.* 2nd Ed., Vol. 1, p. 114.

7 *Selected Works of Karl Marx and Friedrich Engels.* 2nd Ed., Vol. 4, p. 212.

8 *Selected Works of Karl Marx and Friedrich Engels.* Beijing: People's Publishing House, 1995: 2nd Ed., Vol. 3, p. 481.

To really comprehend this viewpoint of Engels, it needs to understand fully the nature of traditional philosophy and Marx's concept of world.

Relative to "modern philosophy", "traditional philosophy" refers to the philosophical form during the historical period from ancient Greece to the mid-nineteenth century, including ancient philosophy and early modern philosophy. The traditional philosophy aims to trace the principle or essentials of the whole world and constitutes a common theme for different schools it covers. It basically belongs to "metaphysics", namely a theory concerning the nature of transcendent being, which tries to understand and grasp the nature of things, as well as the essence and behavior basis of man, based on "ultimate being" or "prime principle".

Early modern materialism had a tendency of rejecting "metaphysics" at the very beginning. According to Bacon, materialism "holds back within itself in a naive way the germs of a many-sided development". However, "in its further evolution, materialism becomes one-sided" and "takes to misanthropy"[9]. That "abstract substance" and "abstract entity" became the subject of all changes and formed "the causa efficiens of the natures and existences of things." In Descartes' opinion, what philosophy pursues is to grasp this "primary cause and true principle" and deduce the natures and causes of all things accordingly. The early modern materialism started from the critique on "metaphysics" but returned to "metaphysics" in the end.

By combining "metaphysics" with German idealistic dialectics, Hegel built a realm of "metaphysics", thereby realizing "the victorious and substantial restoration" of "metaphysics" in the classical German philosophy. The problem is that Hegel restored everything into "absolute reason", which had become a new superstitious belief towering overhead and receiving the worship of men; men themselves become the tool for self-realization of such "absolute reason". Hegelian philosophy recognizes human initiative merely in form, and actually, it deprives man of initiative, creativity and subjectivity thoroughly for it only takes man as a "tool". Thus, a large cycle of "metaphysics" had been completed till Hegel since Aristotle specified "the Beings of beings" as the theme of "the first philosophy".

---

9 *Karl Marx and Friedrich Engels*. Beijing: People's Publishing House, 1959: 1st Chinese Ed., Vol. 2, pp. 163 and 164.

This means that no matter whether in the philosophical system of early modern materialism or early modern idealism, not only the "thing-in-itself" but "mankind" is taken as an abstract being, and human beings and human subjectivity are lost. As a result, after its tragic "restoration" in the classical German philosophy, "metaphysics" "lost all credit in the domain of theory" and "in practice". Marx had ever asserted, "Metaphysics will be defeated forever by materialism, which has now been perfected by the work of speculation itself and coincides with humanism."[10] It was Marx who fulfilled such a task of times. In other words, making materialism "coincident with" human subjectivity is what Marxist philosophy focuses on, and opposing or rejecting "metaphysics" is its basic principle.

In the history of philosophy, Marx and Comte raised the banner of "rejecting metaphysics" at the same time. Marx even believed that the new philosophy he founded was the "real positive science". Marx's "rejection of metaphysics" is consistent with that of Comte with respect to the times, but the two are essentially different in the aspect of directionality. Comte just limited "the rejection of metaphysics" to the scope of experience, knowledge and "verifiability"; Marx, however, brought forward another train of thought – after "the rejection of metaphysics", philosophy should pay attention to "the real world of its times", "existing world", "sensuous world", and "human world", as well as "making real beings and earthly things the center of all interest"[11].

The "existing world" referred to by Marx certainly includes nature, but this nature is not the untouched ecological nature but "the natural world of anthropology". According to Marx, there is a "priority" of nature, but "nature that preceded human history", or nature beyond the range of human activity, means "nothing" or "non-existent nature" to human beings. The reason is that only through exploration and discovery of human beings can the untouched ecological nature acquire the realistic feature for man; only after the practice and transformation by human beings can it constitute the "sensuous world" where men live; through practice, men do not only transform natural beings, but fuse with them and give a new dimension to them – sociality. It is apparent that the "existing world" mentioned by Marx does not refer to the universe embracing nature, society and thought, namely "the whole world", but means

---

10   *Karl Marx and Friedrich Engels.* 1st Chinese Ed., Vol. 2, pp. 159 – 160.
11   Ibid., pp. 161 – 162.

human world. Natural history and human history are closely linked with each other; as long as men exist, the both are dependent on each other. In this existing world, due to interaction and inter-infiltration, what appears before men is social nature and natural society, or "historical nature and natural history". Human world is a "two-in-one" world of nature and society.

The traditional philosophy concentrates its attention on the universe noumenon and the "absolute" or "abstract substance" of God, but just forgets to pay attention to human world; Marx, on the contrary, attached importance to human world and mankind in reality and their development. For Marxist philosophy, "all the issues are for the purpose of revolutionizing the existing world", i.e. remolding the world in coordination with human development, thereby returning "human world and human relation to men themselves"[12]. In this way, Marx shifted the focus of philosophy from the whole world to the existing world, from the universe noumenon to human world, thus accomplishing the fundamental transformation of the theme of philosophy.

The fundamental transformation of the theme of philosophy was completed along with the object change.

Historically, philosophies at different times and even different philosophical schools of the same epoch have their particular study objects. Fichte pointed out, "We want to call the foundation put forward by every philosophy for experience interpretation the object of such philosophy, because this object seems to exist only through and for such philosophy."[13] This is a quite insightful opinion. Throughout the entire span of the history of philosophy, the basis used by every philosophy to interpret the world and build its theoretical system is its object. Feuerbach's philosophy has tried to interpret the world and construct its system in the basic principle of "real man", taking "man, together with nature as the basis of man, the exclusive, universal, and highest object of philosophy"[14]. Hegelian philosophy interprets the world and builds its system on the basis of abstract human rationality – absolute rationality; as a matter of fact, it regards human rationality as study object,

---

12   *Karl Marx and Friedrich Engels*. 1st Chinese Ed., Vol. 1, p. 443.
13   *German Philosophy during Late 1700s – Early 1800s*, compiled by the Department of Philosophy, Peking University. Beijing: The Commercial Press, 1975: p. 187.
14   *Selected Philosophical Works of Feuerbach*. Beijing: The Commercial Press, 1984: 1st New Chinese Ed., Vol. I, p. 184.

so he thought that "philosophy is to explore rational things"[15]. It was based on such cognition that Hegel built a philosophical system of "a science of sciences". "In the sense that philosophy was regarded as a special science standing above the other sciences, Hegel's system was the final thorough form of philosophy. The entire philosophy declined along with this system."[16]

As soon as Marx turned his eyes to human world, he started to seek the basis for comprehending, interpreting and grasping such a world and take it as the study object of new philosophy. At last, this basis was discovered, that is, practical activity of human beings.

As far as Marx is concerned, nature and society in human world integrate with each other in human practice, which plays the role as a converter. Through practice, society infuses its objective into nature, making it the social nature; meanwhile, nature enters society and converts into a constant factor in society, making society the natural society. Human world, of course, cannot be resolved into the consciousness of man, nor should it be restored to the untouched ecological nature. The practical activity of human beings is the foundation and base for the existence of human world or existing world, and plays a guiding role in the movement of human world, that is to say, men "set the mind for Heaven and Earth" by means of their practical activity, and rebuild the world on the basis of their material practice activities. In other words, practice is the real noumenon of human world, a dynamic noumenon in continuous evolution and generation; the human world is therefore made an open system with larger and larger scale and more and more tiers.

For this reason, Marx set the practical activity of human beings as the object of philosophy, and the resolutions to the relationships between man and world, subject and object, and subjectivity and objectivity as the task of philosophy, thereby providing methodology for changing the world. Marxist philosophy was founded aiming to change the practical activity in the existing world, and the contents of practice are its theoretical contents. Marxist philosophy itself is a kind of theoretical reflection on all kinds of contradictory relations in the practical activity of human beings; that's why Marx believed that the new materialism is "the real positive science, the representation of the practical activity,

15 Hegel, *Principles of the Philosophy of Right*. Beijing: The Commercial Press, 1961: p. 10.
16 *Selected Works of Karl Marx and Friedrich Engels*. 2nd Ed., Vol. 3, p. 362.

of the practical process of development of men"[17], and its basic content is from "the study of the actual life-process and the activity of the individuals of each epoch"[18]. In this way, Marx found the point directly bonding philosophy with the change of world.

The theme transformation and object change of philosophy realized by Marxist philosophy are coincident with the development of modern science. "As soon as each special science is bound to make clear its position in the great totality of things and of our knowledge of things, a special science dealing with this totality is superfluous."[19] Marx did not grant the new materialism, at anytime and anywhere, such a privilege, i.e. constructing a comprehensive prospect of whole world relying on the achievements in natural science and social science. As Engels accurately pointed out, along with the generation of modern science, "that which still survives, independently, of all earlier philosophy is the science of thought and its laws – formal logic and dialectics. Everything else is subsumed in the positive science of nature and history"[20]. By the twentieth century, the study on thought had been split from philosophy, and become an independent science. It can be said that up to now, nature, society and even thought itself haven't belong to the study domain of philosophy any longer. It has been demonstrated by modern science that any attempt to reconstruct a world outlook concerning the "universal relation" of the whole world upon science is really "superfluous", and its essence is nothing but the "restoration" of "metaphysics" under modern conditions.

The theme transformation of philosophy realized by Marxist philosophy marks the transition of philosophy – from traditional to modern. What the modern philosophy emphasizes, in general, is the living world and existence of human beings. In Jaspers' words, "the objective of philosophy is striving to comprehend the reality of man in the practical situation". Even the "linguistic turn" achieved by analytic philosophy essentially reflects the search for the connecting point or intermediate link between man and world, and shows the general understanding of modern philosophy on the relationships between thought, language and world, that is, the world is beyond the thought of men, but men can understand the world and express their understanding of the world

17 *Selected Works of Karl Marx and Friedrich Engels*. 2nd Ed., Vol. 1, p. 73.
18 Ibid., p. 74.
19 *Selected Works of Karl Marx and Friedrich Engels*. 2nd Ed., Vol. 3, p. 364.
20 *Selected Works of Karl Marx and Friedrich Engels*. 2nd Ed., Vol. 3, p. 364.

only through language, so "the boundary of language is the boundary of world", and we can only talk about "my world".

This opinion of analytic philosophy is quite reasonable. "Language is the immediate actuality of thought", "the manifestation of real life" and "the language of actual world". The fruits of human cognition of world are accumulated in and expressed by language. Studying the significance of world in the sense of language is actually to understand and grasp the world based on the relationship with man. Of course, the analytic philosophy goes too far after all, where language becomes an independent realm. It seemed that Marx had foreseen such a "linguistic turn", because he pointed out that "just as philosophers have given thought an independent existence, they were bound to make language into an independent realm."[21] As far as I am concerned, the analytic philosophy, in effect, boosts the study on the relationship between man and world in a regressive way.

In respect of content but not manifestation mode, the operation of entire modern western philosophy takes, generally but not individually, the theme transformation realized by Marxist philosophy as its fundamental content. No matter whether other schools of modern western philosophy have realized or acknowledged, Marx is, indeed, the pathfinder and founder of modern western philosophy. Thus, Marxist philosophy falls under "modern materialism".

3 CHARACTERISTICS OF MARXIST PHILOSOPHY

As "modern materialism", Marxist philosophy achieved its development through critique of traditional philosophy; therefore, in order to really understand the substantive characteristics of Marxist philosophy, we need to know the major defects of old materialism and idealism first of all.

The old materialism consists of natural materialism and humanistic materialism.

With origin traced back to ancient philosophy, natural materialism becomes systematic in the theory of Hobbes, and extends to the mechanical materialism in French materialism. It restores the whole world to a natural substance in the principle of "time priority", and makes man

---

21 *Karl Marx and Friedrich Engels.* Beijing: People's Publishing House, 1960: 1st Chinese Ed., Vol. 3, p. 525.

a kind of manifestation of natural substance. In natural materialism, substance is considered as "the subject of all changes", and "both man and nature follow the same rules". It acknowledges material unity of the world, but totally negates the initiative, creativity and subjectivity of man; it studies "the whole world", but does not find a practical standing point for man – the real subject. To put it another way, there is "a vacant land of humanism" in natural materialism. It is because of this that Marx thinks natural materialism is a kind of "pure materialism", and Hobbes had made "materialism become misanthropy"[22].

Humanistic materialism originated from the other school of French materialism, namely "real humanism"[23], and obtained its typical form from Feuerbach. "Feuerbach has a great advantage over the 'pure' materialists in that he realizes how man too is an 'object of the senses'."[24] Concretely speaking, Feuerbach regarded man as the foundation for the unity of thought and nature, and tried to comprehend the world in the basic principle of "real man". He, however, did not realize that practice is the mode of being of man, and could "never manage to conceive the sensuous world as the total living sensuous activity of the individuals composing it"[25]. Feuerbach, for this reason, stopped at abstract man, and still ignored the initiative, creativity and subjectivity of man. The same as natural materialism, humanistic materialism also understands "thing, reality and sensuousness" "only in the form of the object", but not "subjectively". It is in this sense that Marx "included" the materialism of Feuerbach into the category of "old materialism", and held that the chief defect of old materialism was that it did not acknowledge practical activity and its significance.

On the contrary, idealism acknowledges the initiative of subject consciousness, and demonstrates that in the cognitive activity, men grasp external objects relying on their own properties and conditions. The results of such cognition are embodied largely in critical philosophy of Kant and negative dialectics of Hegel. The problem is that both Kant's critical philosophy and Hegel's negative dialectics repudiated the materialistic foundation of active conscious activity, but only "abstractly developed" the "active side" of man. The primary cause for this is that idealism also does not know practical activity and its significance.

22 *Karl Marx and Friedrich Engels*. 1st Chinese Ed., Vol. 2, p. 164.
23 Ibid., pp. 167 – 168.
24 *Selected Works of Karl Marx and Friedrich Engels*. 2nd Ed., Vol. 1, p. 77.
25 Ibid., p. 78.

Thus, it is clear that the common chief defect of old materialism and idealism is that both do not understand the practical activity of man and its significance. It was this chief defect that resulted in the separation of materialism and dialectics in early modern philosophy, and the condition that "materialism and history diverged completely" in old materialistic philosophy, viz., forming materialistic view of nature and idealistic conception of history.

On account of the astonishingly consistent major defect of old materialism and idealism, Marx was impelled to investigate the practical activity of human beings and its significance in a deep and comprehensive manner, and defined Marxist philosophy as "practical materialism". In my opinion, this is a global fundamental definition, and what it intends to manifest is not only a philosophical attitude of putting theory into action, but more importantly, that the view of practice is the primary and fundamental view in Marxist philosophy, and the principle of practice is the principle for construction of Marxist philosophy. Practical materialism constitutes the substantive characteristic of Marxist philosophy, in other words.

In the view of Marx, practice, above all, is the process in which men cause, regulate and control the material exchange between man and nature through their own activity; in this process, it is necessary for individuals to establish definite relations with each other for the exchange of their activities. At the same time, the result that will be obtained at the completion of practice already exists there at the commencement of the process, as the purpose, in the mind of the practitioner in the form of idea, and such purpose is realized, which gives the law to modus operandi" of the practitioner. This means that practice inherently encompasses those relationships between man and nature, man and society, and man and his consciousness, and the integration of these relationships constitutes the fundamental relation in the existing world. Practice, implying all secrets of the existing world, can be described as an epitome reflecting the existing world, as well as the total origin of all real contractions confronting human beings. That's why Marxist philosophy rethinks, probes into and comprehends the existing world based on practice, and "conceives thing, reality and sensuousness" "as practice".

The basic point for understanding the existing world based on practice is to grasp the existing world from the starting point of material practice, and regard the material exchange between man and nature caused by material production as the foundation of existing world. According to Marx, the integration of existing world is realized through the normalization of various relations and structures of the existing world by the material exchange between man and nature, which always is the deep structure in the existing world, fundamentally determining social structure, political structure, conceptual structure, etc. "Definite individuals who are productively active in a definite way enter into definite social and political relations. Empirical observation must in each separate instance bring out empirically, and without any mystification and speculation, the connection of the social and political structure with production."[26]

This means the "priority" of natural substance is recognized; this, however, is merely the common character of new materialism and old materialism, and is not the exclusive characteristic of new materialism. The material exchange between man and nature caused by human practical activity forms the foundation of existing world, which is the "novelty" of new materialism, or the "materialistic character" of Marx's materialism.

Practice is the mode of being and the essential activity of man. The existing world is "conceived as practice", or "subjectively" in fact, in Marxist philosophy. It is also in Marxist philosophy that both practice principle and subjectivity principle are inherently consistent, thereby providing a new way of thinking for understanding the human essence and the relationship between man and world.

As far as Marx is concerned, man comes from nature originally; and "in the same way the existence of the human race is the result of an earlier process which organic life passed through. Man comes into existence only when a certain point is reached. But once man has emerged, he becomes the permanent pre-condition of human history, likewise its permanent product and result, and he is pre-condition only as his own product and result."[27] That is to say, man is the result of self-creation and self-shaping through his own activity.

26 *Selected Works of Karl Marx and Friedrich Engels.* 2nd Ed., Vol. 1, p. 71.
27 *Karl Marx and Friedrich Engels.* Beijing: People's Publishing House, 1974: 1st Chinese Ed., Vol. 26 III, p. 545.

This is exactly true. Animals realize unity with nature and maintain their survival depending on their negative adaption to surroundings, so they are only a part of nature. Men, differently, achieve unity with nature, maintain their survival and continuously develop themselves through transformation and creation of circumstances by themselves; that's why men are sui generis as the unique human beings. Human evolution is not only biological heredity and variation but also historiographical continuation and innovation, and the unification of the two is accomplished exactly in the practical activity. Practice is the mode of being and the essential activity of man. According to Marx, the substantive characteristics of man are formed in his survival activity, and the secrets of man are also hidden in his practical activity. "As individuals express their life, so they are. What they are, therefore, coincides with their production, both with what they produce and with how they produce."[28] As a result, to judge what mankind is, the first thing is to know how man exists and acts. This doubtlessly provides a way of thinking for comprehending and grasping the human essence based on man's own activity.

Man performs activity and enters into relation with nature in the mode of substance during practice, and what he obtains is the existence of nature or substance in the mode of human being, thereby making man the subject and nature the object. "The entire so-called history of the world is nothing but the creation of man through human labor, nothing but the emergence of nature for man."[29] It indicates that practice makes the relationship between man and nature a relationship that "exists for me"[30], which is a negative contradictory relation. Marx believed that with the aim to maintain his existence – affirming himself, man must take negative actions towards nature, i.e. changing the original ecology of nature, and making it "humanized nature" and "thing-for-me".

Unlike animals, men are always realizing the unification with nature by constantly establishing opposite relations with nature – negation against nature as object is just the affirmation of subject. The dialectical relationship between affirmation and negation puts subject and object into a bidirectional movement. While continuously transforming and creating the existing world, practice is also transforming and creating mankind constantly. "The coincidence of the changing of circumstances

28   *Selected Works of Karl Marx and Friedrich Engels.* 2nd Ed., Vol. 1, pp. 67 – 68.
29   *Karl Marx and Friedrich Engels.* Beijing: People's Publishing House, 1979: 1st Chinese Ed., Vol. 42, p. 131.
30   *Selected Works of Karl Marx and Friedrich Engels.* 2nd Ed., Vol. 1, p. 81.

with human activity or self-changing can be conceived and rationally understood only as revolutionary practice."[31] As the mode of being and the essential activity of man, practice certainly embodies the inherent measure of man and the criticalness on the existing world, and also involves self-development of man.

It can be observed that the negative relationship that "exists for me" between man and nature is the most profound and complicated contradictory relation, which is like the "Waterloo" for many master philosophers before Marx, making materialism "powerless and frustrated" with respect to the subjectivity of man, and separating materialism far from dialectics. The wisdom of Marx lies in his unity of materialism and human subjectivity, and his integration of materialism and dialectics consequently, through deep and comprehensive analysis on the practical activity of man and its significance. In other words, dialectical materialism is another important characteristic of Marxist philosophy.

When materialism and human subjectivity, as well as materialism and dialectics, is organically integrated by Marx on the basis of scientific view of practice, the unity of materialistic view of nature and conception of history is realized, which are the two aspects of a same process.

It is generally thought that the materialistic conception of history is the extension or application of general materialism to social history, but this is not true. Helvetius had long since "envisaged materialism in relation to social life"[32], but he arrived at historical idealism. The particularity of social life is like a "drop leaf" between nature and society. Prior to Marx, even when the firm materialists turned their eyes from nature to society, and started to study social history, almost all of them were pushed to the abyss of idealism by this drop leaf. From the angle of epistemology, the fundamental cause of such a condition is still that previous philosophers did not realize practical activity and its significance, and did not perceive that social life was practical in essence. The genius of Marx is that he comprehended society and the relationship between society and nature based on practice, and thereby founded the materialistic conception of history. The view of practice serves as the primary and fundamental view both of Marxist epistemology and Marxist philosophy.

---

31   Ibid., p. 55.
32   *Karl Marx and Friedrich Engels*. 1st Chinese Ed., Vol. 2, p. 165.

In the opinion of Marx, men must be able to live for creating history, and must conduct material practice and accomplish the material exchange between man and nature for living; with the purpose of accomplishing the said material exchange, men must exchange their activities, and enter into definite social relations necessarily. Such social relations "are nothing but the necessary forms in which man's material and individual activity is realized"[33], and even social productivity is, in essence, formed in the human practical activity of nature transformation. Practice really is the cradle of all social relations and the essence of all social life. Fundamentally speaking, it is during the material exchange between man and nature that society takes its shape and receives its development. The material exchange between man and nature becomes the "eternal natural necessity" for the existence and development of society.

It is because of this that previous philosophers, including old materialists, could do nothing but stepped towards historical idealism after excluding the practical relationship of man to nature from history; but Marx interpreted idea, historical process and its rules based on "material practice" – "the foundation of real history", and created the materialistic conception of history, thereby shattering the myth of the opposition between material nature and spiritual history, and accomplishing the unity of materialistic view of nature and conception of history. "After history was also subjected to materialistic treatment, a new avenue of development had opened."[34] It is true that the creation of the materialistic conception of history had opened up a new path for the development of philosophy, and without it, the generation of Marxist dialectical materialism was impossible. Historical materialism, therefore, also constitutes another important characteristic of Marxist philosophy.

Hence, we can see that the view of practice is exactly the primary and fundamental view of Marxist philosophy, and its two important characteristics – historical materialism and dialectical materialism – are derived from the substantive characteristic of practical materialism as the inherent logic and theoretical representation necessarily developed by the substantive characteristic.

---

33   *Selected Works of Karl Marx and Friedrich Engels.* 2nd Ed., Vol. 4, p. 532.
34   Ibid., p. 228.

By promoting practice to the fundamental principle for the first time in the history of philosophy, and transforming the philosophical way of thinking, Marx founded a kind of practical, dialectical and historical materialism. Thus, the traditional philosophy was ended by Marxist philosophy, and modern philosophy was initiated, which is superior to other schools of modern western philosophy on the whole. According to my understanding, other schools of modern western philosophy all view the human world based on a certain aspect, link or relation, and reduce the human world to such an aspect, link or relation, thus failing to grasp the human world generally and the human being fundamentally; Marxist philosophy, on the contrary, grasps the foundation of human being and human world – practice, and radiates this foundation to all the aspects, links and relations in the human world, thus forming a "holistic vision of society". I have a deeper understanding on the well-known saying of Sartre than Sartre himself – Marxist philosophy is the sole unsurpassable philosophy of our times, in that I have grasped the substantive characteristic of Marxist philosophy, that is, practical materialism.

CHAPTER II

MARX, THE PATHFINDER OF MODERN WESTERN PHILOSOPHY

It is generally believed that Marxist philosophy is fundamentally opposite to modern western philosophy. The basic principle of modern western philosophy, to be specific, is to reject metaphysics, whereas Marxist philosophy, different from or superior to it, still maintains the "essence" of metaphysics, i.e. aiming to trace the principle or essentials of the whole world, and striving to grasp the nature of all things based on such ultimate being – ultimate substance – and then derive social being from natural being. This is actually a misunderstanding. Through profoundly rethinking on Marxist philosophy and modern western philosophy, I realize that opposing or rejecting metaphysics is also the basic principle of Marxist philosophy. Differing from the traditional western philosophy, Marxist philosophy focuses on the mode of being of man, as well as the elimination of their alienated living condition. Marxist philosophy basically interprets the significance of beings based on the existence of human beings, and comprehends and grasps the relationship between man and world based on the mode of being of man – practice. So, metaphysics was terminated by Marx, who, together with Comte, initiated the process of modern western philosophy.

1 REJECTION OF METAPHYSICS AND ESTABLISHMENT OF "MATERIALISM COINCIDENT WITH HUMANISM"

With respect to origin, Marxist philosophy apodictically belongs to western philosophy; put into the development history of western philosophy, Marx is the terminator of early modern western philosophy and the pathfinder of modern western philosophy, and Marxist philosophy undoubtedly falls under the category of modern philosophy; the theoretical symbol is that Marx expressly proposed to "reject all metaphysics" in the mid-nineteenth century. In my opinion, the reform caused by Marxist philosophy in the history of philosophy was initiated and developed at the level of ontology, leading to fundamental finalization of metaphysics and transformation of western philosophy from traditional form into modern form.

"Metaphysics" I mention here does not mean its transferred meaning – a kind of thinking method in the sense opposite to dialectics, but its original meaning – a philosophy about the nature of transcendent being. This philosophy tries to understand and grasp the nature of things, as well as the nature and behavior of man, based on constant "ultimate being" or "prime principle". Metaphysics originated from Platonism, and became systematic in Aristotle's book *The Metaphysics*. In the opinion of Aristotle, metaphysics is the "first philosophy", i.e. the theory about the being of beings, or the theory studying objects that are super-sensuous and beyond experience. In a word, what metaphysics pursues is the ultimate being behind all the real objects; it takes such a being as the foundation – the noumenon – for specific and particular being of things and their various characteristics, and reasons out everything else on this basis. It is in this sense that Aristotle thinks that philosophy is the "supreme wisdom" among all wisdoms because it aims at "seeking the basic principle of highest reason".

During its exploration into the being of beings and the ultimate foundation of world, metaphysics set up an inference rule strictly complying with logic, that is, starting from axiom and theorem to draw an inevitable conclusion as per the inference rule. That was no doubt of positive significance, marking the generation of philosophy in theoretical form. However, from Plato, Aristotle to Hegel, the being in metaphysics was gradually separated from the real things and men and human activity, and became an abstract being and thing-in-itself, even a mysterious dominating force above mankind and the world. "The response of metaphysics is the being of logos; thus seen from its main form, metaphysics is logic, but it is a kind of logic thinking the being of beings, and therefore the logic specified in respect of the differences of difference: Being-God-Logic."[1] Here, being and beings are confused, and the being of mankind is concealed. The creativity and subjectivity of man, together with the freedom and value of man, are all dissolved in such an abstract thing-in-itself, no matter whether it is "absolute reason" or "abstract substance".

Meanwhile, metaphysics gradually evolved into a "science of sciences" over all sciences. It thought itself as having found the most universal, absolutely reliable and self-evident rational concept and principle, and thereby being able to infer all kinds of knowledge and even beings. Philosophy, in other words, was made the foundation of all sciences and knowledge. In fact, that was unfounded "extravagant expectation and requirement for the essence of philosophy", and it became a language hegemony constraining and limiting the development of science. As Engels said, "As soon as each special science is bound to make clear its position in the great totality of things and of our knowledge of things, a special science dealing with this totality is superfluous. That which still survives, independently, of all earlier philosophy is the science of thought and its laws – formal logic and dialectics. Everything else is subsumed in the positive science of nature and history."[2]

Till the mid-nineteenth century, along with the independence of natural sciences and "marking-out of their independent fields", and the prominence of the alienated living condition of man due to the development of social practice, men began to "be the center of all interest", so the metaphysics disconnected with positive science and the existence of man lost its holy aura, and "had become insipid". As time went by, metaphysics did not only "lose all credit in the domain of theory", but also "in practice"[3]. Rejecting metaphysics therefore became a trend and the spirit of times. Marx noticed that trend depending on his keen insight, and clearly proposed to "reject all metaphysics", and he also asserted metaphysics "will be defeated forever by materialism, which has now been perfected by the work of speculation itself and coincides with humanism"[4]. It was Marx who fulfilled such a task of history.

---

1   Selected Works of Martin Heidegger. Shanghai: Shanghai Joint Publishing Company, 1996: Vol. II, p. 840.
2   Selected Works of Karl Marx and Friedrich Engels. 2nd Ed., Vol. 3, p. 364.
3   Karl Marx and Friedrich Engels. 1st Chinese Ed., Vol. 2, pp. 161 – 162.
4   Ibid., pp. 159 – 160.

Early modern materialism, especially French materialism, had historically had a tendency of rejecting metaphysics from the very beginning.
Materialism in Bacon's opinion "still holds back within itself in a naive
way the germs of a many-sided development. Matter, surrounded by a
sensuous, poetic glamour, seems to attract man's whole entity by winning smiles."[5] In the eyes of Condillac, "metaphysics is not science"
but "a mere botch work of fancy and theological prejudice". However,
early modern materialism developed in a contrary way to its original
intention – changing from regarding man as the center of philosophy
and advocating the creative development of man to rendering "matter"
as the subject and becoming "misanthropy"[6]. Man, who had just emancipated from the great pressure of theocracy, became "machine" again,
and the matter separated from the real men and their activity became
"the substratum of all changes". "If it is to overcome its opponent, mis-
anthropic, fleshless spiritualism, and that on the latter's own ground,
materialism has to chastise its own flesh and turn ascetic. Thus it passes
into an intellectual entity; but thus, too, it evolves all the consistency,
regardless of consequences, characteristic of the intellect." In this way,
philosophy was transformed by early modern materialism into an all-
inclusive metaphysical system, a huge "natural system" in which men
and their existence were dissolved in the abstract nature.

This turn has made the diversion of philosophy necessary, turning to
discuss the initiative of cognitive subject, and highlight the effect of
self-consciousness. Such a "diversion" was executed and finished by
Kant and Hegel, both of whom became well-known consequently.
Hegel, moreover, built a huge all-embracing realm of metaphysics. Just
as Marx said, "Hegel linked the metaphysics of the seventeenth century
in a masterly fashion with all subsequent metaphysics and with German
idealism and founded a metaphysical universal kingdom", thereby giving metaphysics "a victorious and substantial restoration in German
philosophy, particularly in the speculative German philosophy of the
nineteenth century"[7]. Marx meant that the metaphysics of Hegel "summarized the whole development of philosophy in a grandest manner",
and fused itself together with conceptual dialectics. In this metaphysics,
the whole world is described as in a course of continuous movement,
change and development.

---

5   Ibid., p. 163.
6   Ibid., p. 164.
7   Ibid., p. 159.

Hegel, however, recognizes human initiative merely in form, and actually, it deprives man of initiative, creativity and subjectivity thoroughly for it only takes man as a tool for self-actualization of absolute reason. That is to say, in Hegelian philosophy, not only the thing-in-itself but mankind is taken as an abstract being, and the human essence does not exist in the real existence of man, but in the concept of "mankind" as an external manifestation of such concept. The subjectivity and creativity of man, as well as his freedom and dignity, are all dissolved in the speculative metaphysics, and the existence of man vanishes into the shadow of "absolute reason". If we say Platonism is the real origin of all metaphysics, then Hegelian philosophy can be thought as the enormous abyss of it. In a word, Hegelian philosophy is the epitome and summit of metaphysics. All modern western philosophy was started from critique of Hegelian philosophy. The critique on Hegelian philosophy means criticizing "all metaphysics".

In the history of philosophy, Marx and Comte raised the banner of rejecting metaphysics at the same time. Marx's rejection of metaphysics is consistent with that of Comte with respect to the times – the critique of both on metaphysics is in fact the critique on early modern western philosophy and even the entire traditional philosophy, i.e. the critique of modern spirit on early modern and ancient spirits; but the two are essentially different in the aspect of directionality. Comte criticized metaphysics in the principle of the verifiability and accuracy of natural science, tried to transform and transcend traditional philosophy with the spirit of positive science, and limited philosophy to the scope of phenomenon, knowledge and verifiability; Marx, however, criticized metaphysics from the starting point of the existence of man, and thought by the rejection of metaphysics, philosophy should transform its theoretical theme to the human world and the existence of human beings, deeply criticize the alienated living condition of man, and pay close attention to the value, freedom and emancipation of man. So for Marxist philosophy, "all the issues are for the purpose of revolutionizing the existing world" and eliminating the alienated living condition of man.

2 STARTING FROM THE EXISTENCE OF MAN AND OPENING UP THE PATH OF "COGNIZING REALITY BASED ON ONTOLOGY"

Metaphysics is closely associated with ontology in the aspect of content. Ontology as a philosophical concept was used by Goclenius in 1613 for the first time. According to its original meaning, it is a theory concerning the being itself as the initial and final foundation of all beings. Such a being is a super-sensuous object, so the two concepts – metaphysics and ontology – are always confused in the history of philosophy. As a matter of fact, ontology is the groundwork or important branch of metaphysics. As Heidegger said, "The definition 'ontology' firstly appeared in the seventeenth century, symbolizing the traditional theory about beings had become a branch of philosophy, a part of the philosophical system."[8]

The critique and finalization of metaphysics by Marx was fundamentally initiated and developed at the level of ontology. From his point of view, the primary premise for human survival is being able to live, and all social life is essentially practical; history is just the development of practical activity of man in time; practice therefore constitutes the foundation and essence of the existence of man and the real world. In this sense, Marxist philosophy is the ontology of existentialism, i.e. practical ontology. This ontology sets the existence of man itself as the noumenon embraced by philosophy. It is a dynamic noumenon in continuous evolution and generation, putting the existence into society or history.

According to Marx, man is not only a natural being but a "human natural being", namely social being. In other words, man is the unity of natural being and social being, and such unity is accomplished during practice. As Marx said, "the existence of man itself is a social activity"; practice is the mode of being of man. To be concrete about it, man performs activity and enters into relation with nature in the mode of substance during practice, and what he obtains is the existence of nature in the mode of human being; meanwhile, human beings always realize their appropriation of nature within and by dint of a definite social form. "The human aspect of nature exists only for social man", and "only then does nature exist as the foundation of his own human existence"[9].

---

8   Heidegger, The Metaphysics. Beijing: The Commercial Press, 1996: p. 41.
9   Marx, Economic and Philosophical Manuscripts of 1844. Beijing: People's Publishing House, 1979: p. 75.

That is to say, man realizes his existence through practice, and endows natural beings with a new dimension – sociality or historicity, making the relationship between man and nature a relationship that "exists for me". Thus, it is clear that Marx does not conceive and grasp the issue of beings in an abstract and sur-real manner, but interprets the significance of beings based on the existence of man, and also highlights the fundamental feature of beings: historicity. This is the starting point for correctly comprehending the ontology of all issues.

In this way, Marx does not only acknowledge the difference between beings and being, but also makes a distinction between social being and natural being, and inquires in detail the significance of beings based on the existence of man. In the words of Heidegger, he "brings being out of beings, and gives interpretation on the being itself", thereby unveiling the concealed significance of beings.

The entire age of metaphysics since Plato was called by Heidegger the "forgetting times of being". According to Heidegger, "metaphysics talks about being in a variety of modes. It shows, and seems to have confirmed, that it has inquired and answered the question about being. Actually it has never resolved this issue, because it has never made a detailed inquiry about such issue. When talking about being, metaphysics just conceives of it as beings. Although it involves being, what it refers to is all the beings. Various propositions of metaphysics always confuse beings with being from beginning to end ... Due to such a permanent confusion, the so-called statement that being is put forward by metaphysics has led us into a totally wrong situation"[10].

That "forgetting times of being" was ended by Marx undeniably, who took philosophy out of "the totally wrong situation". It is because of this that Heidegger thought that "metaphysics is Platonic. Nietzsche labels his own philosophy as the reversed Platonism; along with the reversal of metaphysics accomplished by Karl Marx, philosophy reaches its most extreme possibility and enters into its final stage"[11]. I should say Heidegger's evaluation is impartial.

Along with "the reversal of metaphysics accomplished" by Karl Marx, the theoretical theme of materialistic philosophy and even the entire

10 Heidegger, The Way Back into the Ground of Metaphysics. English Ed., p. 43.
11 Heidegger, The Matter toward Thinking. Beijing: The Commercial Press, 1996: pp. 59 – 60.

philosophy was transformed fundamentally. Engels had ever said that in the wake of the epoch-making discovery of natural science, materialism had to change its form. Actually, in the wake of the significant development of natural science and the great change in social life, materialism did not only need to change its theoretical form, but also its theoretical theme. With respect to the theoretical theme, the ancient materialism and even the entire ancient philosophy focuses on the principle of all things and the being of beings; the early modern materialism has the tendency of rejecting metaphysics, but instead of smashing metaphysics, it has finally returned to metaphysics; early modern philosophy still concentrated its attention on the noumenon of universe and the "absolute" or "abstract substance" of God; both ignored the existence of man and their development. Different from them, Marxist philosophy pays attention to "the real world of its times", the existence of man, and "the genuine resolution of the conflict between man and nature and between man and man"[12].

As far as Marx is concerned, men must carry out material practice and accomplish the material exchange between man and nature for survival and living; with the purpose of accomplishing the said material exchange, men must necessarily exchange their activities, and enter into definite social relations. In order words, the living practical activity and "actual daily life" of man always involve, and are embodied by, the relationships or contradictions respectively between man and nature and between man and man. Hence, the basic issue to be solved by Marxist philosophy as "communist materialism" is the relationships between man and nature and between man and man that are involved and revealed in the living practical activity and "actual daily life".

"The object as being for man, as the objective being of man, is at the same time the existence of man for other men, his human relation to other men, and the social behaviour of man to man."[13] In other words, behind the relationship between object and object is the relationship between man and man, as the labor product objectified by material practice, or we can say in the real world, "object" simultaneously embodies the relationship respectively between man and nature and between man and man. For Marxist philosophy, any object or nature separated from human activity and social history and unrelated to mankind means

12   Karl Marx and Friedrich Engels. 1st Chinese Ed., Vol. 42, p. 120.
13   Karl Marx and Friedrich Engels. 1st Chinese Ed., Vol. 2, p. 52.

"nothing" or "non-existent being". Marx's materialism, differing from "the abstract materialism of natural science, a materialism that excludes history and its process", discusses the material unity of world neither based on "abstract substance" nor in an abstract sur-real way, but starts from practice – the mode of being of man; through the critique on the alienated condition in the existing world, it reveals the social attribute of man concealed by the natural attribute of object and the relationship between man and man concealed by that between object and object, and realizes "reduction of the human world and relationships to man himself" by revolutionizing the existing world[14].

Thus, Marx turns the focus of philosophy from the whole world to the human world, from the noumenon of universe to the living condition of man, thereby fundamentally changing the theme of philosophy. This theme transformation of philosophy realized by Marxist philosophy marks the transition of western philosophy – from traditional to modern.

The modern western philosophy emphasizes, in general, the living world and existence of human beings. In Jaspers' words, "the objective of philosophy is striving to comprehend the reality of man in the practical situation". Marx, indeed, opened up a path of "cognizing reality based on ontology" for western philosophy. Modern western philosophy always, consciously and unconsciously, interprets the significance of beings based on the existence of man, and comprehends and grasps the relationship between man and world based on human activity. Even the "linguistic turn" achieved by analytic philosophy essentially pays attention to the mode of being of man, and reflects the seeking for the linking point between man and world. The fruits of human cognition of world are accumulated and expressed by language. Studying the significance of world in the sense of language is actually to understand and grasp the world based on the relationship with man. Wittgenstein comprehended language and significance from the viewpoint of life style at his late age, and revealed the publicity and practical attribute of language, which is similar to or consistent with Marxist philosophy. Besides, the speech act theory of Searle et al. concretely analyzes the function of "illocutionary act" of language, unconsciously offering Marxist philosophy with the demonstration and proof of linguistic philosophy.

---

14   Karl Marx and Friedrich Engels. 1st Chinese Ed., Vol. 1, p. 443.

Of course, the analytic philosophy goes too far after all, where language becomes an independent realm. It seemed that Marx had foreseen such a "linguistic turn", because he pointed out that "just as philosophers have given thought an independent existence, they were bound to make language into an independent realm."[15] As far as I'm concerned, the analytic philosophy, in effect, boosts the study on the mode of being of man and the relationship between man and world in a "regressive" way.

I notice that metaphysics has not disappeared yet in modern western philosophy. If we say the dialectics of Hegel is a tragic "restoration" of metaphysics in early modern times, then the phenomenology of Husserl can be regarded as a glorious rejuvenation of metaphysics in modern times. The problem lays in the fact that modern western philosophy, which opened up a new road of existentialism after experiencing the movement of phenomenology, re-realized the great originality of Marx in respects of his rejection of metaphysics and directionality. Through studying the relationship between being and beings, Heidegger realized that "being was always the 'Sein' in Dasein", and the significance of beings can only be shown by "Dasein" as the existence of man. Thus, he was aware of "the reversal of metaphysics accomplished by Karl Marx", as well as the profoundness, advancement and great superiority of such a reversal, and he also asserted, "Marx went deep into the dimension of the essence of history while realizing alienation. That's why the viewpoint of Marxism on history is superior to those of other historical theories. However, Husserl failed to find out the essence of historical things from being, so did Sartre, in my opinion; therefore both phenomenology and existentialism do not arrive at such a dimension, but only in such a dimension can they be possibly qualified to talk with Marxism."[16] In front of Marxist philosophy, Sartre did not only realize that the penetrating critique of Marx on modern society provided important theoretical basis for existentialism, but meanwhile was aware of some deficiency of existentialism itself, so he suggested "attaching" existentialism to Marxism, and declared that "Marxist philosophy is the sole unsurpassable philosophy of our times".

From my point of view, the reason why Marxist philosophy is unsurpassable is basically because the "situation" generating Marxist philosophy has not yet been surpassed, that is to say, issues focused by

15   Karl Marx and Friedrich Engels. 1st Chinese Ed., Vol. 3, p. 525.
16   Selected Works of Martin Heidegger. Shanghai: Shanghai Joint Publishing Company, 1996: Vol. I, p. 383.

modern western philosophy have not stepped out of the problem domain of Marxist philosophy, or out of the horizon of Marxist philosophy, and modern western philosophy is still speaking in the words of
Marxist philosophy. Even though postmodernism strongly advocates
"rewriting modernity", its essence is still paying attention to the alienated living condition of man, and the so-called "end of man" of postmodernism is actually the critique on the alienated condition caused by
capitalist system. To put it in the words of Jameson, "the real historical
nightmare is the alienated labor", and we should "draw" it, such an
unbearable fact, away.[17]

After deconstructing the priority and transcendence of man, postmodernism declares that mankind is a "creative being", and tries hard to
eliminate the opposition between man and nature set by "modernity"
and rebuild the relationship between man and world. "Capitalism is one
of the descriptions of modernity."[18] So, during the survey and reflection on modernity and the relationship between man and world, the
critique of Marx on capitalist society and its alienated condition naturally appears in the context of post-modernistic ideologists. Jameson
thinks Marxist philosophy "is a cognitive mode for us today to restore
our relationship with being". And Foucault points out that Marx reveals
a "brand-new discursive practice" "on the basis of political economy",
and "at present, it is impossible for anyone to write history without applying a series of thoughts directly or indirectly connecting with Marx's
thought and putting himself into the thought horizon defined and described by Marx"[19].

The profoundness, advancement and great superiority of Marxist philosophy make it impossible for any other school of modern western
philosophy to avoid and turn a blind eye to it. According to my understanding, other schools of modern western philosophy all view human
activity based on a certain aspect, link or relation, and reduce the human world to such an aspect, link or relation, thus failing to grasp the
existence of man and the relationship between man and world generally and fundamentally; Marxist philosophy, on the contrary, grasps the

---

17 M. Foucault, The Order of Things, An Archaeology of the Human Sciences, New
York, Pantheon Books,1970, p. 21.
18 Lyotard, Post-modernity and Fair Game. Shanghai: Shanghai People's Publishing
House, 1997: p. 147.
19 M. Foucault, The Order of Things, An Archaeology of the Human Sciences, New
York, Pantheon Books, 1970, p. 21.

foundation for the mode of being of man and the relationship between man and world – practice, and radiates this foundation to all the aspects, links and relations in the human world, thus forming a holistic thinking and constituting the motive source of modern western philosophy, including postmodernism. As Jameson has said, other schools of modern western philosophy are merely coincident with "this or that local law of a fragmented social life", whereas Marxist philosophy provides a "holistic vision of society"; it "assigns" other schools of modern western philosophy "an undoubted sectoral validity within itself", "and thus at once canceling and preserving them", thereby being "the untranscendable semantic horizon"[20].

In respect of content but not manifestation mode, the operation of modern western philosophy takes, generally rather than individually, the theme transformation realized by Marxist philosophy as fundamental direction. Marx is, indeed, the pathfinder and founder of modern western philosophy. As modern materialism, Marxist philosophy is not only the interlocutor of creativity in modern western philosophy, but also the vitally important participant and powerful booster in the evolution process of modern western philosophy.

3 CONCLUSION: THE HORIZON TRANSCENDING EARLY MODERN MATERIALISM

In the conclusion part of this chapter, I would like to make a brief comment on the traditional textbook system of Marxist philosophy and its relationship with Marxist philosophy, instead of summarizing my discussion above. This is useful for us to conceive the fundamental characteristics of Marxist philosophy and the fundamental drawbacks of its traditional textbook system.

The traditional textbook system of Marxist philosophy I mention here refers to the Soviet model of Marxist philosophy. With respect to time, such a system was formed in the 1930s; and with regard to content, it took shape in the Second Section "Dialectical and Historical Materialism", Chapter Four of *Soviet Union Communist Party (Bolshevik) Party Concise Guide*. After the

---

20   F. Jameson, Marxism and Historicism, New Literary History, Vol. XI, No. 1, Autumn, 1979, p. 42.

Soviet Union Communist Party (Bolshevik) Party Concise Guide was regarded as the highest authority, "dialectical materialism and historical materialism", the Soviet model of Marxist philosophy formed under that particular historical condition, became the sole or legitimate form of Marxist philosophy, and thus the traditional textbook system of Marxist philosophy was formed. Stalin's *Dialectical and Historical Materialism* and F. V. Konstantinov's *Fundementals of the Philosophy of Marxism-Leninism* uniformly fall under the Soviet model of Marxist philosophy; although the latter deepens the former partially, its overall framework and fundamental feature do not go beyond those of the former; on the contrary, it actually takes the former as the chief source. It is a unified Soviet model of Marxist philosophy.

I do not deny that the traditional textbook system of Marxist philosophy reflects and deepens some viewpoints of Marxist philosophy, but this system or model, generally and fundamentally, does not reflect the real spirit of Marxist philosophy; contrarily, it distorts Marxist philosophy to a large extent. To be specific, in the Soviet model of Marxist philosophy, dialectical materialism becomes a kind of method and theory which study and interpret nature respectively, and historical materialism is just the extension and application of dialectical materialism – a kind of view of nature – to the domain of social history.[21] In this so-called dialectical materialism, nature is separated from human activity and abstracted from history; it is actually "a thing given direct from all eternity, remaining ever the same" mentioned by Marx during his critique on Feuerbach. After such separation and abstraction, a kind of "abstract substance" becomes the cornerstone of the Soviet model of Marxist philosophy, and the ontology based on nature is formed.

On this basis, the Soviet model of Marxist philosophy carries out a series logical deduction from nature to society: "if the connection between the phenomena of nature and their interdependence

---

21   See Soviet Union Communist Party (Bolshevik) Party Concise Guide. Beijing: People's Publishing House, 1975: p. 116.

are laws of the development of nature, it follows, too, that the connection and interdependence of the phenomena of social life are laws of the development of society, and not something accidental"; "if our knowledge of the laws of development of nature is authentic knowledge, having the validity of objective truth, it follows that social life, the development of society, is also knowable, and that the data of science regarding the laws of development of society are authentic data having the validity of objective truths"[22], and so on. In other words, in the traditional textbook system of Marxist philosophy, from dialectical materialism to historical materialism, it is in fact a logic process from natural being to social being.

In this way, the logical direction of Marxist philosophy, i.e. from social being to natural being, is reversed, and the ontological significance of practice – the mode of being of man – and human subjectivity are concealed. This is an involution to the early modern materialism, which takes "abstract substance" as noumenon, a horrendous theoretical retrogression. It indicates that the Soviet model of Marxist philosophy actually interprets Marxist philosophy with the logic of early modern materialism, and it, basically speaking, belongs to "abstract materialism", or "the abstract materialism of natural science, a materialism that excludes history and its process", mentioned by Marx.

I agree and appreciate this point of view: when the traditional textbook system of Marxist philosophy talks glibly about "the materiality of world" while being separated from human activity and social life, it has stealthily gone "in the abstract materialistic direction, or rather idealism" criticized by Marx[23]. Marx rejects all metaphysics, but the Soviet model of Marxist philosophy itself becomes a kind of metaphysics. To really comprehend and grasp Marxist philosophy, we must go beyond the horizons of early modern materialism, early modern philosophy and even the entire traditional philosophy.

22   See Soviet Union Communist Party (Bolshevik) Party Concise Guide, p. 127.
23   Yu Wujin, Being, Natural Being and Social Being, carried in Chinese Social Sciences, 2001 (2).

There is an interesting phenomenon frequently happening in history – a viewpoint or even the whole philosophical theory of a great philosopher always tends to show its intrinsic value and catch the attention of people again after the philosopher's death and a relatively long historical movement, so is the historical destiny of Marx's thought of rejecting metaphysics and his ontology of existentialism, which were put forward and established in the mid-nineteenth century, but did not arouse people's understanding and concern at that time and during a relatively long historical period thereafter. For this reason, when constructing the textbook system of Marxist philosophy, the descendants precisely ignored such thought and ontology of Marx, and exactly abandoned the method for interpreting the significance of beings based on the existence of man, thus resulting in the inherent defect. This is the fundamental defect, rejecting the epoch-making contribution of Marxist philosophy to a quite large extent.

The historical movement and the development of practice, science and modern western philosophy itself in the twentieth century highlight Marx's thought of rejecting metaphysics, his ontology of existentialism, and the intrinsic value of the method for interpreting the significance of beings based on the existence of man, and reveal the modernity and contemporary significance of Marxist philosophy to people again. It can be predicted that constructing a new textbook system of Marxist philosophy that coincides with the "text" of Marxist philosophy by interpreting the significance of beings based on the existence of man and comprehending and grasping the relationship between man and world on the basis of practice will gain "overwhelming popularity" soon, and become an important topic of Marxists again. This makes me think of two famous lines of verses in Faust:

What dazzles, for the moment spends its spirit;

What's genuine, shall posterity inherit.

CHAPTER III

POSTMODERN CONNOTATION OF MARXIST PHILOSOPHY

In the history of philosophy, there are some ideological systems that are formed in certain times but not exclusive to such times, and they contrarily have the cross-era symptom. Marxist philosophy exactly belongs to such few but constantly charming systems. It is impossible for a philosophy that only adapts to a certain era to look far ahead. "Marx could not remain so politically and theoretically central to the later twentieth century, if he had not at times been out of synchrony with the later nineteenth century in which he lived."[1] That is quite true. Marx lived in industrial society, but he had made "accurate" prediction on some important features of "postindustrial society"[2]; Marxist philosophy falls under modern materialism, but it also catches the "postmodern" clue exuded by "modern" relying on its keen insight, and makes critique and review over it; as a result, postmodernism getting prosperous in

---

1 Perry Anderson, *Considerations on Western Marxism*. Beijing: People's Publishing House, 1981: p. 141.
2 Daniel Bell, *The Coming of Postindustrial Society*. Beijing: The Commercial Press, 1984: p. 66.

the later twentieth century cannot neglect and ignore Marxist philosophy generated in the later nineteenth century. Marxist philosophy, for postmodernism, is the necessary ideological bridge from modernity to post-modernity, because it is "the untranscendable semantic horizon"[3]. We are unable to discuss the relation between Marxist philosophy and postmodernism in generalities, nevertheless the meeting of the two in contemporary era is an indisputable fact. Marxist philosophy certainly does not belong to postmodernism, and I flatly disagree with the so-called "postmodern Marxism". However, I believe at the same time that Marxist philosophy has the postmodern connotation, and to discuss the contemporary development of Marxist philosophy, its postmodern connotation must be thoroughly elucidated.

1 MARXIST PHILOSOPHY IN THE POSTMODERN CONTEXT

Since the 1950s, a series of new noticeable phenomena have emerged in western society and its cultural field, and they cannot be interpreted or covered by either traditional theories or modern concepts. Thus, Hassan thinks that these phenomena different from "modernities" can be named as "post-modernities", and points out that "postmodernism is a response of modernism to the unimaginable things that it has glanced at directly or indirectly at its prophetic moment"[4]. In other words, postmodernism is the survey and reflection on modern, modernity and modernism. In the eyes of post-modernistic ideologists, "capitalism is one of the descriptions of modernity"[5]. Hence, during the survey and reflection on modern, modernity and modernism, the critique of Marx on capitalist society naturally appears in the postmodern context. The theoretical pioneer of postmodernism Heidegger, as well as core figures of postmodernism, such as Derrida, Foucault, Lyotard, Rorty and Jameson, attach sufficient importance to Marxist philosophy. So we can grasp Marxist philosophy in the postmodern context.

Postmodernism has upheld the banner of rejecting "all metaphysics" since its generation. We can say that rejecting "metaphysics" is the consensus of post-modernistic ideologists.

---

3   F. Jameson, *Marxism and Historicism, New Literary History*, Vol. XI, No. 1, Autumn, 1979, p. 42.
4   Ihab Hassan, *The Postmodern Turn*. The Ohio State University Press, 1987: p. 39.
5   Lyotard, Post-modernity and Fair Game, p. 147.

Heidegger noticed Marx's efforts in rejecting "metaphysics", and believed Marx accomplished "the finalization of metaphysics": "Metaphysics is Platonic. Nietzsche labels his own philosophy as the reversed Platonism; along with the reversal of metaphysics accomplished by Karl Marx, philosophy reaches its most extreme possibility and enters into its final stage"[6]. In the *Letter on Humanism,* he also thought that Marx had gone deep into the dimension of the essence of history while realizing alienation, so Marxist conception of history is superior to other conceptions of history.

Derrida points out, "If there is a spirit of Marxism which I will never be ready to renounce, it is not only the critical idea or the questioning stance ... It is even more a certain emancipator and messianic affirmation, a certain experience of the promise that one can try to liberate from any dogmatism and even from any metaphysico-religious determination, from any messianic."[7] In Derrida's view, there will be no future without Marx, without "the memory and the inheritance" of Marx.

According to Foucault, three basic sources dominating the critical ideologies of France and even the contemporary times are Nietzsche, Freud and Marx. These three masters play a fundamental "de-centering" role respectively, and jointly open up the path of contemporary hermeneutics. What Marx interprets, from Foucault's point of view, is the interpretation of the bourgeoisie on production, but not the production itself; Marx's *Das Kapital* in fact negates the generally so-called "deep meaning" or "truth" through revealing the essence of the bourgeois values, i.e. the cover-up for ordinary values. Foucault "believes the historical analysis of Marx", and thinks the historical analysis of Marx is not "set up based on any eighteenth-century model", but reveals a "brand-new discursive practice" "on the basis of political economy"; "at present, it is impossible for anyone to write history without applying a series of thoughts directly or indirectly connecting with Marx's thought and putting himself into the thought horizon defined and described by Marx"[8].

---

6 Heidegger, *The Matter toward Thinking*, pp. 59 – 60.
7 *The Future cannot Exist without Marx*, carried in *The Orient*, 1996 (6): pp. 69 – 73.
8 M. Foucault, *The Order of Things, An Archaeology of the Human Sciences*, New York, Pantheon Books, 1970, p. 21.

In the eyes of Lyotard, Capitalism, as one of the descriptions of modernity, has become a "symbol of metaphysics"; "Marx has intensive views on this, especially in *The Communist Manifesto*"[9]; Marxist philosophy, by means of dialectics, has changed into the discourse used to interpret infinite contradiction movement, and the problem precisely lies in the fact that "now it is dialectical logic itself ... that is becoming a pure style language"[10].

Rorty holds dual attitude to Marxist philosophy: on the one hand, he puts Marx into the same category of Nietzsche and Heidegger, and thinks Marx is a civilizing-type philosopher and Marxist philosophy falls under enlightenment philosophy, namely post-philosophical culture, which stands for practice priority and always persists in the consciousness of historicism, and whose purpose is to continuously make dialogues between man and nature, between man and man and between man and text; on the other hand, he also considers that although advocating practice priority, Marx still keeps such two faiths as attempting to reach deep into the reality behind phenomena, and seeking for theoretical foundation for politics. Obviously, Rorty is stressing that there is a gap between the method and the theoretical system of Marxist philosophy.

Jameson commits himself to the contemporary explanation of Marxist philosophy, and believes that Marx has established an "appropriate stance" long ago for us to treat postmodernism; Marxist philosophy is by no means the "concise outdated holistic discourse underlining the unique importance of productivity"; instead, it is a grander and profounder study method, "a cognitive mode for us today to restore our relationship with being". In Jameson's opinion, Marxist philosophy provides a "holistic vision of society", which "subsumes such apparently antagonistic or incommensurable critical operations, assigning them an undoubted sectoral validity within itself, and thus at once canceling and preserving them"; "the authority of other methods springs from their faithful consonance with this or that local law of a fragmented social life, this or that subsystem of a complex and mushrooming cultural superstructure."[11] For this reason, it is impossible for any contemporary critical theory to avoid and turn a blind eye to Marxist philosophy, which, for the contemporary critical theories, is "the untranscendable horizon".

9   Lyotard, *Post-modernity and Fair Game*, p. 148.
10   Jean François Lyotard, Peregrinations, Columbia Press, 1988, p. 50.
11   F. Jameson, *The Political Unconscious*. Cornell University Press, 1981: p. 10.

It can be seen that the expositions of post-modernistic ideologists on Marxist philosophy involve the relationship respectively between Marxist philosophy and "metaphysics" and between Marxist philosophy and contemporary western philosophy, including postmodernism. Although the post-modernistic ideologists have different understandings on Marxist philosophy, and accept or reject different parts of it, the rejection of "metaphysics", the ontological significance of practice, and the contemporary meaning of Marxist philosophy, which had been neglected, restrained and even forgotten, are shown in the postmodern context in general.

The relationship between Marxist philosophy and "metaphysics" is in direct connection with the theme of Marxist philosophy and the relation of Marxist philosophy with the western philosophical tradition since Plato. The prevalent view in the western thought circle is that Marxist philosophy itself is a kind of "metaphysics", which follows the theme of philosophy since Plato, that is, aiming to trace the essence or essentials of the whole world, and trying to understand and grasp the nature of things, as well as the essence and behavior basis of man, based on "ultimate being" or "prime principle". But post-modernistic ideologists stress that Marxist philosophy really "reverses Platonism", and "accomplishes the finalization of metaphysics". This view highlights Marxist philosophy's nature of rejecting "metaphysics", and coincides with the "text" of Marxist philosophy.

"Throughout the history of philosophy, Platonic thoughts always play a crucial role in variable forms. Metaphysics is Platonic"[12], and Marxist philosophy criticizes Platonism and rejects "metaphysics" from the very beginning. According to Marx, Platonism is fundamentally characterized by "the deep pursuit for a higher essence", and during the process of "pursuit", Platonism develops "this abstract determination of the good, of the purpose, into a comprehensive, world-embracing philosophy"[13]; such worship of abstract universality inevitably leads to mysticism, thereby creating theoretical precondition for later Christianity. In this connection, Nietzsche, a theoretical pioneer of postmodernism, happens to hold the same view with Marx, thinking Platonism, which regards the good as the supreme belief, is "antecedent to Christianity but full of the flavor of Christianity".

---

12   Heidegger, *The Matter toward Thinking*, p. 59.
13   *Karl Marx and Friedrich Engels*. Beijing: People's Publishing House, 1982: 1st Chinese Ed., Vol. 40, p. 69.

"Metaphysics is Platonic", so the critique on Platonism certainly impels Marx to criticize the whole "metaphysics". In *The Holy Family*, Marx criticizes "metaphysics" both theoretically and practically, and thinks "the whole wealth of metaphysics consisted only of beings of thought and heavenly things, at the very time when real beings and earthly things began to be the center of all interest"[14] in the wake of the development of science and practice. The fundamental drawback of metaphysics as a philosophical morphology, from Marx's point of view, is that what it focuses on is the universe noumenon or "ultimate being" separated from mankind and their activity; in this philosophy, not only the "thing-in-itself" but "mankind" is taken as an abstract being, and both human beings and human world disappear. Hence, it is needed to "negate existing philosophy" and "abolish philosophy itself"[15], that is, "to finalize metaphysics", and to make philosophy pay attention to "the real world of its times" and "the human world". Marx had asserted that metaphysics "will be defeated forever by materialism, which has now been perfected by the work of speculation itself and coincides with humanism"[16].

It was Marx who fulfilled such a mission. The premise of Marx's materialism is recognizing the "priority" of nature, but what it focuses on is not the abstract thing-in-itself or any abstract substance, let alone the material unity of the world discussed abstractly in the Scholastic way, but is the reveal of the social attribute of man, as well as the relationship between man and man, covered by the natural attribute of object and the relationship between object and object through the critique on the alienated condition of capitalist society and the ubiquitous "fetishism", thereby realizing the "reduction of the human world and relationships to man himself".

That is to say, Marxist philosophy rejects "metaphysics", and realizes the theme transformation of philosophy, i.e. from the universe to human world, emphasizing "revolutionizing the existing world". In the words of post-modernistic ideologists, Marxist philosophy is not for occupying "all truths", but for pursuing truths infinitely, and not "constructed for generation after generation", but "deconstructed for their own times". With Marx, "philosophy entered into its final stage".

---

14   *Karl Marx and Friedrich Engels.* 1st Chinese Ed., Vol. 2, pp. 161 – 162.
15   *Selected Works of Karl Marx and Friedrich Engels.* 2nd Ed., Vol. 1, p. 8.
16   *Karl Marx and Friedrich Engels.* 1st Chinese Ed., Vol. 2, pp. 159 – 160.

In the "traditional" genealogy of Marxist philosophy, the category of practice is only considered as the epistemological category, and beyond epistemology, even the category of practice is mentioned, it is just a kind of social enthusiasm. But the post-modernistic ideologists lay stress on the ontological significance of practice, and hold the opinion that the emphasis of Marx on the practical essence of social life aims to break through the epistemological genealogy of western philosophy, and then conceive social being based on human activity. We should say that this opinion is penetrating and enlightening in that practice really has the ontological significance in Marxist philosophy.

According to Marx, practice is the original activity in which beings and the existence of man are generated and transformed mutually; after coming into the world, man enters into the combination of beings, and endows beings with a new dimension – sociality, thereby giving beings the nature of "existing for me"; men "set the mind for Heaven and Earth" by means of their practical activity, and rebuild the world on the basis of material practice activities; therefore, practice constitutes the foundation and base for the existence of existing world. So, the existence of man is the result and product of man's practical activity. As said by Marx, "the existence of men is their actual life-process"[17]. In Marxist philosophy, the authority of practice is all-around, which does not only exist in epistemology, but can also be found in the view of nature and the conception of history: with respect to the view of nature, practice, as the groundwork for the differentiation and unity between nature itself and humanized nature, sublates the binary opposition between man and nature; while in respect of the conception of history, practice constitutes the essence of society and the mode of being of man as the cornerstone for the unity between "natural history" and "historical nature", and shatters the myth of the opposition between "material nature" and "spiritual history".

It is because of the ontological significance of practice that Marx investigates and conceives the human world, and surveys, evaluates, and changes the category and norms of previous philosophy based on practice. Practice is the real sun around which Marxist philosophy revolves; therefore, only by importing "practice" as main melody into the grand symphony of Marxist philosophy can Marxist philosophy be played in a wonderfully harmonious manner.

---

17 *Selected Works of Karl Marx and Friedrich Engels.* 2nd Ed., Vol. 1, p. 72.

The relationship between Marxist philosophy and "metaphysics" meanwhile implies the relationship between Marxist philosophy and contemporary Western philosophy, including postmodernism. While confirming the nature of "rejection of metaphysics" of Marxist philosophy, the
post-modernistic ideologists will do notice the contemporary significance of Marxist philosophy.

This is really true. "Post-modernity", i.e. some important features of
contemporary society, is foreseen by Marxist philosophy in its critique
on the negative effects of modernization, because the relationship between it and contemporary Western philosophy, including postmodernism, is not as incompatible as ice and hot coals. Meanwhile, other
schools of contemporary Western philosophy all view the human world
based on a certain aspect, link or relation, and reduce the world to such
an aspect, link or relation, thus failing to grasp the human world generally and fundamentally; Marxist philosophy, on the contrary, grasps the
foundation of human world – practice, and radiates this foundation to
all the aspects, links and relations in the human world, thus forming an
"untranscendable" holistic thinking and constituting the motive source
of modern western philosophy, including postmodernism. In the words
of post-modernistic ideologists, other schools of contemporary Western
philosophy are merely coincident with "this or that local law of a fragmented social life", whereas Marxist philosophy provides a "holistic
vision of society"; it "assigns" other schools of contemporary western
philosophy "an undoubted sectoral validity within itself", "and thus at
once canceling and preserving them", thereby constituting "the untranscendable semantic horizon" in the contemporary era. We can suggest
a deeper understanding on this important proposition of Jameson than
Jameson himself in that we have grasped the substantive characteristic
of Marxist philosophy – practical materialism.

Of course, I also notice that there are still half-veiled criticisms of post-
modernistic ideologists on Marxist philosophy mainly in two following
aspects: (1) Marxist philosophy contains strong skeptical and critical
spirits, but it can also be embedded into the "entity" constructed by
Communists, and integrated into a unified theoretical system as an ideological basis and action program of some politics; thus, it is turned into
"meta-narrative" unavoidably, and accordingly, it can hardly escape the
fate of conservativeness and closure; (2) Marxist philosophy advocates
the primacy of practice, and emphasizes the realistic feature of man

and the diversity of life; however, its theory about class struggle and humanity emancipation still belongs to "grand narrative", thus resulting in the bigotry and repression of real socialist movement respectively towards unified whole and heterogeneous elements; though Marx provides a cognition framework for investigating the structure of capitalist society, he is excessively infatuated with and dependent on the "structure" as a kind of cognition paradigm, and consequently dabbles little in the basic plights of human survival like crime, disease, loneliness and death, and so on.

Obviously, the post-modernistic ideologists appreciate the nondeterministic, non-central and non-fundamental side of Marxist philosophy, and criticize its deterministic, central and fundamental side.

For us, the major significance of the praise or censure of post-modernistic ideologists on Marxist philosophy, no matter whether it is impartial or biased, is that a new understanding of Marxist philosophy is presented. The post-modernistic ideologists deconstruct both the Soviet model of Marxist philosophy and the western interpretation system of Marxist philosophy, and face the "text" of Marxist philosophy again, thereby "awakening" the elements in Marxist philosophy which had been neglected, restrained and even forgotten for a long term; the post-modern discourse advocates heterogeneity and marginality, so Marxist philosophy conceived by the post-modernistic ideologists, i.e. Marxist philosophy in the postmodern context, is also helpful for us to rediscover and grasp the Marxist philosophy beyond the "traditional" genealogy of Marxist philosophy, and thereby impels us to rethink Marx's expositions regarding to the relationships between freedom and necessity, between man and nature and between the East and the West, in order to grasp the contemporary value of Marxist philosophy.

It's worth noting that Marxist philosophy in the postmodern context is presented in a scattered and alienated way, and the post-modernistic ideologists tends to stress its methods rather than conclusions, value its train of thought rather than system, and think highly of some fragments rather than the whole. More importantly, the stress of some post-modernistic ideologists on some elements of Marxist philosophy aims to deconstruct Marxist philosophy as a whole, so as to make it take on internal antagonism and self-effacement. The post-modernistic ideologists implicitly and explicitly have such a view, that is, when Marxist philosophy is developed into a critical political idea, the criticalness of its original philosophical ideas is seriously suppressed, thereby being impossible to be reflected from beginning to end. As a result, the text of Marxist philosophy is made fragmented in the postmodern context, no longer having the consistent unified meaning.

2 "POST-MODERNITY" IN THE HORIZON OF MARXIST PHILOSOPHY

The core proposition throughout the twentieth century, in short, was "post-modernity", namely how to "rewrite modernity". The philosophies about universal reason and historical progress since the Enlightenment were smashed by two world wars and their consequences, and the contemporary technological revolution and its results casted doubts upon modernity itself. From then on, modernity became a question rather than a certain answer. The so-called post-modernity and postmodernism is the "rethinking", reinterpretation and re-understanding on modern, modernity and modernism. According to Hassan, there is not an impassable "iron barrier" or "great wall" between post-modernity and modernity, because "history is like a palimpsest on which the old can be erased and the new can be recorded, while culture is permeated with the past, the present, and the future"[18].

That is to say, postmodernism derives from modernism and is the reinterpretation on modernism, and there is no essential difference between the two. In Lyotard's opinion, "post-modernity" manages to express those that cannot be represented by "modernity", transforming the "intangible" into the "tangible", so "post-modernity is always implied in modernity", or "post-modernity" is a part of "modernity". Lyotard thus believes, "From such understanding, postmodernism is not the desperate modernism but the fresh status of modernism, and such a status is repeated."[19] In other words, post-modernity does not refer to a new era, and instead, it is the "rewriting" of modernity. More importantly, the work to "rewrite modernity" has been carried out for a long time within modernity itself.

It's indeed true. "Rewriting of modernity" had become a kind of emotion and appeal throughout the modernization movement. What the contemporary western ideologists, such as Marx, Nietzsche and Freud,

---

18   Ihab Hassan, *The Postmodern Turn. See Postmodern Culture and Aesthetics*, compiled by Wang Yuechuan and Shang Shui. Beijing: Peking University Press, 1992: p. 113.
19   Lyotard, *Post-modernity and Fair Game*, p. 138.

have done is to "rewrite modernity" conscientiously and unconscientiously, so to say. The movement of "modern" as a concept of historical periodization, seen from the angle of history, was initiated in the seventeenth century. The "grand narrative" about theory, freedom and progress established by modernity was synchronized with the Industrial Revolution, technological revolution and social revolution sweeping the West. Although modernity or modernization cannot be equated with capitalism, it's for sure that the modernization movement started in the Industrial Revolution was launched by the bourgeoisie, and the concept of "modern" representing historical periodization and the historical course of capitalism were in a mutually promoting relationship; therefore "capitalism is one of the descriptions of modernity". It is for this reason that the critique by Marx on capitalism simultaneously includes his critique on the negative effects of modernity or modernization, or we can say that it is the "rewriting of modernity". In this sense, Marxist philosophy can be considered as having the postmodern connotation.

Of course I have noticed there is not the concept of "post-modernity" in Marxist philosophy; however, it connotes a "post-capitalist theory". As mentioned before, capitalism is one of the descriptions of modernity, so there is both difference and relation between "post-capitalism" and "postmodernism". To summarize, "post-capitalism" puts particular emphasis on the thinking about social politics and economy, predicting the possibility and prospect of social revolution, while "postmodernism" lays stress on the thinking about the statuses of culture, idea and knowledge, implying the goal and possibility of transformation. Through the elucidation by western Marxists on the cultural theory or meaning of Marxist philosophy, "post-capitalism" and "postmodernism" shows a subtle relationship – the two repel but mix with each other, and parallel to but intersect with each other at the same time.

Postmodernism, basically, is a kind of cultural reflection of the forthcoming "postindustrial society". Daniel Bell is the first person who connects Marx with "post-modernity". In his famous book *The Coming of Post-Industrial Society*, Bell considers that Marx had "accurately" foreseen some important features of "postindustrial society". This is a profound opinion. In our eyes, there is no lack of the postmodern thoughts in Marxist philosophy, though without the concept of "post-modernity". It is demonstrated by the history of human thoughts that there is both connection and difference between concept and thought or theory; the two may be consistent with each other, but are frequently in contradictory relationship; when a thought or theory has been brought forward, the concept summarizing this thought or theory often cannot be correctly expressed, which is a common phenomenon in the history of thought, especially the history of Marxism. For example, Marx set up the theory of historical materialism in 1846, but it was not until 1890 that Engels summarized the theory and put forward the concept of "historical materialism".

According to postmodernism, "post-modernity" is a skeptical and critical attitude to "meta-narrative". The "meta-narrative" refers to the Hegelian thought tradition – "purely speculative and theoretical narrative" – and the thought tradition of French Enlightenment – "freedom and emancipation narrative"; the former lays emphasis on the thinking model of identity value, while the latter focuses on the thinking model of humanistic independence; the two are joint up to serve the institutionalized scientific researches and defend for the occupation of "all truths" and the pursuit of eternal justice. However, the result of defense unexpectedly constitutes a perfect irony against the original intention of "meta-narrative": reason is exaggerated extremely, but individual man is dissolved; science advances rapidly, but the humanistic world tends to rigidity and suffocation.

From the theoretical perspective, Marxist philosophy has committed itself to the critique on the Hegelian thought tradition and the thought tradition of French Enlightenment since the beginning of its establishment. A section in Engels' *Socialism: Utopian and Scientific* reflects the consensus of him and Marx on these two thought traditions, "The great men, who in France prepared men's minds for the coming revolution, were themselves extreme revolutionists. They recognized no external authority of any kind whatever ... everything must justify its existence before the judgment-seat of reason or give up existence. Reason became the sole measure of everything. It was the time when, as Hegel says, the world stood upon its head; first in the sense that the human head, and the principles arrived at by its thought, claimed to be the basis of all human action and association." "We know today that this kingdom of reason was nothing more than the idealized kingdom of the bourgeoisie ... the government of reason, the Contract Social of Rousseau, came into being, and only could come into being, as a democratic bourgeois republic."[20] During the process of "critique on Hegelian dialectics and the entire philosophy" and "critique on French materialism", Marx paid attention to how natural science and the science of man became "a science" respectively, and tended to "personalized individual". In the aspect of the doubt and critique on "metanarrative", Marxist philosophy is similar to postmodernism, and has the directionality of "post-modernity".

Both Marxist philosophy and postmodernism are concerned with the critique on the negative effects of modernity and modernization. If we say postmodernism represents "the logic of constant capitalist revolution", and highlights the crises in the constant revolution, i.e. "narrative crisis, representation crisis and legitimacy crisis", then Marxist philosophy had revealed "the logic of constant capitalist revolution" as early as at the early stage of capitalism, and stated the economic, cultural and social crises confronting the bourgeois epoch with high foreseeability: "constant revolutionization of production, uninterrupted disturbance of all social conditions, everlasting uncertainty and agitation distinguish the bourgeois epoch from all earlier ones. All fixed, fast-frozen relations, with their train of ancient and venerable prejudices and opinions, are swept away, all new-formed ones become antiquated before they can ossify. All that is solid melts into air; all that is holy is profaned." [21] Thus, Lyotard believes that Marx has "intensive views" on "modernity" and "post-modernity". Upon the inspiration from Marx, some post-modernistic ideologists started to study the effects of aforesaid revolutions, for instance, Bell's attack on the propagation of the "cultural profaneness phenomenon", Bourdieu's analysis on the developed mechanism of "the field of cultural production", Giddens' perspective into the modern "knowledge uncertainty" and its consequences, etc. It was in that process that postmodernism immediately faced the crises in front of contemporary capitalism, and astonishingly exclaimed against the "dissolution of center", "collapse of foundation", "fall of reason" and "end of man". With respect to the discussion about "the logic of constant capitalist revolution" and its crisis consciousness, Marxist philosophy is similar to postmodernism, and has the directionality of "post-modernity".

---

20 *Selected Works of Karl Marx and Friedrich Engels*. 2nd Ed., Vol. 3, pp. 719 – 720.
21 *Selected Works of Karl Marx and Friedrich Engels*. 2nd Ed., Vol. 1, p. 275.

The crisis consciousness is closely related to questioning consciousness and critical consciousness. Marxist philosophy and postmodernism both have the feature of "the theory of questioning". The opinion
that "what is actual is what is reasonable" is by no means the thinking
mode of Marxist philosophy. When talking about the relationship between the spirit of times and philosophy, Marx emphasized that "question was the slogan", and thought that question was more significant
than answer: "the fate which a question of times has in common with
every question justified by its content, and therefore rational, is that
the question and not the answer constitutes the main difficulty."[22] It
was based on that questioning consciousness that Marx insisted on "not
anticipat[ing] the world with their dogmas but instead attempt[ing] to
discover the new world through the critique of the old"[23]. Marxist philosophy, to put it another way, takes the problems existing in "modern
society" as its focus, which is the essence of its emphasis on "critique".
Postmodernism also shows a strong questioning consciousness. As a
matter of fact, postmodernism in the West firstly existed as a subject
or question, whose focus was the problems of modernity itself; it does
not intend to "tell" truth to men but instead to eliminate the "obstacles"
on the way to truth, in a bid to "remove" and "get rid of" the "false appearance" and "dense fog" that cover modernism. This is the secret of
postmodernism's emphasis on "deconstruction".

From the times of Marx to the times of Frankfurt School, existentialism and structuralism, and to postmodernism, the critique on modernity
went through a process from the critique on social politics and economy
to cultural and ideological critique, and then to the critique on language.
Such evolution, from the angle of scientific principle, is the constantly
refining, deepening and elaborating process of critique, revealing the
difficulty and complexity of social critique, and also showing the transition logic and realistic meaning of such critique. In handling modernity,
Marxist philosophy is similar to postmodernism, and its "critique" has
the directionality of post-modernistic "deconstruction".

It is beyond doubt that Marx had sufficiently estimated the positive
effects of modernity. He called the new era opened up by the bourgeoisie since the seventeenth century the "modern society" different
from the traditional society, the "modern mechanical industrial age"
different from the period of manufacture, and the times of "personal

---

22 *Karl Marx and Friedrich Engels*. 1st Chinese Ed., Vol. 40, p. 289.
23 *Karl Marx and Friedrich Engels*. 1st Chinese Ed., Vol. 1, p. 416.

independence founded on objective dependence" different from the times featured by personal dependence. *The Communist Manifesto* gives more sufficient evaluation on the positive effects of modern bourgeois society in history than the bourgeois ideologists. However, Marx paid more attention to the "problems" of modernity rather than its achievements. From *Economic and Philosophical Manuscripts of 1844* during the establishing period of the materialistic conception of history to the creating times of *Das Kapital*, the alienated condition in modern society was always one of the focuses of Marx's theoretical activity. The analysis and critique on such alienated condition fully and centrally reflects the postmodern directionality of Marxist philosophy's critique, whose characteristic rests with that it does not seek to "conceive" the operating law of capitalism "within" capitalism itself, but to grasp and disclose its disease "outside" it. In the words of Lyotard, Marx "pursued to show where the symbols of capitalism destruct itself"[24].

To really understand the critique of Marx on the "problems" of modernity and its postmodern directionality, we need to reread the classic discussion of Marx about "the realm of freedom and the realm of necessity". For the convenience of writing, it is necessary to quote that classic well-known paragraph in detail:

"In fact, the realm of freedom actually begins only where labor which is determined by necessity and mundane considerations ceases; thus in the very nature of things it lies beyond the sphere of actual material production. Just as the savage must wrestle with Nature to satisfy his wants, to maintain and reproduce life, so must civilized man, and he must do so in all social formations and under all possible modes of production. With his development this realm of physical necessity expands as a result of his wants; but, at the same time, the forces of production which satisfy these wants also increase. Freedom in this field can only consist in socialized man, the associated producers, rationally regulating their interchange with Nature, bringing it under their common control, instead of being ruled by it as by the blind forces of Nature; and achieving this with the least expenditure of energy and under conditions most favorable to, and worthy of, their human nature. But it nonetheless still remains a realm of necessity. Beyond it begins that development of human energy which is an end in itself, the true realm of freedom, which, however, can blossom forth only with this realm of necessity as its basis."[25]

---

24   Lyotard, *Post-modernity and Fair Game*, p. 148.
25   *Karl Marx and Friedrich Engels.* Beijing: People's Publishing House, 1974: 1st Chinese Ed., Vol. 25, pp. 926 – 927.

This paragraph is superficially the most touching example for the extension of Marxist philosophy's horizon into future, but actually, it is a typical instance for the postmodern connotation of Marxist philosophy. Here, Marx pushes the positive effects of modernity to its limit, and therefore makes its limitations prominent. As far as Marx is concerned, what modernity creates for human beings is merely limited freedom, whose highest achievement is the achievement of socialized man, namely the associated producers, rationally regulating their interchange with nature; such rationality is demonstrated by "achieving this with the least expenditure of energy and under conditions most favorable to, and worthy of, their human nature", but that's all, because it is not the "development of human energy which is an end in itself". So Marx stresses that this sphere "still remains a realm of necessity". That is to say, the logic of modernity is the logic to acquire limited freedom in the realm of necessity, and although having to take it as basis, the all-around free development of man or "personalized individual" is "beyond" it, rather than readily connoted within modernity.

The realm of freedom "beyond" it can certainly be conceived as the communist society in the future; communism, however, does not mean a future thought that reality should adapt to it, but real movement, a critical element used to confront the negative effects of modernity. This unintentionally reminds us of a famous remark of Lyotard, "'Postmodern' would have to be understood according to the paradox of the future (post) anterior (modo)." "The realm of freedom" in effect only shows the critical dimension of Marxist philosophy's horizon. The realm of freedom in Marx's opinion is not the substitute for the realm of necessity on account of the fact that "labor which is determined by mundane considerations" will exist "in all social formations" and "under all possible modes of production". Here, the orientation of Marx's thinking is obviously featured by "critique" and "the theory of questioning". In the post-modernistic words, "the realm of freedom", aiming to "deconstruct" the realm of necessity, is not Utopia in the future, but the critical element resorting to eternal historical process and preventing the rational logic of the realm of necessity from controlling everything.

Marxist philosophy is similar to postmodernism in that Marxist philosophy has the postmodern connotation; however, the "post-modernity" in the horizon of Marxist philosophy greatly differs from that in the context of postmodernism. Concretely speaking, postmodernism covers the

entire social life with intellectual life, or ponders over contemporary society only based on intellectual condition; its "post-modernity" aims at
deconstructing the intellectual condition, and even concentrates the deconstruction on language; furthermore, while applying itself to dispel-
ling the transcendental binary opposition respectively between essence
and phenomenon, between necessity and contingency, and between
center and margin, postmodernism in fact has specific objective and
purport, that is, laying particular stress on the nondeterministic, non-
central and non-fundamental side, thus contributing to the effect and
impact that essence is dispelled by phenomenon, necessity replaced by
contingency, and center segmented by margin; besides, what it affirms
is just the meaning and value of segmented, superficial and uncertain
living mode. As a result, "post-modernity", relative to "modernity", has
walked toward another extreme.

The error and deficiency of postmodernism exactly shows the superiority of Marxist philosophy's postmodern discourse. As far as I'm
concerned, postmodernism perceives the "disease" of western society
but makes a wrong "prescription"; on the contrary, Marxist philosophy
does not only reveal the predicament of western society, but points a
way out of such predicament. The postmodern discourse in the framework of Marxist philosophy, in my opinion, can be summarized as the
follows: (1) taking the idea of modernity running through the whole
modernization course as study object, and the principle of practice as
study method, to go deep into economic critique from the representation
of alienation; (2) against the study background of binary oppositions
between determinacy and nondeterminacy, between center and margin,
between the East and the West, and between history and discourse, aiming at rebuilding "individual ownership" and establishing "personalized
individual"; (3) hammering at preventing extreme swing of objectivism
or objectivism, and creatively thinking and answering the fundamental
question on how human beings can survive in the "post-capitalist" and
"post-metaphysical" times. The "post-modernity" in the framework of
Marxist philosophy represents both a kind of intellectual attitude which
queries and deconstructs the myth of modernity and a kind of historical sphere which is the basis for our times to exist, and establishes the
"personalized individual".

3 THE MEETING OF MARXIST PHILOSOPHY AND POSTMODERNISM IN CONTEMPORARY ERA

As mentioned previously, the meeting of Marxist philosophy and post-modernism in contemporary era is an indisputable fact. After we have discussed Marxist philosophy in the postmodern context and "post-modernity" in the horizon of Marxist philosophy, it is very necessary to sufficiently realize and focus on such meeting, investigate its realistic background, grasp its theoretical origin, and thereby deepen the study on Marxist philosophy.

Seen from the background of real life, the meeting of Marxist philosophy and postmodernism in contemporary era is derived from such a fact that both are for the purpose of criticizing capitalist society.

Criticalness is the basic spirit of Marxist philosophy, which has declared at the beginning of its establishment to ruthlessly criticize everything that exists, and the critique is directed against capitalist society. No matter what the critique is about, "critique on Hegel's dialectics and entire philosophy", "critique on philosophical forms after Hegel", "critique on French materialism" or "critique on political economy", it is the disclosure, analysis and critique on capitalist society and its alienated condition in the final analysis. In the post-modernistic words, it is for the purpose of "deconstructing" capitalist society. Other Marxist philosophies after Marx also stick to and carry out such a critique all along, i.e. devoting themselves to the critique on the continuously expanded and deepened alienated condition in capitalist society during its development. Even with respect to the controversial western Marxism, all of its theoretical work is the application, development and deepening to a certain extent of the alienation theory of Marx. From the critique by Lukacs on capitalist "materialization" at the early stage to the "social critical theory" of Frankfurt School, and then to "new Marxism" of France in recent years, we can say that they are quite keen and incisive exposure and critique of capitalist society and its alienated condition from different sides during different periods. The tenet of western Marxism, in its entirety, is to criticize capitalism rather than safeguard it.

The critique by postmodernism on the negative effects of modernity is based on the critique on the alienated condition in capitalist society as well. In general, postmodernism is for the purpose of "deconstructing" modernity, and in the eyes of post-modernistic ideologists, capitalism coincides with modernity to a certain degree, therefore the "deconstruction" of modernity by postmodernism is linked with the critique on capitalism. Derrida points out, "Deconstruction is not, and should not be, merely the analysis on discourse, philosophical statement or concept and semantics; instead, it must challenge system, social and political structures, as well as most stubborn traditions."[26] Foucault says frankly, "What I am concerned is the peculiar relationship of knowledge, academics and theory with real history."[27] His discussions about the relationships between knowledge and power and between prison and power are all aimed at reveal the oppression mechanism of capitalism. Baudrillard thinks that the development of capitalist mode of production from the nineteenth century to the twentieth century is a process during which the "complete operation over social representation" is achieved; hence, he transits from Marx's commodity conversion theory to the issue of "symbol conversion", and couches critique on capitalism in the domain of "symbol economy" and on the basis of political economic critique of Marx. Jameson explicitly defines postmodernism as "the cultural logic of late capitalism", and believes "ultimate form of 'nightmare of history' is rather the fact of labor itself, the mately scandalous fact of the alienated work and of the irremediable loss and waste of human energies, a scandal to which no metaphysical categories can give a meaning"[28]; therefore, the scandalous fact of alienated labor should be "diverted away". These demonstrate that postmodernism is neither rootless duckweed nor "mutters" of some ideologists, and instead, with specific real background and practical source, it is critically directed against the politics and economy of capitalist society, especially its cultural and intellectual conditions. "Post-modernity is thoroughly anti-originalism – absolutism evading all noumenon, cognition or ethics. Meanwhile, it firmly shows the radical attitude to reform existing western social order."[29]

---

26 Derrida, *Thought is Guarded by a Craziness*. Shanghai: Shanghai People's Publishing House, 1997: p. 21.
27 Foucault, *The Eyes of Power*. Shanghai: Shanghai People's Publishing House, 1997: p. 12.
28 F. Jameson, *Marxism and Historicism*, New Literary History, Vol. XI, No. 1, Autumn, 1979, p. 42.
29 John Mcgowan, *Postmodernism and Its Critics*, Ethaca, Cornell University Press, 1991, p. 9.

It is because both Marxist philosophy and postmodernism are concerned with the critique on capitalism, its alienated condition in particular, that Marxist philosophy precisely foresees some important features
of "post-modernity" and post-modernistic ideologists spontaneously
think of Marxist philosophy during their critique. The two "meet" in
contemporary era, which is not a myth, but an objective fact.

We should pay attention to giving scientific analysis and evaluation on
the "hostility" of postmodernism toward modern capitalism in general.
While touching upon the relationship between material production and
spiritual production, Marx pointed out that the relationship between
the two was not directly corresponding, "as simple as originally conceived – capitalist production is hostile to certain branches of spiritual
production, for example, art and poetry"[30]. This opinion is extremely
profound, which unveils the "hostile" relationship of literature, art and
even the entire spiritual production with the material production mode
of capitalism. The technological alienation and social alienation generated by capitalist system in the twentieth century, compared with the
situation in the nineteenth century, turn more "hostile" to the development of entire spiritual production. Just because of this, uncovering and
criticizing the modern alienation of capitalism becomes one of the major contemporary ideological and cultural topics in the West. An anti-
alienation theme runs through *The Waste Land* of Eliot, *La Nausée* of
Sartre, "non-rationalism turn" of philosophy, and "deconstruction" of
postmodernism, all of which fight the modern alienation of capitalism
in an extreme mode. Since Nietzsche, the modern alienation of capitalism and its "modern conditions of whole life" have become the "target
of critique" by contemporary western philosophy, including postmodernism. Such critique is from the inside of capitalism, so it is more
powerful and better hits home than the critique from the outside.

Certainly, the critiques of Marxist philosophy and postmodernism on
capitalism evidently differ from each other as regards focus and strategy. Marxist philosophy focuses on the critique on the macro condition of capitalism, so it usually appears as a kind of "grand narrative",
whereas postmodernism focuses on the analysis on micro-fields of capitalism, therefore being keen on "little narrative"; Marx focuses on the
critique on the economic base and social system of capitalism, aiming

---

30   *Karl Marx and Friedrich Engels.* Beijing: People's Publishing House, 1972: 1st
Chinese Ed., Vol. 26 I, p. 296.

to radically overthrow the capitalist system, whilst postmodernism majorly expresses critique on the mainstream ideology of capitalism, but hardly involves the economic base, especially the relationship of ownership, based on which the said mainstream ideology is bred, so it is a kind of critique under the premise of not touching the fundamental system of capitalism. Such difference leads Marxists to accuse the "little narrative" critique by postmodernism of inaction on capitalism and innocuousness for capitalist system; the post-modernistic ideologists, however, criticize that the "grand narrative" critique by Marxism on capitalism is still subject to the overall logic of capitalism in the final analysis. We cannot ignore the obvious difference between Marxist philosophy and postmodernism, but cannot deny such a fact either – both are concerned with the critique on capitalism in reality; that's why the two can meet each other by chance in contemporary era.

To grasp the meeting of Marxist philosophy and postmodernism, theoretically, we should take notice of the theory about the relationship between man and nature and between the East and the West, respectively.

Firstly, about the relationship between man and nature

In contemporary times, the occurrence of "global issues" makes men gradually realize that social alienation is not only manifested by the alienation of relationships between man and man and between man and society, but also by the alienation of relationship between man and nature, and these alienations are fundamentally linked with the idea of "rational man" since modern times in the West. There are many common points in Marxist philosophy and postmodernism in treating with "rational man" and the relationship between man and nature.

Western philosophy has established the priority of rationality since Descartes put forward the opinion that "Cogito, ergo sum (I think, therefore I am)". Marxist philosophy does not admit that mankind inherently possesses a general nature of rationality any longer, and believes there is no so-called "inner 'dumb' generality which unites many individuals only in a natural way". From Marx's point of view, practice is the mode of being of man and the substantive characteristic of life activity; the characteristics of man is gradually generated during social practice, and the human essence, in its reality, is the ensemble of the social relations; as individuals express their life, so they are. For this reason, the relationship between man and world is firstly practical, rather than epistemological. Marx had presented such a thought earlier than Heidegger: the substantive characteristic of man is that he is "the existence in the world"; man does not watch the world outside through his lonely self-window, and he has been in the world before he gets to know it.

Corresponding to this, Marxist philosophy also pays great attention to the relationship between man and nature, and thinks that nature itself is converted by human race into humanized nature through practice, translating "thing-in-itself" into "thing-for-me"; in this process, the "revenge" of nature upon human race emerges – "if man, by dint of his knowledge and inventive genius, has subdued the forces of nature, the latter avenge themselves upon him by subjecting him, in so far as he employs them, to a veritable despotism independent of all social organization."[31]. Being the first to bring forward the issues of "the genuine resolution of the conflict between man and nature" and "rational regulation of man's interchange with Nature" in the western history of thoughts, Marxist philosophy emphasizes that "the writing of history must always set out from these natural bases and their modification in the course of history through the action of men"[32], and thinks that nature should be transformed based on the dual correlation between inherent and extrinsic measures of man, making nature a real "anthropological nature". It should be mentioned that the proposal of this mission itself is deeply insightful and advanced, and besides, Marxist philosophy also points out the only way to accomplish it, which undoubtedly demonstrates contemporary significance of Marxist philosophy.

The post-modernistic conclusion of the "end of man" also requires men to rethink the issues of subjectivity and relationship between man and nature, aiming at the idea of "rational man" since Descartes. According to the viewpoints of postmodernism, the soul or spirit of ego cogito has been separated from and become opposite to the external material world since the Enlightenment, leading to "anthropocentrism", which does not only cause contemporary western cultural crisis, but also contemporary global ecological problems. As a result, postmodernism attempts to give a new position of man. In the words of Foucault, postmodernistic ideologists "undertake the mission to build a relationship between man and his sciences, discoveries and the world – a concrete

---

31 *Selected Works of Karl Marx and Friedrich Engels.* 2nd Ed., Vol. 3, p. 225.
32 *Selected Works of Karl Marx and Friedrich Engels.* 2nd Ed., Vol. 1, p. 67.

world"[33]. Postmodernism deconstructs the priority, centrality and transcendence of man, and clearly declares that mankind is a "creative being" and self-image of man is "the image to create but not to discover". In the eyes of Griffin, "an individual is not a self-sufficient entity born with various attributes. He just, by virtue of these attributes, interacts apparently with other things that do not affect his essence. On the contrary, the relationships between individual and ego and between him and vast nature, family, culture, etc. are all the constituents of individual identity"[34]. This means that man in essence is the product of self-creation and self-shaping during his own activity, and for man, the relationships between individual and other persons and objects aren't extrinsic, but inherent, essential and constitutional.

Postmodernism, correspondingly, also pays great attention to the relationship between man and nature. In the "postmodern society" or "postmodern times" within the horizon of postmodernism, "'nature' is gone for good; it is a more fully human world than the older one, but one in which 'culture' has become a veritable 'second nature'"[35]. So, postmodernism does not only strive for "negation" and "destruction", but in fact, it is very concerned about the rebuilding of the relationship between man and nature, and strongly advocates eliminating the opposition between man and nature resulting from "modernity". Starting from this, postmodernism praises highly "ecologism" and "the green movement", and pursues to "provide philosophical and ideological basis for the everlasting view advocated by ecological movement". Hence, it is not hard for us to understand the well-known saying of Griffin that "postmodern thought is thoroughly ecological".

The so-called "end of man" of postmodernism is actually the critique on the alienated man caused by capitalist system. It requires men to take a new look at the ego of man and reestablish a harmonious relationship between man and nature. It is because of this that postmodernism agrees Heidegger's conclusion that "man is the guardian of nature". In my eyes, this conclusion is consistent with Marx's thought about the harmony between man and nature.

---

33 *On the Three Morphologies of Postmodernism, carried in Social Sciences Abroad,* 1995 (1): p. 43.
34 *Spirituality and Society, Postmodern Visions,* David Griffin, ed. State University of New York Press, 1988, p. 14.
35 F. Jameson, *Postmodernism, or The Cultural Logic of Late Capitalism.* Duke University Press, 1991: p. 9.

Secondly, about the relationship between the East and the West

Throughout the twentieth century, the core problem confronting unde-veloped countries and regions is that modernity is an inevitable ori-entation of history. However, does modernity equal to westernization? In other words, is the universal historical discourse based on "western centralism" reasonable? With respect to this question, Marxist philoso-phy and postmodernism happen to have some same views.

The birthplace of Marxist philosophy is Europe, but Marx is by no means "eurocentric". At the beginning of the establishment of the ma-terialistic conception of history, the foothold of Marx was undoubtedly western society; however, as the deepening of research and the elapse of time, Marx turned his sight to the eastern society, and set up his unique oriental society theory. He deconstructed "western centralism" in the process of analyzing the western society, studying "world his-tory", and discussing the structure and historical destiny of the eastern society. During his study on the eastern society, Marx, to be specific, was opposed to applying the evolution model of western society me-chanically to the eastern society, because he believed that the feudal system of western meaning wasn't prevalent in the eastern society. For example, "Kovalevsky forgets about serfdom, which does not exist in India, and it is a basic factor"[36]. This in fact deconstructs the universal-ity of the feudal system in Western Europe. This is the first point.

Second, Marx clearly limited the historical necessity of capitalist primi-tive accumulation to the countries in Western Europe, and objected to "metamorphosing his historical sketch of the genesis of capitalism in Western Europe into a historico-philosophic theory of the *marche gen-erale* (general path)"[37], thereby deconstructing the universality of the genesis of capitalism in Western Europe.

Third, when discussing the development path of Russia's society, Marx put forward the assumption of striding across the "Crafting Gorge" of capitalism, and this assumption actually deconstructs the universal-ity of Western European capitalism, and completely embodies the de-construction of "western centralism" by Marxist philosophy. Thanks to

36 *Karl Marx and Friedrich Engels*. Beijing: People's Publishing House, 1985: 1st Chinese Ed., Vol. 45, p. 284.
37 *Karl Marx and Friedrich Engels*. Beijing: People's Publishing House, 1963: 1st Chinese Ed., Vol. 19, p. 130.

Copernicus, we know that the earth is not the center of universe, and owing to Marx, we know that the West is not the center of world. It was in the process of criticizing the bourgeois "Orientalism" and deconstructing "western centralism" that Marx revealed western economic and political hegemonies, in the opinion that the western society dominated economic and political outputs and, by virtue of war and economic and political contacts, "made barbarian and semi-barbarian countries dependent on the civilized ones, nations of peasants on nations of bourgeois, the East on the West"[38]. In the eyes of Marx, if colonies and the entire eastern society want to get real development, they have to "absorb all the positive achievements of capitalism", and meanwhile transcend capitalism.

The deconstruction of "western centralism" by Marx and his oriental social theory exert long-standing influence in contemporary era. The post-colonialism generated against the background of postmodernism also gives attention to the relationship between the East and the West. At the beginning of Said's *Orientalism*, one famous remark of Marx is quoted – "they cannot represent themselves, they must be represented", so as to describe the relationship between the East and the West in history. In the opinion of post-colonialism, accompanying with the economic invasion and political expansion of western capitalism into the eastern society, there is a synchronous process during which every aspect in the whole world is contextualized and symbolized at the level of culture; it also is the process of the formation of western "culture hegemony" or "cultural imperialism", and post-colonialism aims to "demystify" and "decode" it. Starting from the critique on western "Orientalism", Said devoted himself to overturning the legitimacy of western "culture hegemony", and redefining the relationship between oriental culture and western culture. Jameson thinks that the first world controls the dominant right of culture output and coercively instills its values and ideology, which are encoded into a whole culture machine by means of culture and media, into the Third World, and this is in effect a kind of cultural invasion. Thus, Jameson is greatly concerned with the destiny of the Third World, and seeks to find out a new moment for human cultural development in the binary opposition between oriental culture and western culture in the postmodern atmosphere.

It is thus clear that Marxist philosophy and postmodernism are similar to each other and indeed have common views in respect of the relationship between the East and the West. Certainly the two stress different aspects: Marxist philosophy focuses on the elimination of western

---

38 *Selected Works of Karl Marx and Friedrich Engels*. 2nd Ed., Vol. 1, p. 277.

economic and political hegemonies, while postmodernism pays attention to the "decoding" of western culture hegemony; Marxist philosophy is concerned with how colonies get decolonized through practical
actions, whereas postmodernism stresses the significance of language
to "ideological decolonization", and "indulges itself in discourse, caring nothing about those effective social, economic and political systems
and other social practical forms"[39].

The meeting of Marxist philosophy and postmodernism in contemporary era shows the postmodern connotation of Marxist philosophy,
and at the same time urges me to further ponder over how to develop
Marxist philosophy. "Stone from other hills could be taken as the jade."
The expositions of post-modernistic ideologists on Marxist philosophy
inspire me to discover many elements in Marxist philosophy that have
been shelved, suppressed and even forgotten, and dissociated from
the "traditional" genealogy of Marxist philosophy for a long time. As
Foucault has said, "the comments on the theory of surplus value, as vast
as the open sea, make lots of very important materials of Marx almost
neglected by people completely."[40]

Above all, these suppressed and even completely neglected thoughts
or "heterogeneous elements" often coincide with contemporary social
issues, and show the advancement and "shocking sense of space" of
Marxist philosophy. As a result, to develop Marxist philosophy in contemporary era, we must "reread Marx from the perspective of space",
focus on the "heterogeneous elements" within it, seize its theoretical
growth point in contemporary era, and make those shelved, suppressed
and even forgotten thoughts prominent, in a bid to study them inten-
sively and systematically and give them more adequate meaning. After
deconstructing "the theory of the end of history" of Fukuyama, Derrida
underlines that to understand various conflicts in the world at present,
we "must rely on a traditional questioning mode of Marxism for a long
term", i.e. "an open constantly transformed questioning mode". This
reflects the postmodern connotation or contemporary significance of
Marxist philosophy to the full, reminding me of two famous verses of
Yu Shinan, a poet in the Tang Dynasty:

High perching, far your voice would strew,
To which the autumn wind aids nil.

---

39   Benita Parry, *Problems in Current Theories of Colonial Discourse*. The Oxford
Literary, Review, No. 9, 1997: p. 43.
40   Foucault, *The Eyes of Power*, p. 212.

CHAPTER IV

THE SIGNIFICANCE OF WORLD OUTLOOK OF PRACTICE: A NEW INTERPRETATION OF MARXIST WORLD OUTLOOK

Marxist philosophy, the same as all materialisms, acknowledges the materiality of world and the "priority" of nature; however, different from the old materialism, Marxist philosophy conceives "thing, reality and sensuousness" and grasps the relationship between man and world based on practice not only objectively but also "subjectively". As the mode of being of man, practice in essence is a kind of object activity. It is not only the groundwork to differentiate and unite objective world and subjective world, but also the bridge to differentiate and unite the world-in-itself and the human world; practice does not only transform the world, but also create the world. Therefore, practice has the significance of world outlook. Only after deeply comprehending the essence and effect of practice can we really understand the essence and characteristics of Marxist world outlook.

1 PRACTICE: THE MODE OF BEING OF MAN

Though practice had entered the horizon of philosophers in ancient times, issues concerning its connotation, essence and effect were not really conceived by either materialism or idealism prior to the emergence of Marxist philosophy. In the ancient Chinese philosophy, practice is considered as "doing", a category corresponding to "knowing", which mainly refers to epistemic and moral behavior and practice. The relationship between "knowing" and "doing" had been discussed by Confucius in *The Analects of Confucius* from the angle of philosophy, and he proposed to "judge a person not only by his words, but also by his actions". "Doing" here has the meaning of practice. From the perspective of materialism, Xun-tse did not only parallel "doing" with "knowing", but put forward the viewpoint that "doing" overtops "knowing". He believed, "Not hearing is not as good as hearing, hearing is not as good as seeing, seeing is not as good as mentally knowing, and mentally knowing is not as good as acting; true learning continues up to the point that action comes forth." Wang Shouren, on the basis of idealism, brought forward the theory of "the unity of knowing and doing", thinking that "if we seek after principle beyond mind, knowing and doing are two things; but if we seek after principle in our mind, knowing and doing will be united". However, in the philosophy of Wang Shouren, "doing" is just an "idea", and he had ever said, "My purpose of putting forward the unity of knowing and doing today is to let people know that once they are thinking, they are doing".

In the ancient western philosophy, Socrates had presented the concept of "the practice of philosophy". Aristotle differentiated theoretical activity from practical activity, and thought that practice was the activity including target. But according to Aristotle, practice majorly meant ethical and political behaviors. In the European history of philosophy, Kant, who formally introduced "practice" into philosophy, proposed two concepts, namely "theoretical reason" and "practical reason", and believed that practical reason had the capability or function to act, that is, it governed the moral activity of men by means of normalizing their will, thereby setting them free. Practice in the philosophy of Kant is not beyond the sphere of ethical practice, and is merely a kind of good moral activity reaching freedom under the governance of good will.

In Hegelian philosophy, practice generally refers to "action", "activity of will" and "human activity". As far as Hegel is concerned, "the true being of man is his act"[1], and it is through work that men transform nature, "cultivate things", and establish a "negative relationship" with objects, "making the world what it should be"; meanwhile, human beings separate themselves from nature, and perceive their independence and achieve self-consciousness through the products of labor. The main contribution of Hegel rests with the fact that he conceives practice as labor, and raises labor to the level of philosophy. However, practice and labor in the opinion of Hegel are fundamentally abstract activity of idea, and the real activity of man is just a limited "pattern" of such abstract activity. Negative dialectics of Hegel only gives an "abstract, logical, speculative expression" to the real human activity. This shows that idealistic philosophy does not understand practical-critical activity and its significance, thus abstractly developing the initiative of man.

Feuerbach linked practice with life in the belief that practice was capable of solving the difficulties that cannot be solved by theory. However, he had not really understood the relationship between practice and life, and instead, he simply regarded theoretical activity as the real human activity, but considered practical activity as a kind of behavior of the Jews for private gain; what's more, he merely saw man as "object of the senses", but not "activity of the senses", and did not realize that practice was the real foundation for sensuous world. Similar to natural materialism, humanistic materialism of Feuerbach also conceives "thing, reality and sensuousness" only in the form of the object, and does not understand practical-critical activity and its significance, either. Thus, old materialism has no choice but to "sigh its inadequacy in the face of" the initiative of man.

Marx summarizes the practical spirit of times of modern industry, criticizes and transforms the reasonable factors in labor theory within classical German philosophy and classical British economics, scientifically resolves the inner contradictions of practical activity, i.e. the contradictions between initiative and materiality and between naturality and sociality, and gives scientific specification to the connotation of practice.

---

1   Hegel, *The Phenomenology of Mind.* Beijing: The Commercial Press, 1979: Vol. I, p. 213.

"Men must be in a position to live in order to be able to 'make history'. But life involves before everything else eating and drinking, a habitation, clothing and many other things. The first historical act is thus the production of the means to satisfy these needs, the production of material life itself."[2] Marx is the first person in the history of philosophy who considers the activities in material production as the primary and fundamental form of practice, and raises practice to the level of the mode of being of man for comprehension. In his opinion, the activities in material production constitute the foundation for existence and development of human society, so they are the activities determining all other human activities.

Practice is the purposive creative activity of man with initiative. The initiative of practice indicates that practice is not the activity of animal negatively accommodating to nature, but the activity purposively transforming nature. It is in this process that nature itself is converted into humanized nature, and "thing-in-itself" into "thing-for-us". During practical activity, human beings do not only change the existing forms of natural objects, but inject their purpose into the natural objects, thus creating things that are impossible to generate by the movement of nature itself and then creating the world of human beings. In other words, practice does not only transform the world, but also create the world. However, the initiative of practice cannot be separated from materiality, and cognizing, grasping and exploiting the laws of material motion is invariably the precondition for bringing the initiative of practice into play; the expression of the initiative of practice cannot be realized without material instruments, and it does not create material itself. Practice is the unity of initiative and materiality.

Practice is social activity whose object, scope and mode are all restricted by social relations. It is not only the process of material exchange between man and nature, but also the process of activity exchange between man and man. In this process, men do not only establish a definite relationship with nature, but also enter into definite social relations with each other. "In order to produce, human beings enter into definite connections and relations to one another, and only within these social connections and relations does their influence upon nature operate – i.e., does production take place."[3] Men always carry out practical activity

---

2   *Selected Works of Karl Marx and Friedrich Engels*. 2nd Ed., Vol. 1, p. 79.
3   Ibid., p. 344.

in definite social relations, which are constrained by specific historical conditions all the time. In case such social relations are not adapted to the demand of practical activity, men will be bound to regulate or change the said social relations so as to adapt them to the demand of practical activity, for the purpose of conducting new practical activity in new social relations under new historical conditions. Thus, practice is endowed with historicity. So, practice is the unity of naturality and sociality.

Practice is objective activity, meaning that practice is real-life activity with mankind as subject and objective things as object; more importantly, it means that practice can objectify the essential powers of man, such as goal, knowledge and capability, into objective reality, and create a human world of objects. Practice, as the objective activity, enables human beings to externalize and materialize their own essential powers, condense them into object, and endow them with the form of objective reality. At the same time, human beings cognize and confirm their essential powers through such externalized and materialized object. As Marx said, "The product of labor is labor which has been embodied in an object, which has become material: it is the objectification of labor. Labor's realization is its objectification."[4] "The history of industry and the established objective existence of industry are the open book of man's essential powers."[5]

Being an objective activity and an activity dynamically transforming the world, practice constitutes the mode of being of man. "The whole character of a species, its species-character, is contained in the character of its life activity"[6]. That is to say, the mode of being and substantive characteristics of a species is judged from the form of its life activity. Animals subsist depending on their instinctive negative adaption to nature, so the mode of being of animals is their instinctive activity. Differing from them, men keep their survival during their purposive and positive transformation of nature; therefore practice constitutes the mode of being of man.

First of all, practice remolds and develops the natural attribute of man. The natural attribute of man means the physical and biological desire and need of man. There is no doubt that the labor of men is "conditioned

---

4   *Karl Marx and Friedrich Engels.* 1st Chinese Ed., Vol. 42, p. 91.

5   Ibid., p. 127.

6   ibid., p. 96.

by their physical organization". The problem is that labor, i.e. practice, since the very beginning, has become a powerful impetus that controls the direction of human biological evolution. "The satisfaction of the first need (the action of satisfying, and the instrument of satisfaction which has been acquired) leads to new needs"[7]. Practice results in qualitative changes in the object, content and satisfaction mode of man's natural needs, compared with those of animals, and gives them human social and historical properties, thereby remolding and developing the specific natural attribute of man and making man "an active natural being".

In the second place, practice generates and develops the social attribute of man. "The production of life, both of one's own in labor and of fresh life in procreation, now appears as a double relationship: on the one hand as a natural, on the other as a social relationship"[8]. The social relationship generated during practice in turn restricts and specifies human essence, which, in its reality, is the ensemble of the social relations, and real social relations are established during practical activity. In other words, men "create, produce, the human community, the social entity" during practical activity, thereby making themselves "social beings".

Thirdly, practice generates and develops the spiritual attribute of man. The life activity of man is "conscious activity", which distinguishes man immediately from animal life activity, making man "a conscious species-being". The point is that the consciousness of man is generated, realized and confirmed during practice; thus, language also "is practical consciousness that exists also for other men, and for that reason alone it really exists for me personally as well"[9]. That is to say, it is practice that makes the life activity of man conscious and man "a conscious species-being".

Hence, it can be seen that the natural, social and spiritual attributes of man are all remolded, generated, developed and united during practical activity. So, Marx points out that "what they [men] are, therefore, coincides with their production, both with what they produce and with how they produce. The nature of individuals thus depends on the material conditions determining their production."[10] In sum, practice constitutes the mode of being of man; therefore it is the foundation for the living of man.

---

7 *Selected Works of Karl Marx and Friedrich Engels.* 2nd Ed., Vol. 1, p. 79.

8 ibid., p. 80.

9 *Selected Works of Karl Marx and Friedrich Engels.* 2nd Ed., Vol. 1, p. 81.

10 ibid., p. 68.

2 SUBJECT AND OBJECT OF PRACTICE AND THE RELATIONSHIP BETWEEN THEM

During practical activity, human beings change those beings beyond themselves into the object of their activity, and therefore make themselves the being with subjectivity. These two categories, subject and object, can be highlighted when we investigate the relationship between man and world from the perspective of objective activity. In other words, subject and object belong to philosophical categories that show the specific relationship between actor and active object.

The subject of practice is neither the natural being in biological sense understood by old materialism nor the pure transcendental self-consciousness argued by idealism, but an organic unity composed of multiple factors like material and spirit, emotion and will, nature and society, etc.

Seen from the ability structure of subject, "the intrinsic natural forces of man" form material basis. It is with the help of such material force that man can realize material exchange with nature. However, the material force of man is under the domination of spirit. So, knowledge vs. experience and emotion vs. will constitute the spiritual factor in the subject's ability structure. During practical activity, knowledge and experience play a leading role in giving scope to the ability of subject; meanwhile, emotion and will can get the best from the subject, making him indomitable and able to "overcome all the difficulties in the way" and thereby achieving the purposes of practice. It is in this sense that Marx thinks that "passion is the essential power of man energetically bent on its object"[11].

From the angle of the social structure of subject, there are four forms of subject, namely individual subject, collective subject, social subject and human subject. The precondition for the existence of society is indubitably "the existence of living human individuals". Individuals have their own relatively-independent scopes and forms of practice. In this sense, individual is independent subject, i.e. individual subject. Men who conduct practical activity in the form of a certain collective, team or group compose a collective subject. In class society, class is the main existence form of collective subject. When there has been no violent

---

11   *Karl Marx and Friedrich Engels.* 1st Chinese Ed., Vol. 42, p. 169.

external conflict arising out of the internal confrontation in a certain society, this society is probably engaged in some practical activities as a whole to a certain extent, thereby forming a social subject. Different nations and countries that carry out practical activity as a species whole constitute human subject. However, for natural and social reasons, human subject merely in a definite sense has so far been formed by human beings as a common subject in some aspects under specific conditions. And only when classes and countries wither away in the future can conscious human subject be really formed.

The object of practice means the objective things that enter the activity field of subject and are aimed at or transformed by the activity of subject. Objective things are objective before becoming the object, and their objectivity still survives when they enter into the relational structure of subject and object, but object, as the target aimed at or transformed by practical activity, does not equal objective things. Whether an objective thing can become the object depends on not only its self-nature but also whether the practical level of human beings can aim at or transform it and whether it has obtained human nature and "humanized" form.

Along with the development of practice, object brought into the activity scope of subject is always in a constantly changing state. In general, object is classified into three forms – natural object, social object and spiritual object. Natural object covers both natural objects related to human activity and artificial natural objects transformed or produced by man in some way. Social object refers to social structures in reality, such as economic system, political system, etc., and also includes social relations embodied by objects. Spiritual object refers to the results produced by spirit existing in the form of objects. Spiritual objects have their own "materialized" forms, but what man pays attention to is not their material forms but the spiritual contents reflected or carried by these material forms.

Subject and object of practice interacts with each other; though the interaction between them has the feature of materiality, it cannot be reduced to materiality simply. Both subject and object are a kind of material substance, so the interaction between the two is also between material substances, but such interaction differs from that between general material substances. In practical activity, the subject acts on the object for a definite purpose, and impels the object to change structurally or formally according to the needs and purposes of subject, forming the object of "humanized nature", which comes but differs from nature itself. "Humanized nature" is the materialized form of man's essential powers and the "thing-for-me". Except with man, the interaction of any object with another is unconscious and blind, and by no means is it the specific interaction between subject and object.

The interaction between subject and object of practice is concerned with a new relationship, the relationship between spirit and substance, ends and means, the agent and the affected, or the creator and the created. In such a relationship, subject is at a dominant and central position, whereas object becomes the "thing-for-me" of subject. This indicates that on the one hand, subject is restricted and limited by object, and on the other hand, subject is able to unceasingly break the confinement from object and transcends object by means of initiative activity. Such a relationship of confinement and transcendence, or transcendence in confinement, between subject and object is the essence of the interaction between the two.

The contents and results of the interaction between subject and object are realized by a bidirectional movement, that is, subject objectification and object non-objectification. Subject objectification means that man translates his essential powers into object through practice; object non-objectification means that object is translated from the existence form of objective thing into the internal factor of subject's life structure or essential powers. The translation of object from the existence form of objective thing into the factor in life activity structure of subject, including the extension of the organ of man, is the object non-objectification. "In production persons acquire an objective aspect, and in consumption objects acquire a subjective aspect"[12]. This is the process of subject objectification and object subjectification.

The process of subject objectification is meanwhile the process of object subjectification.

Subject objectification and object non-objectification, i.e. object subjectification, are the premise and medium mutually. The former represents the initiative and transcendence of subject; the latter shows the passivity and confinement of object. The contradictory movement

---

12 *Karl Marx and Friedrich Engels.* 1st Chinese Ed., Vol. 46 (I), p. 26.

formed by initiative vs. passivity and transcendence vs. confinement in practical activity, or the bidirectional movement of the confinement of object to subject and the transcendence of subject over object and the relationship that "exists for me" resulting therefrom, constitutes the essential content of human practical activity.

3 PRACTICAL REASON AND EVALUATING REASON DURING PRACTICE AND THEIR EFFECTS

As the mode of being and the essential activity of man, practice is a movement process in and for itself during which men, for specific purposes, transforms objects with instruments and regulates them based on the feedback of results. This process reflects the dialectical relationship between theoretical reason, practical reason and evaluating reason.

The establishment of any purpose is for the objective of building or realizing a thing that has not existed in the existing world currently. The proposal of practice's purposes means men have had a definite understanding on their own needs, on objective things and their laws, and does not only embody the inherent measure of man but also the extrinsic measure of object. As a result, the establishment of purposes is the idea transformation of object by subject in thinking before object is actually transformed, the negative and critical reflection of subject on object, and the ideal object formed in idea. For this reason, purpose vividly reflects the contradictions between subjectivity and objectivity, ideal and reality and ought and practice.

Practice is the purposive activity remolding the world. Purposes, running through the whole course of practice, are both the initial link and the internal control factor. As Marx said, "At the end of every labor-process, we get a result that already existed in the imagination of the laborer at its commencement. He not only effects a change of form in the material on which he works, but he also realizes a purpose of his own that gives the law to his modus operandi."[13]

However, purpose is after all an ideological form. Instruments must be used to realize purpose. Instead of being natural objects, instruments are the product of human activity, embodying and materializing activity of man in the past and directing the activity in the future. They establish internal connections between activities of predecessors and

13   *Selected Works of Karl Marx and Friedrich Engels*. 2nd Ed., Vol. 2, p. 178.

descendants and between activities in the past and in the future. In this way, while using instruments, each generation is in fact using the activities and fruits of the previous generation as their own means, thereby incorporating the aggregation of human powers created in history into themselves. Relying on instruments, the organ outside of body, men break through the limitation of organs inside their bodies, and make it possible for their essential powers to develop infinitely. What's more, every generation does not stop creating new instruments while carrying forward those of previous generation, and thereby ceaselessly break through the limitations from their own powers and activity scope and carry out new practical activities in the form of society as a whole and in the identity of human "species". Thus, the law of human practical activity, different from the law of biological evolution, is formed, namely the law of social development.

The process of purpose externalization by dint of instruments (means) is a process of continuous self-realization and self-sublation. During this process, subject practically repudiates both the pure subjectivity of purpose itself and the real objectivity of object as the premise of purpose, and conforms object to the requirements of subject, thereby creating an existence unifying subjectivity and objectivity. Then the result of practice is reached. In other words, the result of practice is the embodiment and reflection of human purposes in objective things, as well as the fusion of various elements during practice. Once formed, the result of practice will become a kind of objective reality that does not change with man's subjective will but in turn restricts human activity.

In the course during which purpose becomes result by means, practical reason plays an important role. Practical reason refers to the ideal prototype or blueprint about the result of practice prebuilt by man in advance of the commencement of practical activity. Practical reason is both the highest link in the process of cognition and the intermediary link in the translation from cognitive activity into practical activity; its mission is to sublate the one-sidedness of object and transform existing things according to the purpose of subject. If we say what theoretical reason reveals is the essence and law of existing things, practical reason is the plan and scheme for transforming existing things formulated by men to satisfy their own needs.

Practical reason takes theoretical reason as its basis, but it is not the logical deduction of theoretical reason. It is formed based on the extrinsic measure of object and the inherent measure of man. As the intermediary link in the translation from theoretical reason into practical activity, practical reason is possible to be established only when subject has cognized the essence and law of objective things through theoretical reason and made use of the results of cognition. Meanwhile, practical reason also reflects the ideal purpose of man and contains the cognition of man on his own needs. The practical activity conducted by men does not aim at simply reduplicating and imitating existing things, but changing existing things so as to meet their own needs.

Hence, practical reason is by no means just the reflection of existing things "as they are", but it is also the reflection of existing things "as they could be" according to human scale. The forming process of practical reason is the process during which subject ideally applies his inherent measure to the extrinsic measure of object in a certain way, unifies the two together, and then creates an "ideal purpose" or ideal object.

To rationalize this process, evaluating reason is required for judgment. As far as I am concerned, evaluating reason is a special cognition form that judges the values of things, activities and processes, and its feature is introducing the inherent measure of man into cognitive activity and then judging on this basis whether the thing, activity or process is beneficial or harmful to man and is valuable or not, thereby deciding whether to accept or reject it. Different from theoretical reason pursuing the cognition on existing things "as they are" and practical reason seeking for the cognition on existing things "as they could be", evaluating reason pursues the cognition on existing things "as they should be".

Evaluating reason focuses on evaluation on the result of practice. Such result, as the embodiment and reflection of human ideal purposes and essential powers in objective things, as well as the fusion of various elements during practice, will become a kind of objective reality that does not change with man's will once formed. With the result of practice as a kind of objective existence, man is able to rethink and evaluate the rationality of practical reason, practical activity and practical process. In case there is any deviation between result and purpose of practice, practical reason should be corrected and improved, plan and means of practice changed and practical activity itself regulated, making ideal purpose consistent with objective reality. In fact, it is a self-evaluation, self-feedback and self-regulation process of human practical activity from practical reason to evaluation of the result of practice.

In brief, practice is a movement process in and for itself whose basic framework is composed of subject, medium (instruments) and object and which exploits the feedback and regulation of purposes, means and results. Being the bidirectional movement process of subject objectification and object subjectification, practice gives rise to the formation of human subjective world and creates the human world while transforming the objective world. The foundation for differentiation and unity respectively between subjective world and objective world and between world-in-itself and human world is the practice activity of man.

4 PRACTICE: THE FOUNDATION FOR DIFFERENTIATION AND UNITY BETWEEN SUBJECTIVE WORLD AND OBJECTIVE WORLD

Subjective world means the spiritual and ideal world of man, the ensemble of all spiritual and psychological activities in human mind that reflect and grasp the material world. It includes not only the process of conscious activity but also the ideas created in this process, namely the achievements of conscious activity. Subjective world originates from the mind of subject, and manifests the state of mind of subject. The desire, emotion, will, purpose, idea, belief, thought, and so on of man are all different existence forms of subjective world. Subjective world in general is the unity of cognition, emotion and will.

Objective world refers to the "material, perceivable world", the ensemble of all material motions beyond the conscious activity of man. From a content point of view, objective world consists of two parts – nature and society. The former exists independently from human activity, and the latter is formed in the practical activity of man but does not change with the consciousness of man. Common point of the two consists in their attribute of objective being, but not spiritual and ideal being. The unity between natural being and social being constitutes the "external world" or the "material world", i.e. the objective world.

Subjective world differs from objective world. Objective world, existing beyond the conscious activity of man, has the character of immediate actuality and moves according to its inherent law. The material basis of external natural being lies in itself, while the material basis for social being of man is the material production mode. Subjective world, taking human brain as material (physiological) basis, is based on various elements of consciousness and their movement. Existing in human brain, subjective world is the amplitudes and limits for the sizes and strengths of the intelligence, wisdom and thinking ability possessed by subject's conscious activity, as well as the thinking capacity domain of it to accept, understand and process information. Different subjects have diverse subjective worlds. Subjective world and objective world, for one thing, are heterogeneous.

Secondly, the developments of subjective world and objective world are incompletely synchronous. Objective world basically is the external space of subjective world, and determines subjective world. The relationship of subjective world with objective world is the relationship between the reflector and the reflected. However, subjective world is after all a kind of non-immediate actual being, and the "self-arbitrariness" from inside of mind allows men to assemble and construct object in their minds at will. Thus, it is possible for subjective world to deviate from objective world because of some illusions or mistakes, or to transcend objective world and reflect future beings in advance. Consequently the development of subjective world is incompletely synchronous with that of objective world. Subjective world and objective world are in complex contradictory relationship. Subjective world affirms, manifests and reflects objective world on the one hand, and deviates from, negates and transcends objective world on the other hand. The two interlace with each other all the time.

Subjective world and objective world are unified.

Firstly, subjective world and objective world are isomorphic in the aspect of content, meaning that the two are corresponding to each other with respect to basic elements and structure modes. Isomorphism between the two arises out of the premise, condition and foundation for the formation of subjective world itself. Subjective world is neither a self-existent entity separate from objective world nor an absolutely isolated world beyond objective world. Fundamentally speaking, subjective world reflects objective world, reflecting the content of objective world ideally and concentrating the understanding on the essence of objective world in concept. Subjective world is virtually the objective world reflected by human brain and translated into ideal form, so it stems from objective world regarding content, thus being isomorphic with objective world necessarily.

Secondly, the movement law of subjective world is identical with that of objective world. Because subjective world is isomorphic with objective world in respect to content, the movement law of subjective world is the reflection and sublimation of that of objective world. Therefore, it is also featured by necessity and repeatability. No matter whether or not men have been aware of the requirements of the law of thinking, and whether or not they conduct cognitive activity following the law of thinking, the law of thinking will play a part. The basic law of dialectics is applicable to both subjective world and objective world. When we regard conceptual dialectics as the conscious reflection of real world's dialectical movement, dialectics is resolved into a science concerning the general law of external world and human thinking movement. The laws of the two are identical in essence but different in manifestation form.

Finally, subjective world and objective world are translated mutually. As mentioned above, subjective world is essentially the objective world reflected by human brain and translated into ideal form; subjective world, especially the ideal being in it, is translated into real being through practice, becomes one part of objective world, and continuously updates the content of objective world. It is in this sense that Lenin pointed out that "man's consciousness not only reflects the objective world, but also creates it"[14].

The realistic foundation for the differentiation and unity between subjective world and objective world is the practical activity of man.

The relationship between subjective world and objective world is formed in the practical activity of man. Subjective world is not the product of the automatic differentiation of objective world, or the web of thoughts constituted by a variety of "congenital categories". As far as its genesis is concerned, practice is its closest foundation, and it is "internalized" practical activity in human brain. It is during practical activity that the material world is differentiated, reflected in human mind and translated into subjective world. That is to say, the unified material world is practice differentiated by practice into subjective world and objective world.

---

14   *Collected Works of Lenin.* Beijing: People's Publishing House, 1990: 2nd Chinese Ed., Vol. 55, p. 182.

Practice is the contact point between subjective world and objective world. The conversion of the content of objective world into that of subjective world is realized in the mutual contact process of the two worlds. It is a continuously deepened and expanded process. For the specific subject of every era, not all the contents of objective world can be translated into the contents of subjective world, except those having been brought into the scopes of practical and cognitive activities, or we can say, only the part of objective world that is brought into the scopes of practical and cognitive activities, accepted and cognized by subject, and accumulated and internalized as the capacity framework, amplitude and boundary of consciousness can be translated into subjective world. Practice fundamentally restricts the range of contact between subjective world and objective world, as well as the breadth and depth of subjective world.

Practice is the foundation and approach for mutual translation between subjective world and objective world. Only by virtue of practical and cognitive activities can the two worlds be translated mutually. Practice itself is the activity that subjectivity is reflected by objectivity and the "nodal point" of subjectivity and objectivity. "It has not only the dignity of universality, but also of immediate actuality"[15]. Because of this, practice is the foundation and approach for mutual translation between subjective world and objective world.

Practice is the purposive activity of man. "The activity of the end is not directed against itself ... but aims, by destroying definite (sides, features, phenomena) of the external world, at giving itself reality in the form of external actuality"[16]. In other words, man does not only accept objective world and its laws in practical activity, but takes advantage of objective laws to change the existing condition of objective world according to his purpose, bringing the objective world to a new state meeting the requirements of man's purpose, that is, making it the human world. Thus in the process of differentiation and unity between subjective world and objective world, the differentiation and unity between world-in-itself and human world are formed at the same time.

---

15   ibid., p. 183.
16   ibid., p. 183.

5 PRACTICE: THE FOUNDATION FOR DIFFERENTIATION AND UNITY BETWEEN WORLD-IN-ITSELF AND HUMAN WORLD

World-in-itself and human world are two opposite concepts. World-in-itself is also called natural nature, which has two implications: one is the nature before the formation of human world, i.e. the preexisting world prior to the emergence of human beings, and the other is the nature having not been included into the scope of human activity, i.e. the part of nature that has not been "humanized". Human world is the unity of humanized nature and human society formed based on human practice.

Both world-in-itself and human world have objective reality. The human world is not created by men beyond world-in-itself, but instead, men shows their own essential powers and constructs humanized world and human world on the basis of the materials provided by the world-in-itself. Human practice is able to change the external form and internal structure of natural nature, and even the ways how natural nature's laws function, but it cannot wipe away the objective reality of natural world or world-in-itself. On the contrary, the objective reality of natural nature extends into humanized nature and human world through practice, and constitutes the natural basis for the objective reality of human world.

World-in-itself is different from human world in that it is the nature independent from human activity or having not been included into the scope of human activity, its movement and change are completely spontaneous, and all the things in it interact with each other blindly. Oppositely, human world is inseparable from human activity. Transformed by human activity, humanized nature embodies the needs, purposes, wills and essential powers of man; social relations are objectified human activity. The uniqueness of human world is its dependence on human practical activity. It's true that human world cannot be separate from world-in-itself, and world-in-itself is the foundation for its existence and development, but human world, in the final analysis, differs from world-in-itself, and is not the product of automatic extension of world-in-itself. Fundamentally speaking, human world is objectified practical activity of man, the human world of objects.

There was no classification between world-in-itself and human world originally in the unified material world. In the wake of the emergence of mankind and human activity, "the web of nature" started to crack and divided into two, that is, world-in-itself and human world on its basis, opposite to but unified with it. Practice is the foundation for differentiation and unity between world-in-itself and human world.

Practice does not only change the morphology of natural nature, but meanwhile injects the purposive factors of man into the chain of cause and effect in nature, making this chain operate according to "human nature", which is also objective. Thus, "we can even produce motions which do not occur at all in nature (industry), at least not in this way, and we can give these motions a predetermined direction and extent"[17]. To put it another way, although practice is unable to change the nature and law of natural objects, it can apply the inherent measure of man to material objects, specify the direction and process of material motion in the way of mankind, and then change the "being-in-itself" form of material. During practice, natural nature and "thing-in-itself" are ceaselessly transformed into humanized nature and "thing-for-me", which reflect human purposes and satisfy the needs of man.

The process of transformation from natural nature and "thing-in-itself" into humanized nature and "thing-for-me" is the process of "nature humanization". "Nature humanization" stresses "the emergence of nature for man"[18]. In other words, what "nature humanization" emphasizes is not the change of nature, but the fact that nature is continuously endowed with human properties and transformed into the existence and development conditions for mankind in the process of human practice, and becomes "man's real nature", i.e. "anthropological nature"[19].

The process of nature's "humanization" is the process of the formation and development of human society. While being engaged in material production and nature transformation, men form, transform and create their social ties and relations. There will not be a real relationship between man and nature without the social relations between individuals. The "humanization" of nature is realized within society instead of beyond it. It is in this sense that Marx believes "the human aspect of

17   *Karl Marx and Friedrich Engels.* Beijing: People's Publishing House, 1971: 1st Chinese Ed., Vol. 20, p. 573.
18   *Karl Marx and Friedrich Engels.* 1st Chinese Ed., Vol. 42, p. 131.
19   ibid., p. 128.

nature exists only for social man", and "only then does nature exist as the foundation of his own human existence"[20]. Humanized nature and human society, as well as their unity, formed during the practical activity of man, constitute the human world.

Human beings build the human world on the groundwork of world-in-itself by dint of their practical activity, thereby dualizing world into world-in-itself and human world. The two have internal links, shown in the following two aspects.

On the one hand, world-in-itself is the natural foundation for the existence and development of human world. Natural nature is assimilated by men and converted into their essential powers, and meanwhile men objectify these essential powers in human world; after taking its shape, human world in turn restricts natural nature, and ceaselessly change the boundary of world-in-itself. In practical activity, world-in-itself and human world are closely related to each other. As long as there exists man, natural history and human history will interact on each other. It is demonstrated by the achievements of contemporary sciences that the highest "convergence" in natural history happens at the stage when natural history is being translated into human history; at that time, the natural system at a lower level becomes a part of social system at a higher level, and the social system puts "constraints" on the natural system.

On the other hand, natural nature is translated into humanized nature through the practical activity of man, and continues to exist in humanized nature and human world; at the same time, humanized nature inevitably needs to participate in the movement of the entire nature, or still needs to join in the movement course of world-in-itself, which is under the governance of natural laws. Then, two conditions will arise: first, the movement of world-in-itself, relying on its powerfulness, will forcibly erase the traces of humanized nature, making the activity achievements of man trend toward fading and disappearance; second, humanized nature changes the scope and result of the effects of natural laws, as well as the natural process, especially the circulation and conversion of substances and energies within the biosphere. This will probably exert negative effects on mankind, such as the trouble of ecological unbalance nowadays. Environmental pollution and ecological unbalance, at bottom, are "man-made calamities" shown in the form

---

20   Marx, *Economic and Philosophical Manuscripts of 1844*: p. 75.

of "natural disasters". Just because of this, Engels put forward nature's "revenge upon human beings" and "the genuine resolution of the conflict between man and nature".

In a word, the practical activity of man is a kind of activity that unceasingly differentiates, dualizes and unifies the world. For human beings, the world is both a primitive and objective being. So Marx had pointed out that "thing, reality and sensuousness" should not be conceived only from the angle of object, but also from the perspective of "the human sensuous activity, practice," subjectively.

6 CONCLUSION: THE SIGNIFICANCE OF WORLD OUTLOOK OF PRACTICE

While transforming nature, practice does not only change the morphologies of natural objects, but more importantly injects the needs, purposes and essential powers of man into those objects, turning them from nature itself into humanized nature and from "thing-in-itself" into "thing-for-me" and thereby creating things that cannot be generated by the movement of world-in-itself. The process of world differentiation by practice is actually the process of "organizing the world in a human way"[21]. and creating the world. Hence, practice has the significance of world outlook.

The significance of world outlook of practice is embodied by the fact that practice dualizes the world, and creates the human world, which is opposite to but unified with the world-in-itself.

Regarding its content, human world includes two aspects, nature and society. However, human world is not simply the "sum" of nature and society, but a "two-in-one" world of nature and society formed based on practice. In the human world, due to interaction and inter-infiltration, what appears before men is social nature and natural society, or historical nature and natural history.

Nature in human world is not the nature separate from mankind and his activity, but the nature "machined" by men, who do not only transform natural beings, but fuse with them and give a new dimension to them. All the machining and transformation of nature are carried out "within and with the help of a definite social organization". The nature

---

21 *Karl Marx and Friedrich Engels.* 1st Chinese Ed., Vol. 42, p. 24.

in human world is branded with the mark of society. In human world, the significance of nature, the relationship of nature with man, and the form, content and scope of man's effect on nature are all restricted by social relations. It is impossible to divorce the nature in human world from social relations. Nature in human world does not only keep its natural material character, but is also humanized; it has both objective reality and social historicity. In this sense, nature belongs to social (historical) category.

In human world, just as nature is restricted by society, society is in turn restricted by nature. The forming and development of human society is based on the material exchange between man and nature, and human history is no more than "the emergence of nature for man". For nature as an object in human world, it is impossible to completely dissolve its own laws into the social process that appropriates it; nature is not apart from society, but exists as a constant factor in social history. Only through the medium of natural process can the purposes and needs of society be realized. The material exchange between man and nature constitutes the "eternal natural necessity" for the existence and development of society. Social development is neither a pure natural process nor a supernatural process isolated from nature, but a process "similar to" natural movement. Excluding nature and the relationship of man to nature from society (history) means constructing society (history) on nothingness, and this will inevitably lead to historical idealism.

Social nature and natural society are both the products of human objective activity. Practice, the foundation and base for the existence of human world, plays a guiding role in the movement of human world, that is to say, men "set the mind for Heaven and Earth" by means of practice, and rebuild the world on the basis of the unity between material measure and human measure. Human world, of course, cannot be resolved into the consciousness of mankind, or be restored to natural nature. Human consciousness, human society and even the entire human world are all irreducible to natural nature. Social nature and natural society are realized or expressed by the human practical activity, and human world cannot be anything but an existence in practice.

The significance of world outlook of practice is not only embodied by the dualization of world and the formation of human world, but also reflected in the continuous development of human world.

Human world is an existence in practice, which itself is in a continuous change and development. Human world thus becomes a dynamic open system in a state of continuous generation, development and formation of larger scale and more tiers. In other words, practice endows human world with historicity. Marx had criticized the intuition of Feuerbach on the world long ago: "He does not see how the sensuous world around him is, not a thing given direct from all eternity, remaining ever the same, but the product of industry and of the state of society; and, indeed, in the sense that it is an historical product, the result of the activity of a whole succession of generations, each standing on the shoulders of the preceding one, developing its industry and its intercourse, modifying its social system according to the changed needs."[22] In his eyes, "so much is this activity, this unceasing sensuous labor and creation, this production, the basis of the whole sensuous world as it now exists"[23]. Reality, objectivity, historicity and practical attribute are the general characteristics featuring human world and its relationship with world-in-itself. Among them, practice is the fundamental feature.

An animal "produces one-sidedly, whilst man produces universally"; "an animal produces only itself, whilst man reproduces the whole of nature."[24] At the present times, the practical activity of human beings has extended to the sky, the underground and the ocean, involving the vast universe and the broad oceans, deepening into the bowels of the earth and the molecular structure of organisms. Just as Herbert A. Simon, a famous contemporary scientist, said, "The world we live in today is much more a man-made, or artificial, world than it is a natural world. Almost everything around us is stamped with the mark of human skills." The contemporary practical activity and the change and development of human world more highlight the significance of world outlook of practice.

We acknowledge the significance of world outlook of practice, but it does not mean that we deny the "priority" of nature to human world. Marxist philosophy, the same with all materialisms, acknowledges the "priority" of nature. However, instead of transplanting old materialism's concept of nature into new materialism with the concept unchanged, Marxist philosophy sublates it with scientific view of practice; Marxist philosophy does not extend or apply natural materialism

22   *Selected Works of Karl Marx and Friedrich Engels.* 2nd Ed., Vol. 1, p. 76.
23   ibid., p. 77.
24   *Karl Marx and Friedrich Engels.* 1st Chinese Ed., Vol. 42, pp. 96-97, 97.

into the domain of society (history), but contrarily, it conceives nature in human world within the framework of social practice, and connects nature with the processes of practical activity and social life for survey; it believes "the writing of history must always set out from these natural bases and their modification in the course of history through the action of men"[25], and "conceives the sensuous world as the total living sensuous activity of the individuals composing it"[26].

Practice not only transforms but also creates the world. It inherently encompasses the relationships between man and nature, man and society, and man and self. Practice can be considered as an epitome of existing world, as well as the root of all contradictions in reality confronting human beings. It is based on the practical activity of human beings that Marx reviews the world, and constructs a new world outlook, a materialistic, "actually a critical view of the world"[27], and thinks "for the practical materialist, i.e. the communist, it is a question of revolutionizing the existing world, of practically attacking and changing existing things"[28] . This is a profound reform in the world outlook of philosophy.

---

25   *Selected Works of Karl Marx and Friedrich Engels.* 2nd Ed., Vol. 1, p. 67.
26   ibid., p. 78.
27   *Karl Marx and Friedrich Engels.* 1st Chinese Ed., Vol. 3, p. 261.
28   *Selected Works of Karl Marx and Friedrich Engels.* 2nd Ed., Vol. 1, p. 75.

CHAPTER V

PRACTICAL ONTOLOGY:
A NEW INTERPRETATION OF MARXIST ONTOLOGY

The critique and finalization of traditional philosophy by Marx, basically speaking, is initiated and developed at the level of ontology, and the key point lies in the foundation of practical ontology by Marx. However, Marxist practical ontology has faced all sorts of misunderstandings, distortions and criticisms; therefore correctly and comprehensively understanding Marxist practical ontology is still a major theoretical subject to be resolved.

1 CONTRADICTORY FEATURE OF PRACTICE ITSELF

Practice as a social phenomenon had long since caught the attention of philosophers, but it was Kant who formally introduced the concept of "practice" into philosophy. The problem was that the Kant's concept of "practice" was still within the sphere of ethical practice. Feuerbach linked "practice" with "life" and put forward some instructive opinions, but he did not really grasp the real relationship between practice and life, or the significance of revolutionary, practical-critical activity.

Hegel revealed the creative feature of human practical activity based on abstract speculation, not only pointing out the difference between theoretical activity and practical activity, but also involving the important significance of practice in transforming the world and creating human history. However, practice discussed by Hegel was fundamentally abstract activity of idea, and the real activity of man was just a "pattern" of such abstract activity. Actually, Hegel "conceives labor as man's act of self-genesis within the sphere of abstraction", and human life is regarded as "a process traversed by man's abstract, pure, absolute essence that is distinct from himself".[1]

The reason why old philosophy did not correctly resolve the issue of practice's essence is both due to the subjective reason respectively of idealism and old materialism and the objective reason, namely the contradictory feature of practice as the specific activity of mankind: on the one hand, practice is the purposive activity of man, which is dominated by man's subjective factors, rationality and will, and reflects the pursuit of man for ideal world; on the other hand, practice is also an objective process during which man, the material substance, actualizes material exchange with the material world by physical means of instruments.

Marx found that material production activity was the first historical activity, as well as the basic activity that must be conducted every minute of every day, of human beings. When he regarded material production as the principal and decisive form and fundamental content of practice, practice grasped by him became a kind of activity in and for itself, a social process linked with and different from natural process.

In the opinion of Marx, material production first of all is the process during which human beings regulate and control the material exchange between man and nature; in this process, it is necessary for individuals to establish definite relations with each other for they exchange their activities. The relationship between man and nature restricts the relationship between individuals, whereas the relationship between individuals restricts the relationship between man and nature. At the same time, the material result that is obtained at the completion of material production already exists there at the commencement of the process, as the purpose, in the mind of the practitioner in the form of conception;

---

1   *Karl Marx and Friedrich Engels.* 1st Chinese Ed., Vol. 42, p. 175 – 176.

such purpose "is realized, which gives the law to modus operandi"[2] of the practitioner, and is translated into real existence through practical activity. This is a process of "material translation into spirit" and "spirit translation into material". That is to say, production practice is the process of material exchange between man and nature, the process of activity exchange between individuals, and the process of mutual conversion of material and idea between man and nature.

In this way, Marx found the foundation for unity of initiative, freedom and creativity with reality, objectivity and materiality.

Practice in the view of Marx is an objective activity of man to dynamically transform the world. Such an understanding and specification on the essence of practice affirms the objectivity of practical activity in the first place, i.e. a real-life activity with mankind as subject and objective things as object. More importantly, practice objectifies the essential powers of man, such as goal, ideal, knowledge and capability, into objective reality, and creates things that are impossible to generate, or the possibility of generation is almost nil, by the natural law itself, thus creating the human objective world. As a result, practice is the objective activity specific to man. As Marx mentioned, "The product of labor is labor which has been embodied in an object, which has become material: it is the objectification of labor. Labor's realization is its objectification."[3]

Being an objective activity specific to man, practice enables man to transform his essential powers into object, which is the objectification of subject. During this process, the object changes structurally or formally according to the needs and purposes of subject, forming various objects that do not exist in nature originally. These various objects are created by man in his interaction with the external world, and the materialized embodiment of the physical power and intelligence of man, namely the existence form of static material translated from the essential powers of subject by virtue of activity; that is to say, the essential powers of subject are deposited, concentrated and materialized in object. Hence, subject objectification is the infiltration and translation of subject into object. All the results of human practical activity are the results of subject objectification.

---

2   *Karl Marx and Friedrich Engels*. 1st Chinese Ed., Vol. 23, p. 202.
3   *Karl Marx and Friedrich Engels*. 1st Chinese Ed., Vol. 42, p. 91.

Simultaneous with subject objectification, there is the activity of object non-objectification, which means that object is translated from the existence form of objective thing into the internal factor of subject's life structure or essential powers; it loses the form as an object and turns into a part of subject. During practice, subject changes object depending on the output of material and energy on the one hand, and meanwhile needs to consume partial object as immediate means of livelihood on the other hand, or extends material instruments as a body organ into the life activity of subject. All of these are the infiltration and translation of object into subject, i.e. object subjectification.

The external accumulation of human activity achievements resulting from subject objectification forms a special mode for human beings to accumulate, exchange, pass on, inherit and develop their essential powers – the mode of social inheritance, thus the fruits of material culture and spiritual culture of mankind will vanish with the death of individual. By the dint of object non-objectification or object subjectification, man appropriates and absorbs objects (including the activity achievements of predecessors), unceasingly enrich their essential powers, and thereby improve the ability of subject, making subject capable of transforming object with a new higher performance. Subject objectification and object non-objectification, i.e. object subjectification, are two indivisible aspects of human practical activity in bidirectional movement, and they are the premise and medium mutually. Men continuously resolve the contradictions in the world through such movement mode, which is the vivid manifestations of object's restriction on subject and subject's transcendence over object, as well as the substantial content of human practical activity.

From the perspective of running mechanism, practical activity is realized by the feedback and regulation process of purpose, means and result. Man's practical grasp of material world is just based on these three links, which in fact constitute the running mechanism of the practical activity of man.

Purpose is the result of activity predetermined in the mind of man in advance to the process of practice. With respect to its formation, purpose is at first the consciousness of men of their own needs, and also their cognition on object and object's relationship with subject. External objects cannot readily satisfy the needs of man, so man must transform them according to his internal demands. Such transformation is conducted firstly in mind, that is, exterminating the "currently exist-ing" objectivity in-itself of external objects through "the operation of thinking", forming an "ideal being" that meets man's internal needs and subjective requirements in mind, and ideally establish a new uni-fied relationship between subject and object. Such a transformation by thinking is ahead of actual transformation, and it is a rehearsal of the practical transformation of external objects in mind. The advanced transformation gives rise to the purpose of practice and determines tar-gets for human activity.

The purposiveness of practical activity distinguishes the practical pro-cess of man from the process of natural movement. In the process of natural movement, object, objective state and its development are di-rectly restricted by the law of cause and effect, and the status quo of a thing is majorly dominated by events in the past, so it is the past that restricts the present. The practical process of man, however, is not an ordinary conversion process of "cause − result", but of "purpose − re-sult". Purpose is inserted into the chain of cause and effect connected with each other objectively, and plays a part as a special cause. In this special relation of causality, purpose as the cause does not point to a past event, but an event that has yet to happen. Therefore, human activ-ity is not only restricted purely by the past event, but also by the future event; but the future event has not yet existed in reality, and it's just the result selected by subject. Thus practical process appears as a material motion process in and for itself. Such kind of process changes the natu-ral process of object, putting it under the restriction of subject. This is the essential difference between the objectivity of subject activity and the objectivity of object motion.

"'The movement of the relation of causality' = in fact: the movement of matter, respective the movement of history, grasped, mastered in its inner connection up to one or other degree of breadth or depth."[4] The whole natural sciences can be considered as being built on the basis of the category of causality, and if leaving this category, natural sciences will not exist. However, the practical activity of man always embodies purposive activity, and it will be unexplainable without purpose; the relationship between such purposive activity and objective causality is not as incompatible as ice and hot coals. Just as Engels said, human activity is able to "produce motions which do not occur at all in nature

---

4   *Collected Works of Lenin.* 2nd Chinese Ed., Vol. 55, p. 135.

(industry), at least not in this way, and that we can give these motions a predetermined direction and extent. In this way, by the activity of human beings the idea of causality becomes established ... the activity of human beings forms the test ... the test of causality is so to say a double one"[5].

Purpose is subjective, whilst the object it transforms is objective. So purpose cannot immediately act on objective objects, and "material force must be overthrown by material force"[6]. Objective objects can be changed only by a kind of real objective force, that is, means. Purpose must count on means in a bid to realize itself in external objects, but means is selected as per the requirements of subjective purpose, and only those "things" complying with such requirements can be used as means. Different purposes must be realized by means of different functions. Meanwhile the performance of the functions of means must be obedient to purposes; means is functioning according to purposes and restricted by purposes all the time. The laborer "makes use of the mechanical, physical and chemical properties of some substances in order to make other substances subservient to his aims."[7] Therefore, means is the material motion process that serves purpose and is controlled by purpose.

From Marx's point of view, means is a thing, or a complex of things, interposed by subject between himself and object to conduct his activity to object: "Thus Nature becomes one of the organs of his activity, one that he annexes to his own bodily organs, adding stature to himself in spite of the Bible."[8] Hence, means is a contradictory unity between the function of man's internal organs and the external natural force. In the practical activity of man, the function of means, though constituted by external natural objects, is the externalization of functions of man's internal organs, so means is an organ outside the body of man. It is relying on the effects of this external organ that man occupies and controls a part of natural forces at first, and then makes this part of natural forces his own power and other natural forces subservient to his purposes. This way, men break through the limitation of organs inside, and make it possible for their powers to develop infinitely.

---

5 *Selected Works of Karl Marx and Friedrich Engels.* 2nd Ed., Vol. 4, pp. 328 – 329.
6 *Selected Works of Karl Marx and Friedrich Engels.* 2nd Ed., Vol. 1, p. 9.
7 *Karl Marx and Friedrich Engels.* 1st Chinese Ed., Vol. 23, p. 203.
8 Ibid., p. 203.

As a result, Marx suggested to pay attention to issues of "the productive organs of man" and "a critical history of technology", and pointed out that "Darwin has interested us in the history of nature's technology, i.e., in the formation of the organs of plants and animals, which organs serve as instruments of production for sustaining life. Does not the history of the productive organs of man, of organs that are the material basis of all social organizations, deserve equal attention?"[9] As long as we study carefully the instruments as means, and establish "a critical history of technology", "technology discloses man's mode of dealing with Nature" (*Karl Marx and Friedrich Engels*. 1st Chinese Ed., Vol. 23, pp. 409 and 410.).

The formation of "the productive organs of man" demonstrates that the practical activity of man is characterized by the usage of instruments manufactured by men themselves rather than natural ones. This shows that means is first of all the result of the past activity of man, and then the precondition for the future activity; means is not a crude natural object, but a natural object concentrating and materializing human activity in the past. If the internal organs of man belong to natural organs, means, as an external organ of man, is a kind of artificial organ, "the productive organs of man"[10]. Therefore, the relationship between means and human bodily organs is not only between the external and the internal, but also between the artificial and the natural. Only when a thing simultaneously has such two properties as the result of past activity and the precondition of future activity can it is eligible for means. In other words, means is the contradictory unity between past and future activities of man.

Means unifies past and future activities of man, as well as the activities of predecessors and descendants, giving human activity the characteristics different from those of animal activity. In this way, while using instruments, each generation is in fact using the activities and fruits of the previous generation as their own means, thus every generation breaks through the limitation of their own powers, incorporates the aggregation of powers created in human history into themselves, and carries out new activity in the identity of "species". This makes the development of human ability a constantly upward snowballing process, forming the law of social development different from the law of biological evolution.

9   Marx, *Das Kapital* (Translation of Vol. I of French Edition Revised by the Author). Beijing: China Social Sciences Press, 1983: p. 374.
10   ibid., p. 409.

Purpose is realized by means. The result of practice is the subjective purpose achieved in the objective form in the external world of objects, so it is the unity between subjectivity and objectivity. In this process, subject consciously cognizes, grasps and utilizes the law of object, and conforms object to the properties and states fitting the needs of subject. In this way, the relation of causality potentially existing in nature is optionally realized through the movement of "purpose → means → result".

Compared with the result of natural movement, the result of practical activity has a striking feature, that is, the success-failure attribute. The result of nature just arises from cause, and natural movement itself is governed by natural laws, so there is no possibility for violation of objective laws, and no success or failure problem between cause and result. However, the result of practice originates from purpose, which does not disappear in the whole process of practice and dominates the modes and methods of human activity. In this process, it is possible for man to abide by, or violate, the objective laws; consequently, once the result of practice comes into being, it will be immediately compared with purpose, and such comparison relationship forms the unique success-failure attribute of practical result. For this reason, the result of practice has a feedback effect on the purpose of practice, and men are able to firm or correct the purpose of practical activity and make reflection on the practical activity.

It is thus clear that the reason why the practical activity of man is different from the material motion of nature is because human activity is under the governance of rationality. The basic characteristic of the activity of man, as subject, is that during the activity, rationality shows subject the multiple optional possibilities of object and the estimates on the results of various possibilities; meanwhile, it also reflects the multiple levels of subject's internal needs and the possibilities of their realizations, thereby determining the targets of activity, combining the possibility of object with that of subject, and actualizing such possibility during activity. Therefore the unity between necessity and ought is realized and human world of objects created, namely the human world.

2 CONNOTATION AND SIGNIFICANCE OF PRACTICAL ONTOLOGY

The human world of objects, i.e. human world, is the unity between nature and society. What appears before men is social nature and natural society. Social nature is essentially "humanized nature". It is beyond doubt that men do not create humanized nature beyond nature itself, but show their own essential powers and create humanized nature on the basis of the materials provided by nature itself. Human practice is able to change the external form and internal structure of nature itself, and even the ways how natural laws function, but it cannot eliminate the objective reality of nature itself. The objective reality of nature itself, contrarily, extends into humanized nature through practice, and constitutes the natural basis for the objective reality of humanized nature.

Humanized nature is different from nature itself. Nature itself is the nature independent from human activity or having not been included into the scope of human activity, its movement is completely spontaneous, and all the things in it interact with each other blindly. Oppositely, humanized nature is inseparable from human activity. Resulting from human activity, humanized nature embodies the needs, purposes, wills and essential powers of man, and it is the objectified human activity. The uniqueness of humanized nature lies in its subjectivity and its dependence on the practical activity of subject. Fundamentally speaking, humanized nature is the objectification of human practical activity, the world of objects belonging to human beings.

There was no classification between nature itself and humanized nature originally in the unified material world. In the wake of the emergence of mankind and human activity, "the web of nature" started to crack and divided into two, that is, nature itself and humanized nature on its basis, opposite to but unified with it. Practice is the foundation for differentiation and unity between nature itself and humanized nature.

As mentioned before, practice does not only change the morphology of nature itself, but at the same time injects the purposive factors into the chain of cause and effect in nature, making this chain operate according to "human nature", which is also objective. Though production practice is unable to change the nature and law of natural objects, it can apply the purposes of man to material objects, specify the direction and process of material exchange in a human way, and then change the "being-in-itself" form of material. As Engels said, "not only do we find that a particular motion is followed by another, we find also that we can evoke a particular motion by setting up, the conditions in which it takes place in nature, that we can even produce motions which do not occur at all in nature (industry), at least not in this way, and we can give these motions a predetermined direction and extent"[11]. In practice, nature itself, the "thing-in-itself", is day by day transformed into the "thing-for-me", which reflects human purposes and satisfy the needs of man. This is the process of nature "humanization", which results in the differentiation of humanized nature from nature itself. "Nature humanization" stresses "the emergence of nature for man". In other words, what "nature humanization" emphasizes is not the change of nature, but the fact that nature is unceasingly endowed with human properties and transformed into the existence and development conditions for mankind in the process of human practice, thereby becoming the definite confirmation and presentation of man's essential powers. Hence, humanized nature is "man's real nature", the "true anthropological nature"[12].

The process of nature's "humanization" is the process of the formation and development of human society. While being engaged in material production and nature transformation, men form, transform and create their social ties and relations: "by manifesting their nature men create, produce, the human community"[13]. There will be no the real relationship between man and nature without the social relations between individuals, and "production is always appropriation of nature by an individual within and with the help of a definite social organization"[14]. That is to say, the "humanization" of nature is realized within society instead of beyond it. It was in that sense that Marx pointed out:

"The human aspect of nature exists only for social man; for only then does nature exist for him as a bond with man ... and as the life-element of human reality. Only then does nature exist as the foundation of his own human existence."[15]

---

11   *Selected Works of Karl Marx and Friedrich Engels.* 2nd Ed., Vol. 4, p. 328.
12   *Karl Marx and Friedrich Engels.* 1st Chinese Ed., Vol. 42, p. 128.
13   ibid., p. 24.
14   *Karl Marx and Friedrich Engels.* 1st Chinese Ed., Vol. 46 (I), p. 24.
15   *Karl Marx and Friedrich Engels.* 1st Chinese Ed., Vol. 42, p. 122.

While transforming nature, practice does not only change the morphologies of natural objects, but more importantly injects the essential and social powers of man into nature, turning the essential and social powers of man into natural beings, and endowing natural beings with a new dimension – sociality or historicity. In the real world, the significance of nature, the relationship of nature with man, and the content, scope and form of man's effect on nature are all restricted by social relations. Definite social relations are reflected in humanized nature, and give natural objects a distinct social property. It is impossible to separate humanized nature from practical social form. Nature in the real world does not only keep its natural material character, but is also branded with the mark of mankind; it has both objective reality and social historicity. Humanized nature, falling under social (historical) category, is social nature or "historical nature" in essence.

In the human world of objects, just as nature is the intermediary of society, society is in turn the intermediary of nature. The forming and development of human society is based on the material exchange between man and nature caused by labor, and human history is no more than "the emergence of nature for man". For nature as an object in human world, it is impossible to completely dissolve its own laws into the social process that appropriates it. After entering society through practice, nature is translated into an element of social life, and restricts the development of society. Nature is not apart from society, but exists as a constant factor in social history; only through the medium of natural process can the needs of society be realized in the final analysis. "The universality of man appears in practice precisely in the universality which makes all nature his inorganic body – both inasmuch as nature is (1) his direct means of life, and (2) the material, the object, and the instrument of his life activity."[16]

The material exchange between man and nature constitutes the "eternal natural necessity" for the existence and development of society. Social development is neither a pure natural process nor a supernatural process isolated from nature, but a process "similar to" natural history, including natural movement. In this sense, society is natural society or "natural history". Excluding nature and the theoretical and practical relationship of man to nature from society (history) is equal to constructing society (history) on nothingness.

---

16   *Karl Marx and Friedrich Engels*. 1st Chinese Ed., Vol. 42, p. 95.

Social nature and natural society are both the products of human objective activity. Practice is the intermediary for interaction and inter-infiltration between society and nature, as well as the foundation in reality for both to be the intermediary mutually. In short, practice is the foundation and base for the existence of human world, and plays a guiding role in the movement of human world. Human world, of course, can be neither reduced to the consciousness of mankind, nor restored to nature itself. Human consciousness, human society and even the entire human world are all irreducible to nature itself. Social nature and natural society are realized or expressed by the human practical activity, and human world cannot be anything but an existence in practice. The significance of practical ontology is embodied, first of all, by the fact that practice dualizes the world, and creates the human world, which is opposite to but unified with the world-in-itself.

Besides, the significance of practical ontology is also reflected in the continuous development of human world. As previously discussed, human world is an existence in practice, which itself is in a continuous change and development. Thus, human object becomes a dynamic open system in a state of continuous generation and formation of larger scale and more tiers. Marx had criticized the intuition of Feuerbach's materialism on the world long ago, "He does not see how the sensuous world around him is, not a thing given direct from all eternity, remaining ever the same, but the product of industry and of the state of society; and, indeed, in the sense that it is an historical product, the result of the activity of a whole succession of generations, each standing on the shoulders of the preceding one, developing its industry and its intercourse, modifying its social system according to the changed needs."[17] The unity of man with nature "has existed in varying forms in every epoch according to the lesser or greater development of industry"[18]. "So much is this activity, this unceasing sensuous labor and creation, this production, the basis of the whole sensuous world as it now exists"[19].

Human world has the character of immediate actuality for the survival of man, so Marx calls it "sensuous world", "existing world" and "real world". The reality of human world contains objectivity, and the practical attribute of human world further confirms the objectivity of human world and makes human world and its relationship with world-in-itself

17 *Selected Works of Karl Marx and Friedrich Engels*. 2nd Ed., Vol. 1, p. 76.
18 *Karl Marx and Friedrich Engels*. 1st Chinese Ed., Vol. 3, p. 49.
19 *Selected Works of Karl Marx and Friedrich Engels*. 2nd Ed., Vol. 1, p. 77.

take on historicity. Reality, objectivity, historicity and practical attribute compose the general characteristics featuring human world and its relationship with world-in-itself, among which, practice is the fundamental feature. For this reason, Marx "conceives the sensuous world as the total living sensuous activity of the individuals composing it"[20].

Because human world is realistic to the survival of man and practice constitutes the noumenon of human world, practice is closely associated with the living condition of man. In a word, practice is the mode of being of man, i.e. the living noumenon of man. Marx had said, "The whole character of a species, its species-character, is contained in the character of its life activity."[21] This conclusion is extremely profound, which indicates such a truth that the mode of being of a species is judged from the form of its life activity. Specifically speaking, animals subsist depending on their negative adaption to nature, so the mode of being of animals is their instinctive activity, determined by their physiological structure, especially their active organs. Differing from them, men keep their survival during their positive transformation of nature by exploiting instruments; therefore practice is the foundation for the living of man. The secret of man consists in practical activity. As Marx said, "As individuals express their life, so they are. What they are, therefore, coincides with their production, both with what they produce and with how they produce."[22] Practice thus constitutes the special life form of mankind, namely the mode of being and living noumenon of man. All things of human beings, including the alienation of their living condition and its sublation, happen and finish in the process of practical activity. "Only man himself can be this alien power over man", and "the medium through which estrangement takes place is itself practical."[23]

So when confirming practice is the noumenon of human world, Marx also confirms it is the living noumenon of man. Both are the two sides of the same issue. Because Marx pays attention to the elimination of the aliened living condition of man, Marxist philosophy, in this sense, is the ontology of existentialism, i.e. practical ontology.

---

20   ibid., p. 78.
21   *Karl Marx and Friedrich Engels.* 1st Chinese Ed., Vol. 42, p. 96.
22   *Selected Works of Karl Marx and Friedrich Engels.* 2nd Ed., Vol. 1, pp. 67 – 68.
23   *Karl Marx and Friedrich Engels.* 1st Chinese Ed., Vol. 42, p. 99.

The universe noumenon that traditional ontology pursues is an "un-moved mover", therefore it must conclude that there is a eternal un-moved entity, a forever unchanged independent entity beyond sensuous things. This is an abstract noumenon separate from the real society, real mankind and their activities, the so-called "ultimate being" behind all the real things, and it's in fact a "non-existent being". It is impossible to perceive reality based on such abstract being or noumenon. Idealistic ontology is like this, so is old materialistic ontology, and the two go from one extreme to the other. Just as Marx said, "The weak points in the abstract materialism of natural science, a materialism that excludes history and its process, are at once evident from the abstract and ideo-logical conceptions of its spokesmen, whenever they venture beyond the bounds of their own speciality."[24]

Marx turns the focus of philosophy from the whole world to the human world, from the noumenon of universe to the living condition of man, and confirms that practice is the base for the sensuous existence of man and the profound foundation for the existence of sensuous world that man lives in, and that practice is the ontological activity or activity itself of man and man realizes his existence through practice. For this reason, Marx does not conceive and grasp the issue of beings in an abstract sur-real manner, but comprehends and grasps the existence of human beings based on practice, interprets the significance of beings based on the existence of man, and also highlights the fundamental feature of beings – historicity.

That is to say, the practical ontology of Marx sets the existence of man itself as the goal embraced by philosophy. What is pursued by such ontology is not the so-called "ultimate being", i.e. what on earth the existence of "thing, reality and sensuousness" is, but what makes such existence what it is, namely the significance of their existence. The sig-nificance lies in the living practice of mankind, "for human beings". In other words, "thing, reality and sensuousness" are linked with human beings and their living practice, and the ontology is closely related to the living practice of man. That's why Marx believed that "thing, reality and sensuousness" should not be conceived only in the form of object, but "as practice, the human sensuous activity" "subjectively", and ex-pressly pointed out that "for the practical materialist, i.e. the commu-nist, it is a question of revolutionizing the existing world, of practically attacking and changing existing things"[25].

24   Marx, *Das Kapital* (Translation of Vol. I of French Edition Revised by the Author), p. 375.
25   *Selected Works of Karl Marx and Friedrich Engels*. 2nd Ed., Vol. 1, p. 75.

In this way, Marxist practical ontology opens up a path of conceiving the reality through ontology.

3 UNDERSTANDINGS OF STALIN AND LUKACS ON THE ONTOLOGY OF MARXIST PHILOSOPHY

Now, I have to mention the understandings and expositions of Stalin and Lukacs in the ontology of Marxist philosophy. The understanding and exposition of Stalin on the ontology of Marxist philosophy had dominated for a long term in the history of Marxism as the sole supreme authority and as the classic, creating the Soviet model of Marxist philosophy. The understanding and exposition of Lukacs, the founder of Western Marxism, on the ontology of Marxist philosophy represented the direction of Western Marxists' interpretation on Marxist philosophy, and had begun to influence Chinese philosophy since the 1980s. So I would like to make a brief comment on the opinions of Stalin and Lukacs, and this will help us conceive the fundamental feature of Marxist philosophy and the fundamental drawback of traditional textbook system of Marxist philosophy.

In terms of time, the Soviet model of Marxist philosophy was formed in the 1930s; with respect to content, it took shape in the Second Section "Dialectical and Historical Materialism", Chapter Four of *Soviet Union Communist Party (Bolshevik) Party Concise Guide*. After the *Soviet Union Communist Party (Bolshevik) Party Concise Guide* was regarded as the highest authority, "dialectical materialism and historical materialism", the Soviet model of Marxist philosophy formed under that particular historical condition, became the sole or legitimate form of Marxist philosophy. From Stalin's *Dialectical and Historical Materialism* to F. V. Konstantinov's *Fundementals of the Philosophy of Marxism-Leninism*, although the latter deepens the former partially, its overall framework and fundamental feature do not go beyond those of the former; actually, it takes the former as the chief source.

I do not deny that the Soviet model of Marxist philosophy reflects and deepens some viewpoints of Marxist philosophy, but this system or model, generally and fundamentally, does not reflect the real spirit of Marxist philosophy; on the contrary, it distorts Marxist philosophy and its ontology to a large extent. Specifically speaking, in the Soviet model of Marxist philosophy, dialectical materialism is a kind of method and theory which study and interpret nature respectively, and historical

materialism is just the extension and application of dialectical materialism – a kind of view of nature – to the domain of social history. In
Stalin's eyes, "historical materialism is the extension of the principles
of dialectical materialism to the study of social life, an application of
the principles of dialectical materialism to the phenomena of the life
of society, to the study of society and of its history"[26], and dialectical materialism is such an ideological system that "its approach to the
phenomena of nature, its method of studying and apprehending them,
is dialectical, while its interpretation of the phenomena of nature, its
conception of these phenomena, its theory, is materialistic"[27].

It's not hard to find that Stalin, as a matter of fact, construed dialectical
materialism as a kind of view of nature unrelated to historical process,
and took such so-called dialectical materialism as the theoretical basis for historical materialism. In such dialectical materialism, nature
is separated from human activity and abstracted from history, actually
becoming "a thing given direct from all eternity, remaining ever the
same" mentioned by Marx during his critique on Feuerbach. After the
separation and abstraction, a kind of "abstract substance" becomes the
cornerstone of the dialectical materialism, and a nature-based ontology
is formed.

On this basis, Stalin made a series logical deduction from nature to
society: "if the connection between the phenomena of nature and their
interdependence are laws of the development of nature, it follows, too,
that the connection and interdependence of the phenomena of social life
are laws of the development of society, and not something accidental";
"if our knowledge of the laws of development of nature is authentic
knowledge, having the validity of objective truth, it follows that social
life, the development of society, is also knowable, and that the data of
science regarding the laws of development of society are authentic data
having the validity of objective truths"; "if nature, being, the material
world, is primary, and consciousness, thought, is secondary, derivative;
if the material world represents objective reality existing independently
of the consciousness of men, while consciousness is a reflection of this
objective reality, it follows that the material life of society, its being,
is also primary, and its spiritual life secondary, derivative, and that the
material life of society is an objective reality existing independently of

---

26   *Selected Works of Stalin.* Beijing: People's Publishing House, 1979: Vol. II, p. 424.
27   ibid., p. 424

the will of men, while the spiritual life of society is a reflection of this objective reality, a reflection of being"[28], and so on.

That is, according to Stalin, from dialectical materialism to historical materialism, it is actually a logical operation process from natural being to social being. It's clear that although Stalin did not mention "noumenon" or "ontology" in his *Dialectical and Historical Materialism*, he in fact summed up Marxist philosophy as natural ontology.

In this way, the logical direction of Marxist philosophy from social being to natural being is reversed, the existence mode and state of man is ignored, and the ontological significance of practice and the subjectivity of man are concealed. This is an involution to natural materialism taking "abstract substance" as noumenon, a horrendous theoretical retrogression. The epoch-making contribution of Marxist philosophy is abandoned to a quite large extent. It shows that Stalin actually interprets the materialism of Marx with the logic of natural materialism. The dialectical materialism in the Soviet model is fundamentally the "abstract materialism" referred to by Marx, the material of natural science that excludes history and its process. When it prattles about "the materiality of world" while being separated from human practical activity and social life, it has stealthily gone "in the abstract materialistic direction, or rather idealism" criticized by Marx.

I cannot say that the opinions of Stalin have no sense at all, since he observes, after all, the connection between historical materialism and dialectical materialism, but I do not agree with his opinions. When considering the view of nature as the theoretical basis for the conception of history, Stalin cut the internal connection between theory and method, and confused the essential difference of Marx's materialism from natural materialism. In his discussion about "the basic features of the materialism of Marxist philosophy", Stalin actually showed us the common ground of Marx's materialism and natural materialism, and quoted the sentence that "matter is the substratum of all changes" as the words of Marx, thinking it was one of the fundamental features of Marx's materialism. In fact, that was an obvious misquotation, that is, Stalin took the restatement of Hobbes' thought by Marx for the thought of Marx himself, and misunderstood the viewpoint criticized by Marx as that appreciated by Marx. As far as I am concerned, this is not an accidental

---

28   ibid., pp. 435 and 436

ignorance, but it indicates that Stalin did not clearly perceive the essential differences between Marx's materialism and natural materialism, between new materialism and old materialism.

All in all, the dialectical materialism apprehended by Stalin is in essence a view of nature that separates theory from method, simply adds materialism with dialectics, and has a thick color of natural materialism. Once such a dialectical materialism that "excludes history and its process" is regarded as the theoretical basis for historical materialism or the ontology of Marxist philosophy, the material exchange between man and nature and the "anthropological nature" that Marx focuses on inevitably disappear, the practice of man and its ontological significance are dissolved, and the relationship between man and man is concealed by that between object and object; then the development of the mode of production becomes a mysterious movement process, and historical laws turn to preformed "absolute plan" independent of the practical activity of man. Stalin attempted to expound Marxist philosophy in a vulgar manner, but he comprehended Marxist philosophy and its ontology so simply that he reached the end of logic on that road.

Lukacs held a sharply critical attitude to the philosophical thought of Stalin. One of Lukacs' creative contributions in the history of Marxism is the confirmation of scientific view of practice as the theoretical basis for historical materialism and the specification of historical materialism as the ontology of social being, i.e. the ontology of social practice. From Lukacs' point of view, practice, especially labor as "primary practice", always occupies the fundamental core position in social being, and the entire social being, in terms of its ontological feature, is built upon the groundwork of human practice. "It is the labor theory of Marx, the theory which conceives labor as the exclusive existence mode of the purposive creative being, that establishes the character of social being for the first time."[29] It is for this reason that Lukacs also called the ontology of social being "the ontology of social practice".

Lukacs thought that "the labor of man always has a purpose – it sets a purpose, and this purpose is a selected result, therefore the labor of man represents man's freedom. Such freedom, however, only exists in bringing the objective natural forces subject to the law of cause and effect

---

29   Lukacs, *The Ontology of Social Being.* English Ed., p. 25.

of the material world into operation"[30]. That is to say, objective labor contains the purpose of man, and has the objective material premise. It is an active natural-transforming activity that inserts the link of man's purpose into the objective chain of cause and effect, and by doing this, it does not only changes the form of nature, but realizes the purpose of man in natural objects, thereby making nature ceaselessly "socialized". Meanwhile the "constraints" of natural being on social being will not disappear; "I'm talking about the retreat of constraints from nature, but not the disappearance of nature", and it is impossible for men to "fully sublate these constraints". Thus, Lukacs brought the material exchange between man and nature, as well as the conversion process between material and idea, under the category of practice, thereby giving concrete contents to the concept of practice.

Lukacs' opinion is perfectly consistent with that of Marx. In the *Economic Manuscripts of 1861 – 1863*, Marx points out that labor is purposeful activity aimed at the appropriation of natural material. Marx has emphasized this opinion again and again, and writes it into the final draft of Das Kapital. Lukacs thus believed practice constituted the ontological foundation of human society:

"It is labor that introduces the unified dualism-based correlation between purposiveness and causality into beings, and there was only the process of cause and effect in nature prior to the generation of labor. So this complex composed of two aspects only exists in labor and its social results, in social practice. Consequently, the purposively-set activity that transforms reality becomes the ontological foundation for the existence of human society."[31]

Owing to correct understanding on practice and its status in social history, Lukacs extremely underlined that "material practice", "labor", was the basic category of Marxist philosophy, and connected society with nature by virtue of the category of practice, for the purpose of establishing the ontology of social being. "The concept of labor is the key of my analysis"; "in the light of Marx's thought, I conceive ontology as philosophy itself, the philosophy on the basis of history ... The essence of human society is the purposive activity of man, that is, labor. This is the uppermost new category in that it includes everything"[32]. The

---

30   *Autobiography of Lukacs*. Beijing: Social Science Academic Press, 1986: p. 294.

31   Lukacs, *The Ontology of Social Being*. English Ed., pp. 14 – 15.

32   *Autobiography of Lukacs*, p. 203.

exposition of Lukacs makes me spontaneously think of a famous saying of Marx – "all social life is essentially practical"[33].

At this point, Lukacs returned to Marx, restored the original look of historical materialism, and showed a new ideological horizon.

However, as he showed us a new ideological horizon, Lukacs suddenly took a step back – he considered general ontology, or natural ontology, as the premise and foundation of the ontology of social being. In the sight of Lukacs, "social ontology is premised on general ontology", and "the ontology of social being can be built only based on natural ontology"[34]. "It is based on the ontology of dialectical materialism that historical materialism gets the scientific basis for its inherent necessity and reliability."[35]

Lukacs had stringently criticized the philosophical though of Stalin, and indeed he was different from Stalin while specifically elaborating the basic principles of historical materialism, and even reached a new state concerning the ontology of social being. However, he happened to have the same view with Stalin when it came to the relationship respectively between historical materialism and dialectical materialism and between dialectical materialism and natural materialism; the opinions of them are strikingly similar – Lukacs conceived dialectical materialism as the theoretical basis of historical materialism in the end, and made dialectical materialism natural ontology-based. In this way, natural materialism, natural ontology, criticized by Marx went so far as to become the premise and foundation of Marxist philosophy.

This is really a tragedy, a theoretical tragedy that seemingly should not happen but really happened to Lukacs. The fundamental cause of this tragedy was that there was a shadow lingering in his mind, namely the phylogenetic investigation method in line with "time priority". On that methodological basis, Lukacs "conceives the order of priority" of the three major modes of being – inorganic nature, organic nature and human society – "in the irreversible process of world as the core of self-thinking on ontology"[36]. From this it is not difficult for us to understand why Lukacs finally set natural ontology as the premise and foundation for the ontology of social being.

---

33 *Selected Works of Karl Marx and Friedrich Engels*. 2nd Ed., Vol. 1, p. 56.
34 Lukacs, *The Ontology of Social Being*. English Ed., p. 472.
35 Ibid., p. 151.
36 ibid., p. 10.

There is an interesting phenomenon frequently happening in history – a theory or even the whole philosophical theory of a great philosopher always tends to show its intrinsic value and catch the attention of people again after the philosopher's death and a relatively long historical movement, so is the historical destiny of Marx's practical ontology. The practical ontology of Marx was put forward and founded in the mid-nineteenth century, and "no one had comprehensively studied the ontology of social being like Marx". But the new ontology did not arouse men's concern and understanding at that time and for a relatively long historical period thereafter, thus leading to the inherent drawback in the traditional textbook system of Marxist philosophy. This is the fundamental defect. The historical movement and the development of practice, science and philosophy itself in the twentieth century highlight the intrinsic value of Marx's practical ontology, and reveal the modernity and contemporary significance of Marxist philosophy to people again. As Lukacs said, "Today, if people attempt to make a down-to-earth thinking on the world on the basis of being, they cannot succeed unless taking the road to revival of Marxist ontology." Of course, the Marxist ontology is not natural ontology, but practical ontology, i.e. the ontology of existentialism.

CHAPTER VI

DIALECTICAL NEGATION AND NEGATIVE DIALECTICS: A NEW INTERPRETATION OF MARXIST DIALECTICS

Almost all the textbooks of Marxist philosophy interpret negation of the negation as three related objects, or as the natural development stages of an object, and demonstrate the law of negation of the negation based on the classic specific examples of Engels' expositions in *Anti-Dühring*, namely grain – plant – grain, public ownership – private ownership – public ownership, spontaneous materialism – idealism – modern materialism, etc. The problem is that dialectics is not "the ensemble of examples", so it is a superficial understanding on the law of negation of the negation to demonstrate it with examples. Rereading of the works of Marx, Engels and Lenin enables me to realize that the law of negation of the negation in materialistic dialectics is not used to describe three related objects, or the natural development stages of an object, but it refers to such an inevitable course and development trend in which things develop from the form of potential contradiction to extension of contradiction, to a stage of intensified contradictions, and then to a stage of resolution of contradictions which, in turn, gives rise to new things. This inevitable process and development trend, what's more, is manifested as "negative dialectics" in the movement of human history.

1 DIALECTICAL NEGATION AND NEGATION OF THE NEGATION

In the history of philosophy, Kant explicitly introduced the thought of negation of the negation into the domain of thinking, in the belief that "the number of the categories in each class is always the same, namely, three ... the third category in each triad always arises from the combination of the second with the first"[1]. We can find from Kant's list of categories that he took negation of the negation as the form of transcendental categorical structure, and had already had the thought from affirmation to negation, and then to negation of the negation. Hegel set a high value on that thought of Kant, and believed "it betrays a great instinct for the Notion when Kant says that the first category is positive, the second the negative of the first, the third the synthesis of the two; the triplicity, although it here reappears as a quite external schema only, conceals within itself the absolute form, the Notion"[2].

Hegel consciously and expressly described the process of thinking and world developments as a process of negation of the negation. According to Hegel, negation of the negation is developed in triad stages of thesis – antithesis – synthesis. In thesis, contradictions are under the same condition, whose opposition is potential; in antithesis, the opposition of contradictions is extended, as the negation against thesis; in synthesis, the opposition of contradictions is solved; synthesis is the negation against antithesis, so it is negation of the negation. The reason is that affirmation "contains negativity within itself, so it can transcend itself and cause its own changes".

Meanwhile, "negation is equally positive, or what is self-contradictory does not resolve itself into a nullity, into abstract nothingness, but essentially only into the negation of its particular content; or such a negation is not just negation, but is the negation of the determined fact which is resolved, and is therefore determinate negation"[3]. The "determinate negation" means that negation itself has the positive significance. In other words, the result of negation is not nothingness, but the generation of new determinations. As a result, negation contains affirmation, and in a certain sense, negation equals to affirmation. The process of

1   Kant, *The Critique of Pure Reason*. Beijing: The Commercial Press, 1980: pp. 80 – 90.
2   Hegel, *Lectures on the History of Philosophy*. Beijing: The Commercial Press, 1980: Vol. 4, p. 269.
3   Hegel, Science of Logic. Beijing: The Commercial Press, 1980: p. 36.

negation of the negation is described by Hegel as a course of contradictions from potential form to extension, and then to resolution; Hegel,
on the basis of idealism, revealed the substance of the law of negation
of the negation.

Marx and Engels critically inherited Hegel's thought of negation of the
negation. According to Marx, "what constitutes dialectical movement
is the coexistence of two contradictory sides, their conflict and their
fusion into a new category"[4]. Engels thought that the developments of
things "in their nature are antagonistic, contain a contradiction; transformation of one extreme into its opposite; and finally, as the kernel
of the whole thing, the negation of the negation."[5] The "coexistence",
"conflict", "antagonistic", "transformation … into its opposite", "fusion into a new category" and "the kernel of the whole thing" mentioned here together refer to the process of negation of the negation, the
process of contradictions from potential form to extension, and then to
resolution of contradictions.

Based on deep analysis of Hegelian dialectics, Lenin carried further
forward the thought of Marx and Engels on negation of the negation. In
Lenin's opinion, at the initial development stage of a thing, contradiction is "'in itself' = potentially, not yet developed, not yet unfolded"[6];
the first negation "sharpens the blunt difference of variety … into essential difference, into opposition. Only when raised to the peak of contradiction, do the manifold entities become active (regasm) and lively
in relation to one another, – they receive, acquire that negativity which
is the inherent pulsation of self-movement and vitality"[7]; the extension
and intensification of contradiction will be negated by the consequence
of movement, and this is the second negation, i.e. the negation of the
negation. Negation of the negation "demands the demonstration of
'unity', i.e., of the connection of negative and positive, the presence of
this positive in the negative, from assertion to negation – from negation to 'unity' with the asserted"[8]. This is the process of negation of the
negation.

4   *Selected Works of Karl Marx and Friedrich Engels*. 2nd Ed., Vol. 1, p. 144.
5   *Selected Works of Karl Marx and Friedrich Engels*. 2nd Ed., Vol. 3, p. 483.
6   *Collected Works of Lenin*. 2nd Chinese Ed., Vol. 55, p. 196.
7   *Collected Works of Lenin*. 2nd Chinese Ed., Vol. 55, p. 119.
8   ibid., p. 196.

Thus, it is clear that Marx, Engels and Lenin all think that the process of negation of the negation is the course of contradictions from potential form to extension, and then to resolution. The reason why the law of negation of the negation is regarded, together with the law of unity of opposites and the law of mutual change of quality and quantity, as the universal law of natural, social and thinking developments is because the development process of anything is a development process of contradiction, and the development process of contradiction is bound to go through three stages, namely potential form, extension and intensification, and resolution. The contradictory movement of a thing, to be precise, determines that the development of the thing will be unavoidably manifested as a process of negation of the negation.

The three stages in the development of a thing specified by the law of negation of the negation are related to but also different from the specific natural development stages of a thing classified according to different qualitative states, and the two kinds of stages are not completely equivalent. For example, we can classify the growth process of barley not only into three stages of grain – plant – grain, but also into five, even more, stages of grain – barley grass – straw – grouting – grain; the development of human society can be classified into three social patterns of public ownership – private ownership – public ownership or five social formations of primitive society – slave society – feudal society – capitalist society – socialist society, and so forth. The problem is that no matter whether we divide the growth process of barley into three or five stages and the social development into three or five formations, both are essentially the process of contradictions from potential form to extension and intensification, and then to resolution and generation of a new thing, and contradictions run throughout the whole process and constitute the development impetus of the process. Thus it is easy for us to comprehend the well-known saying of Hegel: in the very essence of objects, to elucidate and reveal the contradiction which it has in itself is dialectics in the proper sense.

It is demonstrated by the law of negation of the negation that the development of a thing is completed through three links and two negations: the three links refer to the commencement, extension and resolution of contradiction, which are inevitably experienced by the thing in the development process; and the two negations mean the negation of the extension of contraction (sharpening of opposition) to the commencement (potential stage of contradiction) and the negation of the resolution of contradiction to its extension. To put it another way, the development of a thing will undergo two transformations of opposites.

However, the two transformations are not the two status inversions between opposites mentioned by the traditional textbook of philosophy, but the transformation of contradiction from the initial potential stage to the stage of contradiction extension and opposition intensification and the transformation from contradiction intensification to resolution and generation of a new thing. During this process, some factors in the origin, the old thing, are affirmatively maintained in a different form in the result, the new thing, thereby achieving "the repetition at a higher stage of certain features, properties, etc., of the lower"[9] and making development "the apparent return to the old" and the seeming "movement back to the starting point"[10]. In fact, it is the reproduction of some features of the lower stage at the higher stage in a transformed form.

I cannot agree with Adorno's opinion that Marx advocates "absolute negation", i.e. pure negation without any affirmation. This is a misunderstanding and even a distortion. Marx had pointed out while evaluating Hegel's thought of negation of the negation that "a peculiar role, therefore, is played by the act of superseding in which denial and preservation, i.e., affirmation, are bound together"[11]. Marx indeed sees such a "peculiar role", and states that the negation of the negation of communism is "no flight, no abstraction, no loss of the objective world created by man – of man's essential powers born to the realm of objectivity; ... not a returning in poverty to unnatural, primitive simplicity."[12], but is the reestablishment of "individual property" "based on the acquisition of the capitalist era". "The capitalist mode of appropriation, the result of the capitalist mode of production, produces capitalist private property. This is the first negation of individual private property, as founded on the labor of the proprietor. But capitalist production begets, with the inexorability of a law of Nature, its own negation. It is the negation of negation. This does not re-establish private property for the producer, but gives him individual property based on the acquisition of the capitalist era: i.e., on cooperation and the possession in common of the land and of the means of production."[13]

---

9   *Collected Works of Lenin*. 2nd Chinese Ed., Vol. 55, p. 191.
10   ibid., p. 295.
11   *Karl Marx and Friedrich Engels*. 1st Chinese Ed., Vol. 42, p. 172.
12   ibid., p. 175.
13   *Karl Marx and Friedrich Engels*. 1st Chinese Ed., Vol. 23, p. 832.

During the development of a thing, negation of the negation is a latter and higher link which contains affirmation and meanwhile has richer content than affirmation; it really reflects dialectics of thing's development, that is, dialectical negation. "Not empty negation ... is characteristic and essential in dialectics ... as a moment of development"[14]. The process of negation of the negation is the link both eradicating the old thing and giving rise to the new thing, the link both disconnecting and demarcating the previous thing from the subsequent thing and connecting the previous with the subsequent.

Of course, I notice that the significance of overcoming is particularly important in dialectical negation. The purpose of dialectical negation is to overcome the old thing, and preservation is realized on the basis of overcoming. The affirmation contained in negation is definitely not the affirmation and preservation of the entire unity of old thing and old contradictions, but of the reasonable factors in such a unity. Even for the reasonable factors having been preserved, they are not moved to the new thing as they are, but are included into the new thing after transformation. As a link in development, negation of the negation is the negation against the unity of old thing and contradictions as a whole, the extinction of old thing and the generation of new thing.

Therefore, dialectics "includes in its comprehension and affirmative recognition of the existing state of things, at the same time also, the recognition of the negation of that state, of its inevitable breaking up; because it regards every historically developed social form as in fluid movement, and therefore takes into account its transient nature not less than its momentary existence; because it lets nothing impose upon it, and is in its essence critical and revolutionary."[15] Critique is to conceive and handle existing things based on the unity between affirmation and negation and between generation and extinction, and revolution is "practically attacking and changing existing things". "In reality and for the practical materialist, i.e. the communist, it is a question of revolutionizing the existing world, of practically attacking and changing existing things"[16]. "In history, progress makes its appearance as the negation of the existing state of things"[17].

---

14   *Collected Works of Lenin*. 2nd Chinese Ed., Vol. 55, p. 195.
15   *Selected Works of Karl Marx and Friedrich Engels*. 2nd Ed., Vol. 2, p. 112.
16   *Selected Works of Karl Marx and Friedrich Engels*. 2nd Ed., Vol. 1, p. 75.
17   *Karl Marx and Friedrich Engels*. 1st Chinese Ed., Vol. 20, p. 553.

2 NEGATIVE DIALECTICS AND NEGATION OF THE NEGATION

The law of negation of the negation shows different forms in different realms. In practical activity, man realizes the unity between himself and world in a negative manner, thereby forming "negative dialectics" in the movement of human history. In other words, the law of negation of the negation in the movement of human history is manifested as "negative dialectics".

"The outstanding achievement of Hegel's *Phänomenologie* and of its final outcome, the dialectic of negativity as the moving and generating principle, is thus first that Hegel conceives the self-creation of man as a process, conceives objectification as loss of the object, as alienation and as transcendence of this alienation; that he thus grasps the essence of labor and comprehends objective man – true, because real man – as the outcome of man's own labor."[18] For the purpose of defining the essence of man, Hegel introduced the viewpoints of labor and generation, believing that man showed his essence during activity, and "the true being of a man is his act"[19]. Marx thus thought that Hegel "grasps labor as the essence of man – as man's essence which stands the test", as "man's coming-to-be for himself within alienation, or as alienated man"[20]. It was because of his quite deep philosophical thinking on labor and apprehension of negation with labor that Hegel brought forward the negative dialectics as the moving and generating principle.

From Hegel's point of view, labor is the activity of man to "shape" natural objects, namely to transform natural objects, and it constitutes the "negative middle term" between man and nature. It is with the help of this middle term that man separates himself from nature, brands natural objects with the mark of mankind, and negates the primitive morphologies of them; in this process, man externalizes his powers while appropriating and acquiring natural objects. "I have accomplished something, [and] have [thereby] alienated it from myself; this negative [element] is positive; this alienation is an acquiring."[21]. The negativity of labor externalizes, i.e. objectifies, the powers of man, and the object formed by such objectification in turn conflicts with man, resulting in alienation.

18   *Karl Marx and Friedrich Engels*. 1st Chinese Ed., Vol. 42, p. 163.
19   Hegel, *The Phenomenology of Mind*, Vol. I, p. 213.
20   *Karl Marx and Friedrich Engels*. 1st Chinese Ed., Vol. 42, p. 163.
21   Hegel, *The Phenomenology of Mind*, Vol. I, p. 23.

As a result, negation is not only manifested as externalization and alien-ation, but also as the activity sublating such externalization and aliena-tion. During this process, man directly observes himself, consciously realizes his independence, and restores the alienated object, i.e. the ob-ject, back into man, thereby accomplishing the unity of subject with object and self-actualization of subject. As far as Hegel is concerned, this is the process of negation of the negation. The negativity "is the simple point of the negative self-reference, the innermost source of all activity, of living and spiritual self-movement; it is the dialectical soul which everything true possesses and through which alone it is true"[22].

However, according to Hegel, only abstract thinking activity and spir-itual labor have the initiative and creativity in the sense of ultimate source, and material sensuous labor is just "pattern of spiritual activi-ty"; the real man is radically the self-consciousness in and for itself, and the domain of human relations is "the spiritual daylight of the present". "For Hegel the human being – man – equals self-consciousness. All estrangement of the human being is therefore nothing but estrangement of self-consciousness. ... All reappropriation of the estranged objective essence appears therefore, as incorporation into self-consciousness: the man who takes hold of his essential being is merely the self-conscious-ness which takes hold of objective essences. Return of the object into the self is therefore the reappropriation of the object."[23]

This indicates that the negative dialectics of Hegel is a kind of dialec-tics expressing the movement of human history in an "abstract, logical, speculative" way on the basis of idealism. "Because Hegel has con-ceived the negation of the negation, from the point of view of the posi-tive relation inherent in it, as the true and only positive, and from the point of view of the negative relation inherent in it as the only true act and spontaneous activity of all being, he has only found the abstract, logical, speculative expression for the movement of history"[24].

As a matter of fact, Rousseau had studied the movement of human his-tory with the thought of negation of the negation and possessed the ideology of negative dialectics before Hegel. The movement of human history, in Rousseau's opinion, is a course of equality – inequality – equality. In primitive society, human beings lived under the condition

22 Hegel, *The Phenomenology of Mind*. Beijing: The Commercial Press, 1979: Vol. II, p. 543.
23 *Karl Marx and Friedrich Engels*. 1st Chinese Ed., Vol. 42, p. 165.
24 ibid., p. 159.

of no private property, and the relations between people were free and equal; in the wake of the development of production and technology, human society becomes civilized and private ownership is generated, consequently bringing about inequality between people; this is an era of "individual perfection" and "decline of species"; as the inequality develops to extreme, it will switched to equality, but such equality is not the spontaneous equality between primitive men; instead, it is a higher equality based on social contract. Here, Rousseau spreads a picture of negation of the negation before us, and displays us a dialectical process that transforms into its opposite in confrontation and contradiction.

This shows that Rousseau had consciously and clearly used the thought of negation of the negation to study human history, thus showing his sensitivity to historicism beyond the expectation of his times. "The doctrine in its first presentation bears almost ostentatiously the imprint of its dialectical origin". Engels spoke highly of Rousseau's dialectical thought, and thought that "in Rousseau, therefore, we find not only a line of thought which corresponds exactly to the one developed in Marx's *Das Kapital*, but also, in details, a whole series of the same dialectical turns of speech as Marx used: processes which in their nature are antagonistic, contain a contradiction; transformation of one extreme into its opposite; and finally, as the kernel of the whole thing, the negation of the negation."[25]

Marx critically inherited the negative dialectics of Hegel and the thought of negation of the negation of Rousseau. When he conceived practice as the mode of being of man and material practice as the foundation for the relationships between man and nature and between man and society, the negative dialectics gains its groundwork in reality, and becomes the dialectics with "reasonable morphology".

The relationship between man and nature differs from that between animal and nature. Instead of acknowledging the immediate state of being of nature and negatively accommodating himself to nature like animals, man, relying on his practical activity, negates the immediate state of being of nature and endows it with the form meeting his needs and purposes. However, purpose itself cannot be imposed upon object directly, so a medium that unites purpose with object is necessary, that is, instruments of labor. With a certain instrument or a certain system of

---

25   *Selected Works of Karl Marx and Friedrich Engels*. 2nd Ed., Vol. 3, p. 483.

instruments, man engages himself in practical activity of nature transformation for a certain purpose. Instrument has identity with purpose
and object: on the one hand, as the extension of man's body, instrument
complies with the purpose of man, or we can say it is identical with
purpose; on the other hand, instrument itself is also a material object,
identical with the material objects of practice.

Hence, instrument, under the governance of purpose and based on its
materiality, is able to interact with the materiality of the object of practice, impose the purpose of man on such object and negate its primary
morphology, thus endowing it with human properties, that is, translating nature itself into humanized nature and "thing-in-itself" into "thing-
for-me". In this process, nature "emerges for man", and the relationship between man and nature changes into a relationship that "exists for
me"[26]. Practice contains a kind of negative dialectics within itself, and
the relationship that "exists for me" created during practice marks that
the relationship between man and nature is negatively contradictory.

The private ownership of the means of production emerged when the
negative activity of man to nature developed to a definite extent and
stage, and the existence of private ownership and natural labor division
alienated the activity of man; the formation of alienation marked that
human history has stepped into the stage when man is dominated by alien power. "As long as a cleavage exists between the particular and the
common interest, as long, therefore, as activity is not voluntarily, but
naturally, divided, man's own deed becomes an alien power opposed to
him, which enslaves him instead of being controlled by him"[27].

Capitalist society is the typical and extreme form of alienation. In capitalist society, it is capital, rather than, active individual who has personality;
man is controlled and enslaved by objects instead of controlling them; the
reason why objects are able to control and enslave man is because, in fact, it
is a minority of people who control and enslave the majority with the aid of
the powers of objects. "The emphasis comes to be placed not on the state of
being objectified, but on the state of being alienated, dispossessed, sold; on
the condition that the monstrous objective power which social labor itself
erected opposite itself as one of its moments belongs not to the worker, but
to the personified conditions of production, i.e. to capital."[28]

26   *Selected Works of Karl Marx and Friedrich Engels*. 2nd Ed., Vol. 1, p. 81.
27   *Selected Works of Karl Marx and Friedrich Engels*. 2nd Ed., Vol. 1, p. 85.
28   *Karl Marx and Friedrich Engels*. 1st Chinese Ed., Vol. 46 (II), p. 360.

However, capitalist society, in the final analysis, fosters "personal in-dependence founded on objective dependence", and forms "a system of general social metabolism, of universal relations, of all-around needs and universal capacities"[29], thereby creating and providing precondi-tions for the free development of every individual. In other words, capi-talist society, while pushing alienation to extreme, also creates condi-tions for the sublation of alienation. Along with the huge growth and high development of productive forces, when the opposition between labor and capital reaches its limit, the extinction of private ownership and the sublation of alienation will be ineluctable.

The alienation of man and the sublation of alienation is not a simple contradictory movement process of self-consciousness, but a contradic-tory movement process of practical activity that "transforms the world of objects" and "creates the world of objects". Alienation, "this process of inversion, is a merely historical necessity, a necessity for the devel-opment of the forces of production solely from a specific historic point of departure, or basis, but in no way an absolute necessity of produc-tion; rather, a vanishing one, and the result and the inherent purpose of this process is to suspend this basis itself, together with this form of the process."[30]

From the generation of alienation to its sublation, it is a process of nega-tion of the negation with historical necessity. This negation of the nega-tion, "based on the acquisition of the capitalist era" and "the possession in common of ... the means of production", rebuilds individual prop-erty and establishes "personalized individual". "Communism as the positive transcendence of private property as human self-estrangement, and therefore as the real appropriation of the human essence by and for man; communism therefore as the complete return of man to himself as a social (i.e., human) being – a return accomplished consciously and embracing the entire wealth of previous development; ... it is the genu-ine resolution of the conflict between man and nature and between man and man – the true resolution of the strife between existence and es-sence, between objectification and self-confirmation, between freedom and necessity, between the individual and the species."[31] Undoubtedly, this is a process of negation of the negation, the negative dialectics in the movement of human history.

---

29   *Karl Marx and Friedrich Engels*. 1st Chinese Ed., Vol. 46 (I), p. 104.
30   *Karl Marx and Friedrich Engels*. 1st Chinese Ed., Vol. 46 (II), p. 361.
31   *Karl Marx and Friedrich Engels*. 1st Chinese Ed., Vol. 42, p. 120.

It can be found that in Marxist philosophy, the negative dialectics is based on the view of practice, and organically integrated with the conception of history. Marcuse thus believes in Marxist philosophy, "the negativity of reality becomes a historical condition which cannot he hypostatized as a metaphysical state of affairs. In other words, it becomes a social condition, associated with a particular historical form of society." "The historical character of the Marxian dialectic embraces the prevailing negativity as well as its negation. The given state of affairs is negative and can be rendered positive only by liberating the possibilities immanent in it."[32] I should admit that the evaluation of Marcuse is pertinent and reasonable.

3 BRIEF CONCLUSION

The negative dialectics is different either from that of Hegel in early modern times or the "negative dialectics" of Adorno in modern times.

According to Adorno, among the contradictions of a thing, identity and non-identity are absolutely opposite, and the negative dialectics is to replace identity with non-identity; because "contradiction is nonidentity under the aspect of identity", "dialectics is the consistent sense of nonidentity"[33]; the negative dialectics is to replace negation of the negation with "absolute negation", because there is no positive negation, negation and re-negation in the development of thing, and "what is negated is negative, until it has passed away"[34]; the negative dialectics is the "logic of disintegration", the critique and destruction, which negates and abolishes reality through interpreting it; "negative dialectics equals to devastating destruction".

Adorno attempted to "think dialectically" and "in contradictions"; he underlined "heterogeneity and particularity" in the critique of identity, objected to "the abstract identity that submits to the world", and grasped the fundamental defects of traditional western philosophy, as well as the non-thoroughness of Hegel's negative dialectics, to a certain degree; all of those were surely reasonable. But Adorno did not have a true understanding on contradiction, or on the dialectical relationship between negation and affirmation, and reach the "depth of negation" that he had yearned for.

32　Marcuse, *Reason and Revolution*. Chongqing: Chongqing Publishing House, 1993: 1st Chinese Ed., pp. 284 and 285.
33　Adorno, *Negative Dialectics*. Chongqing: Chongqing Publishing House, 1993: p. 3.
34　Adorno, *Negative Dialectics*, p. 157.

The critique of Adorno on identity is not only philosophical, but also political and social, on the capitalist system. This critique realizes that the "materialized world" is the "managed world" integrated by the logic of capital identity, and that "under the all-subjugating identity principle, whatever does not enter into identity, whatever eludes rational planning in the realm of means, turns into frightening retribution for the calamity which identity brought on the nonidentical"[35]. Adorno therefore connected negation with "revolution", and strived to negate the reality of capitalism, thereby being positively ideal. However, he merely revealed the negative dialectics gingerly under a specific historical context, denied the dependence of human freedom on practical activity, and did not really comprehend the connotation of "revolutionizing the existing world" proposed by Marx; thus, negation in his mind does not only mean "revolution", but "extinction, fear, despair". With Adorno, the negation dialectics is directly manifested as aesthetic romanticism and religious messianism.

From the angle of time, Marxian negative dialectics was later than the negative dialectics of Hegel but earlier than that of Adorno; but regarding logic, the negative dialectics of Marx is "the late philosophy", which, owing to its tremendous advancement, sublates the opposition between the negative dialectics of Adorno and that of Hegel, thus having the inherent contemporary significance.

---

35   ibid., p. 319.

CHAPTER VII

"THE PROCESS OF NATURAL HISTORY" OF SOCIAL DEVELOPMENT: A NEW INTERPRETATION

For a long term, the textbook of Marxist philosophy regarded the statement that "the development of social formation is a process of natural history" as the cornerstone and general principle of historical materialism. This is actually a misunderstanding on Marxian theory of social development. Marx never expressed the opinion that the process of social history was equal to "the process of natural history", and he only pointed out that the development of the economic formation of society had "similarity" with natural history. However, similarity does not mean equality. We therefore need to make a new investigation and survey on the opinion that the development of social formation is the process of natural history.

1 RAISING OF THE ISSUE

The statement that "the development of social formation is the process of natural history" is put forward by Marx in Preface to the First German Edition, Volume I of *Das Kapital*. To fully understand the issue, let's firstly look at the original German text and Chinese translations.

In the German edition of *Das Kapital*, the original sentence of Marx is "Mein Standpunkt, der die Entwicklung der ökonomischen Gesellschaftsformation als einen naturgeschichtlichen Prozeß auffaßt", which should be translated into "my standpoint, from which the evolution of the economic formation of society is viewed as a process of natural history". Guo Dali and Wang Yanan translated it into: "我的观点，是把经济社会形态的发展，理解为一个自然史的过程 (my standpoint is that the development of the economic formation of society is viewed as a process of natural history)"[1]. In the translation by the Central Compilation & Translation Bureau, this sentence is "我的观点是：社会经济形态的发展是一种自然历史过程 (my standpoint is that the development of the economic formation of society is a process of natural history)"[2]. After comparison with the original German text, we think the translation of Guo Dali and Wang Yanan is more accurate, because they "view" the evolution of the economic formation of society as the process of natural history, but do not say that the former "is" the latter.

In order to make it clearer, let's also review the Chinese version of Volume I of *Das Kapital* in French edition, which was revised by Marx, translated by the Central Compilation & Translation Bureau. Here, it is pointed by Marx that "my standpoint is that the evolution of the economic formation of society has similarity with natural course and natural history"[3]. Obviously, Marx conceives the development of the economic formation of society as the process of natural history, but he does not mean the development of the economic formation of society itself is a process of natural history, but it has similarity with natural history. Because of this, Marx expresses the aspect of "similarity" more explicitly and prominently in Volume I of *Das Kapital* in French edition.

1　Marx, *Das Kapital*, trans. by Guo Dali and Wang Yanan. Beijing: People's Publishing House, 1963: Vol. I, p. XII.
2　Marx, *Das Kapital*, trans. by the Central Compilation & Translation Bureau. Beijing: People's Publishing House, 1975: Vol. I, p. 12.
3　Marx, *Das Kapital* (Translation of Vol. I of French Edition Revised by the Author), p. 4.

It is thus not difficult for us to make a conclusion that Marx himself never said the development of social formation was the process of natural history, and it was also not the original intention of him to regard the evolution of the economic formation of society as the process of natural history; his original intention was that such evolution could be comprehended from the perspective of "natural course and natural history" for the reason that the economic structure of society and its running mechanism, especially the technological process of society, have similarity with natural course and natural history. Considering social development as "the process of natural history" is evidently a misunderstanding, which is caused by the following skips in thinking at least:

First, skipping from the economic formation of society said by Marx to social formation; the economic formation of society said by Marx especially refers to the composing formation of "the productive organs of man"[4], namely the economic activity structure of society, which is not the same concept with the social formation as the unity of economic base and superstructure that we understand today.

Second, skipping from "similarity" between the economic formation of society and "the process of natural history" to sameness between the two; social development is the process of the subject behaviour of real man, so it should not be equated with natural process. What should be thought seriously is that in what sense the economic formation of society is "similar" to the process of natural history, and in what sense the former is dissimilar to the latter.

Last but most important, the emphasis of Marx in *Das Kapital* is not the interpretation of historical materialism, but the dissection of the economic formation of capitalism, as well as the communication and production relationships in line with them, i.e. analysis on a special stage and particular aspect of social movement. It is beyond doubt that this special stage and particular aspect are very important, but it is inadequate to use this to replace and skip to the general viewpoint of historical materialism. The basic thought of historical materialism was formed in *Economic and Philosophical Manuscripts of 1844* and comprehensively expounded for the first time in *The German Ideology*. The thoughts of Marx thereafter have been elucidated in an all-around basis in *A Contribution to the Critique of Political Economy*, *Das Kapital* and

---

4   ibid., p. 374.

other philosophical, political economic and scientific socialist works, as well as anthropological manuscripts in his later years. We should not stay at one aspect during research.

2 WHAT IS MEANT BY "THE PROCESS OF NATURAL HISTORY"?

In a bid to get the issue clear, we should at first make clear what "historical process" is and what "process of natural history" is.

"Historical process", or history for short, is a concept that has extraordinary significance according to Marx. Marx endowed history with the meaning of inherent change and development, and frequently used expressions like "excludes history" and "without historical elements" to criticize those "abstract" viewpoints, including not only various idealisms, metaphysical materialism and natural scientific materialism, but Feuerbach's contemplative materialism. Marx thought, "This connection is ever taking on new forms, and thus presents a 'history'."[5] If there is "no development", there will be "no history".

In the eyes of Marx, history means change, the process during which the new forms of connection continuously emerges, i.e. the process of development. Although there are same repetitions without any change in form and content, there is no history. For instance, when talking about India, the model of the Asiatic mode of production, Marx stated that "Indian society has no history at all, at least no known history."[6], and believed "no history", in essence, meant "" and "immutability". In the Asiatic mode of production, "the simplicity of the organization for production in these self-sufficing communities that constantly reproduce themselves in the same form, and when accidentally destroyed, spring up again on the spot and with the same name, this simplicity supplies the key to the secret of the unchangeableness of Asiatic societies"[7].

Hence, Marx believes that "we know only a single science, the science of history. One can look at history from two sides and divide it into the history of nature and the history of men", that is to say, history can be divided into the process of natural history and the process of social history. In "the existing world", during human practical activity, the

---

5   Marx and Engels, *Feuerbach*. Beijing: People's Publishing House, 1988: p. 25.
6   *Selected Works of Karl Marx and Friedrich Engels*. 2nd Ed., Vol. 1, p. 767.
7   Marx, *Das Kapital*, p. 361.

history of man and the history of nature are inseparable. The two sides "are dependent on each other so long as men exist". But for the convenience of analysis, we separate them for the time being.

"The process of natural history" conceived by Marx at that time referred to the process of the diversification of connections in nature. Judging the scientific conditions at the times of Marx, he conceived that process based on Darwin's theory of evolution – considering the process of the diversification of connections in nature as "the process of biological evolution". Marx pointed out that "Darwin has interested us in the history of nature's technology, i.e., in the formation of the organs of plants and animals, which organs serve as instruments of production for sustaining life."[8]

So "the process of natural history" mentioned by Marx does not generally refer to "natural necessity", but to the "history of formation", the "history of generation", of the "organs" of plants and animals, but such "history of formation" or "history of generation" is characterized by the followings: (1) it is self-organized by plants and animals during their interaction with surroundings in their life; (2) this process appears as a generating process of continuous diversification of the "organs" of plants and animals, and it is essentially the development history of plants and animals; (3) this process is also pushed forward by plants and animals blindly and unconsciously. However, in this blind process, a path of development, a course in diversified forms, emerges.

"The process of natural history" mentioned by Marx, in a manner of speaking, is quite different from that understood by current textbook of Marxist philosophy. As far as Marx is concerned, the process of natural history is objective, and does not change with man's will; it has inherent regularity, which, however, exists in the self-organized activity of plants and animals and is reflected by the diversification of the "organs" of plants and animals; natural regularity and necessity mean the irresistible trend of the diversification in the self-organized activity of plants and animals.

I notice that the apprehension of Marx on "the process of natural history" had deepened into geology: "as in geological formations, these historical forms contain a whole series of primary, secondary, tertiary

---

8 Marx, *Das Kapital*, p. 374.

types, etc."[9] But it should be also pointed out that his apprehension on "the process of natural history" had not extended into, and was impossible to extend into, the mechanical, physical and chemical processes in nature for the sciences at his times had not developed to that level. At that time, the principle of "entropy increase" for the development of nature based on the second law of thermodynamics just proved that the physical process of nature was spontaneously trending toward "disorder". In this connection, Engels criticized "the theory of heat death", which applied the principle of "entropy increase" to the whole universe.

However, in respect of how physical and chemical processes achieved their "historical developments", the problem was not proved at the times of Marx and Engels, and there was only, at most, philosophical logical derivation correspondingly. It was not until the 1970s that the "historical process" of physical and chemical movements was proved by the "non-equilibrium thermodynamics" of Prigogine and the "synergetics" of Haken. While dealing with the evolution of dissipative structure, Prigogine pointed out, "Bifurcation introduces in a sense 'history' into physics. ... In this way we introduce in physics and chemistry a 'historical' element, which until now seemed to be reserved only for sciences dealing with biological, social, and cultural phenomena."[10] It was not until that time that we got an understanding on the overall meaning of "the process of natural history" – "the process of natural history" simply refers to the fact that the development of nature is a self-organizing process of the movement of nature itself, whose development is shown as a generating process during which the forms of nature turn to more and more diversified and complex.

The "historical process" of nature is a process formed by nature itself during blind movement rather than a development process predetermined, but it is shown as an irreversible movement process with an arrow. This movement process goes roughly like this: what was generated earliest in nature was low equilibrium structure, which moved spontaneously toward "disorder" and "entropy increase"; due to specific fluctuation conditions, far-from equilibrium state was formed; as a result, equilibrium structure negated itself and gave rise to self-organizing dissipative structure. Since then, the historical process of nature is manifested as a self-organized diversifying process of dissipative

9　*Karl Marx and Friedrich Engels.* 1st Chinese Ed., Vol. 19, p. 432.
10　Prigogine, *Time, Structure and Fluctuations*, see *Collected Nobel Lectures of 1977*, p. 42.

structure from simplicity to complexity, especially as an unceasingly complicating and upgrading process of "organs" in the system of plants and animals. The overall movement process of nature conforms to the concept of "history" meant by Marx, that is, connection is ever taking on new forms.

3 IN WHAT SENSE DOES THE ECONOMIC LAWS OF SOCIETY EQUAL TO NATURAL LAWS?

The thinking skip that takes social development as the process of natural history is premised on the opinion that views the economic laws of society as natural laws. It is true that Marx mentions the economic laws of society equal to natural laws in many places; for example, in *Das Kapital*, he repeatedly refers to "the natural laws of capitalist production", "even when a society has got upon the right track for the discovery of the natural laws of its movement – and it is the ultimate aim of this work"[11]. Lenin had stated, "Marx speaks of the economic law of motion of society, even referring to this law as a Naturgesetz – a law of nature"[12]. However, the problem is that in what sense Marx considers the economic laws of society are natural laws.

The economic laws of society are the laws of men's economic activity. As the most important laws of society, they reflect the sociality, historicity and epochal character of human activity most deeply. The economic laws of society are different from natural laws: (1) the economic laws of society run through the relationship between man and man through the exchange between man and nature; (2) the economic laws of society are a process of the appropriation of "material exchange" in the form of man and by means of the inherent measure of man; (3) the economic laws of society are essentially practical, as the activity laws of man in economic practice, changing continuously along with the changes in the pattern of men's economic practice, and their realization also depends on the practice of man. Natural laws are the mechanical, physical, chemical and biological laws of nature, existing themselves blindly; when they are not cognized by men, natural laws appear to be opposite to men; once they are discovered, they can be utilized by men to conquer natural forces with sciences. Obviously, natural laws and social laws are different in essence.

11   Marx, *Das Kapital* (Translation of Vol. I of French Edition Revised by the Author), p. 4.
12   *Collected Works of Lenin*. Beijing: People's Publishing House, 1984: 2nd Chinese Ed., Vol. 1, p. 105.

As a matter of fact, Marx regards the economic laws of society as natural laws in dual sense: one is the particularity of the economic laws of capitalist society; the other is the particularity of the foundation of entire economic laws.

From Marx's point of view, the economic movement of capitalism is a typical social movement. "In all forms where landed property rules, the natural relation still predominant. In those where capital rules, the social, historically created element."[13] Capitalism is a social formation that has an advantage in the historical factors of society, and meanwhile it is a antagonistic social formation. It is because of such antagonism that the economic laws of society choose to appear in the particular form of natural laws, which are opposite to man. That is to say, when the producers lose the right to control their own social relations and autonomous activities, "the social character of the means of production and of the products today reacts against the producers, periodically disrupts all production and exchange, acts only like a law of nature working blindly, forcibly, destructively"[14]. "What are we to think of a law which can only assert itself through periodic upheavals? It is certainly a natural law based on the unconsciousness of the participants."[15] Thus, it is clear that the appearance of the economic laws of society in the form of natural laws, which are opposite to man, in essence, is the reflection of the "social character" of capitalist society, of the antagonism in capitalism and other social formations before it. In other words, the social formation where the relationship between man and man is antagonistic makes social laws have to take the form of natural laws. This is the first point.

Second, Marx thinks that economic laws have their eternal basis, that is, the process of "material exchanges" between man and nature. As Marx pointed out, "As labor is a creator of use value, is useful labor, it is a necessary condition, independent of all forms of society, for the existence of the human race; it is an eternal nature-imposed necessity, without which there can be no material exchanges between man and Nature, and therefore no life."[16] Only in this "general" sense, i.e. in the sense of the creation of "use value", can the economic laws of society be considered as a natural law embodying the "material exchanges" between man and nature. However, since such "material exchanges" are

---

13 *Karl Marx and Friedrich Engels*. 1st Chinese Ed., Vol. 46 (I), p. 45.
14 *Selected Works of Karl Marx and Friedrich Engels*. 2nd Ed., Vol. 3, p. 629.
15 *Karl Marx and Friedrich Engels*. 1st Chinese Ed., Vol. 23, p. 92.
16 *Karl Marx and Friedrich Engels*. 1st Chinese Ed., Vol. 23, p. 56.

the foundation for all social movements, it has to take on a social form. Therefore the economic laws of society will not appear in the form of pure "natural laws", and the movement of them is always a process of social movement based on the natural law of "material exchanges" between man and nature.

This thought is elaborated more thoroughly by Marx in Volume III of *Das Kapital*. According to Marx, the "material exchanges" between man and nature compose a realm of nature-imposed necessity, the foundation for "all social formations" and "all possible modes of production", and the production of human beings in future is just "rationally regulating their interchange with Nature", and "achieving this ... under conditions most favorable to, and worthy of, their human nature"[17]. Evidently, Marx acknowledges the natural process of economic laws in the sense that all possible modes of production are abstracted away from the process of material exchange between man and nature – the foundation for the laws of economic activity.

But as long as any specific social form is involved, Marx will immediately view economic laws from the perspective of society. In his opinion, the mark to differentiate social stages is not what is produced, but how to produce. He firmly opposes to interpret social development with natural laws. In the letter to Kugelmann, Marx criticized the naturalization of social laws by Lange, and said:

"Mr. Lange, you see, has made a great discovery. All history may be subsumed in one single great natural law. This natural law is the phrase (– the Darwinian expression becomes, in this application, just a phrase –) 'struggle for life', and the content of this phrase is the Malthusian law of population, or rather over-population. Thus, instead of analyzing this 'struggle for life' as it manifests itself historically in various specific forms of society, all that need be done is to transpose every given struggle into the phrase 'struggle for life', and then this phrase into the Malthusian 'population fantasy'."[18]

Here, the issue Marx is concerned with is what is manifested "historically in various specific forms", and he always interprets society with "historical" methodology. More importantly, he believes economic

17 *Karl Marx and Friedrich Engels*. 1st Chinese Ed., Vol. 25, pp. 926 – 927.
18 *Karl Marx and Friedrich Engels*. Beijing: People's Publishing House, 1975: 1st Chinese Ed., Vol. 32, pp. 671 – 672.

laws are not preformed, but are generated during human "material practice", during history; there is no an existing unchanging economic law
available in front of men for cognition, and economic laws also have
historicity. The grasping of social laws (including economic laws) is
changing historically, and "man's reflections on the forms of social life,
and consequently, also, his scientific analysis of those forms, take a
course directly opposite to that of their actual historical development.
He begins, post festum, with the results of the process of development
ready to hand before him."[19]

As a result, to forecast a road of social development in advance and
believe there preexists an economic law of society is not the opinion
of Marxism on social laws. With respect to the opinion that the process of human history is restricted by the economic laws, I admit that
there is a general trend for social development; all social life (including economic life) is essentially practical, and in this sense, I think the
realization of economic laws is also a historical process, the process of
"material practice" and human autonomous activity. Social laws, fundamentally different from natural laws, are "the laws of man's own social action"[20]. Equating the economic laws of society with natural laws
will beget nothing but abstraction, logicalization and preforming of the
economic laws of society, which, in essence, regress to the "absolute
plan" of Hegel.

4 IN WHAT SENSE IS THE DEVELOPMENT OF THE
ECONOMIC FORMATION OF SOCIETY SIMILAR
TO THE PROCESS OF NATURAL HISTORY?

Just as "material exchange" as an intermediary between the economic
laws of society and the natural laws, economic technology of society
is the intermediary between the development of the economic formation of society and the process of natural history. To put it another way,
they are in such relationships: economic laws of society – material exchange – natural laws, and economic formation of society – economic
technology of society – process of natural history. Here, the economic technology of society has direct relation with material exchange.
However, current historical materialism system does not deal with the
concepts of material exchange and economic technology of society; the
economic formation of society is traditionally viewed as the relations

---

19   Marx, *Das Kapital* (Translation of Vol. I of French Edition Revised by the Author), p. 55.
20   *Selected Works of Karl Marx and Friedrich Engels*. 2nd Ed., Vol. 3, p. 634.

of production directly, as economic base, and even as social formations. This is the cognitive origin of the skip from "similarity" between
the economic formation of society and the process of natural history to
sameness between the two, that is, the opinion that "social formation is
a process of natural history".

It should be pointed out that abstracting the economic formation and
technology of society out of social development is a tremendous deepening of Marx in social cognition. In *The German Ideology*, Marx had
considered the division of labor as an intermediary between productivity and ownership: "division of labor and private property are, moreover, identical expressions: in the one the same thing is affirmed with
reference to activity as is affirmed in the other with reference to the
product of the activity"[21]. But the concept of the economic formation of
society had not been stripped from "activity" at that time, and Marx was
more interesting in the relationship of ownership. He therefore classified historical stages, based on ownership, into "tribal ownership", "ancient communal and State ownership", "feudal or estate property" and
"capitalist ownership". It was not until 1895 that Marx brought forth
the concept of "social economic formation" for the first time in *Preface
to A Contribution to the Critique of Political Economy*. From then on,
he made a survey on society with the idea of economic formation all
along. He made two advancements in *Preface to A Contribution to the
Critique of Political Economy*:

Firstly, dividing history according to the economic formation of society instead of ownership. He pointed out, "In broad outlines Asiatic,
ancient, feudal, and modern bourgeois modes of production can be des-
ignated as progressive epochs in the economic formation of society."
Thus, the coordinates for surveying history was transformed.

Secondly, giving a definition to the economic formation of society,
namely "economic structure of society". The content of the concept
of social economic formation is more deepened in *Das Kapital*. Marx
analyzed the history of instrument development in the economic movement of society, and compared the instruments of production of man
with the organs of plants and animals, reaching the conclusion that the
theory of evolution of Darwin revealed "natural technology" – the history concerning how the organs of plants and animals as instruments

---

21   Marx and Engels, Feuerbach, p. 28.

of production for sustaining life were formed, and the history of how social technology – "the productive organs of man" – was formed was of equally important significance. "Technology reveals the mode of activity of man to nature, the production process of man's material life, thus the social relations and the origin of spiritual concepts resulting therefrom."[22] Seen from this point, the concept of the economic formation of society should be the economic structure of society on the basis of social technology.

So, by saying that the development of the economic formation of society is "similar" to the process of natural history, Marx means that just as the development of plants and animals in nature is the process of formation and development based on their own organs, the development of the economic formation of society is also a process of formation and development based on "the productive organs of man". Any overstatement of this similarity, misunderstanding of "the process of natural process" as preformed and linear social development, and opinion that the development of all nations is subject to a sole path will bring about catastrophic consequences for society and human development.

The development of social technology is manifested as an orderly evolution process of economic structure, to which various approaches are available, including "spontaneously-generated", "derivative", "intermediate", "typical" and other formations. Here, we must make a distinction between the following points:

Firstly, those epochs of economic formations of society mentioned by Marx, i.e. Asiatic, ancient, feudal, and modern bourgeois, are not the common development path of all nations. It is a path with specific coordinate system and particular conditions. Marx, specifically speaking, deals with this issue by focusing on the development of capitalism in Europe. In other words, this path takes Europe as the coordinate system, relative to the typical path of European capitalism. As Marx said, what he studied was the mode of production of capitalism, and the typical case he studied was England.

Marx had not ever asked all nations to take the same path, and on the contrary, he set himself against that. In the letter to Editor of the *Otecestvenniye Zapisky*, Marx stated, "He feels himself obliged to

---

22   Marx, *Das Kapital* (Translation of Vol. I of French Edition Revised by the Author), p. 374.

metamorphose my historical sketch of the genesis of capitalism in Western Europe into a historico-philosophic theory of the marche generale [general path] imposed by fate upon every people, whatever the historic circumstances in which it finds itself ... He is both honoring and shaming me too much."[23] In dealing with social development, He often said "this ... does not apply to ... the orient", "which is so considered only from the European point of view", and so on.

This indicates that Marx does not conceive "the process of natural history" as the development path of Asiatic – ancient – feudal – capitalistic – socialistic, or as a general development path that is preformed for all peoples. Those who conceive "the process of natural history" as a trans-historical "necessity", as the sole path to which the development of all nations is bound, i.e. the path going through primitive – servile – feudal – capitalistic – socialistic society, are imposing the development of Europe on other nations, and such act means nothing but the abstraction and preforming of historical necessity.

Secondly, Marx views social development as the self-organizing process of human beings, and believes the specific path of this process is diversified. He never studied history in a single track, and besides "typical", "original" relations of production he was concerned with, Marx frequently raised questions to himself, "Secondary and tertiary matters; in general, derivative, inherited, not original relations of production. Influence here of international relations."[24]

Apparently, here involves a grander path of social development. From Marx's point of view, the approaches and paths for the formation of capitalism is diversified, for example, American "bourgeois society did not develop on the foundation of the feudal system, but developed rather from itself"[25]. "In real history, wage labor arises out of the dissolution of slavery and serfdom – or of the decay of communal property, as with oriental and Slavonic peoples – and, in its adequate, epoch-making form, the form which takes possession of the entire social being of labor, out of the decline and fall of the guild economy, of the system of Estates, of labor and income in kind, of industry carried on as rural subsidiary occupation, of small-scale feudal agriculture etc."[26] Here,

---

23   *Karl Marx and Friedrich Engels*. 1st Chinese Ed., Vol. 19, p. 130.
24   *Karl Marx and Friedrich Engels*. 1st Chinese Ed., Vol. 46 (I), p. 47.
25   ibid., p. 4.
26   *Karl Marx and Friedrich Engels*. 1st Chinese Ed., Vol. 46 (I), p. 14.

there is no a fixed model or a trans-historical necessity, or a so-called "process of natural history".

Thirdly, if we focus on the process of social technology, namely the specific composing model of social production, then we will find there really exists an orderly historical process from low level to high level in it, and this process really "can be determined with the precision of natural science", because social technology marks in what specific mode man realizes material exchange with nature and the shaping process, and indeed it is not subject to the will, emotion, need and selection of man.

The irreversibility of the development of social technology is manifested by no duplication of the road that has been walked in history; this is a "transforming" process that happens during the autonomous activity of mankind, continuously under the "general illumination" of the highest level of era development. For example, if we are designing the social development of China, it will be certainly unnecessary to go through the stage of naturally formed capitalism. However, it is also impossible to skip from backward social technology of natural economy to modern social technology. Therefore, the necessity and rationality of the stage of commodity economy must be confirmed according to the process of technology, which is an ineluctable "process of natural history". Of course, we can make this course shorter and faster on the basis of modern world pattern and technology pattern. This obviously involves the "derivative", "inherited", "not original" processes in the development of technology, as well as the influence of world intercourse and international relations.

5 NATURAL, DERIVATIVE AND TRANSCENDING FORMATIONS IN SOCIAL DEVELOPMENT

In the process of social development, social formation goes through three different types, namely natural formation, derivative formation, and transcending formation. When every nation or state was secluded, the historical development of each repeated "identical historical necessity", and the model of social development largely took on natural formation. After the factor of communication arose, especially when communication became regional or worldwide, "in place of the old local and national seclusion and self-sufficiency, we have intercourse in every direction, universal inter-dependence of nations"[27], thereby forming the situation that the change of every nation started to be dependent on that of other nations. Since then, the development model based on natural formation had been sublated, and derivative or transcending formation began to appear and gradually became the general or conventional phenomenon in social development, which gained its speed accordingly.

In a nation or state with natural formation, external factors or relations exert very little impact on social development, so they are negligible, and its development is mainly subject to its internal factors and relations. In the words of contemporary social development theory, natural formation belongs to endogenous development. The ancient civilizations, such as China, India, the Tigris and Euphrates, Greece and Egypt, almost developed endogenously, and the development respectively of Chinese feudal society and capitalist society in Western Europe also fell under endogenous development. Such development was basically finished under a situation of mutual isolation and non-interference. In general, before capitalism created the world history, natural formation was dominant in social development.

The dominate position of natural formation was premised on an isolated and closed environment. According to Marx, natural formation is a "spontaneous generation" process of various elements and relations in the society; each stage in this development process is "a naturally developing stage" of the society. "Specialization" of society formed by "spontaneous generation", i.e. different genetic "code" mechanisms among different spontaneous generation types, determines the independence of different communities; the "specialized" genetic "code" is also the source of the diversification of social development. Due to different genetic "codes", different communities have different paths, emphases and growth points in their developments. Marx laid much importance on the analysis of the "spontaneous generation" of society. As far as he is concerned, "relations of personal dependence (entirely spontaneous at the outset) are the first social forms"[28], and men in ancient times were "the original men produced by generatio aequivoca [spontaneous generation]"[29]. The analysis on "spontaneous generation" is the starting point of Marx's analyses on all social organics, because

27   *Selected Works of Karl Marx and Friedrich Engels*. 2nd Ed., Vol. 1, p. 276.
28   *Karl Marx and Friedrich Engels*. 1st Chinese Ed., Vol. 46 (I), p. 104.
29   *Selected Works of Karl Marx and Friedrich Engels*. 2nd Ed., Vol. 1, p. 77.

even though the society has developed into an advanced formation, it still shows the traces of "spontaneous generation".

Even the society developing in an isolated and closed environment, i.e. natural formation in social development, has its own typical formation, such as the typical of Asiatic or oriental society, the typical of Western European capitalism, etc. The Chinese feudal society is the typical case, "the living fossil", of oriental society in that it embodies "the common feature of all oriental movements"[30]. There were three paths to the generation of capitalism, that is to say, capitalism arose out of the "decay" of communal property, the "dissolution" of slavery, and the "decline and fall" of feudalism. Among them, capitalism arising out of the decline and fall of feudalism is the typical case of the spontaneous generation of capitalism. And more than that, different aspects of capitalism also have their respective typical cases. In Marx's opinion, England is the model of the economic development of capitalism and France the model of political development.

When communication goes beyond adjacent areas and serves as an indispensable factor in the daily life and act of all peoples, "derivative formation" in social development emerges. While investigating social development, Marx came up with another crucial thought – "secondary and tertiary matters; in general, derivative, inherited, not original relations of production. Influence here of international relations."[31] In Marx's view, those spontaneously generated social relations are original, i.e. primary, and the derivative and inherited relations belong to secondary and tertiary matters, produced by communications between nations or states. As to the relationship between the primary relations and the secondary and tertiary relations, the primary is the starting point, and the subsequent development deviates from the "original relations of production". Marx had ever described such deviation, "The original form of this property is therefore itself direct common property (oriental form, modified in the Slavonic; developed to the point of antithesis, but still as the secret, if antithetical, foundation in classical and Germanic property)."[32]

---

30   *Karl Marx and Friedrich Engels.* Beijing: People's Publishing House, 1963: 1st Chinese Ed., Vol. 15, p. 545.
31   *Karl Marx and Friedrich Engels.* 1st Chinese Ed., Vol. 46 (I), p. 47.
32   Ibid., 498.

That is to say, there exists such a movement in the original formation or primitive form of society: typical oriental form, modified form in the Slavonic, and antithetical form in the Germanic, all of which constitute differences in the "original relations of production". In the process of intercourse among nations, the differences in the "original relations of production" are transformed into the secondary matters, and different original forms result in large differences. "Slavery, serfdom, etc., where the laborer himself appears among the natural conditions of production for a third individual or community ... is always secondary. (This character of slavery does not apply to the general slavery of the orient, which is so considered only from the European point of view.)"[33] This means that in the derivative, secondary relations, formal dissimilarity has arisen.

Regarding the tertiary relations, the condition is more complicated. There are three basic forms: (1) brought by the conqueror to the conquered at a lower development stage; (2) brought by the conqueror to the conquered at a higher development stage; and (3) both of the conqueror and the conquered in the same social formation but at different development stages. These three conditions have different impacts on the development of derivative social formation. As Marx pointed out, "The feudalism introduced into England was formally more complete than the feudalism which had naturally grown up on France."[34] That was because "whereas in its home it (the form of intercourse) was still encumbered with interests and relationships left over from earlier periods, here it can and must be established completely and without hindrance, if only to assure the conquerors' lasting power (England and Naples after the Norman conquest, when they received the most perfect form of feudal organization.)"[35] On the contrary, there was also a plenty of "destruction of an old civilization by a barbarous people and the resulting formation of an entirely new organization of society (Rome and the barbarians; feudalism and Gaul; the Byzantine Empire and the Turks.)"[36]. All of these constitute a certain variant of social formation, respectively, namely "secondary form introduced and transmitted"[37].

---

33 Ibid., 496.
34 Ibid., pp. 489 – 490.
35 *Selected Works of Karl Marx and Friedrich Engels*. 2nd Ed., Vol. 1, p. 125.
36 ibid., p. 125.
37 *Karl Marx and Friedrich Engels*. 1st Chinese Ed., Vol. 46 (I), p. 489.

The rising of the capitalist mode of production has opened a new era of "world intercourse", which is participated in by all nations and states consciously or unconsciously, thus realizing the comprehensiveness of intercourse's subject and forming "all-sided production", "all-around dependence", and "world-historical co-operation"; every nation or state is facing a whole based on the globe and composed of other nations and states, thus leading to the universality of intercourse intermediary.

Intermediary involves every nation or state in the world intercourse, so a worldwide, global intermediary form and correlation are formed. Owing to such universal intermediary, each nation or state is able to compare itself with others on a universal basis so as to absorb nutrients in various aspects. As intercourse become worldwide, the characteristics of social development take a fundamental change: the one-sidedness and limitation of every nation in the past are sufficiently uncovered during the intercourse, and it is by virtue of intercourse that the one-sidedness of a nation is developed into an all-sided force.

"The further the separate spheres, which interact on one another, extend in the course of this development, the more the original isolation of the separate nationalities is destroyed by the developed mode of production and intercourse and the division of labor between various nations naturally brought forth by these, the more history becomes world history."[38] As intercourse become worldwide, history is transformed into "world history", and the phenomenon of "transcendence" during social development becomes into a universal or conventional thing. If the "secondary and tertiary" relations in social development are still the product of regional intercourse, then transcending formation, as a universal phenomenon in social development, is a product of world intercourse.

Before world intercourse and world history resulting therefrom, transcending formation had occurred in social development; for instance, after conquering the Roman Empire through "martial intercourse", the Germanic nation stepped over slavery, and directly entered feudalism from primitive society. That, however, was after all a particular phenomenon prior to the formation of world history. Then, after world history came into being, transcending formation in social development became a universal phenomenon. North America was still in primitive society before European immigrants arrived there, but following the

---

38 *Selected Works of Karl Marx and Friedrich Engels.* 2nd Ed., Vol. 1, p. 88.

arrival of European immigrants, capitalism was established rapidly there. So Marx thinks that in America, "the bourgeois society did not develop on the foundation of the feudal system, but developed rather from itself"[39]; the similar road was also taken by Oceania; in Africa, there were nations directly enter capitalist society, some from primitive society and some from slave society; "as with oriental and Slavonic peoples", capitalism arose out "of the decay of communal property"; and in Asia, some relatively backward states strode across the "Crafting Gorge" of capitalism, and directly took the way of socialism.

Throughout the world history, slave society, feudal society and subsequent capitalist society have been leapt over by different nations in different regions at different stages, therefore we can see that "transcendence" itself exists universally as a conventional repeatable phenomenon in social development.

The reason why "transcendence" itself could become a conventional phenomenon in social development is closely related to world intercourse, and meanwhile it is premised on the spatial coexistence of several social formations. The changes of social formation in different nations are unsynchronized – when some have entered feudal or even capitalist society, some might still stay at slave or even primitive society, thereby forming the situation that several social formations coexist spatially. At the same time, world intercourse makes different nations correlated with one another in an all-around manner, meaning that nations entering the intercourse process will influence, interact on, and infiltrate into each other. When nations with different social formations communicate with each other, three "transcendences" will occur:

First, when a backward nation conquers a relatively advanced one, it will consciously or unconsciously adapt to the higher level of productive forces of the conquered and form a new social structure, and thereby consciously or unconsciously transcend a certain social formation.

Second, when an advanced nation conquers a backward one, it will "introduce" the higher productive forces and social relations of itself into the backward nation, thus impelling the backward to transcend a certain social form and take on a more advanced social formation; in this case, the advanced nation is an "unconscious tool of history".

---

39   *Karl Marx and Friedrich Engels.* 1st Chinese Ed., Vol. 46 (I), p. 4.

Third, when a nation is at its historical turning point, the advanced social formation is more attractive to it, and under the "historical enlightenment" of advanced nations, the backward nation is able to consciously take advantage of their experience and fruits, and select and design its own development form in the framework of social formation of advanced society, thereby consciously transcending a certain social formation. Therefore, Marx pointed out, "The whole internal structure of the nation itself depends on the stage of development reached by its production and its internal and external intercourse."[40]

Thus it is clear that world intercourse and the correlation generated by it cause the variation of social development. Although the object and the approach of "transcendence" of every nation is particular, as long as there exist different social formations in the same times, as long as there exists world intercourse, "transcendence" will happen ceaselessly and repeatedly, becoming a conventional phenomenon in social development.

The reason why world intercourse is able to change the progress of social development and accelerate social development increasingly is because there is the law of additive effect for intercourse activity in human society, that is to say, what is put into intercourse tends to be the latest fruits or spare things of a nation; by changing spare things for needed things, the nation gains a new strength and obtains the "explosive power" for its development. In this way, nations participating in intercourse are able to share the latest achievements with all mankind, avoiding time waste in "starting right over again from the beginning" and passive consequences of loss, so that they can continuously create newer things based on the achievements having been gained by mankind. Thanks to the fundamental extrication from repeated labor, social stagnation is gotten rid of, and development is more and more accelerated. The condition under the state of self-seclusion, or when intercourse is limited to adjacent areas, is completely different. In such case, "every invention must be made separately in each locality, and mere chances such as irruptions of barbaric peoples, even ordinary wars, are sufficient to cause a country with advanced productive forces and needs to have to start right over again from the beginning", and "every invention had to be made daily anew and in each locality independently"[41]. This gives

---

40   *Selected Works of Karl Marx and Friedrich Engels.* 2nd Ed., Vol. 1, p. 68.
41   *Selected Works of Karl Marx and Friedrich Engels.* 2nd Ed., Vol. 1, pp. 107 – 108.

rise to repeated labor, and forms the law of repetition effect of closed behavior, leading to the stagnation of social development. "Only when commerce has become world commerce and has as its basis large-scale industry, when all nations are drawn into the competitive struggle, is the permanence of the acquired productive forces assured."[42] This is the precondition for the acceleration of social development.

"Transcendence" becomes a universal or conventional phenomenon in social development. The diversification of the paths of social develop- ment is neither "antinomy" of the integrity of world history nor negation to the "internal cause determinism" of materialistic dialectics. All so- cial development originates from the contradiction between productive forces and intercourse form, but because of the existence of intercourse, especially of world intercourse, the revolution of a specific state does not need to wait this contradiction to develop to the extreme situation in the state. "The competition with industrially more advanced countries, brought about by the expansion of international intercourse, is suffi- cient to produce a similar contradiction in countries with a backward industry."[43] For this reason, social development is not only a "process of natural history", but also "can shorten and lessen the birth-pangs", thus speeding up itself.

In this way, the social development of specific nation takes on its own particularity in terms of the path, form and model. Diversification does not mean pluralism. Social development is unitary in essence – the con- dition of material life is the original cause, and economic premise and condition are decisive in the final analysis. Economic necessity is a red thread running through all social development and leading us to funda- mentally apprehend this development process, including the historical course of socialism's first realization in oriental society.

The emergence and universalization of transcending formation is not the negation against the overall succession of human historical devel- opment, and we cannot thus think that the development of social for- mation is like a bottle falling down on the ground, whose fragments are scattered everywhere without a definite direction. During social development, some nations or states may transcend a certain historical stage, but their histories are impossible to go against the overall process

---

42 Ibid., p. 108.
43 Ibid., pp. 115 – 116.

of human history. The direction of "transcendence", contrarily, is consistent with the direction of human history and its running law. The "transcendence" of a nation's historical development takes insurmountability of the process of human history as premise, and the limit of "transcendence" is determined by real existing social formations. So far the transcendence of a nation over a definite social formation is realized under the condition that there has been more advanced social formation in the world, especially in neighboring countries. If there had been no the Roman Empire, the Germanic could not been able to skip slavery and directly enter feudal society from primitive society; without the existence of capitalism and the world history it created, some nations could not have leapt over feudalism or slavery and directly enter capitalist society from slavery or primitive society, some backward oriental nations could not have skipped over the historical stage of capitalism to socialism directly, and "transcendence" could not have been the universal phenomenon in social development.

That's why Marx thinks that the comparatively advanced social relations reached by a nation after "transcendence" is not generated spontaneously within itself, but is "introduced and transmitted". When there coexist several different social formations at the same time, the real existing advanced social formation, or the more advanced social formation pointed to by the development of times, plays a guiding role for the transcendence of backward nations. The limit of "transcendence" of a backward nation is, in a definite sense, dependent on the developed mode of production of the advanced nation and the degree of its "transmission" or "introduction" into the backward.

CHAPTER VIII

HISTORICAL NECESSITY: A NEW INTERPRETATION

Since the establishment of the philosophy of history by Vico, the issue of historical necessity had been a crucial problem focused by western philosophy of history, and up to now it is still the bone of contention of contemporary western philosophy of history; comprehensively and scientifically solving the problem of historical necessity is one of the great contributions of Marxian philosophy of history – historical materialism – to the human history of thoughts. However, Marx's view of historical necessity has been confronted with various distortions, criticisms and challenges at the present times. Therefore, we need to have a new investigation and survey on the idea of historical necessity in the western philosophy of history and the evolution of this concept, in order to deepen the research on historical necessity.

1 ESTABLISHMENT OF THE IDEA OF HISTORICAL NECESSITY

In the human history of thoughts, Italian ideologist Vico was the first person to explore historical necessity. In his groundbreaking works concerning the philosophy of history – *Principles of the New Science Concerning the Common Nature of Nations*, Vico emphasizes the survey of the "common nature" of nations, namely historical necessity, and brings forward two significant viewpoints: (1) the human history is created by human beings themselves; (2) historical development has its necessity, and the history of any nation is bound to go through three stages, i.e. theocracy, hero and human rights.

Prior to Vico, the theological conception of history reigned supreme, and people were convinced of the opinion that "the history of men is an order determined by God". Vico shifted the center of human history from God to mankind himself, and affirmed the existence of historical necessity from the angle of humanism, which is the uniqueness of Vico's philosophy of history and his contribution to the human history of thoughts. However, when declaring that "history is created by human beings", he also claimed that "nature is created by God". Thus the myth of opposition between nature and history was made in a new form, setting a precedent for the opposition between humanism and scientism.

French enlightenment philosophy probed further into historical necessity. In Rousseau's opinion, the development of production and technology is the major motivation of historical development; the process of history is irreversible, and history is transiting to its opposite just in confrontation and contradiction. Rousseau had studied history and its necessity from the point of view of interaction, thus showing his sensitivity to historicism beyond the expectation of his times. "The doctrine in its first presentation bears almost ostentatiously the imprint of its dialectical origin"[1].

The dialectics of Rousseau was accepted by French utopian socialists, and Saint-Simon and Fourier pushed the idea of historical necessity greatly forward.

---

1 *Karl Marx and Friedrich Engels*. Beijing: People's Publishing House, 1971: 1st Chinese Ed., Vol. 20, p. 152.

First of all, historical development has its inherent necessity. Fourier asserted, "Social movement ... is going on in line with laws", and "these laws of social movement have been seen through by me"[2]. Saint-Simon classified human history into five periods, namely civilizing period, slavery, theology-feudalism, "new feudalism" (capitalism), and future "industrial system", and thought the generation of these five systems was necessary; Fourier divided human history into five ages, i.e. age of unenlightenment, age of patriarchy, age of barbarism, age of civilization, and age of "série" in future, and he also thought the generation of these five ages were necessary, "economically destined".

Next, the inner contradictory movement of society constitutes historical necessity. From Fourier's point of view, the contradictory movement between man's inherent appetite and external material wealth constitutes historical necessity, and "the changes of society are subject to living and economic behaviors"[3]. Saint-Simon classified history into two formations – phenomenon and essence, thinking that the former was restricted by the latter; the change of regime was merely the superficial phenomenon, the form, of history, and the essence of history was the distribution of property and the arrangement of economy.

We can see that the historical philosophy of French utopian socialism had taken a vitally important step towards materialistic apprehension of historical necessity, and it also embraced rich dialectical thoughts, which was really a progress in history. Of course, the historical philosophy of French utopian socialism adopts a kind of scientistic conception of history and conceives historical necessity according to the characteristics of natural necessity, so it does not have a genuine grasp of historical necessity. Saint-Simon called his conception of history "social physics". Fourier affirmed that historical laws "accord with the law of material gravitation expounded by Newton and Leibniz in all aspects"[4].

The reason for such situation is the success of the classical mechanics of Newton, which, accepted by numerous French ideologists, constituted the general theoretical background of the changes in the philosophy of history from the eighteenth century to the early nineteenth century. It aroused a strong emotion of scientism, stimulating Saint-Simon and Fourier to attempt to change their historical theories into a science as

2   *Selected Works of Charles Fourier*. Beijing: The Commercial Press, 1982: Vol. 1, p. 35.
3   ibid., p. 29.
4   ibid., p. 60.

precise as natural sciences, and to conceive historical necessity according to the characteristics of natural necessity. If Vico is believed as the founder of the humanistic philosophy of history, then Saint-Simon and Fourier are the pioneers of the scientistic philosophy of history. Comte's positivistic philosophy of history just arose out of the dissolution of the historical philosophy of French utopian socialism.

"In this system (Hegelian system) – and herein is its great merit – for the first time the whole world, natural, historical, intellectual, is represented as a process, i.e., as in constant motion, change transformation, development."[5] Meanwhile, upon the awareness of certain differences between nature and history, Hegel put forward a unique interpretation on historical necessity.

Firstly, historical necessity is the development of "absolute reason" in time, embodied as "the progress of free consciousness". In the sight of Hegel, it is an irreversible process from the orient to the West, from Greece to the Germanic. The four periods in the world history, i.e. oriental countries, the Greek state, the Roman state and the Germanic state, shows the particular principles of historical necessity respectively in their own histories.

Secondly, historical necessity can be realized only through human activity, and absolute reason and human activity are "the one the warp, the other the woof of the vast arras-web of Universal History"[6]. In Hegel's eyes, without human activity, any great cause in the world is unlikely to succeed. But he also believes historical necessity is a preformed "absolute plan" antecedent to history, and man is just a "living tool" to realize such trans-historical "plan".

Thirdly, historical necessity has "its absolute final purpose", and the unswerving intention to achieve this purpose constitutes the inner connection of history. Hence, the decisive effect of historical necessity is shown in the diachronic one-way process. There is one chance for it to fall upon a nation, and there is no history in a nation that is beyond its track or has experienced its definite principles. That is to say, historical necessity only has the feature of purposiveness, diachronism or linearity, but does not have repeatability and conventionality. Because of this, and because it shows its existence under the imprecisely restricted

---

5   *Selected Works of Karl Marx and Friedrich Engels.* 2nd Ed., Vol. 3, pp. 736 – 737.
6   Hegel, *Philosophy of History.* Beijing, Joint Publishing Company, 1956: p. 62.

condition that countless individuals pursue their particular purposes, it cannot be grasped with the precision of natural sciences. In Hegel's opinion, only by means of philosophical speculation can the essence of history be perceived and the historical necessity grasped through the uproarious surface of history.

The concept of historical necessity after Vico was systematized, but also mystified, by Hegel. In Hegel's idea of historical necessity, so to say, lives a pair of twins called remarkableness and evil consequence.

On the one hand, Hegel dared to think history in generality, and deeply investigated historical necessity in an all-around way; "however abstract and idealist the form employed, yet his evolution of ideas runs always parallel with the evolution of universal history"[7]. Hegel's idea of historical necessity, as a "grand conception of history", an "epoch-making conception of history", exerted a huge influence, and reigned exclusively during the period from the late eighteenth century to the early nineteenth century, "to a greater or lesser extent infected even its opponents"[8]. Hegel started the era of "absolute reason" in the history of philosophy, thereby establishing the authority of historical necessity on the basis of objective idealism.

On the other hand, with Hegel historical necessity boiled down to trans-historical "absolute plan", "absolute reason", thus he made a mistake of importing necessity into history outside of it. At both starting and ending points of his idea of historical necessity, history and man were divorced, and he merely acknowledged the initiative of man in form but in fact thoroughly deprived history of its human nature. Taking off the mysterious cloth of Hegel's idea of historical necessity and revealing historical necessity in the activity of man, the real subject of history, is the "absolute command" for the further development of the philosophy of history.

2 BASIC FEATURES OF HISTORICAL NECESSITY

The revolutionary change in the idea of historical necessity is realized by Marxian philosophy of history. Historical materialism believes history differs from nature: what happens in nature is the result of blind effect; "in the history of society, on the contrary, the actors are all endowed

---

7   *Selected Works of Karl Marx and Friedrich Engels*. 2nd Ed., Vol. 2, p. 42.
8   *Selected Works of Karl Marx and Friedrich Engels*. 2nd Ed., Vol. 4, p. 220.

with consciousness, are men acting with deliberation or passion, working towards definite goals; nothing happens without a conscious purpose, without an intended aim."[9] As far as Marx is concerned, history is no other than the activity of man who is pursuing his own objectives. However, history is inseparable from nature, and society in reality is the unity of dual relationship between man and nature and between man and man. "The entire so-called history of the world is nothing but the creation of man through human labor, nothing but the emergence of nature for man."[10] Without taking the relationship between man and nature into consideration, society can only be built on nothingness; excluding the relationship of man to nature from history will inevitably lead to historical idealism.

In Marx's eyes, what differentiates history from nature but meanwhile connects the two is the practical activity of man. As the primary and fundamental form of practice, labor is the process of man to cause, regulate and control his material exchange with nature through his activity; in this process, it is necessary for individuals to establish definite relations with each other for they exchange their activities. At the same time, the result that will be obtained at the completion of practice already exists there at the commencement of the process, as the purpose, in the mind of the practitioner in the form of idea. That is to say, practice inherently embraces triple relationships, respectively between man and nature, between man and man, and between man and consciousness; and the ensemble of these relationships compose the basic social relations. Practice, in a manner of speaking, condenses all social relations into itself, and it is the cradle of all social relations and the realistic foundation of human history, thus constituting the essence of history.

Fundamentally, history is just the development of practical activity of man in time. So Marx argues, "As soon as this active life-process is described, history ceases to be a collection of dead facts as it is with the empiricists (themselves still abstract), or an imagined activity of imagined subjects, as with the idealists."[11] On the premise of this, historical materialism establishes the scientific idea of historical necessity.

---

9   ibid., p. 247.
10 *Karl Marx and Friedrich Engels.* 1st Chinese Ed., Vol. 42, p. 131.
11 *Selected Works of Karl Marx and Friedrich Engels.* 2nd Ed., Vol. 1, p. 73.

Historical materialism first of all ascribes historical necessity to the process of material practice, and believes historical necessity is not only realized, but also formed, in the activity of man. As mentioned before, practice inherently embraces the material exchange between man and nature, activity exchange between man and man, as well as the conversion between material and idea. The first is commonly possessed by human activity and natural movement, while the latter two are unique to the practical activity of man. Practical activity involves material exchange, indicating human activity also must observe the common law of material motion; the activity exchange between man and man and the conversion between material and idea that are particular to it reflect its new, special law of movement that is not found in other natural objects, which is the characteristic featuring the activity of subject, the law of human practical activity covering material motion. Social life is essentially practical, therefore the law of human practical activity is actually the law of historical movement, i.e. historical necessity.

History is the development of practical activity of man in time, and historical necessity is realized and formed in the activity of man. Then we encounter the proposition that "freedom is the appreciation of necessity". According to the materialistic conception of history, this never means that there is an existing historical necessity or law for the convenience of cognition in advance of any historical activity of men; on the contrary, "man's reflections on the forms of social life, and consequently, also, his scientific analysis of those forms, take a course directly opposite to that of their actual historical development. He begins, post festum, with the results of the process of development ready to hand before him"[12], because:

Firstly, there is no a preformed, pure, constant historical necessity or laws, and any specific kind of historical necessity is formed in a definite historical activity and social formation; when such historical activity and social formation come to an end, the specific historical necessity will be no longer in existence.

Secondly, previous historical traditions and established historical conditions serve as preconditions, and determine the general direction, for the historical activity of new generation; but these historical conditions are changed constantly in the historical activity of new generation, and

12   *Karl Marx and Friedrich Engels.* 1st Chinese Ed., Vol. 23, p. 92.

it is during the activity which changes the previous conditions that the new historical necessity determining the destiny of the new generation is formed.

Thirdly, only when a certain historical activity and social relation are sufficiently developed and revealed can a certain historical necessity be really formed in an all-around manner; only at such moment can men understand and grasp such historical necessity. It is in this sense that Marx thinks that the general historical laws abstracted out in the process of "thinking post festum" can be by no means used as the prescription or formula for all other historical ages, and instead, such abstracted history has no value at all once leaving reality.

The relationship between human freedom and historical necessity is essentially an issue concerning practice, not only about cognition.

According to historical materialism, historical necessity has the character of totality. Fundamentally speaking, historical necessity is the restriction of economic movement on human historical process; the contradictory movement between productive forces and relations of production determines the general running trend of history, and constitutes the "central axis" of historical movement. But we cannot equate historical necessity with economic necessity. In the whole history, there is no significant historical event whose origin cannot be explained by economic necessity, and meanwhile there is no significant historical event which is not steered, accompanied and followed by definite political factors and consciousness. The evolution of history, in no case, happens in the dimension of economy. It is impossible for economic necessity to either act as an independent entity divorced from the material practice of man, or purely exert its effect separated from such social elements as politics and culture. Economic necessity itself possesses the characters of sociality and historicity, thus historical necessity based on it has totality, i.e. the product of interactions between economy, politics, culture and other social elements.

According to historical materialism, historical necessity also has the characters of repeatability and conventionality, meaning that under a certain condition, a certain historical necessity will exert effect repeatedly and become a conventional phenomenon. Marx proposed the theory of "five social formations", in the belief that same economic, political and social formations could happen to different nations in different historical periods. However, as a kind of law, the repeatability of historical necessity is different from a natural law in aspect of manifestation. Seen from the manifestation forms, natural laws are more manifested as the laws of dynamics, and historical laws mainly as the laws of statistics.

The notion of the laws of dynamics were generated on the basis of the study on the laws of mechanical motion by classical mechanics, and the characteristic of such laws is that with them, men can be sure of the entire motion of a system according to certain initial materials, and of the status and moving speed of this system at every timing point. For example, according to Newton's Second Law of Motion, as long as we know the momentum of an object at initial position and the force acting on the object, we are able to correctly figure out the motion track of this object, and infer its status at any time from past to future. Generally speaking, the regularity relation between objects reflected by the laws of dynamics is a definite connection of one-to-one correspondence, and demonstrates that the existence or occurrence of a thing must bring about the existence or occurrence of another thing. Under the effect of the laws of dynamics, contingency is negligible.

The laws of statistics reveal the necessary connections between things with the method of statistics, and what they reflect is the regularity relation between a kind of necessity and multiple random phenomena. With respect to the laws of statistics, contingency and random phenomena cannot be ignored, but contrarily, they are exactly presented in a large amount of contingencies and random phenomena. In other words, if things or phenomena do not happen "in a large amount", they will show an indefinite mutual connection; but if the amount is "large", a definite connection will be shown. Taking a coin with even mass for instance, if it is thrown to the air, the chance for head or tail is random, but if it is thrown for plenty of times, the probability for head or tail is 50%. This is regularity. In social life, it is the laws of statistics that play a leading role, or we can say, historical necessity is majorly manifested as the laws of statistics.

In *Das Kapital*, Marx did not only praise Belgian statistician Quetelet for his application of the method of average statistics to study social phenomena, but also uses the method of statistics by himself to reveal a series of laws of capitalist economic movement; he also points out, "inherent laws impose themselves only as the mean of apparently lawless irregularities that compensate one another."[13] The "mean" laws mentioned by Marx are actually the laws of statistics. Because natural laws are more manifested as the laws of dynamics, and historical laws mainly as the laws of statistics, natural sciences are capable of accurately predicting the occurrence of a natural event, whereas social sciences are only able to foresee the trend of social development, but not the occurrence of any historical event.

From Marx's point of view, to analyze economic, political and social forms and grasp historical necessity and its repeatability and conventionality, neither microscope nor chemical reagent is advisable, and both should be substituted by abstract force. Besides, because social relations are ascribed to the relations of production and the relations of production to the relationship between man – the productive force – and nature, historical materialism does not only find out the repeatability and conventionality, as well as the secrets, of historical necessity, but can point out the material changes in society depending on "the precision of natural sciences". This indicates that the materialistic conception of history also encompasses the positiveness of natural sciences to a certain degree. For this reason, historical materialism is valued as "the real positive science"[14] by Marx and Engels. The emergence of notions of "repeatability", "conventionality" and "precision" makes historical materialism a science, a mature science.

In this way, historical materialism shatters the myth of the opposition between material nature and spiritual history, and realizes the genuine resolution of the conflict between natural science and historical science.

Historical necessity is acknowledged as historical determinism, but the determinism of the materialistic conception of history is dialectical, which admits economic necessity will be "transformed" to a certain extent under the reactions from social elements like politics, culture, and so on, and argues historical necessity can be realized only through contingencies.

"It (world history) would, on the other hand, be a very mystical nature, if 'accidents' played no part. These accidents themselves fall naturally into the general course of development and are compensated again by

---

13   *Karl Marx and Friedrich Engels.* 1st Chinese Ed., Vol. 23, p. 120.
14   *Selected Works of Karl Marx and Friedrich Engels.* 2nd Ed., Vol. 1, p. 73.

other accidents."[15] Historical necessity is nothing but an unavoidable trend in social development, which can only be realized under the action of definite conditions. However, historical necessity itself cannot freely select these conditions, and the conditions happening to it are just a kind of "chance" or "accident", namely contingency. So, definite historical necessity must be realized by indefinite contingency, which thus becomes the realization form of historical necessity and brands different features in the manifestations of the same necessity.

In addition, the dialectical determinism of the materialistic conception of history also acknowledges man as the subject of history, and believes historical necessity must be realized through human activity. In terms of the mode of realization, natural necessity exerts its effect spontaneously during the blind interactions between various factors in nature, and it is also realized by such blind interactions; the essential condition for the existence and functioning of historical necessity is human activity, and historical necessity can only be realized through purposive conscious activity of man. Leaving the practical activity of man and the interaction between individuals, historical necessity will lose the carrier by which it exists and the place for it to work, let alone its realization.

Contemporary critics of Marxism usually confuse the determinism of the materialistic conception of history with mechanical determinism, and then attack it greatly. On the one hand, it shows that such critics do not grasp the essential difference between Marx's historical determinism and mechanical determinism; and on the other hand, this is not the fight of Quixote who takes windmill for a demon, but the opposition between two concrete conceptions of history, namely idealist conception of history and materialistic conception of history.

3 CAUSES AND LINKS OF THE APPEARANCE OF IDEA OPPOSED TO HISTORICAL NECESSITY

From Vico to Hegel and then to Marx, it was an age of rapid development of the idea of historical necessity, and more and more ideologists admitted the existence of historical necessity. However, since the late nineteenth century, many ideologists started to suspect, negate and even abandon the idea of historical necessity. If we think the idea of historical necessity reigned over the early modern western philosophy

---

15   *Karl Marx and Friedrich Engels.* Beijing: People's Publishing House, 1973: 1st Chinese Ed., Vol. 33, p. 210.

of history, then the idea negating historical necessity was the dominant ideological trend in the modern western philosophy of history. There were three causes for that cognition reversion:

First of all, the rebellion of Hegel against the philosophy of history; as previously mentioned, Hegel's idea of historical necessity was remarkable, and it had ever exerted a tremendous influence. But Hegel rationalized everything, making reason a new superstition. For the purpose of proving his rationalistic conception of history, he frequently showed no hesitation to crudely cut and distort history, and degraded historiography to the status as the servant of philosophy. For historiography, the idea of historical necessity of Hegel played an arbitrary role. That presumptuous demand and outrageous act evoked the strong dissatisfaction and instinctive resistance of historians. The rebellion against Hegel's philosophy of history became a distinctive feature of western historiography in the second half of the nineteenth century.

Next, the influence of Comte's positivism; from the positivistic point of view of Comte, science can only narrate facts rather than interpret facts. "To explore those so-called initial cause or final cause, for us, is out of the question, and meaningless"[16]; the so-called necessity is nothing but a "constant sequence relation and similarity relation" in experience or between feelings. Achieving a certain success in the second half of the nineteenth century, the positivism of Comte took by historians and philosophers at that time as the "antidote" for Hegel's philosophy of history. It was under the influence of Comte's positivism that western historiography in the second half of the nineteenth century developed towards positivism, becoming "the historiography of positivism". Most of the historians during that period were very keen on ascertaining new facts, but seldom cared about the discovery of laws.

Finally, the fear of historical materialism; within the positive apprehension by the idea of historical necessity of historical materialism on the existing society, there coexists the negative apprehension simultaneously, that is, the understanding on the ineluctable ruin of existing society. The opinion that "what is actual is what is reasonable" is by no means the thinking mode of Marxist philosophy. According to the materialistic conception of history, the generation of capitalism was

---

16 *Collection of Modern Western Bourgeois Philosophical Works*. Beijing: The Commercial Press, 1982: p. 30.

necessary in history, and the failure of it and the victory of socialism are also inevitable trends of history, i.e. historical necessity. It seemed that the establishment of such a scientific idea of historical necessity issued a death notice to capitalist society. The bourgeois ideologists shivered, so they changed from acknowledging historical necessity to negating it.

The transformation from the establishment of the idea of historical necessity to the prevalence of the opposition to this idea roughly went through three links in the western philosophy of history.

Firstly, the historical objectivism of Ranke; the tenet of Ranke's historical objectivism is to "write down the truth", that is, just recording history as it is but not exploring why it is like this. Ranke was a turning point. The historical theory before him focused on the exploration of historical necessity, while the historical theory after him committed itself to describing historical phenomena.

Secondly, the theory of historical understanding of Dilthey; as far as Dilthey is concerned, history is what has gone, what cannot be studied and grasped with the method of objectivism and the precision of natural sciences; the sole method that works in historical science is "experiencing", "understanding"; there is no objective history and its necessity, at least no cognoscible objective history and its necessity. Just like a "Trojan Horse" placed in the traditional history, the theory of historical understanding of Dilthey destructed the historical objectivism internally and fundamentally, and bred a new philosophy of history – critical philosophy of history.

Thirdly, the historical subjectivism of Croce; Croce negated historical necessity by analyzing historical knowledge and data. In his eyes, historical knowledge and data are subjective rather than objective, because every generation of people always research the past history according to the needs and values of their own times, and in this process, historians inevitably interpose the consciousness and needs of their times into historical events. As a result, all history is contemporary history. Since there is no objective history, seeking for historical necessity becomes meaningless nonsense. This viewpoint of Croce had an extensive impact on the western philosophy of history and even the whole western academic circles. Since then, the idea opposed to historical necessity turned into the leading ideological trend of the modern western philosophy, to such an extent that it almost became an "epidemic".

4 NEGATION OF MODERN WESTERN PHILOSOPHY OF HISTORY TO HISTORICAL NECESSITY AND ITS ERRORS

Modern western philosophy of history negates historical necessity on the grounds of the unicity of historical events. In the opinion of modern western philosophy of history, only things that occur repeatedly are able to form necessity or regularity; in nature, same events occur repeatedly, so there exists necessity; however, in history, everything is "purely one-off", and every historical event is particular, unrepeatable, so there is no historical necessity. Windelband pointed out, "in the study on nature, thinking grasps general relation by confirming special relations, whilst in history, thinking amiably copies particular things all the time." "The former pursues laws, whilst the latter goes after forms."[17] Rickert asserted, "The concept of 'historical laws' is ... a contradiction in wording."[18]

History is different from nature; indeed every historical event is unique, and the French Revolution, Meiji Restoration, Hundred Days' Reform, Xi'an Incident, etc. are all unrepeated existences, but it is unacceptable to thus negate historical necessity. The Hundred Days' Reform is "unique", but such historical phenomena as improvement and reform are not rare at all times and in all countries, they are "many"; the French Revolution is "unique", but the bourgeois revolutions can be found repeatedly as a historical phenomenon in early modern and modern histories, they are "many" ... This demonstrates that it is necessary to make a differentiation between the three notions of historical event, historical phenomenon and historical necessity. Historical event is "unique", but historical phenomena are "many", behind which there is historical necessity that will exert repeated effect as long as given definite conditions.

Historical necessity belongs to the deep structure of history, hiding behind the unicity of historical events, while the difference of natural events deeply hides behind their similarity. When observing nature, we should find difference from similarity, but while studying history, we should discover sameness from difference, and perceive necessity through the unicity of events. Only in this way can we walk deep into history. However, contemporary western philosophy just stays at the surface of history, and confuse historical event with historical phenomenon and historical law.

---

17   *Collection of Modern Western Bourgeois Philosophical Works*, p. 59.
18   Rickert, *Cultural and Natural Sciences*. Beijing: The Commercial Press, 1986: p. IX.

The repeatability of historical necessity is not equal to that of historical events. Any historical event is the product of the synergy of necessity and contingency; the contingency makes historical events distinctive and unrepeatable, and the necessity only repeats common essence of the historical events of the same kind; it does not, and can never, repeats the accidental factors. In fact, the repeatability of historical necessity is exactly embodied in the unrepeatable historical events. The English Revolution in 1640, the French Revolution in 1789, the Revolution of 1911 in China ... does not the successive occurrence of the unrepeatable historical events precisely reflect the historical necessity of bourgeois revolutions?

To put it strictly, any event, including natural event, is the result of the synergy of necessity and contingency. Natural event is also unrepeatable, and natural necessity is also embodied in a series of unrepeatable natural events. Modern western philosophy magnifies the difference between natural events and historical events, and equates the repeatability of historical necessity with that of historical events. When it negates historical necessity with the repeatability of historical events, it just shows that it does not really perceive the relationship between necessity and contingency, or the inner connection between repeatable historical necessity and unrepeatable historical events.

Another argument of modern western philosophy of history against historical necessity is that the historical activity of man is selective, and different nations are able to select different social systems based on their respective needs, thereby making historical development have multiple ways; thus there is no historical necessity. As far as Sartre is concerned, "anything is possible", and the key lies in the free choice of man. Hook thinks the entire human history is the result of men's continuous selection, and such selection is the representation of the freedom of man rather than objective necessity, "it is the unique and irreducible representation of man's essence"[19].

Selection is an important link in historical creation activity of human beings, especially when the history of a nation is at a turning point, there tend to be multiple possible paths shown for the further development of history; among so many possibilities, which one is realizable

---

19 Hook, *Towards the Understanding of Karl Marx*. Chongqing: Chongqing Publishing House, 1989: p. 153.

depends on the conscious selection of this nation and the ratio between class forces within it. However, it is wrong to then make historical selectivity against historical necessity and negate the latter on the grounds of the existence of the former, because:

The formation of "possible space" – the premise for historical choice – has the character of necessity. The object of historical choice can only exist in an established "possible space", so the formation of a definite "possible space" is the premise for historical choice of men; but the formation of such space is dependent of productive forces, which cannot be chosen by men freely, and the condition of "possible space" is fundamentally determined by the condition of productive forces. Men in primitive society are unable to choose capitalist society. If men can choose freely, why the West had chosen a "Dark Middle Age"? The fact that both western society and oriental society have taken the path of absolutism argues that the historical choice of men is based on an established premise and restricted by historical necessity.

What's more, historical choice is unable to change the overall progress of human history. Historical choice can help a nation transcend a certain social formation and rank among the advanced in human history by virtue of "leapfrog" development, thus making historical development diversified. However, such selectivity and diversification cannot change the overall process of human history and its monism – economic necessity. Throughout the whole history of human beings, the "five social formations" are indeed successively replaced: the generation of capitalism did not, and was impossible to, precede feudalism; the emergence of socialism did not, and was impossible to, precede capitalism, either, and on the contrary, the generation of the former was the inevitable result of the inner contradictory movement of the latter. The first establishment of socialist system in some backward oriental countries was exactly the inevitable result of the conflict, influence and infiltration of capitalist society's inner contradictory movement with, upon and into oriental society through the "world history" created by capitalism.

Negating historical necessity with the relativity of historical cognition is a prominent feature of modern western philosophy of history, which is sufficiently reflected in the historical philosophy of Croce. According to him, only the interests in real life can impel people to study the past, and people usually cognize and evaluate history based on their contemporary consciousness, therefore "contemporariness" is the inherent feature of all histories. Croce thus believed such "contemporariness" made people only know limited, specific history that was related to real life, and "that 'remaining' history is eternal illusion of 'thing-in-itself'; being neither 'thing' nor 'itself', it is just the embodiment of the infinite imagination of our actions and knowledge"[20]. This means that "it will never succeed" to seek for a "universal history" in the limited, specific history branded with "contemporariness", and history "has no rules to follow", so the idea of historical necessity must be discarded.

It is true that Croce put forward an important issue, that is, the particularity of men's cognition on history. The reasonability of the statement that "all histories are contemporary history" is: it reveals that historical cognition of men is always a reverse process tracing the present back to the past. As mentioned before, Marx also thinks man's reflections on the forms of social life, and consequently his scientific analysis of those forms, are begun, post festum, with the results of the process of development ready to hand before him. But Croce had gone too far, to the extent that he made everything relativized and subjectified, so that he negated objective history and its necessity. From the view of epistemology, Croce had made two mistakes at least:

In the first place, he cut the link between reality and history. System is the assembly of processes, and history is always spread in a section of society. That is to say, although belonging to the past, history does not disappear, but exists in the real society in a concentrated or stunted form; the real society is the continuation and epitome of history, so it is the key to cognizing history. It is in this sense that Marx thinks the comprehension of the social structure of capitalism "also allows insights into the structure and the relations of production of all the vanished social formations out of whose ruins and elements it built itself up, whose partly still unconquered remnants are carried along within it, whose mere nuances have developed explicit significance within it, etc."[21]

Meanwhile, the real social form has historical difference from the past one, and the two should not be treated equally. "Since bourgeois society is itself only a contradictory form of development, relations derived from earlier forms will often be found within it only in an entirely stunted form, or even travestied."[22] In Marx's opinion, only under the

---

20   Croce, *History: Its Theory and Practice*. Beijing: The Commercial Press, 1982: p. 38.
21   *Selected Works of Karl Marx and Friedrich Engels*. 2nd Ed., Vol. 2, p. 23.
22   *Selected Works of Karl Marx and Friedrich Engels*. 2nd Ed., Vol. 2, p. 23.

condition that the real social form is able to criticize itself can the past social form be understood "objectively"; otherwise it should be conceived "one-sidedly".

Seen from a timeline, "the method of thinking post festum" of Marx is earlier than "the method of thinking from contemporary era" of Croce; with regard to logic, "the method of thinking post festum" of Marx is superior to Croce's method, because it reveals the inner link between reality and history by means of a dialectical thinking mode, not only declaring the possibility to cognize history from the reality but also pointing out the necessary condition for realizing "objective understanding" of history – "self-criticism" of real society.

In the second place, he cut the connection between finiteness and infiniteness. As long as given definite conditions, necessity is able to play a role in infinite things repeatedly. In this sense, necessity is truly infinite, but its infiniteness needs not to be testified in infinite events in reality; instead, once its infiniteness is proved in certain finite events, its existence and repeatable effectiveness in infinite events of the same kind is proved, as well. It is actually metaphysical to require people to validate historical necessity in infinite historical events. It shows that Croce had cut the inner connection between finiteness and infiniteness, returned to the idea of "bad infinity" having been criticized by Hegel long ago, and reached the end of logic on that wrong road.

It is another distinctive feature of modern western philosophy of history to negate historical necessity on the grounds of the unpredictability of historical events. From the viewpoint of Popper, the core of historical determinism is to predict the future evolution of human history based on the so-called historical necessity, but the problem is that there is no necessity in history, and historical movements have no objective rules to follow.

In Popper's eyes, the evolution of human society is a separate historical process, whose description is just a singular historical proposition rather than a general historical law; what is found from successive historical events is merely the trend of social changes, but trend is not law in that people can make scientific prediction based on laws but are unable to do so based on trends; in other words, history is unpredictable; prediction is a cognitive activity of man, and man is the subject of history, so if history is predictable, then the prediction itself will participate in and impose impact on the historical process. In history, a prediction can even lead to the occurrence of the historical event it has predicted, and without this prediction, the historical event may never happen. In turn, the prediction of a forthcoming historical event can prevent the event from happening. As a result, historical necessity does not exist, scientific historical prediction is impossible, and historical determinism is untenable.

Here, Popper makes at least one epistemological mistake, that is, confusing forecasting with foreseeing. Forecasting is the judgment on the inevitable or possible occurrence of a thing within defined time and space ranges, whilst foreseeing is the judgment on the development trend in line with laws, or a law-based judgment only concerning development trend. Natural sciences can make both forecasting and foreseeing, whereas social sciences can only make foreseeing but not forecasting. In front the objective fact, Popper had no choice but to admit that "the prediction of Marx may also come true", and the development of modern capitalism "verifies the prediction of Marx, that is, trade cycle will inevitably be one of the factors resulting in the collapse of unconfined capitalist system"; but he also found a excuse to console himself, thinking that what contributes to the success of Marx's foreseeing "is not his method of historicism but the analytic method of institutional theory all the time"[23]. As a matter of fact, no matter which method Marx had used, the method of historicism or the analytic method of institutional theory, his foreseeing was premised on the discovery and grasp of historical necessity.

The conclusion of Popper is wrong, but his thinking is profound, leaving some valuable problems: (1) the relationship between historical law and historical relation; specifically speaking, a trend that is increasingly intensified will finally turn into a necessity and thereby a law, and some trends contain a certain necessity within themselves originally; in turn, along with the change of conditions, a law may be translated into a trend in the end as a result of its increasingly weakened effect, and so forth; (2) the relationship between historical prediction and historical process, that is, whether or not historical prediction can influence, and how it will, historical process, historical events and historical laws, as well as the relationship between historical process and the cognitive subject of history.

---

23   Popper, *The Open Society and its Enemies*. Beijing: China Social Sciences Press, 1999: Vol. 2, p. 303.

The negation against historical necessity pushes modern western philosophy of history into quagmire and makes it toss around irresistibly. This theoretical error, in turn, implies to us that the Marxist idea of historical necessity is the truth of our times. The real way leading modern western philosophy of history out of the quagmire is to return back to Marx, and deepen, reconstruct and develop the idea of historical necessity of historical materialism based on modern practices and sciences.

CHAPTER IX

CONTRADICTORY MOVEMENT BETWEEN PRODUCTIVE FORCES AND RELATIONS OF PRODUCTION: A NEW INTERPRETATION

Fundamentally, the decisive factor for social development is economic necessity, i.e. the decisive effect of the contradictory movement between productive forces and relations of production on the process of human history. The reform of socialism and the new changes of capitalism make people greatly interested in reexamining the principles of the contradictory movement between productive forces and relations of production. Here, we plan to have a new investigation and discussion on the features of productive forces and the internal impetus for their development, as well as on the internal mechanism and modern characteristics of the contradictory movement between productive forces and relations of production.

1 FEATURES OF PRODUCTIVE FORCES AND INTERNAL IMPETUS FOR THEIR DEVELOPMENT

Productive forces are doubtlessly the final dominant force for the development of human history, but they are anything but a kind of trans-historical being that has independent personality and volition and always control the destiny of human history with "invisible hands". Existing within, but not beyond, the activity of man, they are the practical ability of men formed during productive labor to resolve the contradiction between society and nature.

"The first premise of all human history is, of course, the existence of living human individuals. Thus the first fact to be established is the physical organization of these individuals and their consequent relation to the rest of nature."[1] The object of human needs exists in nature in the final analysis, so for the purpose of existence and development, men will necessarily enter into a definite relationship with nature. However, nature will never satisfy the needs of man automatically, or provide ready-made material means of livelihood for man, thus determining that the relation between man and nature is a contradictory relationship.

To resolve this contradiction and appropriate nature in a bid to satisfy their internal needs, men must carry out labor. Therefore the first historical activity of mankind is the activity of material production. Meanwhile, it is also the basic activity that must be conducted every minute of every day by men for the purpose of their existence and development. To what extent men can resolve the contradiction between man's needs and nature during material production activity, i.e. labor, or the ability of men in resolving the contradiction between man's needs and nature, is regarded productive forces. That is to say, productive forces are formed during the translation of men's needs into labor, and material production activity is the real foundation for their formation. Omitting the needs and labor of man, productive forces are nothing but an inane abstract category.

From the view of historical materialism, productive forces symbolize the relationship in reality between man and nature, and they are the ability of man as the subject to cause, regulate and control his material exchange with nature through his activity. In the process of material

---

1   *Selected Works of Karl Marx and Friedrich Engels.* 2nd Ed., Vol. 1, p. 67.

exchange with nature, man, the subject, does not only expend physical power and intelligence, but also resorts to natural forces; he does not only change the nature outside, but also transforms "the nature of his own". This is a process of "nature humanization" realized through the objectification of man's essential powers, and meanwhile a process during which natural forces are assimilated into human physical power and natural laws are transformed into human intelligence; the two form a bidirectional movement in interdependence and interaction. The productive forces in reality are formed in this bidirectional movement. The unity between "man and his labor on the one side, and Nature and its materials on the other"[2] constitutes the essential content of productive forces, and the productive forces in reality will not be formed without either of them.

The essential content of productive forces determines they have four features:

Firstly, productive forces have human nature.

Productive forces are the power formed by man during labor and under immediate control of man. Man is the subject of productive forces. From a static angle, productive forces are the product of men's previous activities, representing the practical ability of men and indicating the essential powers of man and his active relation with nature; seen dynamically, productive forces are the activity mode of men to acquire the means of livelihood, "the only possible form" of men to resolve the contradiction between society and nature, and to appropriate nature and sustain and develop themselves.

Hence, productive forces are not a trans-historical preformed entity, but the product of human practical activity; they embody the essential powers of man, therefore having the human nature. For this reason, Marx declares the history of the development of productive forces is "the history of the development of the forces of the individuals themselves"[3], and the development of human productive forces "is the development of the richness of human nature as an end in itself"[4].

---

2   *Karl Marx and Friedrich Engels*. 1st Chinese Ed., Vol. 23, p. 209.
3   *Selected Works of Karl Marx and Friedrich Engels*. 2nd Ed., Vol. 1, p. 124.
4   *Karl Marx and Friedrich Engels*. Beijing: People's Publishing House, 1973: 1st Chinese Ed., Vol. 26 (II), p. 124.

Secondly, productive forces have sociality.

The labor capacity of individual is the element of productive forces, and the effect, operation and development of productive forces are inseparable from the labor capacity of individual as a "cell". "The relation of the productive forces to the form of intercourse is the relation of the form of intercourse to the occupation or activity of the individuals"[5], and "real wealth is the developed productive power of all individuals"[6]. But productive forces are not the "arithmetic sum" obtained by simply summing the labor capacities of individuals up; instead, they are the collective force and social force composed of the labor capacities of individuals through definite social combination modes, including intermediary links like division of labor, cooperation, etc. This is an overall productivity, namely "social productive forces", qualitatively different from the "arithmetic sum" of individuals' labor capacities. "The social power, i.e., the multiplied productive force, which arises through the cooperation of different individuals as it is determined by the division of labor."[7]

Because of this, Marx thinks that only in the intercourse of individuals and their interrelation can productive forces become a real power; and only as "social individual", "social being", can individuals really occupy the productive forces. It is one of the unique features of historical materialism's theory about productive forces to lay stress on the all-around general development of the labor capacity of individual and on the study of social productive forces formed on that basis, and to maintain that social productive forces are qualitatively superior to the labor capacity of individual.

Thirdly, productive forces have objectivity.

In reality, the material objects can only be transformed effectively by material forces. As the real power of men to transform and conquer nature, productive forces, of course, have objectivity and materiality. They above all are objective and material power formed during the material exchange between man and nature. In this sense, they are called by Marx "material productive forces". The objectivity and materiality of productive forces are centrally embodied in the instruments of

---

5 *Selected Works of Karl Marx and Friedrich Engels.* 2nd Ed., Vol. 1, p. 123.
6 *Karl Marx and Friedrich Engels.* 1st Chinese Ed., Vol. 46 (II), p. 222.
7 *Selected Works of Karl Marx and Friedrich Engels.* 2nd Ed., Vol. 1, p. 85.

production, which are the "humanized" natural forces, the material strength contained in "humanized nature", and the means of man to put his intelligence into good use.

Acknowledging the objectivity and materiality of productive forces does not mean denying the "social intelligence" of man condensed in productive forces. Marx believes since the date of formation of human productive forces, there have been "special forces of production, both objective and subjective, … appearing as qualities of the individuals", and "all productive forces are material and spiritual productive forces". However, "objective productive forces", or "spiritual productive forces", are after all in intellectual form, so they cannot become the real productive forces, or turn into the real power with "material creativity" to transform nature, unless "materialized" into the instruments of production. Just because of this, we should attach importance both to scientific research and translation of sciences into technology and productive forces. Only in this way can we make society function in an all-around scientific way and promote the practical development of productive forces.

Fourthly, productive forces have historicity.

As what has been mentioned, productive forces are formed during the translation of men's needs into labor. However, not only the translation into labor is needed, but labor also needs translating, because "the satisfaction of the first need (the action of satisfying, and the instrument of satisfaction which has been acquired) leads to new needs"[8]. The needs of man are increased and multiplied during his interaction with labor; therefore the motivation of man's labor is objectively everlasting. No matter how the productive forces formed in labor are developed, there always is an internal impetus driving them, and they will be inevitably in constant change and development along with the change of man's needs and the development of labor, thus they possess historicity.

Productive forces are formed during the translation of men's needs into labor. The needs referred to here do not mean the instinctive needs of animals, but the needs of social men. Such needs do not only include the needs for means of livelihood, but the needs for manufacturing and improving instruments of production, as well as other various social

---

8   *Selected Works of Karl Marx and Friedrich Engels.* 2nd Ed., Vol. 1, p. 79.

needs; instead of being the pure subjective intention, they, first of all, belong to a kind of objective necessity to which man is subject and that does not change with man's will, meaning that the needs having been satisfied, the activities of satisfying, and the improvement of instruments will inevitably lead to new needs. The contradiction between man's needs and nature is an eternal contradiction in human society. It is this contradiction, as an objective forcible strength, that drives the continuous development of productive forces. In other words, the reason why productive forces have an irresistible trend of development forward is because of the objective necessity that the contradiction between man's needs and nature is under the condition of continuous resolution and continuous generation. The contradiction between man's needs and nature constitutes the fundamental cause or source of the ceaseless development of productive forces.

The source of development is the contradiction at a deeper level, while impetus is the contradiction at a shallower level; the contradiction at a deeper level usually tends to be resolved based on the contradiction at a shallower level. Generally speaking, the source or fundamental cause of development creates the possibility for realizing the development of a thing, and impetus "paves the way" for this possibility and makes it come true. From the perspective of the relation between possibility and reality, the contradiction between man's needs and nature merely gives possibility to the continuous development of productive forces, but to translate this possibility into reality, direct impetus is required.

The direct impetus for the development of productive forces is the contradiction between laborer and instruments of production. This is because: new instruments of production are required to satisfy new needs, and when original instruments of production are incapable of adapting to the new situation, laborers will improve original instruments of production, or create new ones; the emergence of new instruments of production, in turn, will necessitate new laborers with new labor skills. The mutual promotion and conversion between the two sides of contradiction – laborers, new instruments of production, new laborers, and newer instruments of production ... – ceaselessly resolve the contradiction between man's needs and nature, thereby directly driving the continuous development of productive forces.

This shows that productive forces constitute a self-organized system with internal impetus, and the development of productive forces is a systematic movement with inseparable integrity. In the revolution of productive forces, a significant change of a factor will inevitably arouse a chain reaction, which will rapidly spread to and influence other factors, and even change the overall condition of productive forces.

The integrity of the development of productive forces does not mean that all the factors therein should be at an absolutely balanced state, and contrarily the development of factors will inevitably takes on an unbalanced character to a certain degree; productive forces in different periods have different growth or breakthrough points in development. Marx points out that the revolution of productive forces "in manufacture ... begins with the labor-power, in modern industry it begins with the instruments of labor"[9]. In modern times, the growth point of productive forces' development is "spiritual productive forces". The field of microelectronic technology oriented by computer technology, the new material field guided by superconducting technology, and the achievements of bioengineering researches become the growth or breakthrough points of the modern development of productive forces. This characteristic of productive forces' development requires us to possess high abilities of foreseeing and judgment, to be good at selecting the growth or breakthrough point and grasping the totality of development, and to rapidly extend any achievement gotten from the growth or breakthrough point to other factors of productive forces. Only by dint of such translation and transplanting can brand-new productive forces be formed.

2 INTERNAL MECHANISM OF THE INTERACTION BETWEEN PRODUCTIVE FORCES AND RELATIONS OF PRODUCTION

The principles of the interaction between productive forces and relations of production is well known to people; however, "well knowing does not mean truly knowing", and almost all the textbooks of Marxist philosophy totally ignore, or mention vaguely, the intermediary and internal mechanism of the interaction between productive forces and relations of production. But what interests me is none other than this issue, which plays a very significant role in the reform of economic system.

---

9   *Karl Marx and Friedrich Engels*. 1st Chinese Ed., Vol. 23, p. 408.

The intermediary between productive forces and relations of production must have dual attribute, i.e. both the attribute of productive forces and the attribute of relations of production; otherwise it will be unqualified to be the joint part, link and "bridge" of productive forces and relations of production. The division of labor has such duality: in terms of the mode of combination between man and "things" during production, it belongs to the category of productive forces; with respect to the mode of combination between man and man, it falls under the category of relations of production. Such a duality makes the division of labor the intermediary between productive forces and relations of production.

Being a link in the social productive forces, the division of labor has the attribute of productive forces. The division of labor, first of all, is directly related to instruments of production – one of the essential factors of productive forces. "The concentration of the instruments of production and the division of labor are inseparable one from the other", that is to say, "as the concentration of instruments develops, the division develops also, and vice versa". It means that the properties and development of instruments of production determine the properties and development of the division of labor, and the development of the latter also influences and boosts the development of the former. "This is why every big mechanical invention is followed by a greater division of labor, and each increase in the division of labor gives rise in turn to new mechanical inventions."[10] In fact, the division of labor, premised on particular instruments of production, breaks the unified production up into sections independent of and meanwhile linked with one another; social divisions of labor in various types are actually the combination modes of different processes in material production.

Therefore, the division of labor is in essence the specific combination mode of laborer and instrument in the process of production, symbolizing the technology structure of production. Marx had pointed out, "labor is organized, is divided differently according to the instruments it disposes over."[11] At the same time, the division of labor "creates a qualitative gradation, and a quantitative proportion in the social process of production; it consequently creates a definite organization of the labor of society, and thereby develops at the same time new productive forces in the society"[12]. Because of this, the division of labor constitutes a link

10   *Selected Works of Karl Marx and Friedrich Engels.* 2nd Ed., Vol. 1, p. 166.
11   Ibid., p. 161.
12   *Karl Marx and Friedrich Engels.* 1st Chinese Ed., Vol. 23, p. 403.

in the social productive forces, as the comprehensive embodiment of the levels of productive instruments and laborers, thus being the representation of the level of productive forces. "How far the productive forces of a nation are developed is shown most manifestly by the degree to which the division of labor has been carried."[13]

The organic combination of division of labor with distribution, exchange and other links constitutes the relationship of ownership, thus it has the attribute of relations of production. The division of labor at first separates individuals in the process of production, but meanwhile it is a kind of combination between man and man; "division of labor is, in one sense, nothing but coexisting labor"[14]. Division of labor is the modes of combinations both between man and instruments and between man and man in the process of production. Relations of distribution, exchange, and so on between individuals are established on the basis of division of labor, which is the external manifestation of the necessary connection between individuals engaged in different labors.

"The division of labor implies from the outset the division of the conditions of labor, of tools and materials, and thus the splitting-up of accumulated capital among different owners, and thus, also, the division between capital and labor, and the different forms of property itself."[15]

In *Das Kapital*, Marx reveals, based on the theory mentioned above and through analyzing average profit, how all kinds of capitalists unceasingly achieve profit equalization during the appropriation, domination and application of the means of production, thereby forming a class in terms of economic interests; as for the laborers, because the mode of social combination of production changes – not only combining with the capitalists in their own enterprises but also with the means of production of the capitalists in other enterprises and industries, thus the relationship to capitalist is no longer the opposite relation between individuals, but an antagonistic relation between different classes.

To put it another way, the division of labor is the form of social organization of production. In this sense, Marx thinks the division of labor is a "synonym" of ownership, and different development stages of the division of labor are different forms of ownership, "i.e. the existing stage in the

---

13   *Selected Works of Karl Marx and Friedrich Engels.* 2nd Ed., Vol. 1, p. 68.
14   *Karl Marx and Friedrich Engels.* 1st Chinese Ed., Vol. 26 (III), p. 295.
15   *Selected Works of Karl Marx and Friedrich Engels.* 2nd Ed., Vol. 1, p. 127.

division of labor determines also the relations of individuals to one another with reference to the material, instrument, and product of labor"[16]. Clearly, the division of labor has the attribute of relations of production.

The duality of the division of labor makes it the intermediary for the interaction between productive forces and relations of production. On the premise of the properties of productive instruments, the division of labor itself embodies the technology structure form of production, and meanwhile forms specific mode of economic activity. Thus, such an interactive chain is created: productive forces (instruments of production) $\rightarrow$ technology form of production $\rightarrow$ modes of the division of labor and the economic activity $\rightarrow$ relationship of ownership (relations of production). This chain demonstrates the internal mechanism of the interaction between production forces and relations of production. The decisive action of productive forces on relations of production and the reaction of relations of production on productive forces, generally speaking, are realized through the division of labor as the intermediary. The interaction between the both realized through the division of labor gives rise to the contradictory movement between the both.

The investigation on the intermediary and the internal mechanism of the interaction between productive forces and relations of production causes such a reflection: the relationship of ownership is the relations of production, and the investigation on it should be in no case separated from the survey on the process of production and reproduction. As a matter of fact, ownership is closely bound up with production process, so it cannot be correctly perceived in any case once separated from the process of production and reproduction.

The relationship of ownership is certainly the relationship between man and means of production, and more importantly, it is the economic relationship between man and man reflected by the relationship between man and means of production. The essence of ownership is as the follows: a definite social organization wants to realize appropriation of products based on its appropriation of means of production; for this end, various links, namely production, distribution, exchange and consumption, are necessary in the process of production and reproduction, and only in this process can definite relationship of ownership be maintained and developed. Marx points out:

---

16   *Selected Works of Karl Marx and Friedrich Engels.* 2nd Ed., Vol. 1, p. 68.

"Capitalist production, therefore, under its aspect of a continuous connected process, of a process of reproduction, produces not only commodities, not only surplus-value, but it also produces and reproduces
the capitalist relation; on the one side the capitalist, on the other the
wage laborer."[17]

That is to say, seen from the whole production process, ownership is
the premise of production on the one hand and the result of production
on the other. Ownership is not an independent entity dissociated from
the production process, and it is unable to preset an unchanged frame
and external premises for the economic activity of men; on the contrary,
such premises are reproduced continuously in the process of production
and reproduction. Without the four links in the process of production
and reproduction – production, distribution, exchange and consumption, the ownership of the means of production is unrealizable, is out of
the question, and is bound to be nothingness.

For this reason, Marx believes ownership and relations of production
are the same concept, and "thus to define bourgeois property is nothing
else than to give an exposition of all the social relations of bourgeois
production". "To try to give a definition of property as of an independent relation, a category apart, an abstract and eternal idea, can be nothing but an illusion of metaphysics or jurisprudence."[18] We cannot really
apprehend the essence of ownership or relations of production, or the
mechanism of the action of productive forces on relations of production, unless we put them into the process of production and reproduction and the process of social economic movement.

Since the relationship of ownership is confirmed to be inherently included in the process of production, it should be conceived from angles
of production, distribution, exchange and consumption, the four links
in the process of production and reproduction, and the form and reform
of ownership should be apprehended based on the technology structure
and the labor division of production, as well as the mode of economic
activity arising therefrom. The ownership of the means of production
is realized through the four links of production, distribution, exchange
and consumption. In a capitalist society, division of labor and competition, monopoly, trade, etc., "the ensemble of these relations, constitute

17   *Karl Marx and Friedrich Engels.* 1st Chinese Ed., Vol. 23, p. 634.
18   *Karl Marx and Friedrich Engels.* 1st Chinese Ed., Vol. 4, p. 180.

the thing called ownership today". As mentioned before, specific division of labor embodies specific technology structure of production, and at the same time forms specific mode of economic activity or specific form of economic organization; then, any change in the mode of economic activity will certainly result in the change of ownership's form, until the fundamental nature of ownership is transformed. For example, on the premise that the fundamental nature remains unchanged, the capitalist ownership has successively gone through several forms of ownership, i.e. individual ownership, joint ownership and state ownership; all these changes have ever met the requirement of the economic activity mode formed by specific division of labor in a definite period to a definite extent, and are realized through the links of production, distribution, etc. Omitting the process of production and reproduction and the economic activity mode formed by specific division of labor, the form changes of capitalist ownership will become incomprehensible.

Therefore we get the following enlightenment: the mechanism of the action of productive forces on the relationship of ownership or the relations of production develops as a process of entire social economic movement along with the continuous development of production. The reform of economic system should not only aim at ownership itself, or merely focus on the issue of "retaking of power" or "delegation of power"; instead, its starting point should be the real production process, and the mode of economic activity formed by the division of labor, and its focus of attention should be the economic movement mechanism. It is in the reform of economic movement mechanism that the form of ownership is changed, and the socialist relations of production are able to obtain new continuous development on a higher basis.

3 CONTEMPORARY CHARACTERISTICS OF THE CONTRADICTORY MOVEMENT BETWEEN PRODUCTIVE FORCES AND RELATIONS OF PRODUCTION

The interaction between productive forces and relations of production brings about the contradictory movement between the two, which takes on different characteristics in different eras. In modern times, what features the movement between productive forces and relations of production is the manifestation in the mode featured by national character against the background of worldwide development.

The farther the history is traced back, the more prominent the national character of the contradictory movement between productive forces and relations of production is. In the ancient times, the contradictory movement between productive forces and relations of production usually happened "separately" in each narrow locality of every nation, and its distinctive characteristic was that the formation of each kind of production mode must "start right over again from the beginning" with each nation. Marx points out:

"As long as there exists no commerce transcending the immediate neighborhood, every invention must be made separately in each locality, and mere chances such as irruptions of barbaric peoples, even ordinary wars, are sufficient to cause a country with advanced productive forces and needs to have to start right over again from the beginning. In primitive history every invention had to be made daily anew and in each locality independently."[19]

As the intercourse between nations developed into a definite condition, the original "separate" modes of production of different nations will start to influence, infiltrate into, and interact on each other. For instance, after the Roman Empire was conquered by the Germanic nation, the more advanced productive forces of the conquered interacted on the original relations of production of the conqueror, and consequently, the Germanic nation was enabled to directly establish the feudal system. "The feudal system was by no means brought complete from Germany, but had its origin, as far as the conquerors were concerned, in the martial organization of the army during the actual conquest, and this only evolved after the conquest into the feudal system proper through the action of the productive forces found in the conquered countries."[20] At that time, the "cosmopolitan character" of the contradictory movement between productive forces and relations of production had sprouted.

Along with the further development of productive forces and intercourse, especially the formation respectively of "world market" and "international relations of production", "in place of the old local and national seclusion and self-sufficiency, we have intercourse in every direction, universal inter-dependence of nations"[21]. Thus, the previous secluded state of every state "naturally brought forth" was eliminated,

19   *Selected Works of Karl Marx and Friedrich Engels.* 2nd Ed., Vol. 1, pp. 107 – 108.
20   *Selected Works of Karl Marx and Friedrich Engels.* 2nd Ed., Vol. 1, p. 126.
21   ibid., p. 276

giving a cosmopolitan character to production and consumption in every country. From then on, world became a unified entirety, and history changed into world history. The contradictory movement between productive forces and relations of production really jumped over the boundaries of nations, stepped onto the world "arena", and therefore possessed the cosmopolitan character, i.e. entering into the historical stage of all-around mutual influence, inter-infiltration and interaction.

Cosmopolitan character of the contradictory movement between productive forces and relations of production is based on its national character, but it is not the simple repeated addition of national characters. As a kind of integration, it is relatively independent, being able to impel national character to "transform" to a certain degree, in order to coordinate it with cosmopolitan character. In the context of world history, the contradiction between productive forces and relations of production of a nation or state may be intensified rapidly. All historical conflicts root in the contradiction between productive forces and relations of production, but "incidentally, to lead to collisions in a country, this contradiction need not necessarily have reached its extreme limit in this particular country. The competition with industrially more advanced countries, brought about by the expansion of international intercourse, is sufficient to produce a similar contradiction in countries with a backward industry"[22].

Under such historical conditions, the backward nations do not have to "start right over again from the beginning" and blindly follow the historical path of developed states. Upon the "historical enlightenment" of advanced states, the backward nations can consciously exploit the cosmopolitan character of the contradictory movement between productive forces and relations of production, with a view to shortening the process of their contradiction resolution and ranking among the advanced in the world by virtue of "leapfrog" development. This is the secret why China and some backward oriental countries are able to leap over the complete or typical capitalist stage and directly enter socialism.

Following the modern development of productive forces, the intercourse between different nations are increasing day by day, with level continuously expanded and pace continuously speeded up. From the martial intercourse, contractual intercourse and consanguineous intercourse in

22   ibid., pp. 115 – 116.

ancient times to the material intercourse, spiritual intercourse, political intercourse, scientific intercourse, etc. nowadays, the "system value" of intercourse is formed, and "world market", "international relations of production" and international coalition with grander scales are generated, so are the global circular material flow, capital flow, technological flow and information flow; the integration of world has reached an unprecedented level, giving rise to the emergence of "global village". The present world is indeed an open world. The openness of modern world strengthens the symbiosis between all nations and the cosmopolitan character of the contradictory movement between productive forces and relations of production. Such openness, cosmopolitan character and symbiosis determine that there is no way for any nation to be isolated from the process of world history for long, just as the "organs" of a man cannot be isolated from his blood circulation system. In modern times, any nation or state cannot survive unless it concretely associates itself with the "production of the whole world", and does its best to develop itself by utilizing the contradictory movement between productive forces and relations of production.

After the formation of world history, the condition of national seclusion cannot stand, but this does not mean the individual characteristics of a specific nation have disappeared. Modern intercourse and openness more and more highlight the cosmopolitan character of the contradictory movement between productive forces and relations of production on the one hand and the individual characteristics of every component in the system on the other hand. To be specific, every nation is involved in the tide of world history with its "individual" traditions and particular hobbies and needs, as well as distinguishing values, and shows the characteristics of diversity and individualization in mutual competition, thus making the contradictory movement between productive forces and relations of production manifested in the mode featured by national character against the background of worldwide development. In modern times, a nation that does not enter the world history is futureless; a nation that does not maintain and carry forward its own "individual" characteristics and only blindly follows and "imitates" others is also futureless. We must change those things with universal worldwide significance into the conditions for our autonomous activities, into the foundation for us to create our "characteristics", so as to build the socialism with Chinese characteristics in the openness to the world.

CHAPTER X

INEVITABLE REPLACEMENT OF CAPITALISM BY SOCIALISM AND ITS HISTORICAL PROCESS: A NEW INTERPRETATION

In the system of Marxism there is the theory about the inevitable replacement of capitalism by socialism and the inevitable victory of socialism (hereinafter referred to as "two inevitabilities"), which centrally reflects the truthful, critical and revolutionary characters of Marxism and also the unity between Marxist philosophy, political economy and scientific socialism. We can say the entire Marxism is focused exactly on this core. However, the theory of "two inevitabilities" has been confronted with various misunderstandings, distortions and challenges in contemporary times. In front of such a significant issue which is directly relevant to the truthfulness of all Marxist doctrines and the reform direction of contemporary China, we must profoundly rethink, carefully discuss and cognize anew the "two inevitabilities" at the height of contemporary practice and reevaluate the contemporary value of Marxism on that basis.

1 OBJECTIVE BASIS FOR THE INEVITABLE REPLACEMENT OF CAPITALISM BY SOCIALISM

Capitalist system has received different critiques from different stand-points and different directions since the first day of its establishment, and the development of capitalism is accompanied by the critique as a shadow. Especially in the early nineteenth century, the "critical-utopian socialism" represented by Saint-Simon, Fourier and Owen criticized capitalism thoroughly, providing "the most valuable materials for the enlightenment of the working class". However, this critique is passionate rather than rational, where illusion prevails over science and which aims at result but not cause, and it does not work out the inevitability of the replacement of capitalism by socialism and the objective basis of this inevitability. The reason why scientific socialism is regarded to be scientific is because it fundamentally reveals the inevitability of the replacement of capitalism by socialism and its objective basis in terms of both cause and result, by taking the laws of social development as the foundation and the economic analysis on the capitalist mode of production and its inner contradiction as the basis.

The development of society has its inherent law, which is not subject to the will of anyone. Throughout the history of China, although the feudal emperor of each generation was taught how to rule and warned of the admonition that "while water can carry a boat, it can also overturn it", and even books like *History As A Mirror* were specially compiled for them to read, with the hope of keeping an unbroken imperial line generation after generation, there were still peasant uprisings, still dynasty changes, and still bourgeois revolutions. "In acquiring new productive forces men change their mode of production; and in changing their mode of production, in changing the way of earning their living, they change all their social relations. The hand-mill gives you society with the feudal lord; the steam-mill, society with the industrial capitalist."[1]

This indicates that the rise and fall of a certain social formation is a regular phenomenon. Capitalist society arising out of the fall of feudal society is the product of a series of changes in the mode of production, thus having historical necessity; capitalism therefore "historically has played a most revolutionary part". However, any kind of social formation will not last forever, and just like the feudal dynasty that had

---

1   *Selected Works of Karl Marx and Friedrich Engels.* 2nd Ed., Vol. 1, p. 142.

tried to keep an unbroken imperial line generation after generation but eventually collapsed, capitalist society generated in history will inevitably fall historically and be replaced by a new social formation. The inevitability of the replacement of capitalism by socialism is rooted in the historical process itself, in the nature of the inner contradiction of capitalist mode of production.

The inner contradiction of capitalist mode of production is the contradiction between the socialization of production and the capitalist private ownership of the means of production. As the special manifestation of the contradiction between productive forces and relations of production in capitalist society, this contradiction is the basic one among all the contradictions in capitalist society, and creates the basic economic law of capitalist society – the law of surplus value. "The essential conditions for the existence and for the sway of the bourgeois class is the formation and augmentation of capital"[2], and the process of capital's formation and augmentation is precisely the process of unceasing production and realization of surplus value. Endless pursuit for surplus value is just the natural character of capital.

Hence, the pursuit and greed for surplus value becomes the internal impetus of capitalists – the "personalized" capital – to continuously expand reproduction and infinitely develop productive forces. "The development of the productive force of labor – first the positing of surplus labor – is a necessary condition for the growth of value or the realization of capital. As the infinite urge to wealth, it strives consistently towards infinite increase of the productive forces of labor and calls them into being."[3] In other words, the development of productive forces in capitalist society is restricted by the regularity of the value augmentation of capital.

Specifically, the value augmentation of capital or the realization of surplus value rests upon the conversion from production process to circulation process, and once leaving the production process and reentering the circulation process, capital will be subject to two restrictions:

One is the restriction from current consumption or consuming power on capital as the product produced. The production and accumulation of capital is essentially the production and reproduction of the capitalist relations of production, which will inevitably lead to the opposition

---

2   ibid., p. 284.
3   *Karl Marx and Friedrich Engels*. 1st Chinese Ed., Vol. 46 (I), p. 306.

between the two poles, namely the minority that continuously accumu-
lates wealth on the one side and the majority that continuously sinks
into poverty on the other side, or the developed countries becoming
more and more developed on the one side and the developing countries
more and more difficult to get rid of poverty on the other side, thus
resulting in extremely limited consuming power, and causing the huge
contrast between productive power and consuming power and the deep
opposition respectively between the bourgeoisie and the proletariat and
between developed countries and developing countries.

The other is the restriction from the quantity of current equivalent, first
of all from the quantity of money, on the product produced by capital as
a new value. The realization of surplus value requires a "surplus equivalent"; just like product, as a use value, it is subject to the restriction
from others' consumption, whilst as a value, it is restricted by others'
production. Because capitalist production is for the purpose of pursuing
the surplus value, manifested as the opposition between the organiza-
tional character of individual enterprise production and the weak organ-
izational character of entire social production and world market, with
respect to the exchange in general, there is no equivalent for all surplus
value, which will unavoidably bring about the restriction of exchange
value on use value. So Marx points out that capital is in the first place
subject to "the restriction from the quantity of money", and "this (surplus equivalent) now appears as a second barrier [for capital]"[4].

Fundamentally speaking, these two restrictions are the barriers for the
infinite development trend of productive forces, but capital always tries
to break through these barriers in the process of continuous development
of productive forces and continuous change of relations of production.
"The bourgeoisie cannot exist without constantly revolutionizing the
instruments of production, and thereby the relations of production, and
with them the whole relations of society."[5] But the problem is that every
"creative destruction" pushes capital into crises greater each time. The
bourgeoisie does not understand, or it forgets, that no matter whether it
is from the consumption or the "surplus equivalent", it is the restriction,
in the final analysis, from the capitalist private ownership on the infinite
development trend of productive forces, which is the "major limit" that
the bourgeoisie is unable, and also unwilling, to break through.

---

4   *Karl Marx and Friedrich Engels*. 1st Chinese Ed., Vol. 46 (I), p. 388.
5   *Selected Works of Karl Marx and Friedrich Engels*. 2nd Ed., Vol. 1, p. 275.

The economic crisis in 1825, as the beginning, and the repeated periodical economic crises occurring subsequently, as well as the social crises caused by them, made the bourgeoisie aware of the fact that it could not survive without the reform in relations of production and social relations, without the change in economic movement mechanism and without the establishment of an anti-crisis social mechanism that prevented economic crisis. Thus capitalism entered the stage of state monopoly capitalism, whose features include the intervention and control of the state over the economic activity, the coexistence of state intervention and private enterprise, the coexistence of monopoly and competition, a certain socialization trend of the appropriation mode of means of production, and the enhancement of planning for capitalist production to some extent. From this, some western scholars assert that such a kind of economic system activates the interaction between the authority of state and the driving force of private enterprise, not only retaining the advantages of free capitalism, but also overcoming its defects, thereby showing the eternality of capitalism.

I do not deny that the new changes in contemporary capitalism strengthen the social adaptation ability of capitalism or that the expansion ability of the capitalist mode of production has not yet weakened, but I disagree with the negation to the inevitability of the fall of capitalism on that account. Engels had put forward long ago, "Capitalist production by joint-stock companies is no longer private production but production on behalf of many associated people; and when we pass on from joint-stock companies to trusts, which dominate and monopolize whole branches of industry, this puts an end not only to private production but also to planlessness."[6]

In capitalist society, no matter which form the state adopts for economy, laissez-faire or planned intervention, its foundation is private enterprise system, and the economic activity of government is majorly arranged on the basis of the activity of private enterprise; the purpose of state intervention into economy is to ensure the normal operation of private enterprise's business activities within the scope of the whole society, and to reliably guarantee the accumulation of capital. No matter what monopoly form is adopted, capitalism can never make capital give up its greed for surplus value, or eliminate the capitalist private ownership of the means of production and its restriction on the infinite development

---

6   *Selected Works of Karl Marx and Friedrich Engels*. 2nd Ed., Vol. 4, p. 408.

trend of productive forces. As said by Marx, "the real barrier of capital-ist production is capital itself"[7].

Of course, contemporary developed capitalist countries can alleviate social contradictions by acquiring high profits from the developing countries, regulate class relations by means of various social guaran-tee policies, and "relieve" "institutional crisis" and obtain "the method for aging delay" by "reform and improvement of system", but such "alleviation", "regulation" and "delay" are still realized in the histori-cal framework of capitalist private ownership and "restricted by capi-tal itself", with the result that it is impossible to eliminate the inner contradiction of capitalist mode of production and the economic crises resulting from it. The series of crises ranging from the oil crisis in the 1970s, the stagflation crisis and the structure crisis in the 1980s, and the financial crisis in the 1990s to the global financial crisis in the early twenty-first century show that the economic crises of capitalism is tak-ing on new patterns of manifestation on the one hand, and reflect, on the other hand, the inner contradiction of capitalist mode of production is ceaselessly accumulated and intensified. It indicates that capitalism will be irresistibly replaced by socialism, just as day is followed by night. The theory for this is objectively based on the inner contradiction of capitalist mode of production. It is fairly pointed out by Heilbroner, a famous contemporary western scholar, that "as long as capitalism ex-ists, I do not believe we can declare any fault in his (Marx's) analysis on the intrinsic nature of capitalism at any time"[8].

It is true that in capitalist countries "there is no any kind of social for-mation that can be thought as Marxist socialism" up to now. Mills thus alleges that "two inevitabilities" are "fictional", and that "the huge his-torical framework of Marx's theory and prediction"[9] should be modi-fied. It will be a quite long historical process for socialism to replace capitalism, so it is either a kind of "shortsightedness" or "prejudice" to negate "two inevitabilities" merely based on the capitalist condi-tion in a definite region within a definite time period. Such opinion does not understand the theory of "two inevitabilities" is not a discov-ery of historical event, but is a revelation of historical trend. The in-evitable replacement of capitalism by socialism, as a historical trend, will be confronted with "real resistance" or "opposite tendency" that

---

7   *Karl Marx and Friedrich Engels.* 1st Chinese Ed., Vol. 25, p. 278.

8   Heilbroner, *Marxism: For and Against.* Beijing: China Social Sciences Press, 1982: p. 62.

9   Wright Mills, *The Marxists.* Beijing: The Commercial Press, 1985: p. 128.

hinders its realization. As Marx said, "under capitalist production, the general law acts as the prevailing tendency only in a very complicated and approximate manner, as a never ascertainable average of ceaseless fluctuations"[10]. Along with the historical changes in social relations and class contradictions, the realization form of the inevitable replacement of capitalism by socialism is also being transformed. As the inner contradiction of western capitalist mode of production impacts, infiltrates into, and influences oriental countries, and the social contradictions in oriental countries are sharpened, the inevitable replacement of capitalism by socialism starts its historical process of realization.

2 REALIZATION PROCESS OF THE INEVITABLE REPLACEMENT OF CAPITALISM BY SOCIALISM

The inevitability of the replacement of capitalism by socialism at first came into being in western developed countries, but was firstly actualized in oriental backward countries. The cause of this historical "inversion" is still the capitalist mode of production itself, as the result of the impact, influence and infiltration from the inner contradiction of western capitalist mode of production upon and into oriental countries.

The contradictory process of the capitalist mode of production began in the West, but in the wake of the formation of world history, the capitalist mode of production takes the whole world as the stage for its contradictory movement, and impacts, infiltrates into, and influences oriental countries during this process. The "world history" mentioned here does not refer to that in a general historiographical sense, but the history since world integration resulting from mutual influence, restriction, interpenetration and interdependence of various nations and countries in an all-around way. As an experienced fact in the twentieth century, the world history took its form in the nineteenth century. Marx noticed this historical trend relying on his extraordinary insight, and pointed out that capitalism, through expanding world market, "produced world history for the first time", thus "in place of the old local and national seclusion and self-sufficiency, we have intercourse in every direction, universal inter-dependence of nations"[11]. Since the world history is formed, the interdependence, mutual influence, interpenetration and interaction between all nations and countries have been shown in various

---

10   *Karl Marx and Friedrich Engels*. 1st Chinese Ed., Vol. 25, p. 181.
11   *Selected Works of Karl Marx and Friedrich Engels*. 2nd Ed., Vol. 1, p. 276.

aspects. Among them, most importantly, the contradictory movement of the mode of production steps out of the "separate" condition in a nation or state, and then becomes the dialectical unity between national character and cosmopolitan character.

National character of the contradictory movement of production mode means that the contradictory movement has different properties, structures and movement mechanisms in different nations or states; and its cosmopolitan character means that in the wake of the formation of world history, the contradictory movement steps out of the original narrow locality of its nation or state, and integrates itself into the complete movement of mutual restriction, influence and interaction under the vast background of the entire world. During such a complete movement, the national character of the contradictory movement will "transform" to a certain degree, the inner contradiction of mode of production of some backward nations or states, i.e. the contradiction between productive forces and relations of production, will be sharpened rapidly, and "a similar contradiction" to that of the developed countries will be brought about. Marx points out that all historical conflicts root in the contradiction between productive forces and relations of production, but "to lead to collisions in a country, this contradiction need not necessarily have reached its extreme limit in this particular country. The competition with industrially more advanced countries, brought about by the expansion of international intercourse, is sufficient to produce a similar contradiction in countries with a backward industry"[12]. It is under the guidance of this "similar contradiction" that backward nations or states can shorten a certain historical process or leap over a certain social formation and directly enter a more advanced one. This is the reason why such oriental countries as Russia, China, and so on are the first to realize the inevitability of the replacement of capitalism by socialism.

Russia was facing a new era in the early twentieth century. Seen from the overall process of world history, capitalism had developed from the stage of free competition to the stage of monopoly, and the inner contradiction of capitalist mode of production had been in an intensifying state, which was marked by the frequent occurrence of economic crises. At the same time, the development of capitalism in various countries had shown imbalance, and the contradictions of the capitalist world system arose everywhere, which was the inescapable consequence of

---

12   ibid., pp. 115 – 116.

the development of commodity production in the context of world market. Profound analysis on the era helped Lenin realize that "the imbalance of economic and political development is the absolute law of capitalism", and that absolute law would inevitably form a weak link in the capitalist chain, so that socialist revolution might achieve its victory first in a minority of countries, or even a single country. Judged from its domestic situation, Russia at that time had embarked on the capitalist road, and "the most advanced industrial capitalism" and "the most backward land ownership" coexisted there, but for Western Europe, Russia was still a backward country, so it politically belonged to oriental countries. Besides, it had been involved into the war system of world imperialism and strongly impacted, broadly permeated and profoundly influenced by the inner contradiction of capitalist mode of production from Western Europe.

The combination of international and domestic conditions forced "a similar contradiction" to that of the western developed countries to emerge in Russia, and the "similar contradiction" was the contradiction between the proletariat and the bourgeoisie, encompassing the contradiction between the bourgeoisie and the landlord class, the contradiction between the bourgeoisie and the peasant class, and the contradiction between the landlord class and the peasant class. All of those contradictions intertwining with each other in an intensifying state, making Russia the concentrating point of all inner contradictions of the capitalist world system and the weak link in the capitalist chain at that time. That situation offered Russia a possibility, that is, shortening the historical process of capitalism in Russia and marching towards the historical process of socialism. The proletariat of Russia grasped that historical trend, seized "the best opportunity" given by history, and successfully launched the October Revolution, thus leading the development of Russia onto a "peculiar path" – an economically backward country went to the forefront of world history. In fact, the formation of that "peculiar path" was the result of the interaction between national and cosmopolitan characters of the contradictory movement of production mode, as well as the result of the impact, influence and infiltration from the inner contradiction of capitalist mode of production upon and into Russia. What was deeply hiding behind that "peculiar path" was the historical law that capitalism would inevitably be replaced by socialism.

The October Revolution of Russia was the beginning in the realization process of the inevitable replacement of capitalism by socialism, and opened up a new epoch of socialism; however, the Drastic Changes of Soviet Union and Eastern Europe brought socialist movement into a low tide. Fukuyama et al. thus negated the October Revolution and the "two inevitabilities", alleging that the liberal democracy of capitalism had become "the end point of mankind's ideological evolution and the final form of human government, and as such constituted the end of history"[13]. That was historical nihilism. We cannot negate a previous success with a present failure, just as we cannot negate the birth of a man with his death. In the powerful developed capitalist world, the socialist practice starting from backward countries will certainly face huge difficulties, and it is impossible that there is no vortex, setback or repetition; and there will even be reversal and regression. The key point is that in a country where reversal or regression happens, along with the formation of the bourgeoisie, the working class that is hired will certainly emerge; and as the bourgeoisie regains its dominant position, the working class will surely be dominated. Then, the contradiction that has been resolved is resumed, and the "two inevitabilities" will re-function under the changed historical condition; therefore history has not been, and will impossibly be, ended.

Russia shortened the historical process of capitalism and entered socialism, while China directly leapt over the historical process of capitalism and entered socialism from a semi-colonial and semi-feudal society. The cause of this more "peculiar path" is also the dialectics of the interaction between national and cosmopolitan characters of the contradictory movement of production mode. This is a special manifestation of the inevitability of the replacement of capitalism by socialism.

During the first half of the twentieth century, the social productive forces of China had a distinctive feature, namely coexistence of backwardness and advancement: individual agricultural economy and manufacture occupied 90%, and modern industry took up 10%; the former belonged to backward productive forces, "similar to the ancient times", or "staying at the condition of ancient times", and the latter belonged to advanced productive forces, which centrally controlled the economic lifeline of the country and trained 3 million's modern industrial workers. Those two kinds of productive forces, through interaction and mutual

---

13   Fukuyama, *The End of History*. Hohhot: Yuanfang Publishing House, 1998: p. 1.

restriction, constituted the overall productive forces of China and endowed them with duality. It was the economic movement of that duality that brought about "China's two possible destinies" and determined that the future development of China had two possibilities, i.e. developing and establishing capitalist relations of production or establishing socialist relations. "China's two possible destinies" were the result of the impact, influence and infiltration from the inner contradiction of western capitalist mode of production upon and into China. So which possibility for China's future development would come true hinged on, to a large extent, the relationship between China and world and the tendency of world history.

Seen from its history, China was forcibly dragged by western capitalist countries onto the track of world history. During that process, the western capitalism created "new industry" in China, destructed the groundwork of feudal economy and unconsciously accelerated capitalist development of China to a certain degree on the one hand, and oppressed the capitalist development of China in collusion with Chinese feudal force, putting the capitalist development of China into a deformed condition. "It is certainly not the purpose of the imperialist powers invading China to transform feudal China into capitalist China. On the contrary, their purpose is to transform China into their own semi-colony or colony."[14] That is to say, the western capitalist countries did not allow China to turn into an independent capitalist country. That seemed to be a contradiction, but it was a fact. The self-interest of western capitalism led to the generation of that historical phenomenon.

Seen from the world history, in the first half of the twentieth century, the inner contradiction of capitalist mode of production had been in an intensifying state, economic crises occurred frequently, and the scale of war was larger and larger, thereby unfolding the "future prospect" of capitalism to the undeveloped countries. Meanwhile, the tendency of world history was changed by the October Revolution, inspiring the economically backward countries to "take the path of the Russian". During that period of time, the labor movements in socialist and developed capitalist countries and the national liberation movements in colonies echoed each other across the world, forming "the age of world socialist revolutions". China was in that "age of world socialist revolutions" at that time.

---

14 *Selected Works of Mao Zedong*. Beijing: People's Publishing House, 1991: 2nd Ed., Vol. 2, p. 628.

The combination of international and domestic conditions, such as the duality of China's productive forces, the impact, influence and infiltration from the inner contradiction of western capitalist mode of production upon and into China, and "the age of world socialist revolutions", made the socialist revolution historically necessary in China.

The historical necessity is the fundamental restriction of social economic movement on historical process. The historical necessity of socialist revolution in China determines the general trend of China's future development, whose actualization is presented as the practical process of Chinese people and whose actualization mode rests with the contrast between domestic class forces in China. In China during the first half of the twentieth century, there arose not only "a similar contradiction" to that of western capitalist countries, namely the contradiction between the proletariat and the bourgeoisie, but also a particular "group of contradictions" that could not be found in western capitalist countries, including the contradiction between Chinese nation and western "bourgeois nation", the contradiction between the broad masses of people and feudalism, the contradiction between the peasant class and the landlord class, the contradiction between the national bourgeoisie and the foreign bourgeoisie as well as the bureaucrat bourgeoisie, etc.

All of those contradictions interweaved with the contradiction between the proletariat and the bourgeoisie, forming a huge social web. In that web, the contradiction between western "bourgeois nation" and Chinese nation, feudalism and the broad masses of people constituted the major contradiction in society, which gave a special realization form to the inevitability of the replacement of capitalism by socialism in China. And it is indeed true. The socialist revolution in the original sense is realized in China through the intermediary of new-democratic revolution, and the new-democratic revolution and the construction of the socialism with Chinese characteristics find a concrete path for China to realize the "two inevitabilities".

While studying Chinese history, some people always give no consideration to historical necessity but indulge in the hypothetic judgments of "if... then...". In their eyes, if the Hundred Days' Reform had succeeded, then China could not have been so backward; if China had chosen capitalism in the 1950s, then it would have ... today. However, the development of history has its inherent law, which is not subject to the formula of "if... then...". As a matter of fact, in historical researches, the judgment of "if... then..." can never be verified, thus it has no sci-entific significance. By indulging in such a study model, we can only learn illusory, rather than true, history. This is not the fight of Quixote who takes windmill for a demon, but the opposition between two con-crete conceptions of history, namely idealist conception of history and materialistic conception of history.

3 FULL REALIZATION OF THE INEVITABLE REPLACEMENT OF CAPITALISM BY SOCIALISM

The first realization of socialist revolution in oriental countries marked the inevitability of the replacement of capitalism by socialism had changed from a historical trend into a social reality. However, that was just the starting point but not the end. The capitalist mode of production in essence "has the international nature", thus it will has a worldwide stage. This means that the inevitability of the replacement of capitalism by socialism can be separately realized in a country first, but its full realization, i.e. the ultimate victory of socialism against capitalism, will be a long-term worldwide development process of world history.

Marx pointed out, "The proper task of bourgeois society is the creation of the world market, at least in outline, and of the production based on that market."[15] Indeed, the commercialization of production and the in-finite pursuit for surplus propelled the bourgeoisie into rushing around the globe and making every effort to build up a world market. The es-tablishment of large-scale industry, the advancement of communication media, the invasion into India and China, the colonization of America and Africa, and so forth all provided condition for the formations of world market and "international relations of production". "The bour-geoisie has through its exploitation of the world market given a cos-mopolitan character to production and consumption in every country." While expanding the world market, the bourgeoisie strived to make all nations "adopt the bourgeois mode of production" and meanwhile vio-lently "made barbarian and semi-barbarian countries dependent on the civilized ones, nations of peasants on nations of bourgeois, the East on the West"[16], thereby creating a capitalist world system. As regards its essence, the formation and development process of capitalist world system is a capital accumulation process of world capitalism, and the

15 *Karl Marx and Friedrich Engels*. Beijing: People's Publishing House, 1972: 1st Chinese Ed., Vol. 29, p. 348.
16 *Selected Works of Karl Marx and Friedrich Engels*. 2nd Ed., Vol. 1, pp. 276 – 277.

primitive accumulation of capital is just the beginning of capital accumulation. Just as the primitive accumulation of capital, the world accumulation of capital is also "written in the annals of mankind in letters
of blood and fire".

The capitalist world system is structurally a "center-periphery" or
"center-satellite" system, in which the developed countries constitute
the "center" and the developing ones are "satellites". Engels had vividly pointed out, "England, the great manufacturing centre of an agricultural world, with an ever-increasing number of corn and cotton-
growing Irelands revolving around her, the industrial sun."[17]

In such a "center-satellite" capitalist world system, the developed countries cruelly exploit and plunder the developing countries by various
means, such as immediate investment in developing countries to make
use of their cheap labor resource; debt exploitation that causes debt
crisis in developing countries; bidirectional monopoly, namely seller's
monopoly (monopoly of high price) and buyer's monopoly (monopoly
of low price), during international trades relying upon their advanced
science and technology and powerful economic strength to form a
long-term unequal exchange beyond the action of the law of value, etc.
During this process, capital flows to the whole world, whereas profit
flows to the "center". The bourgeoisie of developed countries obtains
dual benefit through dual exploitation, of workers not only in their
countries but also in developing countries; consequently, it cannot only
achieve a high profit rate abroad, but also maintain a high surplus value
rate domestically. As the developed countries enjoy the "bonus" of globalization, the developing countries are still suffering from poverty and
backwardness to the fullest extent, giving rise to the situation that the
rich countries are richer and richer, whilst the poor countries are poorer
and poorer. On the one side, the wealth of developed countries is accumulated continuously, and on the other side, the poverty of developing countries is aggravated unceasingly. The globalization of modern
scientific technology and economy, instead of universally benefiting all
countries in the world, exacerbates the imbalance in the development
of world.

---

17   *Selected Works of Karl Marx and Friedrich Engels*. 2nd Ed., Vol. 4, p. 425.

According to relevant statistics, there are currently 1.3 billion of people living below the absolute poverty line around the world, with an average daily living cost less than one US dollar. The developed countries take up 86% of the global GDP and 82% of the export market share, but the developing countries, where the vast majority of world population live, only amount to 14% and 18%, respectively. Twenty years ago, there were 20 most undeveloped countries among the member states of the United Nations, but so far the number has increased to 48; forty years ago, the income ratio between the richest population and the poorest population in the world was 30:1, but now the ratio has risen to 74:1. The increasingly widened "digital gap" indicates that capitalism does not put an end to class opposition and gap between the rich and the poor. On the contrary, it exploits the working class around the world while exploiting the working class in the developed countries, and despoils the "peasants' nation"; while continuously widening the gap between the rich and the poor within the developed countries, it also produces the same gap throughout the world and widens it with each passing day; it does not eliminate the original backwardness of the third-world countries, but puts these economically backward countries into a condition of deformed development or "undeveloped development" and makes them confront unprecedented pressure and challenge in terms of economic security and economic sovereignty; instead of relieving the economic crises in the developed countries, it tries hard to transfer the crises to the developing countries with the aim of putting the developing countries into serious economic and social crises.

In contemporary times, the development of the developed countries is at the cost of the underdevelopment of the undeveloped countries, or we can say, the "underdevelopment" of the undeveloped countries is a kind of distorted development form resulting from the exploitation, plunder and control of developed countries in the capitalist world system. "Underdevelopment does not arise out of the existence of old systems and the capital shortage in those areas isolated from the mainstream of world history. On the contrary, either in the past or at the present, what results in underdevelopment is exactly the same historical process that creates economic development (the development of capitalism itself)."[18] In a word, the capitalist world system causes the opposition between development and underdevelopment.

18   Frank, *Issues about Development and Underdevelopment*. Beijing: China Social Sciences Press, 1986: p. 151.

The contradiction between developed countries and undeveloped countries also interweaves with the contradiction respectively between the proletariat and the bourgeoisie and between socialism and capitalism. As mentioned previously, the bourgeoisie of developed countries exploits the working class both in developed countries and developing countries, so the contradiction between developed countries and undeveloped countries in contemporary times interweaves with the contradiction between the proletariat and the bourgeoisie. In addition, the generation of oriental socialist countries is the result of the impact, influence and infiltration from the inner contradiction of capitalist mode of production upon and into oriental countries, and such oriental socialist countries fall under the developing countries concerning their economic development level, so the contradiction between developed countries and developing countries in contemporary times also interweaves with the contradiction between capitalism and socialism.

All in all, the inner contradictions of capitalist world system are manifested as interweaved contradictions between the bourgeoisie and the proletariat, between developed countries and developing countries or between the "peasants' nation" and the "bourgeois nation", and between capitalism and socialism. The emergence and interweaving of these contradictions is basically the consequence of the globalization of capitalist mode of production and its inner contradiction.

In fact, capitalist economy needs an external non-capitalist or "quasi-capitalist" space and market for its expansion, and the economic "subordinate" or "dependent" relation of undeveloped countries to developed countries, namely the "center-satellite" relationship, is the necessary condition for the worldwide establishment and development of capitalist mode of production. For this reason, the poor and backward condition of undeveloped countries can never be relieved through the capitalist expansion of developed countries. What's more, the capitalist development in contemporary undeveloped countries has a different nature from the capitalist development in the history of developed countries in that the capitalist world system needs developing countries to keep their underdeveloped status, so developing countries are prevented by developed countries from taking the same development road with them.

That is to say, it is impossible for contemporary undeveloped countries to make any economic progress by following the road that has been taken by developed capitalist countries; on the contrary, only by the aid of socialism can they get over the economic "subordination" or "dependence" on the developed countries and really realize economic and social development. Contemporarily, the contradiction between developed countries and undeveloped countries is still the manifestation, the prominent manifestation, of the inner contradiction of capitalist mode of production. It shows that the inevitable replacement of capitalism by socialism still has its objective basis and still works.

The entry into socialism of some oriental countries is a special manifestation of the inevitability of the replacement of capitalism by socialism and a conscious selection of backward countries in the capitalist world system for revivification. Reform, as a process in which socialism is finding a specific path, is also a conscious selection of socialist countries in the capitalist world system for rejuvenation. In this process, socialism has indeed learnt from and absorbed some advanced management methods of capitalism; and during its development, capitalism also learns from and absorbs some advocacies of socialism, such as establishment of social insurance system and welfare system, "participation of workers in management", planning to a definite extent, etc. However, negating the "two inevitabilities" on this ground in the belief that "socialism and capitalism are converging" is unacceptable.

As two social formations, socialism and capitalism are different in essence, so the two cannot converge: capitalism will never give up the private ownership of the means of production, which is its "sacred and inviolable" principle, and socialism will never change its economic structure centered on public ownership of the means of production because its ultimate goal is to abolish private ownership; capitalism cannot eliminate exploitation and polarization and realize common prosperity of people, whereas socialism essentially aims to liberate and develop productive forces, eliminate exploitation and polarization, and ultimately realize common prosperity.

The reason why socialism can learn from and absorb some management methods of capitalism is because socialism and capitalism have a common material foundation, i.e. large-scale socialized production, within a definite period of time; and the reason why capitalism learns from and absorbs some advocacies of socialism is, to a large degree, because of the strong influence of socialism and the long-term struggle of the working class in the capitalist countries, both of which force it to carry out some reforms in order to withstand socialism and relieve domestic class contradiction. No matter whether it is "hot war" or "cold war", coexistence or competition, or even mutual learning, they are actually different effects of the "two inevitabilities" under different historical conditions.

Throughout the overall human history, "no social order is ever destroyed before all the productive forces for which it is sufficient have been developed, and new superior relations of production never replace older ones before the material conditions for their existence have matured within the framework of the old society"[19]. The "two nevers" here and the "two inevitabilities" are inherently uniform. To be specific, the more developed the productive forces of capitalist society are, the more mature the material existence conditions for socialist society will be; the day when the best of the productive forces contained in capitalist society is gotten out will be the moment when the material existence conditions for socialist society become completely mature. Then, the "two inevitabilities" will be fully realized.

In other words, the development of capitalism is not opposite to its inevitable fall. The more developed capitalism is, the more it indicates that the means of production and the results of production are appropriated commonly by the entire society, which is not only necessary but also feasible. The "two nevers" here and the "two inevitabilities" are a theoretical integral, reflecting the high unity between materialism and dialectics. This materialistic dialectics tell us that when firmly believing the "two inevitabilities", we should not ignore the "two nevers", and when facing the "two nevers", we should not forget the "two inevitabilities".

In contemporary times, socialism is full of vitality, and all the productive forces contained in capitalism haven't yet been completely developed, so capitalism has not reached its limit. However, not reaching limit does not mean there is no limit. The capitalist ownership of the means of production fundamentally determines the limit of capitalist development, and the inner contradictions of capitalist world system, i.e. the contradictions between the bourgeoisie and the proletariat,

---

19 *Selected Works of Karl Marx and Friedrich Engels.* 2nd Ed., Vol. 2, p. 33.

between developed countries and developing countries, and between capitalist society and socialist society, determine the space of capitalist development. Because the existence and development of capital itself is based on the contradiction between infinite promotion of productive forces' development and infinite pursuit for surplus value, or it can be said that capital itself is the expression and extension of this contradiction, once the development productive forces reaches a definite stage, once capital expansion reaches the "saturated" state in the world, the development of capitalism will reach its limit. The limit of capital expansion in space is the time of the fall of capitalism as a "worldwide system". Meanwhile, to really be a "worldwide system", socialism can only be established in a new world system. As Marx said, "The proletariat can thus only exist world-historically, just as communism, its activity, can only have a 'world-historical' existence."[20] That is to say, the replacement of capitalism by socialism is a process of world history, and the full realization of the "two inevitabilities" is cosmopolitan.

How long capitalism can last cannot be predicted. Marxists are not fortune-tellers, and what the theory of "two inevitabilities" reveals is the trend of historical development rather than its schedule. The key point is that capitalism should not be regarded as the ultimate formation of social development or temporary relative steadiness as an everlasting absolute form. Besides, the temporary setback of socialism should not be deemed as the permanent failure or twists and turns in movement as the end of movement. Judged from the overall historical process of human beings, the replacement of capitalism by socialism just starts its historical process, and the magnificent and mighty historical drama of the realization of "two inevitabilities" has just begun. It is a historical illusion to take beginning for end and prologue for curtain call. Just as Deng Xiaoping said,

"Feudal society replaced slave society, capitalism supplanted feudalism, and, after a long time, socialism will necessarily supersede capitalism. This is an irreversible general trend of historical development, but the road has many twists and turns. Over the several centuries that it took for capitalism to replace feudalism, how many times were monarchies restored! So, in a sense, temporary restorations are usual and can hardly be avoided. Some countries have suffered major setbacks, and socialism appears to have been weakened. But the people have been

---

20   *Selected Works of Karl Marx and Friedrich Engels*. 2nd Ed., Vol. 1, p. 87.

tempered by the setbacks and have drawn lessons from them, and that will make socialism develop in a healthier direction."[21]

The prospect is bright, while the road is tortuous. The fall of capitalism and the victory of socialism are both inevitable, which is still our conclusion.

---

21 *Selected Works of Deng Xiaoping.* Beijing: People's Publishing House, 1994: 1st Ed., Vol. 3, pp. 382 – 382.

CHAPTER XI

GENESIS, ESSENCE AND PROCESS: A NEW INTERPRETATION OF MARXIST EPISTEMOLOGY (I)

The term "cognition" refers to the acquisition of knowledge. Human beings need not only to cognize the external world as the objective object, but also to make reflections on their own cognitive activity, so as to improve the consciousness of the cognitive activity. This is the task of epistemology. With respect to time, epistemology was generated in ancient times, with a history as long as the entire philosophy, but it did not obtain a real development until the modern times. Marxist epistemology, starting from practice, combines the natural and social factors of the genesis of cognition together, and scientifically interprets the genesis, essence and process of cognition, thus bringing about a revolutionary change in the history of epistemology and exerting great and far-reaching influence on the development of epistemology.

1 RECAPITULATION: THE ESSENTIAL RELATIONSHIP BETWEEN ONTOGENY AND PHYLOGENY OF COGNITION

From Marx's point of view, labor enabled the ancestors of human beings to more and more deeply and extensively contact the attributes and relations of world of objects, thereby forming a uniform nervous physiological structure taking brain as the center and sense organs as gateways, which provides a natural premise for man's absorption, processing and integration of various information and for the realization of the coincident reflection of object by subject. However, the symbol of man's cognitive ability is the social cognitive structure of man rather than the biological structure of his brain.

Labor has been a social activity since the outset. The more it developed, the more men needed to communicate, thus language was produced. Intercourse expansion and language development, as two powerful impetuses, caused the cognitive activity of man to become a kind of social activity and formed the social mode of inheritance, different from biological mode of heredity, for the cognitive activity of man. Such social cognitive structure and social mode of inheritance gradually came into being through the "internalization" of activity under the interaction between man and object.

Specifically speaking, in the process of applying instruments to actually transform object, man gradually converts external actual action mode into internal ideal action mode, which is called internalization, and brings the latter into correspondence with the former. In this way, the cognitive schema specific to man is formed, fixed and accumulated in logical form. The generation of language plays an important role in this process. Language, as the common mode for the expression of human thoughts, brings cognition out of the narrow scope of individual experience; the application of language enables men to ideally process and transform object, thereby making it possible for man to ideally grasp the material world, i.e. making the genesis of human cognition possible.

The genesis of cognition conceived by Marx concerns both phylogeny and ontogeny of cognition. The former refers to the process during which mankind forms the social reflection model specific to man along with getting rid of the psychological reaction model of animals and thereby give rise to the human cognition; the latter refers to the process experienced by every individual person in human society after his birth, during which his cognition is developed from the level of children to the level of adults along with his physiological and psychological maturation. Ontogeny and phylogeny of cognition are coincident with each other regarding the restriction and determination from practical activity on them. Meanwhile, ontogeny of cognition has a recapitulation relationship with phylogeny of cognition, meaning that the genesis process of ontogeny reproduces the genesis process of human cognition in a concentrated form. Recapitulation is the essential relationship between ontogeny and phylogeny of cognition.

Recapitulation refers to a similarity, correlation or isomorphism in process between individual development and phyletic evolution of biological organism. The development process of a biont always recapitulates or reproduces the historical process of biological phyletic evolution in a certain manner and to a certain extent in aspects of its extension mode, sequence, development stage, dynamic model and evolutionary law, thus being the recapitulation or reproduction of phyletic evolution. So, the recapitulation relationship between ontogeny and phylogeny of biological organism is called by biologist Haeckel et al. "biological recapitulation law".

Recapitulation law is a general law in the process of biological organism's existence, continuation and development. The recapitulation relationship between ontogeny and phylogeny of mankind, the supreme form in the evolution of life, as the movement process unifying individuality with totality, biological nature with sociality, and materiality with spirituality, is exceptionally prominent, and the effect of recapitulation law is particularly significant. More importantly, the recapitulation relationship and the recapitulation law do not only lie in the organism development of man, but also consist in the intelligence development and cognition genesis of man. As Engels said, "Just as the development history of the human embryo in the mother's womb is only an abbreviated repetition of the history, extending over millions of years, of the bodily development of our animal ancestors, starting from the worm, so the mental development of the human child is only a still more abbreviated repetition of the intellectual development of these same ancestors, at least of the later ones."[1]

---

1   *Selected Works of Karl Marx and Friedrich Engels.* 2nd Ed., Vol. 4, p. 383.

From the perspective for history, the phylogeny of human cognition is realized in the process of the cognition genesis of innumerable primitive individuals. It is the continuous psychological, ideological and intellectual genesis, development and evolution of the innumerable primitive individuals that constitute the process of the phylogeny of human cognition and drive man to transcend the psychology and senses of animals step by step and then become "a conscious species-being". In this process, the cognition genesis of every individual is recapitulating, in a definite mode, the genesis and development process of human cognition prior to him. Owing to this recapitulation relationship, the existing cognitive ability and results of human beings can be preserved, continued and consolidated, and at the same time, the cognition of individual can fuse into the overall structure of human cognition, playing a boosting and promoting role in the overall evolution of human cognition. The historical process of the phylogeny of human cognition is exactly realized in the process of the cognition genesis and development of countless primitive individuals.

In reality, the genesis and development process of individual cognition is recapitulating the genesis and development process of human cognition in the form of "epitome". Such a procedural recapitulation is fundamentally caused by the fact that each genesis of individual cognition in reality is premised and based on the results having obtained by the phylogeny of human cognition. During this process, biological genetic genes and social inheritance factors, together with their unity, as the chain for the continuation and preservation of human species, predetermine the pattern and level that can be reached by individual in respect of organism structure and function, and determine the road that individual will necessarily take to reach such a pattern and level. Hence, the genesis and development process of individual cognition inevitably recapitulates the spiritual development history of mankind in a definite mode.

However, the recapitulation of the phylogeny of human cognition by the ontogeny of human cognition is after all made under the natural and social conditions different from those of the original genesis process and on the premise of relatively mature and complete results, making the real ontogeny of cognition recapitulate the long process of the phylogeny of human cognition in the form of "epitome". Here, "epitome" has a significant epistemological meaning.

With respect to space structure, "epitome" has the connotation of concentration, contraction, gathering and constriction, meaning that the species origin and cognition phylogeny of human beings are reflected concentratedly in the formation and cognition genesis of individual organism. Correspondingly, by grasping and magnifying the process of the formation and cognition genesis of individual organism, we can learn more about the species origin and cognition phylogeny of human beings.

With respect to time structure, "epitome" has the connotation of simplification, acceleration and shortening, meaning that the long progressive process of human species origin and cognition phylogeny is recapitulated or reproduced in a brief and short form by the process of the formation and cognition genesis of individual organism. Men thus are able to apprehend and sketch the whole process of the species origin and cognition phylogeny of human beings by extending and expanding this brief and short process.

From the angle of content, "epitome" has the connotation of summarization, abbreviation and conciseness, meaning that the complex evolutionary process of human species origin and cognition phylogeny is reproduced in a concise form by the process of the formation and cognition genesis of individual organism. Recapitulation does not mean the formation and cognition genesis of individual organism must repeat all details and all aspects of historical process, but only reproduce main aspects, key links and basic stages of historical process in a simplified way. Then, men are able to understand the main aspects, key links and basic stages in the process of human species origin and cognition phylogeny by grasping this simplified process.

Cognition is in fact the product of the interaction between hereditary factors and environmental factors; its genesis is both endogenous and exogenous. The interaction between man and environment does not only change the cognitive structure of man and promote the systematization of internal structure, but also change external materials and facilitate the systematization of external materials. Cognition cannot be realized without the systematization respectively of external materials and internal structure.

In view of the above, the genetic epistemology of Piaget investigates the process of the cognition ontogeny of children and reveals that the cognition genesis of children is a dual construction process unifying the internalization of children's operational activity as cognitive schema with the externalization of this cognitive schema and the assimilation of external stimuli into the cognitive schema. To explain the ontogeny of cognition from such two aspects as the internalization and externalization of activity is undeniably reasonable, but the genetic epistemology of Piaget ignores the effect of social inheritance in the genesis process of cognition to a very large degree, and understands neither that practical activity with instruments is the realistic basis for the differentiation between subject and object and the genesis of cognition, nor that cognition is essentially the active reflection of object by subject on the basis of practice.

2 UNITY OF REFLECTION AND CREATION: THE ESSENTIAL FEATURE OF COGNITIVE ACTIVITY

During the survey on cognition, the first issue in front of us is how to understand the essence of cognition. This is an issue highly focused by philosophers and causing endless controversies. Seen from the history of philosophy, the understanding on the essence of cognition can roughly be divided into two lines: one is transcendentalism dating from Plato in ancient times and developing into the tradition of Continental European rationalism in early modern times, and the other is empiricism dating back to Aristotle in ancient times and developing into the tradition of British empiricism in early modern times.

The epistemological transcendentalism believes the cognition of man comes from a certain sacred enlightenment and congenital idea, or it is a kind of subjectively spontaneous, innate ability. In Plato's opinion, cognition is the memory of soul about "the world of ideas"; Kant asserts that cognition is the process in which mankind sorts out empirical materials depending on the a priori form of his innate skills and establishes regular associations among them; Hegel points out that the inherently existing "absolute idea" is the source of cognition, and human cognition is no more than a self-cognition process of "absolute idea" through human thought as an externalized form. It is undoubtedly reasonable that the epistemological transcendentalism underlines the active effect of cognitive schema on cognitive activity, but it overlooks the practical foundation for the initiative of human cognitive schema, and turns cognition into a pure spiritual being unrelated to the real world.

The empiricism of epistemology is classified into idealistic empiricism and materialistic empiricism. Idealistic empiricism asserts that experience is the ensemble of man's senses, and senses belong to a kind of subjective experience unrelated to objective object. Materialistic empiricism argues that the prior existence of objective object is the premise of cognition, experience is men's feeling to external stimuli, and cognition is the reflection of objective object in human brain. But when interpreting how human brain reflects the objective object, materialistic empiricism merely considers the subject of cognition as a biological being, and thinks the reflection of objective object in human brain is the result of passive and negative acceptance of external stimuli. In materialistic empiricism, cognition is simplified into the result of subject's passive acceptance of object stimuli and object's "stamping" of itself into the brain of subject, and interpreted as a linear process of the passive mechanical response of subject to object; the initiative and creativity of subject are thus dissolved. Obviously, this is an intuitive theory of reflection.

Despite different routes, different schools and different viewpoints, the epistemologies before Marx all have a fatal common defect, that is, not grasping that practice is the foundation for differentiation and unity between subject and object and not apprehending cognition is the active reflection of object by subject based on practice. Idealistic epistemology extremely commits itself to defining the essence of cognition from the angle of subject, either making the cognitive schema of subject transcendental or the sensory experience of subject isolated; old materialistic epistemology places extreme emphasis on discussing the essence of cognition from the perspective of object, and conceives cognition as a passive mechanical response of subject to object. Both of the two do not really apprehend the essence of cognition.

According to Marx, the relationship between man and world is above all the relationship between the transformer and the transformed, on which basis the relationship between the reflector and the reflected is generated. In such a dual relationship, man transforms not only the external nature but also the nature of himself, not only the objective world but also his subjective world, thereby constantly improving his cognitive ability and modifying his cognitive schema. As Engels pointed out, "It is precisely the alteration of nature by men, not solely nature as such, which is most essential and immediate basis of human thought, and it is in the measure that man has learned to change nature that his intelligence has increased."[2]

The subject of cognition is not the abstract individual isolated from society. Though the cognitive activity of human beings is composed of the cognitive activities of countless individuals, the cognitive activity of any individual cannot be done beyond society, because cognitive activity is generated and developed under the interactions between individual and society and between individual and species. The cognitive schema of subject, the social being, is formed on the basis of prior activity, but once formed, it will continue all along by means of social inheritance, becoming a relatively fixed framework or model and constituting a knowledge background. The cognitive activity of man is always under the knowledge background of a definite cognitive schema, and extends and applies the fixed cognitive schema to the object of cognition. Cognitive schema, being the social cognitive organ of man, determines that different subjects of cognition sort out and process object information from different angles of view and at different levels and give their own interpretations on the significance of object.

In cognitive activity, object is information source, the giver of information, while subject is receiver and processor of information; instruments help subject impel object to release messages, or assist subject with operation and processing of information. On the one hand, information about the existence, attributes and laws of object enters into the brain of subject, and is reflected by subject, meaning that object has exerted influence and restrictive effect on the consciousness and ideas of subject; on the other hand, while reflecting and cognizing object, subject is ideally transforming and creating object, which is not only represented by that subject always transforms the information of object into the cognitive content and thinking form specific to man, but also by that in the process of receiving and processing information, subject forms such practical reasons as purpose, plan, etc. for object transformation, and also creates ideal object. These are the embodiment of the initiative of subject in cognitive activity.

In cognitive activity, object will not spontaneously "present" its internal information to subject, and subject will not passively wait and receive the information of object either; instead, subject acquires the information of

---

2   *Selected Works of Karl Marx and Friedrich Engels*. 2nd Ed., Vol. 4, p. 329.

object by positively acting on object with instruments. Above all, subject does not only stimulate object to release messages with a certain method, but also processes these messages in his mind, constructs an idea model of object through multi-level thinking operation, and thereby cognizes and grasps object. The thinking operation of subject, the active processor of object information, is the decisive condition for the formation of cognition. Subject exerts effect and influence on object with cognitive instruments, and reconstructs or constructs object through thinking; this is the initiative unique to the cognitive activity of man.

We must know that the specific interaction between subject and object of cognition is not formed naturally, but is generated in the process during which subject, through his own activity, brings a certain part, a certain level or a certain aspect of the objective world into the scope of his practical and cognitive activities. Besides, in cognitive activity, subject is the positive and active party, whereas object is the passive and reactive party. The cognition relationship between subject and object is the result of the selection and setting of object by subject under a definite condition; in other words, object is selected and set by subject.

We should also see that the cognitive activity of subject is restricted and restrained by object. Object has its inherent laws of existence and development, and the selection and setting of object by subject must comply with the features of object; when subject acts on object by virtue of cognitive instruments, the selection and application of cognitive instruments must conform to the properties and state of object, as well; otherwise the purpose of stimulating object to release messages will not be achieved. The aim of cognition is to correctly reflect the attributes, state, innate characters and laws of object, and the selection, reflection and construction of object information by subject is all for the purpose of ideal reproduction of object.

The active process of man's cognition on the objective world is permeated with the reflection and creation of object by subject from beginning to end. Marxist epistemology grasps the concept of cognition just based on these two aspects – imitation and creation. The moon in water is actually the moon in the sky, and the man in your eyes is actually the man in front of you. Cognition cannot be divorced from reflection, and reflection must take objective things as prototype. The imitating character of reflection determines the objectivity of cognition. Therefore, reflection is one of the basic connotations of concept "cognition".

However, as the imitation and reflection of objective things, cognition does not intuitively imitate, or reflect like a mirror, the objective things; instead, subject actively explores, transforms and creates object during practice and cognition, not only involving active selection of object or some aspects of object according to his needs, but also including ideal reconstruction or construction of object. Cognition is creative, because through the selection, processing and production of sensuous materials by the aid of his thinking, man reveals the essence and law of things, and constructs the ideal object, which is actually the advanced reflection and ideal creation of realistic object, in his mind according to his needs and the laws of things. Creation is another basic connotation of concept "cognition".

If we negate the reflective character of cognition and the imitating character of reflection, we will be entrapped in the idealistic epistemology; turning a blind eye to the creativity of cognition, we will fall into the intuitive theory of reflection of old materialism. In the process of man's cognition on the objective world, cognition is creative reflection rather than mechanical imitation or simple reflection by a mirror; creation is based on reflection rather than being arbitrary and divorced from imitation. Cognition, being both objective and subjective and both reflective and creative, is the unity of reflection, selection and construction. In short, the unity of reflection and creation is the essential feature of cognitive activity, which is the Marxist concept of cognition.

3 LANGUAGE: THE ELEMENT OF COGNITIVE ACTIVITY

The cognitive activity of man is realized by means of language. It is by virtue of language, the symbolized thinking, that a child grows from the state of self-centralization to the state of the differentiation between subject and object, and turns from pure emotional attitude to theoretical attitude. Language is the premise for the genesis and maturation of individual cognition and the execution of human cognitive activity.

Concerning the relationship between language and thought, thought is the content of language, and language is the carrier of thought. Only with the help of language can men make abstract summarization and thereby reflect the essence and law of things. As Lenin said, "Every word (speech) already universalizes"[3]. Only on the basis of language can men make judgment and inference and thereby form theoretical systems as per concepts and their relations. Language is an element of thinking, as well as an element of cognitive activity. No language, no human cognition. "Language is as old as consciousness."[4]

Consciousness itself is immaterial, but it cannot be separated from material, so it must be expressed by language as a special form of material. As Marx said, "From the start the 'spirit' is afflicted with the curse of being 'burdened' with matter, which here makes its appearance in the form of agitated layers of air, sounds, in short, of language."[5] Language is the immediate actuality of consciousness or thought. Man fixes his consciousness or thought in language, and studies and rethinks it as an ideal object, thereby forming self-consciousness.

Language has been relatively independent and exerted influence on cognitive activity since its formation. Especially, the development of written language expedites the formation of "objective knowledge world" defined by Popper, namely the objectified knowledge world manifested in various forms. The formation of "objective knowledge world" essentially ensures the preservation and continuation of human civilization. Specifically speaking, human individuals will die and disappear, but the cognition fruits obtained by individuals will enter the "objective knowledge world" due to the recording with linguistic signs, thereby being preserved, continued and developed. So the cognition fruits will survive the death of individuals.

It is beyond doubt that world exists beyond the thought and language of man. However, men can only understand the world and express their understanding on the world through language. The proficiency of their language directly influences and restricts the width and depth of their understanding on the world. In this sense, the boundary of language is also the boundary of cognition. Language is involved in cognitive activity all the time, and linguistic signs are a kind of sensuous instrument of man used for carrying out cognitive activity, expressing cognition results and conducting thinking operation. Linguistic signs and cognitive activity have a history of the same length, share the same source, and jointly develop during interaction, thereby constituting an inseparable

3 *Collected Works of Lenin*. 2nd Chinese Ed., Vol. 55, p. 233.
4 *Selected Works of Karl Marx and Friedrich Engels*. 2nd Ed., Vol. 1, p. 81.
5 Ibid., p. 81.

unity. In a word, language reflects the contradictory relationship respectively between thinking and being, between subjectivity and objectivity, and between self-consciousness and object-consciousness. Therefore, correctly understanding and grasping language, in a definite sense, is the key to opening the door of the relationship between man and world.

Just because of this, analytic philosophy pays high attention to language, and realizes the "linguistic turn" in the history of philosophy. Wittgenstein asserted, "All philosophy is linguistic critique."[6] Russell pointed out, "Logic is the essence of philosophy."[7] The "linguistic turn" essentially reflects the search of modern western philosophy for the connecting point or intermediate link between man and world, and shows the general understanding of modern western philosophy on the relationships between thought, language and world, that is, the world is beyond the thought of men, but men can only express their understanding of the world through language, and the world becomes human world in the language of men, so "the boundary of language is the boundary of world", and we can only talk about "my world".

This opinion of analytic philosophy is quite reasonable. The fruits of human cognition on world are accumulated in and expressed by language. Studying the world from the angle of language is actually to understand and grasp the world based on the relationship with man. However, the analytic philosophy goes too far after all, where language becomes an independent realm. It radically reverses the relationship between practice and language. It seemed that Marx had foreseen such a "linguistic turn", because he clearly pointed out that "just as philosophers have given thought an independent existence, they were bound to make language into an independent realm."[8] It seems that practice does not determine language, but language determines practice.

"Language is practical consciousness that exists also for other men, and for that reason alone it really exists for me personally as well; language, like consciousness, only arises from the need, the necessity, of intercourse with other men"[9]. Language structure is basically the internalization and sublimation of practice structure in human brain, "the

6 Wittgenstein, *Tractatus Logico-Philosophicus*. London Ed., p. 44.
7 Russell, *Our Knowledge of the External World*. New York Ed., p. 33.
8 *Karl Marx and Friedrich Engels*. Beijing: People's Publishing House, 1960: 1st Chinese Ed., Vol. 3, p. 525.
9 *Selected Works of Karl Marx and Friedrich Engels*. 2nd Ed., Vol. 1, p. 81.

manifestation of real life". Practice, rather than language, is the fundamental connecting point of between man and world; it is not language that determines practice, but it is practice that determines language. Only based on practice can we fundamentally comprehend the formation, evolution and development of language, and can we explain the contradictory relationship respectively between thinking and being, between subjectivity and objectivity, between subject and object, and between man and world.

With respect to the relationship between language and thinking mode, language influences thinking mode, and nations applying different language systems tend to have different thinking modes. Of course, language is not the decisive factor of thinking mode, but it indeed has influence on the latter. The amount of vocabulary, grammatical structure, syntactic expression, etc. all influence and restrict the thinking modes of different nations in different ways; the application of concept, category and reference in language is the process of differentiating, integrating and summarizing experience, and the different sequences of the said concept, category and reference show different understandings of different nations on the relationship between man and world. Through frequent use of language, such difference intensifies the difference in cognitive structure, causing different nations to form different thinking modes and cognitive schemas.

Regarding the relationship between language and symbol, language itself is a form of sign. Signs refer to the abstract indications or marks of things and their relations, the man-made referents about object. For example, the totems of prehistoric primitive tribes, the national flags of modern countries, etc. belong to symbol signs; the bonfire on the beacon tower in ancient times, the radio waves emitted by a radio station in modern society, etc. are signal signs, and so forth. Language is a basic form of sign, the foundation for other various kinds of forms of sign. Only after understanding language can we understand other forms of sign.

This signified cognitive mode is from reality but beyond reality. Linguistic signs, as a kind of meaning sign, are the material carrier of various abstract concepts, including a series of sign units (sign elements), and representing various determinations and relations of objective things. By applying linguistic signs, we can break down objective things with many determinations in thinking, carry out thinking operation on these linguistic signs standing for definite information and contents with the method of encoding, and then realize the reflection of objective things by combining the sign units. Furthermore, men combine and recombine the sign units based on the meanings of signs and according to definite logic rules, and establish a symbolic system with strict logical structure, thereby forming the knowledge or theoretical system concerning objective things.

Various concepts and categories expressed by linguistic signs are the summarization and abstraction of the general characters of things. Linguistic signs are the basic unit of men's logical thinking; just like the mathematical scientific signs used by men to abstract and deduce the quantitative relations in the real world, linguistic signs are used by men for logical deduction, so as to raise thinking from sensuous cognition to rational cognition, from abstract determination to thinking concreteness, and from theoretical reason to practical reason, for the ultimate purpose of revealing the relationship between man and world.

4 FROM SENSUOUS COGNITION, THINKING CONCRETENESS TO PRACTICAL IDEA: THE BASIC PROCESS OF COGNITION

Judged from its process, the cognition of man goes through two stages, that is, from sensuous cognition to rational cognition. The reason why the process of cognition goes through these two stages is not only related to the relationship between phenomenon and essence of object, but also closely associated with the relationship between sense organ and thinking organ of man. In other words, the differentiation between phenomenon and essence is based on not only objective thing but also man himself; it falls under both the category of ontology and the category of epistemology.

Sensuous cognition has two basic characteristics: for the subject of cognition, sensuous cognition cannot exist without the experience of man, and empirical knowledge commonly referred to basically belong to sensuous cognition; as to the object of cognition, sensuous cognition is the cognition of things' phenomena and external relations. The problem is that the sensuous cognition of man is different from the sensory activity of animals, because it is always linked with the cognitive schema specific to man. The sensation of man is by no means the pure perception without reason in any case, and it is restricted by the established cognitive schema all the time; the values and social relations of subject additionally permeate and influence the formation of sensuous cognition. As Marx said, "The forming of the five senses is a labor of the entire history of the world down to the present. … The care-burdened, poverty-stricken man has no sense for the finest play; the dealer in minerals sees only the commercial value but not the beauty and the specific character of the mineral: he has no mineralogical sense."[10]

Rational cognition is the cognition about things' essence and internal connections acquired by man through processing, sorting out and generalizing the sensuous cognition by virtue of abstract thinking. It is not only manifested as the forms of concept, judgment and inference, but also as the theoretical system made up of such concept, judgment and inference. The theoretical system, as the systematic form of the thinking reflection, assumes the task to reproduce the essence and law of things generally and concretely in the thinking.

There is an inherent logic in the process from phenomenon to essence, from sensuous cognition to rational cognition, that is, from sensuous concreteness to thinking abstraction, and then to thinking concreteness. Marx thinks there are two paths in cognition: along the first, "the full conception was evaporated to yield an abstract determination", and along the second, "the abstract determinations lead towards a reproduction of the concrete by way of thought"[11]. The two paths are connected end to end, constituting a process of negation of the negation of "sensuous concreteness – thinking abstraction – thinking concreteness".

Sensuous concreteness belongs to sensuous cognition, which results in the formation of a concrete thing, a sensuousness-based thing in front of the sense organs of man, in the brain of man as a "full conception" and "intuitive entirety" through the sensation and perception of man, namely the formation of the general impression of the thing's external relations. Abstract determination and thinking concreteness belong to rational cognition. The former refer to every single determination, essential determination in particular, abstracted by thinking through analysis on the sensuous concreteness; the latter refers to rational concreteness reproduced and constructed on the basis of abstract determination, and it is "the concentration of many determinations, hence unity of the diverse"[12].

---

10   *Karl Marx and Friedrich Engels*. 1st Chinese Ed., Vol. 42, p. 126.
11   *Selected Works of Karl Marx and Friedrich Engels*. 2nd Ed., Vol. 2, p. 18.
12   ibid., p. 18.

Thinking concreteness and sensuous concreteness are different. Sensuous concreteness is just a kind of chaotic conception not reaching the essence level of object, whilst thinking concreteness, through the intermediate process of abstract determination, does not only go deep into the essence level of a thing, but also concentrates and unifies the determinations of the thing, so it is the overall cognition of a thing regained after rational analysis. To put it another way, thinking concreteness is the organic concentration of many abstract determinations about an object, achieving the cognition of the essence, law and overall condition of things at rational level.

Thinking concreteness and abstract determination are different. Abstract determinations have included the cognition of the essential determinations of things, but the single abstract determinations are not enough for man to grasp the laws of things and their general relations. Only by adopting the method of concentration to link the abstract determinations of things with each other and form a unified cognition of things as a whole can man really and fundamentally grasp the objective things, and really achieve the conformity between subjectivity and objectivity.

Rational cognition, including thinking concreteness, reflects the essence and law of objective things, and has the characters of abstractness and universality, but practical activity is concrete, therefore the results of rational cognition cannot be directly applied to practical activity. In other words, to realize the so-called leap from rational cognition to practical activity, we must concretize the rational cognition according to specific practical activity, and form and establish practical reason, i.e. practical idea.

Practical idea refers to the idea model, the ideal object, about practice established by men before practical activity. Marx pointed out, "A spider conducts operations that resemble those of a weaver, and a bee puts to shame many an architect in the construction of her cells. But what distinguishes the worst architect from the best of bees is this, that the architect raises his structure in imagination before he erects it in reality. At the end of every labor-process, we get a result that already existed in the imagination of the laborer at its commencement."[13] Such result of practice that already existed in the imagination is practical idea. In other words, practical idea is the ideal prototype of the real object to be created by practical activity, and the practical result of the real object is the objectification and materialization of practical idea.

---

13   *Karl Marx and Friedrich Engels.* 1st Chinese Ed., Vol. 23, p. 202.

Practical idea and theoretical reason both belong to the category of con-sciousness and idea, but the two also have large differences. If theo-retical reason is considered as the cognition on the essence and laws of an object itself, then practical idea is the purpose, plan, scheme, etc. formulated by men for transforming the object in a bid to satisfy their needs. As for the content, apart from the knowledge about the existence condition, internal structure, essential attributes, movement laws and so on of object revealed by theoretical reason, practical idea also con-centrates the cognition on the needs, purposes and activities of subject; besides the knowledge about "what" and "how" the object is, practical idea also includes judgments, made by subject for achieving his purpos-es, on the object and "how" the relationship between subject and object "could and should be", and includes the evaluation on the significance of object. Therefore, in the process of cognition, practical idea is a stage higher than theoretical reason.

Practical idea cannot be established without theoretical reason, but it is not simple logical deduction of theoretical reason. Practical reason is formed and established on the basis of the unity between extrinsic measure of ob-ject and inherent measure of man. On the one hand, practical reason is pos-sible to be established only when subject has cognized the essence and law of objective things. Without theoretical reason and the grasp of the extrinsic measure of object, there will be no practical idea; on the other hand, the es-tablishment of practical idea is premised on the cognition of the needs and essential powers of man. The transformation of world by men does not aim at simply reduplicating and imitating the existing forms of objective things, but changing the existing forms of objective things and creating "things-for-me" and "relations that exist for me" which are satisfactory to the needs of men and suitable for the development of men.

The forming process of practical idea is the process in which subject forms an "ideal purpose" and creates the ideal object by ideally apply-ing his inherent measure to the extrinsic measure of object in a definite mode. Practical idea does not only include the cognition on the uni-versality of essence and law of object, but also concerns the needs of subject, combines the specific requirements of practical activity, and unifies the three together. Hence, practical idea is the highest link in the process of cognition and the intermediary link in the translation from rational cognition into practical activity; it is the practical conscious-ness with a strong sense of reality.

CHAPTER XII

CONSTRUCTION, REFLECTION AND REFLEX: A NEW INTERPRETATION OF MARXIST EPISTEMOLOGY (II)

The important significance of the epistemological revolution in the twentieth century rests in the revelation of the constructive character of human thinking and its relationship to the theory of reflection. Concepts like "schema", "paradigm", "Gestalt", "conceptual structure", "model", etc. flooded into the sphere of epistemology at a time, giving a fatal blow to the intuitive theory of reflection. But it is wrong to believe the constructive character of thinking destructs the theory of reflection on this ground. The constructive character of thinking only embodies that cognition is the unity of reflex, reflection and construction, and instead of negating the theory of reflection, it caused a revolution in the theory of reflection. As far as I am concerned, cognition is indeed the processing of external information, and without external information, cognition cannot be formed, which is one side of the problem; on the other side, in respect of why cognition is what it is, we must find the answer in the construction and reflection of thinking, so as to reveal the sociality, historicity and designability of cognition.

1 CONSTRUCTIVE CHARACTER OF THINKING AND ITS ESSENCE

The constructive character of thinking was one of the controversial hot issues of epistemology in the twentieth century. In my eyes, the emergence of the constructive character of thinking as a theory marked the deepening of people's understanding on the structure of cognition, namely expanding cognition from two-dimensional structure into three-dimensional structure.

Before the generation of Kant's philosophy, the constructive character of thinking as a theory had not been highlighted. Thinking was conceived by men as a simple two-dimensional structure, in which there was only a relationship of the determinant and the determined. Just as Engels had said, scientists and philosophers before then knew "only nature on the one hand and thought on the other", and they either used nature to interpret thought, or used thought to explain nature. It is known to all that old materialism takes the path of "nature → thought", and idealism reversely follows the path of "thought → nature". One is the determinant, and the other is the determined; how simple and clear!

In the early twentieth century, Watson, the founder of US behaviorism, simply summarized thinking as a binomial of stimulation → reflection. This is the famous binomial schema S→R (stimulation → reflection). Centering on the study of human subjectivity, modern epistemology changed the binomial S→R into a trinomial S→O→R by interposing a middle tern (O) into the structure. Thus, the model from nature to thought, or from thought to nature, understood by men originally was broken, and a trinomial "object-in-itself → subject → ideal object" was generated. In this trinomial, subject becomes the converter between object-in-itself and ideal object, that is, object-in-itself is converted by subject into ideal object. Here, subject is active, being the processing and adjusting system for information conversion.

The structure of this trinomial in fact highlights the constructive character of thinking: (1) the formation of ideal object is determined on the one side by object-in-itself as the input system and on the other side by the thinking structure of subject; only when the two sides function simultaneously can the ideal object as the output system be created; (2) in the trinomial, subject is the sole active side, which selects and processes the input system with the thinking structure he has already possessed and then forms the output system. Considered from the aspects of form and function, it appears that object is being constructed by subject, meaning that by using his own thinking structure, subject decomposes, filters and converts the information of object-in-itself, and constructs the ideal object.

In the history of philosophy, the issue concerning the constructive character of thinking was initially put forward by Kant in the concepts of "a priori form", "schema" and "apperception". Kant thinks that there are three opinions on why cognition is possible to take shape, namely "abiogenesis" represented by Locke's empiricism, "theory of preformation" represented by Leibniz's theory of innate ideas, and his advocacy "epigenesis", i.e. constructivism. In Kant's opinion, constructing a concept means a priori providing an intuition corresponding to the concept; for instance, to construct an isosceles triangle, man should not either "only follow what he has seen in the figure", or "rigidly focus on the pure concept of the figure". In other words, construction should not be only based on experience in that experience cannot provide universal validity, or just based on pure concept because pure concept cannot provide expanded knowledge. Fundamentally, construction is "to extract out all sorts of features of the figure by means of a thing a priori imagined and shown (through drawing) by man according to concept"[1].

Hence, "construction" is created by reason, "a priori imagined and shown according to concept", and it includes four links: (1) construction should be based on reason rather than experience or concept, but it cannot be separated from experience and concept; (2) construction is to imagine intuition according to concept; (3) this intuition is both predetermined by reason and procedural; (4) the extension process of this predetermined intuition is to "extract out" the features connoted in experience.

The concept "construction" of Kant is a historic summarization of scientific cognition; it is actually the construction of thinking. In Kant's philosophy, the construction of thinking means that thinking establishes laws in the mind in advance, and then asks nature to give an answer. In the words of Kant, "it (reason) is only the principles of reason which can give to concordant phenomena the validity of laws, and it is only when experiment is directed by these rational principles that it can have

---

1   *Studies on Kant and Hegel*, 2nd Ed., p. 411.

any real utility; reason must approach nature with the view, indeed, of receiving information from it"[2].

It is obvious that this thinking constructivism is Kant's opinions of "human being's legislation for nature" and "schema", and it is the extension of the basic thought of "synthetic a priori judgment". From Kant's point of view, in the analytic a priori judgment advocated by continental rationalism, object is contained in subject, so its weakness is that it cannot expand knowledge; in the synthetic a posteriori judgment advocated by British empiricism, object is beyond subject, thus knowledge is expanded, but it cannot prove the universal validity of knowledge. In his eyes, seeking for necessity in perception is tantamount to getting water from stone, because objective validity "cannot be acquired from the direct cognition of object". The chaotic sensuous materials obtained from the external world through sensation do not constitute knowledge; they first of all need to be sorted out by the a priori forms (time, space) of sensuousness to form a conception with space-time certainty and synthesized by the a priori intellectual forms (category); then they have the universal validity. Therefore, "object is the conjunction of the given manifold of intuition in the concept", that is to say, synthetic a priori judgment is a process during which thinking conjoins sensuous manifold through a priori form (category), i.e. the construction process of thinking.

The premise of Kant is wrong – the so-called "a priori form", the category, is not a priori in fact, but is the fruit acquired by mankind in practice and cognition after birth. As a matter of fact, the transcendental time and space of Kant are the manifestation of the relative independence of objective time and space, and his opinion that Euclidean geometry is a priori given to subject has already been subverted by Lobachevsky, Polya and Riemannian geometry long ago. However, his theory of thinking construction brings forth a liberating thought, that is, theory, law and necessity cannot be solely summarized from repeated experience, which fired the first shot on the way to modern sciences in modern times dominated by the classical mechanics of Newton with "I make no assumptions" as motto, and has also been proved by the development of modern psychology.

---

2   *Studies on Kant and Hegel*, 2nd Ed., p. 412.

Basically speaking, the constructive character of thinking means that the process of man's reflection of world is the process of the social and conceptual grasp of world by man in the mode of subject. Besides factors like race, culture, historical knowledge background, etc., it mainly refers to the followings: (1) experience, intuition and daily consciousness are different in essence from theory, knowledge system and scientific consciousness, and there is an intermediary process of a series of abstraction, imagination and evaporation, as well as thinning and idealization; (2) man always grasps the world with his own conceptual structure and thinking model, and subsumes the world into his own understanding and interpreting system; (3) subject is a special converting unit, in which all sensuous, intellectual and rational things are "transformed", or constructed, so to speak.

The constructive character of thinking shows that cognition is the process of interaction between subject, by means of various intermediary systems (instrument operation system, conceptual logic system, social relation system), and object, and reflection is dually determined. There will be surely no ideal object without object-in-itself, which is the objective premise of cognition; without apprehension and creation by subject, without decomposition of object-in-itself by conceptual structure, there will be no ideal object. In any case, ideal object is the product of subject's particular understanding and grasp of object-in-itself, the product of thinking construction.

Here, two opposite sides in cognition movement appears: on the one side, object-in-itself determines ideal object, and on the other side, the physiological, empirical, intellectual, social and practical modes specific to subject determine the width and depth of the conversion from object-in-itself to ideal object, and subject possesses specific modes for selecting, understanding and interpreting object. Moreover, object-in-itself will not show its pure essence directly, and will instead conceal such essence in one way or another with the help of the interaction between illusion, hierarchy and interlacing. So cognition is the movement from immediacy to indirectness, from outside to inside, from phenomenon to essence, and from the first essence to the second one. It should not be immediately obtained from phenomena and experience just by using inductive method, but should be sublated through the intermediary relations and the idealization process of concept. This is the active role of thinking construction at a higher level. In Marx's opinion, thinking construction refers to the process of active reflection of object by man in the form of subject based on practice.

The constructive character of thinking highly embodies the initiative of subject, and most distinctively and immediately reflects Marx's glorious thought that "thing, reality and sensuousness" should be conceived "as practice, the human sensuous activity" "subjectively". According to Marx, the reflection of world by man is shown through thinking construction of ideal object, and the world is reflected by man through concept, category and logical idea. Lenin also points out, "Knowledge is the reflection of nature by man. But this is not simple, not an immediate, not a complete reflection, but the process of a series of abstractions, the formation and development of concepts, laws, etc." "Man is confronted by a web of natural phenomena. Instinctive man, the savage, does not distinguish himself from nature. Conscious man does distinguish, categories are stages of distinguishing, i.e. of cognizing the world, focal points in the web, which assist in cognizing and mastering it."[3]

The generation and application of category therefore is the sublimation of human cognition, marking the differentiation between subject and object. Besides, the differentiation between subject and object is manifested by the differentiation between object-in-itself and ideal object; ideal object refers to the object logically and ideally grasped by subject. Once categorical relation is interposed by man between subject and object, reflection has the characteristic of construction. The web of natural phenomena is grasped by man by the aid of the "knotting" effect of category. So it appears that the constructive character of thinking has three meanings:

Firstly, thinking construction refers to the process of conversion from object-in-itself to ideal concept by thinking through conceptual and categorical relations.

The differentiation process of object-in-itself, happening in the imagination, is the process of its decomposition and understanding by logical idea and conceptual structure, as well as the process of sensuous material ordering by conceptual structure. Here such a relationship is displayed: object-in-itself → logical structure → ideal object. Since ideal object is converted from object-in-itself by logical structure as the intermediary,

---

3   *Collected Works of Lenin.* 2nd Chinese Ed., Vol. 55, pp. 152 and 78.

logical structure is the converter between the two. Different logical structures will lead to different reflections of object-in-itself; to be specific, different ideal objects will be created by different selections of information input, different processing angles and extents, and different modes of message specification and construction. Taking the falling of stone as example, the same fact of a stone's falling from a height, from ancient times to modern times, is considered respectively by Aristotle as that the stone is looking for its natural position, by Galileo as the circular motion of stone the same as a celestial body, by Newton as the result of gravity, and by Einstein as the shortest route of the stone along Riemannian space in the gravitational field. This indicates that conceptual structure plays a constructive role in converting object-in-itself to ideal object.

In the view of the theory of information, the constructive effect of thinking is the role played by specific conceptual structure in processing and converting information. Information is bidirectional; the viewpoint of Wiener is that "information is a name for the content of what is exchanged with the outer world as we adjust to it, and make our adjustment felt upon it"[4]. Conceptual structure resembles a kind of information converter, converting the external information input to the thinking element of subject and meanwhile reflecting the structure, attribute and law of the outside world to a definite degree. Once fixed, the converting process will form a certain thinking model or mode. A specific conceptual structure is merely the grasp and conversion of object to a definite degree, and it is unable to encompass all messages, structures and attributes of object. For this reason, the selectivity of subject and his thinking is the embodiment of his initiative on the one hand and his passivity on the other. Selection, on the one side, shows definite differentiation and autonomy, and on the other side, indicates that subject is confined within definite limits, within the bounds understandable and selectable to him, and he has been restricted dually by external object and internal conceptual structure.

The constructive character of thinking embodies the bidirectional movement between subject and object with conceptual structure as the intermediary: subject decomposes object-in-itself by using his conceptual structure, and object is then converted to ideal object to a definite degree, hence reflection process is manifested as the construction process, as the process of conceiving "subjectively".

---

4   Wiener, *The Human Use of Human Beings*. Beijing: The Commercial Press, 1978: p. 9.

Secondly, thinking construction refers to the process during which thinking grasps the world in the mode from the abstract to the concrete and by forming "a priori construction".

In the history of philosophy, Marx had explicitly and profoundly revealed the special path of thinking construction. From his point of view, the concreteness grasped by men is a theoretical concreteness, realized by the concentration of thinking; "the concrete is concrete because it is the concentration of many determinations, hence unity of the diverse"[5]. During this process, the formation of the abstraction and diversity of determinations and the concentration of determinations are both dependent on the constructive effect of thinking. This process is realized through two paths: "along the first path, the full conception was evaporated to yield an abstract determination", "from the imagined concrete towards ever thinner abstractions until the simplest determinations had been arrived at"; along the second, the route of thinking is reversed, and "the abstract determinations lead towards a reproduction of the concrete by way of thought"[6]. This is the construction of thinking, thinning the chaotic concreteness into abstractions and various determinations and then concentrating the said determinations; once the work is done, "if the life of the subject-matter is ideally reflected as in a mirror, then it may appear as if we had before us a mere a priori construction"[7].

Therefore, the purpose of thinking construction is to form an apparent "a priori construction". Thinking is different from experience at the very start, and it has to form certain "determinations" for object-in-itself. The said determination refers to the purification of a certain aspect, and this abstract process only happens in thinking, and cannot be found in actual life. Even the simplest determination, such as a dot without area, a line without width, and a plane without thickness, as well as a line formed by the motion of dot, a plane formed by the motion of line, and a solid formed by the motion of plane in Euclidean geometry, is the product of thinking construction, a kind of thinking abstraction highly purified. The entirety formed based on these abstractions is just a purified entirety, seeming to be "a priori construction". Here indeed occurs the "free creation of thinking" repeatedly emphasized by Einstein, because "human concepts are subjective in their abstractness,

---

5   *Selected Works of Karl Marx and Friedrich Engels*. 2nd Ed., Vol. 2, p. 18.

6   ibid., p. 18.

7   ibid., p. 111.

separateness"[8]. For the cognitive activity of man, such subjectivity is necessary in that "the method of rising from the abstract to the concrete is only the way in which thought appropriates the concrete, reproduces it as the concrete in the mind"[9]. This process is, in effect, the process of thinking construction, and thinking can subjectively reproduce object only with the method of rising from the abstract to the concrete, which is the specific "reflex" mode of man. This subjectivity, of course, will be "sublated" by practice.

Thirdly, thinking construction refers to the "objective form of thought" conventionalized in a definite era.

Thinking construction is not only done in the mind subjectively, but in fact, it is always manifested as a certain "objective form of thought". When a constructive form of thinking, i.e. specific conceptual structure, is acknowledged by society, it seems to have certain objective effectiveness and become a certain fixed model. Marx thinks the categories of bourgeois economy, relative to the capitalist relations of production, "are forms of thought expressing with social validity[10]. Categories and their relations will be translated into "objective forms of thought", which is the process of the conventionalization, modeling and objectification of thinking construction. Originally, categorical structure is no more than the product of "relations of production" and "practical relations", but once "objectified", it will form a kind of "inertial motion", give rise to a phenomenon as if though is determined by "categorical structure", and generate "mystery" and "magic and necromancy".

However, "the whole mystery, all the magic and necromancy ... vanishes therefore, so soon as we come to other forms of production"[11] and investigate it from the viewpoints of historicism and phylogeny. Though the constructive character of thinking has its specific objectivity in different times, it also has historicity. Engels thinks that it is also necessary for theoretical natural sciences to cognize the historical development process of man's thinking and various opinions on the universal relation of external world occurring in different times, because they provide a measure for the theories put forward by theoretical natural sciences. As far as I am concerned, this measure is historicity, meaning

---

8   *Collected Works of Lenin.* 2nd Chinese Ed., Vol. 55, p. 178.
9   *Selected Works of Karl Marx and Friedrich Engels.* 2nd Ed., Vol. 2, p. 19.
10 *Karl Marx and Friedrich Engels.* 1st Chinese Ed., Vol. 23, p. 93.
11 ibid., p. 93.

that any thinking construction – theory – is historical, and will be inevitably superseded by new theory. The constructive character of thinking manifests the characteristic of man's cognition of world, and its effect is necessary to reveal the intrinsic essence of world; but the constructive character of thinking is not unique, and it is also constructed and replaced by new theory. We should consciously grasp this point and do not sink into some definite forms of thinking construction. In this connection, we should further grasp the reflective character of thinking.

2 REFLECTIVE CHARACTER OF THINKING AND ITS EFFECT

Thinking is not only constructive but also reflective. In the history of philosophy, the "method of general doubt" of Descartes was the first to carefully raise the task of reflective thinking. Descartes divides thinking into two parts: in one part, thinking, like Euclidean geometry, deduces the entire knowledge system on a "clear" "plain" premise, similar to constructive thinking; the other part is "general doubt", similar to reflective thinking, through which thinking examines itself and removes all thinking prejudices and thought obstacles. Descartes unifies the two parts with the aim to form a unified thinking process, in which thinking, through doubt, finds out the unimpeachable starting point of thinking and then constructs knowledge system with deductive method. Obviously "general doubt" here plays a different role from deductive thinking, that is, making reflection on thinking. Reflective thinking and constructive thinking has been vaguely differentiated in the philosophy of Descartes.

The two concepts of Kant, "dogmatic thinking" and "critical thinking", further show the difference between constructive thinking and reflective thinking. With Kant, reflection breaks through the "general doubt" of Descartes, and is equated with critique, and constructive thinking is regarded as dogmatic thinking. "This critical science is not opposed to the dogmatic procedure of reason in pure cognition; for pure cognition must always be dogmatic, that is, must rest on strict demonstration from sure principles a priori – but to dogmatism." "Dogmatism is thus the dogmatic procedure of pure reason without previous criticism of its own powers."[12] Kant takes critique (reflection) as a kind of thinking that prevents dogmatism but enables thinking to correctly carry out dogmatic procedure; in other words, dogmatic procedure, the thinking

---

12   *Studies on Kant and Hegel*, 2nd Ed., p. 425.

process resting on "strict demonstration", must use critique to prevent it from making the mistake of dogmatism. Kant achieves the characteristics of his philosophy just through three critiques, namely *The Critique of Pure Reason, The Critique of Practical Reason* and *The Critique of Judgment*. In the philosophy of Hegel, reflection is given a higher position, and acquires its relatively independent meaning.

Reflection of thinking is, in fact, the product of thinking development. In early modern times, thinking reflection did not receive attention from people. Space and its relations were interpreted by Euclidean geometry so perfectly that it became the sole space that was never doubted by men. Newtonian mechanics believed it had constructed the basic framework of world and the macroscopic hall of universe once for all, and what was left was only to calculate some minor questions. At that very moment, the building of early modern sciences was shook by the establishment of non-Euclidean geometry, the definition of concept "field" of Faraday, and the discovery of electron and radioactive elements. People found that the thinking originally considered to be absolutely complete was just under a definite condition, and it was a mistake made by thinking itself – blindly taking the thinking under a definite precondition for the sole. It was not until then that people realized that any thinking had its specific angle, coordinates and level and grasped the world at a definite specialized level, and that the premise and level of thinking developed along with the development of practice.

In this way, the so-called direct premise of thinking and the starting point of judgment and inference are changing relatively, conditionally and historically. Thus, examining the premise of thinking and criticizing every link of thinking becomes a link in human thinking; doubt, critique, negation and thought on thinking itself become realistic aspects of thinking movement. In my opinion, reflection, as an independent form of thinking, does not only have objective basis for existence but also specific object, function and method; more importantly, reflection fully embodies the characteristic of modern thinking, that is, we should not only conceive thinking as a cognition process, but also decompose it as an independent object, as the "knowledge object".

Judged in general, the reason why reflective thinking can be considered as a modern independent form of thinking is first of all because of the hierarchy of material world, which is the objective foundation of reflective thinking.

There are various levels related to each other in the material world. Human cognition of the objective world spans 44 orders of magnitude from 10-10cm to 1,023m. From fundamental particle, nucleus, atom and molecule to object, star and galaxy, they all have their respective spatial and temporal scale, mass and energy level, corresponding structure and mode of motion, and particular information communication mode. The material world is a multi-level huge system composed of these greatly different levels and orders, and these levels also form new motions by interweaving, such as motion from macrocosm to microcosm and the movement of the condensation of history into reality. The hierarchy and difference of the motions in the world and the interweaving among them require thinking to be reflective.

The hierarchy of world is the objective foundation of reflective thinking, because it is impossible for men to simultaneously grasp all the levels of world in an all-around manner; contrarily, men always go forward level by level, and use an old level to explain the new one before they have cognized the new, thus bringing about "paradox" in thinking. The fundamental error of the world outlook of modern metaphysics is that it absolutizes the mechanical level of world and explains all other levels with mechanical level. To erase this error, thinking needs to make reflection, i.e. critically dealing with mechanical properties and making them only speak for the mechanical level of world. In this way, reflection plays a critical role in thinking, and the reason why this role can be realized is, again, because of the hierarchy of world.

Next, the particularity of the translation between thinking and being is the special reason for the existence of reflective thinking.

The reason why reflective thinking exists is also because the grasp of being by thinking is a particular process of contradictory movement. Lenin had pointed out long ago, "We cannot imagine, express, measure, depict movement, without interrupting continuity, without simplifying, coarsening, dismembering, strangling that which is living."[13] This is a contradiction in the nature of thinking. Without simplifying the complicated, strangling the moving, and interrupting continuity, thinking cannot work, and the "continuity" and "that which is living" cannot have the reality that is expressible, quantitative and describable.

---

13   *Collected Works of Lenin.* 2nd Chinese Ed., Vol. 55, p. 219.

In the process of thinking there exists the possibility and reality to linearize and strangle the thinking curve, manifested as the contradictions between finite and infinite, the static and the moving, phenomenon and essence, form and content, interruption and continuity, etc. Because thinking has to enter into infinite from finite, into the moving from the static, and into continuity from interruption, it is required to be capable of self-cognition, self-negation and self-development. This is the special reason for the existence of reflective thinking.

Finally, the inner contradiction between logic and non-logic of thinking is the immediate cause for the generation of reflective thinking.

The immediate cause for the generation of reflective thinking consists in the contradiction between logic and non-logic in the movement of thinking. Thinking is the process of judgment and inference based on definite concepts and spread out from definite conceptual structures and logic rules. This is essential for thinking, but thinking cannot actually work without strangling the moving and interrupting continuity, thus forming its unavoidable limitation.

Thinking operates pursuant to certain logic rules and forms its "thinking framework", "thinking set" and "thinking circle". In the "framework" and "circle", thinking that operates according to logic rules forms its constructive character; "thinking set" itself becomes exclusive, rejecting information that does not conform to its thinking requirements, but thinking can only grasp infinite based on finite, so once a "thinking circle" is formed, thinking itself will fall into simplification and linearization; thinking cannot break through itself within its logic circle, therefore when it faces fresh information, "blind zone of thinking", "state of ignorance" or "paradox" will emerge, entrapping thinking in the unsolvable contradiction. Marx had talked about this issue generally – "Human history is like paleontology. Owing to a certain judicial blindness even the best intelligences absolutely fail to see the things which lie in front of their noses. Later, when the moment has arrived, we are surprised to find traces everywhere of what we failed to see."[14] This "judicial blindness" results from the premise limitation and the inference stylization of thinking. That is to say, once thinking is entrapped in a "thinking circle", a "blind zone of thinking" will be generated and thereby a certain "judicial blindness", making men "fail to see

---

14 *Selected Works of Karl Marx and Friedrich Engels*. 2nd Ed., Vol. 4, p. 579.

the things which lie in front of their noses", i.e. making men unable to correctly comprehend new information.

Thinking framework, thinking set and thinking circle form a correlated process. The concept of "thinking framework" was first proposed by Engels, referring to the space for the operation of thinking. It is like a scaffold determining the horizon, depth and capacity of thinking. Engels believes any thinking is carried out in a definite framework, which determines the "boundary of thinking", namely the "thinking circle" known by us today; there is an intermediary called "thinking set" between "thinking framework" to "thinking circle". Thinking set refers to the movement of thinking towards a kind of "integrity" and "stability", a process that thinking is bound to move like this generated in a definite thinking framework. The formation of thinking set marks the formation of thinking circle and the conventionalization of thinking mode.

Just because of these characteristics of the operation of thinking, reflective thinking is necessitated for the development of thinking. The significance of reflection lies in its critique and negation against original thinking framework, thinking set and thinking circle, and its help for forming new thinking framework, thinking set and thinking circle. Reflection grows out of "state of ignorance" and "problems". Engels thinks due to the epochal character of thinking, it needs to break and transcend its original "framework" sooner or later, and under such circumstance, the original thinking mode will be entrapped in the "unsolvable contradiction" as to the issues beyond its "framework", which is the objective condition for the emergence of "state of ignorance" and "problems". The "state of ignorance" itself is not ignorant, and it is only "ignorant" relative to the original thinking circle. In fact, it is the beginning of new "knowledge".

To reach the knowledge from the ignorance, the criticalness of thinking needs launching to criticize original thinking framework and thinking set, and understand why the original thinking structure leads to the "state of ignorance". The process from the "state of ignorance" to "problems" is the movement process of reflective thinking. "Ignorance" resembles a simple negation, and "problems" have stripped contradiction out and makes it the center of reflective thinking; the creative process of thinking extending along with the "problems" is the higher level of reflective thinking, i.e. forming a new constructive thinking.

The importance of reflection in the movement of thinking is thus demonstrated. Reflection is referred to by Hegel as the "negativity which is the inherent pulsation of self-movement and vitality" of thinking in the belief that reflection is "a positive moment of the Absolute" in thinking, which is indeed extremely profound. Combining criticalness and creativity into one, reflection is the specific embodiment of dialectical negation during thinking. No reflection, no self-movement of thinking. For this reason, it is a necessary requirement of the high development of human subjectivity to make reflection an independent form of thinking.

3 EXISTENCE FORM OF THE REFLEX OF THINKING

With respect to its derivation, reflex has different meanings, such as reflection of light, reverberation, introspection and rethinking. It is just a special apprehension of modern mechanical materialism to regard reflex with the same meaning as mapping-into, shining-into or mirroring and conceive cognition as the purely objective one-time reflex reflected as in a mirror, and such a mechanical theory of reflection has been subverted by modern sciences and modern philosophy. Marx points out, "For not only the five senses but also the so-called mental senses, the practical senses (will, love, etc.), in a word, human sense, the human nature of the senses, comes to be by virtue of its object, by virtue of humanized nature. The forming of the five senses is a labor of the entire history of the world down to the present."[15] Obviously, negating mechanical form of reflex is the difference of Marxist epistemology from the epistemology of old materialism and the historical contribution of Marxist philosophy.

The reflex of being by thinking reveals the content of thinking, and how thinking reflects being shows the mode, dimension and orientation of thinking to reflect being, namely in what mode and way, from what angle, at what level and within what scope thinking and being achieves their unity. According to Marxist epistemology, the reflex of being by thinking is not only completed through practice and the interaction between subject and object, but also through the self-constitution of thinking. Mao Zedong had stated, "Every difference in men's concepts should be regarded as reflecting an objective contradiction. Objective contradictions are reflected in subjective thinking, and this process constitutes the contradictory movement of concepts, pushes

---

15   *Karl Marx and Friedrich Engels*. 1st Chinese Ed., Vol. 42, p. 126.

forward the development of thought, and ceaselessly solves problems in man's thinking."[16] Here apparently involves two problems: first of all, subjective contradictions are the reflex of objective contradictions; next, subjective contradictions are relatively independent, "constituting the contradictory movement of concepts" and "pushing forward the development of thought". Hence, the dialectical relationship of practice to cognition is manifested by the "contradictory movement of concepts", which is the process of relatively independent self-constitution of thinking.

It is true that Marx and Engels had "neglected" the self-constitution of thinking. As Engels said, "This side of the matter, ... we have all, I think, neglected more than it deserves. It is the old story: form is always neglected at first for content." "There is only one other point lacking, which, however, Marx and I always failed to stress enough in our writings and in regard to which we are all equally guilty. That is to say, we all laid, and were bound to lay, the main emphasis, in the first place, on the derivation of political, juridical and other ideological notions, and of actions arising through the medium of these notions, from basic economic facts. But in so doing we neglected the formal side — the ways and means by which these notions, etc., come about — for the sake of the content."[17] In view of the importance of this issue, in his *Philosophical Notebooks*, Lenin reinterprets Hegel's thought of "the self-constitution path of thinking" and remolds Hegel's viewpoint of "the pure movement of thought in Notions", thereby pointing the way for us to probe into the problems in this aspect.

Modern philosophy pays close attention to the self-constitution of thinking. Hook stresses, "The process of reason studying all beings is both a discovery process and a creation and reconstruction process." (*Collection of Modern Western Bourgeois Philosophical Works*, p. 209.) Lévi-Strauss thinks the cognitive activity of man is determined by language structure. Piaget believes cognitive schema determines the cognitive activity of man. Russell, Wittgenstein and Carnap consider the relationship between thinking and being as an issue about logic structure and language structure. The interest of philosophy is thus turned from general relationship between thinking and being to the specific relationship between the two, which is grasped from a certain perspective

16 *Selected Works of Mao Zedong.* Beijing: People's Publishing House, 1991: 2nd Ed., Vol. 1, p. 306.
17 *Selected Works of Karl Marx and Friedrich Engels.* 2nd Ed., Vol. 4, pp. 727 and 726.

and in a certain form of language structure, cognitive structure, logic structure and experience structure.

Here are two problems: on the one hand, it is of course one-sided to subsume the relationship between thinking and being into a certain aspect; on the other hand, it is unadvisable to merely stay at the general relationship between the two, because the two are not generally identical, and their identity always needs to be expressed in a special form; form has its own relative independence. Therefore, the reflex of being by thinking is inevitably presented by the contradictory process of self-constitution of thinking on the one side, and the self-constitution of thinking is the historical presentation form of the reflex of being by thinking on the other side; the two are the unity of contradiction.

Not only the self-constitution of thinking is the presentation form of the contradictoriness of the reflex of being by thinking, but the advancement, construction and selection of thinking are also the forms and characteristics of reflex, the embodiment of the self-organization of subject. It is indicated by the researches of modern anthropology, genetic epistemology, child psychology and artificial intelligence that thinking is really constituted by itself, and it has inherent inner contradictions and development logic, thus being a typical self-organization process. It is an orderly development process from behavioral thinking to mythical thinking, and then to conceptual thinking; and the conversion of human conceptual structure is also an orderly development process. We should for one thing reveal the development of thinking based on the development of practice, and for the other thing study thinking based on the extension of its inner contradictions. In other words, we should step from the first-level study on the cognition of practice into the second-level study on the inner contradictory movement of thinking, and combines the studies of the two levels together. Actually, this is the higher requirement put forward by modern practice and sciences and the development of philosophy itself for epistemology. This is the first point.

Second, the reflex of being by thinking is achieved through specific subject coordinates. The reflex of being by thinking has its direction and center. To put it another way, men always pursue the identity between thinking and being from specific angle and based on specific coordinates. The identity between thinking and being is the identity of contradictions in specific direction and angle. The understandings and interpretations of object by different subjects are restricted by the unique knowledge backgrounds, cognitive schemas, thinking frameworks and conceptual structures of the subjects, therefore they all have their own special cognitive coordinates.

To be concrete, the purpose of men to cognize nature is not only for knowing its mechanical, physical, chemical and biological characteristics, but for governing, controlling and appropriating nature and translating "thing-in-itself" into "thing-for-me". Marx points out, "In practice I can relate myself to a thing humanly only if the thing relates itself humanly to the human being."[18] The meaning of "the thing ... humanly to the human being" is that the thing becomes the object of the objective activity of man, and the meaning of "in practice I can relate myself to a thing humanly" is that man appropriates object through objective activity. During this process, man transforms things with his inherent measure with the aim to give human nature to things and translate "nature itself" into "humanized nature".

Here, two kinds of measures are involved – "material measure" and "inherent measure". The "inherent measure" of subject translates "nature itself" into "humanized nature" and "thing-in-itself" into "thing-for-me", and the grasp of "material measure" is the objective foundation for the functioning of "inherent measure". It is shown by modern epistemology that the cognition of world by man has its own coordinates and direction. As a matter of fact, Marx had suggested long ago that "thing, reality and sensuousness" should be conceived "as practice, the human sensuous activity" "subjectively", which is exactly the direction of cognition, the subject coordinates for the reflex of being by thinking.

Third, the reflex of being by thinking continuously develops in the form of practical reflection. From Marx's point of view, "man's reflections on the forms of social life, and consequently, also, his scientific analysis of those forms, take a course directly opposite to that of their actual historical development. He begins, post festum, with the results of the process of development ready to hand before him"[19]. This is the fundamental law of thinking development, namely the law of practical reflection. Practical determines the development of thinking at bottom. "The question whether objective truth can be attributed to human thinking is

---

18   *Karl Marx and Friedrich Engels.* 1st Chinese Ed., Vol. 42, p. 124.
19   *Karl Marx and Friedrich Engels.* 1st Chinese Ed., Vol. 23, p. 92.

not a question of theory but is a practical question. Man must prove the truth, viz., the reality and power, the this-sidedness of his thinking, in practice. The dispute over the reality or non-reality of thinking which is isolated from practice is a purely scholastic question."[20]

"Human anatomy contains a key to the anatomy of the ape. The intimations of higher development among the subordinate animal species, however, can be understood only after the higher development is already known"[21]. So, the movement of human thinking is not from "ape" to "human", or from "subordinate animal species" to "higher development", but from "human" to "ape", from "higher development" to "subordinate animal species". That is to say, the process of thinking is "reversed", and always "begins, post festum, with the results of the process of development", from "end" to "outset", and from "result" to "cause". In other words, thinking is a process, based on modern practice, of transformation, reflection and reconstruction of historical conceptual structure. Therefore Marx points out, "It would therefore be unfeasible and wrong to let the economic categories follow one another in the same sequence as that in which they were historically decisive. Their sequence is determined, rather, by their relation to one another in modern bourgeois society, which is precisely the opposite of that which seems to be their natural order or which corresponds to historical development."[22]

The understanding of current textbook system of Marxist philosophy on rational cognition totally overlooks the viewpoint of "practical reflection" put forward by Marx; instead, it stresses the decisive effect of practice on cognition, but ignores this decisive effect will go through the intermediary link of "thinking in reverse"; neglecting "thinking in reverse" means simplifying and linearizing the decisive effect of practice on cognition. For development thinking needs to break original conceptual, judicial and inferential systems and break up original conceptual structure and cognition schema, which makes it necessary for thinking to make reflection on itself. Regarding this issue, Kant only suggests critique on the cognitive ability of subject, and Hegel only resorts to the inner contradictory movement of thinking; both are weak and feeble. Only the theory of practical reflection of Marx proves not only that practice is the fundamental impetus of thinking development,

20 *Selected Works of Karl Marx and Friedrich Engels.* 2nd Ed., Vol. 1, p. 55.
21 *Selected Works of Karl Marx and Friedrich Engels.* 2nd Ed., Vol. 2, p. 23.
22 Ibid., p. 25.

but also that the specific process of thinking is "reversed", that is, "taking a course directly opposite to that of its actual historical development". Indubitably, by taking the mode of "reversal", thinking does not only need to criticize the original conceptual structure, but also to set up new conceptual structure on the premise of critical reflection. The "practical reflection" of Marx does not only sublate the critical reflection of Kant and the conceptual reflection of Hegel, but predicts the creativity of the reflex of being by modern thinking based on its tremendous advancement.

So it follows that to reasonably resolve the problem of epistemology, we should divide reflex into two levels:

The first level is that thinking reflects being. Here, reflex indicates the essence of cognition that no matter whether it is correct or wrong, visual or logical, cognition contains objective content. The fundamentality of reflex is that no matter what or how it is, cognition is formed on the foundation of reflex. Specifically speaking, reflex is the process in which subject, based on his own form of reflex, processes and transforms the partial information he receives from object during interactions between subject, object and reflex form.

The problem is that the content of reflex is simultaneously related to and different from the attributes of the reflected object. It means that the content of reflex is not completely identical with the reflected object and is relatively independent from the attributes of the reflected object. It is just because of this that the generation of abstraction, concept and logic, including cognitive schema and conceptual structure, is possible. All of these are based on the fundamental characteristic of the content of reflex, that is, it is both the object and not the object.

The second level is how thinking reflects being, which should be conceived not only "subjectively", but also based on the practice of subject first of all. In other words, how thinking reflects being is primarily directed by the need of practice, and the effects of selection, construction and advancement are all normalized by the need of practice. It is the need of practice that makes reflex develop along a special and complex path. Hence, practice is taken by Marx as the life of reflex, and Marxist epistemology thus becomes an active revolutionary theory of reflection.

CHAPTER XIII

PRACTICAL REFLECTION:
A NEW INTERPRETATION OF MARXIST EPISTEMOLOGY
(III)

Reflection is the movement of thinking aiming at thoughts. In the history of thoughts, the reflection of mankind, after going through two historical morphologies, namely the critical reflection of Kant and the speculative reflection of Hegel, took on its modern morphology with Marx – the practical reflection. Practical reflection occupies an extraordinarily important position in the huge system of Marxist philosophy in that it does not only embrace the reasonable factors of previous reflection morphologies, but also embodies the fundamental feature of Marxist epistemology and predicts the modern trends of epistemology and even the whole philosophy. However, due to various reasons, Marx's theory of practical reflection is neglected by us to a large extent, but its great significance has been highlighted in the development of modern practice and epistemology. As a result, we need to investigate and survey the theory of practical reflection of Marx so as to deepening the study on Marxist epistemology.

1 FROM THE CRITICAL REFLECTION OF KANT AND THE SPECULATIVE REFLECTION OF HEGEL TO THE PRACTICAL REFLECTION OF MARX

Kant is the first to raise the banner of critique in the history of philosophy and state that "I do not mean by this a criticism of books and systems, but a critical inquiry into the faculty of reason, with reference to the cognitions to which it strives to attain without the aid of experience"[1]. That is to say, the "critique" of Kant is targeted at cognition itself for the purpose of clearly conceiving the source, boundary and scope of cognition and determining how scientific cognition will be possible. "Criticism is the necessary preparation for a thoroughly scientific system of metaphysics."[2] Kant requires to cognize cognition itself before the cognitive activity, that is, cognizing the cognitive ability and limitation of man, cognizing what to cognize and what not to cognize, and cognizing the reliable approach to cognition. In Kant's eyes, "they are far from having attained to the certainty of scientific progress and may rather be said to be merely groping about in the dark"[3].

The critical reflection of Kant expands the scope of reflection, and targets reflection to cognition and subject, thereby opening up a new realm of reflection. It is also proved by the fact that since thinking is the process of subject's grasp of object, it is impossible to comprehensively grasp cognition without considering the ability of subject. The merit of Kant's critical reflection is that it points out the needs to criticize the cognitive ability of man as the subject and the possibility and boundary of cognition, which is a coordinate transformation in the development of reflection.

Hegel shows a particular interest in reflection. In all his works of philosophy, especially *Shorter Logic* and *Science of Logic*, the concept of "reflection" appears frequently. It appears that according to Hegel, reflection has multiple meanings, which have no inner links with one another, but in fact, "reflection" has a definite connotation in Hegel.

Firstly, reflection "brings thoughts into consciousness", a positive intermediary link in the development of thinking.

---

1 Kant, *The Critique of Pure Reason*. Beijing: The Commercial Press, 1960: p. 3.
2 Quoted from *Studies on Kant and Hegel*, 2nd Ed., p. 425.
3 Quoted from *Studies on Kant and Hegel*, 2nd Ed., p. 408.

According to Hegel, "'reflective' thinking has to deal with thoughts as thoughts, and brings them into consciousness"[4]. So the object of reflection is thought, and reflection is for the purpose of cognizing thought. Hegel investigates the development thinking from the angle of "the pure movement of thought in Notions", and thinks "the rise of thought beyond the world of sense, its passage from the finite to the infinite, the leap into the supersensible which it takes when it snaps asunder the chain of sense, all this transition is thought and nothing but thought."[5]. The problem is that such thought takes reflection as its intermediary.

"We misconceive therefore the nature of reason if we exclude reflection or mediation from ultimate truth, and do not take it to be a positive moment of the Absolute. It is reflection which constitutes truth the final result, and yet at the same time does away with the contrast between result and the process of arriving at it."[6]

Thus, reflection in general can be conceived as such a form of thinking – a form of thinking that takes thoughts as object. As far as Hegel is concerned, reflection is an intermediary link in the development of thinking, and by means of it, thinking cognizes itself and develops to a higher level. Therefore reflection results in the ceaseless "transition" and the movement of "self-constitution" of thinking. In respect of its effect, reflection is "a positive moment of the Absolute", actually a link of dialectical negation, in the development of thinking.

Secondly, reflection is manifested as different forms at different levels of the development of thinking.

As an intermediary in the movement of thinking, reflection has its particular manifestations at different levels, which are classified into "Being", "Essence" and "Notion" in *Science of Logic* of Hegel. Reflection operates differently at these three levels. For example, in the "Essence", different categories are linked together through reflection. In other words, various determinations in the "Essence" are the determinations of reflection. "The point of view given by the Essence is, in general, the standpoint of 'Reflection'. This word 'reflection' is originally applied, when a ray of light in a straight line impinging upon the surface of a mirror is thrown back from it. In this phenomenon, we

---

4   Hegel, *Shorter Logic*. Beijing: The Commercial Press, 1980: p. 39.
5   ibid., p. 136.
6   Hegel, *The Phenomenology of Mind*, Vol. I, p. 13.

have two things – first an immediate fact which is, and secondly the deputed, derivated, or transmitted phase of the same."[7]

Hence, reflection will not occur unless being develops towards essence and immediacy towards the derivative or mediated, reflection appears. That's why Hegel thinks that in the "Essence", all sorts of determinations of thinking are explored and fixed by reflection. "The point of view given by the Essence is, in general, the standpoint of 'Reflection'"[8]. It can thus be seen that reflection is manifested as different forms at different levels.

Thirdly, reflection itself, the intermediary of thinking movement, needs to be sublated, thereby forming the movement of thinking as a whole.

In the "Notion", reflection itself is sublated. At this moment, essence has been derived or mediated through the intermediary of reflection. "Notion is the unity of 'being' and 'essence'." So, reflection is analyzed by Hegel in two aspects: "first, the determination is positedness, negation as such; secondly, it is reflection-into-self". Here a dual relationship is generated, that is, reflection as positedness is negation, "but as reflection-into-self it is at the same time the sublatedness of this positedness, infinite self-relation"[9].

In other words, reflection is the negation to immediate being, and the infinite movement of thinking as a whole is the negation to such a negation, i.e. the reflection of negation itself. In this way, reflection includes both immediacy and derivation, both reflection of others and self-reflection, and both outward appearance and inward appearance. Meanwhile, this process is the development process of reflection, as the intermediary link, to "whole reflection".

The contributions of Hegel to the theory of reflection lie in the revelation of the object, i.e. the thoughts, of reflection, this specific form of thinking; the revelation of the intermediary effect of reflection in thinking development, which is the concrete embodiment of dialectical negation in thinking; and the revelation of the various morphologies of reflection, which are linked from low level to high level according to the historical clue of "self-constitution" of thinking. Of course, the

---

7   Hegel, *Shorter Logic*, p. 242.
8   Ibid., p. 242.
9   Hegel, *Science of Logic*. Beijing: The Commercial Press, 1976: Vol. II, p. 26.

reflection of Hegel on thinking is made in the sphere of pure speculation, and reflection reaches the peak of speculation in Hegelian philosophy.

Marx's theory of practical reflection is the product of materialistic transformation of the speculative reflection at its historical peak.

Since Marx, reflection, this form of thinking, has entered into its modern morphology. From Marx's point of view, the reflection of thinking is determined by the development of practice, and the main source of its vitality is practice, but its direction is "directly opposite to that of its actual historical development", that is, "man's reflections on the forms of social life, and consequently, also, his scientific analysis of those forms, take a course directly opposite to that of their actual historical development. He begins, post festum, with the results of the process of development ready to hand before him"[10]. This process of reflection is also critical, that is, continuously "deconstructing" previous modes of thinking in history. The greatest contribution of Marx to the theory of reflection is that he breaks the mystery of reflection, and makes reflection return to social movement from the realm of pure speculation and become a link conceived "as practice".

2 GENERAL FEATURES OF THE THEORY OF PRACTICAL REFLECTION OF MARX

The development of social practice and history is from one-sided to all-around all the time. "The so-called historical presentation of development is founded, as a rule, on the fact that the latest form regards the previous ones as steps leading up to itself, and, since it is only rarely and only under quite specific conditions able to criticize itself – leaving aside, of course, the historical periods which appear to themselves as times of decadence – it always conceives them one-sidedly."[11] Such one-sidedness of practical and historical development results in certain one-sidedness and limitation of human cognition, but the "category" corresponding to the one-sided form of practical and historical development tends to become a thinking set, an "objective form of thought", governing the thinking of mankind.

---

10 *Karl Marx and Friedrich Engels*. 1st Chinese Ed., Vol. 23, p. 92.
11 *Selected Works of Karl Marx and Friedrich Engels*. 2nd Ed., Vol. 2, pp. 23 – 24.

Hence, as social practice and history develops from "one-sidedness" to "all-roundness", the original category system should be criticized, rethought and broken in order to establish a new category system adapting to the all-around form of practice. The critique of new category system on the old one is, in effect, the product of the continuous development of practical activity. Therefore reflection must be investigated on the basis of practical and historical development.

Reflection in the theoretical horizon of Marx is meanwhile the critique on the basis of self-criticism. As far as Marx is concerned, real reflection is based on self-criticism. "The Christian religion was able to be of assistance in reaching an objective understanding of earlier mythologies only when its own self-criticism had been accomplished to a certain degree. Likewise, bourgeois economics arrived at an understanding of feudal, ancient, oriental economics only after the self-criticism of bourgeois society had begun."[12] This means that reflection is a form of critique based on "self-criticism" of practice and subject when they have developed to a certain degree, and only such reflection has the significance of "objective understanding". The profoundness of Marx's thoughts just rests with its rooting of reflection in practical activity and subject development.

Here, we can interpret the general features of Marx's theory of reflection by studying the analysis of Marx on the category of "labor" of Aristotle.

Aristotle is the first ideologist who analyzes the form of value. He correctly saw that "5 beds = 1 house" can be converted into "5 beds = so much money". However, he ceased to advance, because he believed "exchange cannot take place without equality, and equality not without commensurability". So he realized there was "equality" between "five beds and one house" on the one hand, but thought on the other hand that "it is, however, in reality, impossible, that such unlike things can be commensurable".

The immediate cause for this result is that Aristotle had no "concept of value". Aristotle lived in Greek society founded upon slavery. The one-sidedness of that social practice made it impossible for him to have the concept of labor equality, and he could only have the idea of unequal

---

12   *Selected Works of Karl Marx and Friedrich Engels*. 2nd Ed., Vol. 2, p. 24.

human labor. So Marx points out, "The peculiar conditions of the society in which he lived, alone prevented him from discovering what, 'in truth', was at the bottom of this equality."[13] One-sided practice gives rise to one-sided idea, and even the ideologist as great as Aristotle is unescapable. "If the conscious expression of the real relations of these individuals is illusory, if in their imagination they turn reality upside-down, then this in its turn is the result of their limited material mode of activity and their limited social relations arising from it."[14] Thus it is clear that the actual form of practical development determines the form of reflection, and the limitation of reflection stems from "limited material mode of activity". For this reason, the reflection on thinking is always necessary.

Through the analysis on the historical understanding of the category of "labor", Marx further explains that reflection is based on practice. According to Marx, "labor" itself is ancient, but the meaning of "labor" is genuinely grasped in modern society. This process is roughly divided into five stages: (1) monetarism took wealth as a completely objective thing, an object existing in money; (2) industrialism and mercantilism converted the source of wealth from object to the activity of subject, namely industrial and commercial labor, but they just stopped at "activity itself"; (3) physiocrats took agriculture, which was just a specific form of labor, for the labor creating wealth; (4) Adam Smith made further abstraction − "wealth-creating activity − not only manufacturing, or commercial or agricultural labor, but one as well as the others, labor in general"[15], and then the concept of "labor in general" was abstracted out and "the labor theory of value" established; (5) on the basis of "the labor theory of value", Marx firstly makes a distinction between two concepts − "labor" and "labor power", and points out that labor is the application of labor power during production, while labor power is the intelligence and physical strength existing in human body, thereby revealing that the existence of capital is on the premise of depriving the laborers of the means of production and making labor power a commodity, which lays a scientific foundation for the theory of surplus value.

---

13   Marx, *Das Kapital*. Beijing: People's Publishing House, 1975: Vol. I, p. 75.
14   *Selected Works of Karl Marx and Friedrich Engels*. 2nd Ed., Vol. 1, p. 72.
15   *Selected Works of Karl Marx and Friedrich Engels*. 2nd Ed., Vol. 2, p. 21.

Concerning the relationship between labor and value, there are five levels in the development of abstraction: pure object → activity of subject → labor in a certain form → labor in general → separation between labor and labor power, surplus value. As to these five levels, there are always two sides: one is the development of practice, and the other is the critique and reflection on the abstraction having been formed previously, namely the critique of industrialism and mercantilism on monetarism, the critique of physiocracy on industrialism and mercantilism, the critique of Adam Smith on physiocracy, and the critique of Marx on Adam Smith. Here, the development of practice is the premise and foundation for the realization of critique and reflection. Just as Marx said, "The most general abstractions arise only in the midst of the richest possible concrete development, where one thing appears as common to many, to all. Then it ceases to be thinkable in a particular form alone."[16]

Marx actually points out the features of practical reflection: (1) "the most general abstractions" are determined by practice, meaning that the abstracted object has went through "the richest possible concrete development"; (2) before "the most general abstractions" are made, the object has been thought by men "in a particular form"; and (3) the process of making "the most general abstractions" is a process rising from "particular form" to "general form", i.e. the process of criticizing the conventionalized modes of thinking.

As a result, Marx takes "the labor theory of value" of Adam Smith as the product not only of the critique on physiocracy but also of social practice. In the view of Marx, the abstraction of "labor in general" cannot be made unless the following conditions are met: (1) "indifference towards any specific kind of labor presupposes a very developed totality of real kinds of labor, of which no single one is any longer predominant."[17]; (2) "indifference towards specific labors corresponds to a form of society in which individuals can with ease transfer from one labor to another, and where the specific kind is a matter of chance for them, hence of indifference[18]; (3) so, labor, as "the simplest abstraction, then, which modern economics places at the head of its discussions, and which expresses an immeasurably ancient relation valid in all forms of society, nevertheless achieves practical truth as an abstraction only as a category of the most

---

16   Ibid., p. 22.
17   *Selected Works of Karl Marx and Friedrich Engels.* 2nd Ed., Vol. 2, p. 22.
18   Ibid., p. 22.

modern society"[19]. That is to say, the abstraction of "labor in general" can only be made in modern times, when the form of labor is developed in an all-around way. This is the essence of the issue.

However, Marx does not linearly view the relationship between practice and thinking. In his eyes, thinking develops with the development of practice, but due to the particularity of thinking movement, a reverse movement of thinking arises, that is to say, thinking in turn cognizes the lower stage at the higher stage; only based on the developed specific category can man grasp the simple category more deeply; the forming process of higher category is meanwhile the "transforming" process of lower category. In other words, the development of thinking is relatively independent, and the significance of reflection cannot be deeply conceived unless we grasp the crux of the problem that "human anatomy contains a key to the anatomy of the ape".

The development of society and category is a process of unceasing expansion of scope and unceasing formation of new tiers. In Marx's opinion, the connections in this respect are like this: "the simple categories are the expressions of relations within which the less developed concrete may have already realized itself before having posited the more many-sided connection or relation which is mentally expressed in the more concrete category; while the more developed concrete preserves the same category as a subordinate relation." "The simpler category can express the dominant relations of a less developed whole, or else those subordinate relations of a more developed whole which already had a historic existence before this whole developed in the direction expressed by a more concrete category."[20] Here two categories are involved: (1) simple category, (2) undeveloped concrete (whole), (3) simpler category, (4) less developed concrete (whole), (5) more concrete category, and (6) more developed whole.

These six categories are horizontally corresponding to each other: simple category – undeveloped whole; simpler category – less developed whole; and more concrete category – more developed whole. At the same time, there are also vertical relations among them, from independence to "subordinate": simple category → simpler category → more concrete category; undeveloped whole → less developed whole →

---

19   ibid., p. 22.
20   Ibid., p. 20.

more developed whole. Marx thinks "to that extent the path of abstract thought, rising from the simple to the combined, would correspond to the real historical process."[21], meaning that logic is consistent with history.

The problem is that the particularity of the development of logic cannot be fully interpreted if we only stay at the level of consistency between logic and history. What's more important is that in the development of cognition from the lower stage to the higher stage exists a process of "transformation" and "thinking in reverse", that is, the evolution from simple category to simpler category, and then to more concrete category is a special process of structure transformation. During this process, the simple category becomes a subordinate factor of the more concrete category, an element and constituent in the system at a higher level; the more concrete category, in turn, changes the specific gravity and structure of the simple category originally at a lower level. There exists a kind of "general illumination" in the development of category, the same with the development of practice; such "illuminated light" is the conceptual structure that reflects the characteristics of the supreme practical activity of mankind and dominates the previous conceptual structure, just as said by Marx that "it is a general illumination which bathes all the other colors and modifies their particularity; it is a particular ether which determines the specific gravity of every being which has materialized within it"[22].

In the theoretical system of Marx, therefore, the categories are not sorted in the same sequence as that in which they were historically decisive, but are arranged "reversely". The new conceptual structure, "the more concrete category", is always criticizing the original one, changing the specific gravity of every element in it, and making it subordinate.

Through the study on such a forward and reverse movement in the development of category, it will be not hard for us to understand why Marx proposes that man's reflections and scientific analysis on the forms of social life always "begin, post festum, with the results of the process of development". The reason for this is because "the latter" has been different from "the former", and "the results" have been different from "the beginning" – a leap has happened in structure, level and stage; on

21   *Selected Works of Karl Marx and Friedrich Engels.* 2nd Ed., Vol. 2, p. 20.
22   ibid., p. 24.

the opposite, if starting from "the former" and "the beginning", man will be limited into the "simple category" and the "undeveloped whole" followed by "the former" and "the beginning", and thinking itself cannot rise to "the more concrete category" within such a "thinking circle". So the process of thinking is reversed, starting from "the latter" and "the results". If so, thinking is based on "the more concrete category" and "more developed whole" and thereby able to exert its critical effect, making the original conceptual structure "transformed".

This is also the reason for why "human anatomy contains a key to the anatomy of the ape". "Human" is the advanced morphology in the development of "ape", and the relationship between the two is similar to the relationship respectively between "the more developed whole" and "the less developed whole" and between "the more concrete category" and "the simple category". So "the intimations of higher development among the subordinate animal species, however, can be understood only after the higher development is already known"[23]. Here exists such a relation that development is from "ape" to "human", but deeper cognition is from "human" to "ape". The developments of social science, humanistic science and natural science are all the same. For instance, the development is from Euclidean geometry to non-Euclidean geometry, from Newtonian mechanics to modern non-classical mechanics, but deeper cognitions of Euclidean geometry and Newtonian mechanics are achieved after the generation of non-Euclidean geometry and non-classical mechanics. Only at this time can men find the "relations" respectively between them through reflection and realize the achievements and deficiencies, the advantages and weaknesses, of Euclidean geometry and Newtonian mechanics. The "thinking in reverse" runs through the whole process.

The important significance of Marx's theory of practical reflection is that it reveals the real cause for reflection to become "a positive moment of the Absolute" in thinking, that is, the development of practical activity; besides, it also reveals the process of "thinking in reverse" in the movement of thinking, that is, criticizing and "transforming" the original category system with the more advanced category system established. The theory of practical reflection of Marx reveals that thinking moves in both forward and reverse directions, thereby supplying the key for us to grasp the movement of human history.

---

23   *Selected Works of Karl Marx and Friedrich Engels.* 2nd Ed., Vol. 2, p. 23.

3 THE THEORY OF PRACTICAL REFLECTION OF MARX AND HISTORICAL EPISTEMOLOGY

In historical epistemology, the theory of practical reflection of Marx is concretized as the method of "thinking post festum", which is brought forward by Marx in the analysis of the fetishism of commodities and the secret thereof in *Das* Kapital. From Marx's point of view, commodities have existed in the ancient Asiatic and ancient Greek and Roman modes of production and "have already acquired the stability of natural, self-understood forms of social life", but the scientific cognition of men on commodities is achieved post festum, in the capitalist mode of production. It is because the production of commodities "held a subordinate place" in ancient Asiatic and ancient Greek and Roman societies, but occupied a dominant position in capitalist society and obtained the "typical form". For this reason, Marx clearly put forward the method of "thinking post festum", that is, "man's reflections on the forms of social life, and consequently, also, his scientific analysis of those forms, take a course directly opposite to that of their actual historical development. He begins, post festum, with the results of the process of development ready to hand before him."[24].

It can be seen by studying and reading the works of Marx that though the method of "thinking post festum" is proposed by Marx in the analysis of the fetishism of commodities and the secret thereof in *Das Kapital*, it is the method of thinking that has been constantly advocated by Marx.

In his *Doctoral Dissertation*, Marx has adopted the method of "thinking post festum" to analyze the ancient Greek philosophy, i.e. "reasoning back from the Epicurean philosophy to Greek philosophy". The reason is that in Marx's opinion, the self-consciousness philosophy in the late ancient Greece is the highest morphology of the development of ancient Greek philosophy; "with the Epicureans, Stoics and Sceptics all moments of self-consciousness are represented completely, but every moment as a particular existence", and "these systems in their totality form the complete structure of self-consciousness", so "these systems are the key to the true history of Greek philosophy"[25]. Just because of this, Marx reasons "back from the latter (the Epicurean philosophy) to draw conclusions about the former (Greek philosophy)"[26] instead of presenting moments out of the Greek philosophies preceding to Epicurus.

---

24   Marx, *Das Kapital* (Translation of Vol. I of French Edition Revised by the Author), p. 55.
25   Marx, *Doctoral Dissertation*. Beijing: People's Publishing House, 1961: pp. 3 and 2.
26   *Karl Marx and Friedrich Engels*. 1st Chinese Ed., Vol. 40, p. 138.

In *A Contribution to the Critique of Hegel's Philosophy of Right,* Marx stated that the social system of Germany in 1843 was lower than the level of world history at that time, because "people are, therefore, now about to begin, in Germany, what people in France and England are about to end". "There it is a case of solution, here as yet a case of collision."[27] So, it will inevitably be anachronistic to negate the social system of Germany in 1843 based on "the German status quo". To correctly and comprehensively grasp the historical development of Germany, we must start from "what people in France and England are about to end", viz., to apprehend the historical development of a relatively backward nation based on the advanced practice at that time.

In the *Economic Manuscripts of 1857 – 1858*, Marx expressly points out that "bourgeois economy as a merely historical form of the production process points beyond itself to earlier historical modes of production", and "these indications, together with a correct grasp of the present, then also offer the key to the understanding of the past"[28]. He also points out in the *Preface of A Contribution to the Critique of Political Economy* that "the bourgeois economy thus supplies the key to the ancient, etc." [29]

Thus it is clear that Marx constantly believes only based on reality can we find the key to correct understanding of history. The method of "thinking post festum" has a general meaning for the historical science. Due to this, Marx thinks the discussion about the method of "thinking post festum" is "a work in its own right which, it is to be hoped, we shall be able to undertake as well"[30]. The method of "thinking post festum" should be considered as the core in the historical epistemology of Marx.

As to the cognition of history, "thinking post festum" is rendered possible on the objective basis that although history has passed, it does not disappear, but exists in the real society in a concentrated or distorted form. In this sense, reality is the extension of history, and history is always spread in a section of society. So we are able to see through the real society to perceive the past history. In the view of Marx, capitalist society is built up out of "ruins and elements" of the past social formations; among the "ruins and elements", some are "unconquered remnants" carried along within capitalist society, some are mere "nuances"

---

27   *Selected Works of Karl Marx and Friedrich Engels.* 2nd Ed., Vol. 1, p. 6.
28   *Karl Marx and Friedrich Engels.* 1st Chinese Ed., Vol. 46 (I), p. 458.
29   *Selected Works of Karl Marx and Friedrich Engels.* 2nd Ed., Vol. 2, p. 23.
30   *Karl Marx and Friedrich Engels.* 1st Chinese Ed., Vol. 46 (I), p. 458.

in the past social formations that "have developed explicit significance" within capitalist society, etc.

Therefore, in capitalist society, "the categories which express its relations, the comprehension of its structure, thereby also allow insights into the structure and the relations of production of all the vanished social formations[31]. In historical epistemology, "thinking post festum" is to "see through" the real society to perceive the past history.

The reasons why "thinking post festum" is necessary for historical epistemology are as follows:

Firstly, social development is from past to present, from low level to high level. However, history has passed, in the activity of cognizing history, it is impossible for the cognition subject to immediately face the cognition object, or to simulate the past history with laboratory methods, thus the cognition of history cannot be conducted from past to present and from low level to high level; it, on the contrary, has to "take a course directly opposite to that of its actual historical development" through "thinking in reverse", i.e. from high level to low level, from present to past, and from result to cause.

Secondly, various elements and relations in history cannot be fully cognized until they are sufficiently developed and revealed, and following their sufficient revelation, they have negated themselves and translated into more advanced things. Therefore, the investigation of past low-level social formations should use the real high-level social formation as reference. "Human anatomy contains a key to the anatomy of the ape". The intimations of higher development among the subordinate animal species can be understood only after the higher development is already known.

"Human history is like paleontology. Owing to a certain judicial blindness even the best intelligences absolutely fail to see the things which lie in front of their noses. Later, when the moment has arrived, we are surprised to find traces everywhere of what we failed to see."[32]

---

31   *Selected Works of Karl Marx and Friedrich Engels*. 2nd Ed., Vol. 2, p. 23.
32   *Letters of Karl Marx and Friedrich Engels about Capital*. Beijing: People's Publishing House, 1976: p. 258.

So, we can see that "thinking post festum" is to, based on "the results of the process of development", grasp the inherent logic of historical movement through "insights into" history and regression from result to cause.

Such "insights" are certainly restricted by the process of history all the time, so it has comparatively great relativity. However, we should never give up the principle of objectivity, or give up understanding history "objectively". In the eyes of Marx, to understand history "objectively", we must first of all get "a correct grasp of the present", make self-criticism of real society, and in the observation of real society, work out some "primary equations – like the empirical numbers e.g. in natural science – which point towards a past lying behind this system. These indications, together with a correct grasp of the present, then also offer the key to the understanding of the past"[33].

However, "probing into" and making reflection on the past social formations at present, definitely, never mean "smudging over all historical differences" and identifying all relations in reality with "relations derived from earlier forms", because "relations derived from earlier forms" will often be found "in a developed, or stunted, or caricatured form etc." in the real society, which always contains the past social formations "with an essential difference". The method of "thinking post festum" of Marx "indicates the points where historical investigation must enter in".

The first requirement of "thinking post festum" is to choose the starting point of thinking. As far as Marx is concerned, though philosophers and historians are unable to do experiments under the condition of pure morphology, because there is no society in a "pure morphology", they can investigate historical process with a society model – a social unit in which a certain social relation is expressed most sufficiently and some experience and facts developed in an more all-around manner. This method is called by Marx model analysis. According to my understanding, the model analysis is the starting point of "thinking post festum", and the selection and identification of the model as the starting point of "thinking post festum" is aroused and determined by real practice. The model analysis is a "scientific experimental method" for the study of history. Just like the laboratory methods of natural science that

---

33   *Karl Marx and Friedrich Engels*. 1st Chinese Ed., Vol. 46 (I), p. 458.

continuously deepen men's cognition on natural process, the method of model analysis in historical study ceaselessly deepen men's cognition on historical process.

Seen from the angle of essence, "thinking post festum" is to trace the cause reversely. An important feature of historical study is that it takes pursuing the causes of historical process and historical events as its unremitting mission. Historical study is for the purpose of scientific interpretation of history, while the causes of historical process and historical events should be found out to this end, which is, "ultimately", the common requirement of ancient historians and the consensus of modern historians and philosophers. "The study of history is a study of causes." "Every historical argument revolves round the question of the priority of causes."[34] The opinions of Carr, a famous modern historical philosopher, are quite insightful, summarizing a significant feature of the study of history.

But during actual cognition of history, man is unable to reason out the result from cause, because history has passed, and the causes of historical process and historical events have vanished; it is also impossible to simulate these causes in laboratory just like what natural science does. In order to truly cognize historical movement and the causes of major historical events, man has no choice but to "take a course directly opposite to that of actual historical development", that is, tracing the cause reversely from "the results of the process of development", "post festum".

Tracing the cause reversely is not performed strictly in the reverse order like today → yesterday → the day before yesterday ...; what should be done first is to analyze the process of real society, and based on the "materials absolutely identified", find some "primary equations – like the empirical numbers e.g. in natural science – which point towards a past lying behind this system". Then, we can leap immediately from the real society to the object of investigation, analyze the object on the footing of the unity between logic and history, and "resolve the visible, merely external movement into the true intrinsic movement"[35]. In this way, the causes of major historical events and historical movement can be discovered.

---

34   Carr, *What Is History?*. Beijing: The Commercial Press, 1981: pp. 93 and 97.
35   *Karl Marx and Friedrich Engels*. 1st Chinese Ed., Vol. 25, pp. 349 – 350.

In the process of "thinking post festum", both model analysis and reverse tracing of cause must employ the method of scientific abstraction. For economic analysis, and even in the entire historical science,
scientific abstraction is "the sole force that can be used as the analysis
tool"[36].

In Marx's opinion, scientific abstraction is an orderly developing process along two paths: "along the first path the full conception was evaporated to yield an abstract determination; along the second, the abstract
determinations lead towards a reproduction of the concrete by way of
thought"[37]. Here are two problems: in terms of the process of cognition, it begins with "the full conception" and arrives at some "simplest
determinations" by dint of "abstraction"; in respect of the formation of
theoretical system, cognition is the beginning of "abstract determination"; in other words, theory takes "abstract determination", rather than
"conception", as its element.

In Marx's view, only by dint of "abstract determination" can theoretical
thinking run; only by dint of "abstraction" can man find the "primary
equations" for grasp of the past in the real society and "indicate the
sequence of separate strata" of historical material, thereby "resurrect-
ing things that have died" and making the historical material of the past
"speak". Thus, "the life of the subject-matter" is "ideally reflected as in
a mirror" and thereby deeply, accurately and theoretically "reproduces"
the objective history, bringing about a critical effect of theory. It is in
this sense that Marx argues the method of rising from the abstract to the
concrete is a correct method for scientific research.

It must be pointed out that "thinking post festum", even the whole reflection movement, is by no means an absolutely free spiritual impulse;
it, as a matter of fact, is the product of the contradiction between the
"changed economic facts" and the original theoretical system[38]. The
new forms shown by practice and the emergence of "changed economic
facts" in large number will push the old theory into "crisis". Theory
itself is a system constructed by initial concepts in line with definite
logical principles, a conventionalized theoretical structure; therefore reflection needs to be made on the original theoretical system and change
its structure so as to generate the theory corresponding to the "changed

36   Marx, *Das Kapital* (Translation of Vol. I of French Edition Revised by the Author), p. 2.
37   *Selected Works of Karl Marx and Friedrich Engels*. 2nd Ed., Vol. 2, p. 18.
38   *Selected Works of Karl Marx and Friedrich Engels*. 2nd Ed., Vol. 4, p. 727.

economic facts", thereby causing the reflection movement of thinking. Hence, reflection, in essence, is targeted by men at the original theoretical system on account of the "changed economic facts".

This means that "thinking post festum" is essentially reflex, but in a particular form. If theory is regarded as the primary reflex, then reflection is the reflex of the primary reflex, namely the secondary reflex. The excellence of Marx's method of "thinking post festum" is that it acknowledges the particularity of the cognition of history, in the belief that there is neither an abstract process of reflex or imitation nor a process of pure "self-consciousness" construction in the cognitive activity of history; it subsumes cognitive activity into practical activity, regards the real society as extension and expansion of the past history, and real practice as "converting measure" and "presenting measure" for the transition of past history to the real society, and discusses the past history, as well as the process and laws of men's cognition of history, based on real practice, thereby laying a reliable foundation for establishing a scientific historical epistemology. The method of "thinking post festum" of Marx profoundly embodies the inner unity of historical ontology and historical epistemology; it, owing to its "advanced consciousness", presaged the "convergence" trend of historical philosophy in the twentieth century – deepening of the study on historical epistemology on the basis of "resurrection" of historical ontology.

4 THE THEORY OF PRACTICAL REFLECTION OF MARX AND MODERN EPISTEMOLOGY

The theory of practical reflection of Marx reveals the law of thinking movement and the essence of reflection. Marx thinks in every epoch, thinking forms the ideological mode meeting the requirement of the epoch; when such a logical ideological mode becomes unsuited to the development of practice, thinking is required to criticize and transform the original logical structure and form a new one. That is to say, the necessity of reflection roots in the developments of practice and thinking. This opinion has been testified by the development of modern science.

It is demonstrated by the dissipative structure of Prigogine that as system moves away from the equilibrium state, the fluctuations will cause its instability and thereby qualitative change at bifurcation, forming a new structure; the upgrading of system is a continuously breaking and differentiating process of symmetry; it is not only manifested as a more and more diversified process, but more importantly, it contains the past. So, to know the current status of a thing, we should know the process of its continuous differentiation and evolution in history. "Bifurcation introduces in a sense 'history' into physics. ... In this way we introduce in physics and chemistry a 'historical' element, which until now seemed to be reserved only for sciences dealing with biological, social, and cultural phenomena."[39] In my view, the "evolution of dissipative structure" of Prigogine coincides exactly with the "concept evolution" and "general development" of Marx.

It is indicated by the developments of modern science and thinking that development of reflection has four characteristics:

First, reflection criticizes and reconstructs the original theoretical system based on "the new information emerging in practice", and thereby upgrades theory to a theoretical system with new structure. The reason why the original theoretical system still exists is because it can explain some existing information, in which scope it is valid.

Second, the original theoretical system can understand and grasp merely a portion of the existence information, and a large amount of information, especially the new information emerging in practice, are rejected, so that such information has to arise in the forms of various "problems", "contradictions", "paralogisms", "paradoxes", "the incomprehensible", and "the unreasonable". Thus, the original theoretical system is criticized and rethought by men based on the new information emerging in practice.

Third, reflection is followed by the "abolition" of original theoretical principles and the rapid dissemination of new theoretical principles, which form new laws, rules and new theoretical system. The new theoretical system makes the information rejected by the original system, i.e. "problems", "contradictions", "paralogisms", etc., and other new information explained.

Fourth, the new theoretical system encompasses the old theoretical elements, or we can say that the original theoretical principles and conceptual structure become a part or a subordinate subsystem of the new theoretical principles and conceptual structure. However, the principles of thinking and logic will not be reversed, that is, the new theoretical

---

39   Prigogine, *Time, Structure and Fluctuations*, see *Collected Nobel Lectures of 1977*, p. 42.

system will not be deduced from the original one; for example, dialectical materialism will not be deduced from mechanical materialism, or
quantum mechanics from Newtonian mechanics, and so on. In the wake
of new practice, new theoretical system and the conceptual structure
thereof will be bound to the reflection of men.

This shows that the contradiction between practice and cognition do
not move linearly, and the resolution of the contradiction requires the
reflection by men, through the negation against old conceptual structure
and the construction of new conceptual structure. That is to say, the
resolution of the contradiction between practice and cognition needs to
be realized by self-negation and "self-constitution" of thinking itself.
The particularity of the development of thinking structure is highlighted here, namely that the thinking structure in history is always changing
into a subordinate element of the thinking structure in reality, which,
or to say, is the "transformed" thinking structure in history, and built
upon it. The so-called "thinking in reverse", thinking "post festum",
is a simple indication that thinking should stand at the highest end of
practice and the frontier of development, because as long as it does so,
thinking will necessarily "transform" the original theory and the structure thereof and render them subordinate to modern social movement
and thinking movement.

Introducing practical reflection into modern epistemology is demanded
by the developments of Marxist philosophy and even the whole epistemology. The involvement of reflection makes the relationships between thinking and being and between subject and object complicated.
Originally, thinking is linked with being through a variety of intermedi-
aries, but now, reflection aims at objectifying thinking and the relationship between thinking and being. In this process, subject is dualized – it
is not only the subject, but is also translated into object; additionally,
thinking itself is thought, thus highlighting the crucial role played by
practical reflection in modern epistemology.

As an important link in modern thinking, reflection has a relatively long
advancement effect on practice. Thinking generally has the character of
advancement. But if thinking is merely based on experience and corresponding summarization, its advancement will be extremely limited,
only having a relation to the direct needs of practice. Reflection is apparently a kind of thinking simply targeted at thinking itself and theoretical knowledge, but in fact it goes deep into practice and exerts a

relatively long advancement effect on practice. The advancements of the two are not identical: the advancement of general thinking is always translated into technical, strategic and schematic specific operating processes, with remarkable effectiveness, whereas the advancement of reflection often means the breakthrough of thinking, whose effectiveness will take a long time to emerge. For example, Engels demonstrates the generation of dots, lines, planes, constants and variables, and points out that "only at the very end do we reach the free creations and imaginations of the mind itself, that is to say, imaginary magnitudes"[40]. This shows that the generation of imaginary magnitudes has no experience basis, and it is no more than a reflection of thinking on mathematical form. The reason why imaginary magnitudes were thought to be "imaginary" was because men at that time did not know their reality. Until the nineteenth century, "imaginary magnitudes" obtained their own interpretation, based on which the function of complex variable was created. The "imaginary function" generated out of "imaginary magnitudes" is no longer "imaginary", and on the contrary, it becomes a realistic mathematical tool that plays an important theoretical role in issues like the rise of airfoil and the water seepage of dyke. So we can see that once reflection forms a movement in deep thinking, it will open up new fields for the thinking of human beings and show a relatively long advancement effect on practice.

As an important link in modern thinking, reflection also has internal logical organization effect on thinking movement. The immediate product of reflection's effect on thinking is the generation of language logic, sign logic, object theory and meta-theory. Language, sign and knowledge construction are the logical parts in the operation of thinking; without these elements, there will be no thinking and theory, and without the study on these logical parts – meta-theory, it will be impossible to properly apply language and sign and correctly construct theoretical system so as to form internal logical networks between knowledge and knowledge and between system and system. The "linguistic turn" in modern western philosophy is the product of thinking development. That is to say, men have to think how thinking works. Wittgenstein pointed out, "All philosophy is linguistic critique."[41] Russell believed, "Logic is the essence of philosophy."[42] The "linguistic turn" of phi-

---

40   *Selected Works of Karl Marx and Friedrich Engels.* 2nd Ed., Vol. 3, p. 377.
41   Wittgenstein, *Tractatus Logico-Philosophicus.* London Ed., p. 44.
42   Russell, *Our Knowledge of the External World.* New York Ed., p. 33.

losophy, semiology and semantics are certainly one-sided to a definite extent, but they are also reasonable, that is, thinking should make a reflection on thinking itself and study the movement of thinking itself. One of the significant features of modern thinking development is that thinking is oriented to thinking itself, to the internal logical organization of theoretical system. As long as such orientation is not absolutized but is only investigated in its relatively independent sense, it will be very meaningful work.

Logical analysis, semantic analysis, word sign, symbol, language structure, theoretical constitution, etc. are not pure conceptual games, but the scientific analysis and reflection on thinking, whose importance deserves our sufficient attention. Engels had ever profoundly pointed out, "Only when dialectics is accepted by natural science and historical science, can all waste of philosophy – except the pure theory of thinking – be turned into unnecessary thing, disappearing in positive science."[43] The correctness of this prediction of Engels is increasingly verified by the development of modern thinking, so is the importance of "the pure theory of thinking" in modern epistemology.

As an important link in modern thinking, reflection, in addition, has the effect of showing the new angles and new forms of thinking. The angle and form of human thinking are in constant change, and men always adjust the angle of thinking as per the developments of practice and science and bring those forms that are originally unimportant or ignored into focus, thereby continuously improving the thinking level of human beings and their ability to grasp the world. In this point, reflection plays a crucial role – the generation of a series of modern emerging science branches is all in connection with the reflection of thinking. For instance, Bertalanffy turned to system theory while studying biological organisms, and when that thinking point came out, he then started to explore the history of human thinking and found that the viewpoint of system had existed in ancient times. The idea and viewpoint of system was at a subordinate position in ancient times, so did not catch sufficient attention of men, but when modern practice becomes systematized, such idea and viewpoint begin being taken seriously by men. Thus, thinking highlights them through reflection and brings them from naive morphology into scientific morphology. Cybernetics is created in the same way. Judged from its substantivity, the study of Wiener on cybernetics

---

43   *Selected Works of Karl Marx and Friedrich Engels.* 2nd Ed., Vol. 20, p. 552.

was initially as the result of the actual combat needs in the Second World War. After the idea of "control" was created, Wiener found that it was an ancient form; Plato referred to politics as "steering", which precisely contained multiple meanings like "control", "feedback", etc. Hence, reflection arouses the emergence of "control type" and changes it from "daily expression" into "scientific expression", from simple morphology into scientific morphology. Evidently, the formation of any new angle or form of human thinking is always due to the effect of reflection.

"Practical reflection", "thinking post festum", seems to face the past, but its purpose and significance is future-oriented to guide and standardize the development of real society with future. The futurology, the theory of forecasting and so on emerging in modern times are sciences related to reflection, whose reality lies in the long-term needs of practice development. The theory of practical reflection and the method of "thinking post festum" of Marx, which think in reverse based on the long-term needs of practice development, have a guiding effect on real practice, the real society and real thinking. From the standpoint of Marx, making a reflection on history by starting from real practice and real society "leads ... to the points at which the suspension of the present form of production relations, and gives signs of its becoming – foreshadowings of the future"[44]. In other words, the theory of practical reflection and the method of "thinking post festum" of Marx do not only fall under "historiography" but also "futurology"; they are associated with the future development of mankind.

---

44   *Karl Marx and Friedrich Engels.* 1st Chinese Ed., Vol. 46 (I), p. 458.

CHAPTER XIV

INNER CONTRADICTIONS OF THINKING:
A NEW INTERPRETATION

The contradiction between practice and cognition is the fundamental contradiction in the cognitive activity of men. Practice is indubitably the decisive factor of the developments of cognition and thinking, but practice itself does not belong to thinking, and the contradiction between practice and cognition tends to be manifested by the inner contradictions of thinking. Throughout the entire history of thinking, there are mainly three inner contradictions of thinking, namely the contradiction between object consciousness and self-consciousness, the contradiction between constructive thinking and reflective thinking, and the contradiction between intellectual thinking and rational thinking. However, previous studies on Marxist epistemology only discuss the contradiction between practice and cognition, which is necessary but not enough, because if only staying at this level, we cannot enter into the sphere of thinking's self-constitution, or really realize the arduousness and complexity and the epoch-making contribution of the epistemological revolution accomplished by Marxist epistemology. Therefore, we should go deep into the inner contradictions of thinking from the contradiction between practice and cognition and specifically discuss how the contradiction between practice and cognition is manifested by the inner contradictions of thinking, thereby entering into the sphere of thinking's self-constitution from the contradiction between subject objectification and object subjectification during the cognitive activity in order to deepen the study on Marxist epistemology.

1 CONTRADICTION BETWEEN OBJECT CONSCIOUSNESS AND SELF-CONSCIOUSNESS: CONSCIOUSNESS IS CONSCIOUS

Men usually conceive consciousness merely as the consciousness about object, but as a matter of fact, object consciousness and self-consciousness both are the initial elements of consciousness, being the premise mutually: there is no object consciousness that is not self-conscious; while cognizing the object, man is conscious of the fact that he is cognizing the object; object consciousness is always self-conscious, whilst self-consciousness is always the product of the reflection on object consciousness.

I notice that self-consciousness is a multi-level concept, body-sensitive ego, behavioral and operating ego, mental set ego and conscious ego, but its core is the self-consciousness about consciousness. This is because no matter whether it is behavior, psychology or feeling, as long as an ego is to be formed, it must be self-conscious; therefore self-consciousness about consciousness best represents the original meaning of self-consciousness. What's more, self-consciousness is able to cognize subject himself and self-interest, self-purpose and self-ability, thus it constitutes a special intermediary link in the promotion of cognition development by practice, viz., the decisive effect of practice on cognition cannot really function unless it is self-conscious. In other words, problems, contradictions and laws cannot have conscious promoting effect unless they are self-conscious; otherwise they are blind unconscious cognition.

The reflection on the history of human cognition makes me know that self-consciousness constitutes the initial factor of consciousness and the internal impetus for consciousness development. Self-consciousness is one of the important differences of man from animal. In The German Ideology, Marx called the initial human thinking the "mere herd-consciousness", but he does not equate human consciousness with "herd-consciousness". Here, Marx is actually making a bidirectional comparison: he thinks the initial human consciousness is "mere herd-consciousness" compared with modern consciousness on the one hand, and on another hand, he compares the initial human consciousness with real herd-consciousness and makes a conclusion that "man is only distinguished from sheep by the fact that with him consciousness takes the place of instinct or that his instinct is a conscious one"[1].

The so-called "conscious instinct" refers to a bottommost self-consciousness; that is say, man knows his own abilities. So this comparison of Marx is very significant, which in practice indicates the essential difference between human consciousness and animal psychology: the behavioral thinking of man generated originally is similar to animal consciousness with respect to the level; but since it is the "conscious instinct", it has constituted the sprout of self-consciousness that distinguished from animal psychology and become "human consciousness".

Marx emphasizes, "Where there exists a relationship, it exists for me: the animal does not enter into 'relations' with anything, it does not enter into any relation at all. For the animal, its relation to others does not exist as a relation."[2] It is because animal has no "self-consciousness", its relation to environment is mere a freely spontaneous relation, but does not exist for "me"; on the contrary, man has "self-consciousness", so his relation with environment is the relation exists for "me". For this reason, Marx points out that "my relation to my environment is my consciousness"[3].

This thought of Marx has been demonstrated by modern psychology and ethology. Animal can identify sensitive ego and psychological ego, but cannot rise to conscious ego; animal cannot spontaneously have "self-consciousness" under natural conditions. In psychological practice, some animals even learn more than 200 words, become capable of expressing some simple requirements with words, and can say "this is me" when seeing its image in a mirror, but these animals have been trained into particular advanced animals living in social environment. Basically speaking, self-consciousness arises along with labor, society and object consciousness, and constitutes the fundamental difference between human consciousness and animal psychology.

1   *Karl Marx and Friedrich Engels.* 1st Chinese Ed., Vol. 3, p. 35.

2   Ibid., p. 34.

3   ibid., p. 34.

From the perspective of the existence and development of human con-sciousness, self-consciousness is one of the initial elements of con-sciousness, and "ego" had been one of the coordinates for men to cog-nize the world. Marx points out, "Consciousness is at first, of course, merely consciousness concerning the immediate sensuous environment and consciousness of the limited connection with other persons and things outside the individual who is growing self-conscious."[4] That is to say, the initial consciousness of man has two features: one is individual who is growing self-conscious, and the other is the limited connection of individual who is growing self-conscious with other persons and things, i.e. the relationship between man and environment. The former is self-consciousness and the latter object consciousness. It is indicated by the history of thinking, anthropology and linguistics that the initial human consciousness is more "autistic" process in which man expands his cognition of self to other things; "animism" and "totem" are both associated with "autistic thinking".

Marx had never defined consciousness without self-consciousness. It can be found from studying the works of Marx that he has made two classical definitions on consciousness: one is "consciousness can never be anything else than conscious existence"[5]; the other is "the idea is nothing else than the material world reflected by the human mind, and translated into forms of thought"[6]. These two definitions share a com-mon characteristic, that is, besides emphasizing consciousness is about object, both underline that consciousness is "conscious", "translated by the human mind".

The so-called "conscious" means being grasped by the consciousness of man, namely being realized by ego; the statement of "translated by the human mind" refers to "the material world" translated by the structures of human brain and knowledge and the historical experience, or the reality understood from the standpoint of subject; both are of the same meaning. So self-consciousness is the inherent element of conscious-ness, and as long as being "realized" or "conscious", self-consciousness must be contained in it. In other words, as long as thinking is conducted by subject, it must be self-conscious. It is shown by the history of hu-man cognition that man's cognition of ego is invariably deepening his cognition of world.

---

4   *Karl Marx and Friedrich Engels*. 1st Chinese Ed., Vol. 3, pp. 34 – 35.

5   ibid., p. 29.

6   *Karl Marx and Friedrich Engels*. 1st Chinese Ed., Vol. 23, p. 24.

Considered from the essence and activity of man, self-consciousness is the reflection of the species essence of man and the primary condition for striving for "freedom". According to Marx, the species character of man is the free and conscious activity, and self-consciousness is exactly the primary condition for this free activity. "The first essential condition for freedom, however, is self-knowledge."[7] "His own life is an object for him. Only because of that is his activity free activity."[8] Marx therefore does not conceive self-consciousness in a general sense, and he actually regards self-consciousness as the reflection of the species essence of man and the primary condition for the freedom of man.

The reason is quite simple: unless being conscious of his consciousness, man cannot objectively evaluate his consciousness, or reveal the inner contradictions and boundary of consciousness. Self-consciousness is more important when human knowledge enters into microcosmic and cosmoscopic systems from macrocosmic system in that the coordinates of microcosmic and cosmoscopic systems are different from those of macrocosmic system. To cognize microcosmic and cosmoscopic systems, men have to make use of the "projection" of self-macrocosmic coordinates. In short, only with self-consciousness can man cognize, negate and transcend himself for the purpose of freedom.

Laying stress on self-consciousness does not mean negating object consciousness. Just as object consciousness is inseparable from self-consciousness, self-consciousness is also inseparable from object consciousness. To be specific, the formation of self-consciousness is premised on object consciousness, and "man's relation to himself becomes for him objective and actual through his relation to the other man"[9]. As a result, self-consciousness is not generated out of thin air, and its existence should be based on object consciousness. Without object consciousness and objective activity, there will be no self-consciousness. This is the first point.

Second, object consciousness and self-consciousness constitute a particular relationship of mutual reflex. Object consciousness and self-consciousness peculiarly reflect each other – the existence of the former is because of the latter, and the existence of the latter is premised on the former. Disregarding this relationship, self-consciousness is merely

---

7   *Karl Marx and Friedrich Engels*. 1st Chinese Ed., Vol. 1, p. 35.
8   *Karl Marx and Friedrich Engels*. 1st Chinese Ed., Vol. 42, p. 96.
9   ibid., p. 99.

the consciousness with ego as object, thus it also becomes the object consciousness, but another relationship is formed here, because object consciousness is after all a kind of consciousness, and self-consciousness can also take the relationship between object consciousness and self-consciousness as object. Hence, this is an exceedingly particular mutual reflex, and it is the particularity of such mutual reflex that enables consciousness to evaluate consciousness.

Third, self-consciousness develops along with the development of object consciousness. The more sufficient the object consciousness of man is, the more comprehensively man knows himself; the more sufficiently man appropriates object, the more deeply he knows himself. Therefore, ego confirms himself through object, and makes objective being "perceptibly existing" as man's essential powers, thereby fundamentally determining the dialectical relationship between self-consciousness and object consciousness.

Object consciousness and self-consciousness constitute the inner contradiction of cognition, which shows that man, on the basis of practice, reflects not only the world but also ego, as well as the relationship between ego and world. Taking such relationship and reflexes as the object of cognition is the reason why cognition is able to transcend itself. Of course, such transcendence originates from practice in the final analysis. The existence and development of ego can only be embodied by the development of practice, and meanwhile, this is also realized by self-consciousness. The development of practice offers self-consciousness with the abilities of negation and critique, so that self-consciousness is able to take ego and consciousness as object and logically find out the inner contradiction between the premise, relation and logical structure of original thinking, thereby continuously creating new logical structure. Self-consciousness fully incarnates the development of practice. Without self-consciousness, consciousness will not consciously step into new fields. Marx's thought that "the first essential condition for freedom is self-knowledge" is incisive. No self-consciousness, no freedom.

2 CONTRADICTION BETWEEN CONSTRUCTIVE THINKING AND REFLECTIVE THINKING: THINKING IS REFLECTED

As consciousness is dualized into object consciousness and self-consciousness, thinking is dualized into constructive thinking and reflective thinking. The so-called constructive thinking refers to the process of concept, judgment and inference of thinking, that is, thinking grasps the world rationally through judgment and inference based on definite concepts and conceptual structure and in the light of definite logical relations. The thinking commonly mentioned means this process of concept, judgment and inference, but investigated according to the actual movement of thinking, constructive thinking is only one side of thinking. The other side is reflective thinking. Reflection, as an original part of thinking, stems from reflex, and it is meanwhile needed by men to cognize the world more deeply when reflex develops to a certain degree. In other words, reflex is bound to give rise to reflection.

Reflective thinking refers to the self-thinking of thought, namely the thinking targeted at thinking, which takes thought as the object of thinking. The starting point, mission and purpose of reflective thinking are all different from those of constructive thinking. With the established logical premise and structure of thinking as its object, reflective thinking aims to reflect on and criticize existing premise, relation and structure of thinking and incorporate them into a larger thinking system to form a new conceptual structure. Then we can see that reflection is self-cognition, self-criticism, self-negation and self-updating of thinking. Without reflective thinking, thinking will be unavoidably run in the original conceptual structure and never transcend itself.

The foundation of reflective thinking is the flexibility of concepts. It is beyond doubt that the objective basis for the flexibility of concepts is the universal connections in the world. However, the achievement of concept flexibility necessitates the movement of concepts, reflection, and the art of operating concepts. In the view of Lenin, "Dialectics in general is 'the pure movement of thought in Notions' (i.e., putting it without the mysticism of idealism: human concepts are not fixed but are eternally in movement, they pass into one another, they flow into one another, otherwise they do not reflect living life. The analysis of concepts, the study of them, the 'art of operating with them' (Engels) always demands study of the movement of concepts, of their interconnection, of their mutual transitions)."[10]

10 *Collected Works of Lenin.* 2nd Chinese Ed., Vol. 55, p. 213.

This opinion of Lenin is very profound, having three connotations: firstly, dialectics should be conceived as a mutual translation movement of concepts; secondly, the cause for the movement of concepts is the flexibility of concepts, and such flexibility is the reflex of "living life"; and thirdly, "living life" itself cannot spontaneously constitute the flexibility of concepts, because what "living life" spontaneously forms is empirical thinking or naive dialectics; besides, the flexibility of concepts can be operated both objectively and subjectively.

"This flexibility, applied subjectively = eclecticism and sophistry. Flexibility, applied objectively, i.e. reflecting the all-sidedness of the material process and its unity, is dialectics, is the correct reflection of the eternal development of the world."[11]

As a result, thinking should not only operate in experience and intuition, but also in concepts; to objectively, rather than subjectively, realize the movement of concepts "demands study of the movement of concepts, of their interconnection, of their mutual transitions", i.e. the study of "the art of operating them". To put it another way, to realize all of these, thinking itself should be thought, so should concepts and the conceptual thinking. However, we only considered subjective dialectics as the reflex of objective dialectics and the flexibility of concepts as the reflex of universal connections in the world in the past, and ignored that such reflexes are accomplished by "the movement of thought in Notions", and that reflection is the thinking targeted at thinking itself. With respect to its content, reflection is actually "study of the movement of concepts, of their interconnection, of their mutual transitions", but the movement, interconnection and transition of concepts are conducted in the pure thinking sphere, and the reflection on this process happens within thinking, thus seemingly constituting quadratic thinking.

The key point is how to objectively realize the flexibility of concepts. As far as I am concerned, the flexibility of concepts is achieved within contradiction; "every notion occurs in a certain relation, in a certain connection with all the others" on the one side, and the other side is "mutual dependence of notions all without exception, transitions of notions from one into another all without exception"[12]. Clearly, a concept is in "certain relation" and "certain connection" with all the others under

---

11   Ibid., p. 91.
12   ibid., p. 167.

certain conditions, and here "certain" refers to "definite", but dialectics focuses on the transitions or translations of concepts all without exception, namely the translation of "certain" concept into another. Such translation constantly negates the "certain", points out its defect, forms the new "certain", and then re-negates the new "certain" and generates a more advanced "certain". In view of this, concepts and their relations must be reflected, which is the essence of this problem. Without reflection, mutual translation of concepts will be unachievable, so will the flexibility of concepts.

This is because reflection is an inherent element and general factor of thinking. "To understand means to express in the form of notions"[13], and even "as soon as men speak, there is a Notion present"[14]. Hegel thus believes that natural scientists think what they are discussing and debating is what they see, but the truth is that "unconsciously they transform what is immediately seen by means of the Notion"[15]. We should admit this viewpoint of Hegel is quite profound, because what is immediately seen belongs to sensation, whilst what is spoken has been concept, having containing certain abstraction and universality. That is to say, as long as what is immediately perceived is expressed, it has been changed by concept; to understand means to express in the form of concepts.

Hence, as long as man expresses object with language and concept, he has become the intermediary of conceptual structure, has conducted information processing, and has included object-in-itself into a certain conceptual structure. Moving from the original conceptual structure into a new one also requires reflection, viz., thinking over the conceptual structure; otherwise the conceptual structure will not change spontaneously.

In addition, reflection is the art of operating concepts. A certain conceptual structure is just a certain modeled reflex of world, which only reflects a "certain" level of object. On account of its conventionalization, modeling and structuralization, it is exclusive, and does not accept the other thoughts, for example, Euclidean geometry does not accept non-Euclidean geometry. Reflection undertakes the mission of criticizing the old conceptual structure and setting up a new one. This pure thinking critique is a process of rethinking logical relations, with the development of

---

13 *Collected Works of Lenin.* 2nd Chinese Ed., Vol. 55, p. 217.
14 ibid., p. 223.
15 ibid., p. 223.

practice as coordinates; it establishes new starting point and bifurcation of logic, forms new logical relations, and renders the original logic subordinate to the new. Apodictically, this is a special art of operating concepts.

The level of human thinking is presented by both constructive thinking and reflective thinking. Marxist philosophy grasps the essence of reflection – the activity of negation and translation in thinking, connects reflection with the development of cognition, and reveals the development of reflection from the angle of cognition development, thus indicating that reflection, originally an embodiment of thinking activity, is in turn a measure for cognition development and its level.

Reflection runs through the whole process of cognition, manifested as the conceptual, intellectual and rational aspect and link in logics and as various forms and types in history; from negation, suspicion, critique, dialectical negation to the method of "thinking post festum" of Marx, it shows that reflection is not fixed, and its forms are ever increasing. No matter whether it is the critique against thinking premise, logical relation or logical structure, the proposal of new conceptual structure, or the resolution of any paradox, breaking or incompleteness, reflection is necessary all the time. The reason why thinking can constitute itself is because reflection, this "positive moment of the Absolute", plays a critical role. Just because thinking is both constructive and reflective, it is able to reflect on object and itself, being both affirmative and negative. In this way, thinking "moves and has impulse and activity", and forms "the inherent pulsation of self-movement and vitality".

3 CONTRADICTION BETWEEN INTELLECTUAL THINKING AND RATIONAL THINKING: THINKING OPERATION IS TO STRANGLE THE MOVING

To express things and their movement with concepts, man must interrupt continuity and strangle that which is living, which inevitably leads to the contradiction between intellectual thinking and rational thinking, namely dialectical thinking. This contradiction is also embodied as the contradiction between expression and operation of thinking.

In terms of the history of philosophy, Hegel had consciously realized the contradiction between intellectual thinking and rational thinking, between expression and operation of thinking. While analyzing the paradox of "Achilles and the tortoise" of Zeno, Hegel pointed out, "What makes the difficulty is always thought alone, since it keeps apart the moments of an object which in their separation are really united."[16] Lenin realized the significance of this problem, and incisively grasped and developed this thought of Hegel:

"We cannot imagine, express, measure, depict movement, without interrupting continuity, without simplifying, coarsening, dismembering, strangling that which is living. The representation of movement by means of thought always makes coarse, kills, – and not only by means of thought, but also by sense-perception, and not only of movement, but every concept."[17]

Here, Lenin in fact raises the contradiction between intellectual thinking and rational thinking or dialectical thinking to the inner contradiction of the entire thinking, all concepts and all senses. As to its direct meaning, the contradiction between intellectual thinking and rational thinking is the reflection of statics and dynamics in thinking movement. Laying emphasis on the stationarity, discontinuity, formalization and procedure of thinking, intellectual thinking takes a path of formal logic, mathematical logic, consistency, and verification and falsification, and is applied extensively in science. Because intellectual thinking mainly reflects things from the angles of discontinuity, stationarity and aspect, it is just the reflection of thinking movement in a certain aspect, putting aside the motility, continuity and richness of things. The investigations from stationarity to motility, from discontinuity to continuity, and from aspect to whole are majorly finished by rational thinking. It is evident that both kinds of thinking are necessary, and the two complement each other. The contradiction between the two arises out of the characteristics of thinking operation.

For a long time, we equate intellectual thinking with metaphysics. This is a historical misunderstanding that has its historical cause – the metaphysical method of thinking is the result of the absolutization of intellectual thinking and the raising of it to the height of world outlook. In fact, intellectual thinking is a necessary part of thinking, and only such form of thinking is absolutized can it result in metaphysics. It is valid under the conditions of static state, quantification and discontinuity of

---

16 Hegel, *Lectures on the History of Philosophy*. Beijing: The Commercial Press, 1959: Vol. 1, p. 290.
17 *Collected Works of Lenin*. 2nd Chinese Ed., Vol. 55, p. 219.

a thing. Rational thinking needs to be complemented with intellectual thinking, and rational thinking divorced from intellectual thinking will become meaningless.

This is because judged from the contradiction respectively between continuity and discontinuity and between motility and stationarity, intellectual thinking and rational thinking are two independent but interconnected sides in contradiction; regarding the expression of thinking, interruption, stationarity, decomposition and strangling are required in thinking, therefore intellectual thinking is necessary; as for its movement, thinking must develop from discontinuity to continuity and move from stationarity to motility, from aspect to whole, and from the strangled to the living, otherwise we are unable to reflect the living life. Both intellectual thinking and rational thinking are the needs of the reflection of reality, but from different angles. We should combine the two together, making thinking closer to the living life in the contradictory movement.

Rational thinking cannot be formed without practice and inner contradictions of thinking being the foundation. There will certainly be no rational thinking without practice, but even though there is practice, rational thinking still cannot be formed without exploring the inner contradictions of thinking and studying the nature of concepts. The objectivity and millions and millions' repetition of practice make us "well know" the phenomena, morphologies and external connections of different things, but "well knowing does not mean truly knowing". To achieve "true knowing", we must probe into the essence of things and take practice itself and various phenomena as object, entering inside from outside and going deep into essence from phenomenon. Only after revealing the essence of a "good knowing" can we say that we have gotten the "true knowing" of the "good knowing". Hegel points out two thinking determinations: one instinctively and unconsciously runs throughout our spirit, and even it enters language, it is still not object and noticed; the other is explored and fixed by reflection as a subjective form outside of material and content. That is to say, from "good knowing" to "true knowing", the transformation of rational thinking is a must.

In my eyes, what practice spontaneously produces cannot be anything but intellectual thinking and operational thinking. Specifically speaking, intellectual thinking originates from the internalization of the "patterns" of behavior and activity, and the procedural activity operation forms the operational thinking. However, practice cannot spontaneously form rational thinking, because dialectical thinking "presupposes investigations of the nature, of concepts themselves"[18]. Therefore the immediate precondition for the formation of rational thinking is the study of the nature of concepts, and practice is the premise of this precondition. We cannot open the door of rational thinking unless entering the precondition from its premise, i.e. entering the study of the nature of concepts from practice. The inner contradiction of the self-constitution of thinking is developed exactly on the premise of the study of concepts themselves, so it is directly related to the formation and development of rational thinking.

Rational thinking is a thinking activity based on the nature of concepts, a form of thinking used to logically reconstruct object. In respect of is specific process, rational thinking must be abstracted and evaporated first of all to yield simple determinations. These determinations have been existed in thinking instead of in reality. Taking circle, angle, point and force for example, what exist are specific circles, things with angles, points covering area, and various specific forces in specific movement; to carry out theoretical reconstruction of logic, we must abstract the circle, angle, point or force and then form a certain thinking concreteness in the principle of "from the abstract to the concrete". Therefore rational thinking itself is a thinking concreteness logically reconstructed. Seen from its form, such a thinking concreteness seems to be ""a priori construction"".

The reason why I transfer my interest from the relationship between practice and cognition to the inner contradictions of thinking is because only through studying the inner contradictions of thinking between object consciousness and self-consciousness, between constructive thinking and reflective thinking, and between intellectual thinking and rational thinking can we get "true knowing" out of "good knowing", enter into theoretical thinking from empirical thinking, and develop thinking from low morphology to advanced morphology, thereby pointing out the secret to the self-constitution of thinking.

---

18 Hegel, *Science of Logic*. Vol. I, p. 18.

4 PHILOSOPHICAL THINKING IS ALL-AROUND THINKING INCLUDING REFLECTION

Self-constitution of thinking cannot be realized without philosophical thinking. The development of philosophy is manifested as a special process. The history of philosophy "appears to be a process in which the most various thoughts arise in numerous philosophies, each of which opposes, contradicts and refutes the other". "The whole of the history of Philosophy becomes a battlefield covered with the bones of the dead; it is a kingdom not merely formed of dead and lifeless individuals, but of refuted and spiritually dead systems, since each has killed and buried the other."[19] But this is merely a superficial phenomenon, and in fact, the history of philosophy is an orderly development process during which the descendants continuously critically inherit the predecessors. The philosophy appearing earliest in history is "the most abstract, and thus at the same time the poorest", and "the latest birth of time is the result of all the systems that have preceded it, and must include their principles", thus being "the fullest, most comprehensive, and most adequate system of all"[20].

The contradiction between form and content of philosophy itself shows that philosophical thinking is special reflective thinking, which makes reflection on itself and negates a certain form or system of itself along with the developments of practice and science. In other words, the development of the content of philosophy is realized by the replacement of forms through reflection, so it is apparently shown that in the history of philosophy each system "has killed ... the other". Reflection always has the connotation of "killing", that is, criticizing and negating the original premise and establishing a new one. In this sense, Engels points out, "With each epoch-making discovery even in the sphere of natural science, it (materialism) has to change its form."[21] Such a change of form is, in effect, the process of self-reflection based on the development of times. The strong point of philosophical thinking is that it is able to change itself constantly along with the development of times.

Of course, the reflection of philosophy is not the reflection in general sense, i.e. on substantivity or on a certain condition, but is a theoretical thinking based on the development of times and from the view of

---

19   Hegel, *Lectures on the History of Philosophy*. Vol. 1, pp. 21 – 22.
20   Hegel, *Shorter Logic*, p. 55.
21   *Selected Works of Karl Marx and Friedrich Engels*. 2nd Ed., Vol. 4, p. 228.

the relationship between man and world and the status of man in the world; sciences aim at the object, whereas philosophy alone investigates the status of man in the world, as well as the relationship between man and world, which is irreplaceable by the thinking of other sciences. Generally, philosophical thinking is most profoundly reflective. The reflection of philosophy is the deepest reflection in reflective thinking in that it always needs to criticize its own original principle and premise. Philosophical thinking is actually the reflection on the whole history of thinking, "the essence of the spirit of its own times", thus having different forms and contents in different times. Meanwhile, philosophical thinking has the most general comprehensiveness for what it investigates is the macroscopic, whole and most general relationship between man and world, playing a comprehensively integrative role in times.

Philosophy can be divided into two parts in general: on the one hand, investigated statically, it is the knowledge about the relationship between man and world, the summarization and concentration made by philosophical thinking on the basis of practice; on the other hand, investigated dynamically, it is the thinking process continuously criticizing the old principle and forming a new one, and at the same time ceaselessly reflecting and constructing new modes of thinking. The former is philosophical knowledge, and the latter is philosophical thinking ability. Both are closely correlated: there will be no philosophical thinking ability without philosophical knowledge, but having philosophical knowledge does not mean having philosophical thinking ability; philosophical thinking ability is different from philosophical knowledge in terms of function, content and characteristics, so the two cannot be confused. The effect of dialectical philosophical thinking, which turns to be more immediate, more pressing and more important in modern times, is purified and intensified by the developments of philosophy, science and practice, and is manifested in three paths.

The first path is the differentiation of philosophy itself. In ancient times, philosophy was manifested as "all-embracing unity", taking the place of everything and regarded as the "science of sciences"; in early modern times, philosophy was translated into "fancied unity", that is, "putting in place of the real but as yet unknown interconnections ideal, fancied ones, filling in the missing facts by figments of the mind and bridging the actual gaps merely in imagination"[22]; and in modern times, philosophy is

---

22 *Selected Works of Karl Marx and Friedrich Engels.* 2nd Ed., Vol. 4, p. 246.

the "summing-up of the most general results" about times. Marx points out, "Empty talk about consciousness ceases, and real knowledge has to take its place. When reality is depicted, philosophy as an independent branch of knowledge loses its medium of existence. At the best its place can only be taken by a summing-up of the most general results, abstractions which arise from the observation of the historical development of men."[23] Engels had also expressed the same thought, pointing out that for philosophy having been expelled from nature and history, if there is still anything left, it is the pure thinking sphere: the theory concerning the laws of thinking process itself, namely logic and dialectics. It is obvious that along with the development of philosophy from "all-embracing unity" to "fancied unity", and then to "summing-up of the most general results", the philosophical thinking becomes more and more significant; in turn, the study of philosophical thinking itself and the study of dialectics become increasingly important.

The second path is the differentiation of thinking science. When philosophy thought it still had say in thinking process, the differentiation of thinking science was started. Since the twentieth century, thinking science has developed roughly in four directions: first, the study on physiological and psychological mechanisms of thinking; second, the study on genesis of cognition and development of individual and whole thinking; third, the study on the external form of thinking – language and semantics in close association with language; fourth, the study on procedures and characteristics of the formalization, quantification and information processing of thinking process. Along the first direction, neuropsychology, thinking psychology and neuroethology are generated; along the second direction, various well-known achievements have been made, such as the study of Lévy-Bruhl on primitive thinking, of Piaget on children thinking, of scientific philosophy on scientific thinking, etc.; along the third direction, semantic analysis and language logic are created; and along the fourth direction, cognitive psychology is generated, "artificial intelligence" with thinking simulation as content created, and a new era of amplified human intelligence opened up. The differentiation of thinking science "narrows" the domain of philosophy on the one side, and more highlights the effect of dialectical philosophical thinking on the other.

---

23 *Karl Marx and Friedrich Engels.* 1st Chinese Ed., Vol. 3, p. 31.

The third path is the high differentiation of sciences. Modern sciences have become a multi-level, multi-structure and multi-sequence tremendous network composed of more than 2,000 branches. The more sciences are differentiated, the more they need the synthesis by philosophical thinking, in order to know respective position and development direction in the whole system. As Einstein has said, "Once formed and widely accepted, however, they (philosophies) very often influence the further development of scientific thought by indicating one of the many possible lines of procedure."[24]

In modern times, the three paths intersect at the same point, requiring us to investigate philosophy from the angle of the movement process of philosophical thinking. In other words, philosophy is not the collection of a bulk of knowledge, but a movement process with its unique thinking function. The function of philosophical thinking is primarily the function of dialectical integration, referring to the integrative thinking including reflection, which is the biggest characteristic of philosophical thinking. The specific functioning process of this form of thinking is the "summing-up of the most general results, abstractions which arise from the observation of the historical development of men" mentioned by Marx. Philosophy, through self-reflection and integration, produces the knowledge and principles at a higher level.

Einstein believes a scientific truth possesses external verifiability and internal perfection, but such internal perfection must be achieved during the integration of world. Exactly, the studies of different sciences are at different levels, and the authenticity of a certain inference of a system cannot be evaluated unless it is brought out of its own scientific system and put into a larger one. So the integrity of scientific laws cannot be recognized within existing scientific systems, and only the integration of philosophy is able to link different systems at different levels together, making a specific science aware of its development law under a broader and deeper background. The integration of philosophy "can ... serve to facilitate the arrangement of historical material, to indicate the sequence of its separate strata"[25], that is, linking up various sciences and practices at different strata in the ordering principle at a higher stratum, for the purpose of making general planning and prediction for the directions, connecting points and breakthrough points of the developments of science and practice.

---

24 Einstein and Infeld, *The Evolution of Physics*. Shanghai: Shanghai Science & Technology Press, 1962: p. 39.
25 *Karl Marx and Friedrich Engels*. 1st Chinese Ed., Vol. 3, p. 31.

Prediction in general includes foreseeing and forecasting. The so-called forecasting refers to the judgment on the inevitable or possible occurrence of a thing within defined time and space ranges, whilst foreseeing is the judgment on the development trend in line with laws, or a law-based judgment only concerning development trend. Sciences can make both forecasting and foreseeing, whereas philosophy can only make foreseeing but not forecasting. As a kind of thinking about the comprehensiveness and integrity of the relationship between man and world, philosophy provides a whole prospect of the relationship between man and world, therefore with philosophical thinking, it is easier for us to find which things are in the bud but have promising future, which levels and links are missing in the whole, which things are going to decline, and so on, thereby giving certain foreseeing for the social activity of men.

The particularity and complexity of social life renders philosophy impossible to forecast the time, location and participants of a specific event, but philosophy can foresee the development trend, namely foreseeing the ultimate end of a historical phenomenon and the future direction of social development. Philosophical foreseeing is the prediction of the totality, directionality and integrity of human development, so it occupies a unique position irreplaceable by scientific prediction. In contemporary times, the tentacles of science and practice have stretched to every corner of the world, natural science, social science and humanistic science interact on, infiltrate into and cross with each other, the relationships between "biosphere", "technoshpere" and "noosphere" become more and more complex, economic globalization and problems resulting therefrom are increasingly prominent, and so forth. For such conditions, partial prediction is obviously insufficient, what is needed is philosophical thinking and prediction, without which it is hard to form a tendentious comprehensive and integrative opinion. Because of this, philosophical prediction receives more and more attention from people today, and it will become an important topic of philosophers in the near future.

CHAPTER XV

OBJECT CONSCIOUSNESS AND SELF-CONSCIOUSNESS: A NEW INTERPRETATION

How to cognize and grasp the relationship between object consciousness and self-consciousness is an extremely important and fundamental theoretical problem in the study of epistemology. In the most intuitional and immediate sense, object consciousness is the cognition of man on the states, attributes, characteristics, structures and laws of external things, i.e. epistemic cognition of "material measure", the reflex of object; self-consciousness is the cognition of man on his own state, characteristics, attributes and his status in the objective world, namely the cognition of man's "inherent measure". Any cognition of man is a kind of "relationship", the unity between object consciousness and self-consciousness. The relationship between object consciousness and self-consciousness is much more complex than its intuitive meaning. The contradiction between the two indicates that consciousness is dualized at the outset, directing both to object and self, and both to outside and inside. More importantly, consciousness itself is also an object of consciousness, forming "the thinking targeted at thinking", "the reflex of reflex", and "the consciousness of consciousness". To put it another way, the contradiction between object consciousness and self-consciousness directly shows the particularity of thinking measure, that is, the contradiction and unity respectively between human measure and material measure, between the measure of internal demand and the measure of external objective necessity, between the measure of reflection and the measure of material reflex. This issue is so profound that numerous philosophy masters before Marx had really resolved it, but its importance is increasingly highlighted by modern science, philosophy and practice. The problem is that during previous study on Marxist epistemology, we summed up cognition only as the cognition on object, viz., on the cognitive relationship of world, and completely ignored the study on such a critical issue as self-consciousness, or the study on the contradiction between object consciousness and self-consciousness. The issue of self-consciousness is an intermediary link between Marxist philosophy and classical German philosophy, and also an important content in Marxist epistemology. The thousand-year's mystery of self-consciousness can be really resolved only by the epistemology of Marx. If ignoring the study on self-consciousness and its relationship with object consciousness, we will fail to get a true understanding on the revolutionary change realized by Marxist epistemology in the history of epistemology.

1 IDEAS OF OBJECT CONSCIOUSNESS AND SELF-CONSCIOUSNESS IN THE HISTORY OF PHILOSOPHY

In ancient times, Protagoras, a famous ancient Greek sage in ancient Greece, was the first to propose self-consciousness and its relationship with object consciousness. According to Protagoras, "Man is the measure of all things, of the existence of things that are, and of the non-existence of things that are not"[1]. This opinion still arouses interest and dispute of men today, and has been misinterpreted all the time. For a long time, the opinion that "man is the measure of all things" has been considered as the pronoun of subjective idealism and absolute relativism. As a matter of fact, Protagoras' viewpoint that "man is the measure of all things" has two connotations at least:

---

1   *Ancient Greek and Roman Philosophy*, compiled by the Department of Philosophy, Peking University. Beijing: The Commercial Press, 1961: p. 138.

First, the sensation of man depends on the physical conditions of man. Protagoras thought, "material is mobile, and continuously metabolizes during motion; senses constantly readjust and change according to age and other physical conditions", and "men have different feelings at different times due to their different conditions."[2]

Second, man is the measure of the thing created by him. Protagoras pointed out, "material is the cause of all things; because all things are dependent on material, material can become all things (for us)"[3], meaning that "thing" does not refer to material itself, but is relative to us, namely "artificial thing". Therefore, the opinion that "man is the measure of all things" actually means "man is the measure of (artificial) things", or man is the measure of the thing created by him. This is the key and core of the opinion that "man is the measure of all things".

It can be seen that when putting forward the opinion that "man is the measure of all things", Protagoras did not deny the objective existence of material, and meanwhile he emphasized that "knowledge is perception". So it is improper to simply and qualitatively determine the opinion that "man is the measure of all things" as subjective idealism. The proposition that "man is the measure of all things" of Protagoras, in effect, raised the question about the relationship between object consciousness and self-consciousness, and pointed out a new direction for the development of ancient Greek philosophy, giving rise to the emergence of "self-consciousness philosophy" during the period of Hellenization. In other words, ancient philosophy started with the study on the "primordium" of all things, namely grasping the world through object consciousness, but "ended up with self-consciousness philosophy". Of course, the "self-consciousness philosophy" did not resolve the problem of the relationship between object consciousness and self-consciousness, and finally led to skepticism.

Opposite to the ancient self-consciousness philosophy, early modern materialism neglected "ego" and "self-consciousness", as well as the initiative and particularity thereof, and brought forward the opinion that "man is machine". Thus, man retrogressed from "the measure of all things" to taking "material as his measure". For this reason, early modern materialism was criticized by Marx: "the chief defect of all

2   Dynnika, *Ancient Dialectics History*. Beijing: People's Publishing House, 1986: p. 131.
3   Ibid., p. 131.

hitherto existing materialism – that of Feuerbach included – is that the thing, reality, sensuousness, is conceived only in the form of the object or of contemplation, but not as sensuous human activity, practice, not subjectively."[4] The essence of "conceiving only in the form of the object or of contemplation" is that the practical relation of man to the world and the initiative of man to apply inherent measure to change the material measure are rejected, and the cognitive relationship between man and world is merely considered as a relation of passive reflection.

The early modern materialism emphasizes objective consciousness. In the view of early modern materialism, the cognition of man is the reflection of world, and "senses are the source of all our knowledge"[5]. However, reflection mentioned by early modern materialism is intuitive, just consistent with "reality". As Locke said, "Our knowledge, therefore is real only so far as there is a conformity between our ideas and the reality of things."[6] Reflection certainly coincides with reality, but it also is a movement process from phenomenon to essence, from immediacy to indirectness, by applying concepts and logic. Early modern materialism just stays at the coincidence with "reality", refuses to leave "reality" even by one step, and thinks "we have no knowledge beyond that, much less of the internal constitution, and true nature of things, being destitute of faculties to attain it"[7].

This defect of early modern materialism is pointed out by Engels, "It restricted itself to the proof that the content of all thought and knowledge must derive from sensuous experience, and revived the principle: *nihil est in intellectu, quod non fuerit in sensu* (nothing is in the mind which has not been in the senses)."[8] This comment indeed strikes home. It is thus clear that although early modern materialism insisted on the theory of reflection, such a theory of reflection is one-sided, mechanical and intuitive. It only starts with the form of senses, and regards all thinking as the combination and subtraction of senses; and the standard for judging the truth of cognition is the conformity to "reality". As a result, with

---

4   *Selected Works of Karl Marx and Friedrich Engels.* 2nd Ed., Vol. 1, p. 54.
5   *French Philosophy in the Eighteenth Century*, compiled by the Department of Philosophy, Peking University. Beijing: The Commercial Press, 1963: p. 337.
6   Locke, *An Essay Concerning Human Understanding*. Beijing: The Commercial Press, 1959: Vol. II, p. 555.
7   Locke, *An Essay Concerning Human Understanding*. Beijing: The Commercial Press, 1959: Vol. I, p. 286.
8   *Selected Works of Karl Marx and Friedrich Engels.* 2nd Ed., Vol. 4, p. 364.

early modern materialism, the creativity, initiative and selectivity of subject and ego are all discarded, and the initiative, jumping character and constructive character of consciousness and self-consciousness all become meaningless nonsense.

I notice that early modern materialism does not completely rejected self-consciousness. Locke put forward two kinds of experience of cognition: external experience and internal experience, pointed out the difference between primary and secondary qualities of a thing, and thought that internal experience and secondary quality were directly related to ego and self-consciousness. Descartes proposed the concept of "cogito" and identified self-consciousness with reason in the belief that "Cogito, ergo sum (I think, therefore I am)". The problem is that either Locke or Descartes, or even the whole early modern materialism, only takes self-consciousness as the cognition of ego, namely introspection or cogito, and does not understand that we cannot deal with object consciousness without self-consciousness, or with self-consciousness without object consciousness; what's more, self-consciousness is not only the consciousness of ego, but also a thinking activity in which the consciousness of ego is immediately translated into subject. Therefore the investigation on ego with the so-called method of introspection is nothing but the closing of ego, and is only limited to ego.

On the contrary of early modern materialism, classical German philosophy arrived at subject and his cognitive initiative by the specific way of highly upholding "self-consciousness". The first person is Kant. He was the first in the history of philosophy to clearly put forward object consciousness and self-consciousness as a pair of concepts and investigate object consciousness from the perspective of self-consciousness, regarding object consciousness as what is constructed by self-consciousness. From the point of view of Kant, material is scattered, and it is solely owing to the effect of self-consciousness' "a priori form" that the cognition of object and the "objective validity" thereof can be constituted. That is to say, object consciousness is constituted by self-consciousness, and it is the result of material summarization by self-consciousness through utilizing its "a priori form".

It can be found through reading the works of Kant that Kant considered self-consciousness as the comprehensive application of human "apperception", and as a kind of activity full of initiative. In his opinion, apperception is self-consciousness, the comprehensive unity of consciousness, and apperception can only be done by ego. "Amongst all ideas, linkage is the only one that cannot be obtained from object. Since integration is an active activity of subject himself, linkage can only be made by subject."[9] In other words, the linkage between a priori form and material, the unity of the two, is possible only by the way of self-consciousness, i.e. apperception, thus we say that self-consciousness constitutes object consciousness and makes cognition possible.

Kant's idea of apperception or self-consciousness was highly evaluated by Hegel, who held "The word 'I' expresses the mere act of bringing-to-bear-upon-self: and whatever is placed in this unit or focus is affected by it and transformed into it. The 'I' is as it were the crucible and the fire which consumes the loose plurality of sense and reduces it to unity. This is the process which Kant calls pure apperception"[10]. That is to say, Kant had laid sufficient stress on self-consciousness and its effect.

Taking Kant's idea of apperception or self-consciousness as his "science of knowledge", Fichte pushed the philosophy of self-consciousness to the extreme. Schelling then developed the subjective idealist self-philosophy of Fichte into the identical philosophy of objective idealism, thinking that "self-consciousness is an act", "an absolutely free act"[11], which was manifested as a creative activity that continuously set boundaries and limitations on itself and then continuously transcended such limitations. Hegel epitomized the thought development of self-consciousness and summarized the entire spiritual development as the self-consciousness activity of absolute spirit. In his opinion, the absolute spirit is originally externalized into nature, and then by negating nature, it gradually realizes ego and returns to ego in the process of spiritual development. Undoubtedly, "Hegel fell into the illusion of conceiving the real as the product of thought concentrating itself, probing its own depths, and unfolding itself out of itself, by itself"[12]. For this reason, classical German philosophy just abstractly developed subject and the initiative of self-consciousness.

---

9   *German Philosophy from the Late Eighteenth Century to the Early Nineteenth Century*, compiled by the Department of Philosophy, Peking University. Beijing: The Commercial Press, 1960: p. 66.
10   Hegel, *Shorter Logic*, p. 122.
11   Schelling, *System of Transcendental Idealism*. Beijing: The Commercial Press, 1976: p. 31.
12   *Selected Works of Karl Marx and Friedrich Engels*. 2nd Ed., Vol. 2, pp. 18 – 19.

However, Hegel's theory of self-consciousness is still reasonable in certain aspects:

Firstly, Hegel thought self-consciousness was the fundamental difference between man and animal. In the eyes of Hegel, "the animal too is by implication universal, but the universal is not consciously felt by it to be universal: it feels only the individual". "It is man who first makes himself double so as to be a universal for a universal"[13], and the bifurcation happens "when man knows that he is 'I', ... the term 'I' I mean myself". Thus, Hegel took whether having self-consciousness, whether knowing "'I' means myself", as the qualitative difference between man and animal.

Secondly, Hegel thought self-consciousness was multi-level and specifically discomposed "ego", in the belief that "in the 'Ego' there are a variety of contents, derived both from within and from without". From Hegel's point of view, based on different natures of the contents derived both from within and from without, ego may be described as perception, or conception, or reminiscence. If these egos are abstracted, we will obtain an ego of thinking, because "in all of them the 'I' is found: or in them all thought is present, Man ... is always thinking"[14].

Thirdly, Hegel thought self-consciousness was in continuous development. As far as Hegel is concerned, self-consciousness continuously extends itself from being-in-itself to being-for-itself with every step full of contradiction, and meanwhile it also continuously sublates the contradiction to make itself develop continuously.

Since classical German philosophy, self-consciousness and its effect has gained universal attention of people, and become one of the key contents dealt with by contemporary philosophy. The "intention movement" of consciousness of Husserl, Piaget's theory of schema construction, Freud's "ID", "ego" and "superego", and "being" of existentialism are all closely related to ego and self-consciousness. However, these opinions are reasonable only with respect to a certain link and certain aspect in the relationship between man and world, and do not reveal the essence of the relationship between self-consciousness and object consciousness. Marxist philosophy fulfils this mission. From the angle of time, Marxist philosophy was later than classical German philosophy

---

13   Hegel, *Shorter Logic*, p. 81.
14   ibid., p. 82.

but earlier than contemporary western philosophy; but regarding logic, Marxist philosophy is "the late philosophy", which, relying on its great comprehensiveness and advancement, scientifically answers the question about self-consciousness and its relationship between object consciousness.

2 ESSENCES, STRUCTURES AND FUNCTIONS OF OBJECT CONSCIOUSNESS AND SELF-CONSCIOUSNESS

Different from previous philosophies, Marxist philosophy reveals the essences of object consciousness and self-consciousness, as well as the relationship between the two, based on practical activity. According to Marx, the reasons for the formation of the "ego" of man and the dualization of human consciousness into object consciousness and self-consciousness lie in the objectivity of practical activity and the purposiveness of consciousness. The objectivity of practical activity means that practice will not be generated out of nothing, and it must aim at object, actually change objective things and their forms; the purposiveness of practical activity's consciousness means practice is conducted according to the modes and needs of man; it translates the needs of man into the purpose of practice, which has already existed in the imagination of man before the commencement of actual practical activity. In other words, there is both "the mode of thing" and "the mode of man" in a practice process, and practice is the activity of transforming "the mode of thing" in "the mode of man" and subordinating the former to the latter.

Specifically, judged from practice itself, practice is the activity of "things" conducted by subject to actually change the outside world on the one hand, and practice is the object realized by subject on the other hand; subject is conscious of his own activity, namely that the activity of subject becomes the object of subject's cognition. As to the purpose of practice, purpose must be subject to the objective conditions and the object on the one side, and it must ideally exist in the mind of man before the commencement of practice and play a role of basis for regulating man's activity and determining the direction of self-movement on the other, thereby becoming a "volitional movement" that is self-conscious and must be complied with. Regarding the result, i.e. product, of practice, on the one hand, product is an objective thinking independently existing beyond man, and on the other hand, product must satisfy certain needs of man and have "the mode of man".

Therefore, practice inherently includes two aspects: the understanding both on object and practitioner, and the control over things and ego; it is the activity both outwards transforming the objective world and inwards transforming the subjective world. The object transformation, the control over the objective world and the activity directed to the outside world by practice needs and forms object consciousness; and in turn, the understanding on practitioner himself, the control over ego and the transformation of subjective world by practice also requires and forms self-consciousness. The "self-consciousness" of man and the "self-identification" of animal are thus distinguished qualitatively, and man and animal go their separate ways at this point.

So the dualization of consciousness into object consciousness and self-consciousness, in the final analysis, is the embodiment of the development and differentiation of practice structure. Practice does not only bring about the dualization of consciousness, but also the dualization of activity: one side is the control and regulation of things and the other side is the control and regulation of man. The dualization processes of consciousness and activity caused by practice are then fixed as certain social modes during the intercourse of men, thereby having a firm sociality, that is, object consciousness and self-consciousness and their essences.

Self-consciousness constantly shows new content along with the development of practice. The farther back we trace history, the less developed the production was, and the less independent the ego was. As Marx said, "The further back we trace the course of history, the more does the individual, and accordingly also the producing individual, appear to be dependent and to belong to a larger whole."[15] As productive forces had made certain development and mental work was separated from physical labor, the "ego" of individual begun to be independent, and then "self-consciousness" in a strict sense was generated; the "ego of experience" and the "ego of thinking" were formed on the basis of "real ego"; Descartes' "Cogito, ergo sum", Feuerbach's "I desire, therefore I am", Freud's "ID", "ego" and "superego", etc. emerged.

Self-consciousness basically develops along with the development of practice. Marx regards the transformation of world by man as the reflection of ego's essential powers, thinking that "the history of industry

---

15   *Karl Marx and Friedrich Engels.* 1st Chinese Ed., Vol. 46 (I), p. 21.

and the established objective existence of industry are the open book of man's essential powers, the perceptibly existing human psychology"[16]. Thus we can see that "self-consciousness" mystified by idealism does not mysterious at all, and instead, it roots in ordinary practical activity, and is manifested by objective existence and developing along with the development of objective activity.

In the aspect of structure, object consciousness and self-consciousness are quite different, but the fundamental difference rest with other-reflectivity and self-reflexivity, viz., object consciousness is in the other-reflective structure, whereas self-consciousness is in the self-reflective structure. The other-reflectivity of object consciousness means that the object of cognition is external, and it is the reflection of object beyond subject himself. The other-reflective structure determines that the route of cognition must go through object-in-itself, empirical object and ideal object. Object consciousness realizes the development of object-in-itself in consciousness, forms simple determinations through various abstract processes, and then gives rise to the concreteness in mind. The so-called self-reflexivity of self-consciousness means that the object of cognition is subject himself. If object consciousness needs to answer "what objects are", self-consciousness has to answer "what I am", and must cognize "myself" through "I". This seems to be a self-cycling thinking: the question "what I am" must be answered by me, but "I" must be defined by the answer to the question "what I am". The characteristic of this structure is self-reflectivity, or self-dualization. To put it another way, self-reflective cognition takes self as the object of cognition, and the self-reflective structure is sure to be a dualized structure. It is demonstrated by modern psychology, especially personality psychology, social psychology and child psychology, that "ego" is always one of the centers in the cognitions of individuals and human beings. Either the self-cognition of individual or the human cognition of society is structurally different from object consciousness; that is to say, in a bid to cognize "myself", "I" must dualize "myself" into "me as object" and "me as subject", or "reflected me" and "self-reflective me". Thus, a activity structure different from that of object consciousness are produced.

Studied in the aspect of structure, object consciousness and self-consciousness are uniform but also different. The uniformity is that both are objective activity with subject and object, thus both having a

16   *Karl Marx and Friedrich Engels*. 1st Chinese Ed., Vol. 42, p. 127.

process of information input, processing and output; the difference is that object consciousness takes environment as object, which is external, but self-consciousness takes self as object, differentiates self from thinking and forms a self-reflective structure. With self-reflective self-consciousness, man reviews the ego of himself based on the egos of others, "sees himself in a world that he has created" through his own objective activity, or cognizes ego through the historical activity of ego.

Here exists, anyway, the process of ego dualization. Self-consciousness could be not only the cognition of ego but also the reflex of reflex and the thinking targeted at thinking. The condition differs according to the object of dualization, and also relies on the development of object consciousness. However, in the complex changes, the dualized structure of self-reflectivity is unchanged. As a result, to apprehend the fundamental difference between object consciousness and self-consciousness, the essential difference of other-reflectivity and self-reflectivity must be grasped.

The formation of the contradiction between object consciousness and self-consciousness, the structures of other-reflectivity and self-reflexivity, is based on "two forms of the objective process: nature (mechanical and chemical) and the purposive activity of man"[17]. Both the activity of nature itself and the purposive activity of man are objective, but the former is in-itself, whilst the latter is for-itself. Such a difference forms other-reflectivity and self-reflexivity of consciousness: the objective existence of things and the objectivity of practical activity forms object consciousness, and self-consciousness is formed by the purpose of practice and expressed by the regulation of means by purpose.

The specific activity process of object consciousness and self-consciousness and their effects in the activity of consciousness are represented by the functions of the two. From a transversal look, the unity between object consciousness and self-consciousness constitutes reflection and cognition, both of which are formed during the interaction of object and subject instead of being determined solely by object, and have to reflect the movement of subject and ego; from a vertical look, there is a relationship of primary reflex and secondary reflex between object consciousness and self-consciousness.

---

17   *Collected Works of Lenin.* 2nd Chinese Ed., Vol. 55, p. 158.

In the specific activity process, the functions of object consciousness and self-consciousness are different. The first difference consists in directionality. Generally speaking, object consciousness is directed to the world external to man, while self-consciousness is to the internal world of man. There is always the objective existence of cognition, but what kind of information cognition is specifically directed to, or which train of thought should be adopted to grasp information, is regulated by self-consciousness. Self-consciousness concentrates thinking on events and relations related to the needs and interests of ego, and makes the cognition meeting the needs of man spread broadly and deeply rooted in the consciousness and behavior of men; thus it plays a directing role in the development of cognition, and thereby determines the establishment of cognition targets.

It is thus evident that object consciousness and self-consciousness have different functions. The former reveals the "material measure", the mechanical, physical, chemical and biological characteristics of things; the latter reveals the "inherent measure" of man and how men transform the world, as well as how men make world humanized and in what sense can the world be a human world. These two directions are unified during the actual activity of world transformation.

The functional difference between object consciousness and self-consciousness is also represented by the hierarchy of reflex. According to the hierarchy of consciousness activity, object consciousness is the primary reflex of object, while self-consciousness is the secondary reflex. The hierarchy of reflex is one of the characteristics of reflex. The mind of man is not only directed to the external world but also to himself, so it is able to reflect both material object and the process of reflecting the object. In other words, since the consciousness of man is self-cognition, man is to realize both primary reflex (reflex in the first order) and secondary reflex, namely self-reflex (reflex in the second order).

The so-called primary reflex refers to a sensuous and empirical process in which subject deals with and processes the information of object, cognizes object different from himself, conducts theoretical processing on this basis and outputs the results of cognition. The secondary reflex takes this process as the reflex process of the object of cognition, meaning that subject separates out the process of object reflex by subject and makes reflection on this process itself; therefore it is a process of cognizing reflex itself. The summary of experience, brief summary of thoughts and self-criticism we usually talked about are the process of secondary reflex. Such a secondary reflex, originating from the species essence of man and the objectivity of practice, is the activity process of self-reflective cognitive structure. Reflex can be further divided, generating the reflex of secondary reflex, i.e. tertiary reflex. The hierarchy of reflex, in principle, is infinite; however in every age, due to the restrictions from practice and reality, the deepening of such hierarchy will become "discontinuous" in some way.

The progress from primary reflex to secondary reflex embodies the improvement of human cognition. What is produced by primary reflex is the knowledge about object, manifested as material attributes, movement laws and so forth revealed by all sorts of specific sciences; and what is generated by secondary reflex is the knowledge about how knowledge is used, namely the knowledge about inherent logic, relations and procedures of knowledge, such as methodology, epistemology, meta-logic, meta-science, etc. generally known to us, all of which fall under the process of secondary reflex. Mankind in the twentieth century had a huge interest in language and sign, reference and meaning, formalization and inherent logical structure, as well as methodology, which indicated and highlighted the significance of secondary reflex.

3 SELF-CONSCIOUSNESS AND OBJECTIVITY

With respect to its form, self-consciousness is the consciousness about the modes of being and activity of subject different from those of object, and its function is to reveal the particularity of the senses, perceptual time and space, thinking model and inherent measure of subject. This gives rise to a paradox: objectivity refers to "the content not dependent on subject, on man, and on human beings" in the cognition of man, but the existence of self-consciousness shows that cognition is also dependent on subject, on man, and on human beings. In other words, the paradox of self-consciousness and objectivity is featured by the contradiction that on the one hand, since objectivity is "the content not dependent on subject, on man, and on human beings" in the cognition of man, human beings, the subject, cannot grasp it; on the other hand, since man has to cognize the world from the view of human beings, the subject, the objectivity is certainly dependent on subject. This is, indeed, a tricky epistemological problem difficult to solve.

It is demonstrated by modern science that human senses, space-time coordinates and reference frame of objective thing are based on a tri-dimensional macroscopic system. In this system, subject, object and instruments are naturally unified. The cognition of man on the world is started from the four-dimensional space-time manifold of Minkowski, and the living space and perceptual space of man is tri-dimensional, which are the natural measure, natural coordinates and natural back-ground for self-consciousness of man, as well as the inherent character-istics and attributes of the ego of man.

However, the cognition of man is limited by the tri-dimensional mac-roscopic system of man, disabling man to directly perceive the cos-moscopic and microcosmic system. The direct experience and intuitive hierarchy of man have boundaries, but they are not the boundary of hu-man cognition. Just as Einstein had said, man cannot see and intuitively imagine the fourth dimension in physics, but can imagine the fourth dimension in mathematics. So it is clear that as long as man is conscious of the tri-dimensional and macroscopic characteristics, he can step over such a limitation on ego and enter into a deeper level.

Initiative and objectivity of self-consciousness are not contrary to each other. To be specific, the object selection of self-consciousness is not finished at a time, but is realized during the continuous "feedback" and "interaction" with the outside world; feedback regulates, corrects and filters the selection by subject, and it does not only check whether the selection is correct and consistent with the needs of subject, but also verify whether the selection complies with the material measure. At the same time, such a selection is also standardized by social conditions, and if there are no social conditions condensed by historical develop-ment, there will be no selection. As Marx said, "history does not end by being resolved into 'self-consciousness as spirit of the spirit', but in it at each stage there is found a material result: a sum of productive forces, an historically created relation of individuals to nature and to one another"[18]; human senses and man himself are also "labor of the entire history of the world"[19]. More importantly, the concrete selection determined by practice must be implemented practically by objective activity, and then become perceptible.

---

18   *Karl Marx and Friedrich Engels.* 1st Chinese Ed., Vol. 3, p. 43.
19   *Karl Marx and Friedrich Engels.* 1st Chinese Ed., Vol. 42, p. 126.

However, there is contradiction between self-consciousness and objectivity, which is a basic starting point, because ego "starts with himself", but things move in line with their own laws – the two are originally contradictory. All cognition and practice of human beings is for the purpose of resolving the relationship between man and world and the contradiction between self-consciousness and objectivity, and human beings are developing during the resolution of this relationship and contradiction. But this contradiction can only be solved at a definite level within a definite scope in every era. Therefore, acknowledging this contradiction does not aim at suppressing the effect of self-consciousness; on the contrary, only when the effect of self-consciousness is given play to can the contradiction mentioned above be solved in a unceasing manner.

Here involves the problem of understanding on objectivity. Engels had described the characteristics of objectivity in detail, which is still of classical significance till now. From Engels' point of view, objectivity should be explored based on the actual cognition process. "What can be discovered by our thought is more evident from what it has already discovered and is every day still discovering. And that is already enough both as regards quantity and quality."[20] So objectivity should be investigated in combination with the movement of cognition, from the starting point of the regularity and intercommunity actually grasped by cognition rather than from other principles. This is the first point.

Second, objectivity has direction and center. In Engels' eyes, objectivity is not a pure thing. Man can only investigate the objectivity of world "geocentrically" in the direction of the earth, thus this objectivity is just relative to the earth. "Our whole official physics, chemistry, and biology are exclusively geocentric, calculated only for the earth."[21] The activity of cognition always has its direction and center; we can only "geocentrically" cognize the world from the angle of mankind. Without this direction, there will be no cognition, let alone the objectivity of cognition.

Third, objectivity is the universality and regularity in cognition. Engels thinks, "In fact all real, exhaustive knowledge consists solely in raising the individual thing in thought from individuality into particularity and from this into universality, in seeking and establishing the infinite in the

---

20   *Selected Works of Karl Marx and Friedrich Engels*. 2nd Ed., Vol. 4, p. 332.
21   *Selected Works of Karl Marx and Friedrich Engels*. 2nd Ed., Vol. 4, p. 338.

finite, the eternal in the transitory." "The form of universality in nature is law."[22] For this reason, particularity in individuality, the infinite in the finite, and the universality in particularity are the objectivity in cognition, which is expressed in the form of "law".

In a nutshell, objectivity is not "pure"; it is what is reflected in cognition, with universality and regularity in various specific cognitions. It does not depend on the cognition of man, and meanwhile has relativity, i.e. relative to human activity.

Thus it is obvious that to correctly apprehend and grasp the contradiction between self-consciousness and objectivity, we should not one-sidedly emphasize the particularity of ego and self-consciousness, or abandon ourselves to the "purity" of objectivity, but should resolve this contradiction from the starting point of the dialectical relationship between object consciousness and self-consciousness. The contradiction between self-consciousness and objectivity is rendered more prominent by the development of modern science: men can observe the cosmoscopic and microcosmic system only by means of instruments, and given no radio telescope, optical spectrum analyzer, electron accelerator, etc., man is unable to perceive them; the observation with instruments has become the intermediate of instruments, and at this time, men have converted cosmoscopic and microcosmic scale into macroscopic scale. This is a "relation within relation", meaning that what man has observed is the relation confined by instruments, and different instruments will give different relations. Indeterminacy, relativity, coordinates and so on all refer to the same problem, and the resolution of this problem necessitates dialectical thinking.

The relationship between "projection" and "invariant" put forward by Born should be considered as the application of dialectical thinking in modern physics. As far as Born is concerned, the changes from macroscopic view into cosmoscopic and microcosmic view can be explained with the relationship between "projection" and "invariant". Projection refers to every concrete interrelation, namely that in physics, "an observation or measurement does not refer to a natural phenomenon as such, but to its aspect from, or its projection on, a system of reference"[23]. That is to say, projection is the manifestation of the interaction between

---

22   Ibid., p. 341.
23   Born, *Physics in My Generation*. English Ed., p. 190

subject, instrument and object. The reason why projection is so called is because natural phenomenon is individually manifested by it, and it is not natural phenomenon itself, but a manifestation distorted, restricted by various relations. The so-called invariant refers to the common rule in different projections. "In every physical theory there is a rule which connects the projections of the same object on different systems of reference, called a law of transformation, and all these transformations have the property of forming a group, i.e. the sequence of two consecutive transformations is a transformation of the same kind. Invariants are quantities having the same value for any systems of reference, hence they are independent of the transformations."[24]

Evidently, the relationship between "projection" and "invariant" is the relationship respectively between phenomenon and essence, relation and law, form and content, and the individual and the general in the dialectical thinking. Phenomenon, relation, form, or the individual is variable, and just circuitously represents something inherent under certain conditions; it is the manifestation of interaction, that is, "projection"; after entering into the general from the individual, from relation into law, the cognition of man grasps the inherent essence in relations, that is, "invariant". Born used them to resolve the cognitive contradiction between macroscopic system and cosmoscopic and microcosmic system, thereby endowing them with modern physical significance. As a matter of fact, human cognition is always deepened from "projection" into "invariant" unceasingly, and then, in the wake of the expansion of the cognition scope, the original "invariant" becomes the "projection" at a new higher level, thus cognition moves towards a higher essence. This process is manifested as the movement from individuality to particularity and then to universality, from phenomenon to essence, and from primary essence to secondary essence. Such a movement of cognition constantly resolves the contradiction between self-consciousness and objectivity.

If we say the contradiction between self-consciousness and objectivity is theoretically resolved by dialectical thinking, then it is practically resolved by practical activity, meaning that the cognition of self-consciousness on objectivity is verified and adjusted by practice. Viewed from the angle of process, the contradiction between self-consciousness and objectivity is specifically shown as the contradictory movement

---

24 Born, *Physics in My Generation*. English Ed., p. 189

of purpose, means and result. Marx always takes practice as the contradictory movement process of purpose, means and result, namely self-consciousness and objectivity, with the belief that in the process of practice, the laborer "makes use of the mechanical, physical and chemical properties of some substances in order to make other substances subservient to his aims"[25].

Hence, the whole process can only be: self-consciousness is conscious of self-need and establish purpose on this ground. To achieve this purpose, self-consciousness changes into "the cunning of reason": it first of all realizes objectivity, i.e. the mechanical, physical and chemical properties of things; next, it makes the properties of things move according to "purpose", with a part of the properties translated by "purpose" into instruments and means and the other part into object; then, it makes "things" as means and "things" as object move and interact on each other according to purpose, thereby changing the forms of things as per the needs of man and making things meet human needs.

The problem is that the purpose achievement of ego presupposes objectivity. "The latter (man) can work only as Nature does, that is by changing the form of matter. Nay more, in this work of changing the form he is constantly helped by natural forces."[26] So the realizations of purpose, means and result are all based on objectivity, unified in the practical activity of man. Fundamentally speaking, men confirm themselves through practice as the objective activity and its objective existence, and man himself can only be manifested by this historical activity. It is indicated by the whole history of human cognition, the history of practice and the development of mankind that the development of mankind is shown by the development of practice, the contradiction between self-consciousness and object consciousness is in this movement process, and the resolution of this contradiction can only be based on and started with practical activity and dialectical thinking.

---

25 *Karl Marx and Friedrich Engels*. 1st Chinese Ed., Vol. 23, p. 203.
26 *Karl Marx and Friedrich Engels*. 1st Chinese Ed., Vol. 23, pp. 56 – 57.

CHAPTER XVI

INTELLECTUAL THINKING AND DIALECTICAL THINKING: A NEW INTERPRETATION

At the turn of the nineteenth century and the twentieth century, Engels pointed out that when natural science had accumulated a huge amount of experience and knowledge, a movement "returning" to dialectical thinking would be inevitable in order to establish the inner connections among knowledge materials. In Engels' eyes, the movement "returning" to dialectical thinking may take two different paths: "it can come about spontaneously, by the sheer force of the natural-scientific discoveries themselves", and it can also resort to dialectical philosophy. The development of science and philosophy at the turn of the twentieth century and the twenty-first century verifies the truthfulness and predictability of this opinion of Engels and proves the two paths – "coming about spontaneously" and resorting to dialectical philosophy – are functioning simultaneously. Along with the conversion from classical science to non-classical science, intellectual thinking is more and more featured by dialectics under the promotion of its own force, specifically manifested by the transformations of scientific thinking, from negating "contradiction" and "paradox" to acknowledging "contradiction" and "paradox", from requiring "completeness" and "formalization" to acknowledging the existence of factors like "incompleteness" and "non-formalization", and from one-sidedly "rejecting metaphysics" and requiring to thoroughly implement the principles of positivism and falsificationism to acknowledge "historicism" and the reasonable effect of "metaphysics". The boundary between intellectual thinking and dialectical thinking becomes vaguer and vaguer: the former is moving towards the latter, and the latter is continuously intellectualizing what should be intellectualized, that is, the latter is also moving towards the former. For instance, "contradiction", "non-formalization" and "incompleteness", which are originally the categories only belonging to dialectical thinking, have now become the elements of intellectual thinking. We should see that intellectual thinking and dialectical thinking is in the movement process of convergence in modern times, so we should not scrupulously abide by the classification of intellectual thinking and rational thinking made by Kant and Hegel; we must realize that in the wake of the conversion from classical science to non-classical science, in the wake of the generation of new ideas in scientific thinking like system theory, cybernetics, theory of information, etc., and in the wake of the acknowledgement and application of "relativity principle", "indeterminancy principle", "complementarity principle", etc. by scientific thinking, intellectual thinking does not take on its classical historical form any longer, but is full of dialectical feature and "returning" to dialectical thinking.

1 "REJECTING METAPHYSICS" AND VERIFIABILITY

The great change in thinking development in the twentieth century is the "return" of intellectual thinking to dialectical thinking through its inner contradictions, and scientific thinking jumps out of the framework of early modern intellectual thinking and takes on a new form. This "return" path is full of contradictions: in the beginning, men "rejected metaphysics" and required to thoroughly implement the principles of positivism and falsificationism, but later they realized that "metaphysics" could not be rejected completely, and positivism and falsificationism could not be "completed", either. The fact of history is that "metaphysics" that is rejected at the front door returns at the back door in a distorted form; positivism is confronted with its opposite – falsificationism and updated to a new trend of historicism and scientific realism.

Metaphysics mentioned here does not refer to the way of thinking that is relative to dialectical thinking and investigates the world in an isolated, static and one-sided manner, but a kind of transcendent thought. Metaphysics rejected by modern western philosophy exactly refers to such way of thinking. According to Schlick, "The most terrible mistake made in the past times was the opinion that the true meaning and final content of philosophical proposition could be re-expressed with statements, i.e. be expounded with knowledge; this is a 'metaphysical' mistake."[1] And according to Carnap, "I think the proposition referred to as the properties of metaphysics can be clearly explained most easily with the following examples: Thales said 'the essence and principle of the world is water'; Heraclitus said 'it's fire'; Anaximander said 'it's the infinite'; Pythagoras said 'it's number'. And the theory of Plato is that 'all things are nothing but the shadows of eternal ideas, which exist in a timeless and spaceless realm'."[2] From the point of view of Carnap et al., the ancient discussion about ontology is meaningless metaphysics, and the discussion on epistemology in early modern times also belongs to metaphysics and makes no sense; cognition should be confined to experience and knowledge, to the verifiable scope.

"Rejection to metaphysics" by Carnap et al. is reasonable to a certain extent. Marx had pointed out long ago that as "the positive sciences broke away from metaphysics and marked out their independent fields", "the whole wealth of metaphysics now consisted only of beings of thought and heavenly things, at the very time when real beings and earthly things began to be the centre of all interest. Metaphysics had become insipid". Thus "metaphysics had in practice lost all credit" and meanwhile "in the domain of theory"[3]. In modern times, when science becomes non-classical, it is certainly inadvisable to still pursue the changeless ontology or study material in general and spirit in general not based on the development of modern practice and science. But the problem is that Carnap et al. unreasonably understood the reasonable factors, did not understand generality in individuality and the infinite in the finite, and could not make a reflection at a higher level by breaking away from the partial whole and standing at different levels. As far as I am concerned, this is not the problem about "rejecting metaphysics", but about real human practice and cognition.

1   Logical Empiricism, edited by Hong Qian. Beijing: The Commercial Press, 1982: Vol. I, p. 9.
2   Quoted from: White, The Age of Analysis. Beijing: The Commercial Press, 1981: p. 215.
3   Karl Marx and Friedrich Engels. 1st Chinese Ed., Vol. 2, pp. 161 – 162.

Of course, it is impossible to reject the "metaphysics" making a whole reflection on the world. Engels had long since pointed out that "researchers of nature believe: as long as they turn their back on or humiliate philosophy, they can be emancipated from philosophy. However, because they cannot move forward once leaving thinking, and thinking requires thinking determinations", the name of the game is not whether to reject "metaphysics", and "the problem is only that: whether they are willing to be dominated by a crappy fashionable philosophy or by a theoretical form of thinking based on the history and achievements of the thinking of cognition"[4].

In the final analysis, science cannot be divorced from philosophy completely, because (1) science itself is the fruit of thinking, and real scientific thinking is bound to involve the object, process, form and method of thinking, all of which are finalized by the summarization of philosophy. Therefore, the scientific thinking is bound to consciously or unconsciously involve "metaphysics"; (2) the thinking of scientists should not always stay at the fact, but should rise to a higher level and form certain "abstractions", and the cross of a science with another also requires the integration of sciences; such abstractions and integration is inseparable with "metaphysics". As a result, men cannot reject theoretical thinking and philosophical thinking.

After logical empiricism of Schlick, Carnap, Hempel and Cohen, the philosophy of science turned from positivism to falsificationism, bringing out the critical rationalism of Popper and Lakatos; later, due to the difficulty of verification and falsification, it turned to scientific historicism. Then, "metaphysics" became a realistic issue again and accepted by modern western philosophy. It seems to be a process of negation of the negation. In the opinion of Wartofsky, a philosopher of scientific historicism, scientific thinking must employ conceptual framework. "Conceptual framework is a mode we use to rationally collate our knowledge."[5] This is the first point.

Secondly, philosophy realistically "has, under the general topics of (1) metaphysics, (2) epistemology and (3) logic, interposed in the issues mentioned above". Therefore, scientists cannot reject "metaphysics", and they just spontaneously "bring the impacts of previous metaphysics,

4   Selected Works of Karl Marx and Friedrich Engels. 2nd Ed., Vol. 4, p. 308.
5   Wartofsky, Conceptual Foundations of Science Thought – An Introduction to the Philosophy of Science. Beijing: Qiushi Publishing House, 1989: p. 10.

epistemology and logical formalization into their work"[6]. From Descartes, Newton and Leibniz to Planck and Einstein, "all of these persons did not only help the reforming of the conceptual framework of science, but also the reforming of the basic concept of philosophy"[7].

It is not hard to find that the opinion of Wartofsky is the same with that of Engels, but such sameness is not a historical coincidence: Engels had foreseen this point at the height of the development of human thinking with a farsighted view as early as over one hundred years, while Wartofsky realized it after repeated discussions and reflections of science in the twentieth century. These are two cognition processes along two paths but naturally reaching coincident result. This shows that this issue is "unavoidable" and "irresistible" in cognition.

Verifiability is connected with the issue of "rejecting metaphysics". From the view of logical empiricism, whether a question is meaningful depends on whether the theory of the question could be verified or falsified; if it can be neither verified nor falsified, it is a meaningless question, i.e. a "metaphysical" question. Schlick is the first to put forward the issue about verification and meaning and classify verifiability into "empirical possibility" and "logical possibility". Ayer further divided verifiability into "the verifiability of practice" and "the verifiability of principle".

The problem was that verifiability itself had faced logical difficulty. In fact, on account of the continuous development of cognition, science and practice, absolute verification and absolute falsification are impossible, so Carnap brought forward "confirmation" and made distinctions between "confirmation" and "verification", between "verifiability" and "confirmability", and between the principle of meaning and the principle of verification. From the viewpoint of Carnap, the so-called verification is "decisively and finally determined to be true"[8], and confirmation only means being confirmed at current stage and does not guarantee the confirmation subsequently. "There theoretically exists the possibility for the sequence of verifying observation to go ahead, so any absolute verification is also impossible, and it is merely a process of increasingly intensified confirmation."[9]

6   Wartofsky, Conceptual Foundations of Science Thought – An Introduction to the Philosophy of Science. Beijing: Qiushi Publishing House, 1989: pp. 14 – 25.

7   ibid., p. 25.

8   Logical Empiricism, edited by Hong Qian. Vol. I, p. 69.

9   Ibid., p. 75.

The principle of falsification from critical rationalism gave a crushing blow to the principle of verifiability. Popper first of all criticized the inductive method, thinking that induction could only summarize history, but could not predict the future or give a necessary or even occasional knowledge about future; therefore the inductive method could not be considered as a scientific method. On the basis of anti-induction, Popper proposed the principle of falsificationism of critical rationalism, that is to say, all scientific propositions are general or universal propositions, and any verification is about an individual; what's more, the individual cannot be raised by induction to the general, so scientific theories cannot be verified, nevertheless the general scientific proposition can be falsified by falsifying the individual proposition.

Popper consequently believed, "Scientific progress turned out not to consist in the accumulation of observations but in the overthrow of less good theories and their replacement by better ones, in particular by theories of greater content."[10] In Popper's opinion, there is no "verifiable" theory but the theory being "confirmed" at present, and even the theory having been "confirmed" at present will be falsified one day; any theory will be bound to be falsified ultimately.

The development of history is peculiar. Logical positivism "rejects metaphysics" and requires verifiability; its one-sided requirement is fully negated by the falsification on the other side. As a matter of fact, it is impossible for the thinking without "metaphysics" and totally limited to verification and falsification, because both verification and falsification are extraordinarily complex issues which must be clarified with "metaphysical" thinking. Marxist philosophy does not absolutely negate falsification or verification; on the contrary, it stresses the importance of "empirical observation", which "must in each separate instance bring out empirically, and without any mystification and speculation, the connection of the social and political structure with production", and regards historical materialism as "the real positive science"[11].

Marxist philosophy, fundamentally speaking, regards the verification by practice as a historical process, a complex process both with integrity and one-sidedness, absoluteness and relativity, and immediacy and indirectness; during this process, we should not only see the certainty

---

10   Popper, Unended Quest. Fuzhou: Fujian People's Publishing House, 1984: p. 82.
11   Selected Works of Karl Marx and Friedrich Engels. 2nd Ed., Vol. 1, pp. 71 – 73.

and repeatability of verification and falsification but also the conditionality, relativity and uncertainty of the two; thinking has no solid foundation and realistic character unless the certainty of verification and falsification is seen and acknowledged, and meanwhile thinking and practice cannot develop unless their uncertainty is observed. We can say that only based on the movement of practice, this complex historical process, can we transcend the principle of positivism or falsificationism, as well as the principle of omnipotent anarchism.

It is shown by the development of modern science and philosophy that scientific thinking also makes reflections on itself; the reflections on issues like "metaphysics", "verification" and "falsification" belong to historical movement, indicating scientific thinking has taken on a new form of dialectical thinking that includes "paradox", "relativity", "indeterminacy" and "human selectivity". All of these prove one thing, that is, we should not interpret scientific thinking at the original level of intellectual thinking any more.

2 "PARADOX" AND CONSISTENCY

The existence of intellectual thinking and dialectical thinking is the product of the inner contradictions of thinking. It is indicated by the development of modern thinking that there is contradiction in any thought and conclusion. Modern thinking itself grows out of the dialectical nature of the contradictions in thinking; it consciously acknowledges dialectical contradiction and takes this contradiction as the principle of its activity. The dialectical contradiction is reflected, for example, by the theorem of incompleteness, indeterminacy principle, relativity principle, human selectivity principle and so on of modern scientific thinking. The theorem of incompleteness embodies the contradiction between integrity and non-integrity, the indeterminacy principle reflects the contradiction between absoluteness and relativity, and the human selectivity principle shows the contradiction between subject and object. The emergence of a series of "paradoxes" during the development of modern science demonstrates the "frustration" in the development of human thinking and the tortuosity of its process on the one hand, and indicates that the existence of positive thinking and dialectical thinking is the necessary product of the development of inner contradictions of thinking.

I cannot agree with the opinion that the concept of contradiction originates from the apprehension of "force", and it is the logical abstraction of acting force and reacting force; and modern system theory has sublated the idea of "contradiction". This opinion absolutizes the apprehension of contradiction in early modern times, and it is considered to be one-sided for the following reasons: (1) the contradiction as a concept is not generated by abstracting "force", and before Newtonian mechanics came about, the concept of contradiction had been formed in an intuitive and empirical morphology; (2) the concept of contradiction abstracted from the polarization of "force" is merely a reflection of early modern mechanical thinking, just a particular historical understanding on contradiction; and (3) system theory will by no means sublate the theory of contradiction, and what it has sublated is mechanism's view of contradiction; contrarily, it reflects the deep contradiction in cognition; no contradiction, there will be no system. System itself is the product of contradictions between whole and part, aspect and element, and structure and function, and the presentation of "system paradox" precisely demonstrates that system itself cannot escape from contradiction. Instead of negating contradiction, system theory deepens the connotation of contradiction, develops new tiers of contradiction, and embodies the in-depth understanding of modern science on contradiction.

"Dialectics is a property of all human knowledge in general."[12], and contradiction is an inherent factor of human cognition. As long as man is thinking and applying language, sign and logic, contradiction will be created inevitably. Contradiction is the essence of thinking, determined by multiple relationships, such as between subject and object, between subjectivity and objectivity, between continuity and discontinuity, and between comprehensiveness and aspect.

From the angle of the relationship between subjectivity and objectivity, thinking is the activity process of subject, so it certainly has the coordinates, angle and direction of subject and the inherent measure of man, thus subjectivity and objectivity, namely subject and object, can never be absolutely identical, and instead, both are always unified historically, specifically and contradictorily. The width and depth reachable by the thinking of a generation is limited all the time. However, the infinite is invariably expressed by the finite, and absoluteness exists in infinite relativity; they themselves are contradictions, which are then translated

---

12   Collected Works of Lenin. 2nd Chinese Ed., Vol. 55, p. 308.

into unified but non-identical contradictions between thinking and be-ing, between subjectivity and objectivity, and between subject and ob-ject. This shows that cognition is by no means purely objectivist.

From the perspective of the relationship between continuity and discon-tinuity, for the purpose of expressing a thing, thinking must interrupt continuity, strangle the moving, abstract the object of thinking from the whole, and temporarily cut off its connections with other things. Interrupting continuity itself connotes the inner contradiction of for-malized and signified thinking. Taking the simplest equation $1+1=2$ for example, this equation is logically self-explanatory, but in practice, $1+1$ never makes 2, not only because there will never be two completely equal 1 in the world, but also in that 1 is just the reasonable abstraction of thinking, and specific 1 in practical life is always moving and chang-ing. So even in the operation of $1+1=2$, the moving has been strangled and the continuity interrupted, which has already been a contradictory process. Taking the simplest word "this" for another example, "this" can be used to refer to an event or a moment at present; it may represent specific "this matter", "this person" or "this book", i.e. manifesting "in-dividuality", and it may also represent "this" commonly appearing in "this matter", "this person" and "this book". As a result, the word "this" itself is a contradiction – the contradiction between individuality and generality running through the application of word "this".

Since the simplest relations and words have implied all sprouts of dia-lectics, advanced inference and creative thinking inevitably rely on the application of dialectical contradiction. Just because dialectical contra-diction is the running mechanism of thinking, the degree of this contra-diction's application marks the level of human thinking. System theory in fact only grasps certain aspects, such as the aspect of structure, of function, of correlation, of input-output, etc. The adjective "omnibear-ing" in omnibearing thinking is relative. "Bearings" can never be abso-lutely "complete", and to make "bearings" absolutely "complete", the movement must be stopped, but this is impossible. As long as the world is moving, new bearings and aspects will arise. Therefore the compre-hensiveness of thinking only exists in the contradiction between com-prehensiveness and aspect, and thinking is a historical process unceas-ingly approaching to comprehensiveness in the contradictory movement of comprehensiveness and aspect. The "omnibearing" thinking is no more than a thinking movement with ever increasing "bearings".

Modern thinking is a kind of dialectical thinking, which gets rid of the modes of thinking of pure objectivism and objectivism and meanwhile sublates the modes of thinking of subjectivism and relativism, thereby moving in contradictions between subject and object, absoluteness and relativity, possibility and selectivity, whole and part, completeness and incompleteness, and certainty and uncertainty. In this connection, we cannot grasp the essence of modern thinking if not understanding contradictions.

One of the characteristics of modern thinking is the entry of the idea of contradiction into the sphere of intellectual thinking, transforming thinking from excluding "paradox" by all means to acknowledging the reasonable existence of "paradox", and from pursuing "completeness" and "certainty" to acknowledging "incompleteness" and "uncertainty". This fact indicates that intellectual thinking is consciously trending towards dialectical thinking and more and more featured by dialectics. In other words, the modern morphology of "paradox" and the proposal of "relativity", "indeterminacy" and "human selectivity" give a common language to intellectual thinking and dialectical thinking for the first time. This is the exact historical manifestation of the return of science to dialectics.

"Paradox" is an old problem, directly meaning that a theory originally thought to be correct results in two conclusions contradicting with each other. Numerous "paradoxes" have been created from ancient times to modern times, among which typical ones are "Pythagoras' paradox", "Zeno's paradox", "Berkeley's paradox", "Russell's paradox", "semantic paradox", and so forth. Amongst them, "Pythagoras' paradox", "Berkeley's paradox" and "Russell's paradox" had aroused three crises in the development history of western mathematics, resulting in three major progresses in mathematical theory.

In general, paradox should be divided into two categories: one arises out of wrong premise, and the other has a correct premise.

"Pythagoras' paradox" falls under the paradox with a wrong premise. The Pythagorean School adhered to such a belief that all things came down to the ratio of integer to integer, but they found the ratio of the diagonal of a square to its side length was 2, and the ratio of the two could not be integral. The correctness of 2 negated their belief that all things came down to the ratio of integer to integer, thus causing the first crisis in the history of mathematics. That "crisis" was actually a false alarm, and its essence was the stepping of man over the boundary of his cognition of world, as well as the negation to the false premise.

"Russell's paradox" and "Berkeley's paradox" belong to the paradoxes with correct premise. "Berkeley's paradox" is bent on the infinitesimal analysis of calculus. Berkeley proved that infinitesimal was 0 but not 0 in actual application. That was a correct thought, but due to its contradiction with formal logic, it gave rise to the second crisis in the history of mathematics. "Russell's paradox" is the famous "set paradox", namely that any set can constitute a new set through the predicate "not belonging to itself", and this new set is composed of sets not belonging to themselves, but every set can be considered as a set belonging to itself. Therefore, we can infer that a set "does not belong to itself" from the premise that it "belongs to itself", and infer that a set "belongs to itself" from the premise that it "does not belong to itself". Thus, whether or not "a set belongs to itself" has two equivalent answers opposite to each other.

It is clear that "Berkeley's paradox" and "Russell's paradox" are different from "Pythagoras' paradox". To solve "Pythagoras' paradox", we only need to elucidate its premise is wrong. However, we cannot solve "Russell's paradox" in the aspect of premise or logical inference for its premise and logical inference are not wrong, and this "paradox" is logically reasonable. That is to say, the premise, inference and logical process of "paradox" all have no problem, but its conclusions are mutually opposite and contradictory, and equivalently true.

"Reasonable paralogism", or "logical paradox", equals to "correct error". So "Russell's paradox" aroused successive responses from various circles and led to "Burali-Forti's paradox", "Cantor's paradox", "Richard's paradox", "Perry's paradox" and "Grelling's paradox", as well as "paradox cluster", "paradox web" and "paradox series", thereby fiercely impacting the original framework of intellectual thinking and pushing mathematicians into terror and uncertainty. Great mathematician Hilbert thus believed, "Admittedly, the present state of affairs where we run up against the paradoxes is intolerable. Just think, the definitions and deductive methods which everyone learns, teaches, and uses in mathematics, the paragon of truth and certitude, lead to absurdities! If mathematical thinking is defective, where are we to find truth and certitude?"[13]

---

13   Hilbert, A Collection of Mathematical and Philosophical Papers. English Ed., p. 141.

As a matter of fact, the problem is not complicated, and what is complicated is the idea of consistent and purely objective "certitude" and "truth" adhered to by Hilbert and other great mathematicians. As long as they insist on the thinking of consistency, deeper contradiction will be caused inevitably, rendering thinking worried and shocked. Actually, as long as we give up adhering to "consistency", acknowledging "contradiction" and "paradox" will become a common phenomenon in cognition. "Paradox" is the "paralogism" to the thinking of consistency, because "consistency" itself is a "paralogism"; as long as we go forward along "consistency", "paradox" will arise in any route or from any angle, without exception. Hegel had long since stated that there would be as many antinomies as there were concepts.

In my opinion, what we should be shocked at is not "paradox" or "the reasonability of paradox", but the shock at "the reasonability of paradox". We should accept such a fact that "paradox" is reasonable, and "contradiction" cannot be eliminated. Scientists declare the "certitude" and "truth" of their science, but in fact the understanding on such "certitude" and "truth" is subject to the historical conditions of them. Every historical period is limited, so there is no absolute "certitude" and "truth", or constant "certainty".

The essence of "paradox" is fundamentally the reflection of the contradictions between the infinity of world and the finiteness of cognition, and between the diversity of things and the linearity of thinking method and logical means. Lenin pointed out, "We cannot imagine, express, measure, depict movement, without interrupting continuity, without simplifying, coarsening, dismembering, strangling that which is living. The representation of movement by means of thought always makes coarse, kills, – and not only by means of thought, but also by sense-perception, and not only of movement, but every concept."[14] "Paradox" just stems from how thinking imagines, expresses, measures and depicts the "reality"; there are always strangling, simplifying and linearizing factors in thinking.

As far as I'm concerned, the cause of "paradox" does not rest with the unstrictness of thinking, and on the contrary, it is precisely caused by the excess strictness and normalization of intellectual thinking. "Paradox" is unavoidable in human thinking. The development of modern scientific

---

14   Collected Works of Lenin. 2nd Chinese Ed., Vol. 55, p. 219.

thinking rectifies mankind's preference to the thinking of consistency and corrects the historical idea equating "paradox" with "error", thereby acknowledging the reasonable existence of "paradox". If intellectual thinking in history is thought to be featured by excluding "paradox" and pursuing consistency, then along with the acknowledgement of the reasonability of "paradox", modern intellectual thinking begins to consciously recognize contradiction and take dialectical contradiction as its starting point. This is a key step of intellectual thinking's "return" to dialectical thinking.

3 FORMALIZATION AND NON-FORMALIZATION, SYSTEM AND NON-SYSTEM

The "return" of intellectual thinking to dialectical thinking is also embodied by its thorough resolution of formalization in logics. The theorem of incompleteness of Godel buries Hilbert's ideal of formalism, and reveals the reasonable existence of incompleteness and non-formalization in logics.

The so-called form refers to internal and external structures, order and quantity proportionality of a thing. Formalization attempts to comprehensively express the essence of a thing with its structures, order and quantity proportion. The formal method had been used in ancient times, materialized by Euclidean geometry, formal logics, etc. As non-Euclidean geometry broke through Euclidean geometry, the study on formal method entered a new level. Hilbert brought forward his theory of formalism in the early twentieth century, with the belief that the formalization in the past just started with an intuitive object, induced an axiom, and then made a deduction on the basis of axiom, but modern formal system should abandon obvious intuitiveness and become a "hypothesis–deduction system".

Thus the problem was reversed – the importance did not lie in what kind of object was studied, but in what kind of premise and relation, i.e. "the domain of discourse", was set; different "domains of discourse" would reveal different aspects. Hilbert dealt with Euclidean geometry with the form of premise and relation and thereby eliminated the intuitiveness of Euclidean geometry. Hilbert proposed five relations, namely "above ..." – connecting relation, "between ..." – ordering relation, "congruent with ..." – congruence relation, "parallel to ..." – parallel relation, and "continue" – continuing relation, and strived to prove Euclidean geometry by deducing the five relations. Obviously, the formal method of Hilbert was more universal than the axiomatic method of Euclidean geometry. And he also suggested that a formal system should embrace consistency, completeness and axiomatic independence.

The formalistic method of Hilbert changed the object of mathematics. That is to say, mathematics, in a certain sense, could take things, such as sign series, other than "quantity" and "shape" in the objective world as object. Men endowed sign series with various "determinations", "domains of discourse" and "models" through definition. Although those sign series and formal system were abstract, they all represented the structures of things. The thought of formalism of Hilbert was evidently profound, and deepened Pythagorean School's thought of "harmony of number" and the thought of "nominalism" of the Middle Ages in modern times, but his thorough formalistic method was not realized, and instead destroyed by the theorem of incompleteness of Godel.

Incompleteness is relative to completeness. Completeness means that within a complete formal system, all universally valid propositions can be proved when and only when they are in this system. If there is a universally valid proposition cannot be proved in the formal system, then this formal system is incomplete and unfinished. In 1931, Godel proved the theorem of incompleteness: if all propositions in a formal system including elementary number theory are true, there exists contradiction in the system; if there is no contradiction in the system, it is incomplete.

That is to say, a simple system including formal arithmetic is bound to be incomplete. Thus, the systems more advanced than those including natural number series and arithmetic relations are of course more incomplete, and they all contain the propositions that cannot be proved by themselves; in other words, proof of such propositions cannot be done in their own system, and they must be placed into a larger system for proof; to justify the proof by the larger system, this larger system must be put into a further larger system. This work cannot be completed in practice, and we must do it infinitely, infinitely putting a system into "a further larger system". It is an infinite endless work.

Thus, men are required to admit that in logics, any formal system including elementary number theory cannot be consistent and complete simultaneously – consistency inevitably shows incompleteness, while completeness inevitably indicates contradiction. This is obviously a devastating blow to the three pillars of Hilbert's formal system, namely "consistency", "completeness" and "axiomatic independence". To put it another way, the thought of formalization itself is based on a contradiction – it is impossible to simultaneously meet the requirements for consistency and absolute completeness.

The theorem of incompleteness of Godel destroys not only the ideal of formalization, but also the pursuit of intellectual thinking for its ideal of independence. In modern times, intelligence is broken, and its breaking is generated in line with the principle of certainty; it is the destroying of certainty complying with certainty. In this way, the "return" of intellectual thinking to dialectical thinking does not take the way of simple negation of reason against the limitation of intelligence any longer, and contrarily, the "return" happens within the sphere of intelligence. This is the "return" in a real sense.

What is in connection with formalization vs. non-formalization and completeness vs. incompleteness is system vs. non-system. The progress of modern thinking is also manifested by that after sublating mechanism, system theory consciously realizes the existence of non-systems, such as unconsciousness theory, oscillation theory, disorder theory, indeterminancy principle, incompleteness theorem, relativity principle, subjectivity principle and non-organization theory, as well as mentality, inspiration, intuition, illusion, passion, will, etc., all of which reveal a world with different specifications and types from systematic world and systematic connection, viz., non-systematic connection and non-systematic world.

The generation of non-system is an inevitable reflection on the inner contradictions of system, because to truly know system, we must cognize non-system, which is the reverse side of system. The connotation of non-system is relatively complex, and the prefix "non-" itself implies three meanings, namely different from system, not falling under system, and opposite to system. In a general sense, non-system refers to no system, loss of systematic connection, expansion of the broken point in system that begets system collapse, or the opposite to system, i.e. disorder, chaos and vagueness. System is interrelated to non-system. In terms of their identity, both are the subcategories under the "connection" category of dialectics, the extension, differentiation and development of the "connection" category, as well as the representation of the particularized "connection" category. From the connection viewpoint of dialectics, one thing can lose a "system", but cannot lose its "connections" with other things, and it may be translated into another form of "connection" – "non-system".

From a general view, system and non-system are manifested as two movement processes with different characteristics and directions: (1) non-system is a directional (downward) movement process of a thing in a chaotic, disordered and non-systematic direction contrary to the systematic (upward) direction constituted by integration, order, self-organization and diversification; (2) non-system is an aspect of material motion, namely the disordered aspect opposite to the ordered aspect; with respect to the development of thinking, it is the non-rational aspect opposite to rational aspect, and non-logical aspect opposite to logical aspect; (3) non-system is a state (stage) of material motion; relative to system, it is a kind of disordered, chaotic and oscillatory state, belonging to the type different from system state; and (4) non-system is also manifested as a thinking principle, i.e. non-system principle, different from system principle. The characteristic of such thinking principle is to prevent the formation or completion of system, or negate the established systems. Without such non-system principles as relativity principle, incompleteness principle, indeterminacy principle, paradox principle, subjectivity principle and complementarity principle, "missing links" will occur in the modern thinking.

As a state of material motion, non-system is first of all manifested as a chaotic and disordered state. People usually investigate problems from the angle of system, and summarize disorder and chaos merely as the extremely low state of system, which is actually one-sided. It is demonstrated by the Boltzmann's formula of free energy that chaos as an independent state is tenable theoretically. The formula of free energy is $F=E-TS$, where F represents free energy, E represents internal energy, S refers to the entropy of system, and T is absolute temperature. The validity of this formula has been verified by practice, leading to the following conclusions: (1) if T is absolute zero, then TS (entropy) will be zero; in this case, the amount of information is infinitely great, and the thing is in the standard, ideal, absolutely ordered state, viz., $F=E$ (TS is 0); and (2) if T is infinitely high temperature, then TS will be infinitely great; under this condition, the amount of information equals to zero, and the thing is in the standard, ideal, absolutely disordered state. Therefore, theoretically, we are able to obtain the state of polarized opposition between system and non-system.

The fundamental feature of non-system is the breaking of system. The reason why system is called system is because it has integrity formed by the interactions of elements, thus it is the reflection of system nature and relation nature. However, the generation of system results in "system paradox", that is, any system itself must be a whole, which is the precondition for system; meanwhile, any whole is an element in a larger system; it is an infinite quantity, showing system can never be completed; in other words, system is not a system. Thus, the so-called system is only relative to its elements, and once placed into a larger one, it is translated an element, as well. So we can see that system itself is a paradox, and system itself cannot be the system; once a system is systematized, the interrelations and interactions between things are cut off.

Any system, in a manner of speaking, has three non-system acting forces: (1) "entropy increase" spontaneously existing inside the system destroys the existence of system; for the purpose of existence, system must make exchanges with the outside world for substance, energy and information and absorb "negentropy flow" to cope with "entropy increase"; (2) the higher system always incorporates the lower system into its operating scope and makes the lower one subordinate to it; thus in the development of things, the systematization of the higher system is premised on the non-systematization of the lower one, which constitutes the polarized movement of systematization and non-systematization; and (3) systems are interacting on each other; a system certainly exists in a horizontal network of all different systems, and this horizontal network causes the deformation of the system; that's why system is always relative, always broken and incomplete.

The development of modern thinking reveals the breaking and incompleteness of system, thereby setting non-system as the opposite to system. The change between "right" and "wrong" comes out in the modernization of intellectual thinking. "Wrong", as the boundary of "right", has become something similar to "entropy", the opposite of "right". Shannon's formula of information amount is identical with the formula of the second law of thermodynamics in form, but the two formulas are totally contrary in terms of sign, that is, one is negative and the other is positive, both of which peculiarly unified.

As a result, information is just equivalent to the eliminated entropy. In this sense, information is negentropy. Judged from the development of modern thinking, system vs. non-system and formularization vs.

non-formulization have become the measure for the width and depth of thinking. The revolution of the idea of "wrong" in modern thinking is a midpoint of intellectual thinking's "return" to dialectical thinking.

4 SUBJECTIVITY PRINCIPLE AND THREE LEVELS OF MODERN THINKING MOVEMENT

The history of thinking development tells us that thinking should not only be dealt with from the angle of the relationships between thinking and being and between practice and cognition, but also from the perspective of thinking's self-constitution, from the development of subject. What's more, modern thinking is the thinking showing the subjectivity of mankind, and the thinking used by subject to amplify his control over object. So it is necessary to investigate the "return" of intellectual thinking to dialectical thinking from the angle of subject's activity.

The so-called subject is "socialized man", "the participant in history". Starting from "subject" – "the participant in history" – is the key to the revolution of philosophy realized by Marxist philosophy, the core of Marxist philosophy. In the system of Marxist philosophy, the category of subject reveals how man, through "activity", turns object into humanized object and reasonably adjusts and controls his relationship with the world in the light of human nature.

From the view of self-organization theory, subject is a socialized "self-organized system" having self-consciousness and reflection ability and implementing conscious purposes; he transforms material measure with his own inherent measure, and converts, controls and adjusts object for the purpose of appropriating it. However, subject is qualitatively different from general self-organized systems. The formation of subject, a special self-organized system, requires for conditions: (1) the relationship has not been the general relationship between the controller and the controlled, but has been self-conscious; thus the activity is "free and conscious"; (2) the behavioral process has not been generally "purposive"; instead, the "purposiveness" has been conscious, employed to control the behavior, will and means of subject; (3) subject does not only enter into the control relationship with object, but also such control relationship has become the object of subject's cognition and study; thus a new relationship is formed; subject is able to control, and consciously and reasonably expand, this control relationship; and (4) all these relationships cannot only be deposited in social forms and arrived at through society, but also every individual can have them by virtue of education and training after birth; in other words, all these relationships are reproduced no longer through biological heredity or experience accumulation of individuals, but through socialization among total social relations, in the form of social development. Hence, subject is a socialized system transforming and controlling object, namely "the participant in history".

Marx had repeatedly emphasized that "thing, reality and sensuousness" should be conceived "as practice, the human sensuous activity" "subjectively". In this connection, subjectivity principle roots in practical activity. It requires us to apprehend man, thing and human cognition based on practical activity. That is to say, the apprehension of world, man and the relationship between the two should be based on practical activity, the objective activity of subject. The subjectivity principle of Marx, in general, contains four aspects:

First, real man is subject, and there is no abstract man. This means that man and his development should be investigated based on his transforming and controlling relationship with the world. Of course man is the product of the long-term development of nature, whose activity should follow the laws of nature, so in this regard, man is passive; but on the other hand, man has self-consciousness, reflection ability and conscious initiative, and is capable of making all things in the world the object of his cognition and transformation and the useful things for him, thus he becomes the subject – a conscious purposeful "self-organized system" existing for controlling object.

Second, object is appropriated by man as subject, and there is no abstract object. Investigating object from the perspective of the appropriation of object by subject means conceiving "thing, reality and sensuousness" as practice, interpreting them based on practical activity and objective and subjective needs of man, and regarding them as the constituent part of practical activity. Man grasps things in practice through the objective activity of appropriating object in various aspects of his inherent measure, including his needs, desire, pursuit for beauty, and value relation. Object "taken abstractly", or "nature fixed in isolation from man is nothing for man"[15].

---

15   Karl Marx and Friedrich Engels. 1st Chinese Ed., Vol. 42, p. 178.

Third, cognition and sensuousness should also be investigated from the objective activity of subject's appropriation of object. "The forming of the five senses is a labor of the entire history of the world down to the present."[16] "Consciousness can never be anything else than conscious existence."[17] Only in the objective activity of subject can there be cognized nature and consciousness different from nature, and "my relation to my environment is my consciousness"[18]. Therefore abstract consciousness does not exist. Just as nature fixed in isolation from man is "nothing" for man, cognition, sensuousness, consciousness and spirit isolated from nature and subject's objective activity of controlling nature are all "nothing" for man, either.

Fourth, the developments of society and thinking should not be abstractly discussed in separation from the development of individuals. According to Marx, we should avoid placing society as an abstract thing in opposition to individual. In *The Communist Manifesto*, Marx stresses that the free development of each is the condition for the free development of all. So it is clear that the development of every man is the condition and premise for the developments of society, subject and his thinking.

In other words, in the subjectivity principle, the relationship between subject and object should be investigated based on the practical activity of man and the development of subject; we should regard nature not only as the object of cognition but also as the object of transformation, as our "inorganic body", and inject our needs, appetites and interests into it, thereby making it the human nature that emerges for man. Marx points out, "Man appropriates his comprehensive essence in a comprehensive manner, that is to say, as a whole man. Each of his human relations to the world – seeing, hearing, smelling, tasting, feeling, thinking, observing, experiencing, wanting, acting, loving – in short, all the organs of his individual being, like those organs which are directly social in their form, are in their objective orientation, or in their orientation to the object, the appropriation of the object, the appropriation of human reality."[19] To implement subjectivity principle means carrying through the fundamental feature of the comprehensive appropriation of object by subject in all fields.

---

16   Karl Marx and Friedrich Engels. 1st Chinese Ed., Vol. 42, p. 126.

17   *Karl Marx and Friedrich Engels.* 1st Chinese Ed., Vol. 3, p. 29.

18   ibid., p. 34.

19   *Karl Marx and Friedrich Engels.* 1st Chinese Ed., Vol. 42, pp. 123 – 124.

Considered from the view of subjectivity principle, thinking is a link in the objective activity of subject. As Engels said, "It is precisely the alteration of nature by men, not solely nature as such, which is most essential and immediate basis of human thought, and it is in the measure that man has learned to change nature that his intelligence has increased."[20] The understanding on the essence of modern thinking is exactly based on such activity of subject. In other words, the development of modern thinking should be apprehended from three levels of the activity of subject.

The first level is the level of subject's objective activity, i.e. the level of subject objectification and object subjectification constituted during the interaction between subject and object. At this level, a bidirectional movement of mutual translation is caused due to the activity of subject:

On the one hand, object is subjectified. (1) Object is translated into the thinking of subject. Through practical activity, object is cognized by subject, and the laws and characteristics of things are translated into the concepts, formulas, categories, and rules in the thinking of subject, internalized into the sensory tier, thinking tier and conceptual tier of subject, and changed into the theoretical weapon of subject to further cognize and transform the world. (2) Object is translated into the actual possession of subject. During human activity, object is appropriated by subject, and nature is humanized, becoming the extended part of subject, the instrument and means for his activity, and the "inorganic body" of man, and thus leading to "the emergence of nature for man"[21]. (3) The mode of activity of man is internalized as the mode of thinking of man. The "pattern" of practice, after "generalized", "simplified" and "verbalized" by thinking, is ultimately "internalized" as the "pattern" of the thinking of subject.

On the other hand, subject is objectified. (1) Thinking is objectified. The thinking tier of subject is translated into objective knowledge tier, namely the accumulation of science and spiritual civilization. (2) Activity is objectified. The purposes and requirements of subject are translated into plans, schemes, and behavior rules, which ensure the smooth progress of purposive behavior through continuous information–feedback adjustment. Under this condition, the thinking of subject

---

20   *Selected Works of Karl Marx and Friedrich Engels*. 2nd Ed., Vol. 4, p. 329.
21   *Karl Marx and Friedrich Engels*. 1st Chinese Ed., Vol. 42, p. 131.

serves as an adjusting factor for actual operation, giving rise to the controlled behavior; thus subject becomes the subject in practice. (3) The spirits and plans of subject are finally externalized as objective being. Subject realizes his transformation of object through conscious activity, and injects his purpose, requirement, desire and pursuit for the true, the good and the beautiful into material forms; thus material is turned into humanized material, namely the materialization respectively of science, logics and man's inherent measure, and the world of objects is made the human world.

It is then obvious that the thinking of man is an intermediary link in object subjectification and subject objectification, and it develops along with the developments of the practical activity of man and the interaction between subject and object.

The second level is the level of self-consciousness and reflection. At this level, subject, by dint of self-consciousness and reflection, objectifies the process of subject objectification and object subjectification, that is, objectifying the processes of practice and thinking and translating them into the object of cognition. In consequence, the objective activity of subject towards object at the first level becomes the object of self-consciousness and reflection at the second level. The product of the second level is man's cognition on self, on the necessary conditions for his objective activity. In the eyes of Marx, the activity at this level has an essential significance in that during this activity, "man makes his life activity itself the object of his will and of his consciousness", and "his own life is an object for him; only because of that is his activity free activity"[22]. Similarly, the objective activity of man is made the object of self-consciousness and the thinking of man the object of reflection, and only because of this can the objective activity and thinking of man be "free activity".

Self-consciousness and reflection can generally be considered as the level of self-criticism of subject, only through which can man "objectively" understands self, his own objective activity and thinking activity and thereby transcend himself and realize "free activity". Just on this ground, human consciousness is differentiated into object consciousness and self-consciousness, and human thinking is dualized into constructive thinking and reflective thinking.

---

22   *Karl Marx and Friedrich Engels*. 1st Chinese Ed., Vol. 42, p. 96.

The third level is the level of complete subjectivity and complete objectivity. On the basis of the first two, thinking can become complete. At this level, man "duplicates himself not only, as in consciousness, intellectually, but also actively, in reality, and therefore he sees himself in a world that he has created"[23]. Only on the basis of self-criticism can man completely achieve the reasonable unity between his inherent measure and the extrinsic measure of object. This is not a process abandoning subjectivity principle, and contrarily, the active role of subject should be given full play to for the purpose of realizing complete objectivity. This is a process "rationally regulating" the material exchange between man and nature "under conditions most favorable to, and worthy of, their human nature", a process standardizing the extrinsic measure of object with the inherent measure of man, i.e. a process "transforming" the "material measure" in the way most favorable to human nature. This process must bring the initiative of subject into full play, but such initiative is based on self-criticism.

As a result, modern thinking is moving at these three levels. It is relatively independent, and meanwhile is a constituent part of social movement and human development. We must combines thinking with social movement and human development and regard it as a guiding system, feedback system, regulating system, and controlling system for the latter two. The development of social formation is inseparable from the way of thinking, from the self-consciousness of and reflection on the way of thinking. The development of thinking is a crucial measure for the spiritual civilization of human beings, the necessary condition for free and conscious man, and the spiritual leverage for mankind's leap from the realm of necessity to the realm of freedom. Self-consciousness and reflection bring all of these under the consciousness and control of men themselves. Only on this basis can we really arrive at self-knowledge, self-control, autonomy, self-consciousness, and freedom, and not only reflect ourselves in thinking but also see ourselves in the objective activity and the world of objects, thus realizing the high-level unity between object control and self-control.

---

23   ibid., p. 97.

CHAPTER XVII

THE REALM OF NECESSITY AND THE REALM OF FREEDOM: A NEW INTERPRETATION

The development process of society is also the development process of mankind. From the angle of subject, freedom and necessity constitute two poles of human activity, and the relationship between the two constitutes primitive structure of human activity. The development of human society is the process in which men continuously resolve this contradiction and rises from the realm of necessity to the realm of freedom. During this process, after the historical morphologies of "personal dependence" and then "personal independence founded on objective dependence", the development of man will ultimately take on a new historical morphology – the free individuality of man. It will be a very long historical process. The establishment of socialist system brings us to the starting point of it. Promoting the all-around development of man is the essential requirement of socialist society, and communism is the social formation aiming at realizing the free individuality of man.

1 RELATIONSHIP BETWEEN FREEDOM AND NECESSITY: THE PRIMITIVE STRUCTURE OF HUMAN ACTIVITY

Engels had profoundly expounded the relationship between freedom and necessity, "Freedom does not consist in any dreamt-of independence from natural laws, but in the knowledge of these laws, and in the possibility this gives of systematically making them work towards definite ends. This holds good in relation both to the laws of external nature and to those which govern the bodily and mental existence of men themselves – two classes of laws which we can separate from each other at most only in thought but not in reality. Freedom of the will therefore means nothing but the capacity to make decisions with knowledge of the subject. Therefore the freer a man's judgment is in relation to a definite question, the greater is the necessity with which the content of this judgment will be determined; while the uncertainty, founded on ignorance, which seems to make an arbitrary choice among many different and conflicting possible decisions, shows precisely by this that it is not free, that it is controlled by the very object it should itself control. Freedom therefore consists in the control over ourselves and over external nature, a control founded on knowledge of natural necessity."[1]

That is to say, laws or necessity, for one thing, is mandatory to the existence and activity of man, and human activity is impossible to get out of the scope determined by necessity, which is the limit of human freedom; for the other thing, there are many possibilities within the scope determined by necessity, and men are able to know necessity and the scope determined by it, to grasp the possibility space constituted by determinations of this necessity and many possibilities, to make choice among so many possibilities according to their needs and knowledge about necessity, and to actualize these possibilities through practical activity, in order to "control ourselves and external nature" and achieve freedom. This means that freedom opposite to necessity is possible as long as there is cognitive activity, choosing activity and practical activity.

Man is not only a natural being and social being, but also "a conscious species-being". As a natural being, man is from nature, and originally takes on natural attribute; his activity must conform to natural necessity, which does not only control nature, but also restricts the existence of

---

1   *Selected Works of Karl Marx and Friedrich Engels*. 2nd Ed., Vol. 3, pp. 455 – 456.

man. The essence of man as a social being, in its reality, is the ensemble of the social relations, and the activity of man must comply with historical necessity; both social relations and historical necessity does not only restrict the natural attribute of man, but also determines his social attribute. As "a conscious species-being", man is able to understand and grasp necessity, construct a human ideal world on that premise, and change this ideal world into a real existence through his practical activity, thereby arriving at freedom.

Man is a being in practice, and practice constitutes a unique life activity of man. Therefore, in Marx's opinion, only when man makes his life activity "the object of his will and of his consciousness" and forms object consciousness and self-consciousness to grasp the extrinsic measure of object and the inherent measure of man can the activity of man be free. In this sense, freedom is the cognition on necessity and the transformation of world. In other words, we cannot really understand the relationship between freedom and necessity unless starting with practice, this unique life activity of man.

On the one side, practice is the process of man to cause, regulate and control his material exchange with nature through his activity, and meanwhile, such material exchange is carried out among definite social relations and realized during the activity exchange between man and man. For this reason, the practical activity of man is restricted and controlled respectively by natural necessity and historical necessity.

On the other side, practice is the activity of men transforming the world as per their own needs and desires, which, realized by men, govern the activity of men as the purposes of practical activity and in the form of human will. As Marx once said, the result that will be obtained at the completion of labor already exists there at the commencement of the process, as the purpose, in the mind of the practitioner in the form of idea, and "he also realizes a purpose of his own that gives the law to his modus operandi, and to which he must subordinate his will"[2]. In this connection, practice is the conscious purposive activity of man.

That is to say, human activity is both natural and supernatural, both law-compliant and purposive, and both necessary and free. During human activity, purposiveness must be based on law-compliance and included with the content of laws, since simple purposiveness will only

---

2 *Karl Marx and Friedrich Engels*. 1st Chinese Ed., Vol. 23, p. 202.

lead to imaginary freedom; at the same time, law-compliance must be combined with purposiveness and infiltrated with the content of purposiveness, because simple law-compliance will only result in natural necessity lacking of subjectivity and push freedom out of reach.

In this sense, the development of mankind is the process of men to ceaselessly solve the contradiction between freedom and necessity and emancipate themselves from the constraints of nature and society. While talking about the alienation of man and the inverted relationship between subject and object in capitalist society, Marx pointed out that "this process of inversion is a merely historical necessity, a necessity for the development of the forces of production solely from a specific historic point of departure, or basis, but in no way an absolute necessity of production; rather, a vanishing one, and the result and the inherent purpose of this process is to suspend this basis itself, together with this form of the process"[3]. In Engels' eyes, the result of this sublation is that "man, at last the master of his own form of social organization, becomes at the same time the lord over Nature, his own master – free"[4].

2 TRANSFORMATION FROM THE REALM OF NECESSITY TO THE REALM OF FREEDOM

As far as Marx is concerned, nature has the "priority" to human beings, and natural necessity is mandatory to human practical activity; the immediate purpose of material production is to meet the material needs of man so as to maintain and reproduce the life existence of man, and this is also a kind of natural necessity and therefore is mandatory to the practical activity of man. "As labor is a creator of use value, is useful labor, it is a necessary condition, independent of all forms of society, for the existence of the human race; it is an eternal nature-imposed necessity, without which there can be no material exchanges between man and Nature, and therefore no life."[5] "Just as the savage must wrestle with Nature to satisfy his wants, to maintain and reproduce life, so must civilized man, and he must do so in all social formations and under all possible modes of production. With his development this realm of physical necessity expands as a result of his wants; but, at the same time, the forces of production which satisfy these wants also increase."[6]

---

3   *Karl Marx and Friedrich Engels*. 1st Chinese Ed., Vol. 46 (II), p. 361.
4   *Selected Works of Karl Marx and Friedrich Engels*. 2nd Ed., Vol. 3, p. 760.
5   *Karl Marx and Friedrich Engels*. 1st Chinese Ed., Vol. 23, p. 56.
6   *Karl Marx and Friedrich Engels*. 1st Chinese Ed., Vol. 25, p. 926.

It is in this sense that Marx calls in Das Kapital the field of material production "the realm of necessity" of man, and holds that "freedom in this field can only consist in socialized man, the associated producers, rationally regulating their interchange with Nature, bringing it under their common control, instead of being ruled by it as by the blind forces of Nature; and achieving this with the least expenditure of energy and under conditions most favorable to, and worthy of, their human nature. But it nonetheless still remains a realm of necessity"[7]. "In fact, the realm of freedom actually begins only where labor which is determined by necessity and mundane considerations ceases; thus in the very nature of things it lies beyond the sphere of actual material production. ... Beyond it begins that development of human energy which is an end in itself, the true realm of freedom, which, however, can blossom forth only with this realm of necessity as its basis."[8] The words "this" and "beyond" Marx uses here are not simple concepts of space, but historical categories with time meaning, actually referring to the relationship between labor time and free time.

According to Marx, labor time is the time used by mankind to produce material goods for the purpose of maintaining and reproducing life; free time is the time that can be disposed freely, i.e. the time used for the production of non-material goods like science, art, philosophy, and so on. When the productive forces in society have developed to a certain degree, the laborer is able to provide surplus labor for society beyond his needs, namely that the labor time of laborer can be divided into necessary labor time and surplus labor time; then human beings no longer need to spend all time on the production of material goods, and may spare some time to carry out non-material production in science, art, philosophy, etc., that is to say, man has had free time.

The emergence of free time on the basis of surplus labor has a decisive significance for the development of human beings. As Marx said, "The whole of human development, so far as it extends beyond the development directly necessary for the natural existence of human beings, consists merely in the employment of this free time and presupposes it as its necessary basis."[9] Only with free time can human beings develop. The realm of freedom is built up depending on the free time.

---

7   ibid., pp. 926 – 927.
8   Ibid., pp. 926 – 927.
9   *Karl Marx and Friedrich Engels*. 1st Chinese Ed., Vol. 47, p. 216.

That is to say, the realm of necessity and the realm of freedom are historical categories reflecting the development process of human society, the categories revealing the essential features of different social formations. From Marx's point of view, the realm of necessity refers to the social formation in which mankind is governed by the natural necessity for maintaining existence and consequently by the materialized social relations, namely the social formation in which object control man; the realm of freedom means the social formation in which human beings commonly control the material production activity and thereby consciously govern social relations and the relationship between man and nature, namely the social formation in which object is controlled by man. In primitive society, men had to spend all time on material production for subsistence, so the whole human beings lived in "the realm of necessity". In class society, "All emancipation carried through hitherto has been based, however, on restricted productive forces. The production which these productive forces could provide was insufficient for the whole of society and made development possible only if some persons satisfied their needs at the expense of others, and therefore some – the minority – obtained the monopoly of development, while others – the majority – owing to the constant struggle to satisfy their most essential needs, were for the time being (i.e., until the creation of new revolutionary productive forces) excluded from any development. Thus, society has hitherto always developed within the framework of a contradiction – in antiquity the contradiction between free men and slaves, in the Middle Ages that between nobility and serfs, in modern times that between the bourgeoisie and the proletariat."[10] This means that in class society, the minority get out of the field of material production at the cost of appropriating the surplus labor of the majority, i.e. appropriating the free time of society, whereas the majority are forced to bear the heavy labor burden of the whole society and engaged in material production all their life. In other words, laborers occupying a majority of the population create free time but cannot enjoy free time, and the time disposable to them all becomes labor time, "personified labor-time"[11]. "Historical development, political development, art, science etc. take place in higher circles over their heads."[12] The "higher circles" monopolize the free time and obtain the monopoly of the development of human ability, and the time disposable to the "lower circles" becomes

---

10   *Karl Marx and Friedrich Engels.* 1st Chinese Ed., Vol. 3, p. 507.
11   *Karl Marx and Friedrich Engels.* 1st Chinese Ed., Vol. 23, p. 271.
12   *Karl Marx and Friedrich Engels.* 1st Chinese Ed., Vol. 46 (II), p. 88.

labor time, so they "lose room for intellectual development, for that is time"[13]. In capitalist society, the contradiction between labor time and free time gains its typical form. "Its (capital's) tendency is always, on the one side, to create disposable time, on the other, to convert it into surplus labor."[14]

Thus it is clear that in class society, the opposition between labor time and free time deeply reflects the opposition between the bourgeoisie and the proletariat; the development of exploiting class is premised on the loss of development of laboring class, and the development of general human ability is at the sacrifice of the development of laborers taking up a majority of the population. Except primitive society, other social formations have developed within the framework of contradiction, and so far human beings have been living in the realm of necessity on the whole.

Human beings cannot arrive at the realm of freedom until the productive forces are greatly improved and highly developed, the private ownership is eliminated, man becomes the real conscious master of his own social organization and the lord of the relationship between him and nature, and society is able to supply physical means and free time enough for the all-around development of all members. "With the seizing of the means of production by society, production of commodities is done away with, and, simultaneously, the mastery of the product over the producer. Anarchy in social production is replaced by systematic, definite organization. The struggle for individual existence disappears. Then, for the first time, man, in a certain sense, is finally marked off from the rest of the animal kingdom, and emerges from mere animal conditions of existence into really human ones. The whole sphere of the conditions of life which environ man, and which have hitherto ruled man, now comes under the dominion and control of man, who for the first time becomes the real, conscious lord of nature, because he has now become master of his own social organization. The laws of his own social action, hitherto standing face-to-face with man as laws of Nature foreign to, and dominating him, will then be used with full understanding, and so mastered by him. Man's own social organization, hitherto confronting him as a necessity imposed by Nature and history, now becomes the result of his own free action. The extraneous objective

---

13   *Karl Marx and Friedrich Engels*. 1st Chinese Ed., Vol. 47, p. 344.
14   *Karl Marx and Friedrich Engels*. 1st Chinese Ed., Vol. 46 (II), p. 221.

forces that have, hitherto, governed history, pass under the control of man himself. Only from that time will man himself, more and more consciously, make his own history – only from that time will the social causes set in movement by him have, in the main and in a constantly growing measure, the results intended by him. It is the ascent of man from the kingdom of necessity to the kingdom of freedom."[15]

The transformation from the realm of necessity to the realm of freedom marks the fundamental transformation of the mode of being of human beings. In the realm of necessity, the mode of being of man has been in essence different from that of animals: animals survive relying on instinct but human beings on practical activity. However, the practical activities of individuals are mutually conflicting, and there is still struggle for existence between individual members; the final result always comes out of the mutual conflict between many single wills, and this result can be considered as the product of a force that functions unconsciously and involuntarily as a whole. To put it another way, mankind conducts activity consciously and purposively in individual and partial fields, but is living blindly and spontaneously on the whole. In this sense, the mode of being of human beings is similar to that of animals. After the transformation from the realm of necessity to the realm of freedom, man can emerge from mere animal conditions of existence into really human ones.

The transformation from the realm of necessity to the realm of freedom means the fundamental transformation of the goal of social development. In the realm of necessity, men have to set the growth of material wealth as the highest goal of social development, and material production becomes the central sphere of human activity, which is determined by the material needs of man, or to say, by the natural law of "struggle for existence" applicable to the whole biological world. So at this historical stage, "production is the aim of man and wealth the aim of production"[16]. The activity of man, the same with the instruments of production, is taken as the means for the increase of material wealth. The value coordinates of social development cannot take a fundamental change until it enters the realm of freedom – the goal will be transformed from the growth of material wealth to the all-around development of man, really people-oriented. Then, material production will be

---

15   *Selected Works of Karl Marx and Friedrich Engels.* 2nd Ed., Vol. 3, pp. 633 – 634.
16   *Karl Marx and Friedrich Engels.* 1st Chinese Ed., Vol. 46 (I), p. 486.

converted, merely as the means of livelihood of man, into the inner need of the self-development of man. The transformation from the realm of necessity to the realm of freedom means the thorough emancipation of human race, so that every man can get an all-around and free development. In the realm of necessity, most of the social members undertake the material production activity for maintaining human existence, and only a minority of the social members has the opportunity of all-around development. In such case, society is developing at the sacrifice of the development of majority; in other words, the development of the minority is at the cost of the loss of development of the majority. In the realm of freedom, "the free development of each is the condition for the free development of all"[17]; since everyone has the opportunity for all-around free development, all human beings are thoroughly emancipated. Promoting the all-around development of man is the essential requirement of socialist society, and communist society is "a society in which the full and free development of every individual forms the ruling principle"[18].

3 DEVELOPMENT FROM ONE-SIDED MAN INTO ALL-AROUND MAN

The process of the transformation from the realm of necessity to the realm of freedom is also the process of the transformation from the personal dependence and the personal independence founded on objective dependence to the free individuality of man. Marx points out, "Relations of personal dependence (entirely spontaneous at the outset) are the first social forms, in which human productive capacity develops only to a slight extent and at isolated points. Personal independence founded on objective dependence is the second great form, in which a system of general social metabolism, of universal relations, of all-round needs and universal capacities is formed for the first time. Free individuality, based on the universal development of individuals and on their subordination of their communal, social productivity as their social wealth, is the third stage."[19]

The stage during which personal dependence is dominated is corresponding to the natural economic form in social development. In this historical form, an individual is not an independent man, but a member

17   *Selected Works of Karl Marx and Friedrich Engels.* 2nd Ed., Vol. 1, p. 294.
18   *Karl Marx and Friedrich Engels.* 1st Chinese Ed., Vol. 23, p. 649.
19   *Karl Marx and Friedrich Engels.* 1st Chinese Ed., Vol. 46 (I), p. 104.

of a certain natural community, directly dependent on this community. "The further back we trace the course of history, the more does the individual, and accordingly also the producing individual, appear to be dependent and to belong to a larger whole."[20] The personal dependence on natural community is concretely reflected by the subordination of individual to the representative of natural community, and social relations established based on patriarchal hierarchy within the natural community produce the general personal dependence. Every social member in such a relation is neither independent nor free.

The stage of the personal independence founded on objective dependence is corresponding to the commodity economic form in social development. In this historical form, individual shakes off personal dependence and becomes independent. However, such independence is founded on objective dependence, and the social relation between man and man is opposite to individual in the form of the relation with alien object; individual cannot obtain independence unless he grasps capital. In this sense, Marx thinks that in such a social formation, "capital is independent and has individuality, while the living person is dependent and has no individuality"[21].

According to Marx, the development of productive forces to a certain degree brings about surplus products on the one side and social divisions of labor on the other. The division of labor makes it possible for material activity and spiritual activity, labor and enjoyment, and production and consumption to be shared by different persons, and the emergence of surplus products makes this possibility a reality. In addition, "As long as a cleavage exists between the particular and the common interest, as long, therefore, as activity is not voluntarily, but naturally, divided, man's own deed becomes an alien power opposed to him, which enslaves him instead of being controlled by him"[22]. The social power arising out of the activity of men in turn becomes "an alien force existing outside them", "opposed to" them, and enslaves and dominates them, which is the alienation of man.

The alienation of man has appeared since human beings enter into the civilized society. In the social form of "personal dependence", individual has no independence, and laborer is just taken as a natural condition

20 *Karl Marx and Friedrich Engels*. 1st Chinese Ed., Vol. 46 (I), p. 21.
21 *Selected Works of Karl Marx and Friedrich Engels*. 2nd Ed., Vol. 1, p. 287.
22 ibid. p. 85.

of labor. As Marx said, "in the relationship of slavery and serfdom there is no such separation; what happens is that one part of society is treated by another as the mere inorganic and natural condition of its own reproduction. The slave stands in no sort of relation to the objective conditions of his labor. It is rather labor itself, both in the form of the slave as of the serf, which is placed among the other living things as inorganic condition of production, alongside the cattle or as an appendage of the soil"[23]. Thus the relation between a part of men and the other part is alienated as the relation between man and thing, that is, the laborer is taken as a thing (a natural condition of labor) appropriated and controlled by the exploiter who does not work. For labor and laborer, this is alienation; nevertheless, such alienation only happens to a part of members in society but not to everyone.

At the historical stage of personal independence founded on objective dependence, the social relation between man and man becomes commodity relation, and money is the medium for commodity exchange between man and man, so the social relation between man and man is materialized as money relation. In other words, the immediate purpose of personal labor is to get money, and the needs of individual must be satisfied by purchasing commodity with money; the social dependence between man and man is converted into the dependence on money, which turns into the materialized form of the social relation between man and man.

Originally, such a materialized social relation is the product of men's intercourse, but after it comes into being, it becomes an external relation for every individual, and dominates the destiny of individual as "an alien force existing outside", rendering individual "incidental individual" manipulated by external factors. From the perspective of classes, the working class is not only governed by money as a materialized social relation but also exploited by capital as another materialized social relation; from the view of individual, every individual is governed and dominated respectively by money and capital as materialized social relations. "Capital is a collective product, and only by the united action of many members, nay, in the last resort, only by the united action of all members of society, can it be set in motion."[24] This is a historical stage of general alienation of man.

---

23 *Karl Marx and Friedrich Engels.* 1st Chinese Ed., Vol. 46 (I), p. 488.
24 *Selected Works of Karl Marx and Friedrich Engels.* 2nd Ed., Vol. 1, p. 287.

In the state of the general alienation of man, the development of man enters into the generally one-sided stage, making every individual "one-sided man", "one-dimensional man".

First of all, private ownership and mandatory division of labor fix the activity scope for every individual, thus the development of individual ability becomes one-sided. "For as soon as the distribution of labor comes into being, each man has a particular, exclusive sphere of activity, which is forced upon him and from which he cannot escape. He is a hunter, a fisherman, a herdsman, or a critical critic, and must remain so if he does not want to lose his means of livelihood."[25] Consequently, this historical stage "makes one man into a restricted town-animal, the other into a restricted country-animal", the part of men into mental workers with well developed brain and another part into manual workers with well developed body. The application of machine makes the one-sided development of man more deformed.

Next, in large-scale industry and competition, all the existence conditions and all one-sidedness of man are merged into two simplest forms – private ownership and labor, and man is divided into the man of property and the proletarian, namely the capitalist and the employed laborer. Not only the worker but also the capitalist is unable to develop in a comprehensive way: "the empty-minded bourgeois (is made subject) to his own capital and his own insane craving for profits; the lawyer to his fossilized legal conceptions …; the 'educated classes' in general to their manifold species of local narrow-mindedness and one-sidedness, to their own physical and mental short-sightedness, to their stunted growth due to their narrow specialized education and their being chained for life to this specialized activity"[26]. Private ownership makes man only focus on his difference from society but disregard his connection with society; individual one-sidedly develops his individuality but ignores his sociality.

Finally, the materialized social relations change the social relation between man and man into one-sided pure money relation and the purpose of human activity into one-sidedly and purely pursuing money. "Money is the universal self-established value of all things. It has, therefore, robbed the whole world – both the world of men and nature – of its

---

25   Ibid., p. 85.
26   *Karl Marx and Friedrich Engels.* 1st Chinese Ed., Vol. 20, p. 317.

specific value. Money is the estranged essence of man's work and man's existence, and this alien essence dominates him, and he worships it."[27] Thus, the demand of man becomes one-sided, and all feelings of man becomes the pure feeling of object appropriation; man becomes "one-dimensional man".

The stage of "free individuality based on the universal development of individuals and on their subordination of their communal, social productivity as their social wealth"[28] is corresponding to time economy or product economy in social development. At this historical stage, society is "an association of free men", which is "a real collective", rather than "a false collective", for individuals; social relations haven't dominate man as an alien power any longer, but are brought under the common control of men as a form for the realization of free individuality. Only in such a social community, "[with others has each] individual the means of cultivating his gifts in all directions; only in the community, therefore, is personal freedom possible. In the previous substitutes for the community, in the State, etc. personal freedom has existed only for the individuals who developed within the relationships of the ruling class ... In a real community the individuals obtain their freedom in and through their association"[29]. In this social community, the free development of everyone is the condition for the free development of all.

Sublating the alienation of man for the all-around development of man calls for highly developed productive forces on the one hand, and on the other hand needs the "united individuals" to appropriate the ensemble of productive forces and eliminate private ownership, thereby putting the productive forces of society under the common control of men instead of being governed by them as a blind power. Only in this way can man abandon the alienation of man, achieve the universal development of man, and create the free individuality of man.

We should understand that the alienation of man does not mean the transformation to nonhuman nature, but is caused by the fact that men have not created highly developed productive forces of society and universal social relations and not brought such productive forces and social relations under their conscious control; the all-around development of man is not the return to human nature, or the regaining of the universal

---

27 *Karl Marx and Friedrich Engels*. 1st Chinese Ed., Vol. 1, p. 448.
28 *Karl Marx and Friedrich Engels*. 1st Chinese Ed., Vol. 46 (I), p. 104.
29 *Selected Works of Karl Marx and Friedrich Engels*. 2nd Ed., Vol. 1, p. 119.

essence of man; instead, it is the creation and appropriation of man's essence in all directions by creating highly developed productive forces of society and universal social relations, and the realization of man's free individuality through reasonable application of the free time by all social members. Practice is the mode of being of man, and the human essence, in its reality, is the ensemble of the social relations. The all-roundness of human development, in the final analysis, rests with the universality respectively of the development of practice and the social relations. As Marx mentioned, "not an ideal or imagined universality of the individual, but the universality of his real and ideal relations"[30].

4 TIME: THE MEASURE AND DEVELOPMENT SPACE OF HUMAN LIFE

Different from early modern science, early modern philosophy and ancient philosophy, Marx conceives time starting from real man and his activity, emphasizing that "time is the active existence of man", i.e. the significance and value of time for the existence of man, and clearly pointing out that "time is in fact the active existence of the human being; it is not only the measure of human life; it is the space for its development"[31]. The reason why time can be regarded as the measure and development space of human life is because it can reflect the characteristics and value of human life. To be specific, man is able to reduce the time of activity that cannot reflect the nature and development requirement of his life and increase the time of activity that can embody such nature and development requirement based on his own standards, thereby creating conditions for the realization of the meaning of his life.

The measure of human life, time, is manifested as the generation of the value of human life. In biology, man tends to be investigated as a life phenomenon "in the same category" of animals, but in fact the life phenomenon of man is essentially different from that of the animal. "The animal is immediately one with its life activity. It does not distinguish itself from it. It is its life activity. Man makes his life activity itself the object of his will and of his consciousness. He has conscious life activity." "Conscious life activity distinguishes man immediately from animal life activity."[32]

---

30   *Karl Marx and Friedrich Engels.* 1st Chinese Ed., Vol. 46 (II), p. 36.
31   *Karl Marx and Friedrich Engels.* 1st Chinese Ed., Vol. 47, p. 532.
32   *Karl Marx and Friedrich Engels.* 1st Chinese Ed., Vol. 42, p. 96.

Specifically speaking, the life activity of animal shows the essence of a "species", whilst the life activity of man reflects the essence of "species-character". The essence of animal is immediately identical with its life activity, and animals have gotten their essence since they get their lives. The character of animal species is a naturally endowed innate determination in no direct relation with the postnatal activity of animal. Man is "a being that treats the species as his own essential being, or that treats itself as a species-being"[33]. As the existence character of man, "species" is where the essence of man consists in, highlighting the postnatal generation of human essence. "In creating a world of objects by his personal activity, in his work upon inorganic nature, man proves himself a conscious species-being"[34].

The "conscious species-being" is able to make his life activity "the object of his will and of his consciousness", and to uniformly transform and create the world in compliance with "species standard" and "human measure". As Marx said, "an animal forms only in accordance with the standard and the need of the species to which it belongs, whilst man knows how to produce in accordance with the standard of every species, and knows how to apply everywhere the inherent standard to the object"[35]. Therefore, man is the dominator of his life activity and becomes "an active being" beyond the measure of natural life in time.

The life activity of man, differing from the "existence" activity of animal, is the "living" activity unique to man, the activity in which man "makes his life activity itself the object of his will and of his consciousness". It is in such an activity that the problem of life measure arises, i.e. the question that whether the life activity of man has value or not. In my eyes, the reason why Marx stresses that "an animal forms only in accordance with the standard and the need of the species to which it belongs, whilst man knows how to produce in accordance with the standard of every species", and knows to measure the object with his inherent standard anytime and anywhere, "therefore also forms objects in accordance with the laws of beauty"[36] is for the purpose of showing that only after getting the "value life" and transcending the natural life can man be called "man". Regarding time as the "measure" of human life does not mean regarding it as the "length" of human life. The

33 ibid., p. 96.
34 ibid., p. 97.
35 ibid., p. 97.
36 ibid., 97.

fundamental defect of the opinion conceiving time as the "length" of human life is that it fails to realize the essential difference between human life and other ordinary lives and merely conceives man from the nature of things, from the predefined, give, absolutely unchanged aspect, and it actually conceives man as animal.

"Labor time itself exists as such only subjectively, only in the form of activity."[37] The reason why time can be the life measure and active existence of man roots in the practical activity of man, first of all, labor. It is labor constitutes the noumenon of the value of human life and makes time the active existence of man. As the life measure and active existence of man, time obtains its reality to man and becomes a form of human activity during practical activity.

Since time exists in the form of human activity, the space of human activity will inevitably expand along with the development and differentiation of practical activity. As productive forces develop, the activity of man is gradually differentiated: intercourse activity is differentiated from production activity, spiritual intercourse from material intercourse … new fields of activity are being differentiated from every kind of activity. Such a continuous differentiation of activity and continuous expansion of activity fields will certainly give rise to continuous space expansion of human activity and development. Each activity differentiation and intercourse expansion also means the generation of new relation between man and nature and the establishment of new social relation between man and man, in short, the establishment of new activity and development space for man.

As far as Marx is concerned, the amount of free time immediately determines the scale of the development space for man, but free time is immediately and quantitatively dependent on surplus labor time; "surplus labor is on the one hand the basis of society's free time, and on the other hand, by virtue of this, the material basis of its whole development and of civilization in general"[38]. To develop productive forces and raise labor productivity is in effect to shorten necessary labor time and increase free time in a bid to expand the activity and development space of man. For individuals, the increase of free time in fact provides them a new stage of activity, and the larger the stage is, the greater the possibility is

---

37   *Karl Marx and Friedrich Engels*. 1st Chinese Ed., Vol. 46 (I), p. 118.
38   *Karl Marx and Friedrich Engels*. 1st Chinese Ed., Vol. 47, p. 257.

for their development; as to the human being, the development of entire human beings is no other than the application of free time, and the whole society cannot make greater progress and the human capability cannot have greater development unless there is more free time.

"Just as in the case of an individual, the multiplicity of its development, its enjoyment and its activity depends on economization of time. Economy of time, to this all economy ultimately reduces itself."[39] For this reason, the law of the economy of time is "the first economic law" for regulating social life. This law will not disappear due to the change of social system, and what can be changed is just the social form for its realization. "Economy of time, along with the planned distribution of labor time among the various branches of production, remains the first economic law on the basis of communal production"[40]. The primary significance of time factor in the human development is precisely determined by the primacy of this law, that is to say, the law of the economy of time is also a primary law of human development. Economizing labor time by raising labor productivity is actually creating the development space for man.

In the class society, the creation and appropriation of free time are not unified but opposite on the contrary. "The free time of society is produced through the production of unfree time, the labor time of workers prolonged beyond that required for their own subsistence. Free time on the one side corresponds to subjugated time on the other side"[41]. Private ownership and old division of labor force laborers to bear the heavy labor burden of the whole society. They create free time but cannot enjoy free time, and do not obtain corresponding development space; however, those social members who do not work appropriate and control the free time by seizing surplus labor relying on their ownership of the means of production, thus acquiring corresponding development space.

In other words, in the class society, the development of the minority is based on depriving the laborers – the majority – of surplus labor time and free time and at the cost of no development or one-sided development of the majority. The separation between creation and appropriation of free time reaches an extreme degree in capitalist society. From Marx's point of view, labor is the sole fountainhead of value, and the surplus

39 *Karl Marx and Friedrich Engels.* 1st Chinese Ed., Vol. 46 (I), p. 120.
40 *Karl Marx and Friedrich Engels.* 1st Chinese Ed., Vol. 46 (I), p. 120.
41 *Karl Marx and Friedrich Engels.* 1st Chinese Ed., Vol. 47, pp. 216 – 217.

labor of workers produces surplus labor time and free time; however, such free time is not appropriated and controlled by the working class in capitalist society. "What appears as surplus value on capital's side appears identically on the worker's side as surplus labor in excess of his requirements as worker, hence in excess of his immediate requirements for keeping himself alive."[42] Surplus product "simultaneously provides free time, gives them (all the classes apart from the working classes) disposable time for the development of their other capacities. Thus the production of surplus labor time on the one side is at once the production of free time on the other. The whole of human development, so far as it extends beyond the development directly necessary for the natural existence of human beings, consists merely in the employment of this free time and presupposes it as its necessary basis"[43].

The essence and goal of human emancipation is the realization of all-around free development of human beings; however, for the purpose of human emancipation and all-around free development, free time must be passed under the appropriation and control of the united individuals. "All free time is the time available for free development," and the free development of man is "beyond the development directly necessary for the natural existence of human beings". The free activity supporting free development and producing free time is no longer the spontaneous activity maintaining "pure existence" and reflecting the "natural necessity" of man's existence, but the conscious activity of man to develop his ability and appropriate his universal essence.

In the sight of Marx, to translate from spontaneous activity to "free and conscious activity", namely active activity, "the shortening of the working-day is its basic prerequisite"[44]. "The shortening of working-day" provides sufficient free time that is appropriated and controlled by the united individuals, ultimately transforming labor from a way of man to survive into the purpose of life and thereby realizing the revolutionary change in the meaning of labor. This revolutionary change will eliminate the alienated labor, achieve the free development of all conditioned on the free development of each, and ultimately realize the emancipation of the working class and whole human beings. "On the one hand, no individual can throw on the shoulders of others his share in productive labor, this natural condition of human existence; and in

42   *Karl Marx and Friedrich Engels*. 1st Chinese Ed., Vol. 46 (I), p. 287.
43   *Karl Marx and Friedrich Engels*. 1st Chinese Ed., Vol. 47, p. 216.
44   *Karl Marx and Friedrich Engels*. 1st Chinese Ed., Vol. 25, p. 927.

which, on the other hand, productive labor, instead of being a means of subjugating men, will become a means of their emancipation, by offering each individual the opportunity to develop all his faculties, physical and mental, in all directions and exercise them to the full"[45].

It is thus evident that in Marxist philosophy, time is not an abstract category unrelated to real man and his activity, but a theory immediately concerning the emancipation of the working class and human beings, as well as the realization of all-around free development of man. Or we can say that in Marxist philosophy, "time" is closely associated with and fused into the emancipation of the working class and human beings and the all-around free development of man. Therefore we should, and must, reinterpret the theory of time of Marx.

---

45   *Karl Marx and Friedrich Engels*. 1st Chinese Ed., Vol. 20, p. 318.

PART TWO

CHAPTER I

TWO SCHOOLS OF FRENCH MATERIALISM AND THE ENLIGHTENMENT THEREOF

France was in a turbulent and changeable situation in the eighteenth century. Kant asserted that that was an age of critique. Cassirer thought it was an age of reason. In my eyes, it was an age when reason was loaded with critique. French materialism emerging in that era, depending on distinctive reflective spirit, critical attitude and enlightening thought, sufficiently showed its own theoretical appearance, and took an indelible part in the history of human philosophy. However, French materialism is misunderstood and distorted from different aspects. Generally, French materialism in the eighteenth century (hereinafter referred to as "French materialism") is called mechanical materialism or metaphysical materialism. But there are actually two schools in French materialism, namely mechanical materialism and humanistic materialism, both having different theoretical features, sources and destinations. Thus we are enlightened to take a new look at the historical morphologies of materialism and rethink the theoretical space of historical materialism.

1 THE SCHOOL OF MECHANICAL MATERIALISM IN FRENCH MATERIALISM

When the human history entered the eighteenth century, "real beings and earthly things began to be the centre of all interest"[1] in the wake of the development of anti-feudalism and anti-religion struggles, and man started to attract the attention. In general, what French materialism is concerned with is the problems of man, and extends from the reflection on man to the critique of existing society. Hegel believed that French materialism had "negative side, as to everything else", "the attack of reasoning instinct against a condition of degeneracy"[2]. However, the key point is not whether man is studied, but how man is studied. In the process of studying man, French materialism was bifurcated into mechanical materialism and "real humanism", i.e. humanistic materialism, both having different theoretical sources and destinations. Marx points out:

"There are two trends in French materialism; one traces its origin to Descartes, the other to Locke. The latter is mainly a French development and leads directly to socialism. The former, mechanical materialism, merges with French natural science proper."[3]

As a matter of fact, the school of mechanical materialism originated from two sources, scientifically from the classical mechanics of Newton and philosophically from the natural philosophy of Descartes. In other words, the school of mechanical materialism, represented by La Mettrie, was formed in French materialism under the dual influence of Newton and Descartes, or to say, science and philosophy at that time.

The classical mechanics of Newton made a great success from the seventeenth century to the eighteenth century, and established two mature principles of natural science: one was the principle of repeatability, namely that the world submitted to the system of mechanical laws, and repeatability was the fundamental feature of the mechanical laws and even the overall natural laws; the other was the principle of precision, namely that the laws governing the world could not only be known, but also be grasped with precise relations of quantities. The belief of

---

1　*Karl Marx and Friedrich Engels.* 1st Chinese Ed., Vol. 2, pp. 161 – 162.
2　Hegel, *Lectures on the History of Philosophy.* Beijing: The Commercial Press, 1978: Vol. 4, p. 222.
3　*Karl Marx and Friedrich Engels.* 1st Chinese Ed., Vol. 2, p. 160.

Newton was accepted by French scientists in the eighteenth century; besides, through the systematic introduction by philosopher Voltaire, the scientific thought and philosophical idea of Newton had enjoyed a very high reputation in France in the eighteenth century. The strong emotion of scientism and rationalism created by it stimulated quite a lot of scientists, including French materialists, to introduce the idea of natural laws directly into the social domain, or to restore society and man back to nature.

Generally, natural science has no intention of flattering philosophy, but it tends to determine the appearance of philosophy. The success of the classical mechanics of Newton imposed allure, pressure, and power all in all, on French philosophers. It was the power of science that called a large batch of French philosophers together under the banner of scientism, conceiving nature, society and man himself with the viewpoints of mechanism. The success of the classical mechanics of Newton constituted the general theoretical background of the French philosophical revolution and the formation of mechanical materialism in the eighteenth century.

With its scientific source traced to Newtonian mechanics of Britain, mechanical materialism traces its philosophical origin to the philosophy of Descartes, in which the nature of substances is extension, and the feature of motions is displacement. Descartes "constructed the whole physical world" relying on abstract substances and abstract motions, and constantly advocated using the terms of mechanism to interpret natural phenomena. Descartes, in fact, applied the principles of mechanics obtained on the ground to celestial phenomena and even the whole world on the basis of the laws of mechanical motion, thereby drawing a picture of mechanical materialistic world with the significance of anti-religious theology.

The study of Descartes on nature "by feat of the concepts of mechanism" "made natural philosophy take on an entirely new look, and he had put forward a new world outlook arising out of independent spirit and embracing the whole nature"[4]. The evaluation of Feuerbach is quire fair. Cartesian natural philosophy paved the way for anti-religious theology in early modern times, laid a new theoretical foundation for

---

4   *Selected Works of Philosophical History of Feuerbach*. Beijing: The Commercial Press, 1984: Vol. 1, p. 202.

the further development of French materialism, and exerted an influ-ence until the times of La Mettrie. Meanwhile, it unavoidably restricted French materialism, keeping it at the level of mechanism. In fact, it was Descartes that transplanted the idea of mechanism in natural science into philosophy and created mechanical spirit of the times.

La Mettrie spoke highly of Newton and Descartes, arguing that "without him the field of philosophy might perhaps still be waste land, like the field of right thinking without Newton"[5]. Marx thus thought La Mettrie "makes use of Descartes' physics in detail. His *L'homme machine* is a treatise after the model of Descartes' animal-machine."[6] Indeed, it was Descartes' ideas that "world is machine" and "animal is machine" that lead La Mettrie into a world view of both materialism and mechanism. Along Descartes' train of thought of "animal-machine", he brought for-ward the thought of "man-machine", and also deepened the opinion of Descartes. La Mettrie believed substances also had sentience and men-tioned sensation in the same breath with extension and motion, together as the basic attributes of substance.

Based on that, La Mettrie further pointed out that the basic unit of man and animal was atom; the two were similar in structures and modes of functioning but different in quantity, not in quality. In his book *Discourse On Happiness*, La Mettrie explicitly pointed out, "The struc-ture of atoms composes man, the motion of atoms pushes man forward; atoms, independent on the conditions of man, determine the proper-ties of man and guide his destiny." As a result, "man is machine". La Mettrie actually applied Descartes' theory of animal structure to human body, and totally investigated man and man's essence from the view of mechanism. That enraged Lange, a new Kantian, who once used vi-cious words and denounced La Mettrie as the worst French materialist.

But the fact was that Lange lacked of the consciousness of historicism and did not apprehend all connotations of La Mettrie's opinion. As far as I'm concerned, the opinion of "man-machine" has double connota-tions: it is backed on the thought of material unity of the world, and it has the significance of anti-religious theology. Fundamentally speak-ing, the opinion of "man-machine" underscores natural man. It is both a natural scientific study on man and a kind of ideology claiming the

5   *French Philosophy in the Eighteenth Century*, compiled by the Department of Philosophy, Peking University, p. 271.
6   *Karl Marx and Friedrich Engels*. 1st Chinese Ed., Vol. 2, p. 166.

dignity, value and heaven-born power of man. By means of natural man, La Mettrie emancipated man from the entanglement of religious theology and made man obtain natural independence; however, because the horizon of La Mettrie was limited by mechanism, man, who was just emancipated from the pressure of theocracy, was turned into a machine, dissolving both man and man's subjectivity.

This indicates us that philosophy does not equal politics, but it indeed contains politics. The philosophical proposition formally appears to be abstract and otherworldly, but once it is put into a political background in connection with it, its distinct political feature will show up vividly. That is to say, the theoretical meaning of a philosophical proposition is not equivalent to its political effect. The same philosophical proposition will have different political effects under different historical conditions. An ordinary and even wrong philosophical proposition may have an unexpected huge political effect under a specific historical condition and in combination with definite social group, so does the proposition of "man-machine" of La Mettrie. While investigating a philosophical proposition, we should correctly grasp the relationship respectively between its scientific connotation and ideology and between its theoretical meaning and political effect.

Of course, I notice that mechanical materialism originating from Descartes played a promoting role in the natural science development at that time, and its theoretical destination was natural science. That was because Descartes studied nature with the "explicit concepts" of natural science and discovered some natural laws, "laying a foundation for subsequent invention and correction"[7], and "providing the framework and foundation for natural science"[8]. In this sense, Marx thinks that Cartesian materialism, as well as mechanical materialism formed on this basis, "passes into natural science proper"[9].

---

7   *Selected Works of Philosophical History of Feuerbach.* Vol. 1, p. 202.
8   Selected Works of Philosophical History of Feuerbach. Beijing: The Commercial Press, 1984: Vol. 3, p. 123.
9   *Karl Marx and Friedrich Engels.* 1st Chinese Ed., Vol. 2, p. 166.

2 THE SCHOOL OF HUMANISTIC MATERIALISM IN FRENCH MATERIALISM

The other school in French materialism is "real humanism"[10], i.e. humanistic materialism, which traces its theoretical origin to Locke's philosophy and is represented by Helvetius.

As mentioned above, the school of mechanical materialism stems from local Cartesian philosophy, which has obvious limitations, not only reflected by its system of dualism but also by Descartes' confinement of the anti-feudal struggle within the scope of thought. Descartes had ever clearly pointed out that his "maxim was to try always to master myself rather than fortune, and change my desires rather than changing how things stand in the world"[11]. Evidently, this opinion is incompatible with the philosophy of materialism as the precursor of the political transformation in France. French materialism belongs to the category of the philosophy of enlightenment. "The basic tendency and main effort of the philosophy of the enlightenment is not reflecting and depicting life" but is "molding life itself", and its "mission does not only lie in the analysis and dissection of the order of the things that it deems as necessity, but also in the production of such order, thereby proving its reality and truth"[12].

Hence, the other part of French philosophers hoped to find a doctrine that could be used as the basis for French revolution. Thus they turned their eyes to Britain at the other side of the strait, because capitalism in Britain at that time was leading the continent of Europe, and new spirits of times always emerged firstly in Britain. Then, the breeze of British philosophy blew across the English Channel and reached France – Locke's philosophy was introduced into France. That import was warmly welcomed by the bourgeoisie of France just like they were welcoming a "long-expected guest". In the eyes of French philosophers, they could reach the conclusion of transforming environment and society by starting from Locke's philosophy, thus the materialistic empiricism of Locke could be taken as the philosophical basis for French revolution.

---

10   ibid., pp. 167 – 168.

11   *Philosophies in Western European Countries during the Sixteenth Century – the Eighteenth Century*, compiled by the Department of Philosophy, Peking University. Beijing: The Commercial Press, 1975: p. 146.

12   Cassirer, *The Philosophy of the Enlightenment*. Jinan: Shandong People's Publishing House, 1988: p. 4.

Locke is a turning point in the history of western philosophy. Since Locke, the western philosophy consciously turned from nature to man and his inner life. Fundamentally, man is first of all doing activity, rather than thinking, but man does not only do activity, but also is conscious of this fact; the existence, activity and other different aspects of man are all visualized by the consciousness of man. The issue of man himself is immediately shown as the problem of human consciousness and self-consciousness. So the study of early modern western philosophy on man was first manifested as an "epistemological turn". Locke's philosophy precisely adapted to such necessity: it discussed the origin and boundary of cognition and the certainty of knowledge on the premise of thoroughly investigating the cognitive ability of man, and centrally and systematically criticized "the theory of innate ideas" from two aspects – epistemology and moral practice.

According to Locke, there are no innate ideas for either speculative reason or practical reason, and moral idea results from education and environment; society is not natural, but is created by men; the natural tendency of hedonism of man is directed to man's interests, whose realization needs society and moral principle as the tie of society maintenance. Therefore man creates society and moral principle according to his interests. It can be found that opposing to religious theology, affirming the sensuousness of man, and raising the status of individual are the significance of Locke's critique on "the theory of innate ideas". His opinion obviously has both important epistemological significance and political connotation.

Locke's materialistic empiricism deeply touched the heart of Helvetius with its double meaning, namely epistemological character and political connotation, and directly became the starting point and forerunner of Helvetius' materialism. Marx pointed out, "In Helvetius, who also based himself on Locke, materialism assumed a really French character."[13] Man became the topic especially focused on and meticulously studied by Helvetius, who raised and resolved the questions of philosophy revolving around man and centered all the questions on the issue of how man could enjoy a happy life. "Philosophers study man, and the object is the happiness of man, which hinges not only on the laws governing man's life, but also on the education man receives."[14]. If we say

13   *Karl Marx and Friedrich Engels*. 1st Chinese Ed., Vol. 2, p. 165.
14   *French Philosophy in the Eighteenth Century*, compiled by the Department of Philosophy, Peking University, p. 478.

La Mettrie studied man mainly based on the relationship between man and nature, then Helvetius was majorly based on the relationship between man and society. That's why Marx thought Helvetius "conceived it (materialism) immediately in its application to social life"[15].

Based on Locke's philosophy, Helvetius mainly extracted the concept of "sensation" from the materialistic empiricism of Locke, and regarded sensation as the mode of being of man, namely that "I sense, therefore I am". In accordance with the belief of Helvetius on the basis of Locke's viewpoint, sensation is the bridge linking consciousness and the outside objective world, and through sensation, man continuously cognizes the external world, and forms and develops his own sensation and knowledge on the one hand, and on the other hand, translates his desire and requirement for freedom inside his heart into the external activity of fight for freedom. In other words, with materialistic sensualism, freedom is no longer pursued in the inherent spirit, but in the external environment, in the activity changing the external environment.

According to the first aspect, Helvetius reached the conclusion that "man is the product of environment", and according to the second, he proposed the proposition that "opinion dominates environment". What he laid stress on was social environment, different from the natural environment emphasized by Montesquieu. By putting forward those two propositions, he aimed to prove such a truth that men's intelligences were naturally equal, and the character of man was subject to the external environment, so to transform man, the external social environment must be transformed first. Just as Marx said, "if man is shaped by environment, his environment must be made human"[16].

In that way, through the transformation of Helvetius, Locke's materialistic empiricism, the breeze of philosophy from Britain mingled with the drizzle of politics, together with the humanistic materialism of Helvetius like heavy rain and wind, aroused a huge storm in France. Thanks to them, French revolution found its philosophical basis, and "logical foundation" was laid for utopian socialism later.

It is generally believed that the two propositions simultaneously brought forward by Helvetius, namely that "man is the product of environment" and "opinion dominates environment", are logically

15 *Karl Marx and Friedrich Engels.* 1st Chinese Ed., Vol. 2, p. 165.
16 ibid., p. 167.

contradictory and viciously circular, sinking into "antinomy". This is in effect a misunderstanding. Man and environment are indeed in interaction with each other: "circumstances make men just as much as men make circumstances"[17]. So the two propositions simultaneously raised by Helvetius actually reveal the interaction between man and environment, and they are a naive viewpoint of interaction.

Interaction exists in all aspects in social life. "Only starting from the general interaction can we reach causality in reality."[18] Historical materialism definitely does not rule out interaction, but requires to give reasonable interpretation on interaction; it definitely does not abolish interaction, but requires to find out the foundation of interaction. The opinion on interaction of "reasonable form" is an internal principle of, and the dialectical logic required by, historical materialism. From my view, the error of Helvetius does not consist in his simultaneous proposal of the two propositions that "man is the product of environment" and "opinion dominates environment", but in his stay at the interaction between man and environment instead of further exploration into the "third party" that both determines social and environmental development and will development; consequently, he failed to find out the foundation of the interaction between man and environment.

The superiority of Marx is that he does not only see the interaction between man and environment, but also discovers the foundation of this interaction, that is, the practical activity of man, thus he transcends the naive opinion of interaction and gives a reasonable interpretation on the interaction between man and environment. "The coincidence of the changing of circumstances and of human activity or self-changing can be conceived and rationally understood only as revolutionary practice."[19]

With regard to theoretical destination, the "real humanism" represented by Helvetius "leads directly to socialism" "directly to ... communism"[20] It is because further studying the theory of Helvetius will inevitably obtain "logical foundation" for socialism and communism. Marx points out that "if man draws all his knowledge, sensation, etc., from the world of the senses and the experience gained in it, then what has to be done is

17 *Selected Works of Karl Marx and Friedrich Engels.* 2nd Ed., Vol. 1, p. 92.
18 *Selected Works of Karl Marx and Friedrich Engels.* 2nd Ed., Vol. 4, p. 328.
19 *Selected Works of Karl Marx and Friedrich Engels.* 2nd Ed., Vol. 1, p. 55.
20 Karl Marx and Friedrich Engels. 1st Chinese Ed., Vol. 2, pp. 160 and 166.

to arrange the empirical world in such a way that man experiences and becomes accustomed to what is truly human in it and that he becomes aware of himself as man", so "there is no need for any great penetration to see from the teaching of materialism on the original goodness and equal intellectual endowment of men, the omnipotence of experience, habit and education, and the influence of environment on man, the great significance of industry, the justification of enjoyment, etc., how necessarily materialism is connected with communism and socialism"[21].

The communism or socialism mentioned by Marx here majorly refers to utopian socialism in the nineteenth century. But scientific socialism is also theoretically associated with the "real humanism" represented by Helvetius to a certain extent. Just as Engels said, in terms of theoretical form, modern socialism "originally appears ostensibly as a more logical extension of the principles laid down by the great French philosophers of the 18th century"[22].

The humanistic materialism of Helvetius had a significant impact at that time, and Helvetius was praised as "Bacon in moral circle". Famous French writer Stendhal spoke highly of Helvetius' philosophy, thinking "Helvetius has opened a double gate of man for me". In the development history of materialism, Helvetius is a turning point. At the watershed of "real humanism", natural materialism began to decline, and humanistic materialism started to rise.

We can perceive such a historical clue through the two schools of French materialism, that is to say, the study topic of materialistic philosophy is not changeless. If we say the mechanical materialism in French materialism focuses on nature, and in it man is just a form of natural substances, then the school of humanistic materialism is concerned with man himself, with a view to "making environment human". Thus, we are enlightened to restudy the historical morphologies of materialism.

---

21   *Karl Marx and Friedrich Engels.* 1st Chinese Ed., Vol. 2, pp. 166 – 167.
22   *Selected Works of Karl Marx and Friedrich Engels.* 2nd Ed., Vol. 3, p. 719.

3 A NEW LOOK AT THE HISTORICAL MORPHOLOGIES OF MATERIALISM

From traditional standpoint, naive or spontaneous materialism, mechanical or metaphysical materialism, and dialectical materialism are three historical morphologies of materialism, all of which are fundamentally the same with respect to study topic or the theoretical perspective of observing the world, that is to say, the three all take "the whole world" as study object, and the only difference is that naive materialism regards the world as a chaotic whole, metaphysical materialism conceives the world as a static and isolated thing, and dialectical materialism understands the world as a system of substances with universal connections and in eternal development and defines historical materialism as the extension and application of dialectical materialism to the domain of social history. Such a classification has its reasonable factors, but the reasonable factors are dissolved into unreasonable understanding. It ignores the theme transformation in the development course of materialism, and discards the epoch-making contribution of historical materialism to a quite large extent.

Evaluating the essential issue of historical transformation of study theme, the development of materialism goes through three historical stages, forming three historical morphologies, i.e. natural materialism, humanistic materialism and historical materialism.

With its origin traced back to ancient Greek philosophy, natural materialism becomes systematic in the theory of Hobbes, and extends to the mechanical materialism in French materialism. It either seeks for "the unity of all things" based on directly asserting the significance of world itself and reduces the principle of all things to a certain form of natural substances, or based on the empirical study of experimental science on natural phenomena, discusses the unity between man and nature in the process of "epistemological turn" and classifies the material world and man into a certain level of natural substances.

In general, it restores the whole world to a natural substance in the principle of "time priority", and conceives man as a manifestation of natural substance. In natural materialism, substance is considered as "the subject of all changes", and "both man and nature follow the same rules. Power is identical with freedom". It acknowledges material unity of the world, but totally negates the initiative, creativity and subjectivity of man; it studies "the whole world", but does not find a practical standing point for man – the real subject. To put it another way, there is "a vacant land of humanism" in natural materialism. It is because of this that Marx thinks natural materialism is a kind of "pure materialism", and Hobbes had made "materialism takes to misanthropy"[23].

Humanistic materialism originated from the other school of French materialism, namely "real humanism", and obtained its typical form from Feuerbach. The philosophy of Feuerbach makes "man, together with nature as the basis of man," as "exclusive, highest object"; it "resolves all supernatural things into nature by means of man and all superhuman things into man by virtue of nature"[24], and pursuits to "establish a philosophical critique of man" through speculative philosophy and the critique on theology. It is a humanistic materialism system taking nature as foundation and man as core and starting point.

From Feuerbach's point of view, nature is the primary entity, but man is a more important entity in terms of status: "man is the most advanced creature in nature", thus being the key to the apprehension of nature. Therefore, to "make clear the origin and course of nature", "the essence of man must be taken as the starting point"[25]. The essential characteristic of philosophy is consistent with that of man, so Feuerbach regarded man as the foundation for the unity between thought and nature, and pursued to comprehend the world and construct a philosophical system in the basic principle of "real man", thereby constructing a "new philosophy", namely humanistic materialism.

"Feuerbach has a great advantage over the 'pure' materialists in that he realizes how man too is an 'object of the senses'. But apart from the fact that he only conceives him as an 'object of the senses, not as sensuous activity'."[26] In other words, he did not realize that practice is the mode of being of man, and could "never manage to conceive the sensuous world as the total living sensuous activity of the individuals composing it"[27]. Feuerbach, for this reason, stopped at abstract man, and still ignored the initiative, subjectivity and sociality of man. The sensuous world in his mind therefore could not be anything but an abstract nature separated from man and his practical

---

23   *Karl Marx and Friedrich Engels.* 1st Chinese Ed., Vol. 2, p. 164.
24   *Selected Philosophical Works of Feuerbach.* 1st New Chinese Ed., Vol. I, p. 249.
25   ibid., p. 248.
26   *Selected Works of Karl Marx and Friedrich Engels.* 2nd Ed., Vol. 1, pp. 77 – 78.
27   ibid., p. 78.

activity and from social history. "As far as Feuerbach is a materialist he does not deal with history, and as far as he considers history he is not a materialist. With him materialism and history diverge completely."[28] Hence, transcendence over humanistic materialism and establishment of materialism amalgamated with "history", namely historical materialism, were the dual requirement of both theory and history.

I cannot agree with Plekhanov's opinions that the materialism of Feuerbach and the materialism of Marx both belong to "the newest materialism", that Marx's "opinion on materialism is developed in the same direction pointed by the inner logic of Feuerbach's materialism", and that "Marxist epistemology is in fact the epistemology of Feuerbach"[29]. In my opinion, these are silly unprincipled ideas, which show that Plekhanov had fundamentally confused the materialism of Feuerbach with Marxist materialism, and did not understand the former was humanistic materialism, whilst the latter was historical materialism, or the former only conceived man as "object of senses", whilst the latter conceived man as "activity of the senses" and grasped the relationships between man and nature and between man and man on that ground. Because the materialism of Feuerbach does not understand "the human sensuous activity", and conceives "thing, reality and sensuousness" "only in the form of the object or of contemplation", Marx "includes" it into the category of "old materialism", and calls the historical materialism he founds up "the new materialism"[30].

According to Marx, the standpoint of historical materialism is "social humanity", and it is "a summing-up of the most general results, abstractions which arise from the observation of the historical development of men"[31]. Social life is essentially practical, and human history, i.e. social history, is basically no other than the development of practical activity of man in time. Therefore, investigating human history is fundamentally analyzing human practical activity and its development. In this sense, Marx argues that historical materialism is "the real positive science, the representation of the practical activity, of the practical process of development of men"[32].

---

28 Ibid., p. 78.
29 *Selected Philosophical Works of Plekhanov*. Beijing, Joint Publishing Company, 1961: Vol. 3, pp. 148, 154 – 155, and 146 – 147.
30 *Selected Works of Karl Marx and Friedrich Engels*. 2nd Ed., Vol. 1, pp. 54 and 57.
31 *Selected Works of Karl Marx and Friedrich Engels*. 2nd Ed., Vol. 1, pp. 73 – 74.
32 ibid., p. 73.

Seen from the angle of form, historical materialism merely studies human society or human history, but the problem is that society is formed and developed in the process of material exchange between man and nature, which constitutes the "eternal natural necessity" for the existence and development of society. "Society is the complete unity of man with nature", and history is nothing but "the emergence of nature for man"[33]. So "excluding the relation of man to nature from history" will inescapably create the myth of the opposition between "material nature" and "spiritual history", make social history nothingness, and thereby move towards historical idealism. Taking the practical relationship between man and nature as "the realistic foundation of history", historical materialism pursues to change the relations between man and man by changing the relationship between man and nature and by sublating the appropriating relationship (private ownership) of man to material, thereby returning "human world and human relation to men themselves". For this end, the basic issue focused on and to be solved by historical materialism is the relationship respectively between man and nature and between man and man contained and embodied in the living practical activity and "actual daily life" of men. As a result, "history" in the concept of historical materialism refers to the sphere where human activity and inner contradictions thereof are developed.

A new philosophical space, i.e. a self-contained and complete, materialistic and dialectical picture of world, is shown by historical materialism by scientifically resolving the relationships between man and nature and between man and man, i.e. the relationship between man and world, with "social men" – the subject – as thinking coordinates and practice as the starting point and the system-constructing principle. This means that historical materialism is not only a conception of history, but more importantly, a "materialistic world outlook", "actually a critical view of the world" connoting "negative dialectics"[34]. As "a critical view of world", historical materialism is dually concerned with the real existence and the real value of man, and in my eyes, this is the most exciting realistic concern in the whole history of philosophy.

---

33 *Karl Marx and Friedrich Engels.* 1st Chinese Ed., Vol. 42, pp. 122 and 131.
34 *Karl Marx and Friedrich Engels.* 1st Chinese Ed., Vol. 3, p. 261.

CHAPTER II

HISTORIOGRAPHY OF THE FRENCH RESTORATION PERIOD AND ITS RELATIONSHIP WITH THE MATERIALISTIC CONCEPTION OF HISTORY

The historiography of the French Restoration period refers to the new historiography school of French bourgeoisie during the restoration period of the Bourbon Dynasty from 1814 to 1830, and its representatives are François Guizot (1787–1874), Augustin Thierry (1795–1856) and François Mignet (1796–1884). Engels had pointed out, "While Marx discovered the materialist conception of history, Thierry, Mignet, Guizot, and all the English historians up to 1850 are the proof that it was being striven for."[1] Plekhanov thought Marx had employed "the theoretical materials accumulated by French historians during the Restoration period"[2] when he was founding historical materialism. The expositions of Engels and Plekhanov indicate that the historiography of the French Restoration period occupies an important position in the history of human cognition. Here, I attempt to discuss the basic viewpoints

---

1 *Selected Works of Karl Marx and Friedrich Engels*. 2nd Ed., Vol. 4, p. 733.
2 *Selected Philosophical Works of Plekhanov*. Beijing, Joint Publishing Company, 1961: Vol. 3, p. 156.

of the historiography of the French Restoration period and its relationship with the materialistic conception of history with a view to deepening the study on the materialistic conception of history.

1 THEORETICAL CONTRIBUTIONS OF THE HISTORIOGRAPHY OF THE FRENCH RESTORATION PERIOD

Heroic conception of history went back to ancient times and still took a dominant position in the theory of social history. The human history was considered as the history of heroes, but the masses of people were beyond the horizon of historians and philosophers. "Such an opinion was resolutely rejected by French historians during the Restoration period."[3] The first theoretical contribution of the historiography of the French Restoration period lies in its acknowledgement of the masses' effect of creating history.

The masses of people is the protagonist of history, and the study on history should focus on the history of the masses, which is the basic standpoint of Thierry. In his eyes, the past theoretical theory are always centered on emperors, generals, ministers, and heroes, with no room left for the independent activity of the masses of people. Such "history" is not real, and such method for investigating history is not advisable for modern historians.

So, how to study history and absorb experience and lessens from it? In Thierry's opinion, the historical status of the masses of people should be restored in the first place: "the most numerous and most forgotten part of the nation deserves to live over again in history". Only the history studying the masses of people "would present to us at the same time examples of conduct, and that feeling of sympathy which we vainly seek in the adventures of the small number of privileged persons who occupy alone the historical scene. ... the fortune of the great and of princes, ... in which there are no lessons for our use"[4]. It is thus clear that from Thierry's point of view, to truly understand the human history and thereby provide real history of state and nation, we should first study the history of the masses of people and set up their historical status.

---

3 *Selected Philosophical Works of Plekhanov.* Beijing, Joint Publishing Company, 1961: Vol. 2, p. 352.
4 Thierry, *First Letter on the History of France*, see *Research Materials of Marxism-Leninism*, Vol. 20, p. 10.

Seen by the historiography of the French Restoration period, the historical effect of the masses of people lies in their initiative. Thierry expressly pointed out, "There is an extremely particular phenomenon, that is, historians always stubbornly disavow the pioneering spirit and thought of the masses of people."[5] According to Thierry, the initiative of the masses of people is shown in all sorts of aspects: they create skill, language, music and poetry; more importantly, the initiation of a social undertaking, or the will to establish a social system, first sprouts among the masses of people, who are also the main participants in the realization of a social system.

Guizot pointed out in *History of the English revolution of 1640* that in the bourgeois revolutions in Britain and France, "people handled their own things by themselves", came out boldly to undertake the duties that the past leaders had not performed any more, and "possessed the title of leader". As far as Guizot is concerned, this is the real action process and genuine characteristic of the English Revolution and the French Revolution.

The masses of people creates history; then, what is their motive and purpose to carry out historical activity? The historiography school during the French Restoration period answered: for guaranteeing their interests. The masses of people participate in a social undertaking, or establishing a social system in line with their interest needs. Mignet pointed out, "Feudal system actually had existed in the needs of people before its real existence – that was the first age; in the second age, it existed in reality but gradually went against needs, so that its substantial existence was ended at last."[6]

That was a vital breakthrough in the previous conception of history, and demonstrated that the historiography of the French Restoration period diverted the direction of historical study and began to guide the history of human thoughts to the land of hopes. Plekhanov so appreciated it that he believed that was "an earthshaking result worth being kept in mind"[7].

---

5   Thierry, *Ten Years of Historical Studies*. English Ed., p. 348.
6   Mignet, *The Theory of Feudalism*. English Ed., pp. 76 – 77.
7   *Selected Philosophical Works of Plekhanov*. Vol. 2, p. 736.

The fact that there is class struggle existing in society had been discovered and acknowledged by some ideologists in ancient Greece and Rome. The historiographical contribution of the French Restoration period rests with its systematic and in-depth study on this fact and discussion about the economic root and historical effect of class struggle. Class struggle is the central concept in the historiography of the French Restoration period. Affirming that class struggle is the driving force of historical development is the second major theoretical contribution of the historiography of the French Restoration period.

What is the root of class struggle? This is a question extremely concerned by the historiography of the French Restoration period, involving the deep structure of class struggle. Thierry explicitly pointed out that class struggle was "the war for the real interests. All the rest is nothing but cover-up or excuse"[8]. Guizot held that class struggle rooted in the irreconcilable contradiction of property interest between various classes, so there could be no peace among all the classes. "Reconciliation between them is an unachievable intention. Agreement between them is also an unrealizable illusion."[9] Mignet pointed out, "The annals of nations have not as yet presented any instance of such prudent sacrifices." Revolution attacks interests, "interests form parties, parties enter into contest"[10].

The expositions of Thierry, Guizot and Mignet are completely consistent with each other, bringing forth two basic arguments: (1) class struggle roots in economic interest, so it should be observed based on "the realistic interests" of all classes; (2) since class struggle roots in economic interest, it is inevitable and irreconcilable, and force is the sole effective means to resolve this contradiction. Such understandings of the historiography of the French Restoration period are undeniably incisive.

The historiography of the French Restoration period does not only analyze the economic root of class struggle, but also dissects the history of Europe, especially the history of the French Revolution, since the Middle Ages from the viewpoint of class struggle.

---

8   Thierry, *Ten Years of Historical Studies*. English Ed., p. 52.
9   Guizot, *On French Government since the Restoration and Current Cabinet*, see *Research Materials of Marxism-Leninism*, Vol. 20, p. 11.
10   Mignet, *History of the French Revolution*. English Ed., pp. 5 and 105.

First of all, the European history since the Middle Ages was in fact the history of class struggle. Thierry, who was praised by Marx as "the father of class struggle in French historiography", had been close to the understanding on the role played by class struggle in the development of feudal society and the establishment of capitalist system. Guizot also thought class struggle determined the destiny of world and furthered the civilization in Europe. Revolution, instead of interrupting the natural course of things in Europe, boosted the cause of human beings on the contrary. In Guizot's eyes, class struggle was the formula of the progress of civilized society.

Next, the French Revolution was a class struggle, the unavoidable life-and-death struggle between the third estate and the feudal nobles. Guizot pointed out that the French Revolution of 1789 was the most universal and powerful representation of class struggle. "I just want to briefly relate the political history of France. The whole history is full of, or more correctly, constituted by class struggles."[11] Revolution was the right to ask the imperial power for freedom, the nobles for equality, and the monks for human intelligence. According to Mignet, the period of the French Revolution constituted the age of the struggle for political power between several classes of French nation, and "these various phases were almost inevitable, so irresistible was the power of the events which produced them". It was that "irresistible power" that made the feudal system "inescapable from revolution" and the restoration of the Bourbon Dynasty a transient historical phenomenon.

"The past cannot be recalled; and it was not more possible for the nobles to rise from their defeat than it would now be for absolute monarchy to regain its position. ... The third estate, which increased daily in strength, wealth, intelligence, and union, was destined to combat and to displace it (the court)."[12]

The exposition of the historiography of the French Restoration period fairly shows how specific its understanding is on the historical significance of class struggle, and how explicit its apprehension is on the necessity of the French Revolution, that is, class struggle will ineluctably cause revolution and thereby determine the course of political history, change social formation, and promote the social development. Briefly

---

11   Guizot, *On French Government since the Restoration and Current Cabinet*, see *Research Materials of Marxism-Leninism*, Vol. 20, p. 12.
12   Mignet, *History of the French Revolution*. English Ed., pp. 10 – 11.

speaking, the law of history is that class struggle is the driving force of historical development.

Class struggle does not only determine the historical course of social politics, but its influence also touches upon thought. Class struggle determines and restricts the thought of people, which is another profound insight of the historiography of the French Restoration period. Thierry believed religious movement was no more than the reflection of realistic interest. The religious belief of British in the seventeenth century was contingent on their social statuses. "In the camp of subjects were mostly the Presbyterians, that is to say, they did not expect any religious oppression on them. Those who struggled against them in the opposite camp were the bishop and the advocators of the pope, because even in the religious form, they were also seeking for any power useful for them and any duties and taxes they could squeeze from people."[13] Mignet showed the same view, pointing out that "an affair of private interest became first a matter of religion and then a matter of party"[14]. Thus we can see that both Thierry and Mignet believed religion was by no means a simple belief and inevitably determined and restricted by class struggle.

This is religion, so what about art? Guizot was good at reviewing the impact of class struggle on art. He thought the literary activity in Britain depended on the development of industrial wealth and the change of property relations, and the destiny of drama reflected the change of social relations. In early modern times, society was rendered the combination of various classes, therefore drama was unavoidably influenced by class struggle.

The analysis above indicates that the historiography of the French Restoration period had seen the relationship between class struggle and economic interest and clearly understood the historical significance of class struggle. In spite of different horizons and perspectives, Thierry, Guizot and Mignet all deliver the same cognition, namely that class struggle is the driving force of historical development and the basic clue of the historical course of the bourgeois revolutions in Britain and France. Engels points out, "The historians of the Restoration period, from Thierry to Guizot, Mignet, and Thiers, speak of it everywhere

---

13   Thierry, *Ten Years of Historical Studies*. English Ed., pp. 91 – 92.
14   Mignet, *History of the French Revolution*. English Ed., p. 87.

as the key to the understanding of all French history since the Middle Ages."[15] In addition, interpreting religion and art based on the class struggle arising out of economic interest is a significant advancement in the conception of history, laying a sound foundation for interpreting the human history from the standpoint of materialism.

The opinion of the historiography of the French Restoration period occupies an important position in the history of human cognition. The traditional European historiography from Herodotus in ancient Greece to Ranke in the nineteenth century and the traditional European philosophy from Anaxagoras in ancient Greece to French materialists in the eighteenth century either search the inner connections of history from thought motive or take history as the accumulation of accidental events. However, the historiography of the French Restoration period surpasses the views of traditional European historiography and philosophy by considering the historical development of Europe as a "natural course" having its inherent laws and trying to reveal the objective laws of this course.

This is a leap in thought, as said by Engels that "the question was not asked as to whence the ideas come into men's minds and what the driving causes of the political changes are. Only upon the newer school of French, and partly also of English, historians have forced the conviction that, since the Middle Ages at least, the driving force in European history was the struggle of the developing bourgeoisie with the feudal aristocracy for social and political domination."[16] Plekhanov also thought that "the new opinion viewing history as a regular process had been thoroughly expressed by French historians during the Restoration period in their works on the French Revolution"[17].

The third theoretical contribution of the historiography of the French Restoration period is its acknowledgement of property relation as the foundation of political system. Political system is the result before becoming the cause – system has been created by society before it changes due to the influence of system. The historiography of the French Restoration period does not deny the interaction between political system and national customs, but it argues both are determined, in the final analysis, by a third profounder decisive factor, that is, the civil life and property relations of people.

15   *Selected Works of Karl Marx and Friedrich Engels*. 2nd Ed., Vol. 4, p. 250.
16   *Selected Works of Karl Marx and Friedrich Engels*. 2nd Ed., Vol. 3, p. 334.
17   *Selected Philosophical Works of Plekhanov*. Vol. 2, p. 352.

Guizot pointed out, "To know political system, we have to understand various social strata and their correlations. To understand various social strata, we should apprehend the properties and condition of land ownership."[18] In *History of the English revolution of 1640*, he made a further development of that thought, thinking that apart from "the condition of land ownership", the general property condition was also the foundation of political system, and thoughts, theories and constitution itself were the products of social condition and class interest. Mignet showed an identical opinion, thinking that "the broadest and strongest interests order about laws and realize their purposes". "The constitution of 1791 was based on principles adapted to the ideas and situation of France. This constitution was the work of the middle class, then the strongest; for, as is well known, the predominant force ever takes possession of institutions."[19]

The expositions of Guizot and Mignet tell us that class interest and property relation determine thought, theory and political system. Moreover, Mignet also believed property relation also determined the lifestyle of people. "The lifestyle of every individual is dependent on his social condition, relation with various classes, – in a word, civil life of people."[20]

French materialism in the eighteenth century puts forward the opinion that "man is the product of environment" but does not understand what on earth restricts social environment. The social environment in the context of French materialism in the eighteenth century mainly refers to political system, institution, etc. The historiography of the French Restoration period brings forth the viewpoint that property relation is the foundation of political system and national customs, thus initially separating economic sphere from social environment, which is the superiority of the historiography of the French Restoration period to French materialists in the eighteenth century.

This conclusion is a distinctly important contribution to the theory of history. It assumes the character of the materialistic conception of history and derives social structure and historical law from property relation. This is a crucial change, foreboding a new direction to address the mystery of history. From Plekhanov's point of view, this opinion of the

18   Guizot, *An Introduction to French History*. English Ed., pp. 25 – 26.
19   Mignet, *History of the French Revolution*. English Ed., p. 103.
20   Guizot, *An Introduction to French History*. English Ed., p. 74.

historiography of the French Restoration period is an "overall revolution to the historical views"[21] of French materialism in the eighteenth century. Besides, it is also highly rated by Engels, who points out that "the idea that political acts, grand performances of state, are decisive in history is as old as written history itself. ... This idea dominated all the conceptions of historians in the past, and the first blow against it was delivered only by the French bourgeois historians of the Restoration period"[22].

I have discussed the main theoretical contributions of the historiography of the French Restoration period above, and below, I will analyze the reasons why it is able to make these theoretical achievements.

Firstly, the blueprint and cornerstone provided by the French Revolution of the bourgeoisie. The French Revolution of 1789 is unprecedented and magnificent, showing the pioneering spirit of the masses of people, proving that history is not made by some great figures, revealing the effect of class struggle, and demonstrating history is not the accumulation of accidental events. Additionally, classes in this revolution had taken off the cloak of religion and publicly announced their worldly purposes at the very start, and struggled against each other in a completely worldly way, thus revealing the dominant effect of economic interest and property relation. That great change of society originally had no intention of flattering the philosophy of history, but unconsciously determined the appearance and even the general tendency of it. The historical dialectics of Hegel is just the tortuous reflection of the great social change caused by the French Revolution under the conditions of Germany. Hegel warmly eulogized the French Revolution as "a magnificent sunrise. All thinking Beings have participated in celebrating this holy day"[23]. Since the French Revolution can make the German philosopher cheer for it, why cannot it strike a chord with French historians? Thierry et al. did not take part in the French Revolution, but they still felt its mighty impact, so they consciously used it as the blueprint and cornerstone of their historical theory.

Secondly, the urgent need of the French bourgeoisie. The French Revolution "went through a period of tempestuous storm" in "a fierce and turbulent situation". On the one side, it ended the government of

---

21 *Selected Philosophical Works of Plekhanov.* Vol. 2, p. 157.
22 *Selected Works of Karl Marx and Friedrich Engels.* 2nd Ed., Vol. 3, p. 502.
23 Hegel, *The Philosophy of History*, p. 493.

feudal dynasty with a series of heavy blows; on the other side, it diluted the sacred "halo of reason" of French philosophy in the eighteenth century. This great revolution evoked wide debates. The panic and ignorance on the former aspect was shown by the attack from the scholars used by the Bourbon Dynasty on the French Revolution and their refutation against the necessity of the revolution; the incomprehension and confusion on the latter aspect resulted in the condition that some bourgeois figures thought the French Revolution was difficult to be controlled like a natural disaster, although they opposed feudalism. Therefore, systematically and clearly expounding the French Revolution and its necessity from an anti-feudal point of view was urgently needed by the French bourgeoisie.

Thirdly, the enlightenment of the theory of French utopian socialism in the nineteenth century. Compared with French materialists in the eighteenth century, the uniqueness of Saint-Simon is that he touches upon the important issue of the decisive effect of ownership on social system on the one hand, and on the other hand, he uses class struggle to interpret the historical process of Europe since the fifteenth century. The viewpoint of Saint-Simon had a significant impact on the historiography of the French Restoration period. Plekhanov correctly pointed out that the historiography of the French Restoration period "holds the historical views no other than those having been first systematically disseminated by Saint-Simon"[24].

Fourthly, the lesson from the slip of French materialists in the eighteenth century. If we say the viewpoints of Saint-Simon are the positive enlightenment for the historiography of the French Restoration period, then the theoretical slip of Helvetius et al. is the lesson on the negative side. French materialists in the eighteenth century had sunk into the inextricable antinomy between that "man is the product of environment" and that "opinion dominates environment", and finally reached the heroic conception of history. This theoretical slip gives the descendants a profound exhortation, with the enlightenment that to surmount the antinomy between opinion and environment, we must go beyond the standpoint of mutual determination between the two and investigate the decisive factor behind them.

---

24 *Selected Philosophical Works of Plekhanov.* Vol. 3, p. 615.

All in all, the social background, class need, theoretical enlightenment, and lesson from theoretical slip, together with the talents of Guizot et al., all contribute to the glorious achievements made by the historiography of the French Restoration period in the field of the study on social history.

2 THEORETICAL LIMITATIONS OF THE HISTORIOGRAPHY OF THE FRENCH RESTORATION PERIOD

Just as the strengths of a person are always accompanied with his shortcomings, the limitations of the historiography of the French Restoration period hide behind its theoretical contributions. Its limitations, on the whole, are mainly shown in three aspects:

The first aspect is that it does not solve the question that how the masses of people create history.

The historiography of the French Restoration period does not solve the question that how the masses of people create history, mainly because it does not understand the relationship of the creating function of the masses to the objective historical conditions, especially to material production. If this is not resolved, the fact that the creating activity of the masses will lead to different results in different countries and different eras is also incomprehensible. Meanwhile, because the historiography of the French Restoration period does not understand the relationship of the masses of people to individuals, especially the prominent figures, it is unable to explain the creation of history by the masses of people by combining the historical effect of individual and prominent figures.

Both the materialistic conception of history and the historiography of the French Restoration period recognize that history is created by the masses of people, but both are seriously divergent with respect to the apprehension on the connotation of this standpoint. Though putting forward the proposition that history is created by the masses of people, the historiography of the French Restoration period does not understand that the existence of men himself is their practical material life, or that different social and historical conditions and different modes of production for the historical activity of the masses of people will result in different width and depth of the history created by the masses of people.

From the view of the materialistic conception of history, the status of the masses of people and the condition of their functioning, in the final analysis, are determined by the development of productive forces, as well as the conditions of economy, politics, culture, etc. finally determined by productive forces. The masses of people cannot create history at will, and what they can only do is starting with the realistic objective conditions and translating the possibility created by objective situation into reality. As Marx said, "men make their own history, but they do not make it as they please; they do not make it under self-selected circumstances, but under circumstances existing already, given and transmitted from the past"[25]. According to the materialistic conception of history, the activity of history creation by the masses of people is the unity between initiative and passivity. This is the first point.

Secondly, in the opinion of the historiography of the French Restoration period, the history created by the masses of people is ended with the establishment of capitalist system, and the subsequent history only belongs to the bourgeoisie, whereas according to the materialistic conception of history, the creativity of the masses of people is the unity between finiteness and infiniteness. The creativity of the masses is of course finite within a certain era because it is subject to the restriction of the historical conditions in this era, but in respect of the continuity generation after generation, it is infinite. "Historical action is the undertaking of the mass. Together with the thoroughness of the historical action, the size of the mass whose action it is will therefore increase."[26]

Thirdly, the historiography of the French Restoration period does not know the relationship of the masses of people to individuals, especially the prominent figures, or the relationship of the masses' creating function to the historical role of individuals, especially of the prominent figures. The materialistic conception of history is different, which believes that "history is made in such a way that the final result always arises from conflicts between many individual wills"[27]. An "individual will" is relatively independent; although unable to achieve its own aspiration, every will tries to improve or transcend the old historical conditions. In this way, individual wills are merged into a resultant which gives rise to an overall result – historical event. Every will is not equal to zero in the resultant, and on the contrary, each contributes to the resultant and is to

25   *Selected Works of Karl Marx and Friedrich Engels*. 2nd Ed., Vol. 1, p. 585.

26   *Karl Marx and Friedrich Engels*. 1st Chinese Ed., Vol. 2, p. 104.

27   *Selected Works of Karl Marx and Friedrich Engels*. 2nd Ed., Vol. 4, p. 697.

this extent included in it. Depending on this, social history can cease-lessly develop. Therefore the activity of history creation by the masses of people is the unity between group and individual.

The materialistic conception of history also holds that the trend of the masses' sentiment reflects the mainstream of history and predicts the basic direction of social development, and the activity of great figures is the conscious representation of the inevitable course of social devel-opment. As the initiators, participants and directors of historical mis-sion, great figures play an accelerating or retarding role in historical course, and brand historical event with the mark of distinct personality. Meanwhile, the success of great figures is because they get the sup-port from the masses of people by conforming to the basic desire and requirement of them, thus both are highly unified on the basis of the conformity to the trend of historical development.

The second aspect is that it does not formulate a scientific, thorough theory of class struggle.

Concerning the origin of class, the basic viewpoint of the historiog-raphy of the French Restoration period is the conquering theory, but does not touch upon the fundamental cause of class – private ownership of the means of production. From its point of view, class "has been generated since the era of conquest, and all are based on conquest"[28]. Attributing the generation of class to conquest cannot solve the problem in that "force may be able to change the possession of, but cannot cre-ate, private property as such"[29].

As to the issue of class classification, the basic viewpoint of the histo-riography of the French Restoration period is the theory of distribution, and it does not know that class is the community of men at a specific status in a specific economic structure. For example, Mignet based class classification on the source and amount of income, showing that he had not distinguished the concept of "class" from the concept of "estate".

With respect to the trend of class development, the basic viewpoint of the historiography of the French Restoration period is the theory of eternity, and it does not understand class is a historical category. For in-stance, Guizot stated, "There were, and will be, rentiers, entrepreneurs

---

28   Thierry, *Ten Years of Historical Studies*. English Ed., p. 18.
29   *Selected Works of Karl Marx and Friedrich Engels*. 2nd Ed., Vol. 3, p. 505.

and salary earners everywhere in the past and the future. Such classification is not an accidental phenomenon, or a particular phenomenon in a country, at all; it is a naturally repeated general phenomenon in any human society."[30] The historiography of the French Restoration period passionately eulogizes and sufficiently affirms the struggle of the bourgeoisie against the feudal aristocracy, but strongly repudiates and belittles the fight of the proletariat against the bourgeoisie and thinks it is a disaster and shame.

The materialistic conception of history and the historiography of the French Restoration period both acknowledges that class struggle is the principal impetus of the development of class society and thinks class struggle results from economic interest. However, in respect to the generation and development trend of class or class struggle, both are different in principle. Marx points out, "Long before me bourgeois historians had described the historical development of this class struggle ... What I did that was new was to prove: (1) that the existence of classes is only bound up with particular historical phases in the development of production, (2) that the class struggle necessarily leads to the dictatorship of the proletariat, (3) that this dictatorship itself only constitutes the transition to the abolition of all classes and to a classless society."[31] This exposition of Marx centrally demonstrates the essential difference between the materialistic conception of history and the historiography of the French Restoration period in their opinions on class and class struggle.

The third aspect is that it does not find out the real root of historical development.

Property relation is the foundation for political system and ruling thought. We should admit this view is profound. But what determines property relation? This is a key question to resolve the mystery of history, to which the answer of the historiography of the French Restoration period is very dissatisfactory. In the opinion of Guizot et al., "conquest" is the root of property relation; they believe one nation occupies the property of another and some residents appropriate the property of some other all as a result of conquest. However, ascribing property relation to conquest will necessarily bring about two questions: why the social results of conquest are different? And what is the cause of conquest?

---

30   Guizot, *Democracy in France*, see *Research Materials of Marxism-Leninism*, Vol. 20, p. 21.
31   *Selected Works of Karl Marx and Friedrich Engels*. 2nd Ed., Vol. 4, p. 547.

The answer of the historiography of the French Restoration period to the first question is that during different periods, the social systems of nations conflicting with each other are different, so the results of conquest are different. This answer does not solve the question. In the eyes of Guizot et al., social system is determined by property relation, but now they think property relation originates from conquest, while the result of conquest lies on social system. This, beyond of doubt, is a vicious circle.

The historiography of the French Restoration period gives two answers to the second question: (1) the cause of conquest is "actual interest"; and (2) the cause of conquest is "the desire for conquest" in human nature. The first answer does not solve the problem of property relation's origin either, because on the one hand it says property relation results from conquest, and on the other hand it thinks conquest is for "actual interest", which in turn rests with property relation; consequently, it is still trapped in contradiction: using conquest to interpreting property relation and interest, but also explaining conquest with property relation and interest.

Interpreting conquest, property relation and thereby history by using "the desire for conquest" in human nature does not really resolve "the mystery of history", and on the contrary, such theory itself is the idealist conception of history. The materialistic conception of history is in essence different from the historiography of the French Restoration period in the understanding on historical law. According to the latter, there exists an invariable "natural character" or "natural instinct" of man, which is the ultimate cause of historical development, the foundation for class struggle and property relation, and the deep structure of historical law. This indicates that the historiography of the French Restoration period does not truly grasp the internal mechanism of historical law. From the standpoint of the materialistic conception of history, practice, the interaction between subject and object of history, and its development process are the premise and foundation depended by historical law, which, fundamentally, is the general influence of social economic movement on history process and mainly manifested by the propositions that productive forces determines relations of product and that economic base determines superstructure; history is shown as the general course of human practice.

It is thus obvious that the key supplied by the historiography of the French Restoration period to understanding historical event does not open the door of history palace. Such a condition is caused by two reasons:

First, the prejudice of class; being the bourgeois ideologists, Guizot et al. take arguing the reasonableness and eternality of capitalist system as their bounden duty. For this purpose, they seek for the foundation of a social organization in "human nature". Plekhanov considers that this method could "kill two hawks with one arrow", namely explaining capitalist system with the good aspect in human nature and pursuing the whole movement to establish this system, and interpreting the origins of feudal system and all other social organizations that were somewhat strange in the mind of capitalists with the bad aspect in human nature. The opinion of Plekhanov is absolutely right and extraordinarily incisive.

Second, the reason of cognition. For one thing, the historiography of the French Restoration period "has a very confused perspective on human economic history"[32], which means that the historical school of the French Restoration period conceives feudal system based on its collapse rather than its real origin and regards capitalist system as a natural thing, and surplus value is mysterious to them; for the other thing, they do not understand production practice is the source of the whole social history, and the duality of production practice, i.e. the relationships of man to nature and to another man, is still a "riddle of the Sphinx" for them. Therefore, the fact that property relation is just a legal manifestation of relations of production is consequently incomprehensible to them.

---

32 Plekhanov, *Thierry and the Materialistic Conception of History*, see *Research Materials of Marxism-Leninism*, Vol. 20, p. 20.

3 THE INFLUENCE OF HISTORIOGRAPHY OF THE FRENCH RESTORATION PERIOD ON THE FORMATION OF THE MATERIALISTIC CONCEPTION OF HISTORY

The influence of the historiography of the French Restoration period on Marx's establishment of the materialistic conception of history is mainly shown in two aspects, historical and logical.

The historical influence of the historiography of the French Restoration period on the materialistic conception of history is shown in promoting Marx to foster the viewpoint that "civil society is the foundation of a state".

In the period of *Rhine Newspaper*, the thought development of Marx was full of contradictions: he started to doubt Hegelian philosophy on the one side, but had not yet broken away from it on the other; he saw the decisive effect of "objective relation" on the one side, but had not yet made a distinction between economic relation and thought relation on the other. Marx was still hesitating in Hegelian philosophy at that time. *The Critique on Hegel's Philosophy of Right* written by him in 1843 symbolized he had turned from doubting to criticizing Hegelian philosophy and terminated his hesitation. He entered the sphere of economic relation from general "objective relation", and put forward the first initial principle, namely that "civil society is the foundation of a state", in the forming history of the materialistic conception of history.

However, how did that leap of thought happen on earth? It is not adequate to use the actual struggle in the period of Rhine Newspaper to explain this question. The actual struggle at that time only impelled Marx to find the problems but not solve them. In order to dispel the "assailing doubts", Marx "withdrew from the public stage to his study" for theoretical research. In that process, the historiography of the French Restoration period had a significant influence on Marx to reach the conclusion that "civil society is the foundation of a state".

In *Kreuznacher Notes*, Marx directly studied the works of Guizot, Thierry and Mignet. Judged from his extracts and remarks, Marx was interested in the form of ownership and its impact on political system, as well as the issue of class and class struggle. Relevant expositions of Guizot et al. provided empirical arguments for Marx to criticize Hegel's philosophy of right and correctly conceive the relationship between civil society and state. Mehring thought the study on the French bourgeois revolution impelled Marx to investigate the historical literatures of Guizot et al. and thereby find out the decisive effect of economic fact. At that time, "the French Revolution, for Marx, and the British industry, for Engels, became the instruments for them to explain the struggle and the wish of times"[33].

Seen from the writing process of *The Critique on Hegel's Philosophy of Right*, the understanding of Marx is gradually deepened. In the first half, "civil society" is mainly conceived as the social relation of men; in the second half, through analyzing the relations of the private ownership of land, Marx studies the relationship between private property and state, thinks that the law-right relationship of primogeniture is no more than the result and presentation of the private ownership of land, and clearly points out, "the constitution here is the constitution of private property" and "private property is the guarantee of the political constitution"[34].

Here involves an important content in civil society – ownership, which is close to be conceived as the material life relation between man and man. The reason why I use words "involves" and "close" is because the apprehension of Marx at that time was still limited to one form – the land tenure. As previously discussed, Guizot et al. believed property relation, largely land ownership, was the foundation of political system, and class struggle based on interest was the driving force of the development of European history. In *The Critique on Hegel's Philosophy of Right*, Marx proposes that civil society is the foundation of a state and enters the field of ownership from civil society, but he is confined to land ownership. Mutual corroboration of the two shows that Marx's conclusion that civil society is the foundation of a state evidently bears the trace of the influence from the historiography of the French Restoration period.

I do not agree with the opinion that Marx reached the conclusion that "civil society is the foundation of a state" through the study on political economy or under the enlightenment of Feuerbach's materialism.

---

33 Mehring, *German History from the End of the Middle Ages*. Beijing, Joint Publishing Company, 1980: pp. 150 – 151.
34 *Karl Marx and Friedrich Engels*. 1st Chinese Ed., Vol. 1, pp. 380 and 381.

It can be seen from the exposition about the formation and staging of the materialistic conception of history in *Preface to A Contribution to the Critique of Political Economy* of 1895 that Marx found the anatomy of civil society had "to be sought in political economy" after he move to Paris in Sept. of 1843, and before that, he only had "the first instance to turn my attention to economic questions". Thus it is clear that Marx reached the conclusion that "civil society is the foundation of a state" before studying political economy.

The critique of Feuerbach on Hegelian philosophy is groundbreaking, and provides a method, i.e. "reversal method", for transforming Hegelian philosophy. This method is methodologically enlightening for Marx to criticize Hegel's philosophy of right and draw the conclusion that "civil society is the foundation of a state". However, the enlightenment from Feuerbach alone is not enough to make Marx reach this conclusion, because Feuerbach criticizes Hegel's theory of religious speculation and general philosophical idea, whilst Marx criticizes Hegel's philosophy of right, viz., the theory of social speculation; Feuerbach is concentrated on nature and "man" and gives no concrete opinion on the relationship between civil society and state, whereas Marx pays attention to and specifically resolves the problem of the relationship between civil society and state. It is just on this aspect that Marx is influenced by the historiography of the French Restoration period. As for the critique on Hegelian philosophy and the conclusion that "civil society is the foundation of a state", if we say the "reversal method" of Feuerbach gives a methodological enlightenment to Marx, then the opinion that "property relation is the foundation of political system" of the historiography of the French Restoration period provides an empirical argument for Marx, and directly guides Marx to obtain this conclusion.

The analysis and demonstration on both positive and negative aspects indicate that the historiography of the French Restoration period plays a significantly promoting role in Marx's turning from the idealistic conception of history to the materialistic conception of history and his arrival at the conclusion that "civil society is the foundation of a state". If we say the basic principle of the materialistic conception of history is the "overall result" obtained by Marx through studying political economy, then the first initial principle in the forming history of the materialistic conception of history is the result acquired by Marx through studying history and criticizing the historiography of the French Restoration period under the influence of Feuerbach's "reversal method". Plekhanov pointed out that Marx's conclusion that "civil society is the foundation of a state" in 1843 "was just the repetition of the conclusion long ago reached by the science of history under the influence of social development and class struggle related to it. All the difference was that men before Marx had not fully made clear the origins of property relation and interest, but Marx knew very well those matters"[35]. We should say the comment of Plekhanov is quite fair.

In *Ludwig Feuerbach and the End of Classical German Philosophy*, Engels points out that there are three basic links in the logical method used by Marx to establish the materialistic conception of history: observing the activity of man, studying the motive of men's historical action, and exploring "driving force of the impetus". It "is the only path which can put us on the track of the laws holding sway both in history as a whole, and at particular periods and in particular lands."[36] This method is then summarized by Lenin as "singling out the economic sphere from the various spheres of social life, singling out production relations from all social relations", and "the reduction of social relations to production relations and of the latter to the level of the productive forces"[37]. Concerning the logical method used for establishing the materialistic conception of history, Marx is also inspired by the historiography of the French Restoration period.

As mentioned before, the historical effects of the masses of people and economic relation were beyond the horizon of traditional European historiography and philosophy of history. Differently, the historiography of the French Restoration period focused on the great role of the masses of people, and following the basic clue of class struggle, traced it back to economic interest and probed from political system into property relation. The wide study scope and unique horizon of the historiography of the French Restoration period gave readers at that time a feeling of novelty, and meanwhile inspired Marx, who was good at critically carrying forward theories of the predecessors. Thierry et al. emphasized the historical effect of the masses of people and hoped the history of the masses be studied, thus starting to change the attention center of historical theory; they also emphasized that class struggle was the main content in history and determined the process of history, and put forward

---

35   *Selected Philosophical Works of Plekhanov*. Vol. 2, pp. 547 – 548.
36   *Selected Works of Karl Marx and Friedrich Engels*. 2nd Ed., Vol. 4, p. 249.
37   *Collected Works of Lenin*. 2nd Chinese Ed., Vol. 1, pp. 107 and 110.

that interest was the origin of class struggle, thus starting to reveal the objective law of historical development. All those viewpoints helped Marx further realize that the masses of people were the creator of history, that all in social life were related to economic interest, and that class struggle arising out of interest was the main content of civilized era and the "direct driving force" of social development.

So while exploring historical law, Marx firstly paid attention to the motive of the masses of people and the motive of classes. As pointed by Engels, "When, therefore, it is a question of investigating the driving powers which – consciously or unconsciously, and indeed very often unconsciously – lie behind the motives of men who act in history and which constitute the real ultimate driving forces of history, then it is not a question so much of the motives of single individuals, however eminent, as of those motives which set in motion great masses, whole people, and again whole classes of the people in each people; and this, too, not merely for an instant, like the transient flaring up of a straw-fire which quickly dies down, but as a lasting action resulting in a great historical transformation."[38] Thus, Marx, on the premise that men make their own history, found out the thought motives of the masses' creative activity and the classes' historical action, and traced from thought motives to economic interest under the enlightenment of the historiography of the French Restoration period.

Actual economic interest is a concrete objective phenomenon. The quantity and quality of material product only provides a premise for economic interest, and do not mean the actual possession of it. So what is the power that determines different economic interests actually gotten by men? The essence of the problem can be grasped, and a solid foundation laid for dissecting social structure and analyzing social relations, so far as the power is discovered. In this respect, Marx is also enlightened by the historiography of the French Restoration period.

Guizot et al. brought forward that property relation was the profound groundwork for the political system and ruling thought of a state, political law rooted in social relations, and the latter was determined by the condition of ownership. Those in fact gave a preliminary description of social structure, namely property relation – thought and theory – political system, and initially differentiated social relations into property

---

38   *Selected Works of Karl Marx and Friedrich Engels.* 2nd Ed., Vol. 4, p. 249.

relation and political relation. In the view of Guizot et al., historians could not have the key to the understanding of historical event unless paying attention to the study on civil life and property relation. That "key" inspired Marx, while probing into the groundwork of social structure and the root of historical development, to first single out the economic sphere from the various spheres of social life, and thereby he found the reigning role of economic interest. "Everything for which man struggles is a matter of his interest."[39] Whether economic interest can be satisfied and to which extent it is satisfied are inseparable from the development level of the mode of production. In-depth exploration into mode of production and its inner contradictions make Marx realizes that interest reflects definite relationship between subject (individual or group) and object (material products) of history, but while distributing and enjoying those objects, subject will necessarily enter into "benefit"-"harm" or "gain"-"loss" relation with others.

For this reason, economic interest is essentially a category of social relation. On the one hand, relations of production reflect economic interest: all activities of men during economic intercourse, mutual cooperation or fighting with each other, are revolved around economic interest without exception; on the other hand, social relation between man and man is, above all, economic and productive relation, which restricts and determines economic interest. The latter aspect is restricted and determined by the real economic relation, especially the relation of ownership. The natures and levels of the economic interests actually obtained by men are quite different in case of men's different ownerships of the means of production (whether possessing the means of production and how to possess). The content and nature of economic interest inevitably changes with relations of production.

Scientific discussion about economic interest helped Marx correctly understand not only the activity of production and all social activities determined by it, but also the relation of production and all social relations established based on it. In this way, Marx singled out the relations of production from all social relations, and took the former as the basic primitive relation determining all other relations. He discovered the relation of production immediately determining economic interest, thereby regarding economic interest as the specific manifestation of the relation of men to the means respectively of livelihood and production.

---

39   *Karl Marx and Friedrich Engels.* 1st Chinese Ed., Vol. 1, p. 82.

It can be seen that the method used by Guizot et al. in the study of history significantly enlightened Marx in logical method for creating the materialistic conception of history.

Above mentioned are positive enlightenments, and I would like to talk about negative ones below.

It is right that property relation is the foundation of political system. But what determines property relation, namely the condition of ownership? Whether this question is correctly solved concerns whether the theory of history can be transformed into the science of history. It is on this point that the historiography of the French Restoration period slips down. It uses the theory of "conquest" to interpret property relation, thus sinking into the idealistic conception of history. As said by Plekhanov, historians of the historiography of the French Restoration period firmly insisted on the conception of law, but they had not fully known what they should do to understand the laws of historical movement. Their theoretical slip negatively enlightens Marx.

Any fact of a conquest will inevitably give rise to such a question that why its social result is like this rather than another. This makes Marx realize that there is an unknown power in social life, which is not restricted by conquest but contrarily restricts the result of conquest and even conquest itself. By specifically studying conquest, Marx finds that this unknown power is the mode of production of material goods.

"In all cases of conquest, three things are possible. The conquering people subjugates the conquered under its own mode of production (e.g. the English in Ireland in this century, and partly in India); or it leaves the old mode intact and contents itself with a tribute (e.g. Turks and Romans); or a reciprocal interaction takes place whereby something new, a synthesis, arises (the Germanic conquests, in part). In all cases, the mode of production, whether that of the conquering people, that of the conquered, or that emerging from the fusion of both, is decisive for the new distribution which arises."[40]

The historiography of the French Restoration period ascribes conquest to "the desire for conquest" in human nature and uses the natural instinct of man to explain property relation and then history. Such a method contains an irreconcilable contradiction: whether the natural instinct

---

40   *Karl Marx and Friedrich Engels.* 1st Chinese Ed., Vol. 46 (I), pp. 34 – 35.

of man changes? If it is unchanged, how the unchanged human nature can be the cause of the constantly changing history? If it is changeable, then what is the cause of its change? In the words of Plekhanov, this is still a new maze, the new source of eclecticism and contradiction in the science of history. It shows that the historiography of the French Restoration period was still wandering in the antinomy between opinion and environment.

However, this enlightens Marx to jump out of the routine of seeking resolution of "the mystery of history" in human nature and find a real path to the exploration of "the mystery of history", that is, starting from social practice to conceive the whole history and man as well as his representation in reality. "The coincidence of the changing of circumstances and of human activity or self-changing can be conceived and rationally understood only as revolutionary practice." By means of the materialistic and dialectical understanding on practice, Marx scientifically resolves the antinomy between opinion and environment that haunts old philosophy for a long term, and raises the philosophy of history to a brand-new height, thus making the theory of history the genuine science of history. As Plekhanov said, "'By thus acting on the external world and changing it, man at the same time changes his own nature.' This sentence implies all the essences of Marx's theory of history."[41] Thus we can see that the theoretical contributions and faults of the historiography of the French Restoration period enlighten Marx in two respects, namely discussing the decisive factor of economic interest and discussing the unknown power behind conquest and the historical cause of the change of human nature. The gathering of discussions on these two aspects in production practice eventually brings all the theories of social history out of the obscure maze.

---

41   Plekhanov, *On Development of the Monistic Conception of History*. Beijing, Joint Publishing Company, 1961: p. 107.

4 BRIEF PERORATION

In this brief peroration, I make two conclusions based on the summarization of the above:

Firstly, I unhesitatingly think that the historiography of the French Restoration period indeed holds some wise ideas and thoughts, containing the bud and factors of the materialistic conception of history. Its historical role in the history of human cognition is that it shakes the dominant position the idealistic conception of history over the theory of history for the first time and provides immediate theoretical and methodological premises for the materialistic conception of history. If the materialistic conception of history is compared to a splendid sunrise in the history of human cognition, the historiography of the French Restoration period is the dawn before it.

Secondly, the theoretical contributions of the historiography of the French Restoration period should not be smudged, but its theoretical limitations should not be neglected either. Due to the inner irreconcilable contradiction of its theory, it was forced to quit from the development of cognition, and then be displayed as a specimen in the museum of thoughts, instead of being thriving in the world, and superseded by the materialistic conception of history finally. I unambiguously declare that only the materialistic conception of history is the first to scientifically present the fundamental cause and general law of the movement of human history and thereby realize a revolution in the history of human cognition.

CHAPTER III

SOCIAL PHILOSOPHY OF FRENCH UTOPIAN SOCIALISM AND ITS RELATIONSHIP WITH THE MATERIALISTIC CONCEPTION OF HISTORY

The status of French utopian socialism in the nineteenth century in the history of socialist ideology has been known to us, but its position in the history of philosophy has not yet gotten the attention of people. Here, I attempt to discuss the social philosophical thought (hereinafter referred to as "social philosophy") of French utopian socialism so as to determine its status in the history of philosophy and its relationship with the materialistic conception of history. Besides, for the purpose of deeply interpreting social philosophy and its relationship with the materialistic conception of history, I will discuss the social philosophy of British utopian socialist Owen in the same times and theoretical association with French utopian socialism.

1 THEORETICAL ORIGIN OF SOCIAL PHILOSOPHY

In the investigation of the theoretical origin of social philosophy, two different traditions of thought must be mentioned: French enlightenment philosophy in the eighteenth century and the classical mechanics of Newton.

Apparently, social philosophy takes a totally repudiating attitude towards French enlightenment philosophy in the eighteenth century and denies the succession relationship between them. As a matter of fact, it is in French enlightenment philosophy in the eighteenth century, especially the philosophy respective of Rousseau and Helvetius, that social philosophy finds its theoretical premise.

Rousseau perceived that private ownership, which was deemed by other enlightenment ideologists as the basis for human existence, was the source of inequality and evil in human beings, and studied social phenomena from the view of interaction, in the belief that man had the ability of self-improvement and this ability could help man break away from the primitive state but would result in the misfortunes of mankind. According to him, progress was regression at the same time. Mankind was in the transition to its opposite in confrontation and contradiction, and progress appeared in the form that was opposite to it.

Meanwhile, Rousseau viewed history with the standpoint of regularity, and thought there were inner connections in history, the development of production and technology was the main instance of historical development, and the process of history was irreversible, "unable to retrace its steps or renounce the unfortunate acquisitions it had made"[1]. The opinion of Rousseau embraces the factor of the materialistic conception of history, and "the doctrine in its first presentation bears almost ostentatiously the imprint of its dialectical origin", showing his sensitivity to historicism beyond the expectation of his times. His dialectical method is accepted by social philosophy, and his standpoint of regularity is introduced as the central historical theory into social philosophy.

---

1   Rousseau, *Discourse on the Origin and the Foundations of Inequality among Men.* Beijing: The Commercial Press, 1962: p. 69.

"Fourier starts directly from the doctrines of French materialism."[2] This evaluation is also suitable for Saint-Simon. On the one side, in social philosophy, French materialism in the eighteenth century was dense with the opinions that "man is the product of environment", "circumstances determine man's idea", "education is universal", and "history is made by geniuses"; on the other side, Helvetius later attempted to interpret history with material needs; though this attempt failed, "but it served as a will left for the ideologists in the next century who are willing to continue with French materialism"[3]. French utopian socialists are the first executor of this will. All in all, French utopian socialism developed French materialism in the eighteenth century "into real humanism and the logical basis of Communism"[4].

Apart from French philosophy in the eighteenth century, the classical mechanics of Newton also has influence on social philosophy.

Newton asserted that the world is subject to a system of mechanical laws. On that ground, he established two mature principles of natural science: one was the principle of repeatability, namely that repeatability was the fundamental feature of natural laws; the other was the principle of precision, namely that the laws governing the world could not only be known, but also be grasped with precise relations of quantities. The opinions of Newton had made a great success, and were accepted by the science circles of France from the eighteenth century to the early nineteenth century.

Natural science has no intention of flattering social science, but it tends to determine the appearance and even the general tendency of sociology. The success of the classical mechanics of Newton constituted the general theoretical background of the revolution in European social science from the late eighteenth century to the early nineteenth century. The strong emotion of scientism and rationalism created by it stimulated Saint-Simon et al. to transform history into science and interpret the movement of social history in line with the characteristics of natural laws. Saint-Simon worshiped Newton so much that he called his philosophy "the philosophy of universal gravitation" and argued that social science might and should become a science as precise as natural science, namely "social physics". Fourier also showed that the laws

---

2   *Karl Marx and Friedrich Engels*. 1st Chinese Ed., Vol. 2, p. 167.
3   Plekhanov, *On Development of the Monistic Conception of History*, p. 12.
4   *Karl Marx and Friedrich Engels*. 1st Chinese Ed., Vol. 2, pp. 167 – 168.

of social movement "accord with the law of material gravitation expounded by Newton and Leibniz in all aspects"[5]. Social philosophy was generated against such a cultural background.

2 MAIN VIEWPOINTS OF SOCIAL PHILOSOPHY

The viewpoint of historical regularity, as the basis and starting point of social philosophy, is the first contribution of social philosophy to the history of philosophy.

"Saint-Simon first looked for regularity in history"[6], and asserted that the development of human society took on objective regularity, and "all that have happened in the past and all that are going to happen in the future constitute a series, whose former term is the past and last term is the future"[7]. Fourier thought the laws of social movement covered the past, the present and the future, and "every phase of society is obedient to the general growth law"[8]. Owen pointed out that the development of human society was a necessary historical process. "The past is unavoidable, and also necessary for creating the present, just as the present is necessary for creating the future form of human existence"[9]. These expositions are strategically concise and comprehensive, and clearly and correctly tell us a truth: social development has its laws, and history has its inherent regularity.

Social philosophy does not only acknowledge the existence of historical laws, but also points out historical laws can be known by men; additionally, it also discusses them in a specific way with an eye to revealing the driving force of historical development.

The laws of social movement in Fourier's eyes are "the law of appetite gravitation". He pointed out that "the instinct of appetite exists in all people, and it is constant no matter in the past, at present or in the future", and meanwhile it could be satisfied "only through frequent conflict with the opposite". The appetite of man is divided into sensory appetite and spiritual appetite; the satisfaction of the latter must be premised on the satisfaction of the former, while the satisfaction of the

---

5   *Selected Works of Charles Fourier.* Vol. 1, p. 12.
6   Plekhanov, *On Development of the Monistic Conception of History*, p. 29.
7   *Selected Works of Saint-Simon.* Beijing: The Commercial Press, 1964: Vol. I, p. 90.
8   *Selected Works of Charles Fourier.* Vol. 1, p. 242.
9   *Selected Works of Robert Owen.* Vol. 2, pp. 68 – 69.

former must be guaranteed by material wealth. Therefore the contradiction between human inherent appetite and external material wealth constitutes the basic impetus and law of social development.

It is idealistic to think that there is an innate constant "appetite" and the laws of social development can only be shown by the appetite of man. But the theory of "appetite gravitation" connotes another opinion, namely that contradiction is the impetus of social development and the production and distribution of material wealth is the basic force of social development. "Social changes revolve around life and economic behaviors, but not administrative system."[10] While dealing with the evolution of social system, Fourier took the status of production development in that times as basic cause and mark. Such an opinion obviously has some features of the materialistic conception of history.

According to Saint-Simon, historians only narrate the alternation history of regimes, which is actually the form and representation of history, and the essence of history still lies in property distribution and economic arrangement. "The form of parliamentary government is better than any other government forms, but it is just a form, and the establishment of ownership is the essence, the cornerstone for the edifice of society." "The existence of society consists in the reservation of ownership rather than the preservation of the law initially formulating it."[11] The ownership mentioned by Saint-Simon in effect refers to the property relation, i.e. economic relation, in society. Hence, by putting forward that ownership is the cornerstone for the edifice of society and government is merely its form, he explicitly proposes the viewpoint that economic relation determines political system, which is a dramatic progress.

So, what determine ownership and its changes? Saint-Simon thought the answer was in the needs of industrial development. That is to say, the status of production development determines the properties of ownership. It is true that Saint-Simon did not really solve the question that how material production determined ownership and moreover idealistically explained the invention of instruments of labor and then the development of industry with the development of human reason, but it is demonstrated by our analysis that he had roughly interpreted the internal relations between material production, ownership and political system, thereby foreseeing some viewpoints of the materialistic conception of history.

---

10   *Selected Works of Charles Fourier.* Vol. 1, p. 57.
11   *Selected Works of Saint-Simon.* Vol. I, pp. 226 and 22.

Owen showed no inferiority and expressed such a belief that productive forces determined social system. From his point of view, productive forces "grow in an endless way". In capitalist society, productive forces grow into a scale much greater than that over a hundred years ago, becoming "novel productive forces". However, this means, which originally can eliminate poverty, is made the tool creating poverty. "Thus it can be judged that the existing social system has been outdated, and a tremendous change is urgently required in the cause of human beings." Therefore the status of productive forces "is another sign with especially important meaning for the forthcoming of the times requiring rapid transformation of society"[12].

In view of the above, Owen demonstrates the transiency of capitalist private ownership and the inevitability of socialist public ownership from the angle of productive forces. This indicates that Owen has precisely aware of the real relationship between productive forces and social system. His opinion was unique at that time, taking a vital step towards materialistically understanding of history.

We can find that utopian socialists like Saint-Simon et al., although being conscious of the important role of economy, do not understand the inner contradiction of material production, thus being unable to really and scientifically uncover historical laws, and they are just close to the fundamental law of the materialistic conception of history, that is, productive forces determine relations of production. This is the first point.

Secondly, utopian socialists like Saint-Simon et al. stress that history has inherent objective laws and that only knowing the laws of social development can men establish the science about society, and such a viewpoint is of great significance. In the view of the traditional European historiography from Herodotus in ancient Greece to Ranke in the nineteenth century, history is either a casual sequence of a series of segments or the accumulation of transient accidental events, therefore their historical theories are merely limited to describing and discussing the history they have personally experienced and witnessed, and they are unable to have a general survey over the whole history; in traditional European philosophy from the philosophy of ancient Greece and Roman to French philosophy in the eighteenth century, most philosophers either take history as the accumulation of accidental events or

---

12   *Selected Works of Robert Owen*. Vol. 2, pp. 51 – 52.

pursue the history in general from the perspective that God is the master of mankind, in the belief that "the history of mankind is an order determined by God". For this reason, the conception of historical law of the three major utopian socialists started to divert the direction of historical study, guiding human thoughts to the land of necessity and progress.

Thirdly, utopian socialists like Saint-Simon et al. perceive that material production determines ownership and ownership is the cornerstone for the edifice of society, and even that productive forces determine the change of social system. Such viewpoints undoubtedly belong to economic determinism, which is the uniqueness of Saint-Simon et al. to all previous utopian socialists, as well as the prominent scientific factor in their utopianism. This shows that the three major utopian socialists have stridden across the boundary of the idealistic conception of history and reached the realm of the materialistic conception of history.

The theory about the dialectical development of history is the second contribution of social philosophy to the history of philosophy.

Fourier regards historical development as a movement process from low level to high level, and thinks human history goes through four phases, namely system of unenlightenment, patriarchal system, barbarous system and civilized system. The civilized system has a narrow sense and a broad sense with Fourier, with the former referring to capitalist system and the latter referring to slavery system, feudal system and capitalist system. All of them are not everlasting in the eyes of Fourier, which "are nothing but some byways beset with sufferings and brambles, nothing but the phases before the rise to a perfect social system, to an economically destined system – the Fourier system (the ideal system of Fourier – noted by the quoter)"[13]. This is the first point.

Secondly, Fourier holds that the course of history is not linear but is tortuous; history is developing in contradictions, and the whole process of social movement has "rising fluctuation" and "declining fluctuation", including four stages, i.e. childhood, growth, decline and fall. Moreover, every historical period also has rising stage and declining stage; the prime period of a society is always followed by the stage of decline, and another vigorous society will take its place. The same is true to capitalist society and even the ideal society in the future, until human society perishes.

13　*Selected Works of Charles Fourier.* Vol. 1, p. 65.

Thirdly, there is not a pure society, and every society contains the remains of old system and the sprout of a new one. "Every period tends to have the characteristics of both lower and higher periods", and "there is always a society mixing the old with the new in different social periods, which is the hybrid of the characteristics of multiple periods"[14]. This shows that Fourier does not only perceive the stage character of historical development but also the continuity of historical development.

Saint-Simon pointed out, "civilization on the one hand refers to the development of human reason and on the other hand means the development of men's influence on nature arising therefrom."[15] This definition of civilization has a duality: it is idealistic in that it puts the development of reason in the first place, nevertheless it also has a reasonable factor, that is, definitely pointing out that civilization has two aspects – spiritual and material.

As per this conception of civilization, Saint-Simon first of all divided human history into three phases according to the evolution degree of reason: (1) the phase from primitive idolatry to polytheism; (2) the phase in which theism replaces polytheism; and (3) the positive phase of transition from eradicating theism to setting up scientific system.

At the same time, Saint-Simon also classified human history into five periods, namely initial civilizing period of mankind, slavery, theology-feudalism, "new feudalism" (capitalism), and future "industrial system". He thought the generation of these five systems was necessary, and even "the Middle Ages" were not "the discontinuation of history", whose generation was also necessary. However, every society was relative, containing both "the disappearing remains of the past" and "the growing sprout of the future", and the struggle between the two would inevitably make history a continuously rising and progressing development process. Here we can find the historicist attitude and dialectical view of Saint-Simon.

Both Saint-Simon and Fourier have expressed a firm belief that human history is continuously moving, changing and developing process from quantitative change to qualitative change, from low level to high level. Saint-Simon's classification of human history into "five periods" is close to historical reality, and Fourier's opinion on the "four ages"

---

14   *Selected Works of Charles Fourier.* Vol. 1, pp. 122 and 271.
15   *Selected Works of Saint-Simon.* Vol. II, p. 170.

in historical development is profound. His classification also has a significant meaning in the history of historiography and predates the historical periodization viewpoint of Morgan. Engels thinks the critique of Fourier on civilized system shows its entire talent because of Morgan. "Please compare the periods of social development proposed by Fourier (i.e. period of unenlightenment, period of patriarchy, period of barbarism, and period of civilization) and their features with the absolute idea of Hegel! The absolute idea of Hegel went through innumerable trials and hardships before opening up a path out of the maze of history", but "Fourier imagined the future according to his own views after correctly knowing the past and the present"[16].

Both Saint-Simon and Fourier consider history as a development process unifying stages with continuity; that is to say, the development of a society is always qualitatively different from another, but it is simultaneously shown as a picture in which the characteristics of the past, the foundations of the present and the sprouts of the future are interlacing with each other; society is developing in contradictions; not only the whole process of human society's movement has rising fluctuation and declining fluctuation, but also every historical stage has its rising period and declining period; every society is in a process of generation, development and extinction, so is the whole human society.

Needless to say, it is clear that the theory of historical process of social philosophy contains rich dialectical thoughts, so it is generally a dialectical outlook on development. In the times when metaphysics reigned exclusively in the view of nature, dialectics had made a glorious achievement in the conception of history – I have to say that it is a historical progress. Fourier and Saint-Simon are worthy of the high evaluation from Engels: they "use the dialectic method in the same masterly way as his contemporary, Hegel".

Pursuing human emancipation and all-around development is the third contribution of social philosophy to the history of philosophy.

Saint-Simon said on his deathbed, "My whole life can be expressed in one thought: all men must be assured the freest development of their natural capacities." This sentence is quoted by Marx in *The German Ideology*. Fourier deemed all-around development of man as the goal of

---

16 *Karl Marx and Friedrich Engels*. 1st Chinese Ed., Vol. 2, p. 658.

future society, and believed human "happiness rests with the all-around development of appetite. This is a civilized system, the happiness far out of the reach of even the richest man"[17]. Owen definitely argued that only the combination of physical labor with mental work could give an all-around play to the talents of man, and thought the ideal society "will cultivate the noble characters of men by all means, and can use appropriate methods to take advantage of the intellectual, moral, physical and behavioral characteristics of men according to the innate capacity and power of every individual in his whole life"[18]. The same with Fourier, Owen also advocated the combination of education with productive labor for the purpose of fostering well-rounded men. Marx gives a high appraisal to this:

"From the Factory system budded, as Robert Owen has shown us in detail, the germ of the education of the future, an education that will, in the case of every child over a given age, combine productive labor with instruction and gymnastics, not only as one of the methods of adding to the efficiency of production, but as the only method of producing fully developed human beings."[19]

Above all, utopian socialists like Saint-Simon et al. investigate the relationship of social economic system with human emancipation and development from the perspective of labor, and hold that only by changing the labor properties under capitalist system and realizing conscious and free labor can the human emancipation and thereby the all-around development of mankind be achieved. They also design respective ideal social economic systems, namely the "industrial system" of Saint-Simon, the "system of guarantee", "system of cooperation" and "system of harmony" of Fourier, the "cooperative commune system" of Owen, etc., in the belief that these systems are basic paths to the all-around development of man.

From Saint-Simon's point of view, labor is originally a happy thing, but it is forced in the civilized system, and workers are made the slave of labor, so labor becomes into a suffering. As a matter of fact, labor should be free and joyful, coinciding with the natural appetite of man and satisfying man both physically and spiritually. In the society in the future, according to Fourier, labor will even "turn into a thing more attractive

17   Selected Works of Charles Fourier. Vol. 1, p. 136.
18   *Selected Works of Robert Owen.* Vol. 2, p. 27.
19   *Karl Marx and Friedrich Engels.* 1st Chinese Ed., Vol. 23, p. 530.

than theatergoing and dancing party nowadays", and men frequently exchange the types of work freely. In the sight of Owen, old division of labor brings about distorted development respectively of workers and labor activity itself; therefore the old division of labor should be abolished, possibility should be made for every member of society to be engaged in both agriculture and industry and exchange the types of work as many as possible, and opportunity should be provided for every person to develop and show all his capabilities in an all-around way.

Seen in general, the theory of human emancipation and all-around development of the three major utopian socialists like Saint-Simon, etc., although failing to jump out of the frame of the theory of human nature, touches on the relationship of practical activity and economic system with human development, thereby providing a theoretical premise that can be used for reference by Marx in his theory of man's all-around development. In 1847, Engels critically carried forward the thought of utopian socialists like Saint-Simon, etc. on the all-around development of man, and even used the discourse very close to those of Owen and Fourier to describe the basic features of communist society in *The Principles of Communism*: "the rounded development of the capacities of all members of society through the elimination of the present division of labor, through industrial education, through engaging in varying activities, through the participation by all in the enjoyments produced by all, through the combination of city and country"[20].

3 THE MATERIALISTIC CONCEPTION OF HISTORY VS. SOCIAL PHILOSOPHY

Historical facts tell us that Marx studied the works of Saint-Simon and other utopian socialists in Paris in 1844. In the view of Plekhanov, the thought of social philosophy is so "novel and broad" that it is accepted by the historiography of the French Restoration period with pleasure. Thierry thinks that interpreting political system with ownership is a key to understanding history. Since social philosophy can render bourgeois historian Thierry rapt with joy, why cannot it strike a chord with proletarian philosopher Marx?

"Ownership is the essence of the form of government and the cornerstone for the edifice of society" – this opinion of Saint-Simon more confirmed Marx in his belief that had established in 1843, that is, "civil

---

20 Karl Marx and Friedrich Engels. 1st Chinese Ed., Vol. 4, p. 371.

society is the foundation of a political state", which is "the essence (of private property) brought to existence"[21].

"The answer to the understanding of ownership can be found in the development of industry" – this opinion of Saint-Simon, so to speak, had the power to make the deaf ear hear and the dimsighted see in the early nineteenth century. It had significant theoretical meaning, and opened up a new path to scientific resolution of "the mystery of history", thus undoubtedly inspired Marx, who was good at critically carrying forward theories of the predecessors.

It is also the fact that in his *Economic and Philosophical Manuscripts of 1844*, Marx makes a vital conclusion: "religion, family, state, law, morality, science, art, etc., are only particular modes of production, and fall under its general law". The proposal of this conclusion shows Marx does not only inherit but also transcend the viewpoint of Saint-Simon. "Inheritance" means that Marx, the same with Saint-Simon, thought that material production was the cornerstone for the edifice of society, and at that time, Marx had not yet known the inner contradiction of material production either. "Transcendence" means that Marx, apart from thinking material production determined ownership, also argued that material production determined total social consciousness, including sciences. The opinion that material production determines ownership can be considered as the contact point between social philosophy and the materialistic conception of history.

Saint-Simon, Fourier and Owen all attach great importance to labor. The apprehension of Fourier on labor is further deeper than that of classical economics. The classical economics takes labor merely as the source of wealth; Fourier regards labor not only as the source of wealth but also as real life need and self-exercise of man, and the emancipation of labor as the precondition for the all-around development of man. In Owen's opinion, productive labor can guarantee the satisfaction of all reasonable needs of mankind like air, but in capitalist system, the method for creating wealth and virtue is made the means of creating poverty and crime, so present social system must be transformed.

With Saint-Simon and Fourier, "private property is first considered only in its objective aspect – but nevertheless with labor as its essence". Saint-Simon "declares ... that industrial labor as such is the essence",

---

21   *Karl Marx and Friedrich Engels*. 1st Chinese Ed., Vol. 1, pp. 252 and 369.

and Fourier "conceives agricultural labor to be at least the exemplary type"[22]. In *Economic and Philosophical Manuscripts of 1844*, Marx critically transforms the doctrines of Saint-Simon, Fourier, Owen and Hegel on labor, sets up the theory of alienated labor by leveraging the concept of alienation, and uses it as the basis for his historical theory then, thereby reaching two significant conclusions: "for the socialist man the entire so-called history of the world is nothing but the creation of man through human labor"; communism abandons the alienated labor, whereupon men are completely emancipated and fully developed, and "appropriates his comprehensive essence in a comprehensive manner, that is to say, as a whole man"[23].

Economic and Philosophical Manuscripts of 1844 is a critical piece of works during the forming period of the materialistic conception of history, the beginning of the revolutionary change in philosophy. Discussions above demonstrate that social philosophy supplies direct theoretical premise for Marx to resolve "the mystery of history" in *Economic and Philosophical Manuscripts of 1844*. Social philosophy, as correctly pointed out by Plekhanov, is the "important material" for Marx to set up the materialistic conception of history.

The positive enlightenments of social philosophy on Marx's establishment of the materialistic conception of history have been expounded above, and below its negative enlightenments.

While probing into the relationship between man and environment, social philosophy slipped down, and was caught deeply in "antinomy": using environment to interpret man and his ideas, and in turn using man and his ideas to explain environment. Of course, this falls under the theory of interaction. The materialistic conception of history does not reject interaction, and on the contrary affirms the principle of Hegel that "interaction is the real ultimate cause of things" and meanwhile another principle of Hegel that "the relationship of interaction itself still needs understanding". Social philosophy has perceived the interaction between man and environment in a definite sense, but it cannot explain where the interaction comes from and how it is generated, thus its ability has fallen short of its wish to interpret historical laws, and it has to stay at the level of superficial interaction and finally raise the white flag to the heroic conception of history. Its theory of interaction is shallow.

---

22 *Karl Marx and Friedrich Engels*. 1st Chinese Ed., Vol. 42, p. 117.
23 *Karl Marx and Friedrich Engels*. 1st Chinese Ed., Vol. 42, pp. 131 and 123.

The relationship between man and environment, this simple but complex problem, confused French enlightenment philosophers like Helvetius and French utopian socialists like Saint-Simon, but it did not confuse Marx. The theoretical faults of Saint-Simon, etc. negatively inspire Marx to transcend their superficial theory of interaction, to find out the realistic foundation both determining environment and man's development. This is exactly the superiority of Marx.

Marx finds that man lives relying on nature; for living, men must engage in material production; production appears as a dual relationship between man and nature and between man and man. The former forms productive forces, whilst the latter forms relations of production, both of which constitute the inner contradiction of production; productive forces determine relations of production, and on the basis of relations of production, men enter into definite political and thinking relations, namely constituting a definite social environment. This is one side of the issue.

On the other side, practice is the mode of being of man, and labor constitutes the essential activity of man; the human essence, in its reality, is the ensemble of the social relations. Hence, along with the development of practice, men do not only transform natural and social environments, but also change themselves, including physical organization, mental structure, thinking mode, and social relations. "The coincidence of the changing of circumstances with human activity or self-changing can be conceived and rationally understood only as revolutionary practice."

In this way, Marx goes from superficial interaction – the interaction between man and environment – into deep interaction – the interaction between productive forces and relations of production. The "antinomy" between man and nature is finally resolved by Marx. In this connection, Plekhanov declared, "'By thus acting on the external world and changing it, man at the same time changes his own nature.' This sentence implies all the essences of Marx's theory of history."[24]

It is thus observable that the positive and negative enlightenments from social philosophy meet with the scientific discussion of Marx in the mode of production of material goods and its inner contradiction, eventually bringing all the theories of history out of the obscure maze. The

---

24   Plekhanov, *On Development of the Monistic Conception of History*, p. 107.

establishment of the materialistic conception of history brings the effulgent dawn in the history of human cognition.

4 BRIEF PERORATION

With regard to the content of social philosophy itself, it reconciles the materialistic conception of history with the idealistic conception of history, but sinks into the latter in the end. As mentioned before, social philosophy holds many viewpoints of materialism, whose focus is that material production determines ownership, and ownership determines political system, thus driving the development of history. It is in this sense that social philosophy falls under economic determinism. However, this does not mean that social philosophy is the materialistic conception of history.

In my opinion, economic determinism is a necessary theoretical step in the transformation from the idealistic conception of history to the materialistic conception of history, but it is not equal to historical materialism. "Only in vulgar lectures can economy be described as the initial cause of all social phenomena." Economic determinism simply stands for the dominant significance of economic factors or relations in social life, but when economic factors or relations are used to interpret history, they themselves need explaining first of all. Economic factors or relations can be understood materialistically or interpreted idealistically. Economic determinism does not reject historical idealism.

Fact is the case. Social philosophy thinks economic factors, which play a dominant role in social life, and even productive forces are the product of human knowledge and idea, the "function" of human intelligence. At this point, it falls into the arms of the idealistic conception of history, and then conceives perfect legislation and ideal society by taking the so-called invariable human nature as the highest yardstick.

Judged by its class attribute, social philosophy is the early proletarian world outlook, the "symbolization, presentation and herald" of the proletariat. Besides, the inclination to the bourgeoisie still has certain influence in social philosophy, either advocating preserving private ownership or placing the hope of transforming society on "the man of property".

Social philosophy is a contradiction, magically combining the proletarian world outlook with the inclination to the bourgeoisie, materialism with idealism, and dialectics with metaphysics. It seems to be a
paradox, but it substantially exists. Its dissolution is inescapable due to
its own inner contradiction. Two different doctrines arise out of its dissolution: Comte's positivism and Marx's materialism. I believe without
hesitation that social philosophy holds some wise ideas and thoughts
and occupies the position as the "herald" of the proletariat in the history
of philosophy; it is the epitome of materialistic factors among social
philosophies before Marx, as well as the direct theoretical premise of
the establishment of the materialistic conception of history. The materialistic conception of history is the direct successor and great reformer
of social philosophy. I unambiguously declare that only the materialistic conception of history is the first to scientifically present the real
cause and general law of the movement of human history.

CHAPTER IV

FROM HEGEL'S HISTORICAL DIALECTICS TO MARX'S HISTORICAL MATERIALISM

Hegel is an absolute idealist, but "negative dialectics" makes him dare to make an overall survey on history and give an "abstract, logical, speculative expression" of historical movement. Marx is a practical materialist, and practical dialectics leads him to the deep of history and really reveal the general law of historical movement. Based on this fundamental characteristic, I plan to make a new investigation and survey on the basic features of Hegel's historical dialectics and Marx's historical materialism and the relationship between the two.

1 BASIC FEATURES OF HISTORICAL DIALECTICS OF HEGEL

History is the development of "absolute reason" in time, which is the first feature of Hegel's historical dialectics.

The noumenon of world in Hegelian philosophy is reason. In his eyes, "Reason is the Sovereign of the World; that the history of the world, therefore, presents us with a rational process"[1]. This "rational process" is for the first thing a development process in accordance with law. The history of the world is a rational and "most concrete reality", therefore history is inevitably governed by the reason of history, and moves complying with its inherent law. Historical law certainly has different features from natural law. "History in general is therefore the development of Spirit in Time, as Nature is the development of the Idea in Space"[2]. As a result, in contrast with the simultaneity and repeatability of natural law, historical law only takes on the feature of diachronism, and the decisive effect of the reason of history is shown in the diachronic one-way process.

However, time in Hegelian philosophy is nothing but a pure formal feature of reason; the reason of history is actually independent of the diachronism of history. In other words, historical law is merely "the plan of God" antecedent to history; and the "ultimate plan" of the world is the goal pursued by historical movement. For this reason, history is no more than a purposive process specified by the plan preformed before history.

History is the development of the consciousness of freedom, which is the second feature of Hegel's historical dialectics.

The primary principle of Hegel, this absolute idealist, is the supremacy of the reason of history. In Hegelian philosophy, man after all is "a live instrument for the substantive cause of world spirit"[3]. As a dialectical idealist, Hegel notices that the reason of history governing the history itself is in effect an abstract universality, which cannot be realized without human activity: "nothing great in the World has been accomplished without passion". "Two elements, therefore, enter into the object of our

---

1 Hegel, *The Philosophy of History*, p. 47.
2 Ibid., p. 115.
3 Hegel, *Principles of the Philosophy of Law*, p. 354.

investigation; the first the Idea, the second the complex of human passions; the one the warp, the other the woof of the vast arras-web of
Universal History."[4]

Therefore Hegel consciously takes solving the problem of the relationship between historical law and human freedom as the fundamental
mission of his historical dialectics. He perceives that "man is free as
the man-in-himself", the whole process of history and its every phase is
showing and realizing man's freedom, and "the History of the world is
none other than the progress of the consciousness of Freedom"; in addition, he also well knows that "the History of the World is not the theatre
of happiness", and the progress of the consciousness of freedom "must
be conceived in the movement of its world history"[5]. The movement
of the entire world history is in two links – necessity and freedom, and
the law of historical development is dialectically unified with human
freedom.

Labor is the true being of man, which is the third feature of Hegel's
historical dialectics.

The dissection on the labor dialectics is the deep structure in Hegel's
historical dialectics. Hegel believes real man must be separated from
nature, since he is the self-consciousness in and for itself. While determining the essence of man, Hegel introduces in the standpoint of
genesis, change and labor, and thinks man shows his essence by act
and activity – "the true being of man is his act"[6]. Labor is the initiative
activity to transform things, namely to "shape" natural objects.

Thus labor constitutes the "negative middle term" between man and
nature, by virtue of which, man separates himself from nature, brands
natural objects with the mark of subject, and sees himself and realizes
his independence through labor products; then subject and object are
unified. Obviously, two effects of labor can be found here: the effect
of practice that changes the form of natural object and the effect of
cognition that helps man achieve self-consciousness. That's why Hegel
views man is the creation through labor and labor is the essence of man.

---

4   Hegel, *The Philosophy of History*, p. 62.
5   ibid., p. 57.
6   Hegel, *The Phenomenology of Mind*. Vol. I, p. 213.

Fundamentally speaking, the reason why Hegel is able to bring forward a grand conception of history and the negative dialectics running through it and to conceive entity as subject, as an internal process, is because he makes a fairly profound philosophical reflection on labor. He understands labor based on labor; "I have accomplished something, [and] have [thereby] alienated it from myself; this negative [element] is positive; this alienation is an acquiring"[7]. Negativity is therefore the activity of labor, the objectification of the powers of man as subject, and the object created by such objectification is bound to be contradictory and opposite to subject. Thus negativity should not only be alienation but also the activity sublating this alienation, retargeting the object of alienation back to man for the purpose of self-actualization of subject.

However, the "subject" in the mind of Hegel is just "reason" after all. So in his view only abstract thinking activity and spiritual labor have primitive initiative and creativity, whereas actual, material, sensuous labor is just the "pattern of spirit"; the real man and the domain of his real relations are "the spiritual daylight of the present". So we can see that Hegel's historical dialectics merely gives an "abstract, logical, speculative expression" of historical movement.

2 THEORETICAL PATH FROM HEGEL'S HISTORICAL DIALECTICS AND MARX'S HISTORICAL MATERIALISM

The materialistic dialectical analysis of labor is the "hinge" from Hegel's historical dialectics to Marx's historical materialism.

From Marx's point of view, the secret and essence of Hegel's historical dialectics and even the whole Hegelian philosophy is that Hegel "grasps the essence of labor and comprehends objective man – true, because real man – as the outcome of man's own labor", and "grasps labor as the essence of man – as man's essence which stands the test"[8]. The discovery of the essence of Hegel's historical dialectics constitutes a decisive link in the whole chain of Marx's critical inheritance of it.

Marx reveals such a real process that subject is the outcome of the interaction between subject and object. In such interaction, on the one hand, mankind acts on and transforms the objective world through initiative

---

7   Quoted from *Thoughts of Young Hegel about Labor and Alienation*, carried in *Philosophical Researches*, 1978(8).
8   *Karl Marx and Friedrich Engels*. 1st Chinese Ed., Vol. 42, p. 163.

activity, rendering his essential powers "objectified" and "external-ized"; on the other hand, the objective world is translated into subject in the form of objective beings, that is, man appropriates and uses the things he has created previously in his activity. In short, the process of human labor is the unity respectively between creating object and ap-propriating object and between transformation of the objective world and self-transformation, and it is a process in which subject and object of history interact on and infiltrate into each other.

Basically, "the only labor which Hegel knows and recognizes is ab-stractly mental labor"; "the object appears only as abstract conscious-ness, man only as self-consciousness"[9]. In this way, the relationship between real subject and object of history becomes the relationship be-tween self-consciousness and consciousness, and labor, the real activity of man, merely becomes a form. That is to say, Hegel cuts off the real connection between idea, consciousness and its initiative and sensuous material activity, and reverses the positions of subject and object, taking object for subject and conceiving the former as the foundation of the latter by replacing the real historical movement with a logical move-ment divorced from reality.

The fundamental reason of this strange "upside-down" phenomenon is that Hegel denies the objective existence of nature and disavows the ontological meaning of material practice. On the contrary, Marx recog-nizes the "priority" of nature in the first place, and meanwhile thinks that the material exchange between man and nature caused by labor constitutes the realistic foundation of human world, the basis for the ex-istence of man as such. During labor, man starts from his internal needs and faces nature at the same time, and uses the two to determine his activity. Labor, the objective activity, is the initiative activity of man, as an objective being, to objectively and concretely transform nature as another objective being. Thus it can bring its objective effect into play and establish objective object. Such an objective product itself verifies that man is an objective being, that human essence and powers are ob-jective beings, and the activity of labor and beings.

The materialistic dialectical analysis of labor helps Marx be aware of the fact that labor is the foundation for the existence and change of the whole human society and human beings, the most genuine, profound, fundamental basis of all ideas and consciousnesses. Then, he gives a

9   *Karl Marx and Friedrich Engels.* 1st Chinese Ed., Vol. 42, pp. 163 and 162.

new life to Hegel's view of labor, and lays a solid foundation for his historical materialism. Lukacs pointed out:

"Only Marx's view of labor can materialistically resolve the insurmountable difficulties in front of Hegel arising as frequently as his talented presentiment. The reason for this is because Marx's view of labor gives content to the material exchange between society and nature, thus making substantial the relationship between the categories of labor and their natural premises, and the changes of these premises resulting from the social development of labor."[10]

The materialistic dialectical investigation of historical law is the premise for Marx's historical materialism to be a science.

According to Marx, the key to rejecting the idealism, teleology and fatalism in Hegel's historical dialectics consists in the restoration of the materialistic foundation in the conception of historical law. This requires regarding man as both the "author" and the "actor" of history.[11] "'History' is not, as it were, a person apart, using man as a means to achieve its own aims; history is nothing but the activity of man pursuing his aims."[12] Man is the subject of history, the "author" of history. This is one side of the issue.

On the other side, Marx also emphasizes that history is a process of natural history. In the view of Marx, man is the "actor" of history, who cannot create history at will. Man as the subject of history, human activity, and the object of human activity are all premised on nature. Man interacts on nature during labor. Nature entering the sphere of labor is translated into the content of history, and exists and shows in society; thus a bidirectional movement of "nature historicization" and "history naturalization" is formed.

In this movement, the movement law of productive forces, the accumulated materialized labor, fundamentally determines social conditions and historical regularity. The purposive practical activity of man produces the objective historical law that does not change with man's consciousness and will. Such objective historical law cannot be an

---

10   *A Collection of Literary Essays of Lukacs.* Beijing: China Social Sciences Press, 1980: p. 432.
11   *Karl Marx and Friedrich Engels.* 1st Chinese Ed., Vol. 4, p. 149.
12   *Karl Marx and Friedrich Engels.* 1st Chinese Ed., Vol. 2, pp. 118 – 119.

independent entity separated from practical activity, but it makes it possible for the historical activity of men, determines the general trend of historical development, and serves as the law of human activity.

The genuine reconciliation of the objectivity of history and the consciousness of man based on practice is thus realized. The regularity of historical development is the regularity of human activity, i.e. the regularity of correlations between men who make up the society. In the study of history, Marx resolves social relations between man and man into relations of production, and relations of production into the relationship between man and nature – the height of productive forces. In this way, historical materialism is able to demonstrate material change happening on the aspect of "social economy with the precision of natural science", and it also points out the features of repeatability and conventionality of historical law, namely that similar production processes and same social formations may exist in different nations or different times. Marx brings forth five social formations on this premise. The emergence of notions of "precision", "repeatability" and "conventionality" makes historical materialism of Marx a science, a mature science.

3 BASIC FEATURES OF MARX'S HISTORICAL MATERIALISM

The scientific view of practice is the theoretical foundation of Marx's historical materialism.

Marx's historical materialism takes history as the development process of mankind, and its mission is to reveal the general law in this process. To fulfill this mission, it must adopt the scientific view of practice as its theoretical basis.

History is formed by the conscious purposive activity of man. The total activities in history involve three essential relationships – between man and nature, between man and society, and between man and consciousness. The course and law of history is always manifested as the interaction between such three factors as "man", "will" and "thing". These three factors and three relationships are virtually subject and object of history and the relationship between the two. The interaction between subject and object of history gives rise to the regularity of history, which cannot become an independent entity separated from the activity of subject but does not change with the consciousness and will of subject. Historical regularity presupposes the dialectics respectively between subject and object of history and between consciousness and existence.

This is an objectively existing contradiction. For history, if it is studied as objective nature only from the angle of object, the trait of history – the creation of man through human labor – cannot be grasped; if it is studied not as an objective process only from the angle of subject, its inherent law will be obliterated, which is precisely the decayed idea of idealism. The wisdom of Marx is that he grasps the basic structure – the relationship between man and nature – between subject and object of history and makes materialistic dialectical analysis on practice.

Through a series of exceedingly tough studies, Marx comes up with the following opinions: "all social life is essentially practical"[13]; labor, i.e. the activity of man to transform nature, is the first and most basic form of practice. Practice connects subject of history with its object (man and nature in the first place) and involves cognition and its object; men do not only transform and cognize nature, but also transform, create and cognize themselves, including physical organization, mental structure, thinking mode, and social relations. Environmental is created by man, and man is also created by environment; the foundation for this mutual creation is practice. As Marx said, "the coincidence of the changing of circumstances and of human activity or self-changing can be conceived and rationally understood only as revolutionary practice"[14]. History, fundamentally speaking, is the development of practical activity of man in time.

Hence, practice, as "the human sensuous activity", is the foundation for the sensuous existence of man, the profound foundation for the existence of the world of objects that man lives in, and the ontological activity or activity itself of real man. Practice is of ontological significance for history. "Practice" is the real foundation of Marx's historical materialism. By selecting practice as the theoretical foundation for his historical materialism, Marx in effect selects the relationship between subject and object of history as the theoretical clue of his historical materialism. Thus Marx's historical materialism is turned into a verifiable scientific theory with revealing the general law of historical development as its content.

---

13   *Selected Works of Karl Marx and Friedrich Engels.* 2nd Ed., Vol. 1, p. 56.
14   *Selected Works of Karl Marx and Friedrich Engels.* 2nd Ed., Vol. 1, p. 55.

The theory of economic necessity is an inherent principle of Marx's historical materialism.

Different from Hegel who reduces historical regularity to historical reason, Marx reduces all historical laws to the practical activity of man, to the economic necessity generated during the movement of the mode of production. The content of economic necessity is that productive forces determine relations of production and thereby the total social relations. Productive forces, as the ability of men conquer nature, substantially result from the interaction between man and nature. There is no any interaction more fundamental that this interaction in the conception of history. It is the real ultimate cause of things. In this sense, the philosophy of history cannot be traced to a realm farther than the interaction between man and nature.

The mode of production of material life restricts the whole process of social life, political life and spiritual life; the basic trend of historical movement is the general influence of economic necessity on historical course, for which economic necessity has a decisive significance, "forming the red thread which runs through them and alone leads to understanding". However, history is made by men, so economic necessity cannot spontaneously function as an independent entity divorced from the practical activity of man, or purely function in separation from social factors like politics, thought, culture, etc. Social factors of politics, thought, culture, etc. interact on each other and meanwhile react upon economic necessity. In this interaction, factors like politics will change economic necessity within a certain limit, and economic necessity will be impacted more or less and "transformed" to a certain degree. Economic necessity also has historicity.

Economic necessity arises out of the interaction between man and nature, takes change to a certain degree in the interaction with factors like politics, and is realized inevitably in the interaction of various social factors. On this basis, Marx gets the reasonable understanding on economic necessity, which is an inherent principle of Marx's historical materialism.

Historical totality is an inherent principle of Marx's historical materialism.

Marx's historical materialism does not study the whole history, but the history as a whole. Its basic features do not only include the principle of economic necessity but also the principle of historical totality. Lukacs points out that the dialectics of "the concrete unity of the whole" must be introduced into the analysis of history, and "only in this context which sees the isolated facts of social life as aspects of the historical process and integrates them in a totality, can knowledge of the facts hope to become knowledge of reality"[15]. Such knowledge is "concept totality".

According to the principle of historical totality, in the whole process of history, there is no significant historical event whose origin cannot be explained by economic relation, and meanwhile there is no significant historical event which is not steered, accompanied and followed by definite political condition and ideology. The evolution of history, in no case, happens in the dimension of economy. Economic change needs to be realized by dint of political change, and ideal change is the guide of political change. The interaction between economy, politics and idea forms a stereoscopic network, and the evolution of history happens in this network structure. Therefore Marx's historical materialism conceives history as a real totality, an organism that is changeable and always changing. The theory of historical materialism is no other than "a summing-up of the most general results, abstractions which arise from the observation of the historical development of men".

"This conception of history depends on our ability to expound the real process of production, starting out from the material production of life itself, and to comprehend the form of intercourse connected with this and created by this mode of production (i.e. civil society in its various stages), as the basis of all history; and to show it in its action as State, to explain all the different theoretical products and forms of consciousness, religion, philosophy, ethics, etc. etc. and trace their origins and growth from that basis; by which means, of course, the whole thing can be depicted in its totality (and therefore, too, the reciprocal action of these various sides on one another)."[16]

---

15   Lukacs, *History and Class Consciousness*, English Ed., p. 7.
16   *Karl Marx and Friedrich Engels.* 1st Chinese Ed., Vol. 3, pp. 31 and 42 – 43.

Thus it can be seen that in respect of the understanding of history, Marx's historical materialism is certainly based on economic necessity, but it does not confine itself to "economic anatomy". Additionally, Marx's historical materialism also pays attention to the ensemble of all social phenomena that are directly or indirectly determined by practice and economic necessity. It is the materialistic "phenomenology" about history as a whole. Historical totality is another inherent principle of Marx's historical materialism.

In a word, Hegel's historical dialectics belongs to speculative philosophy, and it is essentially an "abstract, logical, speculative expression" of historical movement; Marx's historical materialism is the speculation of philosophy, whose essence is the materialistic, dialectical, logical reproduction of historical movement. The labor dialectics links up these two philosophies of history with different essences, and makes Hegel unconsciously point to Marx a way out of the maze of his theoretical system and to the genuine, practical cognition of history. Marx's historical materialism directly inherits the theoretical clue of Hegel's historical dialectics, and meanwhile "sublates" the latter. By the aid of the power of the scientific view of practice, Marx founds historical materialism, leaving the epoch of "absolute reason" created by Hegel far behind.

CHAPTER V

THEORY OF HUMAN ESSENCE FROM FEUERBACH TO MARX: A NEW INTERPRETATION

The essence and mode of being of man is an old but fresh topic, attracting countless scientists, ideologists and philosophers to explore and think it endlessly, like an enormous gravitational field. It is an extremely broad field of thought, where the understandings of Feuerbach and Marx take a distinctive historical position: both of them take the "complete essence" of man as the focus throughout their lives, and discuss the "complete essence" of man from a global perspective. To further show the contemporary meaning of Marx's theory of human essence, I will also discuss the theory of human essence of Scheler, the founder of modern philosophical anthropology in this chapter. As far as I am concerned, Marx grasps the "real, living man" through the materialistic dialectical analysis of labor or practice, with the result of really finding the mode of being of man and that man is essentially the product of human self-creation activity, and sublating the theoretical opposition between early modern philosophical humanism and modern philosophical anthropology based on tremendous advancement.

1 APPREHENSION OF FEUERBACH'S PHILOSOPHICAL HUMANISM: "MULTIPLE IDENTITIES" OF MAN

The exposition of Feuerbach about the essence of man is indeed on a definite aspect from a definite angle, and the wordings are different from and inconsistent with one another. But his concept of the essence of man is accomplished as a whole. He clearly points out that "truth is only the totality of man's life and being"[1], and his new philosophy aims to reveal "concrete and whole entity of man"[2]; and only by investigating "the whole essence" or "complete essence" of man can "concrete man" be grasped.

From Feuerbach's point of view, man has "multiple identities", and the essence of man is the totality of various attributes distinguishing man from animals, and is common in men; it has three levels: natural essence, social essence and spiritual essence, three of which are unified into the complete essence of man. In the humanism system of Feuerbach's philosophy, the fundamental feature of the concept of human essence is the theory of structural level based on natural attribute. It is not only the primary measure for Feuerbach to resolve the central topic of early modern philosophy – the relationship between thinking and being, but also the epoch-making contribution of his view of human essence and even his whole doctrine.

First of all, man is a natural being. Feuerbach lays particular stress on investigating the essence of man based on the relationship between man and nature. Viewing man as the unity of man and nature is the theoretical premise of his view of human essence. Man is a natural being; this opinion has dual meaning: one is that the essence of man is first determined by nature, by the natural conditions which he is in; the other is that the essence of man forms in the relationship of man to nature. The former emphasizes that man is a product of nature, and his essence can only "come from the deep of nature", while the latter emphasizes that man cannot be equated with nature, because "man immediately generated from nature is merely a pure natural essence rather than man"[3]. Feuerbach believes there is "a series of infinite variations and media" from natural man to real man, and the essence of man cannot be thoroughly grasped only from nature.

---

1   *Selected Philosophical Works of Feuerbach*. 1st New Chinese Ed., Vol. I, p. 185.
2   ibid., p. 180.
3   *Selected Philosophical Works of Feuerbach*. 1st New Chinese Ed., Vol. I, p. 247.

Next, man is a social and historical being. In Feuerbach's eyes, the dependence of man on nature is based on his dependence on man, and one distinguishing feature of man is mutual need, interdependence and intercourse. An isolated man does not take on the essence of man, which is included in group, in the unity of man with man; "the entity of man" should be "merely put in sociality"[4]. Leaving the relationship of man to man, the essence of man will become "a fiction without content". "Only social man is man."[5] Moreover, man is "a product of history". The essence of man is not changeless, and instead, it changes and develops with the elapse of times. The pure natural essence is just the "primitive essence" of man, and "a man is truly and perfectly man only when he possesses an aesthetic or artistic, religious or moral, philosophical or scientific sense"[6] . It is thus obvious that Feuerbach's concept of human essence is not an ossified notion of biology, but contains the elements of social relation and historical development.

Finally, man is a rational being. In the view of Feuerbach, the most important feature differentiating man from animal is that man has "consciousness in a strict sense" – reason, namely that man cannot only perceive himself as an individual and realize "ego", but also realize his "species" and take it as "object". That is to say, man can live a conscious "species" life, which differentiates man from animal. Reason always coexists with the life of man; as long as man is alive, he will necessarily use his rational, will and heart powers. Reason, will and heart "are the absolute essence of man"[7]. The spiritual essence of man constitutes an important content in Feuerbach's concept of human essence.

Thus we can find that Feuerbach probes into the essence of man at different levels, on different aspects, and from different angles. The natural essence, social essence and spiritual essence of man jointly constitute the complete concept of human essence of Feuerbach, who expressly brings forward the concepts of man's "complete essence", "the whole essence of man", etc. Therefore, Feuerbach's concept of human essence is a multi-level integrated concept.

In my opinion, this is a structural schema rising from lower essence to higher essence. In this schema, natural essence belongs to the base component at the lowest level, social essence occupies the position as

4   *Selected Philosophical Works of Feuerbach.* 1st New Chinese Ed., Vol. II, p. 435.
5   *Selected Philosophical Works of Feuerbach.* 1st New Chinese Ed., Vol. I, p. 571.
6   ibid., p. 184.
7   *Selected Philosophical Works of Feuerbach.* 1st New Chinese Ed., Vol. II, p. 28.

a medium, and spiritual essence is at the highest level. The three are closely related with one another: the essence at a lower level is the foundation and premise of that at a higher level, and the essence at a higher level embraces that at a lower level in it. For example, Feuerbach thinks the thinking of man cannot be divorced from the sensuous existence of life and flesh, but it is superior to natural attribute. The essential difference of man from animal is that man has thought. It is in this sense that Feuerbach regards "reason, will and heart" as "the absolute essence" of man.

The evaluation on Feuerbach's concept of human essence must be made in two respects: on the one hand, we should give a positive evaluation on his investigation of the complete human essence from a global perspective; but on the other hand, we must see that Feuerbach's concept of human essence is deeply stamped with the mark of naturalism.

The essence of man, basically speaking, forms from the relationship between man and nature, the material exchange between man and nature, and the conversion between material and idea. Feuerbach puts forward two important concepts of "concrete man" and "concrete nature", and discusses the essence of man first of all based on the relationship between man and nature. Such a practice is doubtlessly reasonable, supplying a feasible train of thought for grasping the essence of man in a deep structure. This is one side of the coin.

On the other side, Feuerbach deals with the relationship between man and nature only in a "sensuous intuitive" manner. Though he has realized that a certain "medium" existing between "natural man" and "real man", he does not understand this "medium" is exactly the transformation of nature by man, viz., the sensuous activity, and forgets that this activity has a decisive influence on the relationship between man and nature and on man himself. So he can only resolve the natural attribute of man into the external natural conditions upon which man relies for existence. In this way, he makes a methodological mistake, that is, confusing the conditions upon which man relies for existence with the essence of man, and replacing essence with being. The tragedy of Feuerbach is that he tightly grasps nature and man, but only confirms the natural relationship between the two and do not advance to their practical relationship.

Raising the relationship between man and nature to the relationship between man and man for further discussion is another characteristic of Feuerbach's view of human essence. The relationship of man to nature is inseparable from his relationship to man. Feuerbach proposes that the "species" essence of man be investigated in social history, opening up the path to conceiving the essence of man starting out from real man. However, the limitation of Feuerbach is precisely reflected in the most significant issue he puts forward. While specifically conceiving social relation, Feuerbach is fundamentally talking about an "intercommunity naturally connecting many individuals", and his fault is that although he confirms the natural relationship between man and man, but fails to reach the practical relationship between them.

Man is a conscious species-being; whether having consciousness, especially self-consciousness, is an important difference between man and ape.

In terms of the relationship between man and nature, if we do not discuss the transformation of nature by man in combination with the thinking attribute of man, we will be unable to explain the difference between man and animal. It is because the changes of nature caused by man are fundamentally different from those caused by animal in that the activity of man to transform nature is the activity of "nature humanization" under the guidance of reason. In respect of the relationship between man and society, if we do not discuss the social attribute of man in combination with his thinking attribute, we will be also unable to explain the difference between man and animal, because the group of animals also has social properties in a certain sense. Here, the fundamental difference between the "sociality" of man and that of animal, still, can only be scientifically explained with the thinking attribute of man. Marx points out, "Man's consciousness of the necessity of associating with the individuals around him is the beginning of the consciousness that he is living in society at all. ... at this point man is only distinguished from sheep by the fact that with him consciousness takes the place of instinct or that his instinct is a conscious one."[8]

That is to way, the division of labor or cooperation of animal is unconscious combination, the instinct of animal for existence, whereas human society is conscious combination, and human consciousness takes the place of animal instinct. In this connection, Feuerbach's further discussion about the essence of man based on the relationship between man

---

8   Marx and Engels, *Feuerbach*, p. 26.

and consciousness is unimpeachable, and this is a work of scientific value, a key to interpreting why the activity of man has conscious initiative. But on the other side, Feuerbach views reason and consciousness only as "mental activity", and does not understand consciousness has an identical connection with the sensuous activity of man to "transform the world of objects". His weakness is that he only confirms the natural (biological) relationship between man and consciousness, but fails to arrive at the practical relationship between the two.

Prior to Feuerbach, the essence of man had been investigated by philosophers respectively from the perspective of nature, society or consciousness. The epoch-making contribution of Feuerbach is that he probes into the complete essence of man from a global perspective, i.e. from perspectives of the relationship respectively between man and nature, between man and society, and between man and consciousness. However, his real limitation is precisely reflected in the most significant issue he puts forward. Marx points out, "Feuerbach has a great advantage over the 'pure' materialists in that he realizes how man too is an 'object of the senses'. But apart from the fact that he only conceives him as an 'object of the senses, not as sensuous activity,' because he still remains in the realm of theory and conceives of men not in their given social connection, not under their existing conditions of life, which have made them what they are, he never arrives at the really existing active men, but stops at the abstraction 'man'."[9] Basically, since Feuerbach does not understand practice is the mode of being of man and the "completeness" of man lies in the comprehensiveness of practice, the complete or "concrete" man described by him is still an abstract man.

2 APPREHENSION OF SCHELER'S PHILOSOPHICAL ANTHROPOLOGY: MAN IS THE UNITY BETWEEN "LIFE IMPULSE" AND SPIRITUAL ACTIVITY

M. Scheler (1874–1928) is the founder of modern philosophical anthropology. "Complete man" is the real topic he discusses in his theory all his life. His investigation of the essence of man as a whole renders his philosophical anthropology "the most powerful philosophical strength in whole modern philosophy"[10]. Scheler expounds the complete essence of man in two steps. He probes into man first in natural sphere

---

9   *Selected Works of Karl Marx and Friedrich Engels*. 2nd Ed., Vol. 1, pp. 77 – 78.
10 Landman, *Experience of Scheler in Modern Philosophy*. German Ed., p. 9.

and then in spiritual sphere, thereby setting up the dual essence structure of life and spirit of man, or to say, establishing the complete man
featured by life impulse and spiritual essence. Scheler argues that man,
in the first place, is a natural being associated with life maintenance,
and there inevitably exists "the desire or impulse of life" in man. Such
a life impulse has duality: on the one hand, it is an outward primitive
activity, the "presentation of internal conditions" of man for all time; on
the other hand, it is a limited impulse of self-limitation. In brief, "it is
in self-movement, self-formation, and self-differentiation", as a "being-
in-himself and being-for-himself"[11].

From the viewpoint of Scheler, life impulse itself has a strong ability of
self-activity. When man is doing activity under the driving force of life
impulse, he is a living power of self-promotion and self-actualization.
However, life impulse, falling under the sphere of reality, is a common
phenomenon for both man and animal, so when man is doing activity
under the driving force of life impulse, he is merely a "natural man",
and "a natural man is an animal"[12].

In fact, man is not only a natural being, but more importantly, he is
a spiritual being. The spirit referred to by Scheler has a broad meaning, not only covering reason but also emotion, intuition and experience. In his opinion, spirit belongs to neither the inorganic world nor
the organic world and originally is "pure activity", but man is able to
make reality "non-actualized", i.e. making environment "objectified",
through spiritual activity, thereby creating a special world for himself;
meanwhile, by means of spiritual activity, man "makes his own physiological and psychological states, as well as any single feelings, his
objects"[13], namely objectifying his own physiological and psychological states. Such a double objectifying activity enables man to transcend
his natural being and realize that he exists as an individual rather than
a "species", thus forming "the essence of individual". In this sense,
Scheler believes spirit is the basic decisive attribute of man, and "only
spirit can differentiate man from other beings"[14].

---

11   Scheler, *The Human Place in the Cosmos*. German Ed., pp. 11 – 12.
12   Scheler, *The Human Place in the Cosmos*. German Ed., p. 44.
13   Scheler, *Ideas about Man*. German Ed., p. 19.
14   ibid., p. 49.

However, spirit is just an intention activity and dynamic tendency; it "accepts object", but does not "constitutes object". Pure spirit is weak and feeble, and the more a being is spiritualized, the weaker he is. As a result, reducing man to either life impulse or spiritual activity is an "unfinished description", insufficient to reveal the complete essence of man or the complete man; a complete man is inevitably a combination of life impulse and spiritual activity. Man is both the reflection of life impulse and the place for spiritual activity; he is the tension and intermediary between the two. Scheler thus thinks the complete essence of man must be described on the basis of the process of mutual complementation and transformation between life and spirit.

According to Scheler, life as a blind impulse needs internally guided by spirit, which has its "orderly activity structure" that makes it able to coordinate various desires and needs of man, guide life out of the plight of limitation, and actualize the abundant styles of life; spirit as a "pure activity" needs to be enriched with concrete content, and as a dynamic tendency it needs to internally absorb original power from life impulse, thereby realizing its own ultimate perfection and eternal value.

This is a process of bidirectional movement of "life spiritualization" and "transformation of spirit into life". The dual structure of life impulse and spirit activity as the essence of man is formed in this process. This dual structure helps man break the closed relationship between animal and environment and become "an X that is infinitely opened to the world"[15].

Scheler's theory of human essence has a prominent dual character:

On the one hand, investigating the essence of man in the bidirectional movement of "life spiritualization" and "transformation of spirit into life" is reasonable. A real man is inevitably a combination of life impulse and spiritual activity, a unity between the two. Marx holds that "the first premise of all human history is, of course, the existence of living human individuals"[16], and the existence of living individuals is at the same time the existence of consciousness. In this sense, the essence of man is really a dual structure of life and spirit.

---

15   Scheler, *The Human Place in the Cosmos*. German Ed., p. 49.
16   Marx and Engels, *Feuerbach*, p. 10.

Scheler investigates the essence of man in the dynamic process of self-creation and thinks man is a "being-in-himself and being-for-himself" and his essence is an open system in dynamic development, indicating that Scheler sets himself against solidifying the essence of man. If we say Feuerbach mainly investigates the essence of man from a static perspective and on the aspect of man's passivity, Scheler is majorly from a dynamic perspective and on the aspect of man's initiative. In Scheler's view, the essence of man is formed and realized in human activity. This opinion, which consciously conceives of the essence of man from the angle of man's self-creation and self-development and based on "the existence of man as such", exactly embodies the superiority of Scheler to Feuerbach.

On the other hand, Scheler classifies spirit as a "high-level thing" and life as a "low-level thing", thinks the former is above the latter, and meanwhile does not rest upon the domain of self-consciousness of life, showing an inclination to dualism. At this point there are two defects:

The first is that he does not apprehend the dialectical relationship between "high-level thing" and "low-level thing". In a highly-organized system, the high-level things function as a coordinator and controller, but they cannot be generated without the low-level things, which are their support and executor.

The second is that he does not know the dialectical relationship between spirit and society. In Scheler's eyes, the content of spirit is turned by language into the wealth of individual, and "language, endowed by God, is the primary phenomenon; it is the premise of thinking, and the chief means of whole cognition, i.e. potential history"[17]. Language has a significant effect on spirit in that spirit is interlacing with language and has a history as long as language. But it is not the primary phenomenon, or the product of God. It, the same with consciousness, arises from the need, the necessity, of intercourse of man with other men. "Language is practical consciousness that exists also for other men, and for that reason alone it really exists for me personally as well." Therefore human consciousness or spirit is "a social product", and "and remains so as long as men exist at all"[18]. It is because spirit is a social product that it can play the role as an element of society.

---

17   Scheler, *On the Overthrow of Values*. German Ed., p. 290.
18   Marx and Engels, *Feuerbach*, p. 25.

Fundamentally, the theoretical fault of Scheler is not that he seeks the essence of man in the bidirectional movement of life and spirit, but that he does not find the real medium in the mutual convection between life and spirit and ignores the decisive effect of social practice on the essence of man. For this reason, the complete essence of man in his doctrine has no real foundation. Though starting from the complete man, he still arrives at one-sided man. Famous modern philosopher Bollnow correctly pointed out:

"None of the historical world with all richness enters the image of man established by these philosophical anthropology. ... Here, only a narrow path is slashed through the forest of the essential features and attributes of man. Although some specific images of man are set up, they are one-sided, merely some distorted pictures, thus the definition of completeness is not definitely reached."[19]

3 APPREHENSION OF MARXIST PHILOSOPHY: LABOR CONSTITUTES THE "COMPREHENSIVE ESSENCE" OF MAN

Marx's philosophy of man is formed on the basis of the sublation of Feuerbach's philosophical humanism, and "just as existentialism has a certain connection with but meanwhile objects to anthropology, Marxism also has similar contradictory relationship with anthropology"[20]. Therefore with respect to time, Marx's philosophy of man was later than Feuerbach's philosophical humanism but earlier than Scheler's philosophical anthropology; but regarding logic, it is "the late philosophy", which sublates the theoretical opposition between Feuerbach's philosophical humanism and Scheler's philosophical anthropology, thus accomplishing a huge integration in the investigation history of human essence.

The same with Feuerbach and Scheler, Marx investigates the essence of man from a global perspective, and "complete man" and his "comprehensive essence" are the main concern of Marx for all his life; different from Feuerbach and Scheler, Marx conceives "complete man" as "man engaged in actual activity", whose complete essence is fundamentally featured by the comprehensiveness and openness of labor. Practice is the mode of being of man, and man in practical activity becomes a

---

19   Bollnow, *Methodological Principles of Philosophical Anthropology*. German Ed., p. 30.
20   Landmann, *Philosophical Anthropology*. English Ed., p. 66.

"being of totality", so labor constitutes the essence of man, which is the global definition of human essence given by Marxist philosophy. On this basis, Marx expounds the essence of man respectively from different angles: man is "an active natural being"; "man is a social being"; man is "a conscious species-being"[21]. These conclusions are respectively partial definition of human essence given by Marxist philosophy, reflecting the essence of man in different respects and together showing the complete essence of man, thereby specifically demonstrating that man appearing in history is the unity between the determined being and the active creative being.

From Marx's point of view, "the whole character of a species, its species-character, is contained in the character of its life activity"[22]. In other words, the essence of man is what runs through the life activity of man and is then manifested as the character of this life activity. Hence, the essence of man should be explored in the life activity of man and its special character, starting with "the real living individuals themselves"[23].

This conclusion of Marx is extremely profound, which indicates such a truth that the mode of being of a species is judged from the form of its life activity. To be specific, animals subsist depending on their negative adaption to nature, so the mode of being of animals is their instinctive activity, determined by their physiological structure, especially their active organs. Differing from them, men keep their survival and development during their positive transformation of nature by exploiting instruments. The first premise of the survival of mankind is that men must be able to live, so the first historical act of mankind is the basic activity, namely "the production of material life itself", which must be carried out every minute of every day. It is such practical activity that continuously creates the fundamental conditions for human existence and development. Practice thus becomes the foundation for the living of man and constitutes a special life form of mankind, i.e. the mode of being of man.

The life activity of animal is instinctive, whereas that of man is conscious. "Conscious life activity distinguishes man immediately from animal life activity." The key point is that Marx specifies the concrete

---

21   *Karl Marx and Friedrich Engels*. 1st Chinese Ed., Vol. 42, pp. 167, 122 and 96.
22   ibid., p. 96.
23   Marx and Engels, *Feuerbach*, p. 16.

content of this conscious life activity as the practice transforming nature and actually creating the world of objects. The fundamental and original form of this practice is labor. In Marx's view, this "labor in general" is "the general nature of man"; it is not only the fundamental one among various common attributes of man, but also the internal basis for explaining why man is as such and why he possesses those other attributes. It constitutes the basic difference between man and animal, and fundamentally features man as a real man. In a word, it constitutes the absolute essence of man. It is indeed an abstraction to regard "labor in general" transforming nature and creating the world of objects as the essence of man, but it is a scientific abstraction, a reasonable abstraction encompassing abundant contents.

According to Marx, "labor is, in the first place, a process in which both man and Nature participate, and in which man of his own accord starts, regulates, and controls the material reactions between himself and Nature"; labor is also a process of the conversion between material and idea participated in by man and nature, and "at the end of every labor-process, we get a result that already existed in the imagination of the laborer at its commencement. He not only effects a change of form in the material on which he works, but he also realizes a purpose of his own that gives the law to his modus operandi."[24]

In addition, the material exchange between man and nature is inseparable from the interpersonal intercourse and the interpersonal activity exchange. Intercourse, including material intercourse and spiritual intercourse between man and man, coexists with labor as its premise and element. Marx points out that men "produce only by working together in a specified manner and reciprocally exchanging their activities. In order to produce, they enter into definite connections and relations to one another, and only within these social connections and relations does their influence upon nature operate – i.e., does production take place"[25].

It is thus clear that labor understood by Marx is a flowing historical category that implies three relationships, namely between man and nature, between man and man, and between man and his spirit, all of which together make man the unity of natural attribute, social attribute, and spiritual attribute.

---

24 *Karl Marx and Friedrich Engels.* 1st Chinese Ed., Vol. 23, pp. 201 – 202.
25 *Selected Works of Karl Marx and Friedrich Engels.* 2nd Ed., Vol. 1, p. 344.

The labor of men is "conditioned by their physical organization", and as soon as coming into being, it becomes a powerful impetus that controls the direction of human biological evolution. It qualitatively distinguishes man from animal in terms of the object, content and satisfaction mode of natural needs, and gives them human character different from that of animal needs, thereby forming and developing natural attribute or life impulse unique to man. The natural attribute of man thus becomes a factor or aspect in the essence of man.

Meanwhile, labor also forms and develops spiritual activity (psychological state and thinking structure) unique to man. The spirit or consciousness is both the product of man's naturality and sociality and the principal factor of the difference between man and animal. The naturality and sociality of man both include actualized subjective factors. The spiritual attribute of man thus becomes another factor or aspect in the essence of man.

So we can see that labor coagulates natural attribute and spiritual attribute of man. In other words, only in labor can mutual convection and organic unity between "sensuous man" and "rational man", or between "life impulse" and "spiritual activity" of man, be really realized; both presuppose and permeate into each other, becoming two inseparable aspects of the life activity of man. The essence of man is not only natural but also spiritual; to be precise, it is the unity of naturality and spirituality. G. Cordier, a famous researcher of "Marxology", holds that when Marx uses "practice, labor and productive labor to interpret the essence of man, he has completely denied the necessity to conceive of man from the perspective of spiritual universality"[26]. This is actually a groundless and extremely shallow criticism on the "humanistic thought" of Marx.

Labor does not only coagulate the relationships of man with nature and consciousness, but at the outset it has includes the relationship between man and society. Man creates a humanized natural environment for himself by means of labor, and meanwhile forms the natural attribute unique to him. In a same way, man creates a social relation system for himself through labor and intercourse activity, and meanwhile forms the social attribute unique to him. Social relations and social attribute restrict the natural attribute of man and brands it with the mark of sociality, making the biological organization of man more and more suitable

---

26   G. Cordier, *From Romanticism to Marxism*. English Ed., p. 84.

for the requirements of social life. The famous conclusion of Marx that the essence of man is the ensemble of the social relations methodologically points out the identical relationships of social relations with social attribute and natural attribute. This is one side of the issue.

On the other side, social relations aren't a pool of hydrochloric acid that melts everything. The natural attribute of man does not disappear after man becomes a social being, and instead, it still participates in the development of man and coexists with labor as the premise and factor of the labor and spiritual production made by the real man. The sociality of man contains the biological attribute of man. Man is the unity between biological heredity and social inheritance and between natural evolution order and social evolution sequence. "Natural man" and "social man" are really unified in an organic manner in labor. The essence of man is not only natural but also social; to be exact, it is the unity of naturality and sociality.

"Labor in general" conceived by Marxist philosophy is the "material practical activity", moving in and for itself, of mankind to transform the external world. It connects real man with objective nature and involves cognition and its object; men do not only transform and cognize nature, but also transform, create and cognize themselves, including physical organization, mental state, thinking mode, and social relations. For this reason, the essence of man apprehended by Marxist philosophy is a system nature encompassing multiple elements (natural attribute, social attribute, and spiritual attribute) and multiple relationships (between man and nature, between man and society, and between man and consciousness).

Fundamentally, the relationships between man and nature, between man and man, and between man and his spirit, together with man's natural, social and spiritual attributes, are unified in practical activity. This indicates that man makes himself a subjective being of self-creation by means of practice. The secrets of man are hidden in his practical activity. As Marx said, "as individuals express their life, so they are. What they are, therefore, coincides with their production, both with what they produce and with how they produce"[27].

---

27   *Selected Works of Karl Marx and Friedrich Engels.* 2nd Ed., Vol. 1, pp. 67 – 68.

In a word, Feuerbach's philosophical humanism and Scheler's philosophical anthropology, indeed, make some penetrating judgments on
the essence of man, and both attempt to find the "complete man" or "the
complete essence of man". However, they discuss the essence of man
superciliously putting aside labor, the mode of being of man. This is a
fundamental mistake, unavoidably leading to their tragic result: though
trying to find the "complete man", they finally arrive at abstract or one-
sided man. "The history of industry and the established objective existence of industry are the open book of man's essential powers." In
Marx's opinion, this book is the fruit of human essence that is most realistic, with richest content, and easiest for perception and understanding, but many philosophers just do not study it in the sense of man's
essential powers. In such case, the theory of human essence "cannot
become a genuine, comprehensive and real science"[28]. The superiority
of Marxist philosophy is that it finds practice is the mode of being of
man, thereby grasping the "real, living man" and really discovering the
complete essence of man. This is the real way for Feuerbach's philosophical humanism, Scheler's philosophical anthropology, and even the
entire philosophy about man.

---

28   *Karl Marx and Friedrich Engels*. 1st Chinese Ed., Vol. 42, p. 127.

CHAPTER VI

ONTOLOGY THOUGHTS OF STALIN AND LUKACS: A NEW INTERPRETATION

In the history of Marxist philosophy, Stalin and Lukacs are remarkable. Stalin had ever been identified as the certain successor and epitome of orthodox Marxist philosophy, and his philosophical thought had ever been regarded as the sole supreme authority and constituted the basic framework of the Soviet model of Marxist philosophy; Lukacs had been considered as the rebel of orthodox Marxist philosophy and "theoretical revisionist", whose philosophical thought had once been blamed for "trying to cancel materialism to emasculate dialectical materialism" but then regarded as "the model of modern Marxism" and "the highest achievement of Marxist philosophy in the twentieth century"; then, he was considered the pathfinder of western Marxism. In this chapter, I plan to make a new investigation and survey on the viewpoints of Stalin and Lukacs about the ontology of Marxist philosophy, in order to deepen the study of the ontology of Marxist philosophy.

1 FROM LENIN TO STALIN

To grasp Stalin's thought about the ontology of Marxist philosophy, the thought of Lenin about the same thing needs understanding in the first place, because the former is the direct successor of the latter, and takes the latter to extreme.

Lenin did not clearly point out Marxist philosophy was dialectical materialism and historical materialism, but such a viewpoint is implied in his philosophical works. As far as Lenin is concerned, Marxist philosophy is the first thorough complete morphology of materialism, namely that Marxist philosophy is materialism with respect to both the view of nature and the conception of history; materialism in the view of nature is "Marx's dialectical materialism", and materialism in the conception of history is "Marx's historical materialism"[1].

But in the system of Marxist philosophy, the statuses of dialectical materialism and historical materialism are different. Specifically, dialectical materialism is the theoretical basis, whilst historical materialism has the character of continuation, that is, it is the extension and continuation of dialectical materialism or the principles of materialism. Lenin explicitly puts forward "the theory of extension" in *The Three Sources and Three Component Parts of Marxism*: "Marx deepened and developed philosophical materialism to the full, and extended the cognition of nature to include the cognition of human society". In Karl Marx, he clearly brings forth "the theory of continuation": "the discovery of the materialist conception of history, or more correctly, the consistent continuation and extension of materialism into the domain of social phenomena ...". Thus Marx crowns "the structure of philosophical materialism", so "Marx's philosophy is a consummate philosophical materialism"[2]. Here, the logic of the "continuation and extension" of historical materialism out of dialectical materialism is that "since materialism in general explains consciousness as the outcome of being, and not conversely, then materialism as applied to the social life of mankind has to explain social consciousness as the outcome of social being"[3].

---

1   *Selected Works of Lenin.* Beijing: People's Publishing House, 1995: 3rd Ed., Vol. II, pp. 310 – 311.
2   *Selected Works of Lenin.* 3rd Ed., Vol. II, p. 311.
3   ibid., p. 423.

The problem is that what are the differences between general materialism and "Marx's dialectical materialism" as the theoretical basis of historical materialism, i.e. as "the cognition of nature", having verified by
"the latest discoveries of natural science"? This is the key to grasping
the ontology of Marxist philosophy in the horizon of Lenin.

From the viewpoint of Lenin, in respect of the view of nature, the difference between Marx's materialism and general materialism is that
Marx enriches materialism in the eighteenth century and Feuerbach's
materialism with Hegel's dialectics. "That is why Marx and Engels laid
the emphasis in their works rather on *dialectical materialism** than on
dialectical *materialism*"[4]. That is to say, there is no essential difference
between Marx's materialism and general materialism on the aspect of
ontology. As said by Lenin, "the existence of matter does not depend on
sensation. Matter is primary. Sensation, thought, consciousness are the
supreme product of matter organized in a particular way. Such are the
views of materialism in general, and of Marx and Engels in particular"[5].

Obviously, Lenin equated Marx's materialistic view of nature with general materialism, and took the "materialism that excludes history and
its process" for the theoretical basis of historical materialism, viz., actually taking the "abstract substance" separated from real mankind and
their activity for ontology. Lenin did not really understand the opinion
of Marx – "the chief defect of all hitherto existing materialism – that
of Feuerbach included – is that the thing, reality, sensuousness, is conceived only in the form of the object or of contemplation, but not as sensuous human activity, practice, not subjectively", however, Marx's dialectical materialism is the materialism that comprehends "sensuousness
as practical activity"[6]. As a result, although Lenin saw the ontological
significance of practice and even pointed out that "the view of practice
is the primary and basic view of ontology", he did not apprehend the
ontological significance of practice, thus failing to fundamentally grasp
the ontology of Marxist philosophy.

---

4   ibid., p. 225.
5   ibid., p. 51.
6   *Selected Works of Karl Marx and Friedrich Engels*. 2nd Ed., Vol. 1, pp. 54 and 56.

*) Lenin wrote dialectical materialism in italics to underline his understanding that it
is a complete wholeness.

Stalin knew Lenin very well and took Lenin's viewpoint to extreme. He definitely classified Marxist philosophy into dialectical materialism and historical materialism, and thought dialectical materialism "is called dialectical materialism because its approach to the phenomena of nature, its method of studying and apprehending them, is dialectical, while its interpretation of the phenomena of nature, its conception of these phenomena, its theory, is material"; and "historical materialism is the extension of the principles of dialectical materialism to the study of social life, an application of the principles of dialectical materialism to the phenomena of the life of society, to the study of society and of its history"[7].

It's not hard to find that Stalin, as a matter of fact, construed dialectical materialism as a kind of view of nature unrelated to historical process, and took such so-called dialectical materialism as the theoretical basis for historical materialism. To demonstrate that historical materialism was the extension and application of dialectical materialism to the domain of social history, Stalin made a series logical deduction from nature to society: "if the connection between the phenomena of nature and their interdependence are laws of the development of nature, it follows, too, that the connection and interdependence of the phenomena of social life are laws of the development of society, and not something accidental"; "if our knowledge of the laws of development of nature is authentic knowledge, having the validity of objective truth, it follows that social life, the development of society, is also knowable, and that the data of science regarding the laws of development of society are authentic data having the validity of objective truths"; "if nature, being, the material world, is primary, and consciousness, thought, is secondary, derivative ... is a reflection of this objective reality, it follows that the material life of society, its being, is also primary, and its spiritual life secondary, derivative, ... a reflection of this objective reality"[8], and so on. That is to say, according to Stalin, from dialectical materialism to historical materialism, it is actually a logical operation process from natural being to social being.

But the problem is that nature and human society has essential differences despite their connections. In nature, everything is in blind interaction and happens not for expected purpose, but in human society, men engaged in activity have conscious intentions, and everything happens

7   *Selected Works of Stalin*. Vol. II, p. 424.
8   ibid., pp. 435 and 436

for expected purposes. So the materialistic conception of history is not the "extension and application" of the materialistic view of nature. Helvetius had "conceived it (materialism) immediately in its application to social life"[9] long ago, but reached the idealistic conception of history. Feuerbach is like him. "As far as Feuerbach is a materialist he does not deal with history, and as far as he considers history he is not a materialist. With him materialism and history diverge completely."[10]

Leaving aside whether the view of nature could be taken as the theoretical basis of the conception of history, the viewpoints of Stalin contain a fatal theoretical mistake: the natural being conceived by him is the "abstract nature" separated from real man and his activity and from historical process, actually "a thing given direct from all eternity, remaining ever the same" mentioned by Marx during his critique on Feuerbach. While pointing out natural environment is not the decisive cause of social development, Stalin argued that a change in natural environment of slight important required millions of years, and "which remains almost unchanged in the course of tens of thousands of years cannot be the chief cause of development of that which undergoes fundamental changes in the course of a few hundred years".

At this point, Stalin, in effect, investigated natural environment in an isolated way, and did not understand the deep connotation of "historical nature and natural history" proposed by Marx and the important meaning of Marx's suggestion to "set out from these natural bases and their modification in the course of history through the action of men", thus he made a Feuerbach-style mistake, that is, "he does not see how the sensuous world around him is, not a thing given direct from all eternity, remaining ever the same, but the product of industry and of the state of society; and, indeed, in the sense that it is an historical product, the result of the activity of a whole succession of generations, ... Even the objects of the simplest 'sensuous certainty' are only given him through social development, industry and commercial intercourse"[11].

After the separation and abstraction, a kind of "abstract substance" becomes the cornerstone of Marxist philosophy in Stalin's mind. Although Stalin did not mention the word "noumenon" or "ontology", he in fact summed up Marxist philosophy as natural ontology.

9 *Karl Marx and Friedrich Engels.* 1st Chinese Ed., Vol. 2, p. 165.
10 *Selected Works of Karl Marx and Friedrich Engels.* 2nd Ed., Vol. 1, p. 78.
11 Ibid., p. 76.

Just because of this, Stalin essentially confused Marx's materialism with mechanical materialism. In his discussion about the "basic features of Marxist materialism", Stalin actually showed us only the common points between Marx's materialism and mechanical materialism, but did not know that the essential feature of Marx's materialism is practical materialism and it is this theoretical particularity that distinguishes Marx's new materialism from mechanical materialism and all old materialism. In his *Dialectical and Historical Materialism*, he quotes the sentence that "matter is the substratum of all changes" as the words of Marx, thinking it is one of the fundamental features of Marx's materialism. In fact, this is an obvious misquotation, that is, Stalin takes the restatement of Hobbes' thought by Marx for the thought of Marx himself, and misunderstands the viewpoint criticized by Marx as that appreciated by Marx. From Marx's point of view, materialism in Bacon "holds back within itself in a naive way the germs of a many-sided development. Matter, surrounded by a sensuous, poetic glamour, seems to attract man's whole entity by winning smiles".

However, in Hobbes, materialism "takes to misanthropy"[12]. It is because in Hobbes' view, "matter is the substratum of all changes", and man is just a kind of manifestation of natural substance; "every human passion is a mechanical movement which has a beginning and an end"; "man is subject to the same laws as nature. Power and freedom are identical". Marx thus believes in Hobbes, "sensuousness" has nothing to do with man and thereby "loses its poetic blossom, passes into the abstract experience of the geometrician"[13]. In other words, in the system of mechanical materialism, "abstract substance" or "abstract sensuousness" is made the subject or substratum of all changes, the so-called noumenon of the world.

However, Stalin did not understand that, so he took Hobbes' viewpoint for that of Marx. As far as I am concerned, this is not an accidental ignorance, but it indicates that Stalin did not clearly perceive the essential differences of Marx's new materialism from mechanical materialism and all old materialism.

We can see that the dialectical materialism apprehended by Stalin is in essence a view of nature that simply adds materialism with dialectics, and has a thick color of mechanical materialism. The first person

---

12   *Karl Marx and Friedrich Engels*. 1st Chinese Ed., Vol. 2, p. 164.
13   ibid., p. 164.

who confuses the materialistic view of nature of Marx with mechanical materialism is Mehring, who thinks Marx and Engels "are mechanical materialists in the domain of natural science, just as they are historical materialists in the field of society". Once such a dialectical materialism that "excludes history and its process" is regarded as the theoretical basis for historical materialism, historical materialism will be inevitably "distorted": the "material exchange" between man and nature and the "anthropological nature" that Marx focuses on disappear; practice, the mode of being of man, the essence of social life, and the groundwork of the real world, is concealed; and the subjectivity of man is dissolved. What's worse, in this so-called dialectical materialism, nature is separated from human activity and historical process, and becomes the "abstract nature" or "abstract substance" actually criticized by Marx.

To my understanding, this is an involution to the early modern materialism, which takes "abstract substance" as noumenon, a horrendous theoretical retrogression abandoning the epoch-making contribution of Marxist philosophy to a quite large extent. It indicates that Stalin attempted to expound Marxist philosophy in a popular manner, but he simply and one-sidedly understood Marxist philosophy and its ontology; in fact, he interpreted Marxist philosophy with the logic of early modern materialism.

No matter from which perspective, history or logic, historical materialism is not the "extension and application" of "dialectical materialism" to the domain of social history. In the philosophical system of Marx, there is no dialectical materialism independently as the theoretical basis or historical materialism independently having the character of application. On the contrary, historical materialism is the first great discovery of Marx, and since history is interpreted materialistically, a new development path has been opened up. It can be seen from in-depth investigation of the history of Marxist philosophy that Marx was not a materialist before becoming a historical materialist, and immediately when he became a historical materialist, he also became a dialectical materialist.

To put it another way, historical materialism was founded on the same day with dialectical materialism. Dialectical materialism and historical materialism are not two different doctrines, but different names of the same doctrine, namely Marx's materialism. The so-called dialectical materialism that "excludes history and its process" and is separated from historical materialism is not the dialectical materialism of Marx, and it is in essence the "restoration" of natural materialism under modern conditions and will lead to historical idealism under certain conditions. As Marx said, "The weak points in the abstract materialism of natural science, a materialism that excludes history and its process, are at once evident from the abstract and ideological conceptions of its spokesmen, whenever they venture beyond the bounds of their own specialty."[14]

The Soviet model of Marxist philosophy, whose foundation is laid and whose framework is erected by Stalin, is basically the "abstract materialism", or "the abstract materialism of natural science, a materialism that excludes history and its process", mentioned by Marx. When it prattles about "the materiality of world" while being separated from human activity and social history, it has stealthily gone "in the abstract materialistic direction, or rather idealism" criticized by Marx.

2 FROM *HISTORY AND CLASS CONSCIOUSNESS* TO *THE ONTOLOGY OF SOCIAL BEING*

The understanding of Stalin on Marxist philosophy and its ontology had been regarded as the sole supreme authority, and reigned in the history of Marxist philosophy for several decades, whereas the apprehension of Lukacs on the same thing had aroused fireworks at the very beginning and gone through ups and downs for several decades, and towards it, different peoples held different opinions. Whether Lukacs is a Marxist or a "western Marxist" is still under debate. As a matter of fact, in 1985, the 100th anniversary of Lukacs' birth, Hungarian Socialist Worker Party at that time had made a "final judgment" on him, that is, "Georg Lukacs is a great outstanding representative of Marxist-Leninist thought". I agree with this judgment, and believe Lukacs is one of the most significant and influential philosophers in the twentieth century. The hardships undergone by his thought reflect the vicissitudes in the history of Marxist philosophy in the twentieth century.

Seen in general, the expositions of Lukacs about the ontology of Marxist philosophy can be divided into two stages; the thought at the former stage are centrally reflected in *History and Class Consciousness* and that at the latter stage in *The Ontology of Social Being*. "Ontology is the real philosophical base of Marxism."[15] Either *History and Class*

14   *Karl Marx and Friedrich Engels*. 1st Chinese Ed., Vol. 23, p. 410.
15   *A Dictionary of Western Marxist Figures*. English Ed., p. 268.

Consciousness or *The Ontology of Social Being* focuses on the ontology of Marxist philosophy, but the understandings of the two are quite different.

In *History and Class Consciousness*, the discussion of Lukacs about the ontology of Marx has a noticeable feature, that is, negating natural dialectics, confining dialectics "within the spheres of history and society", and stressing on totality.

According to Lukacs, there is no natural dialectics referred to by Engels, and all dialectical questions left by Descartes, Kant and Hegel, including the contradictions between subject and object, between thinking and being, and between freedom and necessity and the sublation of "antinomies", "guide us to history"[16]. Since nature "is a social category", "in any definite stage of social development, whatever is considered to be natural, this naturalness is related to man; what form the man-related nature takes on, namely the form, content, scope and objectivity of nature, is conditioned by society", and "the growth of knowledge about nature is a social phenomenon"[17]. In this way, Lukacs excluded natural dialectics from historical dialectics, confined Marxist dialectics within the realm of history, and reduced it to historical dialectics.

The resolution of the problem of dialectics "guides" Lukacs to "history", and the exploration of history leads him to the practical activity of man.

In the view of Lukacs, history is the product of human activity, the object created by subject. As object, history is the objective process of human practice; as subject, history is the process of human self-creation. History is essentially the development of practical activity of man in time, namely the "diachronic" social practice; it can be grasped as our act. Lukacs realizes the practical essence of history through the investigation of history and the historical essence of practice through the analysis of practice. He thinks practice is a historical activity rather than abstract activity; it is a historical activity breaking the alienation of man rather than a pure epistemological category.

---

16   Lukacs, *History and Class Consciousness*. Chongqing: Chongqing Publishing House, 1989: p. 161.
17   Lukacs, *History and Class Consciousness*. Chongqing: Chongqing Publishing House, 1989: pp. 252 and 236.

The interaction between subject and object in historical activity constitutes the decisive factor of dialectics and the movement of history as a totality. From Lukacs' point of view, a whole is universally superior to a part, and any part has a meaning only when connected with the whole. "Only in this context which sees the isolated facts of social life as aspects of the historical process and integrates them in a totality, can knowledge of the facts hope to become knowledge of reality." "Action is directed objectively towards a transformation of totality."[18]

On this ground, Lukacs insisted everything should be based on and explained with history, and even the subject of practice was outspread in the dimension of history. Thus he thought he found the foundation for the ontology of Marxist philosophy – history, and affirmed Marx's "critical philosophy implies above all historical criticism"[19].

These opinions of Lukacs are fairly profound. In *The German Ideology*, Marx brings forward the thought of "historical nature", thus cutting the curtain of Feuerbach's "nature worship" and lighting up nature with the sunshine of history. When Lukacs affirmed nature was a social category, he happened to have the same view with Marx, and that view was like an "antidote" for the misunderstandings of Marxist philosophy as general materialism and the ontology of Marxist philosophy as natural ontology; his affirmation of the inner link between history and practice and the totality of history was very meaningful for economic materialism, which criticized the Second International, i.e. for the vulgarization of the materialistic conception of history.

But Lukacs was "overdoing" after all. He affirmed the "historical nature" but overlooked "natural history", and did not understand Marx's thought of "natural history" cut the path of Hegel's absolute idea to history; he affirmed the totality of history but overstated the effect of proletarian consciousness, and even thought it was the standpoint of historical totality rather than economic necessity that constituted the decisive difference between Marxism and the proletarian ideology; he affirmed the inner link between history and practice and introduced practice into ontology, but abolished the relationship of man to nature in practical activity, limited the stage of human practical activity within the relationship between man and man, and reduced it to the class consciousness of the proletariat, thereby casting a shadow of idealism on *History and Class Consciousness*.

18 Ibid., p. 10 and 198.
19 ibid., p. 53.

The mistakes of Lukacs in *History and Class Consciousness*, fundamentally, were because he understood practice one-sidedly and ignored the material exchange between man and nature, the substantial content in practical activity. This again proves the truthfulness and predictability of Marx's opinion that excluding the relationship between man and nature from history is inclined to giving rise to the idealistic conception of history.

Lukacs was highly conscious of this in his later period. Since the 1930s, he had criticized himself for several times, and confessed that in *History and Class Consciousness*, he ignored "labor, the medium of metabolism and interaction between nature and society and the basic category of Marxism", and excluding the practical relationship between man and practice from history "means that the most important real pillars of the Marxist view of the world disappear"[20]. In consequence, *History and Class Consciousness* "is unintentionally colored by an overriding subjectivism", submits to such a tendency that has happened in the history of Marxism, that is, "the tendency to view Marxism exclusively as a theory of society, as social philosophy, and hence to ignore or repudiate it as a theory of nature", and finally like this tendency, strikes "at the very roots of Marxian ontology"[21].

The self-criticism of Lukacs is moving and quite profound. Just due to this, he wrote the important works titled *The Ontology of Social Being*, with the hope to lay a foundation for Marx's thought that "history is the sole science" and "make out the principles of Marxian ontology"[22].

In Lukacs' view, the theoretical work of Marx is directed linked up with the theoretical clue left over by Hegel and meanwhile revolutionarily changes Hegelian philosophy and even the whole traditional philosophy. The secret to this revolutionary change rests with Marx's establishment of the scientific view of practice or labor.

"Only Marx's view of labor can materialistically resolve the insurmountable difficulties in front of Hegel arising as frequently as his talented presentiment. The reason for this is because Marx's view of labor gives content to the material exchange between society and nature, thus making substantial the relationship between the categories of labor and

---

20   Lukacs, *History and Class Consciousness*, p. 21.
21   ibid., p. 53.
22   *Autobiography of Lukacs*, p. 48.

their natural premises, and the changes of these premises resulting from the social development of labor."[23]

In the history of Marxist philosophy, one of the creative contributions of Lukacs is "re-bringing the factor of practice to the attention center of and primary position in Marxist philosophy"[24], affirming the scientific view of practice is the theoretical basis of Marxist philosophy, and specifying the ontology of Marxist philosophy as the ontology of social being, namely practical ontology. From Lukacs' point of view, practice, especially labor as "primary practice", always occupies the fundamental core position in social being. "The entire social being, in terms of its ontological feature, is built upon the groundwork of the purposive enactment of human practice." "It is the labor theory of Marx, the theory which conceives labor as the exclusive existence mode of the purposive creative being, that establishes the character of social being for the first time."[25] It is for this reason that Lukacs also calles the ontology of social being practical ontology.

Lukacs thought that "the labor of man always has a purpose – it sets a purpose, and this purpose is a selected result, therefore the labor of man represents man's freedom. Such freedom, however, only exists in bringing the objective natural forces subject to the law of cause and effect of the material world into operation"[26]. That is to say, labor contains the purpose of man, and has the objective material premise. It is an active natural-transforming activity that inserts the link of man's purpose into the objective chain of cause and effect, and by doing this, it does not only changes the form of nature, but realizes the purpose of man and the need of society in nature, thereby making nature ceaselessly "socialized". Meanwhile the "constraints" of natural being on social being will not disappear; "I'm talking about the retreat of constraints from nature, but not the disappearance of nature", and it is impossible for men to "fully sublate these constraints". Thus, Lukacs subsumed the material exchange between man and nature, as well as the conversion process between material and idea, into the category of practice, thereby overcoming the defects in *History and Class Consciousness* and giving concrete contents to the concept of practice.

---

23   *A Collection of Literary Essays of Lukacs*, p. 432.
24   Vranicki, *History of Marxism*. Beijing: People's Publishing House, 1988: Vol. 2, p. 101.
25   Lukacs, *The Ontology of Social Being*. English Ed., pp. 309 and 25.
26   *Autobiography of Lukacs*, p. 294.

Lukacs' opinion is perfectly consistent with that of Marx. In the *Economic Manuscripts of 1861 – 1863*, Marx points out that labor is "purposeful activity aimed ... at the appropriation of natural material". Marx has emphasized this opinion again and again, and writes it into the final draft of *Das Kapital*, in which Marx points out, "At the end of every labor-process, we get a result that already existed in the imagination of the laborer at its commencement. He not only effects a change of form in the material on which he works, but he also realizes a purpose of his own that gives the law to his modus operandi."

Fundamentally, the transcendence of *The Ontology of Social Being* over *History and Class Consciousness* is that it sets up a correct concept of practice, connects man with nature, social being with natural being, on this basis, unifies the purpose of man with the objective relation of cause and effect, and deeply expounds the relationship between value and "oughtness".

In Lukacs' opinion, the category of value shows the foundation of social being – labor, and the issue of value is inevitably associated with the issue of "oughtness". "Such a value (affirmation or negation) is involved in any practice; if value cannot become such a purpose assumption of object, it can by no means be connected with any ontology in society."[27] Consequently, man raises himself to the height of society, and constantly realizes the translation from "being-in-itself" to "being-for-itself" during practical activity, making himself more and more take on the form and content of society.

"We cannot reasonably discuss social being unless we understand that the formation of social being, its transcendence over its own foundation, and its independence achievement are all based on labor, that is, based on the continuous realization of the enactment of purpose."[28]

Lukacs thus believed practice constituted the existence of man, i.e. the ontological foundation of social being. "It is labor that introduces the unified dualism-based correlation between purposiveness and causality into beings, and there was only the process of cause and effect in nature prior to the generation of labor. So this complex composed of two aspects only exists in labor and its social results, in social practice. Consequently, the purposively-set activity that transforms

27   Lukacs, *The Ontology of Social Being*. English Ed., p. 94.
28   Ibid., p. 12.

reality becomes the ontological foundation for the existence of human society."[29]

Owing to correct understanding on practice and its effect, Lukacs extremely underlined that "practice" or "labor" was the basic category of Marxist philosophy, expressly took practical ontology as the theoretical basis of Marxist philosophy, and connected society with nature by virtue of the category of practice, with a view to establishing the ontology of social being. He definitely pointed out that "the process of labor is the process between man and nature, and the metabolism between man and nature has an ontological foundation"[30], and the concept of labor was the key of his analysis. "In the light of Marx's thought, I conceive ontology as philosophy itself, the philosophy on the basis of history ... The essence of human society is the purposive activity of man, that is, labor. This is the uppermost new category in that it includes everything"[31]. The exposition of Lukacs makes me spontaneously think of a famous saying of Marx – "all social life is essentially practical".

If "history" is considered as the core category in *History and Class Consciousness*, then "practice" or "labor" is the core category in *The Ontology of Social Being*. In-depth exploration of practice made Lukacs realized that the human being was all social being, whose fundamental feature was historicity; additionally, nature entering into social being and its objectivity extended into social being rather than disappeared. Thus he argued, "Practice itself most immediately makes the most important proof for the essence of social being, and as to the real critical ontology, practice is the necessary objective core."[32]

At this point, Lukacs transcended Stalin and his own *History and Class Consciousness*, returned to Marx, restored the original look of the ontology of Marxist philosophy, and showed a new ideological horizon.

However, as he showed us a new ideological horizon, Lukacs suddenly took a step back – he considered general ontology, or natural ontology, as the premise and foundation of the ontology of social being. In the sight of Lukacs, "social ontology is premised on general ontology", and "the ontology of social being can be built only based on natural

---

29   Lukacs, *The Ontology of Social Being*. English Ed., pp. 14 – 15.
30   ibid., p. 72.
31   *Autobiography of Lukacs*, p. 203.
32   Lukacs, *The Ontology of Social Being*. English Ed., p. 13.

ontology". "It is based on the ontology of dialectical materialism that historical materialism gets the scientific basis for its inherent necessity and reliability."[33]

Lukacs had stringently criticized the philosophical though of Stalin, and indeed he was different from Stalin while specifically elaborating Marxist philosophy and its thought of ontology, and even reached a new state concerning the ontology of social being. However, he happened to have the same view with Stalin when it came to the relationship respectively between historical materialism and dialectical materialism and between dialectical materialism and natural materialism; the opinions of them are strikingly similar – Lukacs conceived the ontology of dialectical materialism as the theoretical basis of historical materialism in the end, and made the ontology of dialectical materialism natural ontology-based. In this way, natural ontology criticized by Marx went so far as to become the premise and foundation of the ontology of Marxist philosophy. Lukacs transcended Stalin, but ultimately returned to Stalin. In this sense, both reached the same end.

This is really a tragedy, a theoretical tragedy that seemingly should not happen but really happened to Lukacs. From the angle of epistemology, the fundamental cause of this tragedy was that there was a shadow lingering in his mind, namely the investigation method in line with "time priority", i.e. the method of reductionism. On that methodological basis, Lukacs "conceives the order of priority" of the three major modes of being – inorganic nature, organic nature and human society – "in the irreversible process of world as the core of self-thinking on ontology"[34]. From this it is not difficult for us to understand why Lukacs finally set natural ontology as the premise and foundation for the ontology of social being.

At this point, Lukacs ignored the profound thought of Marx that nature or any substance separated from real man and his activity means "nothing" or "non-existent being", and materialism based on "abstract substance" is "abstract materialism", which connotes "the direction of idealism". In front of the contradiction of "logical priority" between the "time priority" of nature to man and the relationship of man to nature "that exist for me", it seemed that Lukacs was powerless.

---

33   Ibid., pp. 326, 472 and 151.
34   Lukacs, *The Ontology of Social Being.* English Ed., p. 10.

3 BRIEF CONCLUSION

I make some comments on the understandings of Stalin and Lukacs on the ontology of Marxist philosophy in the sections above, and passingly discuss the view of Marx on the same issue. Now I come to the following conclusion upon the summarization of the above.

I do not agree with the opinion that Marx has not discussed the issue of ontology and Marxist philosophy is only a world outlook but not ontology. This is a misunderstanding and a prejudice, a senseless pride and prejudice. In fact, Marx has dealt with ontology in his *Doctoral Dissertation* on the aspects of "the proof of ontology" and "the determination of ontology", discussed "the issue of the affirmation of ontology" in *Economic and Philosophical Manuscripts of 1844*, and in *The German Ideology* focused on the issue of the existence of man, which is actually the issue of ontology, because ontology is to study the essence and significance of existence.

With respect to this point, the viewpoint of Lukacs is correct – though Marx does not write any works specialized in ontology, Marxist philosophy "is the exposition about existence, i.e. the pure ontology, in the ultimate sense"[35]. In my opinion, the revolutionary change realized by Marxist philosophy in the history of philosophy is launched and spread at the level of ontology, with the result that traditional ontology is terminated, and the ontology of new materialism, i.e. practical ontology, is constructed.

According to Marx, practice is both an objective material activity and a purposive creative activity, and what is moving in and for itself is the practical activity of mankind. It is practice that on the one hand provides foundation and basis for human beings to transform, create and conceive the real world and on the other hand supplies final impetus for the self-development of mankind and constitutes the mode of being of man. Through it, men do not only transform and cognize nature constantly, but also transform, create and understand themselves, including biological organization, social relations, thinking mode, and so on. Practice constitutes the essence of the real world and the living noumenon of man. In this sense, Marx holds that "man's feelings, passions, etc., are not merely anthropological phenomena in the (narrower) sense, but truly ontological affirmations of being (of nature)"[36].

35 Lukacs, *The Ontology of Social Being*. English Ed., p. 559.
36 *Karl Marx and Friedrich Engels*. 1st Chinese Ed., Vol. 42, p. 150.

The practical ontology of Marx is directed to "the real world of its times" and emphasized the elimination of the aliened living condition of man, and affirms that "for the practical materialist, i.e. the communist, it is a question of revolutionizing the existing world, of practically attacking and changing existing things"[37], thereby radically resolving the contradictions between man and world, between being and essence, between freedom and necessity, and between individual and species. As a result, Marx brings ontology from "Heaven" down to "Earth", and combines ontology with the sufferings and happiness in the world, with the ideal of communism; or we should say he makes an ontological proof for the emancipation of the proletariat and all mankind, thereby opening up "a path of conceiving the reality through ontology" and finding the point directly bonding philosophy with the change of world. Marxist philosophy is fundamentally practical ontology, namely the ontology of existentialism. It is dually concerned with the ultimate being and real existence of man, the most exciting concern in the whole history of philosophy.

The incisive opinion of Marx did not arouse the attention of people for a long historical period. In regard to the ontology of Marxist philosophy, Lenin had wrongly understood it, but Stalin took to extreme the opinion of Lenin that historical materialism was the extension and application of the principles of materialism to the domain of social history, mistaking Marxist philosophy for general materialism and the ontology of Marxist philosophy thoroughly for natural ontology. He actually interpreted Marxist philosophy with the logic of early modern materialism and abandoned the epoch-making contribution of Marxist philosophy to a quite large extent. That was a horrendous theoretical retrogression in the history of Marxist philosophy.

Lukacs is sharp-eyed, and his ontology of social being predicts a new train of thought to resolve the problem and, on the road of "reviving" the ontology of Marxist philosophy, provides us with a broad thinking space to comprehensively and deeply apprehend it. However, he was eventually guided by improper method to general materialism and its ontology. Lukacs transcended Stalin, but ultimately returned to Stalin, to the early modern materialism. The merit and demerit of Lukacs, his success and failure, both prove a truth that it is necessary to make a new understanding on the ontology of Marxist philosophy and its contemporary significance on the standpoint of contemporary practice, science and philosophy.

---

37   *Selected Works of Karl Marx and Friedrich Engels.* 2nd Ed., Vol. 1, p. 75.

There is a peculiar phenomenon frequently happening in history – a theory or even the whole philosophical theory of a great philosopher always tends to show its intrinsic value and catch the attention of people again after the philosopher's death and a relatively long historical movement, so is the historical destiny of the ontology of Marxist philosophy, i.e. the practical ontology or the ontology of existentialism, which was put forward and founded in the mid-nineteenth century, but did not arouse people's understanding and concern at that time and during a relatively long historical period thereafter. For this reason, when constructing the textbook system of Marxist philosophy, the descendants precisely ignored the ontology of existentialism of Marx, and exactly abandoned the method for interpreting the significance of beings based on the existence of man, thus resulting in the inherent defect in the traditional textbook system of Marxist philosophy, that is, seeking for the basis of all spiritual phenomena in the "abstract substance" separated from historical process.

The historical movement and the development of practice, science and philosophy itself in the twentieth century highlight Marx's ontology of existentialism and the intrinsic value of the method for interpreting the significance of beings based on the existence of man, and reveal the modernity and contemporary significance of Marxist philosophy to people again. It can be predicted that constructing a new textbook system of Marxist philosophy that coincides with the "text" of Marxist philosophy by interpreting the significance of beings based on the existence of man and comprehending and grasping the relationship between man and world on the basis of practice will gain "overwhelming popularity" soon, and become an important topic of Marxists again.

CHAPTER VII

HUSSERL: TURNING FROM TRANSCENDENTAL EGO TO LIFE-WORLD — FROM MARX'S POINT OF VIEW

In his philosophical career, Husserl pays attention to the analysis of the essence structure of transcendental consciousness in his early days, and turns to the discussion of life-world in his later period and clearly put forward that life-world was the substratum of scientific world. This theoretical turn does not only mean the change in the study mode of Husserl, but also has a great theoretical penetrating power, exerting a long-standing influence on the whole modern philosophy. "Not only phenomenologist but also linguistic philosophy in modern philosophy and the representatives of Marxism are influenced by this thinking motive of Husserl, and develop their respective idea in combination with this motive."[1] After the publications of G. Brand's *The Life-word* in 1971 and H. Blumenberg's *Life-world and Life-time* in 1986, the debate about the issue of life-world repeatedly arose and was further expanded, and following the continuous arguments of many ideologists including Gadamer and Habermas thereafter, the movement of phenomenology

---

1 Stravor, *World in Contradictions: About a Phenomenology as the Philosophy of Ethical Basis*. English Ed., p. 69.

"finally broke out of the realm of European culture". In my opinion, the "later turn" of Husserl was not accidental, and it, in effect, reflected the development trend of modern western philosophy, and highlighted the tremendous advancement of Marx's theory of life-world and its contemporary significance from one side.

1 CRISIS OF CONSTRUCTING "PHILOSOPHY AS RIGOROUS SCIENCE": TURNING TO THE LIFE-WORLD

Husserl pursues to establish a "philosophy as a rigorous science" all his life, and in his mind, the so-called "philosophy as a rigorous science" has duality: on one side, for the purpose of being a system of absolute truth, it is required to be absolutely effective, because "philosophy aims at the absolutely, ultimately effective truth that transcends all relativity"[2]; on the other side, just because of the nature of absolute truth, the "philosophy as a rigorous science" is able to lay a foundation for the realization of human value and significance. "In terms of its historical purposiveness, philosophy is the greatest, most rigorous science, which appropriately expresses the ultimate requirement for pure, absolute knowledge, and corresponding to it is the requirement for pure, absolute value and desire."[3]

That is to say, the "philosophy as a rigorous science" is manifested as the dual pursuit for truth and value, for both the absoluteness of knowledge and the possibility of life, and the pursuit for truth is the basis making the ethics of life possible. For this reason, the "philosophy as a rigorous science" simultaneously has the significances of truth and value, reflecting a new reason of philosophy.

From Husserl's point of view, the exploration for the "philosophy as a rigorous science" motivates the philosophy intention of Socrates and Plato, promotes the reflection on subject of Descartes, and is epitomized in the critical philosophy of Kant in a radical form. However, the problem is that "amongst all the periods of philosophy, almost no one could meet the expected requirement for a rigorous science"[4]. By putting it this way, Husserl does not mean that philosophy is a less-than-perfect

---

2   Husserl, *Phenomenology and Anthropology*, see *Backgrounds of Realism and Phenomenology* edited by R. Chisholm. English Ed., p. 131.
3   Husserl, *Philosophy as a Rigorous Science*. English Ed., p. 72.
4   ibid., p. 71.

science, but that philosophy has not been a science at all so far, and the "philosophy as a rigorous science" has not really taken the first step, whose starting point has yet to be sought for.

Husserl thinks highly of his own effort in phenomenology. He thinks the whole history of European philosophy is the history of pursuing the "philosophy as a rigorous science", and phenomenology is the end and summit of this historical process. If we say the efforts of Socrates, Plato, Descartes and Kant in philosophy are three "Copernican revolutions" in the history of European philosophy, the effort in phenomenology can be considered as the fourth "Copernican revolution", the last but most radical revolution.

In this sense, Husserl asserts that phenomenology is "the hushed-up expectation" of the entire early modern philosophy and meanwhile "the secret aspiration" of our times. There are a lot of setbacks in the path of Husserl to establishing such a "philosophy as a rigorous science". In his early days, he proposes the idea of phenomenological reduction, and strives to ensure the purity of philosophical starting point by demarcating philosophy and to find the transcendental ego having Noesis and associated with Noema by structurally analyzing the pure consciousness. However, he also falls into "crisis" or predicament at that moment.

In Husserl's view, to have an absolutely self-evident starting point, philosophy must "suspend" all daily ideas, scientific opinions and biological thoughts and concentrate on the phenomena of pure consciousness. This is the so-called phenomenological reduction. He concludes that after the belief in the external world is suspended and all human knowledge is bracketed, the realm of pure consciousness will be the only thing left, or "pure consciousness can be reached following this path".

But consciousnesses are in a ceaselessly flowing process, and appear one after another in this process, forming a stream of mental processes. In this stream, phenomenon that is appearing at present is clear, phenomenon that has not appeared can be grasped to a certain degree by virtue of inference, and phenomenon that has disappeared can be grasped to a certain degree according to memory. Every time when the content of a consciousness appears, a "conscious" behavior and the subject of behavior – "I" – will appear at the same time. So as long as we are absorbed in the stream of mental processes of consciousness, we will be able to definitely grasp "I" who am thinking. Even though my memory makes a mistake, "I" who am recalling during reminiscence am appearing self-evidently; even though my inference is not definitely right, "I" who am inferring during inference am appearing self-evidently; even though I can suspend or doubt everything, "I" who am doubting during suspension or suspicion am appearing self-evidently.

Consequently, Husserl obtains a starting point of philosophy the same with Descartes: "the stream of mental processes which is mine, of the one who is thinking, no matter to what extent it is not grasped, no matter how unknown it is in the areas of the stream which have run their course and which have yet to come –: as soon as I look at the flowing life in its actual present; and, while doing so, apprehend myself as the pure subject of this life ..., I say unqualifiedly and necessarily that I am, this life is, I am living: cogito."[5]

However, over how to understand "cogito", there is a great disagreement between Husserl and Descartes. Descartes asserts that "cogito" is a spiritual substance not existing in space and time, whereas reason is the substantial reason. Husserl holds that "I" in "cogito" is neither material nor spiritual substance, but emerges as the executor and bearer of the thinking activity. "Cogito" referred to by Husserl is a function of pure consciousness, a kind of transcendental reason different from Descartes' substantial reason.

The consciousness behavior of man is a stream of mental processes. When a consciousness behavior is happening, we can perceive the existence of ego accompanying it. The problem is that when a consciousness behavior takes to transition to another consciousness behavior, or when a consciousness behavior resumes after an interruption, how we know or ensure the "executor" of this continuous behavior or this behavior resuming after interruption is the same ego?

As far as Husserl is concerned, the identity of the content of our consciousnesses is gotten by us through reflection. When "I" am making a reflection on these "thinking" behaviors, "I" will find they are coherent and identity, and such coherence and identity are bound up with "I" as the center; "I" here cannot be divorced from the stream of consciousness, and "I" exist within this stream rather than beyond it; the phenomena presented by the stream consciousness have temporal feature but no

5   Husserl, *General Introduction to a Pure Phenomenology*. Beijing: The Commercial Press, 1992: p. 127.

spatial feature, and their temporal succession exists in pure conscious-ness, so such time can be called "immanental time". Thus, "I", the "free being" who can freely go out of or withdraw into itself, simultaneously face three time dimensions, namely the past, the present and the future, in the stream of consciousness.

"The pure Ego, as the 'free being' which it is, lives in certain intentive mental processes, those which have the universal modus cogito. But the expression, 'as a free being,' indicates nothing else than such modes of living pertaining to freely going out of itself or freely withdrawing into itself, spontaneous doing, being somehow affected by the Objects, suffering, etc."[6]

Although running through the entire stream of mental processes of con-sciousness, "I" am not such a stream of mental processes of conscious-ness behavior and its relevant contents. Instead, "I" am the subject of mental process, the unvarying in the continually varying stream of mental processes of consciousness, being absolutely self-evident, and will not disappear with the vanishing of each mental process of con-sciousness. Husserl points out:

"The Ego seems to be there continually, indeed, necessarily, and this continualness is obviously not that of a stupidly persistent mental pro-cess, a 'fixed idea.' Instead, the Ego belongs to each coming and going mental process; its 'regard' is directed 'through' each actional cogito to the objective something. This ray of regard changes from one cogito to the next, shooting forth anew with each new cogito and vanishing with it. The Ego, however, is something identical. At least, considered eideti-cally, any cogito can change, come and go, even though one may doubt that every cogito is necessarily something transitory and not simply, as we find it, something in fact transitory. In contradistinction, the pure Ego would, however, seem to be something essentially necessary; and, as something absolutely identical throughout every actual or possible change in mental processes, it cannot in any sense be a really inherent part or moment of the mental processes themselves."[7]

That is to say, "I" is the governor of consciousness behavior at the core of the stream of consciousness; consciousness behavior is shot out from and finally returns to "I". The "shooting" function of "I" is the mode of

6   Husserl, *General Introduction to a Pure Phenomenology*, p. 232.
7   Ibid., p. 151.

consciousness behavior, with a directing effect, viz., "intentionality"; the object directed to by the intentionality is not an external objective thing but rather "the intention-related object" within consciousness. "I", as a "pole" in the stream of consciousness, will be directed to the object of consciousness through various consciousness behaviors. "I" perceived in this way is pure ego or transcendental ego.

In Husserl's opinion, "transcendental ego" is prior to the world, and is the exclusive source for us to make "judgments"; external things, nature and even body are existent, but without "I", their existence means nothing; the primary function of "I", the "center" and "emitter" in the thinking activity, is to give object significance. "The Objective world, the world that exists for me, that always has and always will exist for me, the only world that ever can exist for me this world, with all its Objects, I said, derives its whole sense and its existential status, which it has for me, from me myself, *from me as the transcendental Ego*."[8] Husserl beats his brains to establish transcendental ego as the self-evident starting point of philosophical thinking, as the substratum or representation of new philosophical reason, but he in fact still imposes many restrictions on ego. Hence, he entraps himself in the biggest problem of phenomenology: the predicament of solipsism and the problem of inter-subjectivity.

To put it specifically, if there is only one ego in the world, I can make the conclusion that my ego is the "center" or "governor" of the stream of consciousness, but the problem is that there are many egos in the world, so I have to differentiate my stream of consciousness from other streams of consciousness. If I fail to do so, I will be unable to ensure the coherence and identity of my stream of consciousness, and my self-evidence will become a problem; if I can make such a differentiation, I must confirm the identity of different streams of consciousness and then demonstrate different egos – governors of different streams of consciousness. In brief, the confirmation of my stream of consciousness presupposes the confirmation of other streams of consciousness, and vice versa. This vicious circle is the theoretical trouble confronting Husserl.

---

8   Husserl, *Cartesian Meditations*. English Ed., p. 26.

For the purpose of solving this theoretical trouble, Husserl resorts to the psychological concept "sympathy", and believes that it is the interaction between streams of consciousness in the realm of "pure psychology". Through such interaction, many closed streams of consciousness (different self-consciousnesses) are linked with the stream of consciousness of "I". In this way, we can not only interpret strange consciousnesses by using the things having been cognized in our consciousness, but also interpret our own consciousness by utilizing the things cognized by dint of intercourse with strange consciousnesses, thereby answering the question that through what kind of intercourse relationship consciousness exerts impact on a strange consciousness, or in what kind of mode spirit conducts pure interaction. However, this is still a vicious circle.

To break this vicious circle, Husserl discusses "empathy". From his viewpoint, the primordial given physical object should be cognized through simple intuition, our own consciousness status through inherent perception, and "conscious experience of others" through "empathy". The original meaning of "empathy" is that one radiates his emotion into the object of aesthetic appreciation and fuses himself with the object. By using "empathy", Husserl wants to explain how "I" am able to know the conscious experience of others – I know my own behavior is guided by "my" consciousness, so I imagine that there are consciousnesses, as well, behind the behaviors of others. Specifically, since my body is the same with the bodies of others, my behavior is also the same with others'; therefore I will naturally suppose that the behaviors of others, the same with mine, are also guided by consciousness. Under normal conditions, the conception about others' bodies and behaviors and the impression that others also have consciousness appear at the level of my consciousness almost at the same time.

In order to further resolve his theoretical trouble, Husserl also probes into "apperception". To Husserl's understanding, we are not accepting sensuous materials separately, but organize fragmentary and miscellaneous materials together to form a unified perception. For example, I occasionally observe the tree outside the window, and sometimes I notice the leaves and sometimes the trunk, but no matter which part I notice, a unified image of tree will emerge in my consciousness. In this conception, the part of the tree I have seen is shown clearly, and the part that I haven't seen is shown indistinctly through memory and association. Though the clear part and the indistinct part will change correspondingly with the change of my attention, my perceptions of all parts of the tree appear as a unified conception, which is the function of apperception in the sight of Husserl. This characteristic of apperception can also be used for my cognition of others' egos: although I can only see the bodies and behaviors of others instead of their consciousnesses, I consider them to be conscious in my apperception of others, and in this apperception, the bodies, behaviors and consciousnesses of others concur.

By introducing in the concepts of "empathy" and "apperception", Husserl deduces and proves the egos of others related to the ego of "I", and derives the existence of the inter-subjective world from deduction; he asserts, "In any case then, within myself, within the limits of my transcendentally reduced pure conscious life, I experience the world (including others) and, according to its experiential sense, not as (so to speak) my private synthetic formation but as other than mine alone, as an inter-subjective world, actually there for everyone, accessible in respect of its Objects to everyone."[9]

From transcendental ego to inter-subjective world, the theoretical span of Husserl is quite large, and he is gradually aware of the huge difficulty therein, making him irresolute and his exposition vague. So in his later period, Husserl deliberately avoids the topic of transcendental ego in the realm of consciousness, and transfers his study interest to the topics of "the ego of personality" and "the life-world", in the belief that every ego of personality is positively dealing with the surrounding world and shows its unique ability, character, habit, attitude and motive during the intercourse. In a word, the ego of personality is the ego of life-world. This conclusion, beyond doubt, has rationality, because the surrounding world in which man lives is the objectification of the essential powers of man.

The relationship between man and world is a relationship that "exists for me". The point is that such a relationship that "exists for me" is established during practical activity of man, which is the essence and groundwork of the surrounding world in which man lives; besides, man himself is also a being in practice, and the relationship between ego and others is entered into during practical activity. As Marx said, "the relationship of man to himself becomes objective and real for him

---

9   Husserl, *Cartesian Meditations*. English Ed., p. 90.

only through his relationship to other men", and "self-estrangement can manifest itself only in the practical, real relationship to other men"[10]. In other words, the surrounding world in which man lives and the relationship of ego to others are not speculative problems in the realm of consciousness, but the real, practical problems. As long as Husserl limits his vision within the sphere of pure consciousness, he can never philosophically tackle problems of "ego", "the other", "world" and their relationships.

Husserl has been aware of the theoretical trouble in front of him and always doubts whether the pure ego is really self-evident. He is not yet out of the predicament of solipsism even after borrowing the concepts of "sympathy", "empathy" and "apperception". As a matter of fact, such a "borrowing" without "suspension" is what Husserl himself repeatedly rejects, and will probably lead to the dead end of psychologism criticized by him. The theoretical trouble makes Husserl realize that he should turn his eyes to the reality, to the study of life-world.

2 CRISIS OF EUROPEAN SCIENCES: TURNING TO THE LIFE-WORLD

In the history of philosophy, the theoretical turn of any ideologist does not only have its theoretical logic, but also the realistic cause. The formation of any philosophical system, including its turn, is fundamentally the product of times, so is the phenomenology of Husserl, as well as his "later turn".

To be specific, the later period in Husserl's life was in the times when European civilization was in crisis, which was shown as the obsession of western scientism with cultural traditions on one hand and as the concealment of the living value of westerners. Hence, investigating the root of crisis and providing a solution to it became the historical mission of people of vision at that generation, and Husserl was one of the foregoers. It can be seen by studying and reading his later works that what is immediately related to the concept of "life-world" is the topic about "crises", namely "the crisis of European sciences", "the crisis of European man", and "the crisis of European civilization".

---

10 *Karl Marx and Friedrich Engels*. 1st Chinese Ed., Vol. 42, p. 99.

Before that, Husserl only discussed, from the theoretical perspective, the harm of the scientism's mode of thinking to human spirit and philosophy, and used tags like psychologism, naturalism, objectivism and historicism. The word "crisis" indicated that his tolerance for the scientism's mode of thinking had reached the limit and his voice of criticism was raised obviously. The reason for that was fundamentally due to the pressure from real environment: "the aggressive political situation in Germany at that time constituted the background of that whole thinking effort of Husserl", and "crisis consciousness was the real cause of Husserl's sense of historical responsibility in the era of Nazi"[11].

Husserl spends almost all his later days in exploring the root of European civilization crisis and seeking for corresponding solutions. Being regardless of oldness and not afraid of hard work, he makes a series of reports on crisis in the last years of his life and writes the book titled *The Crisis of European Sciences and Transcendental Phenomenology* on that ground. In this book, he sufficiently elaborates the crisis of European man and the crisis of European civilization, and thinks the representation of these two crises is the crisis of European sciences, whose root is the physical objectivism and its evolution variant – positivism – increasingly expanding in the wake of modern industrial revolution.

Thus Husserl turns to the life-world. According to Husserl, in positivism, "as early as Galileo: the surreptitious substitution of the mathematically substructed world of idealities for the only real world, the one that is actually given through perception, that is ever experienced and experienceable – our everyday life-world. This substitution was promptly passed on to his successors, the physicists of all the succeeding centuries"[12]. This substitution makes modern Europeans kneel at the feet of positive science and immerse themselves in the myth of positive science one after another.

Sciences make brilliant achievements in the development process. However, in the respectful praise of sciences and positivism, modern people let their total world outlook be determined by the positive science and be blinded by the "prosperity" produced by it. "The exclusiveness meant an indifferent turning-away from the questions which are

---

11   Ricoeur, *Husserl*. English Ed., p. 231.
12   Husserl, *The Crisis of European Sciences and Transcendental Phenomenology*. Shanghai: Shanghai Translation Publishing House, 1988: p. 58.

decisive for a genuine humanity. Merely fact-minded sciences make merely fact-minded people", but "in our vital need – so we are told – this science has nothing to say to us. It excludes in principle precisely the questions which man, given over in our unhappy times to the most portentous upheavals, finds the most burning: questions of the meaning or meaninglessness of the whole of this human existence. ... In the final analysis they concern man as a free, self-determining being in his behavior toward the human and extra-human surrounding world"[13]. Thus it can be seen that the crisis of European sciences lies in, above all, the oblivion of man, of the mode of being and living value of man. Husserl believes this "oblivion" results in the crises of European man and European civilization.

In fact, in the course of scientific progress, the issue of man is not excluded from the scope of sciences all the time. Galileo established the tradition of the precision and mathematization of early modern sciences, but his biggest fault was his ignorance of man, the creator of the meaning of geometric idea and his extreme pursuit for the purely objectified study method. As a result, the dominant position of new European humanity since the Renaissance was lost in sciences. "That sort of objectivity which dominates our positive sciences in respect to method and which, having its effect far beyond the sciences themselves, is the basis for the support and widespread acceptance of a philosophical and ideological positivism."[14] Even the spiritual science that "developed so prosperously" neglected the self-understanding of individual life, activity and their results, and tended to trace the physical foundation of spirit and make it comply with the interpretation framework of precise sciences. In the view of Husserl, the scientific reason of positivism runs counter to the real reason of philosophy and the crisis of European sciences is essentially the loss of European spirit.

The topic of "European spirit" showed Husserl's exposition of the crisis of European man and his standpoint of "eurocentrism". In his eyes, the so-called Europeans are not classified according to the geographical Europe on the map, but the Europe in spiritual sense, which covers Britain at the other side of the strait and distant North America and excludes Eskimos, American Indians in the rural markets and Gypsies wandering about Europe all the time. The spiritual origin of Europe

13 *Selected Works of Edmund Husserl*. Shanghai: Shanghai Joint Publishing Company, 1997: Vol. II, p. 982.
14   Ibid., p. 983.

is ancient Greece, whose philosophy reflects the primitive image of European spirit, and the fundamental thing that ancient Greeks pursued is the "philosophical" mode of being of man. In such a mode of being, theoretical philosophy is always primary: "freely giving oneself, one's whole life, its rule through pure reason or through philosophy"[15].

Thus, metaphysics, a science about supreme and ultimate question, should enjoy the honor as a queen of science, thereby determining the significance of the knowledge of all other sciences. Husserl holds that such an understanding of philosophical life guides the common pursuit of Europeans from generation to generation.

But by modern times, especially in positivism, the doubt of the possibility of metaphysics has become a turbulent undercurrent. That is a vital problem concerning the existence of mankind, and the path of philosophical "history of fighting for the meaning of man" has been blocked by positivism. "All modern sciences drifted into a peculiar, increasingly puzzling crisis with regard to the meaning of their original founding as branches of philosophy, a meaning which they continued to bear within themselves. This is a crisis which does not encroach upon the theoretical and practical successes of the special sciences; yet it shakes to the foundations the whole meaning of their truth. This is not just a matter of a special form of culture – "science" or "philosophy" – as one among others belonging to European mankind."[16]

The doubt of metaphysics means that philosophy itself becomes a question; and the collapse of the belief in a universal philosophy means the collapse of belief in reason. Related to this, man loses the faiths in the "absolute" reason that gives the world a meaning, in the meaning of history, in the meaning of man, and in the ability of man to secure rational meaning for human existence. "If man loses this faith, it means nothing less than the loss of faith 'in himself,' in his own true being"[17].

In Husserl's eyes, the loss of all these believes at bottom implies the crisis of philosophy, and "the crisis of philosophy implies the crisis of all modern sciences as members of the philosophical universe: at first a latent, then a more and more prominent crisis of European humanity itself in respect to the total meaningfulness of its cultural life, its total

---

15   pp. 983 – 984.
16   *Selected Works of Edmund Husserl.* Vol. II, p. 988.
17   Ibid., p. 989.

'Existenz.'"[18] In consequence, he explicitly connects "crisis" with humanity as such, cultural life, and the existence of man, thereby brining real life into his philosophical horizon.

"There are only two escapes from the crisis of European existence: the downfall of Europe in its estrangement from its own rational sense of life, its fall into hostility toward the spirit and into barbarity; or the rebirth of Europe from the spirit of philosophy through a heroism of reason that overcomes naturalism once and for all."[19]

According to Husserl, in a bid to awaken Europeans from "sleepiness" and help them out of the "crisis", philosophy must strive for the real self-understanding on the possibility of man and thereby show the vigor and vitality of philosophy; if philosophy wants to show its vigor and vitality and reveal "the historical movement of the inherent reason of man", it must return to the life-world. Habermas thus thinks "Husserl introduces in the concept of life-world from the perspective of rational resistance", and the analysis of Husserl on the life-world is combined with "the issue of crisis". "Husserl generalizes the crisis caused by modern sciences from the oblivion of the world and ego by objectivism. Such a pressure of problems produced by the crisis circumstances of world history or life history objectively changes the conditions of topicalization", so Husserl "combines the analysis on the life-world with the topic of crisis"[20].

So before *The Crisis of European Sciences and Transcendental Phenomenology*, Husserl just occasionally mentioned the term "life-world", and mainly used "the environing world" to express its connotation. In Philosophy and the Crisis of European Man, he still calls the life-world "the environing world", and argues that "'Environing world' is a concept that has its place exclusively in the spiritual sphere. That we live in our own particular environing world, to which all our concerns and efforts are directed, points to an event that takes place purely in the spiritual order. Our environing world is a spiritual structure in us and in our historical life"[21]. But in *The Crisis of European Sciences and Transcendental Phenomenology*, he clearly puts forward the concept of "life-world" and focuses on the discussion of the issues related to the

---

18   ibid., p. 988.
19   ibid., p. 977.
20   Habermas, *Postmetaphysical Thinking*. Nanjing: Yilin Press, 2001: p. 78.
21   *Selected Works of Edmund Husserl*. Vol. II, p. 944.

life-world. From then on, the concept of "life-world" obtains a central meaning and becomes a basic issue in Husserl's philosophy.

3 LIFE-WORLD: THE SUBSTRATUM OF SCIENTIFIC WORLD

Husserl refers to the concept of life-world in multiple senses, and he himself does not, indeed, make a clear definition for this concept. In the words of A. Pazenin, a research expert of phenomenology, "even Husserl himself had not made an appropriate definition on life-world". Nevertheless, we can comprehend and grasp the basic connotation of this concept pursuant to various expositions of Husserl about "the life-world".

It can be seen by studying and reading the works of Husserl that according to Husserl, "life-world", "everyday life-world", "every empirical world", "environing world", "everyday surrounding world", and "practical environing world" have the same connotation, and what they express is pertinent to our intuited horizon. More importantly, while introducing in the concept of "life-world", Husserl emphasizes the life-world that underlined the value of man as the foundation of meaning, the primitive world that can be empirically intuited, i.e. "pre-scientific world", "overall sphere of beings", and meanwhile the purely subjective world of meaning, "the intuitive environing world, purely subjective as it is"[22]. As "pre-scientific world" and "overall sphere of beings", the life-world is given to subject during daily sensuous experience; it is "the only real world, the one that is actually given through perception, that is ever experienced and experienceable – our everyday life-world"[23].

From the viewpoint of Husserl, life-world is an "originally self-evident realm", or to say, a pre-scientific fundamental realm. "The life-world is the world that is constantly pre-given, valid constantly and in advance as existing, but not valid because of some purpose of investigation, according to some universal end. Every end presupposes it; even the universal end of knowing it in scientific truth presupposes it, and in advance; and in the course of [scientific] work it presupposes it ever anew, as a world existing, in its own way [to be sure], but existing nevertheless."[24] It is a

---

22 *Selected Works of Edmund Husserl.* Vol. II, p. 972.

23 ibid., p. 1027.

24 Ibid., p. 1087.

"totality of things that can be intuited in principle"[25]. These sentences of Husserl indicate that life-world is the real world encompassing all real life of men, and all things that are assembled in the forms of time and space belong to it. In this sense, Husserl calls life-world "the realm of constituents".

In the horizon of Husserl, the life-world is the world that only has meaning and exists for us in and through experience, the world that is eternally valid for us, with doubtless certainty, and simply given in front of us. The life-world "appears in these intuited horizons which are not included by scientific praxis", and "is immediately given before us" and "pre-given" for us as an intuitive real world perceptible through experience; it is the world appropriated commonly by us and always has valid effect on us; men live in it but do not "focus on" it.

Therefore, men take the existence of life-world as a self-evident apodictic premise, and never doubt it or study it as a scientific topic. "Pre-given", "immediately given", "experienceable", "appropriated commonly by men", "eternally valid" for men, etc. are the "constant foundation" for the "self-evidence" of life-world. In this sense, life-world is an "originally self-evident realm", a "pre-scientific" fundamental realm. As Held said, "Husserl first introduces the concept of 'life-world' in the Crisis as a title for this unthematic, intuited world."[26]

Meanwhile, Husserl also believes life-world is the realm where the subjective value and meaning of man happen, and it is "the totality of things that always exist for me in constant relative movement"[27]. In other words, life-world is the subjective human world rather than the purely objective world beyond men. "Environing world is a concept that has its place exclusively in the spiritual sphere. That we live in our own particular environing world, to which all our concerns and efforts are directed, points to an event that takes place purely in the spiritual order. Our environing world is a spiritual structure in us and in our historical life."[28]

---

25   *Collected Works of Edmund Husserl.* English Ed., Vol. 6, p. 130.

26   Husserl, *Phenomenology of the Life-World.* Shanghai: Shanghai Translation Publishing House, 2002: p. 43.

27   *Collected Works of Edmund Husserl.* English Ed., Vol. 6, p. 462.

28   Husserl, *Phenomenology and the Crisis of Philosophy.* Beijing: International Culture Press, 1988: p. 138.

This exposition of Husserl seems to completely spiritualize the life-world and become idealism, but this is actually not so. It can be found by studying his works that the subjectivity of life-world mentioned by him refers to the participation and planning of man and means the spirituality and creativity of man have permeated and deposited in the world. "The historical environing world of the Greeks is not the objective world in our sense; rather it is their 'representation of the world,' i.e., their own subjective evaluation, with all the realities therein."[29] In his eyes, the common world where we live, rest, plan, and do practice is the life-world, or to say, life-world is "the world appropriated commonly by men".

That is to say, life-world is not a purely objective world beyond men and human activity, but the world of objects for the activity of subject. "The ontic meaning of the pre-given life-world is a subjective structure", and "only a radical inquiry back into subjectivity ... can make objective truth comprehensible and arrive at the ultimate ontic meaning of the world"[30]. Hence, life-world is the human world as "the totality of things that exist for me". Held evaluates it like this: "this concept of the world is essentially richer compared to its earlier formulation; the world of the natural attitude is now a world that enriches itself historically through the praxis that takes place in it and its sedimentation, through 'streaming-in.' It is the concrete, historical world."[31]

On this basis, Husserl probes into the relationship between life-world and scientific world, reaching the conclusion that the latter grows out of the former and takes the former as the basis; thus the life-world has a primitive priority.

According to Husserl, the life-world cannot run without basic necessities of life, and is the empirical world closest to subject, whilst the scientific world is the abstract world composed of notions and logics, relatively far away from subject. The scientific world apparently pays attention to symbolic systems such as physical space-time, quantitative relation, and so on, seeks for objective truth, and seemingly exists fully excluding subjective wills and has nothing to do with the life-world. But its "prototypes" can actually be found in the life-world; for

29 Ibid., p. 138.
30 Husserl, *The Crisis of European Sciences and Transcendental Phenomenology*, pp. 81 and 82.
31 Husserl, *Phenomenology of the Life-World*, p. 44.

example, the pure shapes of geometry are derived from the sensuous shapes in life. The scientific world is essentially the result of topicalization of the experience in life-world.

The problem is that when dealing with researches and giving opinions, a scientist completely devotes himself to the scientific attitude and condition, regards only his occupational area and interest as the universal prior field, and forgets the life-world as the background of his researches. "The investigator of nature, however, does not make it clear to himself that the constant foundation of his admittedly subjective thinking activity is the environing world of life. This latter is constantly presupposed as the basic working area, in which alone his questions and his methodology make sense."[32] Not only scientists themselves live in concrete everyday life, but also the research fruits acquired by them upon mental and physical efforts make no sense unless fed back to the life-world. Anyway, the life-world is the preset starting point and a default premise of scientific world. This is the first point.

Second, the truthfulness of scientific world must be guaranteed on the dependence of life-world. The value of scientific world must be found in the subjectivity of life-world, and "the subjectivity of life world exactly means that it is actually experienceable"[33]. Husserl holds that the validity in every life is still applicable to the scientific world, and any new validity arising in the scientific world must be unceasingly connected back to the validity in the life-world and presuppose it. Microscope is the extension of vision by science, ultrasonoscope the extension of hearing, computer the extension of intuitive judgment ability, and so forth. No matter how the scientific world is complex, its results must be expressed intuitively in the life-world. Leaving the experienceable intuitive life-world, any scientific judgment is impossible for verification or falsification and therefore is meaningless.

The life-world is the "ground of intuition". "Although the modern scientist deals with a world that transcends all the intuited horizons found in the natural praxis of gaining knowledge (because he considers the scientific world to be infinite), his knowledge remains connected back to a world that appears in these intuited horizons which are not included by scientific praxis. This world is the life-world."[34] This validity of

---

32   *Selected Works of Edmund Husserl.* Vol. II, p. 972.
33   *Collected Works of Edmund Husserl.* English Ed., Vol. 6, p. 133.
34   Husserl, *Phenomenology of the Life-World*, p. 42.

life-world roots in its "most universal structure in form", namely "on the one hand objects and world, and on the other object consciousness and world consciousness", both constituting the fundamental validity of life-world. From Husserl's point of view, as the structure made up by objects and world as well as object consciousness and world consciousness, the life-world plays a prerequisite role as the source of evidence, and "provides ultimate demonstrations on the existing validity of theory – logic – for all objective proof".

Third, the scientific world is a constituent part, a special sphere, of life-world. As a "target constituent", the scientific world is different from "naturally" formed life-world, but both are also unified.

Specifically, the life of scientists is guided by their occupational targets, and their life-world is formed through the cooperation and inheritance among researchers. The theoretical achievements of scientists belong to the life-world, constituting a part of life-world.

"All objects gained through scientific idealization sink down into the reserve of unthematic, horizonal, pre-given possibilities of our praxis." "As a consequence of genetic sedimentation, however, the objectified results of any praxis that transcends intuition – and this includes those results of modern technological praxis based upon idealization – flow into the intuitable horizons of non-scientific praxis. The transformed world that appears unthematically in these horizons is also the life-world."[35] This process is called "streaming-in" by Husserl, who thus thinks the scientific world and things therein that are scientifically true also belong to the life-world.

Fourth, the life-world does not only lay the foundations of value and meaning for the scientific world, but also unifies and integrates various peculiar worlds, thus having the priority in regard to value function. For a natural scientist, "the constant foundation of his admittedly subjective thinking activity is the environing world of life; this latter is constantly presupposed as the basic working area, in which alone his questions and his methodology make sense"[36].

---

35 Ibid, p. 43.
36 Husserl, *Phenomenology and the Crisis of Philosophy*, p. 168.

However, during its generation, the scientific world increasingly indulges in that theoretical world of signs and forgets the foundation for its generation and its "prototypes" in the life-world. "As for the 'objectively true' world, the world of science, it is a structure at a higher level, built on pre-scientific experiencing and thinking, or rather on its accomplishments of validity. Only a radical inquiry back into subjectivity – and specifically the subjectivity which ultimately brings about all world-validity, with its content and in all its pre-scientific and scientific modes, and into the 'what' and the 'how' of the rational accomplishments – can make objective truth comprehensible and arrive at the ultimate ontic meaning of the world."[37]

Furthermore, in society, men in different occupational groups tend to have particular interests and targets, but they all cannot live without the basic necessities of life, and even scientists have to live a daily life; additionally, men observe the external world primarily relying on sensory experience; unless there is any disorder with the sense organs, the senses of men are supposed to be generally consistent. Thus, all scientific notions can be explained in the perceivable life-world; what's more, the ultimate goal of scientific achievements is to serve human beings in daily life. So the life-world has a unique function of integration.

While analyzing and describing the life-world, Husserl first interprets how the scientific world grows out of the life-world and strives to reveal the secularity and experienceable character of life-world. In his mind, the life-world is both the world that is immediately experienced by men and the world where men live in. So the "life-world" of Husserl has the ontological significance, or we can say the life-world theory of Husserl is a system of ontology.

As a result, Husserl does not only lay a sound foundation for his phenomenological reduction, but also makes a "prescription" for the crisis of Europeans. Although this prescription cannot cure the crisis thoroughly, it is after all appropriate with certain therapeutic effect. Just owing to this, his theory of life-world has a far-reaching influence on the philosophical movement in the twentieth century.

---

37   Husserl, *The Crisis of European Sciences and Transcendental Phenomenology*. English Ed., p. 1048.

4 BRIEF PERORATION

The turn to the life-world marks the new direction of Husserl's philosophical study, and does not mean the cognitional "fracture" of Husserl. As far as I am concerned, this "turn" is not only a new direction but also the continuation and expansion of the theoretical thoughts of Husserl, needed by theory and methodology.

Kane asserts, "Husserl methodologically views the issue of life-world as a path to transcendental reduction."[38] Waldenfels points out, "Life-world in Husserl does not an immediately depicted object, but an answering object with methodological purpose; and by virtue of such answering men are able to grasp anew the preexisting givenness of life-world."[39] Stravor emphasizes that "the issue of life-world is a path to transcendental suspension", and argues that the interest of Husserl in the life-world absolutely does not mean his deviation from the meaning of his transcendental idea, but means a methodological change, that is to say, Husserl no longer adopts "the thinking method choosing suspension according to free will, but first answers the questions emerging in the realm of world"[40]; such questions include the crisis of European sciences and the issue of life-world.

This is proved by the later works of Husserl, *The Crisis of European Sciences and Transcendental Phenomenology*. It is in this works that Husserl puts forward a proposition: "the path starting from the life-world leads to transcendental phenomenology."

Of course I notice that although "life-world" is the path of Husserl to transcendental phenomenology, the transcendental phenomenology arrived at through this path is greatly different from that established by Husserl in his early days; the former is a new phenomenological form, at least a philosophical form similar to but meanwhile different from existentialism. As American phenomenologist Marvin Farber said, "Possibly some later works of Husserl has properly indicated that he is able to clearly and reasonably point out all (even more) things declared to be completed by existentialistic philosophers in their discourse about existence and survival."[41]

---

38   *Life-world and Science in the Philosophy of Husserl*, edited by E. Stroeker. English Ed., p. 78.
39   Waldenfels, *In the Web of Life-world*. English Ed., p. 16.
40   Stravor, *World in Contradictions*. English Ed., p. 69.
41   *Contemporary American Bourgeois Philosophical Materials*. Beijing: The Commercial Press, 1982: Vol. 2, p. 148.

For this reason, the turn to the life-world is the continuation and expansion of the theoretical thoughts of Husserl, marks the new direction of Husserl's theoretical study, and means the new development of his phenomenology. In this sense, I agree with the viewpoint of Heidegger: "Husserl does not stand still at Volume I of *Ideas Pertaining to a Pure Phenomenology and to a Phenomenological Philosophy* that is criticized: Husserl's phenomenology is in open development"[42].

Besides, the exposition of Husserl on the life-world makes me involuntarily think of the life-world theory of Marx. In Marx's view, the real life process is a real existence that is experienceable and "can be verified in a purely empirical way"; men must be able to live for the purpose of creating history; "where speculation ends – in real life – there real, positive science begins: the representation of the practical activity, of the practical process of development of men"[43]; the relationship between man and world is a relationship that "exists for me", and the real world in which men live is the product of human activity, the objectification of the essential powers of man, thereby being the human world with subjectivity.

It can be found that the life-world theory of Husserl conforms to that of Marx to a definite degree, reflecting the tremendous advancement of Marxist philosophy. It is the conformity and advancement that impels Merleau-Ponty, M. Farber, E. Paci et al. to study Husserl with Marx together and strive to construct "phenomenological Marxism", and Marcuse is called by Habermas a "Husserl's Marxist". The relation between Husserl and Marx, or between phenomenology and Marxist philosophy, deserves elaboration in a more detailed way, but on account of the length of the chapter, I have to leave this important mission to my subsequent works.

---

42   Quoted from *Phenomenology in Disputes*, edited by Ch. Jammer. English Ed., p. 259.
43   *Selected Works of Karl Marx and Friedrich Engels*. 2nd Ed., Vol. 1, p. 73.

CHAPTER VIII

DERRIDA: TURNING FROM DECONSTRUCTIVISM TO MARXISM — FROM MARX'S POINT OF VIEW

At the turn of the century, Derrida, who enjoyed a high reputation for his deconstructivism, still retained his authority in the theoretical domain of postmodernism and gained an extensive attention in the theoretical circle of Marxism. It was because after the drastic changes in Soviet Union and East Europe, when liberalism acclaimed that "Marxism has died" and "vanished as smoke and ashes" together with its discourse theory and practice, Derrida solemnly published a book named *Specters of Marx*. In this book that had made a stir in the western world, he loudly appeals that "not without Marx, no future without Marx, without the memory and the inheritance of Marx: in any case of a certain Marx, of his genius, of at least one of his spirits." "Maintaining now the specters of Marx."[1] So this chapter is going to discuss how to understand the dominant thought of *Specters of Marx*, or how Derrida safeguard the "specters of Marx"; why Derrida turns from deconstructivism to Marxism; and what Marxism is on earth to the understanding of Derrida.

---

1 Derrida, *Specters of Marx*. Beijing: China Renmin University Press, 1999: p. 21.

1 DOMINANT THOUGHT OF SPECTERS OF MARX

Undoubtedly, Derrida as a master of deconstructivism maintains "the specters of Marx" on the ground of deconstructivism, and Marx or Marxist understood by him has been read and rewritten by him in a deconstructive way. But I still notice that his discourse really contains some penetrating judgments and incisive analysis. In his book *Specters of Marx*, he reveals Marxism's function of deconstructing the myth of "new international" and its contemporary significance through analyzing the new order of capitalism, namely "new international", in the contemporary world and intertextually reading Marx's "text" including *The German Ideology, The Communist Manifesto, The 18th Brumaire of Louis Bonaparte* and *Das Kapital*. Therefore, he points out in Specters of Marx that "one must assume the inheritance of Marxism", and "the recourse to a certain spirit of the Marxist critique remains urgent"[2]. Derrida repeatedly refers to the inheritance of Marxism; then what is inheritance of Marxism? How to inherit it?

The inheritance of Marxism mentioned by Derrida mainly refers to the critical spirit of Marxism. It is pointed in *Specters of Marx* that "to continue to take inspiration from a certain spirit of Marxism would be to keep faith with what has always made of Marxism in principle and first of all a radical critique, namely a procedure ready to undertake its self-critique. This critique wants itself to be in principle and explicitly open to its own transformation, re-evaluation, self-reinterpretation"[3].

In the sight of Derrida, self-critique and self-renewal are the inherent spirits of Marxism, and this spirit of critique is the most living part in Marxism; when the spirit of the constantly changing times is inclined to the inertness and complacence of liberalism, the critical spirit of Marxism assumes an extraordinarily significant meaning. Only this critical spirit can show the true face of contemporary capitalist world, and being faithful to this spirit is an "obligatory duty". As long as we inherit such a critical spirit and adapts it to new conditions, "this Marxist critique can still be fruitful ..., whether it is a matter of new modes of production, of the appropriation of economic and techno-scientific powers and knowledge, of juridical formality in the discourse and the practices of national or international law, of new problems of

---

2   Derrida, Specters of Marx, pp. 78 and 122.
3   ibid., p. 124.

citizenship and nationality, and so forth"[4]. In other words, as long as Marxism is combined with the reality in contemporary times, Marxism will still glow with thriving vitality. Here, Derrida has went beyond the "scholarly reading and discussion", and transferred from "scholastic study" of western Marxists on Marxism to "the study closely concerned with reality", marking a new landmark in the study of western scholars on Marxism.

The understanding of Derrida is correct and penetrating – criticalness is indeed the true spirit of Marxism. Marxism treats not only other theories but also itself with such a critical spirit. To put it in the words of Derrida, Marx "requires transforming the conclusions of his own study topics" "in an explicit manner" so as to overcome his own historical limitation; more importantly, Marxism treats real society with a critical spirit. The opinion that "what is actual is what is reasonable" is by no means the thinking mode of Marxism. On the contrary, Marxism always "includes in its comprehension and affirmative recognition of the existing state of things, at the same time also, the recognition of the negation of that state", thus being critical in essence.

In fact, at the beginning of the establishment of Marxism, Marx has proposed to ruthlessly criticize everything that exists and discover the new world through the critique of the old, aiming at "the self-clarification of the struggles and wishes of the age"[5]. Every progress during the establishment and development of Marxism, so to speak, is made through theoretical critique: "critique on Hegel's philosophy of right", "critique on Hegel's dialectics and entire philosophy", "critique on French materialism", "critique on philosophical forms after Hegel", "critique on political economy" ... This series of critiques helps Marx have a more intensive apprehension on theory itself and other various theories and a more profound cognition on the real social contradictions, thereby enabling him to resolve the subject of times with his forward-looking wisdom and predict the development trend of capitalist world system based on tremendous advancement. For this reason, Derrida declares "the recourse to a certain spirit of the Marxist critique remains urgent and will have to remain indefinitely necessary"[6], and believes such a critique can still be fruitful as long as it adapts to new historical conditions. In this sense, Derrida may probably agree with the opinion of Wallerstein:

4   ibid., p. 122.
5   *Karl Marx and Friedrich Engels*. 1st Chinese Ed., Vol. 1, p. 418.
6   Derrida, *Specters of Marx*, p. 122.

"What has died is Marxism as a modern theory, which is produced elaborately together with the modern theory of liberalism and really stimulated by liberalism to a very large extent. What has not died is Marxism that criticizes modernity and its historical manifestation, i.e. the world economy of capitalism."[7]

In the book *Specters of Marx*, the critical spirit of Marxism is connected with its methodology. Derrida thinks the spirit of critique is the most living part in the inheritance of Marxism, and methodology is an aspect of the most valuable essence. The critical spirit is reflected through methodology and meanwhile reflects the value of methodology. Deconstructivism itself is a method. "Deconstruction has never had any sense or interest ... except a radicalization", and "there has been, then, this attempted radicalization of Marxism called deconstruction"[8].

This means that critique, deconstruction and method are categories in the same sequence and with the same function. Just in this sense, Derrida argues that Marxist methodology is always "absolutely and thoroughly determinate", namely that the Marxist methodology was, is, and will not out of date, and we must inherit it; what's more, we should inherit the whole methodology of Marxism rather than just a method of it. Because Marxist methodology is "absolutely and thoroughly determinate", and it is meanwhile the essence of Marxism, Marxism has become a precious heritage of human culture. In this sense, we are "the heirs of Marx and Marxism"[9].

Derrida is not the first person who regards methodology as the essence of Marxism. Lukacs also thinks that the essence of Marxism is its methodology, and even if all the conclusions of Marxism were wrong, as long as its method is right, Marxism would still be insurmountable. At this point, Derrida and Lukacs happen to have the same view. In *Specters of Marx*, Derrida on the one side stresses that essence and critical spirit are the essence of Marxism, the heritage that must be inherited, and on the other side emphasizes that this critical spirit should be differentiated from other Marxist spirits in that the latter is fixed in the basic concepts related to labor, the mode of production, social class, etc., in the history of state apparatus, and should be discarded.

---

7 Wallerstein, *Marxism after the Drastic Change in Soviet Union and East Europe*, see *"Marxism" in the Era of Globalization*. Beijing: Central Compilation & Translation Press, 1998: p. 13.

8 Derrida, *Specters of Marx*, p. 129.

9 Derrida, *Specters of Marx*, p. 27.

The problem is that if other spirits or all conclusions of Marxism are discarded, the critical spirit and methodology of Marxism as its essence will unavoidably have nothing to lean on and become illusory, because the fundamental spirit or essential feature of any "doctrine" is presented in the deductions of other spirits and basic theories; if the entire deduction process and conclusions are questionable, the so-called fundamental spirit or essence will be also questionable, and even should be abandoned.

But I notice that Derrida reasserts the viewpoint that methodology is the essence of Marxism after the drastic changes in Soviet Union and East Europe; since he is a great ideologist famous for his study on methodology, his viewpoint is worthy of deep reflection by us. Engels has pointed ed out long ago that the whole world outlook of Marx is not a dogma but a method. Marxism is "actually a critical view of the world"[10], and reflects a great and profound deconstructive function. The opinion of Derrida, indeed, has its reasonable factors, but the reasonable factors are dissolved into unreasonable understanding.

By turning to the critical spirit and methodology of Marxism, Derrida hopes to renew Marxism in order to save the ramshackle world. Thus for Derrida, Marxism means a kind of utopian spirit:

"If there is a spirit of Marxism which I will never be ready to renounce, it is not only the critical idea or the questioning stance (a consistent deconstruction must insist on them even as it also learns that this is not the last or first word). It is even more a certain emancipator and *messianic* affirmation, a certain experience of the promise that one can try to liberate from any dogmatics and even from any metaphysico-religious determination, from any *messianism*."[11]

In other words, the critical spirit of Marxism is an activity of experience keeping open to the forthcoming absolute future, that is, an activity of experience that is necessarily uncertain, abstract and wild. Such experience is delivered, shown, and consigned to a wait, a wait for another experience, for the coming of incident. In Derrida's eyes, just like the specter of communism haunting Europe in those years, the specter of Marxism is also haunting the contemporary world, and "has always been and will remain spectral: it is always still to come

10 *Karl Marx and Friedrich Engels.* 1st Chinese Ed., Vol. 3, p. 261.
11 Derrida, *Specters of Marx*, p. 126.

and is distinguished, like democracy itself, from every living present understood as plenitude of a presence-to-itself, as totality of a presence effectively identical to itself"[12].

The insight into *Specters of Marx* shows me such an exciting scene that the critical spirit and methodology have become the precious heritage of human culture. No matter whether you have realized or whether you acknowledge, Marxism has exerted influence on you, so men "are heirs of the absolute singularity of a project – or of a promise – which has a philosophical and scientific form"[13]. As Eagleton said, "Marxism, like Darwinian thought and Freud's thought, has fused with modern civilization, and like the important significance of Newton to the Enlightenment, has occupied a major part in our 'historical unconsciousness'"[14]. That's why Derrida thinks capitalism does "no more than disavow the undeniable itself a ghost never dies, it remains always to come and to come-back"[15]. This is true. For Marxism, it is not a matter of whether people need it or not, and the fact is that it already objectively exists since long ago and inevitably influences people.

Generally, the starting point of Derrida's study on Marxism is to demonstrate its reality and contemporary significance based on the opinion that Marxism has become a precious heritage in the knowledge treasure of mankind, which is also the dominant thought in *Specters of Marx*. In my view, this is also an important enlightenment given by *Specters of Marx* to us.

2 THEORETICAL PATH OF DERRIDA'S TURN IN DISCOURSE

The relationship between deconstructivism and Marxism has not been a fresh topic in the western thought circle. *Marxism and Deconstruction* published by Michael Ryan in 1982 can be deemed as the representative book of this topic in the United States. Terry Eagleton, who constantly bears the relationship between deconstructivism and Marxism, can be thought as the "spokesman" of this topic in the United Kingdom.

---

12   Ibid., p. 141.
13   Derrida, *Specters of Marx*, p. 128.
14   Eagleton, *Politics, Philosophy and Eros in History*. Beijing: China Social Sciences Press, 1999: p. 118.
15   Derrida, *Specters of Marx*, p. 141.

In fact, as early as in the 1970s, the relationship between deconstructivism and Marxism had been noticed. Such an issue had been brought forward in the interview of Hood Byrne and Scarpater with Derrida carried in *The Promise* in 1971. Hood Byrne thought there were many common points between deconstructivism and Marxism, and Derrida neither confirmed nor denied at that time. He answered that the "text" of Marx had yet to be read in detail in a bid to draw out the rhetoric and metaphor forms therein, so it was inappropriate to give a simple interpretation or explore the deep meaning under the surface of "text" according to any preconception.

Before the 1990s, Derrida was always vague when talking about Marxism and never expressly mentioned the relationship between deconstructivism and Marxism. His reticent approach to Marxism is shown by *Specters of Marx*. It is in this book that Derrida thinks there will be no future without Marx and proposes the proposition of "the deconstructed Marxist spirit"[16]. In the book, the attitude of Derrida towards Marxism, as well as his apprehension of the relationship between deconstructivism and Marxism, is quite definite.

The turn of Derrida from deconstructivism to Marxism is apodictically an "event" in the history of thoughts, which results in an unavoidable question, that is, why Derrida "liquidates, criticizes and approaches to" Marxism and turns from deconstructivism to Marxism to pursue "the deconstructed Marxist spirit". From my point of view, Derrida's turn from deconstructivism to Marxism is dependent on the inherent logic of deconstructivism, the deconstructive function of Marxism, and the similar political dimension between the two. Derrida has made a clear definition on "deconstruction", namely that "deconstruction is not a kind of criticism activity, and criticism is its object; deconstruction always, at this or that moment, impacts criticism and the confidence of criticism–theory, that is, impacting the authority of decision, the ultimate possibility of the decision of a thing; deconstruction is to deconstruct the dogmas of criticism"[17]. Thus it is clear that deconstructivism is a kind of reading and criticizing pattern targeted at anti-tradition and anti-authority.

---

16   Derrida, *Specters of Marx*, p. 130.
17   V. B. Leitch, *Deconstructive Criticism*. New York, 1983: p. 205.

To put it another way, as a reading and criticizing pattern, deconstructivism regards above all anti-tradition and anti-authority as its duty. With respect to its specific mode and step, deconstruction does not skip from one concept to another, but inverts and displaces conceptual order and the non-conceptual order connected with it; besides, deconstruction, from a certain external angle, "determines what is covered or excluded by the concept, and just through this suppression process closely bound up with it, it creates its historical existence"[18].

From this we can find that deconstructivism is not a term of literature, philosophy, poetry or theology; it does not only touch upon conceptual structure, but also inextricably involves the structures of meaning, politics and society and the ultimate possibilities of law, authority, value, etc. With complicated social factors and historical background behind it, deconstructivism strives to challenge the authority organ of the state by overthrowing the established structure.

"Deconstruction is not, and should not be, merely the analysis on discourse, philosophical statement or concept and semantics; instead, it must challenge system, social and political structures, as well as most stubborn traditions."[19]

The movement of deconstruction is, in effect, the aspiration and pursuit for fairness. In Derrida's view, fairness, the same with deconstruction itself, cannot be deconstructed. Perhaps this is a hope for emancipation, the messianism without religion, or rather that deconstruction is fairness. Deconstructivism of Derrida really implies political dimension. As Eagleton said, "Derrida's deconstructivism is beyond doubt a political project from the beginning"[20]. The overall structure that is attacked by Derrida sparing no effort is actually the specific historical structure of capitalist countries in their later period. Therefore, "Derrida obviously does not only want to develop a new reading method. For him, deconstructive criticism is finally a 'political' practice, which aims to destroy a specific ideological system and the logics used by the whole political structure and social institutional system behind it to maintain their power. Instead of absurdly repudiating relatively definite truth, meaning, identity, intention and historical continuity, he tries hard to view these as the result of a deeper and broader history – the history of language, subconsciousness, social system and customs"[21].

18   Derrida, *Positions*. Paris, 1972: p. 16.
19   Derrida, *Thought is Guarded by a Craziness*, p. 21.
20   Eagleton, *Politics, Philosophy and Eros in History*, p. 120.
21   Eagleton, *Western Literary Theory in the 20th Century*. Xi'an: Shaanxi Normal University Press, 1986: p. 185.

It is evident that the turn of Derrida to Marxism has its inherent thinking clue, that is, the critique of deconstruction movement on capitalism
in reality and the aspiration and pursuit for fairness related to this. In
the sense of theoretical symbolization, if "deconstruction is fairness",
Marxism is fairer, and the fairness explored by deconstruction is just
the fairness unremittingly pursued by Marxism in a certain sense. On
the path of criticizing capitalism and marching forward to fair theory,
deconstruction movement can be nothing but the successor of Marxism,
and is bound to run "in a tradition of Marxism", i.e. the tradition of
Marxism predicted and guided by the specter of Marxism. In *Specters
of Marxism*, Derrida agrees with the critique of Marxism on capitalism,
and states that the "new capitalist order" in contemporary world is still
riddled with problems, just as it was before Marx's death, so "the recourse to a certain spirit of the Marxist critique remains urgent".

The inherent logic of deconstructivism impels Derrida to "approach to"
Marxism, and the deconstructive function possessed by Marxism also
attracts Derrida like an enormous gravitational field. It is true that Marx
only uses the concept of "structure" and never refers to the concept
of "deconstruction" exclusive to deconstructionists, but the critical essence of Marxism embodies its great and profound deconstructive function. It is sure that Derrida has noticed this.

According to Derrida, the deconstruction of the metaphysics in original meaning, of logocentrism or linguisticism, the demystification
or the de-sedimentation of the autonomic hegemony of language,
"would have been impossible and unthinkable in a pre-Marxist space".
"Deconstruction has never had any sense or interest in my view at least,
except as a radicalization, which is to say also the tradition of a certain
Marxism, in a certain spirit of Marxism. There has been, then, this attempted radicalization of Marxism called deconstruction"[22]. In *Marxism
and Deconstruction*, Ryan thinks deconstructivism and Marxism are
positively comparable on the aspects of both philosophy and politics;
Marxism sublates the traditional concept of metaphysics in philosophy,
and employs deconstructive analysis as its weapon in political critique.

Indeed, by means of the deconstruction of the dominant traditions in
the history of western philosophy, Marxism sublates the metaphysics in
original meaning, namely the traditional philosophical morphology that
aims to trace the essentials of the whole world or "the being of beings",

---

22   Derrida, *Specters of Marx*, p. 129.

and holds that metaphysics "will be defeated forever by materialism, which has now been perfected by the work of speculation itself and coincides with humanism"[23]. Heidegger thus believes Marx accomplishes "the finalization of metaphysics", and "along with the reversal of metaphysics accomplished by Karl Marx, philosophy reaches its most extreme possibility and enters into its final stage"[24]. This is the first point.

Second, it determines the principles for interpreting ideas and language starting out from practice, and thinks "language is the immediate actuality of thought", "in which thoughts in the form of words have their own content". In other words, Marxism makes a reflection on the fact that language is enslaved by ideology against a concrete historical class background. Through the deconstruction of ideology, Marxism reveals the secret of language, and criticizes metaphysical "nonsense, which seeks refuge in etymology"[25].

Third, through the deconstruction of the "materialization" phenomenon and fetishism in capitalist society, Marxism reveals the secret of commodities, the social attribute of man covered by the materialized natural attribute, and the social relation between man and man covered by the material relation, thereby creating a historical sphere aiming at the reestablishment of "individual property" and "personalized individual".

Fourth, by virtue of the deconstruction of capitalist running mechanism, Marxism reveals the root of numerous problems of capitalist society and the trend of its social development, and predicts the lesions of "ten ulcers" of contemporary capitalism relying on its tremendous advancement. As said by Daniel Bell, Marx lived in industrial society, but he had made "accurate" prediction on some important features of "postindustrial society".[26]

Today, we are still in the political and historical "field domains" of Marxism, in the "question domain" of it. No matter whether such "field domains" are created by Marxism or constituted by "responses" to the theories and social movements resisting Marxism, Marxism, all in all, is far from being transcended by this era, and Marx is still a contemporary with us. We always spontaneously put our thoughts and actions in

---

23   *Karl Marx and Friedrich Engels*. 1st Chinese Ed., Vol. 2, pp. 159 – 160.
24   Heidegger, *The Matter toward Thinking*, pp. 59 – 60.
25   *Karl Marx and Friedrich Engels*. 1st Chinese Ed., Vol. 3, p. 523.
26   Daniel Bell, *The Coming of Postindustrial Society*, p. 66.

the "problem domain" of Marxism, "in terms of the Marxism code"[27]. To Derrida's understanding, deconstructivism is no exception, which is also running in the tradition of Marxism and certainly carries a certain spirit of Marxism.

Eagleton points out, "Marxism does not only attract Derrida with its marginal position, but the political theories in place of it are so vapid and insipid that its attraction to Derrida is greater."[28]. The opinion of Eagleton is correct. The reason why Marxism is untranscendable in contemporary times, why Derrida still put his discourse "in terms of the Marxism code", is because Marxism has grasps the foundation of human society, that is, "all social life is essentially practical" and radiates this foundation to all the aspects, levels and relations in the human society, thus forming a "holistic vision of society", and in addition, the issues focused by Marxism and some viewpoints of it existing in the form of sprout or embryo coincide with the major problems in the contemporary society. However, other political or social theories all view human society issue merely based on a certain aspect, level or relation, and reduce human society to such an aspect, level or relation, thus failing to generally and fundamentally grasp human society and frequently wandering in the process of continuous negation of one school to another, like a merry-go-round.

In the words of Jameson, another master of postmodernism, Marxism "is a cognitive mode for us today to restore our relationship with being"; by providing a "holistic vision of society", it "subsumes such apparently antagonistic or incommensurable critical operations, assigning them an undoubted sectoral validity within itself, and thus at once canceling and preserving them"; "the authority of other methods springs from their faithful consonance with this or that local law of a fragmented social life, this or that subsystem of a complex and mushrooming cultural superstructure"[29]. Hence, any contemporary critical theory cannot avoid and turn a blind eye to Marxism, and for contemporary critical theories, Marxism is "the untranscendable semantic horizon".

We can say the inherent logical movement of deconstructivism and the inherent deconstructive function of Marxism make the two meet each other by chance in contemporary era, and promote Derrida not only

27   Derrida, *Specters of Marx*, p. 79.
28   Eagleton, *Politics, Philosophy and Eros in History*, p. 122.
29   F. Jameson, *The Political Unconscious*. Cornell University Press, 1981: p. 10.

to "read and reread and discuss Marx" but also "to go beyond scholarly 'reading' or 'discussion'", i.e. "reading", "discussing", "liquidat-
ing, criticizing and approaching to" Marxism by combining theory with
practice, and to construct "the deconstructed Marxist spirit".

3 DOUBLE CONNOTATIONS OF DERRIDA'S "APPROACH TO" MARXISM

The first is to defend Marxism from the standpoint of deconstructivism.
As far as Derrida is concerned, Marxism at the turn of the century is
materially injured, and it is a "trauma" caused in the name of Marxism,
thus being an "internal injury". Then, how to cure such a "trauma" or
"internal injury"? Derrida believes deconstructivism is an effective prescription, because deconstruction itself is "the memory and tradition of
Marxism", and this "trauma" or "internal injury" "is endlessly denied
by the very movement through which one tries to cushion it, to assimilate it, to interiorize and incorporate it"[30]. In this connection, Derrida
defends Marxism, and "attempts to historically save the foundation of
Marxism" in a political environment where radicals have had no choice.
For Derrida, "his own thought is also developed on this foundation in a
peculiar way; all these connect him with Marxism"[31].

The second is to provide circumstantial evidence for deconstructivism
by applying the strategy and method of Marxism. In his book *White
Mythology*, Derrida highly praises Marx's critique on the interpretation
of social ideas with "etymology", and quotes a long paragraph of *The
German Ideology* as the circumstantial evidence of his metaphor theory; then he resorts to the characters and writings about the definition
of Marxist practice concept, and says, "Let's start with the concept of
practice. To make definition on character, writing, differance and text,
I always persist in the value of 'practice', with the result that the general theory of 'signifying practice' can be thereby explained"[32]. From
Derrida's point of view, the work of deconstruction, the same with the
critique of Marx on ideology in those years, is targeted at dissolving
ideology so as to reevaluate the text in a broad sense and determine
new definitions of the correlations in "reality" (including class struggle,
relation of production, etc.).

---

30 Derrida, *Specters of Marx*, p. 140.
31 Jameson, *The Cultural Logic of Late Capitalism*. Beijing: Joint Publishing
Company, 1997: p. 3.
32 Derrida, *Thought is Guarded by a Craziness*, p. 126.

It is true that deconstructivism is similar to Marxism in form, or to say, it can communicate with Marxism in some opinions. For example, Marxist concept of ideology, in terms of its query on the self-evidence of consciousness, is like the central concept differance of deconstructivism, and the concept of contradiction as the motive power of dialectics, in regard to its operation as a kind of powerful heterogeneous force, predicts the strategy of differance. In the book *Marxism and Deconstruction*, Ryan thinks that the "history" of Marx is similar to the "trace" of Derrida in respect of its criticalness and rejection to ideology. If "history" means breaking natural state and starting to construct and produce, then "trace" means cutting the natural link with reality and starting the process of free game.

In the book *Considerations on Reading Marx: After Reading Derrida*, Spivak asserts that the concern of Marx with "money" is comparable to the enthusiasm of Derrida for "character"; money is originally the alienation of ownership, a supplement to product exchange, but it turns from a servant into a master and becomes the supremacy in the world of commodities, which is extremely similar to the story of character, and so forth. This is one of the theoretical basis for Derrida's keenness on the "alliance" between deconstructivism and Marxism.

I certainly notice that during this "alliance", the spirit of Marxism has been rewritten by Derrida through deconstructive reading, and Marxism in such case is the Marxism in deconstructed version. The embrace with Marxism by Derrida is the application of his deconstruction strategy, with a fundamental view to getting rid of the "grand narrative" of liberalism's "new international" discourse and knocking the wedge of decentralization into the context of globalization, or to "appealing for heterogeneity". As Eagleton said, "As Marxism just arrives at the marginal position, Derrida wants to get close to it, which seems more conform to his plan of post-structuralism."[33]

What's more, under such a reading pattern of deconstructivism, the "text" of Marxism is fragmented to the extent that it no longer has the consistent unified meaning. In the words of Derrida, in the "text" of Marxism, contradiction and dialectics cannot escape from the dominance of metaphysics, and Marxism on the one hand breaks the traditions of idealism, especially Hegelian philosophy, and on the other

---

33   Eagleton, *Politics, Philosophy and Eros in History*, p. 120.

governed by the topic of metaphysics; "I do not believe from the perspective of Marxism, pure Marxist text can simultaneously dissociate
the concept of contradiction from its speculative, purposive and es-
chatological horizon"[34]. Even though Derrida most highly praises the
critical spirit of Marxism, it, in his view, should be differentiated from
Marxism as ontology and dialectical materialism, from Marxism as historical materialism, and from Marxism as the state apparatus.

In this way, the critical spirit as the essence of Marxism becomes abstract, and the practical and class characters of Marxism wear off. Ryan
points out in *Marxism and Deconstruction*, "The theory of deconstruction is the philosophical query on some important philosophical concepts and practice, and Marxism is exactly on the contrary, which is
not a philosophy, but is for the purpose of naming revolutionary movement", and its "theory and practice aim at overturning the society based
on private ownership and replacing it with a society whose wealth is
shared by laborers in free cooperation"[35].

The opinion of Ryan is reasonable to a certain extent. It is obviously
ridiculous to think Marxism is not a philosophy, but practical and class
characters are really the inherent attributes of Marxism, irreplaceable
by even more intensive theoretical critique of deconstructivism on tradition, authority and existing social order. At this "basic point", deconstructivism "cannot be connected" with Marxism. Eagleton thus thinks
Derrida "only wants to use Marxism as a critique, a dissent, a conveni-
ent tool for sharp denouncement, and is less willing to touch upon its
affirmative contents. What he wants is actually the Marxism without
Marxism, that is, the Marxism comfortably appropriated by him according to his own conditions"[36].

The problem is that whether the spiritual essence of Marxism can be
really grasped with the reading pattern of deconstructivism. The pattern used by deconstructivism to read Marxism has been interpreted by
Spivak, who thinks that this reading pattern "can be called a 'literary' or
'rhetorical' reading of a 'philosophical' text", and "the reading is 'literary' only in so far as it recognizes that what Marx products is written
in language"[37].

---

34   Derrida, *Thought is Guarded by a Craziness*, p. 117.
35   M. Ryan, *Marxism and Deconstruction*. Baltimore and London, 1982: p. 1.
36   Eagleton, *Politics, Philosophy and Eros in History*, p. 124.
37   D. Attridge, G. Bennington and R. Younged, *Post-structuralism and the Question of History*. Cambridge University, p. 30.

That is to say, the reading pattern of deconstructivism, after all, interprets Marx with word games. Although Spivak repeatedly declares that the reading pattern of deconstructivism aims to reveal how Marx verifies pure philosophy with practice and thereby questions its "fairness" and "elegance" rather than to resolve the works of Marx into the extreme form of characters, i.e. the text unrelated to the outside world, this reading pattern is, in the final analysis, the effort to interpret Marxism with word games, and I hold a prudent and even skeptical attitude towards to what extent it can grasp the spirit of Marxism on earth.

All in all, regarding the works of Derrida as a master of deconstructivism, we should not believe its meaning will be purely and simply "written down in black and white". The separation of the signifier from the signified, a series of signifiers, the procrastination of meaning in infinite differance – all of these are necessary thought preparations for us when reading Derrida's works. Rather than hastily discuss the thought turn of Derrida, it's better to talk about his discourse turn, the turn of his "signifier", because post-structuralism pays no attention to "the signified" and is only interested in the infinite extension of "signifier chain". But anyway, the assertion of Derrida is remarkable:

"It will always be a fault not to read and reread and discuss Marx – which is to say also a few others – and to go beyond scholarly 'reading' or 'discussion'. It will be more and more a fault, a failing of theoretical, philosophical, political responsibility."[38]

4 ENLIGHTENMENTS FROM SPECTERS OF MARX

In peroration, I do not want to simply summarize the expositions above, but plan to tersely discuss the enlightenments from *Specters of Marx* to us from the angle of "discursive practice".

Foucault had, from the perspective of "discursive practice", pointed out that a kind of authors that could be called the "founders of discursive practice" emerged in the nineteenth century; they were not only the authors of their own works, but also created possibilities and rules of other texts. Freud and Marx belongs to such kind of "founders of discursive practice"[39], who do not only create the similarity factor available for subsequent texts, but open the gate for some differences, thereby

---

38   Derrida, *Specters of Marx*, p. 21.
39   Foucault, *What Is an Author?*. Beijing: Peking University Press, 1992: p. 299.

making a room for introducing in some heterogeneous elements. In the sight of Foucault, the founding of a discursive practice is not isomorphic with the transformation arising after it; the expansion of discursive type does not give discourse the universality that it does not have at the beginning, but opens some potential channels of application. In this transforming process, people do not need to declare some propositions in the works of these founders are wrong, and the so-called "errors" are either insignificant statements or pre-scientific or ideological factors in their works. Only in this way can we understand the inevitable necessity of "return to origin" in these discursive fields.

As a matter of fact, the return to discursive field itself never stops. Such a return is not the increase of discourse or a decorative supplement to history, and it contrarily assumes the necessary mission to transform discursive practice. In this sense, we can say that the overall narrative of Marx about real society contains an internal tension, which makes the "text" of Marx leave a huge theoretical space for the descendants. During the interpretation of Marx's "text", it is meaningless to hammer at the so-called places that are incompatible with present needs in that Marx is after all an ideologist living in the nineteenth century. The reason why constantly rereading Marx is required is because the "text" of Marx itself has already condensed as a part of history and culture, a part of times spirit. In this connection, constantly rereading Marx is to constantly return to history, make a reflection on present reality, and thereby make conversation with history and communication with reality.

The interpretation of *Specters of Marx* on the "text" of Marx can be considered as the practice of Foucault's "author theory". Derrida argues that the text of Marx should not be interpreted for seeking the ultimate signified definitions under the surface of "text", and interpretation is transformation; if the readability of inheritance is given, natural, transparent and mono-semantic, and if such readability does not require or conflict with interpretation, we will have nothing to inherit; the deficiency of system is not a disadvantage here, and on the contrary, heterogeneity provides a prospect for understanding; it allows itself to be broken and opened by the unfolded, coming or upcoming thing – particularly the thing from others. The theorem of incompleteness of Godel indicates that it is impossible for a formal system including elementary number theory to have no contradiction while being complete; no contradiction inevitably means incompleteness, whilst completeness necessarily has contradiction. A system as simple as formal arithmetic system is the case, all the more so when it comes to the senior thinking system.

We should not complete identify with Derrida's deconstructive reading of Marxism, but we also should not simply reject it. The emphasis of Derrida on some elements in Marxism is meant to disassemble the "text" of Marx as a whole and show its internal antagonism and self-resolution. Therefore the "text" of Marx becomes fragmented in the postmodern context, and no longer has the consistent unified meaning. This is one side of the coin. On the other side, such a "fragmented" condition does not only mark the symptom for the crisis confronting the existing Marxist interpreting pattern, but also cultivates the sprout for overcoming the crisis. It is under this "fragmented" condition that the "text" of Marx regains fresh vitality.

The intertextual interpretations of Derrida between Marxism and post-capitalism and between Marxism and post-structuralism at least give us the following enlightenments:

Firstly, the internal difference and heterogeneity of a text is not certainly a disaster, but it may open a new infinite source of meaning for the text and provide the possibility of multiple dimensions for the new interpretation of text.

Secondly, the effort to construct a complete system may have been inappropriate; in the postmodern state of knowledge, Marxism in different versions may be generated in different historical situations; every version is worthy of consideration, and there is no pure "original version" or "negative". Thus, there will be no place for dogmatism and bookishness.

Thirdly, it is beyond all questions that we should discuss the contemporary development of Marxism on the premise of adhering to its basic opinions, standpoints and methods. However, the meaning of Marx's "text" is not an invariable thing that can be used infinitely once discovered, and we should continuously identify the times spirit of Marx's "text" along with the change of times. As Ryan says in *Marxism and Deconstruction*:

"History, as another name of uncertainty, is always opened to the development possibility of new theoretical system. If Marxism is said as a science, it is a science about history. At the moment when its axiom is established, it has opened itself to us and developed itself in the movement of history; its axiom is real-time all the time, because history is a changing, modifying and developing field whose purpose is openness."[40]

---

40   M. Ryan, *Marxism and Deconstruction*, p. 2.

CHAPTER IX

POSTMODERNISM: BACKGROUND, ESSENCE AND SIGNIFICANCE — FROM MARX'S POINT OF VIEW

As the critique on the negative effects of modernization, postmodernism has turned from a "specter" into a "widely-known term" and become a cultural trend of thought in the contemporary West. Since the late 1980s, in the wake of the continuous expansion and deepening of modernization in China, postmodernism floods into China like a vigorous wave, fiercely impacts Chinese ideological and cultural circles, and rapidly permeates and spreads throughout Chinese society, to the extent that talking about "post-modernity" has become a new elite culture and the mark of folk ideology. In the academic world, most scholars think postmodernism is a new historical period after modernism, and some even claims that "postmodernism is also found in China". This is a misunderstanding. "Postmodernism literature cannot be imitated in that it belongs to a special and complex tradition."[1] In fact, the whole postmodernism "cannot be imitated". "Postmodernism is not something we can settle once and for all and then use with a clear conscience. The concept, if there is one, has to come at the end, and not at the beginning,

---

[1] *Approaching Postmodernism*, edited by Fokkema and Bertens. Beijing: Peking University Press, 1991: p. 2.

of our discussions of it."[2] The opinion of Jameson is quite insightful, having an important inspirational function for us to understand postmodernism. In my view, postmodernism exists in the West first as a task or question, and ideologists of postmodernism bring forth various different cognition frameworks in the principle of "fallacious inference" and shows a strong consciousness of question. More importantly, the ideologists of postmodernism still have a consciousness of question as to their own consciousness of question. Therefore the introduction and study of postmodernism under the background of contemporary Chinese culture should also, in the first place, have an adequate consciousness of question, that is, regarding the cultural trend of thought of postmodernism as a question rather than accepting or rejecting it an established theoretical result. Only through this can we fairly grasp the theoretical significance of postmodernism and "know the significant development of western world", thereby "impelling us to think"[3].

1 DIFFERENT POSTMODERN DISCOURSES

The first question confronting us during the study of postmodernism is that whether there is a unified postmodern discourse, or whether it is possible for a unified postmodern discourse. The term "doctrine" means a systematic set of socio-cultural theory in Chinese language, so while investigating postmodernism, the domestic academic circle always tries to form a clearly defined concept of postmodernism from a certain perspective or level.

The problem is that postmodernism is different from such thought schools as existentialism, pragmatism, structuralism, etc.; it has no thought leader, no uniform proposition, and even no identical context. As a result, there is no a clearly defined postmodernism. We would rather take it as a dispute centered on some terms, topics and opinions.

In this sense, the so-called postmodernism means different postmodern discourses. In general, postmodernism focuses on "waging a war on identity", on all "grand narratives"; it stresses heterogeneous elements and rejects essentialism and foundationalism. So there is no a unified postmodern discourse, that is to say, a discourse tending to unity cannot be called the postmodern discourse.

2   Fredric Jameson, *Postmodernism, or The Cultural Logic of Late Capitalism*, Duke University Press, 1991, p. xxii.
3   *Approaching Postmodernism*, edited by Fokkema and Bertens, p. 2.

The rise of postmodernism or postmodern discourse rooted in different realizations of western ideologists on capitalist society and its cultural condition since the 1950s. Since then, many new noticeable phenomena have emerged in western society and its cultural field, and they cannot be covered and interpreted by either traditional concepts or modern ideas. Thus, Hassan thinks that these phenomena different from those of modernism can be named as "post-modernities".

It's indeed true. Derrida, Lyotard, Lacan et al. have noticed these phenomena that should be differentiated from those of modernism and made all sorts of discussions on them. Although such discussions of philosophers, historians and literary theorists have not yet formed a movement, paradigm or school, some corresponding cultural trends and intellectual and life attitudes are aroused. In the eyes of Hassan, these cultural trends and life attitudes can be called "postmodernism", and thinks that "postmodernism is a response of modernism to the unimaginable things that it has glanced at directly or indirectly at its prophetic moment"[4], whose typical features are uncertainty and internality. Hassan also prompts us to deeply think that whether postmodernism falls under the descriptive category or the evaluative category in the literary thought, and whether it is an artistic tendency or a social phenomenon and even a change in western humanism. Obviously, postmodernism in the theoretical horizon of Hassan exists first of all as a question or topic.

From the theoretical standpoint of western Marxism, Jameson insists that all cultural analyses, without exception, contain a theory of historical periodization that is covered or repressed, and postmodernism is closely related to late capitalism. According to Jameson, late capitalism belongs to "postindustrial society", where "the modernization process is complete and 'nature' is gone for good; it is a more fully human world than the older one, but one in which 'culture' has become a veritable 'second nature'"[5]. If early capitalism in "modern" times is thought to focus on conquer nature, then late capitalism in "postmodern" times lays emphasis on the expansion at the level of culture and even "unconsciousness".

---

4   Ihab Hassan, *The Postmodern Turn*. The Ohio State University Press, 1987: p. 39.
5   F. Jameson, *Postmodernism, or The Cultural Logic of Late Capitalism*. Duke University Press, 1991: p. 9.

On these grounds, Jameson defines postmodernism as "the cultural logic of late capitalism", and believes market capitalism produces realism, monopoly capitalism gives rise to modernism, and late capitalism creates postmodernism, which is apparently featured by depthlessness, extinction of historical consciousness, loss of subjectivity, disappearance of the sense of distance, and so forth. In short, postmodernism is the study on capitalist culture at its "late" stage. It can been observed that postmodernism in Jameson's mind is a concept of historical periodization for culture, a descriptive category, and he grasps postmodernism as a major cause rather than a style of culture. In his eyes, "the concept of culture's major cause allows a series of distinctions, but is meanwhile the existence and coexistence of the features of subordination"[6]. In other words, postmodernism, as the leading logic of late capitalist culture, does not completely exclude heterogeneous elements like realism, modernism, etc.

Lyotard uses "post-modernity" to represent the intellectual state in the developed capitalist society, and defines it as "the skeptical attitude to meta-narrative"[7]. The "meta-narrative" refers to the Hegelian thought tradition – "purely speculative and theoretical narrative" – and the representative thought tradition of the French Revolution – "freedom and emancipation narrative"; the former lays stress on the thinking model of identity and integrity values, while the latter focuses on the thinking model of humanistic independence and emancipation; the two are joint up to defend for the institutionalized scientific researches, for the pursuit of truth and justice. However, result of defense unexpectedly constitutes a perfect irony against the original intention of "meta-narrative": the subjectivity of man is exaggerated extremely, but individual man is dissolved; science advances rapidly, but the humanistic world tends to rigidity and suffocation.

Lyotard therefore thinks postmodernism applies itself to the dissolution of identity or unity so as to strengthen our sensitivity to difference and facilitate our ability to tolerate incommensurable things; the principle of postmodern knowledge is not the identical inference of experts, but the fallacious inference of inventors. Obviously, postmodernism mentioned by Lyotard is a non-identical spirit, a set of value model despising limitation and specialized in rebellion, and an analytic and evaluative category.

---

6   *Culture and Aesthetics of Postmodernism*, edited by Wang Yuechuan and Shang Shui, p. 76.
7   ibid., p. 26.

It can be seen from the different postmodern discourses that post-modernity or postmodernism has the following features: (1) as a descriptive category, referring to new phenomena arising in western society and its cultural field; (2) as an evaluative category, used to analyze and probe into these new phenomena; and (3) as the result of evaluation, used to generalize and summarize some new angles of view, trains of thought, methods, etc. of cognition.

This demonstrates that though contemporary western ideologists have different opinions on postmodernism, they all acknowledge new cultural phenomena or new intellectual states emerging in the late capitalist society; even Habermas, who holds a resolutely rejecting attitude towards postmodernism, does not deny the various new characteristics in the contemporary western society. It is revolving around the discussions about these new phenomena, new states and new characteristics that postmodern discourses emerge. A variety of debates on postmodernism are conducted among thought schools including new hermeneutics, deconstructivism, new pragmatism, western Marxism and feminism, forming a complicated and confusing postmodern cultural scene. The opinions of these schools mix with or oppose to one another, and the debates among them are mutually inspired, full of purports; in this way, postmodern discourses are accumulated and augmented ceaselessly, and finally step out of the narrow field of literature and become an extensive cultural trend of thought and worldwide topic spreading the whole globe.

There is another important reason for why I grasp postmodernism as a kind of discourse, that is, postmodernism, or post-modernity, is not a concept in the traditional epistemological sense, but a concept of contemporary hermeneutics. From the standpoint of contemporary hermeneutics, there is nothing needing an ultimate interpretation, and interpretation is infinite, because the sign being interpreted does not negatively wait for its interpretation, and it is also the interpretation of other signs; the interpretation of interpretation itself thus sinks into a cycle – interpretation is not caused by the signified, but by the function of the interpreter. Hence, contemporary hermeneutics disowns the traditional epistemology and its so-called "deep meaning" or "truth".

The term "postmodernism" is proposed as the presetting or framework of interpretation; what it confronts is a textual world, linguistic world and intellectual world; what it deals with, instead of the issues of objective world, is the reasonability of the overall human knowledge constructed through language hitherto. For this reason, the "postmodern society" in the postmodern discourses does not refer to the contemporary developed capitalist society, and it's just the intellectual state in this society at the very outside. As to the contemporary developed capitalist society, postmodern ideologists usually call it the postindustrial society, information society, late capitalism, consumer society, media society, and so on.

Postmodernism generally views itself as the sort-out and construction of existing cultural traditions rather than the cultural reflection of contemporary developed capitalist society. "History in traditional form bears the process of 'recalling' the monuments in the past and change them into literatures", whereas "history in our times becomes a thing changing literatures into monuments"[8]. That is to say, "modern" times is mainly the process of cognizing the world and acquiring knowledge, the process of forming literatures and discourses, whilst "postmodern" times, i.e. "our times", is the process of resurveying the existing literatures and discourses.

To put it another way, postmodernism is no other than a resurvey, rethinking, reintegration, and rewriting of western culture, a "decoding" and "recoding" activity of discourse. This is just what Lyotard has done, and what he discusses in his book *The Postmodern Condition* is the state of "knowledge" hitherto. If the constructing process from "nature" to "culture" is "modern" times, then the process from existing "culture" to "reconstruction of culture" constitutes "postmodern" times.

I notice that postmodernism is primarily concerned with matters at levels of idea and consciousness, so postmodern discourses believe in "language-game theory", that is, believing that linguistic signs are not the substitutes of real meanings, and the meaning of language rests with the difference between signs rather than its reproduction and representation of external world. However, this is just the "self-perception" of postmodernism. In fact, for any cultural trend of thought, regardless of the "character" it has, its formation is associated with its times, and it is at bottom the product of definite times. Leaving their own times, the straightforward and fiery "character" of French enlightenment trend of

---

8   Michel Foucault, *The Archaeology of Knowledge and The Discourse on Language.* Pantheon, 1972: p. 7.

thought and the intricate and obscure feature of classical German philosophy are both incomprehensible, so is postmodernism.

To my understanding, postmodernism is by no means groundless, and the cognition and analysis of it cannot be accomplished merely through "language games". As a kind of discourse, postmodernism is apodictically developed step by step through the confrontation among various theoretical trends of thought and the interpretation of humanistic traditions, but the rise of postmodernism, or postmodern discourse, after all happens on definite historical base. So we cannot obtain a relatively definite exposition and grasp unless putting the overall postmodern cultural debates into a specific background of times.

The rise of postmodernism, in its reality, has two major roots: one is the outbursts of two world wars, and the other is the great changes in the scientific and technological field. If we say the former impels western society to doubt its faiths in the idea of reason, the self-control of man, social progress, etc., the latter makes western society confused with and afraid of the separation of man from the world and the shrinkage and even split of man arising from knowledge growth. In a word, capitalism is in a breaking and splitting condition and the ritual collapse after entering into "late stage". In spite of the maintenance or the criticism of it, capitalism is, as always, running on its established track like a galloping train.

This indicates that in the process of modernization, capitalism is not only "legitimized" but also set as the single authority, turned into "a monolithic block"; it "has forgotten how to think historically", namely forgetting the historicity of capitalism itself, thereby becoming an autocratic authority. In consequence, contemporary western ideologists assemble together again to make an "emergency treatment" for the more and more mortally sick capitalist society and give it a prescription anew – "waging a war on identity". Therefore Jameson points out, "It is safest to grasp the concept of the postmodern as an attempt to think the present historically in an age that has forgotten how to think historically in the first place."[9]

---

9   Fredric Jameson, *Postmodernism, or The Cultural Logic of Late Capitalism*, p. ix.

2 REWRITING MODERNITY:
THE ESSENCE OF POSTMODERNISM

American postmodernist Griffin points out that "if the word postmodern-ism can find a common ground on different aspects in use, the common ground refers to an extensive emotion instead of any common dogma – an emotion that thinks mankind can and must transcend modernity."[10] This "emotion to transcend modernity" is the post-modernity in post-modern discourse. Post-modernity is relative to modernity, therefore the interpretation of post-modernity is synchronized with the sort-out of modernity. Judged from the generation and development process of postmodernism, postmodern discourse reveals the basic contexts of postmodernism, post-modernity and enlightenment philosophy exactly by "deconstructing" modernism, modernity and systematic philosophy. In my opinion, deconstruction is a kind of reinterpretation.

The so-called deconstruction is a unique writing style adopted by Derrida, with the aim at disintegrating phonetic writing with philology and resisting logic with rhetoric, in a bid to destroy the meaning of text (at present), obliterate the original norms, and rewrite new characters. Although Derrida's philosophy of deconstruction has its own style, de-construction as a purport is possessed by the entire postmodern dis-course, and we have to recur to the grasp of deconstruction purport for the purpose of smoothly entering postmodern discourse.

Derrida emphasizes that deconstruction is not deterministic certainly, but it is affirmative, and even an affirmative activity in the first place; the opinion that thinks deconstruction is negative is in effect a meta-physical rewriting; deconstruction is not dismantlement or destroy, not the simple decomposition of systematological structure. From Derrida's point of view, deconstruction is fundamentally a kind of thinking about beings, about metaphysics. So deconstruction mentioned by Derrida in-volves not only this or that construction activity but also the topics of systematology, as well as the issues of foundation, of the relationship be-tween foundation and things making up the foundation, of the structural relationship, and of the whole philosophical structure. Deconstruction is doubtlessly related to system, but this does not mean deconstruc-tion smashes system; instead, it opens the possibility of arrangement or

---

10 *Postmodern Science: The Reenchantment of Science*, edited by Griffin. Beijing: Central Compilation & Translation Press, 1995: p. 17.

assembly. In this sense, deconstruction can be deemed as a response to system, i.e. to the closure and opening of system.

After grasping the deconstruction purport of Derrida, we can understand that deconstruction is different from criticism. If criticism is generally directed from subject to external objects, deconstruction is a self-reflection and self-cleaning of subject. For this reason, the deconstruction of modernity is not to criticize modernity outside it, but to sort out modernity within its historical course with a view to "interpreting" and "giving meaning" anew.

"Modern" as a concept of historical periodization was put forward by French Enlightenment in the seventeenth century for the differentiation from the classical times. In the theoretical horizon of French Enlightenment, the concept of "modern" connotes progress, and progress means reason, order and freedom. In history, the grand narrative about reason, freedom and progress established by modernity is synchronized with the Industrial Revolution, technological revolution and earthshaking social changes sweeping the West. Although modernity or modernization cannot be equated with capitalism, it's for sure that it is just in the capitalist era that modernity is given full play to. Hence the concept of "modern" representing historical periodization and the historical course of capitalism are in a mutually promoting relationship. In this sense, Lyotard views capitalism as one of the descriptions of modernity.

As far as I am concerned, modernity in postmodern discourse refers to such idea of "modern". In other words, modernity in postmodern discourse includes the obsession of literary and artistic works with the sacred, distinctive and formalistic features of intention, design, grade and master rule, the craziness of philosophers about grand narratives like capitalized philosophy, absolute truth, foundationalism, essentialism, etc., and the infatuation of politicians with free subject, theory of linear historical progress, laws of liberal democracy, and so on. It can be observed that modernity as an idea penetrates into all realms of value, spirit and meaning in western society and can be called "the mainstream ideology". While constructing the genealogy of the concept "modern", the ideologists of postmodernism explores the essence of the conceptual distinction between modern and postmodern, between modernity and post-modernity, between and modernism and postmodernism, which are respectively opposite and complementary to each other.

It can be seen through investigating their discussions that the reinterpretation of modernity is an intricate process of thought adventure.

When talking about the uncertainty, disorder, depthlessness and unprincipled character of postmodernism, Hassan points out that whether these features can be used to distinguish postmodernism from modernism is still questionable, because the latter is always reserved in the western literature history as an intensive subterfuge, and postmodernism itself is a disputable concept falling under the category of disjunctive logic, and is subject to the dual restriction from the energy of this phenomenon and the continuously changing apprehensions of critics.

Here, Hassan implicitly and explicitly shows such an attitude that modernism is uncertain, and postmodernism is of course uncertain. In his view, there is not an impassable "iron barrier" or "great wall" between modernism and postmodernism, because "history is like a piece of parchment on which the old can be erased and the new can be recorded, while culture is permeated with the past, the present, and the future"[11]. That is to say, postmodernism derives from modernism and is symbiotically unified with modernism. The enlightenment to us given by the viewpoint that "history is like a palimpsest on which the old can be erased and the new can be recorded" is that there is no essential difference between "modern" and "postmodern", and the former can be "erased and rewritten" through the construction of the latter depending on the theoretical perspective of the elucidator.

Hassan has many doubts about how to define postmodernism, while Lyotard definitely returns to the tide of modernism to grasp postmodernism. According to him, post-modernity is indubitably a part of modernity, and a piece of works must be modern before being postmodern, because "post-modernity" manages to express those that cannot be represented by "modernity", transforming the "intangible" into the "tangible". Virtually, "'post-modern' would have to be understood according to the paradox of the future (post) anterior (modo)".

From such understanding, postmodernism is not the desperate modernism but the fresh status of modernism, and such a status is repeated. In view of this, Lyotard emphasizes that post-modernity does not refer to a new era, and instead, it is the "rewriting" of some features of modernity,

---

11 *Culture and Aesthetics of Postmodernism*, edited by Wang Yuechuan and Shang Shui, p. 113.

first of all the rewriting of modernity's declaration that its validity is established on the cause of human emancipation by means of science and technology, and such a rewriting has been carried out for a long time within modernity itself. Fundamentally speaking, the reason why Lyotard holds that post-modernity is always contained in modernity is because he realizes through historical observation of modernity that modernity itself has an impulse of transcending itself and arriving at a thing different from itself; modernity does not only transcends itself in this way, but also wants to fuse itself into an ultimate steady state. So modernity, in essence, continuously breeds post-modernity.

When Lyotard devotes himself to the rewriting of "modernity", Habermas hopes to "revive modernity". Habermas sees the crisis confronting western modern culture, but he does not think the spring tide – enlightenment, reason, justice, subjectivity, etc. – that has led the entire western civilization into the modern society will be exhausted here. Through investigating the process of postmodern trend of thought's attack at modernity since Hegel, Habermas reveals the core of post-modern trend of thought is to completely overturn subjectivity, totality, identity, primitivity, and deeply structural character of language and replace them with non-centrality, non-subjectivity, non-totality, non-essence and non-primitivity, and he insists that post-modernity is impossible in that subjectivity has not been sufficiently developed in western society, the enlightenment ideal of modernity not realized and its mission not fulfilled, and modernity is far from over. Thus Habermas chooses to firmly defend the enlightenment ideal, correct its designing error and practical deviation, and establish a new schema of reason – intercourse reason.

Obviously, Habermas, unlike Lyotard, discusses "modernity" for the purpose of persisting in, revising and thereby propagating the enlightenment ideal, namely enlightenment's "idea of modern". However, his definition of modernity is essentially from the same theoretical perspective with Lyotard. In the sight of Lyotard, "modernity" means that the activity of knowledge discourse in a society is able to set up a set of self-justified game rules with reference to a grand narrative and thereby make the knowledge discourse reasonable. According to Habermas, "modernity" "no longer seeks its direction of advancement in the process of copying the standards of other eras; it only needs to create the criteria demanded by itself. Modernity is to guarantee that it is copied entirely to a right extent"[12]. That is to say, modern society determines its own principles, and does not need any external authoritative narrative to rationalize or legitimatize its existence. Thus it is clear that the "revival of modernity" of Habermas does not has essential difference from the "rewriting of modernity" of Lyotard in terms of cognition perspective.

After we make clear that postmodernism aims at deconstructing modernity, post-modernity is the deconstruction of modernity, and the "modernity" respectively understood by Habermas and Lyotard, the opposition between Lyotard's effort of "rewriting modernity" and Habermas' belief in "reviving modernity" will have no essential or fundamental sense. The former does not hesitate to give up the meta-narrative about freedom and emancipation for the pursuit of the intellectual life of "anarchism", and the latter is unwilling to give up the enlightenment thought despite knowing it has many problems with an aim to avoid social life of "anarchism"; the former would rather not differentiate correct common views from wrong ones so as to avoid coming out with another meta-narrative, and the latter insists on maintaining a rational standard for the purpose of differentiating theory and ideology; the former opposes to separating post-modernity from modernity, with a view to making a reflection on the preconditions of modernity, and the latter objects to the opposition between post-modernity and modernity, in order to stress that modernity is far from over, and so forth.

From my viewpoint, both Lyotard and Habermas are engaged in the deconstruction of modernity, and the differences lie in their starting points, standpoints and concerns: the former tries for transformation, while the latter persists in upholding the flag of modernity; the former is based on "moral narrative", the latter on "historical narrative"; the former is concerned with intellectual state, while the latter focuses on social life. All of these result in different cognitions of them in the process of modernity deconstruction. What's more, both of them believe that post-modernity is operating within modernity. So the primary significance of the debate between Lyotard and Habermas and the "postmodernism debate" in the European and American academic circles since the 1970s consists in a kind of discourse construction. Just during such a construction of postmodern discourse, the modern discourse is simultaneously accumulated and multiplied.

---

12   Jürgen Habermas, *The Philosophical Discourse of Modernity*. MIT Press, 1987: p. 7.

This is also the significance of Rorty's idea of "post-philosophical culture". Rorty divides philosophy into systematic philosophy and enlightenment philosophy, in the belief that great systematic philosophers are engaged in construction for generation after generation, whereas great enlightenment philosophers in dismantlement for their own times; enlightenment philosophers can never render philosophy ended, but they are helpful for preventing philosophy from taking a rigidified path. As a result, the characteristic of systematic philosophy is holding the principles of centrality and identity, with emphasis laid on normal discourse, construction, and philosophical cognition, whilst the characteristic of enlightenment philosophy is adhering to the principles of difference and relativity, with stress laid on abnormal discourse, deconstruction, and enlightenment process.[13] From the view of Rorty, abnormal discourse always relies upon normal discourse, the possibility of hermeneutics upon the possibility of epistemology, and the work of enlightenment always uses the materials supplied by current culture.

The thought of Rorty expressly shows the deconstruction logic of postmodern discourse: postmodernism, instead of negating modernity, aims to argue with modernity with some of its internal imaginations; postmodernism grows out of the complete system that it attempts to overthrow, so it cannot be considered as a new template; although postmodernism challenges modernism seriously, it does not take the place of it. This means that the significance of postmodernism does not rest with its opposition to modernism, but in its reflection of the internal paradoxes of modernism. As Derrida stated, "As a discourse, deconstruction is always about a discourse about parasite."[14] To put it another way, postmodern discourse is developed on the base of modernity or modernization, and once this base is lost or forgotten, postmodernism will really become a homeless "specter", and postmodern discourse will thoroughly descend to the "mutters" without any referentiality.

Upon relatively sufficient understanding on the connotation that postmodern discourse aims at deconstructing modernity, I think the classification of postmodernism into destructive postmodernism and constructive postmodernism, or into negative postmodernism and positive postmodernism is unreasonable. For example, Derrida and Foucault tend to be regarded as the representatives of destructive postmodernism,

---

13   Rorty, *Philosophy and the Mirror of Nature*. Beijing, Joint Publishing Company, 1987: pp. 319 – 324.
14   Derrida, *Thought is Guarded by a Craziness*, p. 183.

but as a matter of fact, the deconstruction of modernity by Derrida is not for the purpose of sealing its own image up, but of making it opened for rewriting, and what Foucault does is nothing but tracing the genealogy of modernity as a problem; both of them are not different in principle from Rorty, the so-called constructive postmodernist. From Lyotard's viewpoint that postmodernism aims at the "rewriting" of modernity, we can say that Derrida and Foucault center their work on "anew" and hammer at how "anew" is possible, i.e. at the preconditions and possibility of "rewriting", whereas Rorty focuses his attention on "writing" and thinks more about the specific operation of "writing", i.e. about the strategy and mechanism of "rewriting". Evidently, there is no difference of "destructiveness" and "constructiveness" between Derrida, Foucault and Rorty, and the only difference is that they hold different opinions on to what extent the "destructiveness" should be developed and the "construction" started. Postmodernism is a phenomenon full of contradictions, where application and abuse, as well as construction and overturn, coexist.

At bottom, postmodernism no longer assumes there is an absolute pivot to legitimatize truth and order, and no longer believes the so-called transcendental authoritative narrative or the so-called inborn hierarchy; instead, it believes what we possess is just what we construct by ourselves, all things are communicated through conversation, all meanings are generated through interpretation, and all cognitions are started from concrete real life, rather than from any transcendentally set framework, and deduced into theory during concrete practice in life.

3 A KIND OF ATTITUDE TO KNOWLEDGE AND MARGINAL DISCOURSE

In view of the complicatedness and intricacy of postmodern discourse, as well as the realization of postmodernism ideologists on the crisis of language representation, the study on postmodernism is not so much the seeking for the tenet of the cultural trend of thought of postmodernism as the grasp of its theoretical significance. Against the cultural background of contemporary China, all my thinking about postmodernism, in practice, involves a more realistic and basic problem, that is, the relationship between postmodernism and contemporary Chinese culture.

With respect to the theoretical significance of postmodernism, we should first note that postmodernism is an attitude to knowledge.

Based on a brand-new historical stage, modernity fully establishes the confidence in the subjectivity of abstract man, and finally creates the myth of reason, order, and the historical conception of linear progress. Such a myth has served as an internal thought impetus for the modernization of western society and veiled all kinds of costs of man, society and environment paid for modernization with rationality, thus making men accept disasters and sufferings with pleasure. Postmodernism raises doubts on the myth of modernity, which surely contributes to men's reflection of modern society. The problems are: while deconstructing the myth of modernity, whether postmodernism is creating the myth of postmodernism? Whether anti-essentialism, anti-foundationalism and anti-representationalism initiated by postmodern ideologists uproot essence, foundation and representation? Whether the advocacies of relativity, diversity, difference and uncertainty by postmodernism are doomed to slip into the quagmire of nihilism, relativism and anarchism? At these points, the discussions of Hoy and Rorty are quite instructive to us.

Hoy thinks, "Foucault and Gadamer do not generally oppose to the concepts of truth and freedom, and what they are interested in is how these concepts that have yet to be enriched are specifically explained in practice."[15] Rorty points out, "Denouncing postmodernism as relativism is alleging that postmodernism is a meta-narrative."[16] In my opinion, postmodernism underlines the hegemony and unfoundedness of absolute reason rather than advocates ant-rationalism, emphasizes the inherent weakness and transiency of humanism rather than proposes anti-humanism, and just wants to demonstrate that the faith in historical progress tends to make men indulge in superstition and lack vigilance rather than to doubt the progressiveness of history.

In fact, postmodernism only wants to clarify that nothing can absolutely ensure the happiness of mankind and the development society, there is no God at all, and humanity is fictitious. In this connection, postmodernism is fundamentally an attitude to knowledge, unrelated to specific selection or the directionality of construction or destruction.

15   David Couzens Hoy and Thomas Mc Carthy, *Critical Theory*. Blackwell, 1944: p. 70.
16   Rorty, *Post-philosophical Culture*. Shanghai: Shanghai Translation Publishing House, 1992: p. 202.

I notice that new "grand narrative", namely postmodern myth, must be avoided in the process of questioning and deconstructing the myth of modernism. Postmodernism does not represent a new historical stage; it is just a new attitude to knowledge, and this attitude is not the sole respectable and laudable attitude to knowledge in present times. The opinion of Hoy is worthy of our consideration: he thinks that in the same individual or the same discipline or setting, some aspects may be traditional, some modern and some postmodern. Hassan even brings forward that "we have the cultural ethos of the Victorian era and modern and postmodern times at the same time"[17].

From my point of view, postmodernism as an attitude to knowledge is the demarcation of modernism; it operates at the "limitations" of modernism and has its specific pertinence, that is, aiming at dissolving the ultrastable systems like "absolute foundation", "pure reason", "capitalized philosophy", etc. Such an attitude to knowledge is the development and refinement of the thought line of rejecting Platonism since Marx and Nietzsche. To avoid still falling into the plight of foundationalism and essentialism at the end of the rejection to Platonism, the ideologists of postmodernism bring forth various assumptions and seek for various paths. They have no intention of creating a new myth. Deconstruction, as said by Derrida, "is a discourse based on the logic of 'super parasite'".

The same is, in effect, true to postmodern attitude to knowledge, whose significance can only be clarified under the historical background of modernity; if the postmodern attitude of knowledge is emphasized in an isolate manner regardless of this historical background, it will be doomed to become the "modern" attitude to knowledge.

Postmodernism is not only an attitude to knowledge but also a marginal discourse, both of which constitute the theoretical significance of postmodernism.

Marginal discourse is relative to central discourse or mainstream ideology. In the intellectual operating mechanism of society, marginal discourse continually erodes and impacts the field of central discourse, and constitutes a threat to it, but it is just a threat. I disagree with such an opinion that "the rise of postmodernism" marks the western world

---

17   *Culture and Aesthetics of Postmodernism*, edited by Wang Yuechuan and Shang Shui, p. 113.

is at the turning point of human civilization, the internal civilization syndrome of western culture that occupies the dominant position for a long term is gradually exposed, and the prospect of human civilization hangs on the development and promotion of oriental culture, including traditional Chinese culture. This opinion catches some reasonable facts, but dissolves these reasonable facts into unreasonable understanding.

There is no doubt that in line with the logic of postmodern discourse, oriental culture belongs to "others'" discourse, a voice having been forgotten and laid aside for a long time, and a kind of "little narrative" relative to western culture. Hence, postmodernism is inevitably "magnanimous to" the orient, and praises it with various flattering words. However, as a kind of marginal discourse, postmodernism objects to all "grand narratives" and has no intention of establishing a new central consciousness while rejecting an old one.

In my eyes, the enlightenment of postmodernism is that we should survey the traditional Chinese culture in detail to find out which voices are suppressed for a long term, which phenomena are conspicuous but also inapparent, and which narratives are misinterpreted, so as to "rewrite" Chinese culture to a certain degree, or we should expound the "question" consciousness of Chinese culture based on the "text" of traditional Chinese culture and the "text" of the historical course of Chinese culture's modernization, thereby destroying the old Chinese cultural idea and establish the new in a bid to "reconstruct it".

I also disagree with such a viewpoint that although the spring tide of postmodernism has not been formed in China, it has constituted a challenge to the existing culture. There are many theoretical misunderstandings contained in this viewpoint. Even in the western society, postmodernism is still at the margin, quite consciously; it never stops impacting the mainstream culture, and is more or less challenging, but it upholds a "logic of parasite" all the time. As Fokkema has said, postmodernism literature cannot be imitated in that it belongs to a special and complex tradition, so is postmodernism culture actually. If postmodernism is said to be challenging to the contemporary Chinese culture, it just awakens some suppressed internal assumptions of traditional Chinese culture depending on its inspiring influence, and makes them argue with current mainstream culture or ideology.

Of course, there is the so-called "postmodern stance" at present in China; some people take a frivolous and irresponsible attitude towards history, society and politics while dissolving some unreasonable, false and ridiculous things in a mocking manner. As an undercurrent in the folk ideology, such a "postmodern stance" is manifested in many aspects like poetry, painting, novel and lifestyle. But even I admit the cultural trend of thought of postmodernism facilitates the "postmodern stance" in Chinese society, I just think that this phenomenon results from the misunderstanding and abuse of postmodernism, and the crux of the problem is that maybe the social life of contemporary China has a certain demand, and postmodernism more or less meets such a demand.

The modernization of China is being boosted rapidly, and modernity, as the core of modernization, is being developed fully. Being a mainstream ideology or central culture, "modernity" is necessary beyond doubt, but we should still hold a reviewing and even alert attitude to it. "Postmodern stance" is no other than the negative expression of this attitude, which will become increasingly prominent along with the sufficient deepening of China's modernization. The "postmodern stance" in China is fundamentally a response to the modernization of China. Therefore I refuse to conceive the "postmodern stance" in Chinese society with the model of "challenge (of the West) – response (of China)", because this model is characterized by "eurocentrism", and itself is an important constituent part of the idea of "modern".

Postmodernism is laudable as an attitude to knowledge and thought-provoking as a marginal discourse, but such an attitude to knowledge and marginal discourse presets, or logically leads to, a life world, which I call the picture of postmodern world for the moment. This picture of postmodern world, in general, dissolves the world picture respectively provided by scientism and traditional humanism, and does not only disregard objective reality but also takes no glance at the objectivity possibly achieved by subjectivity. Such a picture of postmodern world is inescapably fragmented and turbulent.

The problem is that whether a fragmented and turbulent world can be called a "world". What is the foundation for the picture of postmodern world?

Due to "depthlessness", the life world created by postmodernism text is virtually a weightless planar world. In the picture of postmodern world, I witness very strange mixes, i.e. the mix of elite consciousness with folk consciousness and the mix of avant-garde art with mass culture. These mixes can also be found in Chinese society: some elite consciousnesses propose to give up ideal, take no consideration of doctrine, and downplay value, which are all along embraced by folk ideology. Avantgarde art is committing itself to breaking the boundary between art and life, and turning from pursuing meaning to ceaselessly replacing and renovating the text, from conscious combination to unconscious hotchpotch put together accidentally; the so-called "zero-degree writing" is made a fashion, rendering art have no more transcendence, become the pronoun of adaptability and degradation, and thereby fuse into mass culture.

Postmodernism at first is a heterogeneous voice of rebellion. It devotes itself to the establishment of new intellectual state, and tries to transcend the rigidity, blind faith and mediocrity of real life from the standpoint of marginal discourse, but as a result of its dissolution of the differences between life and art, truth and fallacy, origin and duplication, and nobility and vulgarity, it descends to the mediocre circumstances where "whatever is okay" and "nothing matters". Though the ideologists of postmodernism still adhere to a historical critical stance, the text and operation of postmodernism can only be ambiguous and incapable. In my eyes, postmodernism attempts to seek a new ray of light in the dark night, but eventually combines daylight with night.

In conclusion, there are various voices in postmodern discourse, and postmodernism tries to rewrite modernity. They are helpful for Chinese society in the historical process of modernization to keep a clear mind on the idea of modernity and for us to reexamine the relationships between man and world, man and man, theory and practice, language and world, history and fiction, and literature and philosophy from a new perspective, thereby continually breaking the metaphysical way of thinking and enabling men to "face things themselves" and obtain a real, mellow happiness.

The problem is that postmodernism as an intellectual state and marginal discourse is unavoidably dependent on the presetting of the postmodern meaning world, but the picture of postmodern world is rootless and shows radical relativism and nihilism in specific operation. So postmodernism is laudable as an intellectual state, but it may drag the real world into absurd and disorder as a universal life attitude.

Fundamentally, the significance of postmodernism is that it puts forward the question of how to conceive and grasp the "modernity" in contemporary capitalist society and focuses on revealing the spiritual predicament of contemporary western society. However, it does not, and also is impossible to, point a fundamental way out of the predicament. As far as I am concerned, postmodernism perceives the "disease" of contemporary western society but makes a wrong "prescription".

Thus, I spontaneously think of Marx. He had refuted and criticized modernity when it was at its horizon line. Marxist philosophy is certainly not postmodernism, but it indubitably has the postmodern connotation. The relation between Marxist philosophy and postmodernism is a major theoretical issue worthy of investigation, which will gain "overwhelming popularity" soon and become an important topic of philosophers. This issue deserves elaboration in a more detailed way, but on account of the length of the chapter, I have to leave this important mission to my subsequent works.

CHAPTER X

POST-COLONIALISM: ESSENCE, FEATURES AND LIMITATIONS — FROM MARX'S POINT OF VIEW

Post-colonialism is an extremely influential social trend of thought arising in the West in the late twentieth century and rapidly impacting the Orient. Its representatives are Edward W. Said, Gayatri C. Spivak and Homi F. Bhabha. From the theoretical angle, post-colonialism takes over the mantle of postmodernism to make a reflection on modernity, but it changes the perspective of reflection to interpreting the colonialism in modernity and deconstructing Orientalism and cultural hegemonism from the angle of culture, thereby translating the issue of modernity reflection into an issue about the global relationship between the Orient and the West. In terms of constitution, post-colonialism brings forward a new theoretical question domain, that is, the colonial relationship between the Orient and the West in the process of modernization, shows a strong tendency to anti-west-centralism, and reflects the coincidence with Marxism to a certain degree. This chapter, from Marxist philosophy's point of view, discusses the essence, features and limitations of post-colonialism with an expectation to deepen our study on post-colonialism and its relationship with Marxism.

1 RISE AND ESSENCE OF POST-COLONIALISM

Basically, the emergence of any kind of social trend of thought is related to its times. The positive "individuality" of French enlightenment philosophy and the negative emotion of existentialism are incomprehensible once they leave their own times, so is the case with postmodernism and post-colonialism. As Jameson said, "It is safest to grasp the concept of the postmodern as an attempt to think the present historically in an age that has forgotten how to think historically in the first place."[1]

Put against its times background, the rise of post-colonialism has three roots: the first is the vigorously developed national liberation movement after "the Second World War"; the second is the identification with national cultural identity; and the third is the overall reflection on modernity. Echoing postmodernism, post-colonialism is a multi-cultural political theory and a collective discourse of critical methods. It is not only the cultural strategy for the "conversation" between the Orient and the West, but also, as a strategy of "marginal" scholars for dismantling western mainstream discourse, provides oriental culture with a prospect to cognize itself again. In this connection, post-colonialism has both theoretical and practical significances.

The rise of post-colonialism is first closely associated with the vigorously developed national liberation movement after "the Second World War". Following "the Second World War", a large batch of colonial and semi-colonial countries in Africa, Asia and Latin America win the political independence in succession. After becoming independent, they need to devotedly develop national economy and also reconstruct national culture, in a bid to reverse the history reversed by colonialism, reestablish the culture distorted by colonialism, and create new cultural forms on these grounds.

As a result, these newly-independent former colonial countries must on the one hand oppose to western cultural hegemonism and unremittingly struggle for decolonization in the field of culture, and on the other hand use the excellent elements in western culture for reference and achieve interpenetration, interfusion and coexistence between oriental and western cultures during the fight against western culture. Meanwhile, these countries also have to correctly deal with the relationship between

---

1   Fredric Jameson, *Postmodernism, or The Cultural Logic of Late Capitalism*, p. ix.

nationalism and decolonization, that is, not only realizing the significant role of nationalism in the process of decolonization, but also preventing and watching out for the tendency towards narrow nationalism, especially cultural fundamentalism. These certainly promote the formation of the topic of post-colonialism. Post-colonialism's thinking about nationalism, elaboration on cultural resistance during decolonization, and analysis on the strategy against western cultural hegemonism are actually the responses to the abovementioned problems in national liberation movement.

The issue arising from the vigorous development of national liberation movement and the political independence of former colonial and semi-colonial countries is the identification with national cultural identity. The process of the identification with national cultural identity is generally made up by three complementary links, namely expression by self-action and self-words, conscious self-identification, and acknowledgement from others. In the wake of independence of the former colonial and semi-colonial countries, the contradiction between homogeneity and heterogeneity inside a national state and among national states is made prominent, bringing the issue about the identification with national cultural identity to the front.

Therefore, how to reconstruct the cultural identity of oriental nations and how to deal with the relationships of the identification with cultural identity of oriental nations to western colonial rule and to the traditional cultures of oriental nations naturally become the subjects of times that urgently need to be addressed. The reason why post-colonialism can arouse wide public concern lies in its forward-looking involvement of these subjects. It is in this sense that Dirlik points out that "it is more precise to view post-colonialism as the result of the liberation movement of colonies rather than aimlessly connect it with postmodernism in the 1980s"[2].

The rise of post-colonialism is also bound up with the overall reflection on modernity in the western thought circle. It is without a doubt that the most profound and comprehensive reflection on modernity consists in postmodernism, which shows the context of post-modernity by "deconstructing" modernity and whose essence is "the rewriting of modernity"[3].

2 *Interview Record of Cultural Studies*, edited by Xie Shaobo and Wang Fengzhen. Beijing: China Social Sciences Press, 2003: p. 25.
3 See *Collected Works of Yang Geng*. Shanghai: Xuelin Publishing House, 1998: p. 38.

The problem is that the rapid improvement of western modernization is closely related to the foreign colonial aggression and territorial expansion of western powers. We can say without colonial conquest, there will be no western modernity. "The problems of European modernity are always developed in the global colonial sphere"[4].

Seen from history, modernity is a phenomenon simultaneous with the colonial expansion around the world. It is in this process that other regions in the world are imposed by the West, by means of an unequal power, "with a language, a language of modernity, which everyone has to use, no matter whether it can properly describe his reality"[5]. Post-colonialism is exactly the response to the coloniality in the process of modernization. Taking a critical attitude to the coloniality during modernization and the construction of non-west by the West, Bhabha strives to reinterpret modernity with post-colonial experience and question the mode of modernity by rereading the suppressed history of those marginalized in history, and his theory is called "a post-colonial archaeology of modernity". It can be seen that post-colonialism employs the theoretical fruits obtained by postmodernism from modernity reflection; meanwhile, it changes the reflection perspective and the theoretical topic, i.e. translating the issue of modernity reflection originating from the West into an issue about the global relationship between the Orient and the West, and pays close attention to the coloniality in the course of modernization.

The reflection on modernity will necessarily bring about the reflection on globalization. The times of the rise of post-colonialism is the times when globalization tends to be overwhelming and arouses more and more concerns, and concerns about globalization are inseparably linked with modernity reflection. As Giddens has said, globalization is the extension of modernization around the globe. In history, globalization movement was initiated and led by the western bourgeoisie, and its "game rules" were formulated basically as per the western bourgeois interests. In that process, the western bourgeoisie tried to create "a world after its own image", and "made barbarian and semi-barbarian countries dependent on the civilized ones, nations of peasants on nations of bourgeois, the East on the West"[6].

4   Paul A. Bové, *Edward Said and the Work of the Critic: Speaking Truth to Power*. Beijing: China Social Sciences Press, 2003: p. 368.
5   *Interview Record of Cultural Studies*, edited by Xie Shaobo and Wang Fengzhen, p. 248
6   *Selected Works of Karl Marx and Friedrich Engels*. 2nd Ed., Vol. 1, pp. 276 and 277.

In this sense, the process of globalization is the process of oriental colonization by the West. "The process of globalization creates its own imperialism; if globalization is going to become an inescapable phenomenon, it has to make use of colonialism"[7] for self-actualization. The most noteworthy feature of colonialism lies in its connection with the expanding capitalist order; this order nourishes colonialism and renders it a global phenomenon.

Globalization is not only accompanied by political and economic colonization but also cultural colonization. Economic friction, political conflict and other contradictions contained in the process of globalization are in close association with the differences between different national cultural values. In this sense, globalization is a process of social practice and a movement of cultural expansion, involving dual power will of economy and culture. Hence, Dirlik points out, "Globalization narrative is thoroughly hegemonic compared with modernization discourse in that it internalizes the cultures of others, reconstructs other cultures, and makes them return to the original source in the reconstructed form. Globalization may be the grandest in all the grandest narratives."[8]

Such a globalization characterized by coloniality is noticed by post-colonialism. Said remarks globalization in Orientalism and *Culture and Imperialism*; he thinks that in the system of globalization, a minority of economic powers expands its power to the globe, raises the price of commodities and services, and redistributes the wealth from the low-income regions (usually the non-western world) to the high-income ones; accordingly, a new transnational order is generated, no borders exist between states any more, and labor force and income are only under the dominance of globalizing operators; in consequence, the south submits to the north, and colonialism rises again from the ashes.[9]

In fact, post-colonialism makes a reflection on globalization just from the perspective of colonization, and probes into the cultural issues between the Orient and the West – orient "westernization" and cultural hegemony of the West – in view of globalization. In the West, post-colonialism was once comparable with postmodernism, post-Marxism and new historicism. The reason why post-colonialism can stand out from

---

7   Arif Dirlik, *Post-revolutionary Atmosphere*. Beijing: China Social Sciences Press, 1999: p. 9.
8   *Interview Record of Cultural Studies*, edited by Xie Shaobo and Wang Fengzhen, p. 28
9   See Edward W. Said, *Orientalism*. Beijing, Joint Publishing Company, 1999: p. 449.

the numerous "post-" and "new" doctrines and cause a strong interest of men is because it profoundly rethinks modernity and globalization from colonial angle of view, answers in depth the problems like cultural conflict, national cultural construction, etc. of colonial and semi-colonial countries after being independent, and more consciously realizes coloniality in two major tides, namely modernity and globalization, in today's world and the cultural relationship between the Orient and the West. In this sense, the rise of post-colonialism is the inevitable result of historical development in the second half of the twentieth century.

Any theory has its specific theoretical premise, so does post-colonialism. The generation of post-colonialism does not only has its specific times background but also specific theoretical background. The theoretical topics it is concerned include issues like the identification with national cultural identity, reconstruction of national culture, and the relationship between the Orient and the West during colonization and decolonization. While resolving these issues, post-colonialism absorbs African anti-colonialism discourse and Derrida's deconstructivism.

In *On National Culture*, Fanon, a theorist of African anti-colonialism discourse, emphasizes that national culture is an important aspect of anti-colonialism, and brings forward three phases of the cultural development of a nation, i.e. absorbing western culture with analysis, awakening to explore its own traditional culture to some extent, and thoroughly awakening and joining in the national liberation movement. Fanon interprets colonialism from angles of language, psychology and culture; his stress on the effect of national culture during the struggle for national liberation and his analysis on the relationship between western culture and African culture serve as a significant analytical tool for the decolonization of culture, and as the theoretical resource for post-colonialism to disintegrate the authoritative discourse of imperialism.

Post-colonist theorists do not only carry forward Fanon's analytical model of interpreting colonialism from cultural angle and attaching importance to the effect of national culture, but also highly appreciate the thoughts of Fanon. In article *Remembering Fanon: Self, Psyche and the Colonial Condition*, Bhabha makes appeals that "the demand for Fanon is extremely urgent" and we "should turn to Fanon" and "return back to Fanon". From Bhabha's point of view, Fanon, compared with other theorists, reveals the issues of race, history of racialism, colonialism, and cultural identity in a more profound way.

Besides, Derrida's thoughts of anti-foundationalism, anti-essentialism and anti-centralism also provide important theoretical support for post-colonialism to deconstruct Orientalism and its essentialism and west-centralism. The emphasis of Said and Bhabha on the "hybrid" strategy of culture and the exposition of Bhabha on "simulation" and "the third space" all presuppose Derrida's thoughts of "differance", "dissemination", and so forth. Said says frankly, "The works of Derrida is also urgent for my viewpoints." Bhabha points out, "I'm interested in the works of Derrida, because he argues that in the expressions of meanings by the social world, there is no transparency and necessary synchronicity; therefore meaning cannot be constructed unless through mediation, through his so-called 'differance', 'time lag', and 'displacement'. This point, of course, strikes a particular chord with the cultures of colonies. For this reason, I find this way to think about the 'differance" or 'delay' in the text of colony is very interesting."[10]

Spivak is not only the main translator of Derrida's works, but also one of the scholars who grasp most correctly and interpret most thoroughly the thoughts of Derrida. Spivak begins her long career of post-colonialism study taking deconstructivism as main theoretical foundation, so to speak, by starting with the translation of Derrida's works. In Can the Subaltern Speak?, she states, "However, in the context of the problematic I have addressed, I find his morphology much more painstaking and useful than Foucault's and Deleuze's immediate, substantive involvement with more 'political' issues … Derrida marks radical critique with the danger of appropriating the other by assimilation. He reads catachresis at the origin. He calls for a rewriting of the utopian structural impulse as 'rendering delirious that interior voice that is the voice of the other in us.' I must here acknowledge a long-term usefulness in Jacques Derrida."[11]

Derrida sets forth an important feature of deconstruction, that is, the strategy for reading and interpreting text is to resort to difference. Spivak shows special preference to the "difference" thought of Derrida, and thinks the "transcendental signified" – sign, note and character – is a structure of difference; difference exists all the time, and trace cannot be erased. The interest in difference and trace impels Spivak spends lots

---

10   Quoted from Sheng Anfeng, *Expressions of Post-coloniality, Globalization and Literature*, carried in *Southern Cultural Forum*, 2002(6).
11   *Cultural Theory of Post-colonialism*, edited by Luo Gang and Liu Xiangyu. Beijing: China Social Sciences Press, 1999: p. 157.

of energy in her academic career on the studies of the third-world text and "non-mainstream culture".

Another theoretical topic of post-colonialism is the relationship between culture and power, as well as cultural colonization, whose theoretical resource is provided by Foucault's theory of discourse power and Gramsci's thought of cultural hegemony.

Foucault's theory of discourse power is centered on the relationship between discourse, knowledge and power. In his view, knowledge and power are mutually dependent: knowledge relies upon power anywhere and anytime, and meanwhile knowledge is impossible to not give rise to power; without knowledge, power cannot be executed. In *Traveling Theory*, Said admits that the analysis of Foucault on knowledge and power "provides a set of concepts and categories for the discourse of analytical tool"[12] for him. The analytical method and analytical model of Foucault for discourse power are, in effect, used for reference, applied and developed by post-colonialism in revealing the "westernized" orient in the discourse of *Orientalism*, emphasizing the political and ideological natures of culture, studying culture's power effect in imperialistic causes, and analyzing the "collusive" relationship between culture and power.

In addition, post-colonialism is deeply influenced by Gramsci's thought of cultural hegemony, and gives an extremely high appraisal to it. From the viewpoint of Gramsci, capitalist countries control civil society not only by compulsory means, but more importantly, through cultural hegemony (cultural leadership, and make it readily willing to abide by the moral idea and value system established by the governor and agree with the aesthetic taste, codes of conduct, and thinking habits of the governor. Said argues, "The form of this cultural leadership is what Gramsci has identified as hegemony, an indispensable concept for any understanding of cultural life in the industrial West. It is hegemony, or rather the result of cultural hegemony at work, that gives Orientalism the durability and the strength I have been speaking about so far."[13] If we say the focus of Gramsci is on cultural leadership inside a national country, and he discusses the importance of ideology and cultural leadership majorly revolving around the struggles between the governing

---

12   *Selected Works of Edward W. Said*, p. 155.
13   Edward W. Said, *Orientalism*, pp. 9 – 10.

class and the governed class, between the bourgeoisie and the proletariat, post-colonialism extends his thought to the investigation of the cultural hegemonic relationship between the Orient and the West around
the world, in the belief that cultural hegemony runs through the whole
process of the oriental colonization by the West.

The primary reasons for the rapid rise of post-colonialism in the West
are not only because it answers the questions that other theories at that
time cannot answer, but more importantly, it has a unique perspective
for interpreting colonialism. Post-colonialism, in essence, interprets
colonization from cultural perspective, with stress laid on revealing the
conflict between colonial discourse and colonized discourse in contemporary times and the growth and decline of powers of the two, as well
as the colonial cultural relationship between the West and the Orient.

There can be many angles and methods for interpreting colonialism:
political scholars interpret colonial aggression from the angle of international political relations, economists uncover the colonial exploitation of developed countries on the underdeveloped ones from the angle
of economy, Marxism reveals the colonial invasion of western countries
into oriental countries including China and India, and post-colonialism
interprets colonialism with the analytical method of culturalism from
the angle of culture.

Said clearly shows, "I hope (maybe impractically) to reveal history and
prevent history repeating itself by describing ups and downs in the history of empires on the aspect of culture[14]. He believes almost all colonial programs begin with an assumption: the locals are backward and are
generally not in independent and equal conditions. The questions are:
"why the conditions are like that? Why the holy mission belongs to one
side but not to the other; and why rights are accepted by one side but
repudiated by the other"? Said answers these questions like this: "We'd
better understand these questions from the angle of culture, which
has an extraordinarily good moral, economic and even metaphysical
norms as its foundation; such norms only endorses satisfactory partial
or European order, but does not approve of foreign countries' enjoying
the similar one"[15].

---

14   *Selected Works of Edward W. Said*, p. 177.
15   *Selected Works of Edward W. Said*, p. 245.

The cultural analysis paradigm of post-colonialism undeniably originates from the "cultural studies" rising in contemporary western social
science. Seen from time, cultural studies were initiated in Britain in the
late 1950s and then expanded to the United States and other western
countries, gradually forming a fairly influential western academic trend
of thought. Compared with traditional social scientific study, cultural
studies value the study of contemporary culture with opposition to exclusive study on classical history, attach importance to mass culture
and marginal culture or subculture repelled by mainstream culture in
opposition to exclusive study on elite culture, pay attention to keeping
a close connection with society and focuses on the power relation and
its operating mechanism implied in culture with objection to enclosing
academic research into a tower of ivory, and insist on viewing culture
as social life and taking economy and politics merely as the constituent
elements in opposition to economic determinism.

Raymond Willams defines culture as a whole lifestyle. According to
this definition, the purpose of cultural studies is not merely to elucidate the apparent connotations of some texts, but to explicate the value
and significance of a particular lifestyle; the analysis of text should be
combined with that of social system and structure, and cultural studies
just aim to study the relations of various factors in the whole lifestyle,
to "find out the essence of the organization as the complex of these
relations"[16].

By taking example by the achievements of "cultural studies", post-colonialism rereads all kinds of texts, which are the carriers of culture, and
discover behind these texts are the deep-rooted west-centralism idea,
the "fiction" and "distortion" of oriental cultural identity by the West,
and the cultural colonization and cultural hegemony strategy of the
West in the Orient; it also reveals that the colonization of the West in the
Orient is not only political and economic but also cultural, and cultural
colonization has a greater effect, better result, and deeper influence than
the former two. From the view of post-colonialism, cultural colonization and cultural hegemony, which are deep down to the "marrow" of
man, seize man's soul, and assimilate the world outlook, values, way of
thinking, and lifestyle of man, thus achieving an effect that cannot be
achieved by political or economic colonization.

---

16   *The Reader of Cultural Studies*, edited by Luo Gang and Liu Xiangyu. Beijing:
China Social Sciences Press, 2000: p. 126.

With culture as an entry point, post-colonialism demonstrates the political and ideological natures of culture, the distortion and reconstruction of oriental national cultural identity, the "collusive" relationship between culture and power, and the internal consistency between culture and imperialism, explores the evolution and adjustment of cultural hegemonism and its changes during different periods of colonialism, investigates various means and strategies used by cultural hegemonism for controlling and governing the Orient, and advocates overthrowing the western cultural hegemonism by applying various anti-hegemonic cultural strategies by way of cultural resistance. Upon the enlightenment from "cultural studies", post-colonialism walks out the closed tower of ivory of pure academic research and then towards "cultural and social" studies, and enters the study domain of "cultural imperialism"; thus post-colonialism, instead of being a frigid logical inference, becomes a vivid and substantial doctrine internally related to real social life.

2 MAIN CONTENTS AND FEATURES OF POST-COLONIALISM

Reinterpreting and deconstructing Orientalism, the theoretical discourse of the West about the Orient, is a main content of post-colonialism.

In *Orientalism* and his other works, Said makes a new interpretation on Orientalism, and deeply criticizes it as a way of thinking and a mode of power discourse by dint of Foucault's theory of discourse power. In Said's opinion, Orientalism, as a discipline, a way of thinking, and a mode of power discourse, is a kind of mechanism and mode used by the West to control, reconstruct and govern the Orient. Whatever it is – a discipline, a way of thinking, or a mode of power discourse, Orientalism is about writing, studying, constructing, controlling and governing the Orient by the West, and essentially reflects a particular unequal relationship between the Orient and the West.

According to Said, the Orient in Orientalism is an ideological assumption and illusion. The Orient and the West in it aren't demarcated geographically, but their existences are determined by the ceaselessly changing historical and cultural relationship between Europe and the Orient. "As both geographical and cultural entities – to say nothing of historical entities – such locales, regions geographical sectors as 'Orient' and 'Occident' are man-made."[17]

---

17 Edward W. Said, *Orientalism*, p. 6.

That is to say, Orientalism does not points out the truth of the Orient, but mechanically and graphically processes the Orient. This graphical Orient is elaborately constructed – the Orient in Orientalism is, almost without exception, the academic orient and the field of imagination, and even though adopted as the topic of lyric poetry, illusory works or even a novel, it is not a real existence of the real Orient, but is "fabricated". For Orientalism, the Orient is, rather than a graphical space directly contacted by men, a thing read, studied and written by men in the sphere specified by academic groups, universities and seminars. In a word, the Orient in Orientalism is the Orient constructed, imagined, expressed, demonized, and categorized by the West.

To avoid being misunderstood, Said gives three explanations for this opinion: first of all, this opinion does not deny the truth of the real Orient, and no one should make a wrong conclusion that the Orient is essentially an ideal existence based on this opinion; next, the so-called Orient is a man-made construction, which underlines the power, dominant and hegemonic relationships of the West to the Orient, and because of these relationships the Orient is "fabricated", or "domesticated", into the so-called "Orient"; finally, the Orient in Orientalism is not a lie or mythological structure, not the West's pure fiction or fancy of the Orient, but is a set of created theory and practical system in close relation with western politics, economy and their organs.

Revealing and criticizing cultural hegemony, this new form of oriental colonization by the West, is anther main content of post-colonialism. This work is mainly done through analyzing such aspects as the political and ideological natures of culture, the combination of culture with power, and the involvement of culture in imperialistic causes. From the standpoint of Said, there is no pure cultural form, and "culture is the root of national identity, the root leading to blood-shed battles"[18]. Culture is absolutely not a neutral thing, so when we talk about culture, we should first ask to whom, to which country or nation this culture belongs, who is the subject of this culture, whom this culture serves, and so on.

To put it another way, culture is bound to be "contaminated" by the political system, ideology, values, etc. of its subject. In the words of Said, culture is a battlefield where various forces contrast sharply with each other; culture is a stage where a variety of politics and ideologies come into contact with each other, giving culture the political and ideological

18   Edward W. Said, *Orientalism*, p. 164.

natures. It is the combination and interaction of culture with its political and ideological natures and other factors like economy and military affairs that shape the Orient into a "westernized" image.

The political and ideological natures indicate the close correlation of culture with imperialism and power. In a series works of *Orientalism, The World, the Text, and the Critic, and Culture and Imperialism*, Said discusses in detail how imperialism depends on culture, how culture serves the colonial expansion of empires, and the issue about the "collusion" between culture and power, and argues that the West is in essence constituted by various causes of imperialism and it is impossible to imagine how the West will be without these imperialistic causes.

The "imperialism" in the sight of Said refers to "a unique coherence and a special cultural unification", "the practice, theory and attitude to an urban center governing the remote territory". In Said's eyes, imperialism is inseparable from culture, which is its foundation; culture is also inseparable from imperialism in that only by resting upon imperialism can it have a long existence; what's more, with its theme being imperialism, culture has a deep imperialistic complex. In short, culture is interwoven with imperialism.

The connection of culture with imperialism and the thought of culture's involvement in imperialistic causes of post-colonialism extremely challenge the traditional views of culture and imperialism. They virtually put forward a new paradigm and its cognitive standard, viz., the West is in essence constituted by various causes of imperialism and culture makes great contributions in the forming process of imperialistic causes. Said strives to prove that western culture essentially enters into an inextricable relationship – a collusive relationship – with imperialistic causes, and "such a new world outlook goes forward hand in hand with the colonization and governance of Europe over the world"[19].

The fundamental reason why culture can be involved in imperialistic causes consists in its attributes, namely its political and ideological natures. Culture has a "collusive" relationship with power, and power is embodied by culture itself. The combination of culture and power actualizes the service of culture for empires. The considerations of Said in *Orientalism* and *Culture and Imperialism* are in fact based on the

---

19   Luo Gang and Liu Xiangyu, *Cultural Theory of Post-colonialism*, p. 77.

relationships between discourse, truth and power: truth is the explanation of authenticity in definite discourse rules, and power determines and proves truth; truth never exists beyond power, and power makes truth through discourse structure and will no longer exist once leaving discourse and the support from truth made through discourse. As Foucault said, only through the establishment of truth can men execute power through discourse.

Said further points out to carefully study culture, idea and history, we must study their force relations and power structures at the same time, and cannot just regard the Orient as a man-made thing; because there are power, dominant and hegemonic relationships of the West to the Orient, Orientalism, which presents, constructs, imagines, and "westernizes" the Orient, is necessarily infiltrated with the consciousness of power. As far as Said is concerned, discourse generally reflects the unequal relationship between the colonizer and the colonized, between the oppressor and the oppressed; words and texts are permeated with the consciousness of imperialism and the desire for power; along with the expansion of the areas ruled by the West, discourse power is growing accordingly; colonial discourse and colonial power is accompanied by each other.

No matter whether it is interpreting and deconstructing Orientalism or revealing and criticizing the cultural hegemony of the West for the Orient, post-colonialism always focuses on colonization, which at bottom is the relationship between the Orient and the West. For this reason, the reflection of post-colonialism on colonization is another realization on the relationship between the Orient and the West. The feature of this realization is stressing on the interpretation of the relationship between the Orient and the West from cultural perspective. It should be considered as the first feature of post-colonialism. The relationship between the Orient and the West is not a new topic. It is considered by the western academic circle from the angles of politics and economy, with emphasis laid on the political and economic relationships between the Orient and the West. But post-colonialism thinks the relationship between the Orient and the West is not only political and economic, but more importantly, is cultural. Any apparently transcendental and pure culture is dependent on the hegemonic governance of the West on the Orient and involved in imperialistic causes in a certain form. The characteristic of post-colonialism's study on the relationship between the Orient and the West is that it probes into the complex and subtle relations between economy, politics and culture therein, especially the cultural relationship and its unique effect, thereby presenting a three-dimensional picture of the relationship between the Orient and the West.

Post-colonialism strives to reinterpret the relationship between the Orient and the West by deconstructing Orientalism, resist western cultural hegemonism with the strategy of cultural "hybridity", and achieves integration and coexistence of oriental and western cultures through the conversation between the Orient and the West. Both Said and Bhabha praise greatly the "hybridity" of oriental and western cultures, and make the strategy of "hybridity" vitally important in the resistance to western cultural hegemonism. Although doing their utmost to dissolve west-centralism and cultural hegemonism, they do not aim to destroy a western "center" and then build up an oriental "center" and smash western "cultural hegemony" and then establish oriental "cultural hegemony". The theoretical purport of post-colonialism is to totally overthrow the dominant things like "center" and "hegemony" and realize integration and equal coexistence of oriental and western cultures.

The second feature of post-colonialism lies in its strong anti-essentialism tendency while interpreting the relationship between the Orient and the West.

Anti-essentialism thinks that all things on earth do not have any certain inherent essence and their "attributes" cannot be anything but the man-made nomination, the displacement of signifier symbols. Post-colonialism has a strong anti-essentialism tendency while interpreting the relationship between the Orient and the West and resisting western cultural hegemonism. Said highlights in *Orientalism* that he himself is "a definite anti-essentialist". Showing doubts on the so-called "essential feature of India", Spivak does not acknowledge there is "Indian feature", and thinks such an essential feature is artificially constituted. Bhabha raises doubts on the essentialist idea of the binary opposition between the First World and the Third World, and brings forward a new idea about the cultural difference between the First World and the Third World, emphasizing that the cultures of the First World and the Third World, instead of being simply hostile to each other, both respect and preserve the unique and multiple histories and characters of those cultures that are marginalized in history.

Of course, anti-essentialism is not exclusive to post-colonialism, and postmodernism also stresses it. But different from postmodernism, post-colonialism combines anti-essentialism with the reinterpretation of the relationship between the Orient and the West and the resistance to western cultural hegemonism, with the aim at overturning western cultural hegemony through anti-essentialism. Said expounds in detail the process of oriental essentialization by Orientalism: Orientalism first constructs the orient through categorization, demonization and generalization, and then makes this constructed orient eternal, universal and non-historical; thus, an essential orient is fabricated.

From Said's point of view, Orientalism deals with the diverse, dynamic and complex human reality from the standpoint of essentialism, which has no critical consciousness at all. This implies that there is a never changing oriental essence and a western essence opposite to it but also unvarying. Constituting the common basis of all things being investigated, this essence is both "historical" in that it can traced to the early stage in history and "non-historical" because it fixes the things being investigated into a particularity without evolution and development, rather than defines them as the particularity of historical evolution and development, or as nation, state and culture, which are the product and result of historical evolution.

The third feature of post-colonialism is its special attention on "margin", "the other", "subaltern" and "minority" during the interpretation of the relationship between the Orient and the West.

The attention of post-colonialism on "the weak" doubtlessly echoes with contemporary western academic trends of thought, such as the academic changes of postmodernism and new historicism from "great theory" to "little theory", from "meta-narrative" to "little narrative", from "capitalized philosophy" to "lowercase philosophy", from "capitalized man" to "lowercase man", from "large world" to "small world", and from "macro-history" to "micro-history". Said points out that "Orientalism is more regarded as a presentation of the miserable circumstances of the weak"[20]. In The Commitment to Theory, Bhabha states that "the other" is forever a side line that notes difference and never an active expresser; it loses the desire to express, negate and generate its own history and the power to set up its own institutional opposite discourse. According

---

20   Edward W. Said, *Orientalism*, p. 431.

to Bhabha, the "minority", never being a complete citizen, lives in a crevice and only enjoys partial identity of a citizen. What Spivak is mostly concerned with is whether the "subaltern" can speak for itself. In her view, under the context of colonialism, "subaltern" is virtually a lonely "space", or a fundamentally "uncontactable blank"; "subaltern" cannot speak and has no right to speak, so it has to be represented and expressed by the colonizer.

The attention of post-colonialism on "the weak" like "margin", "the other", "subaltern" and "minority" is not only for the purpose of describing the miserable circumstances of the weak or showing sympathy and pity for "the weak", but also revealing the suppression on and deprival of the discourse of "the weak" by cultural hegemonism. Facing up to the western power discourse and in a stance as a challenger to the central discourse, post-colonialism enters into the interwoven contradictions of ideological discourse in culture, interprets discursive tyranny and cultural hegemony covered by "center" and "majority" from special perspectives of "margin" and "minority", shows the destiny of "the weak" between self-expression and expression by power discourse and between self-characterization and repression by power discourse, reviews the relationship between the Orient and the West under the context of hegemony, and rethinks the misplacement and serious characterization crisis of western hegemonistic culture, in order to dissolve the cultural hegemonism of the West.

These viewpoints of post-colonialism are the deepening and development of Marxist thoughts about hegemonism, colonialism and imperialism.

The times of Marxism was dominated by political and economic colonization. Confined by the historical conditions at that time, Marxism interprets colonization mainly from political and economic angles, analyzes the causes of "political and economic hegemonies", interprets the social consequence of colonies caused by western capitalist "political and economic hegemonies", and discusses the "anti-hegemonic" struggle of people in colonies.

The times of post-colonialism is the times when the effect of culture is increasingly highlighted, and culture has important influence and effect in fields of international intercourse, international relations, institutional change, etc. The charm of post-colonialism is that it grasps this feature

of its times, takes over the mantle of Marxist thoughts about hegemonism, colonialism and imperialism, "rewrites" the history of colonization from cultural perspective, and sharply analyzes and relentlessly
criticizes the cultural relationship between the Orient and the West and
the western cultural hegemonism. In this way, it expands the scope and
horizon of Marxist thought of hegemonism, and makes up the shortage
of Marxist thoughts about hegemonism, colonialism and imperialism
to a certain extent. For example, while expounding the social status of
small-holding peasants in *The 18ᵗʰ Brumaire of Louis Bonaparte*, Marx
states, "They cannot represent themselves; they must be represented."
This opinion is quoted by Said at the beginning of his *Orientalism*.
This actually is the extension of Marxist thoughts about the class relations inside a national state and the political hegemony into the global
relationship between the Orient and the West and the sphere of cultural
hegemony. In this sense, the deconstruction of Orientalism by post-colonialism and its critique on cultural hegemonism are the contemporary
response to Marxist "political and economic hegemonies", and activate
some elements in Marxism.

Just because of this, post-colonialism is helpful for us to further conceive the present relationship between the Orient and the West. Since
"the Second World War", especially after "the Cold War", the colonial nature of western capitalism does not take a fundamental change,
and what has been changed is merely the form and pattern of colonization. No matter whether it is the "cultural exchange", "cultural assistance", the output of cultural products, or the extension of cultural
communication media of western developed countries, it is infiltrated
with the "factors" of cultural colonialism and hegemonism without exception. By virtue of their powerful political, economic, technological
and military strengths, western developed countries employ advanced
media forms to make cultural colonial invasion, which has a stronger
infiltrating force and better effect, and strive to impose their political
and economic systems, lifestyle and values onto underdeveloped or undeveloped countries, with an expectation to dominate the world. The
cultural globalization launched and led by western developed countries
is accompanied by the confliction and contest between different ideologies and mingled with cultural colonialism and hegemonism. In a
certain sense, the process of cultural globalization is the process of actualization of cultural colonialism and hegemonism. The interpretation
of post-colonialism on colonization from cultural perspective does not

only broaden our vision in the study of the relationship between the Orient and the West, but also gives us beneficial enlightenment for understanding another dimension – cultural globalization – of globalization and grasping the contemporary form of colonization.

3 THEORETICAL LIMITATIONS OF POST-COLONIALISM

The theoretical contributions of post-colonialism should not be obliterated, but its theoretical limitations should not be neglected either. In general, post-colonialism lays particular emphasis on interpreting colonization from cultural perspective and expounding the relationship between the Orient and the West with the analytic paradigm of "culturalism" so as to dissolve cultural hegemonism. There is nothing wrong with such a practice, but in this process, post-colonialism fails to correctly grasp the relationships of culture with politics and economy and properly handle the relationships of textual discourse critique with political and economic critiques.

Laying stress on textual critique and ignoring political and economic critiques is the first theoretical limitation of post-colonialism.

No matter whether it is Said's interpretation and deconstruction of Orientalism and his critique on cultural hegemonism, the criticism of Spivak and Mohanty on western feminism, or Bhabha's interpretation of "hybridity" and "simulation", they all convert political and economic issues in society into a matter of culture, and think the issues of culture exist everywhere and textual critique has an absolute significance for the dissolution of western cultural hegemonism; therefore, the national liberation movement and its material achievements since "the Second World War" are all changed into textual interpretation, cultural reproduction, mental impulse, etc. This must be considered as a serious mistake of post-colonialism. Post-colonialism critic Clifford points out after evaluating and analyzing the textual critique and discourse analysis of post-colonialism that "the Marxism critics concerned with ideology and culture are interested in expressions of certain political and economic powers", and different from them, "Said, as an academic historian, depicts Orientalism as a series of definite influences and schools of thought"; this discourse analysis "is merely concerned with those comments related to the other presentations in the same sphere"[21]. Abdul R. JanMohamed thinks Bhabha "circumvent[s] entirely the dense history of the material conflict between Europeans and natives ... to focus on colonial discourse as if it existed in a vacuum"[22].

Laying stress on textual critique actually means insisting on the tendency to anti-hegemonic culturalism. The so-called culturalism refers to a thinking method that attributes social problems to the influence of cultural factor and is determined by cultural factor, so it is a cultural determinism. Post-colonialism tries to seek and imagine the possibility of a new social structure from the angle of cultural critique, basically abandons practice on the aspects of politics and economy, and translates and reduces all kinds of problems in the real society into cultural issues.

As a matter of fact, the real society is a complex system made up by political, economic, cultural, etc. factors through interaction and integration. Among these factors, culture is not only restricted and influenced by politics, but also determined by economy in the final analysis. Hence, the critique on Heaven should be turned to the world, the critique on culture to politics, and finally to economy. "The economic relations, however much they may be influenced by the other political and ideological ones, are still ultimately the decisive ones, forming the red thread which runs through them and alone leads to understanding."[23] If this point is overlooked, we cannot really understand the issue of power and power's relationships with knowledge and culture. It is because post-colonialism only sticks to the analytic method of culturalism that Dirlik says "post-colonialism has a conspiring relationship with contemporary power layout"[24].

Furthermore, post-colonialism does not carefully analyze the mechanism for the generation of cultural hegemony, which means that it is unable to explain how the discourse of Orientalism makes itself a kind of knowledge in hegemonic form. The theory of Said aims to deconstruct Orientalism and criticize cultural hegemonism, but he does not reveal the more important issue – the mechanism for the generation of cultural hegemony. At this point, Said makes a mistake of "conclusion first".

---

21 Luo Gang and Liu Xiangyu, *Cultural Theory of Post-colonialism*, p. 37.
22 Bart Moore-Gilbert, *Postcolonial Theory*. Nanjing: Nanjing University Press, 2001: p. 177.
23 *Selected Works of Karl Marx and Friedrich Engels*. 2nd Ed., Vol. 4, p. 732.
24 Arif Dirlik, *Post-revolutionary Atmosphere*, p. 172.

The reason why culture can become "hegemonic" does not consist in the "effort" of culture itself, but in the factors beyond culture, such as politics, economy, science and technology, and so on and their synergistic effect with culture; the reason why cultural hegemony works lies in the powerful support from political and economic hegemonies, without which cultural hegemony has no choice but to become an empty talk and fantasy.

If culture is regarded as a "soft power", it cannot turn into a real one unless established on the groundwork of "hard powers". Culture as a "soft power" is unable to form hegemony without the aid of "hard powers" like politics and economy, and cultural hegemony is implemented, in the final analysis, for obtaining more political and economic benefits; its actual significance is to provide legitimacy for western countries to realize their interests. Pursuing political and economic benefits with the power of culture is the starting point and destination of cultural hegemony. Marx points out "everything for which man struggles is a matter of his interest"[25], and holds that pursuing interest is the motivation of all human activities and interest has a decisive effect on political power. This conclusion of Marx is still realistically pertinent to our understanding on today's cultural hegemony.

Laying stress on discourse resistance and ignoring "revolution" and effective resistance to colonization is the second theoretical limitation of post-colonialism.

Post-colonialism lays stress on cultural resistance and discourse resistance to western hegemony, and believes the western cultural hegemony can be overturned through them: "resorting to theory will pose a destructive threat to materialization and the entire capitalist system relied upon by materialization". It is thus clear that post-colonialism "replaces real experience with concept or theory", downplaying both colonial oppression in material form and effective resistance to colonial power. In the words of Aijaz Ahmed, post-colonialism "is an armchair strategist".

For this reason, Dirlik advocates replacing "post-colony" with "post-revolution", and claims post-colonialism is a "counter-revolutionary" theory. In Dirlik's opinion, post-colonialism replaces history with text, and rejects the revolution substitutes in the history and assimilates them with post-coloniality, or simply turns a blind eye to them usually;

25   *Karl Marx and Friedrich Engels.* 1st Chinese Ed., Vol. 1, p. 82.

what's more, post-colonialism does not view revolution as a meaning-ful historical event at all; it fails to seriously investigate revolutions in the past and make them the possible conditions for itself, but on the contrary attempts to impose its utopian image onto them.

The critique of Dirlik on post-colonialism is not aimless and ground-less, and it indeed hits the lifeline of post-colonialism. With the analytic method of culturalism, post-colonialism takes culture as the decisive force of social change and development, dissolves and overthrows western cultural hegemony by means of culture, and resists the whole western hegemony which is tightly structured and systematized by dint of thought and theory, but it eventually sinks into the condition criti-cized by Marx, that is, "only opposing other phrases" of the world. The weapon of criticism cannot replace criticism by weapons, and material force must be overthrown by material force. "Not criticism but revolu-tion is the driving force of history, also of religion, of philosophy and all other types of theory."[26] Regarding culture as the main cause of the changes in human history and social development as the result of theory is in effect engraving the model of Hegel again, which had been criti-cized by Marx as early as over 150 years ago.

Laying stress on the "hybridity" of culture and covering inequality and power difference is the third theoretical limitation of post-colonialism.

Post-colonialism lays particular emphasis on the "hybridity" of cul-ture, and takes it as an important strategy for resisting essentialism and cultural hegemonism. The "hybridity" of culture appreciated by Said and Bhabha seems to somewhat have a meaning that "the whole world joins in jubilation", or that "all the people of the world are brothers"; however, this is just their wishful thinking. At present, the strengths of the Orient and the West are still unbalanced on the aspects of politics, economy, science and technology, culture, military affairs, etc., so is the relationship between the two. Ahmed argues that the praise of post-colonialism for cultural "hybridity" does not underline the unequal re-lationship between current cultural powers, and the problems are that "whose culture will it be hybridized into? Whose conditions will be abided by?" These two questions of Ahmed indeed hit the point. In other words, who is "hybridized", who is the subject of "hybridity", who has right to "hybridize", and whose conditions will be abided by

---

26   *Selected Works of Karl Marx and Friedrich Engels.* 2nd Ed., Vol. 1, p. 92.

must be made clear in the first place in the discussion of cultural "hybridity". Under today's pattern of unequal relationship, if "hybridity" is talked about glibly without these important questions clarified, it will, in a certain sense, become the reasonable subterfuge of the West as the strong side to promote its colonial aggression in the name of it.

In fact, the so-called cultural "hybridity" is an important strategy of western developed countries to carry out hegemonism, the permeation of imperialistic ideology into non-western society. Therefore cultural "hybridity" alone cannot eliminate the inequality between the Orient and the West, and what's worse, it will universalize and globalize this realistic inequality to a larger extent. The coverage of post-colonialism over inequality means its coverage over the power difference between the Orient and the West. As Dirlik says, the blind adherence to hybridity does not only cover the position of ideology but also the power difference arising from the difference in position.[27] Post-colonialism one-sidedly emphasizes cultural "hybridity", and ignores or conceals the inequality and power difference between the Orient and the West, so it objectively defends western cultural hegemonism and cultural globalization, and finally reaches the same end with western cultural hegemonism.

Ignoring class and not pointing out the subject of anti-colonization is the fourth theoretical limitation of post-colonialism. Busying itself with cultural "hybridity", post-colonialism pays no attention to the class structure inside western countries, and ignores the class relations inside oriental countries; it only focuses on nation, race and gender, neglecting or overlooking the class analysis method. Ahmed thinks a obvious consequence of post-colonialism's refusal to Marxism is that it views the world composed of colonies and suzerains more from the perspective of nation and race but less from class and does not regard imperialism as a system with class structure under the condition of global capitalism, does not reflect the material life condition of culture itself, and does not consider "which classes are in power"; instead, it just anchor its hope on the struggle between nationalism and imperialism[28].

---

27   See Arif Dirlik, *Post-revolutionary Atmosphere*, p. 129.
28   Bart Moore-Gilbert et al., *Postcolonial Criticism*. Beijing: Peking University Press, 2001: p. 353.

Due to this, Ahmed, based on the class theory of Marxism, tries to fuse post-colonialism into class-based analytic model, and stresses that the struggle in present world is neither between the West and the Orient or the North and the South, nor between former suzerain mighty empires and newly independent countries, but is between global allied classes. I should say Ahmed is quite insightful to use Marxist class analysis method to correct post-colonialism's mistakes of refusing class issue with nation and race issues and rejecting class analysis with cultural analysis while analyzing the problems of post-colonization.

Post-colonialism is concerned with "margin", "the other", "subaltern", "minority" and "female", and it seems that it believes its anti-colonization purpose can be achieved by depending on these "subjects". However, these so-called subjects are unable to assume the important historical mission of anti-colonization. Just because it overlooks class and class struggle, post-colonialism cannot grasp the real subject of anti-colonization. Theresa Ebert says frankly that post-colonialism "avoids the issue of class – the sole agent place of history. The first step of it in doing so is to manifest class as an outdated viewpoint, and then places the allied subject into identity politics with a stance conforming to the trend. At last, what we get is a series of subjects: a feministic subject, an African-American, a Latin American and a homosexual subject, ... and these scrappy subjects ... in my eyes are all pretending to be the agent subject"[29]. In the world permeated with capital, the real subject of anti-colonization is neither "minority" nor "female", "nation" or "race", and "the exclusive agent of history is the alternative of capital – the man living on wages"[30].

I notice that post-colonialism is indeed penetrating, to a certain degree, in the "rewriting of modernity" from colonial angle and the reinterpretation of colonization and East-West relationship from cultural perspective. But I also cannot turn a blind eye to its theoretical faults, which do not lie in its interpretation of colonization from cultural perspective, but in its excess reliance on the analytic paradigm of culturalism and the critique of textual discourse, in its improper dealing with the relationships of cultural critique with political and economic critiques. It is not wrong for post-colonialism to focus on "uncovering the secrets of" and "decoding" western cultural hegemony. The problem is that it

---

29 *Interview Record of Cultural Studies*, edited by Xie Shaobo and Wang Fengzhen, p. 54
30 ibid., p. 55.

one-sidedly stresses the significance of language to "ideological de-colonization", and "indulges itself in discourse, caring nothing about those effective social, economic and political systems and other social practical forms"[31]. At this point, post-colonialism goes too far after all, and reaches the end of logic. This makes me involuntarily think of a famous remark of Marx:

"Once upon a time a valiant fellow had the idea that men were drowned in water only because they were possessed with the idea of gravity. If they were to knock this notion out of their heads, say by stating it to be a superstition, a religious concept, they would be sublimely proof against any danger from water."[32]

---

31   Benita Parry, *Problems in Current Theories of Colonial Discourse*. The Oxford Literary, Review, No. 9, 1997: p. 43.
32   *Karl Marx and Friedrich Engels*. 1st Chinese Ed., Vol. 3, p. 16.

CHAPTER XI

POST-MARXISM: HISTORICAL CONTEXT AND MULTIPLE LOGICS — FROM MARX'S POINT OF VIEW

The concept of "post-Marxism" was put forward by Hungarian-born philosopher Polanyi for the first time in *Personal Knowledge: Towards a Post-Critical Philosophy* in 1950. Though appearing only once in *Personal Knowledge*, this concept means that a theoretical project different from traditional Marxism started to sprout. Just due to this, the concept of "post-Marxism" did not vanish as soon as it appeared, but contrarily was spread in the western thought circle in the 1960s and aroused wide concern of people. In 1973, this concept was mentioned again by Bell in *The Coming of Postindustrial Society: A Venture in Social Forecasting*, and Bell thought post-Marxism was to use Marx's "second schema" about capitalist development to analyze the structure of postindustrial society and review the accumulated problems of capitalism. In 1985, Laclau and Mouffe published *Hegemony and Socialist Strategy: Towards a Radical Democratic Politics*, in which post-Marxism is deeply analyzed and systematically demonstrated as a new theoretical project and then forms a significantly influential social trend of thought on this basis. How to profoundly analyze the theoretical logics of post-Marxism and their criticisms on Marxism constitutes an inescapable subject for the construction of contemporary form of Marxist philosophy.

1 HISTORICAL CONTEXT FOR THE GENERATION OF POST-MARXISM

Philosophy is the times concentratedly expressed by thoughts. The generation of any philosophical theory or social trend of thought is inseparable from its times, and has its specific historical context. Unlike literature, which reflects object with figures, plots and stories, philosophy reflects object with concepts, propositions and laws, which appears to be unrelated to times. But in fact, any philosophy is the theoretical answer, directly or indirectly, more or less, to the subject of times. Leaving their own times, either the straightforward and fiery "character" of French enlightenment philosophy or the intricate and obscure feature of classical German philosophy, either the negative and low emotion of existentialism or the enigmatic "individuality" of deconstructivism, is incomprehensible.

The same condition applies to the understanding and grasping post-Marxism. As far as I'm concerned, post-Marxism is a political theory and philosophical trend of thought that overlaps with postmodern trend of thought and deconstructs or reconstructs traditional Marxism and western Marxism. The historical background for its generation is constituted by the transformation of western society during the 1960s – 1970s, i.e. from modern industrial society to "postindustrial society", from modern capitalism to "post-capitalism".

The transformation of western society during the 1960s – 1970s is basically the transformation of the mode of production, which is manifested as the turn from organized production to flexible production.

Prior to the 1970s, organized production based on Fordism was the major structure of western society; it resolved the planlessness of the production during the period of free capitalism on the one hand, and realized the guidance to production by stimulating consumption and brought the consumption activity of individuals into planning, rendering individuals the executor of consumption planning. Such a system of Fordism reached its extreme in the 1970s. The universal inflation exposed the mismatch between excess productive forces and capital market in western society, and resulted in the breakdown of capital market around the world. Meanwhile, the large-scale investment of developed countries into developing ones caused changes in the production form and management mode in western countries; the Organization of Petroleum Exporting Countries raised the price of petroleum, and Arabian countries once prohibited petroleum export to the West, both of which forced western countries to look for the way of energy saving through technical and institutional changes, thus giving rise to the change of spatial layout of capital and forming an economic, political and social regulating system completely different from Fordism. Such a regulating system relies on "the flexibility related to labor process, labor market, product, and consumption model", namely the so-called "flexible production", and makes "flexible accumulation" the capital accumulation mechanism in the era of transnational capitalism.

At the same time, along with the popularization of electronic computer and its application, science becomes a more and more important factor during production, and electronic network becomes the main technical framework of the world market of capital. The advanced computer system is able to save brand-new and powerful mathematical models and execute transactions quickly; in the wake of financialization and virtualization, capital thoroughly breaks away from the physical form, and obtains autonomous right and flexibility to the largest extent, and complex telecom system and the financial system that is instantly connected to the whole globe realize transnational worldwide operation of capital through online management: the production activity based on microelectronic technique facilitates the standardization of components, so that the final product can be customized in the mode of flexible production and organized according to international assembly. "The current social order in the capitalist countries can be conceived as a synthesis of new technologies and capitalism that is characterized by new technical, social, and cultural forms combining with capitalist relations of production to create the social matrix of our limes."[1]

This significant change in the mode of production impels western scholars to rethink the production theory of Marxism.

---

1 Kellner and Best, *Postmodern Theory: Critical Interrogation*. Beijing: Central Compilation & Translation Press, 2006: 2nd Chinese Ed., pp. 337 – 338.

The change in production structure inevitably leads to the change of class formation. As knowledge and technology turn into the major structure of western society and ownership is separated from the right of management, "social relations (property) is supplanted by productive forces (technology) as the main axis of society", which presents a challenge to traditional Marxism. This challenge can be summarized in this way: "the social forces of production have become industrial, but are common to a wide variety of political systems; the social relations of production have become bureaucratic, in which ownership assumes a diminishing role."[2] In consequence, enterprises and the whole society are bureaucratized on the one side, and new strata (especially technical and white-collar strata) are raised to the leading position in society on the other side, thereby changing the formation and properties of class. This is the first point.

Secondly, the formation of global capital brings more and more labor forces of developing countries into the capital market, forming a multi-exploiting relationship; the difference in social material foundation makes the "workers" of developing countries not at the same social level with the "workers" of developed countries, thus "what is the working class" becomes a question hard to answer.

Thirdly, the rise of consumer society makes the subject of society no longer locked at the "general subject" of class, but extended to marginal groups such as students, minority groups, environmental protectionists, peaceniks and even homosexual persons and the unemployed, all of whom oppose to the repression of organized production and even combat the reality through drug abuse. Apparently, consumer society is a society where individuality is sufficiently embodied, but it is actually a society totally controlling the masses and realized by encoded images. On this account, many marginal groups resisting consumer society emerge. The changes in the formation and properties of class, the formation of multi-exploiting relationship, and the emergence of marginal groups, together with the racial problems and the rise of feminism, render the class theory of traditional Marxism questioned.

The change of class formation is also bound to bring about changes in the contents and forms of social struggles. Along with the postwar development of western economy and the generalization of social

---

2　Bell, *The Coming of Postindustrial Society: A Venture in Social Forecasting.* Beijing: The Commercial Press, 1986: p. 92.

control, social struggles are diffused into various fields of social life. "For a modern concept of macro-politics where clashing forces struggle for control over a centralized source of power rooted in the economy and state, Foucault substitutes a postmodern concept of micro-politics where numerous local groups contest diffuse and decentred forms of power spreading throughout society."[3] For instance, as to the movement of ecologism in response to the worsening of environment, its struggle is targeted at the mode of production and the whole planning of social development; student movement combats the individuality repression by consumer society and the marginalization of student's status caused by bureaucracy, and pursues "total man"; for the Negro, the primary issue is apartheid; and as for women, capital governance is a kind of male governance, and the struggle against capital is in effect against male governance, and so on.

The past struggle strategy aiming at class struggle is diffused, so is the subject of class, which is diffused into the struggle groups in different fields. How to join up these struggles has been beyond the theory domain of traditional Marxism. It is pointed out by Laclau and Mouffe that "the rise of the new feminism, the protest movements of ethnic, national and sexual minorities, the anti-institutional ecology struggles waged by marginalized layers of the population, the anti-nuclear movement, the atypical forms of social struggle in countries on the capitalist periphery – all these imply an extension of social conflictuality to a wide range of areas". "The plural and multifarious character of contemporary social struggles has finally dissolved the last foundation for that political imaginary."[4]

The change of historical context inevitably causes the change in thought context. The end of western Marxist logic and the emergence of postmodernism, in general, constitute the thought context for the generation of post-Marxism.

After capitalism entered the system of organized production, western Marxism made a relatively profound critique on it. According to Lukacs, accompanying the popularization of Taylorism, the "materialization" of capitalism infiltrates from social structure into mental structure, thus "materializing" man totally from body to mind; what happens

---

3   Kellner and Best, *Postmodern Theory: Critical Interrogation.* 2nd Chinese Ed., pp. 64 – 65.
4   Laclau and Mouffe, *Hegemony and Socialist Strategy: Towards a Radical Democratic Politics.* Verso: London, 1985: pp. 1 and 2.

in a synchronized step with this materialization and also takes it as the basis is the materialization of capitalist ideology, which is shown as the "antinomy" in the field of thought, i.e. the opposition between subject and object; the bourgeois ideologists are by no means able to resolve this "antinomy", and only the class consciousness formed by the proletariat during historical practice can really solve it – the "antinomy" between subject and object. Lukacs develops Marxist critical theory about social relations into the critical theory about production structure, and combines it with, and even integrates it into, the theories of subjectivity, identity and totality.

Frankfurt School extends the critical spirit of Marxism into the realm of culture, and uncovers the feature of instrument reason of capitalist society. Horkheimer and Adorno not only reveal the deep cultural root of instrument reason, but also, in combination with the rise of mass culture, announce that instrument reason has infiltrated into all fields of the existence of man and made men consciously subjugated to it by dint of mass culture. From the viewpoint of Horkheimer and Adorno, this is the process during which subject consciously moves towards the control and dominance of reason and actively accomplish the "totality" of contemporary capitalist social control. It is under such a context that Lukacs' theory of totality becomes the critical object in *Negative Dialectics*.

In Adorno's view, "contradiction is nonidentity under the aspect of identity", so "dialectics is the consistent sense of nonidentity"; the negative dialectics is to disavow and abolish reality through explanation and critique. The critique of Adorno on identity is not only philosophical, but also political and social, on the capitalist system. This critique strongly emphasizes "heterogeneity and peculiarity", and rejects to "the abstract identity that submits to the world"; it consciously realizes that capitalism, this "materialized world", is the "managed world" integrated by the logic of capital identity, that "under the all-subjugating identity principle, whatever does not enter into identity, whatever eludes rational planning in the realm of means, turns into frightening retribution for the calamity which identity brought on the nonidentical", and that "identity, as totality, takes ontological precedence, assisted by the promotion of the indirectness of the non-identical to the rank of its absolute conceptual Being"[5].

5   Theodor W. Adorno, *Negative Dialectics*, trans. by E. B. Ashton. Routledge & Kegan Paul Ltd: London, 1973: p. 120.

As a result, when Adorno lays emphasis on negative dialectics, on the connecting role of "loose constellation", he has actually broken the totality theory centered on subject-object dialectics and shown the meaning of "fragments". His theoretical model and thinking method for fundamentally negating the subjectivity, identity and totality of western Marxism show us another way of thinking different from that of western Marxism, and have the connotation of postmodernism. In this sense, the formation of Adorno's negative dialectics marks the logical end of western Marxism.

The logical end of western Marxism was concurrent with the rise of postmodernism. Postmodernism stands against the subjectivity, identity and totality established by enlightenment reason, and replaces them with non-subjectivity, non-centrality and fragments, with an aim to recode western culture through reviewing modernity. In its entirety, it is a cultural reflection of the postindustrial society, namely contemporary capitalist society, or the cultural logic of late capitalism.

From the standpoint of postmodernism, in the process of modernization, capitalism is not only "legitimized" but also set as the single authority, an autocratic authority that "has forgotten how to think historically", namely forgetting the historicity of capitalism itself. Hence, "it is safest to grasp the concept of the postmodern as an attempt to think the present historically in an age that has forgotten how to think historically in the first place."[6] In the process of "thinking historically", postmodernism makes a prescription – "waging a war on identity" – for the more and more mortally sick capitalist society.

Postmodernism focuses on "waging a war on identity" and "waging a war against totality"; it stresses heterogeneous elements and rejects centralism, essentialism and foundationalism. In addition, postmodernism is "the skeptical attitude to meta-narrative"[7]. The so-called "meta-narrative" refers to the Hegelian thought tradition – "purely speculative and theoretical narrative" – and the thought tradition of the French Revolution – "freedom and emancipation narrative"; the former lays stress on the thinking model of identity and totality, while the latter focuses on the thinking model of humanistic independence and emancipation. In the view of Lyotard, postmodernism applies itself to the

---

6   Fredric Jameson, *Postmodernism, or The Cultural Logic of Late Capitalism*, p. ix.
7   *Culture and Aesthetics of Postmodernism*, edited by Wang Yuechuan and Shang Shui. Beijing: Peking University Press, 1992: p. 76.

critique of "meta-narrative" or "grand narrative" and to the dissolution of identity so as to strengthen our sensitivity to difference and facilitate our ability to tolerate incommensurable things.

Depending on its "weird" way of thinking, postmodernism became the leading trend of thought in western thought circle for a time, and almost turned into an "epidemic". If traditional Marxism and western Marxism are reviewed by the thinking mode of postmodernism, such significant theories as subjectivity, practical activity, class struggle, revolution strategy, the dichotomy between economic base and super-structure, the freedom and emancipation of man, etc. all have identity or totality, belong to "meta-narrative" or "grand narrative", fall under modern and metaphysical concepts, reflect the control and dominance of reason, and embody essentialism, centralism and foundationalism. In brief, Marxism needs to be deconstructed or entirely corrected in postmodern times.

So we can see that the changes of historical and thought contexts in western society in the 1970s raised a series of fundamental questions to Marxism. The thinking about these questions promoted the generation of post-Marxism. Laclau and Mouffe point out, "We believe that, by clearly locating ourselves in a post-Marxist terrain, we not only help to clarify the meaning of contemporary social struggles but also give to Marxism its theoretical dignity, which can only proceed from rec-ognition of its limitations and of its historicality. Only through such recognition will Marx's work remain present in our tradition and our political culture."[8]

2 THREE THEORETICAL LOGICS OF POST-MARXISM

With respect to its derivation, the concept of "post-Marxism" appears for the first time in Polanyi's Personal Knowledge. In this works, Polanyi refers to "post-Marxism" as the process of thought liberation in Eastern European socialist countries after Stalin passed away. For this reason, the "post-Marxism" brought forward by Polanyi is virtually "post-Stalinism". In the sight of Polanyi, Marxism is the same concept with Stalinism.

---

8 Ernesto Laclau and Chantal Mouffe: New Left Review, No. 166, November/December 1987: p. 106.

After Polanyi, different scholars gave different meanings to "post-Marxism". Jameson asserted Bernstein belongs to "the first generation of post-Marxists"; Touraine tried hard to construct "the analytic paradigm of post-Marxism"; Cohen strived to lay a foundation for "post-Marxist theory of critique stratification"; Bell claims himself as "post-Marxist", but his leading train of thought is obviously different from that of the "post-Marxism" of Laclau and Mouffe. ... As soon as it comes into being, the concept of "post-Marxism" is used in confusion.

In my opinion, post-Marxism is different from thought schools like the Marxism of existentialism, the Marxism of structuralism, and the analytic Marxism; it has no thought leader, no uniform proposition, and even no identical context. So, there is no a clearly defined post-Marxism. I would rather regard it as a dispute centered on some topics and opinions of Marxism. Therefore, different theoretical logics therein should be made clear in the discussion of post-Marxism.

Judged from theoretical logics, there are three leading trains of thought in post-Marxism: once being a Marxist or deeply influenced by Marxism, and then negating Marxism with postmodernism; deconstructing Marxism with postmodernism, and meanwhile inheriting and reconstructing Marxist critical theory in a definite sense; seeking for the theoretical resource of post-Marxism in the thoughts of Marx, and believing post-Marxism is the contemporary form of Marxism.

Lyotard and Baudrillard are the main representatives of the first logic of post-Marxism.

At his early days, Lyotard had been an important member of left-wing organization "Socialism or Barbarism", whose core concern was how to realize revolution in capitalist society. But in later period, Lyotard left the organization "Socialism or Barbarism", and started to repudiate Marxism. In the eyes of Lyotard, dialectical logic in Marx is merely "a pure style language", and the development of contemporary capitalism has not followed the development mode of dialectical logic revealed by Marx any longer; the thinking of Marx is still in the mode centered on reason, and still pursues unity, thus being to "meta-narrative"; it is "meta-narrative" that makes both modern science and social institutional power legitimized. Standing on the ground of postmodernism, Lyotard objected to the totality theory powered by the binary opposition of contradictions, and emphasized "waging a war against totality" and "activating difference".

Under such a context, Marxist theory of class struggle was totally criticized: "The social foundation of the principle of division, or class struggle, was blurred to the point of losing all of its radicality; we cannot conceal the fact that the critical model in the end lost its theoretical standing and was reduced to the status of a 'utopia' or 'hope,' a token protest raised in the name of man or reason or creativity, or again of some social category such as the Third World or the students – on which is conferred in extremes the henceforth improbable function of critical subject"[9]. A kind of postmodern knowledge or Marxism of postmodernism oriented to paralogism became the theoretical orientation of Lyotard for the purpose of evading the restriction of "meta-narrative". Such a so-called post-Marxism is actually a theoretical form repudiating Marxism.

The same with Lyotard, Baudrillard also fundamentally criticized Marxism. In his early days, Baudrillard, under the deep influence of Marxism, strived to achieve the fusion of Marxist critical theory with psychoanalytic theory and semiotic theory, but in that operation process of theory, Baudrillard's train of thought deviated from Marxian logic. In Baudrillard's opinion, by adopting production theory as the theoretical basis for analyzing and criticizing capitalist society, Marxism is in effect criticizing capitalist society in illusion, and it's the ideological proof of real society.

Through five critiques, namely the critique on the concept of labor, the critique on the nature idea of historical materialistic anthropology, the critique on the primitive society analysis of historical materialism, the critique on the analyses of slave society and feudal society of historical materialism, and the critique on the inner link between historical materialism and political economy, Baudrillard thinks that historical materialism and its social critical theory virtually demonstrate the legitimacy of capitalist society on the standpoint of capitalist political economy; what can really supplants the system of capitalist political economy is the symbolic exchange theory centered on consumption model, and only it can transcend modern reason and metaphysics.[10] The critique on Marxist production theory and the deconstruction of the subject of

9   Lyotard, *The Postmodern Condition: A Report on Knowledge*. Beijing, Joint Publishing Company, 1997: p. 25.
10   Jean Baudrillard, *The Mirror of Production*, trans. by Mark Post, Telos Press, 1975. and Jean Baudrillard, *Symbolic Exchange and Death*, trans. by Lain Hamilton Grant, Sage Publications: London, 1993.

class made Baudrillard take various "marginal groups" as the subject of struggle and believe that the ultimate resistance to the world could be in nothing form but virus, cancerization, etc. Thus he gradually moved towards the theoretical construction of nihilism, and left Marxism in the end.

Derrida, Laclau and Mouffe are the main representatives of the second logic of post-Marxism.

Starting from postmodernism, Derrida strives to establish a kind of "deconstructed Marxism", which is in fact a kind of post-Marxism. On the one hand, this "deconstructed Marxism" resorts to "a certain spirit of the Marxist critique", and "keep[s] faith with what has always made of Marxism in principle and first of all a radical critique"[11]. From Derrida's point of view, only the critical spirit of Marxism can show the true face of contemporary capitalism; besides, "there has been, then, this attempted radicalization of Marxism called deconstruction", and "deconstruction has never had any sense or interest ... except a radicalization"[12]. That is to say, critique, deconstruction and radicalization are categories in the same sequence and with the same function. The purpose of Derrida to set up such post-Marxism is for adapting this Marxist critique "to new conditions" and making it "fruitful"[13].

On the other hand, the Marxist critical spirit inherited by such "deconstructed Marxism" is differentiated from other Marxist spirits, because the latter is subsumed into the systems of ontology and metaphysics and fixed in the basic concepts related to labor, class, etc., and should be discarded. The problem is that the fundamental spirit or essential feature of any doctrine is presented in the deductions of other spirits, basic concepts and theoretical systems. If other spirits, basic concepts, or theoretical systems of Marxism are discarded, the critical spirit of Marxism as its essence will unavoidably have nothing to lean on and become illusory, and can be nothing but "a certain emancipator and messianic affirmation", "a certain experience of the promise". For Derrida, Marxism, as a matter of fact, means a kind of utopian spirit, a theoretical image. With him, the political critique in the era of globalization turns into a metaphysical deconstruction in cultural sense.

---

11   Derrida, *Specters of Marx*, pp. 122 and 124.
12   ibid., p. 129.
13   ibid., p. 122.

The post-Marxism of Laclau and Mouffe is similar to Derrida's post-Marxist train of thought. Owing to the efforts of the two persons, "all themes and final conclusions" of post-Marxism are elaborated and summarized, and a trademark effect is thereby caused. Laclau and Mouffe consequently become the flag-bearers and typical representatives of post-Marxism, and *Hegemony and Socialist Strategy* is called "the most profound works of post-Marxism".

In this book, Laclau and Mouffe clearly express their theoretical intention, and make an elaborate planning and meticulous exposition of post-Marxism. According to them, "to reread Marxist theory in correspondence to contemporary problems, its core category is bound to be deconstructed, which is the post-Marxism referred to by us"[14]. Post-Marxism aims at "scaling down the pretensions and the area of validity of Marxist theory", and "breaking with something deeply inherent in that theory: namely, its monist aspiration to capture with its categories the essence or underlying meaning of History". "Only if we renounce any epistemological prerogative based upon the ontologically privileged position of a 'universal class', will it be possible seriously to discuss the present degree of validity of the Marxist categories. At this point we should state quite plainly that we are now situated in a post-Marxist terrain. It is no longer possible to maintain the conception of subjectivity and classes elaborated by Marxism, nor its vision of the historical course of capitalist development, nor, of course, the conception of communism as a transparent society from which antagonisms have disappeared. But if our intellectual project in this book is port-Marxist, it is evidently also *post-Marxist*."[15]

It can be found that Marxist theories of practice, subject, class, capitalism and communism all are the objects reviewed by Laclau and Mouffe and theoretically transformed by the two. In regard to their theoretical target, they attribute their theory to the question domain of Marxism, but such an attribution is realized with the traditions of Marxism deconstructed and Marxism reread under the new historical conditions.

It is the post-Marxist theoretical direction of Laclau and Mouffe to "suture" the struggles of different subjects in different fields together in the mode of "articulation" in order to constitute a new radically critical force. In the opinion of Laclau and Mouffe, society is constituted

---

14   Laclau, *Theory and Practice of Post-Marxism, carried in Marxism and Reality*, 2003 (2).
15   Laclau and Mouffe, *Hegemony and Socialist Strategy*, p. 4.

based on antagonistic relations, and in contemporary capitalist society, the form of antagonism has been diversified, and all kinds of marginal groups, social fields and "new social movements", such as the green movement, feminist movement, peace movement, movement of ethnic minorities and even homosexuality, have become the subjects and places of struggles for opposition to inequality, resistance to oppression, and establishment of new right relations. This is the first point.

Second, in such a postmodern society where subject and antagonism have been diversified, "it is pointless to insist upon the problematic nature"[16] of class struggle, and it has been impossible for a definite class as "general subject" to emancipate all mankind.

Third, the essence of socialism is to construct radical democracy, which admits diversity of social subjects and affirms no subject can become the general subject and eternal center overtopping others; whichever subject is able to articulate multiple subjects together into a "commonwealth", it will acquire the dominant right of political identity, i.e. acquiring "hegemony". Therefore, Laclau and Mouffe try hard to transform and transcend Gramsci's theory of hegemony and "approach to a new concept of hegemony".

In Gramsci's view, with respect to the leading rule, hegemony refers to the cultural leadership with political planning significance in civil society. In the construction of hegemony, economy plays a fundamental role, the proletariat is the subject, and hegemony is the union of classes under the leadership of the proletariat, especially the union between the proletariat and peasants.

Gramsci's concept of hegemony is transformed by Laclau and Mouffe on the standpoint of postmodernism: first of all, hegemony is transformed into a concept featured by discourse articulation by using the discourse theory of Wittgenstein in his later period; next, hegemony is interpreted, in a multi-centralized manner with the plural determinism of Althusser, as an articulation composed of various internal heterogeneous elements at the same plane; finally, any interpretation from the center is objected to with the deconstruction theory of Derrida, and the deconstructions of the decisive effect of economy and the subject role of the proletariat are stressed.

---

16   Laclau and Mouffe, *Hegemony and Socialist Strategy*, p. 159.

In this way, the concept of hegemony has the postmodern connotation. Laclau and Mouffe hold that present society is articulated by discourse and the transformed "hegemony" is exactly an important scheme for articulating various subjects and constructing a radically critical subject, as well as an important strategy for constructing the radical democracy.

"Post-Marxism, ... as in the work of such major theorists as Ernesto Laclau and Chantal Mouffe, attempts to rescue aspects of Marxist thought from the collapse of Marxism as a global cultural and political force in the later twentieth century, and reorient them to take on new meaning within a rapidly changing cultural climate"[17]. This evaluation of Sim is reasonable. Laclau and Mouffe really want to make Marxism "take on new meaning" in contemporary times, and argue that only by virtue of Marxism can "a new political idea be elucidated"; Laclau and Mouffe firmly believe their theoretical exploration "does not reject Marxism", and even "roots in Marxism".

But the problem is that Laclau and Mouffe stand against the analytic paradigm of Marxism, deconstruct the core category of Marxism, and renounce basic Marxist opinions, so in fact they have diverged from the foundation of Marxism. The most particular but also most contradictory point of the post-Marxism of Laclau and Mouffe is that it carries forward the critical spirit of Marxism and reasserts the value goal of socialism in a manner that diverges and breaks from Marxism. This, however, is an unsolvable paradox.

What has a different logic from the two kinds of post-Marxism above is the post-Marxism of Bell.

According to Bell, "post-Marxism" is a concept closely related to "postindustrial society". "The post-Marxist separation of manager from owner, the bureaucratization of enterprise, the complication of occupational structure, all made the once clear-cut picture of property domination and social relations ambiguous"[18], but the key point is that some important features of postindustrial society have been "accurately" foreseen in Volume III of Marx's *Das Kapital*[19], which has implied the

---

17   Smart Sim, *Post-Marxism: An Intellectual History*. Routledge: London & New York, 2001: p. 1.
18   Bell, *The Coming of Postindustrial Society: A Venture in Social Forecasting*. 1st Chinese Ed., p. 58.
19   ibid., p. 66.

train of thought coping with postindustrial society and the theoretical elements of post-Marxism.

To be specific, there are two schemas of social change in Marx: one is the schema in Volume I of *Das Kapital*, which is a purely theoretical one for class differentiation and struggle, followed by the coming of socialist revolution; the other is the schema in Volume III of *Das Kapital*, whose core is that the development of banking system and the emergence of stock companies begin to change the structure of capitalist society: firstly, the emergence of banking system makes all available social wealth handed over to capitalists, and capital accumulation starts to be completed in a social mode; secondly, the generation of stock companies results in the separation of ownership from the right of management, and it is manager, rather than capitalist, that directs the production; thirdly, the number of white-collar workers is increasing, and the middle class is taking shape and growing larger and larger.

From the viewpoint of Bell, in the theoretical system of Marxism, the first schema is the dominant leading thought, but the problem is that contemporary capitalist society does not run in accordance with it; the second schema is the recessive weak thought, but it implies the train of thought coping with postindustrial society, and the development theory of contemporary society is actually "talking" with the second schema. On such a basis of thinking, Bell calls his theory of postmodern society analysis as per Volume III of *Das Kapital* the post-Marxism. I think his post-Marxism assumes duality: on the one side, it questions the class theory and the social development theory of Marxism, and censures Marxism for ignoring the autonomy of politics; on the other hand, it creates a precedent of seeking for the theoretical resource of post-Marxism in the thoughts of Marx.

Bell insists on looking for theoretical resource in the thoughts of Marx, and rethinks the spirit of Marxism in combination with the development of contemporary capitalist society. His practice is extended and reflected by Jameson, Best and Kellner. The same with Bell, Jameson et al. hold fast to Marxism in the context of postmodernism, and firmly believe that Marx has established an "appropriate stance" for us to treat postmodernism; however, different from Bell's demonstration of Marxism, Jameson et al. lay emphasis on the critical spirit of Marxism, and strive to absorb the fruits of postmodernism to update Marxism. Although Jameson denies that he is a post-Marxist, the "postindustrial

Marxism" that he tries to construct and can explain "postindustrial monopoly capitalism" is virtually a kind of post-Marxism.

Best and Kellner on the one side want to establish a multi-dimensional
multi-perspective social critical theory in combination with postmodernism, and on the other focus on constructing a new subject in system,
discourse and practice in consideration of the lack of an active society-
mediated self-theory in postmodernism; and they also restate that the
critique of Marxism on capitalism is an important constituent in the
contemporary theory of social critique and economy must be viewed
as the core element in the framework of social analysis. "Marxian categories are of central importance precisely in analyzing the phenomena focused on by postmodern social theory: the consumer society, the
media, information, computers, and so on. Although theorists of both
the postindustrial society and postmodern society posit the primacy of
knowledge and information as new principles of social organization, it
is arguably capitalism that is determining what sort of media, information, computers, and other technologies and commodities are being produced and distributed precisely according to its logic and interests". In
this connection, Lyotard, Baudrillard, et al., while criticizing contemporary capitalist society, "have made a serious theoretical and political
mistake in severing their work from the Marxian critique of political
economy and capitalism"[20].

3 PERORATION: SIGNIFICANCE AND PREDICAMENT

Post-Marxism consciously realizes the new changes of contemporary
capitalist society, and tries hard to reveal the process of the changes
and their inherent logics. Bell uncovers the new changes in strata and
foundation of capitalist society, and argues "old social relations (which
were property-bound), existing power structures (centered on narrow
elites), and bourgeois culture (based on notions of restraint and delayed
gratification) are being rapidly eroded"[21]. The "Information Age Series"
of Castells analyzes the new changes in capitalist society arising from
the rise of network in a relatively comprehensive manner, from the
evolutions of technical level, production structure and social system,
to the development of national states and the formation of economic

20   Kellner and Best, *Postmodern Theory: Critical Interrogation.* 2nd Chinese Ed., p. 338.
21   Bell, *The Coming of Postindustrial Society: A Venture in Social Forecasting.* 1st
Chinese Ed., p. 47.

globalization, then to the changes in fields like mental structure of ego, social identity, ideology, etc. ... As to us, no matter whether their analyses are correct, their new reflections under the new historical context and their historical consciousness to theory are noteworthy.

Post-Marxism consciously absorbs the new achievements of contemporary social science, and presents a broad domain of question. In a certain sense, it breaks the discipline barriers in the study of traditional Marxism and integrates philosophy, economy, politics, culture, etc. into one, and meanwhile brings many issues that had been paid no, or less, attention to by Marxism in the past into its own theoretical framework. For instance, the thought construction of Baudrillard absorbs not only the major achievements of western Marxism, especially Frankfurt School, but also the trends of thought of semiology, psychoanalysis, sociology and the critical theory of media culture, and the issues discussed by it involve many fields like philosophy, sociology, media culturology, and so forth. In addition, Kautz's critique on ecology and capitalist economy, Soja's reflection on geography, Hartmann's thinking about the relationship between Marxism and feminism, Zizek's analysis of contemporary movies ... together show us a colorful picture of theories. Among these theories, no matter whether it affirms the validity of Marxism in the postmodern context or takes a critical attitude to Marxism, it has inherited the critical spirit of Marxism to a certain degree and melted such a spirit into a specific theoretical analysis. As far as I'm concerned, this is precisely what the study of Marxist philosophy in China lacks.

The theoretical project of post-Marxism is to hold a critical stance in the historical context of contemporary capitalism and present the contemporary significance of Marxist critical spirit. But at this point, post-Marxism falls into a fundamental theoretical predicament. It wants to reestablish a critical radical strategy under the postindustrial and postmodern context and unite the struggles of different subjects in different fields into a "unified" struggle, and has a firm belief that "deconstruction is able to arouse progress, emancipation and revolution in a new way" [22]. The problem is: whether such a radical stance is really confronting contemporary capitalist society, is it merely a discourse revolution?

---

22 *Lectures of Derrida in China*, edited by Du Xiaozhen and Zhang Ning. Beijing: Central Compilation & Translation Press, 2003: p. 102.

Due to this, many western scholars raise questions and criticisms on the theoretical logics of post-Marxism. From Grass' standpoint, the post-Marxism of Laclau and Mouffe in effect rejects the fundamental principle of Marxism, and it is rather revisionism than post-Marxism, because Laclau and Mouffe repudiate three important aspects of Marxism: the negation to the viewpoint of class, the negation to socialism, which has an emancipating role on the capitalist relations of production, and the placement of society and history into a framework of discourse and theory, which is no other than the method of revisionism[23]. In Reynolds' opinion, "post-Marxism assembles together the lengthy and complicated discourses drawn from such fields as linguistics, semiology, philosophy, literature, cultural research and social science. Indeed, this label appears in very diverse contexts, concealing the heterogeneity of various conclusions it adopts. Maybe it is better to view it as a drama concerning struggle, or as a theoretical movement"[24].

Post-Marxism perceives the new changes of contemporary capitalism, the diversity of social subjects presented in the postindustrial society, and especially the diversification, caused by "marginal groups", of resistance movement against capitalism, but it fails to resolve the fundamental issue of how to form a struggle subject bearing collective will for these diversified resistance movements and constitute a critical movement with a definite goal.

What's more, post-Marxism resolves all society-determined contents into a kind of discourse logic, and thinks only discourse logic is the real existence of society, thus translating the practical critical spirit of Marxism into a theory of discourse revolution and making the value goal of socialism unattainable. In my eyes, such a translation embodies a helpless and desolate mood of the intellectuals in contemporary capitalist society. And just because of this, along with the coming of new century, post-Marxism has been displayed as a specimen in the museum of thoughts rather than been thriving around the world.

---

23 Norman Geran, *"Post-Marxism?"*, in *Post-Marxism: A Reader*, ed. by Stuart Sim. Edinburgh University Press, 1998.
24 Reynolds, *Is Post-Marxism the Radical Political Theory and Practice beyond Marxism?*, trans. by Zhang Mingcang, carried in World Philosophy, 2002 (6).

APPENDIX I

GETTING CLOSE TO PHILOSOPHY AND ENTERING INTO MARX*

— A Self-account of My Academic Road

Philosophy is my major, my profession, and my career. If philosophy was chosen by me at the outset, then I was chosen by philosophy later; I am suitable for philosophy, as philosophy is also suitable for me. Today, philosophy has fused into my daily life, thinking mode and life activity, and I do not know how to live without it. Every time when I think of my career of philosophy, my mind will be spontaneously connected with the destinies of myself and our generation.

I was born in an ordinary teacher's family in 1956. I, the same with my contemporaries, underwent the ups and downs, natural calamities and man-made misfortunes, ... of the People's Republic of China, but I do not think that I was born at the wrong time, and on the contrary, I'm so grateful that I have such a special experience in that experience itself is wealth. It is this special experience that enables me to have a profound realization of society and life and exerts a great influence on my career of philosophy. Our generation is different from the older one. The older generation lived through the war times of blood and fire; our generation live in continuous spiritual tempering during the peaceful age; the older generation "discussed the national affairs" and dared to "ask who rules over man's destiny on this boundless land"; our generation "reconstructs our country" and dare to "ask where the road is". Our generation has our own persistent pursuit.

I am grateful to Deng Xiaoping. This old man set things right and brought forward the reform and opening-up, helping the modernization movement of China miraculously "escape by a hair's breadth" from the quagmire of history and opening up a new world for the development of our generation. In 1977, that "thawed" year, I was enrolled by the Philosophy Department of Anhui University as one of the first-session

---

*) Originally carried in *Academic Research*, 2008 (4), and slightly revised when included into this book.

undergraduates after the reform of college enrollment, and in that year, I set foot on the magical land of philosophy. In 1986, Professor Wang Yongxiang introduced me into the School of Philosophy of China Renmin University, where I assiduously studied for my master's degree, and since then, I had stepped on the "fast traffic lane" of philosophical research; in 1988, Professor Chen Xianda let me stay in the School of Philosophy of China Renmin University for teaching and study for a doctor's degree in advance without examination, and from then on, I walk towards the deep of philosophy and develop my research on philosophy on a new platform. The broad vision and selfless help of Professor Chen Zhiliang are also unforgettable to me. From all these professors, I not only appreciate the literary talent of philosophers but also their elegant demeanor, and not only learn the literary quality of philosophers but also their moral quality.

"To be a sage is the highest achievement of man as such. This is the lofty mission of philosophy" (Feng Youlan). It is hard for philosophy to make man "a sage", but it is able to make man lofty; I can never become "a sage", but I admire this "lofty mission" of philosophy. I have no regrets for choosing philosophy; I am still "intoxicated in" my study on philosophy. Of course, I know very well the exceeding hardships of philosophical thinking, and anyone who chooses philosophy and wants to stand at the commanding height of this realm will inevitably live a life like a fakir, both spiritually and materially. "The road of glory is narrow" (Shakespeare).

The reason why I am "keen on" philosophy so much is not because philosophy is "erudite" and omniscient; in fact, "erudition cannot make man wise" (Heraclitus), and only theology is omniscient. It has been proved by history that the thought systems that boast themselves of omniscience all decline without exception, like the feudal dynasty boasting itself of eternity. The reason why I am "keen on" philosophy is not because philosophy "loves" wisdom; as a matter of fact, philosophy itself is a kind of wisdom, giving man the wisdom and courage for survival and development; it is the "extraordinary courage and wisdom"; if we say religion is about the idea of man's death, about how distressed the life is before death and how to go to paradise after death, then philosophy is about the wisdom of man's life, teaching man how to live, how to live in a valuable and meaningful way. The reason why I am "keen on" philosophy is not because philosophy is the generalization and summarization of natural and social sciences and the science about the general laws of natural, social and thinking movements; philosophy actually does not equal to science, and the development of contemporary science has rendered "a special science dealing with this totality" "superfluous" (Engels); in the words of Heidegger, "such an expectation on and requirement for the essence of philosophy's ability is a bit too extravagant".

The reason why I am "keen on" philosophy is because philosophy is closely related to life. No matter whether it turns to the relationship between man and nature or the relationship between man and society, philosophy is, in the final analysis, always focusing on the position of man in the world and showing the self-image of man. The reason why philosophy causes philosophers to think unceasingly and fascinates them is because it is concerned with man and man's mode of being and his development law on the whole. In this sense, I approve of such a viewpoint that "philosophy is hominology". A drama without a protagonist cannot be put on the stage; if philosophy is willing to give up its protagonist – man – to other disciplines, it is making a mistake like performing a drama of the Prince of Denmark without Hamlet.

By saying philosophy is hominology, I do not mean that it studies all aspects of man. In a definite sense, the whole humanities, social sciences, and even some natural sciences all belong to "hominology": ecology studies the relationship between man and nature, economy studies the economic relationship between man and man, medical science studies the physical organization of man, thinking science deals with the thinking structure of man, and love is the eternal theme of literature. ... For philosophy, the major subject of discussion and exploration is the mode of being and the development law of man, with the aim to address the mystery of life. In my eyes, life outlook is a philosophical issue rather than a scientific one for medical science, biology, archaeology, physics, chemistry, mathematics, etc. are all unable to address the mystery of life, which cannot be seen by a telescope no matter how good it is, or observed by a microscope no matter how large its magnification is, or calculated even by a petascale computer. ... Actually, different answers to the mystery of life imply different understandings on the relationships of man with nature and society. The natural instincts of man are a natural phenomenon, whereas the tragic condition that "meat is allowed to spoil in rich men's homes while the poor die of cold by the roadside" and the tragic love respectively of Liang Shanbo and Zhu Yingtai and Romeo and Juliet are social phenomena, reflecting specific social conditions and moral ideas. The famous saying that "everyone must die; let me but leave a loyal heart shining in the pages of history" indicates that the life and death of man are subject to natural law, but the significance of life and death falls under historical law. The boundary between hero and knave, or between leaving a good name forever and leaving a foul reputation for myriad years, lies in whether to comply with or to go against historical law. Once a great man goes against the historical law and takes an opposite position to the masses of people, there will be only one end for him – "failure and death" like Xiang Yu, the King of Chu, in China's history. That is to say, life outlook is not just the attitude to life, but more importantly, it is about how to apprehend and grasp the relationships of man with nature and society, i.e. the relationship between man and world.

In other words, life outlook is world outlook, and world outlook is life outlook. In philosophy, there is no an independent world outlook as theoretical basis, or an independent life outlook with the nature of application; instead, world outlook and life outlook has fused together in philosophy, or we can say philosophy is both world outlook and life outlook. Philosophy is always concerned with the great issue of "man's life on the earth"; as the thought on the relationship between man and nature probing into Heaven, Earth and man, the analysis on the relationship between man and society making reflection on you, me and others, the discriminating analysis of man and life pursuing truth, kindness and beauty, philosophy is fused with the concern for the living noumenon of mankind, the anxiety for the circumstances of human development, and the care for the real destiny of mankind, and condensed into the deep understanding and grasp of the health of life. Therefore, philosophy constitutes "the highest supporting point" of life, or the foundation for man to "settle down and get on with his pursuit".

As a matter of fact, philosophy is neither mysterious nor far from man, and instead, it exists in human life. Men certainly do not live in the light of philosophy, but there is indeed philosophy in life: life and death, fortune and disaster, reason and appetite, success and failure, honor and disgrace, virtue and vice, ... The crux is that philosophy has its unique horizon, which enables us to perceive generality through individuality, identity through opposition, opposition through identity, negation through affirmation, the infinite through the finite, ... and to understand extreme joy begets sorrow, every cloud has a silver lining, a good thing may turn out to be a bad thing, a success may result in failure, … Philosophy is apprehending and grasping life with a reflective spirit, a critical attitude, and a transcending sentiment. Philosophy needs to focus on life, and life needs the horizon of philosophy. Only by focusing on the daily life and the mode of being of man and addressing the mystery of life can philosophy be "both credible and lovable".

From Socrates' "know yourself" to Kant's "human beings are the ends", from Protagoras' "man is the measure of all things" to Feuerbach's "man is the highest measure of man", from Aristotle's "man is a political animal" to Marx's "man is a social being", from Hegel's "human history is the progress of the consciousness of freedom" to Sartre's "the freedom of man is antecedent to essence" …, philosophers are pulling me continuously towards philosophy with an "invisible hand", and philosophy is getting closer and closer to me at the same time. Thank philosophy for making me "thoroughly understand life", "see through the vanity of life", and "always unperturbed" and "undisturbed either by favor or disgrace". As soon as man "learns to walk, he learns also to fall, and only by falling does he learn to walk" (Marx). For me, family affection and friendship, as well as grievance and hardship, are all a fortune, a fortune that is indispensable. "If you do not want to suffer hardships, you cannot think correctly" (Wittgenstein).

The reason why I am "keen on" philosophy is more because Marxist philosophy is a doctrine related to "the real man and his historical development". It is in Marxist philosophy that I find a thoroughly critical spirit against capitalist system, perceive a deep concern for the living condition of mankind, and apprehend a strong sense of mission to achieve the emancipation of the working class and the whole mankind.

Of course, I notice that the debate on Marxist philosophy is persistent and fierce. In history, there is no lack of precedents that the theories of a great philosopher are discussed and debated anew after his death, but few have aroused a debate so extensive, persistent and fierce around the world as Marxist philosophy. The "image" of Marx is constantly changing after his death, and the longer he leaves us, the more the cognitions on him are diverged, just as the farther a man goes away, the more vague his image is. For this reason, I started to reread Marx with the expectation to walk into his mind. I clearly declared to reread Marx in *China Reading Weekly* in 1995.

Rereading Marx is by no means "making trouble out of nothing" or "groaning without pain", but is the need of developments of contemporary practice, science and philosophy itself. There is an interesting phenomenon frequently happening in history – a theory or even the whole doctrine of a great philosopher always tends to show its intrinsic value and catch the attention of people again after the philosopher's death and a relatively long historical movement. So rereading is a common phenomenon in the history of thoughts, for example, Hegel reread Plato, Peirce reread Kant, and Goethe reread Raphael, and so forth. The history of philosophy is, to a certain extent, the history during which the descendants unceasingly reread the predecessors, so it is rewritten constantly. As far as I'm concerned, the purpose of the descendants to unceasingly reread the predecessors is for absorbing great inspiration and outstanding wisdom from the immortal masters, so as to "be comparable to the ancients in terms of both achievement and talent".

During rereading of Marx, I have gone through an exploring process from Marxist philosophy to the history respectively of Marxist philosophy and western philosophy, to modern western philosophy, and then back to Marxist philosophy, aiming at studying Marxist philosophy in a broad theoretical space. In my opinion, the study on Marxist philosophy cannot be separated from the study on the history of Marxist philosophy, and only when grasping the evolution process of Marxist philosophy after Marx can one really understand the true essence of Marxist philosophy, and when and to what extent it had been misread; only by placing Marxist philosophy into the historical evolvement of western philosophy for study can one really grasp the substantial significance of Marxist philosophy on the transformation of tradition philosophy, and really realize its epoch-making contribution; only by comparing Marxist philosophy with modern western philosophy for study can one really know the historical limitation and the greatness of Marxist philosophy, and understand why it is "the sole unsurpassable philosophy" (Sartre) of our times and why "it will always be a fault not to read and reread and discuss Marx ... and to go beyond scholarly 'reading' or 'discussion'" (Derrida).

During my rereading of Marx, I have also dipped into the history of socialist thought, and meanwhile "made up the missed lessons" of historiography, theoretical economy and sociology of development. Seen from the founding process of Marxist philosophy, Marx had critically studied and made philosophical reflection on historiography, economy and politics, and not only classical German philosophy, but also the historiography during the French Restoration period, classical British economics, and the British and French "critical-utopian socialism" all constituted the theoretical source of Marxist philosophy. In regard to the content of Marxism itself, Marxist philosophy was generated in the process of elaborating socialism; realizing the free and all-around development of man is not only the ultimate goal of Marxist philosophy, but also the highest principle of scientific socialism. Marxist economics is not only a theory about capital, but the theoretical critique or critical theory related to capital; the social attribute of man covered by the natural attribute of material and the interpersonal relationship covered by the relationship between materials revealed by Marx's economics are of great philosophical significance.

Spiritual production is different from material production of flesh, since race continuation based on gene as genetic material is congeneric, whereas philosophical thinking can lead to new philosophical form through absorbing, digesting and recreating the fruits of different disciplines. Just as related breeding is prejudicial to species development, a creative philosophy must break through the limitation from one to another. In my view, Marxist philosophy is such a creative philosophy.

In such a process of rereading Marx, a huge statue of heroes appeared in front of my eyes. I deeply feel the solemn beauty of philosophers pursuing truth and faith, and understand at the turn of the century and the millennium, why Marx is rated as "the most influential ideologist over a thousand years".

Rereading Marx helps me to realize that Marx is the terminator of traditional philosophy and the pathfinder of modern philosophy, and Marxist philosophy is modern materialism.

Traditional philosophy is fundamentally "metaphysics". In history, metaphysics had established a strict logical rule for exploring the ultimate being of the world, that is, starting from axiom and theorem to reach an inevitable conclusion following the inference rule. That undeniably was of positive significance, marking the formation of philosophy as a theoretical form. However, the beings in metaphysics were gradually deviated by the philosophers after Aristotle into the beings separated from the real man and his activity, i.e. into an abstract "thing-in-itself".

Hence, till the middle of the nineteenth century, when natural sciences "marked out their independent fields", and the development of society made "real beings and earthly things the center of all interest" (Marx), the western philosophy started a tide of opposing metaphysics.

Comte and Marx raised the banner of "rejecting metaphysics" at the same era, and Marx expressly proposed to "reject all metaphysics". Comte criticized metaphysics in the principle of verification of natural sciences, while Marx's critique was from the starting point of real man. Comte's rejection to metaphysics overlaps with that of Marx with respect to the times – both are the critique by modern spirit on early modern and ancient spirits. In this connection, Comte and Marx both are the terminators of traditional philosophy and the pathfinders of modern philosophy. However, Comte's rejection to metaphysics is essentially different from that of Marx in the aspect of directionality: Comte thought that through rejection of metaphysics, philosophy should tend to natural science, be limited within the scope of phenomenon, knowledge and verifiability, and pursue to transform and transcend traditional philosophy with the spirit of positive science; Marx, however, thought after the rejection of metaphysics, philosophy should scrutinize the existence of human beings, deeply criticize the alienated living condition of man, and pay close attention to the emancipation and all-around development of man. To that end, Marx pursued to establish a new philosophical form, that is, "materialism, which has now been perfected by the work of speculation itself and coincides with humanism" (Marx).

In this way, the theoretical theme of philosophy was transformed by Marx from "how the world is possible" to "how human emancipation is possible". The exploration into "how human emancipation is possible" guided Marx to discuss the existence noumenon of man, turning the focus of philosophy from the noumenon of universe to the existence noumenon of man. "Man is the world of man" (Marx). The discussion about the existence noumenon of man then impelled Marx to probe into how to change the world, thus turning the focus of philosophy from "how knowing the world is possible" to "how transforming the world is possible". In consequence, Marxist philosophy terminated traditional philosophy, namely metaphysics.

"Throughout the history of philosophy, Platonic thoughts always play a crucial role in variable forms. Metaphysics is Platonic. Nietzsche labels his own philosophy as the reversed Platonism; along with the reversal of metaphysics accomplished by Karl Marx, philosophy reaches its most extreme possibility and enters into its final stage". Heidegger is fairly insightful by saying so. This opinion actually indicates the relationship of Marxist philosophy respectively with traditional western philosophy and modern philosophy. When Marxist philosophy turns the focus of philosophy from the noumenon of universe to the existence noumenon of man and comprehends and grasps the relationship between man and world based on human activity, it also marks the theme transformation of philosophy, i.e. from traditional to modern. The modern western philosophy emphasizes, in general, "the real life world" and the mode of being of man. In Jaspers' words, "the objective of philosophy is striving to comprehend the reality of man in the practical situation". Even postmodernism also tries to take human activity as the starting point, and undertakes "the mission to build a relationship between man and his sciences, discoveries and the world – a concrete world" (Foucault). With respect to content but not manifestation mode, the operation of modern western philosophy is, generally but not individually, directed by the theme transformation realized by Marxist philosophy. From my point of view, no matter whether other schools of modern western philosophy have realized or acknowledged, Marx is, indeed, the terminator of traditional western philosophy and the pathfinder of modern philosophy, and Marxist philosophy is modern materialism.

Rereading Marx makes me realize that Marxist philosophy is the ontology of existentialism, i.e. practical ontology.

As soon as Marx turned his eyes from "how the world is possible" to "how human emancipation is possible", from the noumenon of universe to the existence noumenon of man, he started to seek the basis for comprehending, interpreting and grasping the existence of man. At last, this basis was discovered, that is, practical activity. According to Marx, men keep their survival during their transformation of nature by exploiting instruments and realize their self-development during practice; therefore practice is the foundation for their living, and constitutes the special life form of mankind, i.e. the mode of being and the existence noumenon of man. In this sense, Marxist philosophy is the ontology of existentialism.

Besides, Marx reveals man makes nature "the social nature" through practice and thereby creates a "two-in-one" human world of nature and society for himself. Practice is the fundamental path and real foundation for differentiating and uniting the world-in-itself and the human world, and plays a guiding role in the movement of human world, viz., men "set the mind for Heaven and Earth" and rebuild the world by means of practical activity. "An animal forms only in accordance with the standard and the need of the species to which it belongs, whilst man knows how to produce in accordance with the standard of every species, and knows how to apply everywhere the inherent standard to the object. Man therefore also forms objects in accordance with the laws of beauty" (Marx). Practice constitutes the noumenon for the existence of human world. That is to say, practice is the noumenon both of human existence and human world. In this sense, Marxist philosophy is practical ontology.

The revolutionary change caused by Marxist philosophy in the history of philosophy is initiated and developed at the level of ontology, and the key point is its scientific resolution of the ontological issue – the relationship between man and nature. From the viewpoint of Marx, man does activity and enters into relation with nature in the mode of thing during practice, and what he obtains is the existence of nature or substance in the mode of human being, namely "humanized nature" and "thing-for-me". To put it another way, practice makes the relationship between man and nature a relationship that "exists for me" (Marx), which is a negative contradictory relation: for the purpose of maintaining his existence – affirming himself, man must take negative actions towards nature, i.e. changing the original ecology of nature, and making it "humanized nature" and "thing-for-me". As a result, the relationship between man and nature becomes the relationship between subject and object, both of which are a bidirectional movement: while continuously transforming and creating nature during practice, man is also transforming and creating himself, including physical organization, thinking structure, and social relations. They are the two aspects of a same process. That's why Marx thinks that "the coincidence of the changing of circumstances with human activity or self-changing can be conceived and rationally understood only as revolutionary practice".

It should be mentioned that the relationship that "exists for me" between man and nature is the most profound and complicated contradictory relation among all sorts of contradictory relations. This contradictory relationship "has made countless heroes bow in homage", renders materialism "powerless and frustrated" with respect to the subjectivity of man, and makes materialism standing far from dialectics and the materialistic view of nature "so near to yet so far from" the materialistic conception of history. The wisdom of Marx consists in his "unity" be-tween materialism and human subjectivity, between materialism and dialectics, and between the materialistic view of nature and the mate-rialistic conception of history, respectively, through in-depth and com-prehensive analysis on practice and scientific resolution of the relation-ships of man with nature and society.

In Marxist philosophy, the authority of practice is all-around, which does not only exist in epistemology, but can also be found in the view of nature, the conception of history, and dialectics: with respect to the view of nature, practice, as the foundation for the differentiation and unity between nature itself and humanized nature, sublates the binary opposition between man and nature; in respect of the conception of his-tory, practice constitutes the mode of being of man and the essence of society as the cornerstone for the "two-in-one" unity between "natural history" and "historical nature", and shatters the myth of the opposition between "material nature" and "spiritual history"; in dialectics, practice serves as the foundation for the differentiation and unity respectively between subjective dialectics and objective dialectics and between nat-ural dialectics and historical dialectics, whose conflicts are genuinely resolved by practice since practice itself contains the negative dialec-tics; and in the aspect of epistemology, practice constitutes the basis of cognition, and "the method of practical reflection", as the fundamental feature of Marxist epistemology, fills the gap between general episte-mology and historical epistemology.

Just because of the ontological significance of practice, Marx conceives "thing, reality and sensuousness" not only in the form of object, but also "as practice, the human sensuous activity" "subjectively". The focus of Marxist philosophy is not the so-called "ultimate being" of world, but what makes the existence of "thing, reality and sensuousness" what it is. "Thing, reality and sensuousness" are generated in the practical ac-tivity of man, so "it is a question of revolutionizing the existing world, of practically attacking and changing existing things" (Marx). The practical ontology of Marx is directed to "the existing world" and tar-geted at "revolutionizing the existing world", in order to eliminate the alienated living condition of man. Hence, Marx brings ontology from "Heaven" down to "Earth", and combines ontology with the sufferings and happiness in the world, thereby opening up "a path of conceiving the reality through ontology" and making an ontological proof for the emancipation of the proletariat and all mankind.

I do not agree with the opinion that Marx has not discussed the issue of ontology and Marxist philosophy is only a world outlook but
not ontology. This is an unprincipled confused idea. There is no such a
philosophy that does not have its ontology, and at least it has "ontological commitment". Marxist philosophy certainly has its own ontology.
Marx has dealt with ontology in his *Doctoral Dissertation* on the aspects of "the proof of ontology" and "the determination of ontology"; in
Economic and Philosophical Manuscripts of 1844, he brings forth "the
issue of the affirmation of ontology", and argues "man's feelings, passions, etc., are not merely anthropological phenomena in the (narrower)
sense, but truly ontological affirmations of being (of nature)"; and in
The German Ideology, he centrally expounds the issue of the existence
of man, which is actually the issue of ontology. Lukacs correctly points
out that though Marx does not write any works specialized in ontology,
Marxist philosophy "is the exposition about existence, i.e. the pure ontology, in the ultimate sense".

In my opinion, the fundamental difference between the ontology of
Marxist philosophy and the traditional ontology is that the latter conceives and grasps the issue of beings in an abstract sur-real manner, but
the former, the practical ontology, comprehends and grasps the existence of human beings based on practice, interprets the significance of
beings based on the existence of man, and also highlights the fundamental feature of beings – historicity.

Rereading Marx shows me that historical materialism is a world outlook, and Marxist philosophy is historical materialism.

Apparently, historical materialism merely studies human society or human history, seemingly unrelated with nature, but the problem is that
society is formed and developed in the process of material exchange
between man and nature, which constitutes the realistic foundation for
human society. This point is why historical materialism is "materialistic"; meanwhile, for the purpose of the material exchange between man
and nature, men must exchange their activities with each other and enter into definite social relations. This point is the theoretical feature of
historical materialism. In Marx's view, the living practical activity and
actual daily life of man always involve, and are embodied by, the relationships or contradictions respectively between man and nature and
between man and society. "The history of nature and the history of men
are dependent on each other so long as men exist" (Marx), namely that

the relationship between man and man is restricted by the relationship between man and nature, and vice versa. Marx had consciously realized such "identity of nature with man", and pursued to change the relationship between man and man by changing the relationship between man and nature and change social relations by sublating the appropriating relationship (private ownership) of man to material. The basic issue focused on and to be solved by historical materialism is the relationships of man with nature and society.

History is essentially the development of practical activity of man in time. In the words of Marx, history is no other than the activity of man who is pursuing his own objectives. For this reason, "history" in the concept of historical materialism refers to the sphere where human activity and inner contradictions thereof, i.e. the contradictions between man and nature and between man and society, are developed. A new theoretical space, a self-contained and complete, materialistic and dialectical picture of world, is shown by historical materialism by exploring the relationships between man and nature and between man and society, namely the relationship between man and world. This means that historical materialism is not only a conception of history, but more importantly, a "materialistic world outlook", "actually a critical view of the world" (Marx). In my opinion, dialectical materialism and practical materialism are different expressions of this "critical view of the world".

Social life is essentially practical, and practical activity itself is a "negative dialectics". So, as the philosophical reflection of social life, historical materialism connotes "negative dialectics", and is the unity between materialism and dialectics. Dialectics is essentially critical and revolutionary. Regarding dialectical materialism as a different expression of historical materialism, the "critical view of the world", highlights the dialectical dimension contained in historical materialism and its critical and revolutionary characters. That is to say, in Marxist philosophy, there is no an independent dialectical materialism as theoretical basis, or an independent historical materialism with the nature of application. Additionally, deeming practical materialism as another expression of historical materialism highlights its dimension of practice and its primacy and fundamentality. Thus I further understand the profound connotation of the proposition that "historical materialism is the first great discovery of Marx".

I have experienced three stages before getting such a new overall cognition on Marxist philosophy:

The first stage is from the 1980s to the early 1990s. During that period, I thought that historical materialism was not a complete philosophical morphology but just Marx's philosophy of history, a philosophy of history uniting historical ontology with historical epistemology. In 1990, I published an article titled *Principle of Constructing the Modern Morphology of Historical Materialism* in *Academic Monthly*, and in the article, I explicitly proposed a quite novel viewpoint that historical materialism was the unification of historical ontology with historical epistemology; however, it was based on an unconscious theoretical precondition – dialectical materialism was the theoretical basis of historical materialism.

In the second stage from the late 1980s to the late 1990s, I thought Marxist philosophy was practical materialism, and declared that practical materialism was never "isomorphic" with "dialectical materialism". In my article *Practical Materialism: the Modern Morphology of Materialism* published in *Philosophical Trends* in 1989, I clearly brought forward the opinion that Marxist philosophy was practical materialism, and in the article *On the Practical Materialism of Marx* published in *Journal of the Academic World* in 1990, I elaborated the basic features of practical materialism in a relatively comprehensive way. Since then, I had insisted on that opinion until the end of the twentieth century. I intentionally skirted around the relationship between practical materialism and historical materialism in that period. However, the "integration" of Marxist philosophy was impossible to be completely realized as long as that problem was not resolved. Hence, I started to review the theoretical space of historical materialism again.

Since the beginning of the twenty-first century, I has had a new apprehension on the properties and functions of historical materialism, that is, historical materialism itself is a complete philosophical morphology and a world outlook, and Marxist philosophy is historical materialism. In 2001, I published an article *A New Look at the Historical Morphologies of Materialism and the Theoretical Space of Historical Materialism* in *Academic Research*, and expressly stated that evaluated based on the essential issue of theoretical theme's historical transformation, the development of materialism goes through three historical stages, forming three historical morphologies, i.e. natural materialism, humanistic materialism and historical materialism. This opinion is re-stated and further elaborated in my article *Historical Materialism: A Re-thinking* published in *Hebei Journal* in 2003, in which I also com-prehensively demonstrate that historical materialism is a self-contained and complete, materialistic and dialectical world outlook.

"It is, therefore, the task of history, once the other-world of truth has vanished, to establish the truth of this world. It is the immediate task of philosophy, which is in the service of history, to unmask self-estrange-ment in its unholy forms once the holy form of human self-estrange-ment has been unmasked. Thus, the criticism of Heaven turns into the criticism of Earth, the criticism of religion into the criticism of law, and the criticism of theology into the criticism of politics" (Marx). As "the philosophy in the service of history", historical materialism aims to "overthrow all relations in which man is a debased, enslaved, aban-doned, despicable essence, relations" and realize the "reduction of the human world and relationships to man himself" (Marx). Starting out from "living human individuals", taking changing the world as its own duty, and aiming at "rebuilding individual property" and "establishing personalized individual", historical materialism shows a dual care for the real existence and the ultimate being of man, which is the most exciting care in the entire history of philosophy. I resolutely repudiate such a viewpoint that historical materialism "sees only the material fac-tors and ignore the human ones".

I cannot agree with such an opinion that historical materialism has been "outdated" since it is traced back to the Victorian era, which is 150 years ago. This is a "pride and prejudice", a senseless pride and preju-dice. We should not judge whether a theory is "outdated" or not, or or whether it is true or not, according to its establishment time. A "new" theory is not necessarily true, whereas an "old" one is not necessarily false. Archimedes' principle was established ages ago, but today's ship-building, no matter how developed it is, can go against it in no case. If it does so, the ship built is doom to wreck, no matter how "modern" the ship is. Owing to the profound grasp of the relationship between man and world and the general law of human social development, historical materialism, though founded in the mid-nineteenth century, transcends the specific times of the nineteenth century; just because the issues it focuses on and resolves coincide with the major ones in the contem-porary world, historical materialism has an inherent contemporary significance.

In a certain sense, Marx who is resting in peace in London's Highgate is more attractive to the world than Marx who was immersing himself in writing in the British Museum. Due to Marx, I deeply realize that what "dying yet not perishing" means. From the times when Sartre put forward that "historical materialism is the sole unsurpassable philosophy of our times" to the year when Jameson declared that Marxist philosophy is "the untranscendable semantic horizon" in contemporary times, the time span indicates again that historical materialism is still the truth and conscience of our times. At present times, it is doomed to be powerless to resist historical materialism with structuralism, existentialism, Freudianism, new historicism, neo-liberalism, neo-conservatism, postmodernism, post-colonialism, or post-Marxism. In my eyes, such a resistance is just like that of Pompeii against the magma of Mount Vesuvius that year.

Journal *Theory Front* has once published a signed article, saying that my interpretation paradigm of Marxist philosophy "provides a new way for comprehending Marxist philosophy, breaks through the traditional system of Marxist philosophy, and has a groundbreaking significance for the reform and construction of Chinese philosophy system". I think I am overrated, and I really do not deserve this, but I do have my own opinions on Marxist philosophy. I do not resolve the "integration" of Marxist philosophy in a fundamental manner, but I do provide a new path for resolving it and the relationships between dialectical materialism, historical materialism, and practical materialism. Maybe this path is not passable, but "the man who points a blocked road does a good thing for us just like the one who points the correct way" (Heine).

Marx is not an "eminent monk in desert" who hides Buddhist allegorical words in his heart and speaks gatha; on the contrary, he acts as a philosopher and a revolutionist in perfect combination. Marxist philosophy is not "academism", which discusses principles and theories away from the reality; on the contrary, it is the philosophy interpreting and changing the world in perfect unity; "its achievements are so great that it shocks even rain and wind and moves even the gods". Therefore Marx cannot only be reread from text to textology, from philosophy to the history of philosophy, but more importantly, from theory to reality, and then from reality to theory. I persistently believe that philosophy should not merely become the "conversation" between philosophers or the "soliloquy" of an individual philosopher, and instead, it must "have conversation with" reality. So my rereading of Marx was carried out during the "conversation" with reality.

The most essential reality of China at present is reform and opening-up and modernization. The most prominent feature and most significant meaning of such a social practice is that it concentrates three major social transformations, namely modernization, marketization and socialist reform, into the same era and space, forming an extremely special, complex, difficult, unprecedented, magnificent and great social transition. It will inevitably give rise to a series of significant and profound philosophical problems, and provide an extensive social space for the philosophical thinking of men. Any rereading is fundamentally aroused and activated by reality. Personally speaking, I reread Marx under the promotion of the reform and opening-up and modernization of contemporary China, especially the practice of socialist market-oriented economy. In this process of rereading Marx, Marx is walking towards us as he is "alive". On the aspect of time, Marx is becoming more and more distant from us, but spatially, he is closer and closer to us. In a word, Marx is still alive and always with us.

The impressions of obscureness and irrelevance to reality that philosophy gives to us are caused by its demonstration mode, namely that philosophy is formally manifested as an abstract movement of concepts. The key point is that behind such an abstract concept is the issue of realty, meaning that the demonstration mode of philosophy is abstract, but its issues are realistic. Even postmodernism, which seems to be preposterous and embraces "language-game theory", is in fact a reflection of "postmodern society". In the words of Jameson, postmodernism is "an attempt to think the present historically in an age that has forgotten how to think historically". It is true that philosophy should ascend from the Earth to "Heaven", i.e. entering the pure concept realm, otherwise it cannot be called philosophy; however, philosophy must also fall from "Heaven" to the Earth to face reality, otherwise it will be like the rootless duckweed. Philosophers should not do as a spider does – spinning a web and then appreciating the delicate "web of speculation" made by themselves, and also should not "be caught in their own trap", be isolated with reality on their own initiative, pursue "dispassionate self-examination", or mutter "awe-inspiring incantations that no one understands" (Marx). I think the philosophical discourses produced in such case are "superfluous".

The "conservation" of philosophy with reality for sure contains the "conservation" with politics. Philosophy is not politics, and philosophers are not politicians; some philosophers try every means to get away from and even divorce themselves from politics. However, philosophy is impossible to be separated from politics, and it always implies politics in its particular way. As Jaspers says, "philosophy is inseparable from either politics or the consequences of politics". On the other hand, politics also needs philosophy. Either in history or in reality, a political transformation tends to be guided by a philosophical one. If Marxist economics is considered as political economy, Marxist philosophy is political philosophy in a certain sense. In fact, philosophy is both an intellectual system and an ideology, which pursues both truth and a certain faith; it always reflects definite social relations and the interests, aspirations and requirements of a definite class or social group through an abstract conception system, so does straightforward and fiery French enlightenment philosophy, intricate and obscure classical German philosophy, or enigmatic deconstructivism. In the words of Derrida, deconstructivism challenges the established historical tradition and real political structure by deconstructing the established discourse structure.

Any philosophy has its specific political background, implies politics more or less, and assumes this or that political effect. Of course, the theoretical significance of a philosophical proposition is not equivalent to its political effect, but it is beyond doubt that philosophy has political effect anyway, and the same philosophical proposition will have different political effects under different historical conditions. Practice is the fundamental criterion for testing truth. This is a "common-sense" proposition of Marxist philosophy. However, in the social life of China in 1978, it turned into a strongly political proposition that gave a huge political effect and decisive influence on the development of contemporary China. Philosophy cannot become the loud hailer or pleadings of any politics, because it is relatively independent; it also should not be far away from or even divorced from politics in that its unity with times is realized in the first place by its political effect. As far as I'm concerned, only with philosophical consciousness and keen political vision can a philosopher really understand and grasp reality.

Philosophy should not only go deep into but also surpass reality. It is impossible for a philosophy that only adapts to reality to look far ahead. It is the conscience and mission that contemporary Chinese philosophers should assume to, by generally grasping the reform and opening-up and modernization of contemporary China, arouse philosophical thinking on the nation's modes of living, life and thinking and values, as well as social development, and in turn, guide the movement of reality with Marxism with Chinese features oriented to the 21st century.

At bottom, the Sinicization of Marxist philosophy is to combine it with the specific reality of China, use it to analyze problems in reality, and turn real problems into philosophical ones, and meanwhile to analyze traditional Chinese philosophy with Marxist philosophy, absorb its essences, and creatively transform traditional Chinese philosophy to fuse it into Marxist philosophy, thereby making Marxist philosophy "have a national form". If Marxist philosophy, this foreign culture, does not "have a national form", it cannot be Chinesized; if it cannot be Chinesized, it will be hard for it to take root, blossom, and yield fruits on the old land of China.

The Sinicization of Marxist philosophy is not to simply translate the original category of Marxist philosophy into the category of traditional Chinese philosophy, or translate contradiction into *Yin* and *Yang*, law into Taoism, substance into *Qi*, communist society into "society of great harmony" … These are just language games. It is also not to adapt Marxist philosophy to traditional Chinese philosophy and use the latter to "transform" the former, because the adaptation and transformation in this way will only "hollow out" Marxist philosophy and change it into the so-called "Confucian Marxism". We must know that Marxist philosophy is the fruit of modern industrial civilization and traditional Chinese philosophy and Confucianism are the product of ancient agricultural civilization. It was the victory of new-democratic revolution rather than Confucianism and traditional philosophy that saved China and prevented Confucianism and traditional philosophy from declining along with the downfall of early modern Chinese society and nation. It is not Confucianism and traditional philosophy that lead the war-worn, poor and backward China to the world, but is the reform and opening-up and modernization that introduce Confucianism and traditional philosophy into the world. Without the great achievements of the reform and opening-up and modernization, there will be no Chinese nation realizing its great rejuvenation, no China being increasingly powerful, not to mention Confucianism being world-renowned.

Above is my mental journey of rereading Marx, as well as my new cognition on Marxist philosophy during this journey.

Obviously, this cognition of mine is different from the Marxism "well-known" to people, from the "common sense". The problem is that well knowing does not mean truly knowing, and common sense "is the mode of thought of its time", and "contains the prejudices of its time" (Hegel). Thus a peculiar condition arises – what is the most familiar to people is inclined to be least understood by them. I cannot "go with the flow". So I reread Marx, and obtain the above cognition different from "common sense". I do not think my cognition has fully restored the "true colors" of Marx, or my interpretation is completely consistent with the text of Marxist philosophy. I know very well that the reasonability of the saying that "all history is contemporary history", and that my cognition is restricted by my personal philosophical accomplishment, intellectual structure and values, but I have to point out that the above cognition is the result of my exploration over thirty years and also my heart portrayal and honest record of my rereading of Marx. At this point, I "speak with no fear, speak the words that the predecessors dare not to say" (Lu Xun).

"Everyone should pioneer his own way" (Sartre). In the process of rereading Marx, The theoretical goal I'm pursuing is the unity of innovation seeking with truth seeking; the theoretical form I'm pursing is poetic language and rigorous logic; the theoretical state I'm pursuing is constructing the space of philosophy, and molding the individuality of thinking. However, I know well that "my ability falls short of my wishes", and I am also aware of all the defects in my philosophical accomplishment, intellectual structure and values. I sincerely welcome all well-meaning criticisms and censures, but as to any vicious taunt and attack, my reply cannot be anything but:

"I want to faithfully stay on my own earth … I am my own Hell and Heaven." (Schiller)

APPENDIX II

MARX: FROM "HEAVEN" TO "EARTH"*

— About McLellan's book *Karl Marx: A Biography*

Journalist: Professor Yang, China Renmin University Press recently published *Karl Marx: A Biography (Illustrated Edition)* written by British scholar David McLellan, and that book had been included into *Collected Translations of Studies on Marxism*, which is very influential in the domestic academic circle. That series of books was first planned by you. Could you talk about your original intention to plan it?

Yang Geng: Indeed the first planner of *Collected Translations of Studies on Marxism* was me, and at that time I was the chief editor of China Renmin University Press. Only one book in that collection of translations was published before I was transferred out of China Renmin University, and that book was Derrida's *Specters of Marx*. Later, thanks to the efforts of Comrades Li Yanhui, Gao Zilong, Yu Keping and Zheng Yiming, that series of books was constantly enriched and really exerted a great influence in the academic circle. As the initial planner of the *Collected Translations of Studies on Marxism* and a researcher of Marxism, I should say thank you to Comrade Li Yanhui and other relevant comrades.

To summarize my reason to plan the *Collected Translations of Studies on Marxism* in one sentence: Marxism is still the truth and conscience of our times, and still a "dominant theory" in our times.

Marxism was founded in the mid-nineteenth century, one century and a half from now, but we should not judge whether a theory is "outdated" or not, or whether it is true or not, according to its founding time. A new theory is not necessarily true, whereas an old one is not necessarily a fallacy. Today's shipbuilding, no matter how developed it is, can go against the Archimedes' Law in no case. If the Archimedes' Law

---

*) Originally appeared in China Education Newspaper, July 27, 2006, and the subheading is altered when included into this book.

is violated, the ship built is doom to sink, no matter how "modern" it is. Owing to the profound grasp of the general law of human social development, the capitalist mode of production, and the movement law of capitalist society it produces, Marxism, though founded in the mid-nineteenth century, transcends the specific times of the nineteenth century. As McLellan says in *Karl Marx: A Biography*, "for over a century, Marxism has become such a language: millions of people use it to express their hope for a fairer society". That's why I say that Marxism is still the truth and conscience of our times.

No matter whether it is in China and other foreign countries, Marxism is still a "dominant theory", even after the drastic changes in Soviet Union and East Europe. International Marx conference is convened every year, and the works about the studies of Marxism is being published in an immense number every year. We must bear in mind that Marx was not born in the East but in the West, and the homeland of Marxism is not the East but the West. However, though its homeland is the West, Marxism does not exclusively belong to the West, but to the whole world, as the cultural heritage of human beings. So Marxism should be studied in an omni-bearing manner, and we should use the positive achievements of contemporary western Marxism research for reference. "There are other hills whose stones are good for working jade".

This is my original intention to plan the *Collected Translations of Studies on Marxism*.

Journalist: The *Collected Translations of Studies on Marxism* is a series of books composed of academic works. Why a biography is brought into such a collected translations of study? What do you think is the largest feature of *Karl Marx: A Biography?* And what is its academic value in the research field of Marxism?

Yang Geng: Biography is generally regarded as literary works, but the book *Karl Marx: A Biography* of McLellan is not a life biography in ordinary sense, and more importantly, it is a thought biography. McLellan is a famous contemporary western expert of Marxism research, and has a high academic attainment. His *Karl Marx: A Biography*, to put it in philosophical terms, is the unity between history and logic. It is not only the life biography but also the thought biography of Marx; it does not only expound the development course of Marx's thoughts from the angle of history, but also elaborates how Marx founded Marxism from the perspective of logic. Therefore it is appropriate to include such a biography into the *Collected Translations of Studies on Marxism*.

In my eyes, the greatest characteristic and most attractive point of this biography is that it describes a "reasonable and appropriate" "image" of Marx from a multi-dimensional perspective, taking the lifetime career of Marx as premise, the whole western histories of society and thoughts as background, the text or original works of Marx as basis, and questions as the clue.

According to the limited materials accessible to me, there had been no biography of Marx covering the main aspects of his life since Mehring published *Karl Marx: the Story of His Life* in 1918. Then McLellan published *Karl Marx: A Biography*, which focuses on the main aspects of Marx's life, i.e. personal life, political life and spiritual life. McLellan dissects how Marx changed his thoughts, how he turned from an issue to another, and how he turned from a field into another. For example, what issues Marx had studied and left in 1844, which issues among those left by Marx in 1844 had been resolved in 1845, and what new problems arose … This book leads us into an interesting reading step by step like this. For another example, while evaluating *Economic and Philosophical Manuscripts of 1844*, McLellan thinks, "after summing up his concept of communism like this, Marx then divides his exposition into three specific aspects: the historical foundation, social features and respect for individual of communism." Then he points out that *Economic and Philosophical Manuscripts of 1844* "are further developed in the later economic works, especially in *A Contribution to the Critique of Political Economy* and *Das Kapital*. These later economic works, without doubt, explores the themes of *Economic and Philosophical Manuscripts of 1844* in a more systematical and meticulous way and against an extremely pure economic and historical background; nevertheless, the core enlightening thoughts – the alienation of man in capitalist society and the possibility of his emancipation – remain unchanged."

Here, Marx as an ideologist stands vividly revealed on the paper. Besides, through this *Karl Marx: A Biography*, we perceive the "present" image of McLellan as an expert of Marxism research.

McLellan is a responsible scholar. In *Karl Marx: A Biography*, he does not only deeply explore the "hot" issues in the studies on Marx's thoughts, but also emphasizes meticulously analyzing the classical works of Marx, especially deeply and comprehensively analyzing Marx's "four major manuscripts", namely "Manuscripts of the Critique on Hegel's Philosophy of Right of 1843", "Economic and Philosophical Manuscripts of 1844", "Manuscripts of the German Ideology during 1845 – 1846" and "Manuscripts of Das Kapital during 1857 – 1858", in accordance with new materials in hand.

These "four major manuscripts" were not published before Marx's death and mostly released from the 1920s to the 1930s. We cannot apprehend Marx without them. McLellan knows this fact, so he points out in *Karl Marx: A Biography*, "The several books of Marx published in the 1930s have changed people's cognition on Marx's theoretical contributions to a very large extent." In terms of the achievement in the analysis on Marx's four major manuscripts, and of the application and analysis of new materials, McLellan's *Karl Marx: A Biography* is incomparable by any other biographies of Marx, which is also one of the characteristics of *Karl Marx: A Biography*.

I cannot say that the *Karl Marx: A Biography* of McLellan has thoroughly grasped Marx in all aspects, but it is by no means superficial. Especially after the drastic changes in Soviet Union and East Europe and under the new situation in 1995, McLellan "wrote at a sympathetically critical stance", and tried to "present a reasonable and appropriate image (of Marx)", "completely cover three main aspects in Marx's life – personal, political and spiritual" and reflect his persistent belief in and incisive analysis on Marx's thoughts. You can disagree with the author's opinion, but you should but admire the careful exploration of the author in such a broad field; you may not appreciate this picture, but its colorfulness will certainly light up your passion of exploration in this or that respect.

Journalist: People always have different evaluations on Marx over more than one century. *Karl Marx: A Biography* of McLellan also exposes some weak points of Marx as human. You are a famous expert of Marxism research in China, so I want to know how you think about Marx.

Yang Geng: It is normal that the evaluations on Marx are different. For more than a century, the "image" of Marx is constantly changing; the longer he leaves us, the more the cognitions on him are diverged, just as the farther a man goes away, the more vague his image is. This is the first point I want to mention.

The second point I want to say is: there is such a phenomenon frequently happening in history that a great ideologist always tends to arouse the attention of people again after his death and a relatively long historical movement, or people will turn to study some opinions or the entire thought system of this ideologist, reevaluate their theoretical value, and form different schools due to the disputes and different ideas during this process. This is the destiny of Aristotle, Kant and Hegel, as well as of Marx.

Thirdly, different intellectual structures, values, life experiences and class stands of people determine their evaluations on Marx are different. McLellan notices this point, so he points out in *Karl Marx: A Biography*, "Many books discussing Marx are cut and polished by various political tomahawks. It is impossible to pretend to make a completely 'neutral' description for the life of anyone, let alone for the life of Marx. There are a large amount of evaluations and information about Marx, and the selection of anyone itself shows a definite standpoint."

As to the "weak points in human nature" of Marx exposed in *Karl Marx: A Biography*, as you mentioned above, if I have correctly understood, you mean that it is said in the book that Marx had ever been put in confinement due to intemperance and fighting at his young age, Marx had a bastard with Helene Demuth, and so forth. I think here involve some problems: first, we cannot textually prove whether Marx had a bastard or not, or make a paternity test on that bastard; second, even though Marx had these or those "weak points of human nature", it is quite normal in that everyone has weak points, and Marx had said, "I have everything that a human being possesses"; third, the purpose of McLellan to "expose" these details in Marx's life is for highlighting a lively "image" of Marx, or in his own words, "for presenting a reasonable and appropriate image (of Marx) to readers, and avoiding two extremes – idolizing or smudging".

Marx is a human being rather than a celestial being; he may be compared to Prometheus rather than God. Everyone has weak points, and a man without weak points does not exist. At least up to now, we haven't found that any great personage is free of weak points. So the so-called weak points of Marx in human nature exposed in *Karl Marx: A Biography* are quite normal in my eyes. How old was Marx when he wrote *The Communist Manifesto*? Less than 30 years old. As a Chinese saying goes, at thirty, a man should be independent; at forty, he begins to be immune from perplexities; and at fifty, he knows the Decree of Heaven. At that time, Marx had not reached the year at which he "should be independent", not to mention "be immune from perplexities". The weak points of Marx have no affect on his greatness, but contrarily show us a true Marx. In this sense, *Karl Marx: A Biography* of McLellan tells us a true Marx, and brings Marx from "Heaven" down to "Earth".

Journalist: Marx has left us for more than a century, and his theories are confronted with setbacks and disputes during practice. Under the background of globalization and market-oriented economy, what values and significances does Marx have?

Yang Geng: The theories of Marx succeed in some countries but was frustrated and even failed in some other. This is very normal, because history does not move linearly, let alone that some countries may not correctly understand Marxism in their process of Marxist practice. For instance, the goal pursued by Marx in his lifetime is the emancipation of the proletariat and all mankind, and the supreme idea of Marxism is the free and all-around development of man. It is clearly stated in *The German Ideology* that the proletariat must be established as "personalized individual". *The Communist Manifesto* further points out that the fundamental feature of the new society in future is that "the free development of each is the condition for the free development of all". This opinion is restated in *Das Kapital*, that is, the new society in future aims at realizing the free individuality of man. Such an important thought, or to say, fundamental principle, has been neglected by us for many years.

Lenin had written the free and all-around development of man into the democratic program of Russian society in 1902, but he lived in the times of revolution, so he laid more stress on class struggle and dictatorship of the proletariat and less directly touched upon the free and all-around development of man. In the history of international communist movement, it is Chinese Communists that consciously and clearly realized the promotion of the all-around development of man is the essential requirement of Marxism for establishing the new society of socialism and explicitly assert that socialist society should be people-oriented. In his speech at the meeting of the 80th anniversary of the founding of the CPC in 2001, Comrade Jiang Zemin clearly put forward that the promotion of the all-around development of man is the essential requirement of Marxism for establishing the new society of socialism. Later, Comrade Hu Jintao clearly brought forward the people-oriented, scientific outlook on comprehensive, balanced and sustainable development. After the historical movement over one century and a half, based on repeated summarization of the experience of international communist movement and socialist practice, we finally really realize that the orientation to people or the all-around development of man is the supreme proposition of Marx.

We are now conceiving Marx against the background of globalization. As a matter of fact, Marx expressly puts forward the transformation of national histories into world history and forms Marx's theory of world history in *The German Ideology* and *The Communist Manifesto*. Marx argues capitalism and its large-scale industry has "produced world history for the first time", during which not only world market but also "world literature" were formed. Marx's theory of world history can serve as a theoretical guide for us to correctly conceive globalization. His theory of world history, as far as I'm concerned, is actually a kind of globalization theory, or globalization theory is originally an important theory of Marxism that we have ignored for years. After the 1990s, along with the deepening of China's reform and opening-up and modernization, with the expansion of globalization, we finally find out that there is a theory of world history or globalization in Marxism.

The background of market-oriented economy is more needless to say. Marxism was founded against the background of market-oriented economy. Marx did not only acknowledge its positive effects, but also criticizes its negative ones; he had made both fact and value judgments on market-oriented economy. In short, market-oriented economy creates personal independence founded on objective dependence.

Marx's theory of market-oriented economy provides us with scientific methodology for correctly judging the advantages and disadvantages of market-oriented economy and carrying out the practice of socialist market-oriented economy. I do not agree with such an opinion that in the wake with the establishment of Chinese system of market-oriented, Marx has gone away from us. On the contrary, I believe that along with the deepening and expansion of China's practice of market-oriented economy, Marx is getting closer and closer to us, rather than farther and farther. In the words of Jameson, a famous contemporary western scholar, Marxism still has a "shocking sense of space".

Marxism was compared by Mao Zedong to telescope and microscope. The former shows that Marxism can help us to look things that have existed but beyond our sight with a broad and long-term view; the latter indicates that Marxism can help us to perspicaciously see things that are extraordinarily tiny and also beyond our sight. The three historical trends at present, i.e. modernization, globalization and socialist movement, have been initially formed in the times of Marx, who has made profound insights into them and deeply set forth their internal correlations. I appreciate McLellan's viewpoint that "the history of Marxism walking through the nineteenth century is an inseparable eternal part of mankind's pursuit for the new mode of common life". Marxism does not only profoundly change the historical course of human beings, but it is also a greatly significant participant and powerful impeller of contemporary development. Under the background of globalization and market-oriented economy, we still need Marxism, this telescope and microscope.

Journalist: But some people think that the answers to many contemporary problems cannot be found in Marxism.

Yang Geng: The failure to find the answers to contemporary problems in Marxism cannot be attributed to Marx, but to the ignorance of the scientific nature of Marxism. Marx is Prometheus rather than God, and Marxism is science rather than the Revelation. Marxism does not, and is unwilling to, "anticipate the world with their dogmas", and it is impossible for Marxism to provide answers to all social problems in future. The doctrine that boasts itself of omniscience is theology rather than science. The vitality of Marxism does not consist in its specific conclusion or prediction, but in its revelation of the general law of human social development and the movement law of capitalist society, as well as its anticipation of the basic rules of socialist society and its methodology.

For example, Marx criticized capitalist market-oriented economy, but did not propose to establish the system of socialist market-oriented economy. In other words, socialist market-oriented economy was beyond the horizon of Marx, and it was Deng Xiaoping that proposed to establish the system of socialist market-oriented economy. Hence, Marxism is fundamentally a scientific methodology, which only provides the starting point of further study and the method for it instead of a ready answer. We can only expect Marxism to do what it can do according to its scientific nature, but should not ask it to do what it cannot do.

Journalist: China Renmin University Press has repackaged McLellan's *Karl Marx: A Biography* with a view to letting more readers access to Marx and making the academic biography popularized with illustrations and pictures. What do you think about the significance by doing this?

Yang Geng: I have just said that McLellan's *Karl Marx: A Biography* is more a thought biography. In my view, by repackaging it and inserting illustrations and pictures into it, China Renmin University Press has made a good try in making academics popular, in bringing Marx from "Heaven" down to "Earth". This "illustration edition" tries to popularize academics, make "inscrutable knowledge" accessible to ordinary people, and let people know the life details and distinctive features of Marx. To put it philosophically, the textual expression with illustrations enables people to know Marx, his times and his relations with his contemporaries in the unity of perceptual cognition with conceptual cognition, and to grasp the thoughts of Marx during this process.

Marxism is not "academism", and one of the important features of Marxism is its character of "to the masses". Marx has said that together with the thoroughness of the historical action, the size of the mass whose action it is will therefore increase, and theory is capable of gripping the masses as soon as it demonstrates *ad hominem*. For this reason, Marxism should not be confined within books or to rostrums, and instead, it must enter the mind of the masses. Theory also becomes a material force as soon as it has gripped the masses. The illustration edition of *Karl Marx: A Biography* published by Renmin University Press, in my opinion, is for the purpose of bringing Marx close to the masses, and letting them know Marx and know that Marx is a human being rather than a celestial being and Marxism is science rather than the Revelation. However, we should notice that its academic connotation must be maintained during popularization, which should not be realized at the cost of degrading its academic level.

Journalist: You just said that *Karl Marx: A Biography* is a popular academic work, but ordinary readers may not have a knowledge background as profound as yours to read it. Do you think it is abstract and obscure to ordinary people?

Yang Geng: I should say that there are temporal, spatial and theoretical differences between *Karl Marx: A Biography* and general readers. For general domestic readers, to understand this book, they must know the lifetime career of Marx at least and make certain theoretical preparations in advance, such as reading some books that introduce Marx's thoughts. Though its illustration edition published by Renmin University Press aims to help readers to read in the unity of perceptual cognition with conceptual cognition, certain theoretical preparations are still necessary. As Marx has ever said, the most beautiful music has no sense for the unmusical ear.

In fact, a good piece of work should not only adapt itself to the masses but also guide them. It will be impossible to leave a good name forever if it merely adapts to the masses. Any doctrine is the product of definite times, but if it only adapts to its times, it will be impossible to look far ahead and aim high. Any biography having the connotation of thought should not only cater to the masses but also guide them, which is an interactive process.

Experience itself is wealth. The same motto has different connotations in different persons' words. The same novel or biography gives different feelings to different readers. As for the same *Karl Marx: A Biography*, it is for sure that its readers will have different feelings on account to their different experiences, academic backgrounds and standpoints. But anyway, *Karl Marx: A Biography* of McLellan is beneficial to us.

APPENDIX III

THREE MAJOR TOPICS IN CURRENT STUDIES ON MARXIST PHILOSOPHY*

The research field of Marxist philosophy is a realm of questions. Almost all basic opinions of Marxist philosophy are faced with severe challenge, and the studies on them are significantly different. Among all kinds of discussions, the relationship between Marxist philosophy and western Marxism, the Sinicization of Marxist philosophy, and the idea of constructing the Chinese Marxology fundamentally restrict the tendency of current studies on Marxist philosophy. As three major topics in current studies on Marxist Philosophy, they need to be studied and reviewed carefully.

Western Marxism: Positive Enlightenments and Negative Affects

Since the 1990s, there are more and more translations of western Marxist texts, larger and larger scope of study, and higher and higher evaluation on it, so that the impression that only "western Marxism" is "true Marxism" is generated. Some even say that among all the schools of Marxist philosophy, western Marxist philosophy is the most influential and representative, and only western Marxists really understand, study and propagate Marxist philosophy as a modern philosophy. From my viewpoint, this opinion sees some reasonable facts, but understands these reasonable facts unreasonably.

Since Stalin's *Dialectical and Historical Materialism* was set as authority, the Soviet model of Marxist philosophy had reigned for several decades. Over half a century, at the mention of Marxist philosophy, people would think of dialectical and historical materialism. It was through western Marxism that we knew other nominations, other interpretations and other grasps of Marxist philosophy. Although western Marxism was generally criticized in the domestic circle of Marxist philosophy in the first several years after it entered into China, it still exerted a silent transforming influence. The studies respectively on humanism and alienation, on subjectivity and practical materialism, on epistemology and aesthetics, and on intercourse and social ontology, as well as cultural philosophy,

*) Originally appeared in Chinese Social Sciences, 2007 (5).

existence philosophy, theories of everyday life, etc., were all inspired by western Marxism from their discussion topics to their basic arguments.

As the studies on western Marxism is deepened, more and more scholars notice that the significance of western Marxism, in the first place, does not lie in its proposal of new names and features of Marxist philosophy, but in its method for interpreting Marxist text. For instance, the totality method of Lukacs and Korsch enlightens us that the classical Marxist texts should be grasped as a whole instead of being simply divided into philosophical, political economic and scientific socialism. The symptomatic reading of Althusser tells us that we should not stay at the literal meaning while reading Marxist philosophy, but should try to pursue its framework of issues and discover the secret aspects concealed by appearance; the deconstructive reading of Derrida inspires us that there is tension and conflict even in the same text of Marxist philosophy, so we should be good at deliberating the cracks and gaps therein.

All of these enlighten us that believing Marxism is science is one thing, but studying it scientifically is another. Only by adopting scientific and rigorous interpreting method can we completely grasp the text of Marxist philosophy and avoid interpreting out of context or catching the meaning of words literally. Needless to say, the research paths of Chinese scholars since the 1990s, such as "rereading Marx", "returning to Marx", "approaching to Marx", and "entering into Marx", all have been directly or indirectly enlightened and influenced by western Marxism, and have yielded heartening fruits.

While sufficiently acknowledging the significance of western Marxism and its enlightenments to Chinese studies on Marxist philosophy, we should also soberly realize its limitations and its negative impact on Chinese Marxist philosophy.

Having a variety of schools, western Marxism itself is a contradiction, in which we can find multiple faces of Marx, such as Hegelian Marx, Freudian Marx, Existential Marx, Structuralist Marx, Marx of analytic Marxism, and so forth. All of these editions offer us multiple options for conceiving and grasping Marxist philosophy, but the final answer needs to be chosen by ourselves. In a certain sense, an integral Marxist philosophy is broken up in western Marxism. We therefore should think actively based on our specific times context and social practice in order to deeply and meticulously differentiate western Marxism.

In regard to the application of Marxist philosophy, western Marxism had gone through an expansion from method to horizon. Lukacs interpreted Marxist philosophy more from the angle of dialectics; after Sartre, western Marxists more viewed Marxist philosophy as a horizon, an unavoidable horizon for interpreting contemporary thought and society. In that process, the understandings of western Marxism on Marxist philosophy took a great change and even widely diverged, but they had a certain common view, that is, regarding Marxist philosophy as a critical force and a heterogeneous existence. It is indeed commendable to regard Marxist philosophy as the source of critical force, but unfortunately, the criticisms of western Marxism either on capitalism and modernity are more manifested as cultural criticism, literary criticism, and even symbolic and rhetorical criticism today, and thereby go all the way down towards nothingness and decadence. In my opinion, such criticisms are hard to be considered as the inheritance and development of Marxist critical theory.

With respect to the judgment on the value of Marxist philosophy, western Marxism had gone through the transition from science to philosophy, and then to narrative. Till Jameson and Derrida, western Marxism more and more became a project for finding new, better, more interesting, and more fruitful manners of discourse. On the positive side, western Marxism provides some ideal typical constructions; but on the negative side, it lacks materialization and reality, and almost becomes a pre-modern saga. In this sense, though western Marxism gives us these or those enlightenments, it does not point a realistic direction for social development. Even the enlightenment dialectics of Frankfurt School is a false dialectics in essence. Its critique on technical reason and market-oriented economy is at most applicable to developed countries and well-off society to a certain degree, but for us, it more has a utopian ironic meaning.

After Frankfurt School, western Marxists are all university professors without exception and have no connection with revolutionary practice. In their writings, epistemology, methodology and aesthetics take a proportion much higher than economics and politics, making western Marxism the critique in studies to a great extent. As Perry Anderson said, western Marxism was "to speak its own enciphered language", and "the first and most fundamental of its characteristics has been the structural divorce of this Marxism from political practice"[1]. Derrida has realized this, so he specially points out in *Specters of Marx* that we should not return to Marx as if he is a great classical philosopher and finally subsume him into great philosophical tradition, because this will lead to the risk of domesticating and neutralizing Marxian revolutionary instructions.[2] This opinion is quite incisive.

Western Marxism has important enlightening significance for us to get rid of the dogmatic understanding on Marxism, but overestimation on it will hinder our further thinking: generally discussing the height of western Marxism is useless for our studies and may in turn render the internal tension and conflict of Marxism obscured. Western Marxism does have some profoundness, but meanwhile it also has many romantic inappropriate thoughts.

To put it bluntly, western Marxism has a very positive significance for us to interpret Marx in that it pioneers a broad semantic space and provides various possible trains of thought for the apprehension of Marxist philosophy. However, if western Marxism is looked up to as the "supreme realm" and "best angle of view" of Marxist philosophy, it is a bit too disregardful of other foreign schools of Marxist philosophy and too ignorant of the work in the circle of Chinese Marxist philosophy. As to how to conceive the purport of Marx's thoughts and how to grasp Marxist philosophy fundamentally and generally, Chinese Marxists have given, and will continue to give, positive answers.

Sinicization of Marxist Philosophy: Modernization or Traditionalization

Globalization has been advancing irresistibly since the 1990s, and at the same time, the identity of national culture becomes prominent. Globalization and nationalization as two sides of the same process, together with the coexistence of "global consciousness" and "root-seeking consciousness", bring about again people's review and reflection of the social development of China in the twentieth century, and directly bring how to understand and grasp the Sinicization of Marxist philosophy to the front of Chinese Marxist philosophy.

---

1 Perry Anderson, *Considerations on Western Marxism*. Beijing: People's Publishing House, 1981: pp. 44 and 41.
2 See Derrida, *Specters of Marx*, pp. 45 – 46.

It is generally thought that the Sinicization of Marxist philosophy covers two aspects: firstly, combining Marxist philosophy with the specific practice of China, and secondly, combining Marxist philosophy with traditional Chinese culture and philosophy. There is no divergence in the domestic circle of Marxist philosophy in respect of the first aspect, and the core of divergence and dispute rests with how to conceive the second aspect, namely how to combine Marxist philosophy with traditional Chinese culture and philosophy.

For a long time, we are accustomed to think this combination is mainly to explore positive thought resources from traditional Chinese culture and philosophy and interpret them in a Marxist way. Taking the phrase "seeking truth from facts" for example: this phrase, with origin found in the *History of the Han Dynasty*, originally meant to men should seek truth and reality according to factual materials, and evolved into a proposition of philosophical epistemology in the Qing Dynasty, and then raised to the height of world outlook and methodology by Mao Zedong, who determined it as the fundamental method of the CPC to grasp the national condition of China, and to work out and implement correct routes, guidelines and policies. In current discussions, this opinion is reduced by some scholars to "transforming" traditional Chinese culture and philosophy with Marxist philosophy, and they also correspondingly propose to "transform" Marxist philosophy with traditional Chinese culture and philosophy. Thus, probing into the rejuvenation of Confucianism and its impact on materialistic dialectics and exploring the Chinese cultural root of Mao Zedong become the basic contentions of some papers.

From my point of view, it is difficult to Chinesize Marxist philosophy without combining it with the essences of traditional Chinese culture and philosophy, and also difficult to modernize Chinese philosophy if adhering stubbornly to traditional culture and philosophy and using them to "transform" Marxist philosophy. The Sinicization of Marxist philosophy is meanwhile the modernization of Chinese philosophy, both of which are two sides of the same process. It is an indisputable fact that Marxist philosophy, as the product of modern industrial civilization, and traditional Chinese philosophy, as the result of ancient agricultural civilization, belong to two entirely different cultural systems. Entering the twentieth century, the fundamental mission of Chinese society was to save the country, ensure survival, and seek for the transformation into modern society. Marxism and its philosophy introduced into China had played a tremendous times effect, just because it belongs to modern civilization. So far as we soberly realize that the Sinicization of Marxist philosophy is the modernization of Chinese philosophy, the opinion that the Sinicization of Marxist philosophy is to "transform" Marxist philosophy with traditional Chinese culture and philosophy will collapse of itself, and the opinion that we can remold Marxist philosophy with traditional Chinese culture and philosophy will be extremely ridiculous.

The Sinicization of Marxist philosophy is never to adapt Marxist philosophy to traditional Chinese culture and philosophy, because the adaptation in this way will only "hollow out" Marxist philosophy and change it into the so-called "Confucian Marxism"; the Sinicization of Marxist philosophy is also by no means to simply translate the categories, i.e. translating contradiction into *Yin* and *Yang*, law into reason, substance into *Qi* ... These are just language games. The Sinicization of Marxist philosophy, at bottom, is to combine it with the actual problems confronting China and turn real problems into philosophical ones, thereby making it an epistemological method for analyzing and resolving problems, and meanwhile to use Marxist philosophy to analyze and criticize traditional Chinese culture and philosophy, absorb their essences, and creatively transform them so as to fuse them into Marxist philosophy, thereby making Marxist philosophy "have a national form" "so that its every manifestation has an indubitably Chinese character"[3].

There is another issue involved by the Sinicization of Marxist philosophy that has not gotten enough attention of us so far, namely that the masses of people are necessary to practically realize the Sinicization of Marxist philosophy. To this end, Marxism needs to take on "the fresh, lively Chinese style and spirit which the common people of China love"[4]. In my eyes, this is a significance issue concerning the properties and characteristics of Chinese revolution and construction. The Chinese revolution and construction, having nothing to do with the minority cultural nobles and social elites, is a great social change through which the masses of people pursue national liberation and free individuality. "It would be a sheer illusion to try to build a socialist society on the ruins of the colonial, semi-colonial and semi-feudal order ... without the liberation and the development of the individuality of hundreds of millions of

3   *Selected Works of Mao Zedong*. Beijing: People's Publishing House, 1991: 2nd Ed., Vol. 2, p. 534.
4   *Selected Works of Mao Zedong*. 2nd Ed., Vol. 2, p. 534.

people"[5]. For this reason, we should widely mobilize the masses, follow the mass line, and make Marxist philosophy take on "the fresh, lively Chinese style and spirit which the common people of China love".

The problem is that during the specific implementation, we are faced with a tough problem, that is, whether the masses of people are the subject of revolution and construction or the object of enlightenment and education.

"Awakening China" had been the consensus of the persons of insight since the late Qing Dynasty. Chinese Marxists took over such an important historical mission, and consciously realized that "together with the thoroughness of the historical action, the size of the mass whose action it is will therefore increase"[6]. The mass makes history and change the world, therefore all our routes, guidelines and polices must come from the mass and go to the mass, which is the basic meaning of Marxist mass line. Since the masses of people are the subject of the reform and opening-up and modernization in contemporary China, can they be treated as the object of enlightenment and education? We are always emphasizing "propagandizing the mass", "mobilizing the mass", "organizing the mass", and striving to get close to the mass; however, "the mass" as the incarnation of "historical justice" is an abstract signifier in the final analysis. It is ridiculous to assume an air of cultural elite in front of the masses of people, but "receiving the reeducation from the poor and lower-middle peasants" also has many problems. In the discussion about the Sinicization of Marxist philosophy, we should, and must, also make historical combing and realistic grasp of that issue.

The Sinicization of Marxist philosophy concerns a series of problems like scientization, nationalization and popularization. It is an important topic of Chinese studies on Marxist philosophy to comprehensively cognize and correctly grasp the Sinicization of Marxist philosophy. We should know that it was the victory of Chinese revolution rather than Confucianism and traditional culture that saved China and prevented Confucianism and traditional culture from declining along with the downfall of early modern Chinese society and nation; it is not Confucianism and traditional culture that lead the war-worn, poor and backward China to the world, but is the reform and opening-up

---

5   *Selected Works of Mao Zedong.* Beijing: People's Publishing House, 1991: 2nd Ed., Vol. 3, p. 1060.
6   *Karl Marx and Friedrich Engels.* 1st Chinese Ed., Vol. 2, p. 104.

of contemporary China and the great rejuvenation of Chinese nation that introduce Confucianism and traditional culture into the world and make it possible for traditional Chinese culture and philosophy to revive. Without powerful China, there will be no Confucianism being world-renowned. The Sinicization of Marxist philosophy requires us to, based on the needs of times, practice and the masses of people, evaluate, clean, absorb and carry forward traditional Chinese culture and philosophy rather than to "transform" Marxist philosophy with traditional Chinese culture and philosophy, let alone to honor Confucius and read scriptures.

Chinese Marxology: Philology or Textology

Since the 1990s, a series of changes have happened in the Chinese studies on Marxist philosophy. On the one hand, the call for "rereading Marx" is increasingly louder, and on the other side, "the thinkers are fading out, while the scholars are highlighting". Under such a background, some scholars hammer at increasing the academic taste of the studies on Marxist philosophy and appeal to the circle to return to the academic level and view Marxist philosophy as a pure academic object. In consequence, the construction of Chinese Marxology is put into the agenda at the beginning of the new century.

In general, foreign Marxology is the combination of philology with textology, interpreting text based on literature research. However particular it is, Chinese Marxology cannot exclude philology and textology.

In terms of philology, there is no Marx database, no professional research team of classical literatures of Marxist philosophy, and no original-text identifying experts of classical literatures of Marxist philosophy in the strict sense in China. This is really incommensurate to the huge research teams of Marxist philosophy in China. As a result, it is exceedingly necessary to rapidly promote the philology related to Marx studies. But how long we can go along this road has yet to be tested by time. With respect to textology, i.e. the interpretation of Marxian text commonly mentioned, it has been steadily carried out and continually promoted at least since the reform and opening-up, and the interpretation is based on classical texts of Marxist philosophy all along and relatively familiar with the progress of foreign philology related to Marx. Since the 1980s, a large number of translations of foreign Marxian literatures have been published in journals presided by the Central

Compilation & Translation Bureau, including *Compiled and Translated Materials of the Works of Marx and Lenin, Research Materials of Marxism-Leninism, Researches on Marx and Engels, Researches on Marx, Engels, Lenin and Stalin*, etc. All of these translations play a significant role in boosting Chinese studies on Marxist philosophy and facilitating the establishment of the discipline of Marxist philosophy history. Although western Marxology, the same with western Marxism, was regarded as heresy attacking Marxism during a period, both still broaden the horizon of Chinese scholars, and more or less influence our interpretation on the text of Marxist philosophy, which will be further promoted particularly by the introductions of MEGA2 (Marx-Engels-Gesamtausgabe 2) and new progress in foreign Marxology in recent years.

The interpretation on the text of Marxist philosophy cannot be realized without philology as the foundation. The research on the firsthand original textual information is vitally important, and any serious scholar will not deny this. But the problem is that there is no linear relation of causality between edition research and textual interpretation or thought elucidation. Edition research is necessary, but its rigorousness does not necessarily guarantee the objectivity of interpretation and the thoroughness of thought study. Edition research falls under positive science, but textual interpretation can hardly be subsumed into positive science, and thought elucidation is completely subject to hermeneutic efforts. As foreign studies on Marxian literatures are constantly deepened, the textual information of Marxist philosophy may assume "falsifiability", so that it may more and more "approach" the original textual structure of Marx, but this does not equal the objectivity of the interpretation on Marxian text.

At this point, there are always fierce academic disputes within foreign Marxology. Since the 1960s, the theory of "opposition between Marx and Engels" had prevailed among western scholars, but after 1980s the theory of "consistency" suddenly arose. The opinion change from "opposition" theory to "consistency" theory did not result from the discovery of new literatures or the rearrangement of existing literatures, but from the divergence in thought elucidation. For Chinese researchers of Marxist philosophy, it is inconsiderable to frequently talk about "according to Taubert ..." or "Taubert points out ...". Is Inge Taubert forever correct? Does she always know the truth and make no faults?

Weren't the editions before Taubert compiled and edited by western scholars of Marxology? Though, of course, they could be thought as the outdated scholars of Marxology compared with Taubert.

Regarding the history of foreign Marxology, in the 1920s, Ryazanov first put forward the concept of "Marxology" during the period when he was in charge of the Soviet Research Institute of Marx and Engels, and laid stress on treating Marx and studying Marxian literature and thoughts with a strictly scientific attitude in a bid to establish a special rigorous science. His efforts were valued by the party and country of the Soviet Union. It was pointed out in the resolution of the Central Committee of Soviet Union Communist Party (Bolshevik) on June 14, 1929 that the Soviet Research Institute of Marx and Engels had become "the sole scientific research institute of Marxology in the world", which "is the great achievement of the Soviet working class".

Although Ryazanov was deprived of the position as the President of the Soviet Research Institute of Marx and Engels in 1931, the study on Soviet Marxology was continued. In the Soviet Union, the literatures of Marxist philosophy were abundant beyond comparison, and the Soviet Union had taken the lead in publishing many literatures of Marxist philosophy, such as *Critique of Hegel's Philosophy of Right, The German Ideology*, and so on; Soviet scholars had made a lot of fruits in the researches of edition and historical fact, and there were a group of excellent experts of literature research. However, scientific philology did not result in objective textual interpretation in the Soviet Union, and there arose ideological models of textual interpretation and thought analysis, as well as rigid far-reaching Soviet textbook system of Marxist philosophy. The problem may be caused by these or those reasons, but anyway, it is an indisputable fact that there is a considerable distance between philology and textology.

Classical works should be continuously reread. In the history of thoughts, "rereading" is a common phenomenon, for example, Hegel reread Plato, Peirce reread Kant, and Goethe reread Raphael … The history of philosophy is, to a certain extent, the history during which the descendants unceasingly "reread" the predecessors, so the history of thoughts and the history of philosophy are "rewritten" or changed constantly, so is the history of Marx. The problem is that after the later 1990s, some domestic researchers of Marxist philosophy refer too much to and blindly follow modern western philosophy and western

Marxism while interpreting Marxian text. The papers titled the study on Marxist philosophy actually get Marx lost in the matrixes of modern western philosophy and western Marxism.

It is beyond doubt that introducing in foreign Marxology and its achievements have a positive significance. However, we should not exceed the proper limits in correcting a wrong. It is a bit too extreme to set foreign Marxology against domestic Marxology, praise the former whereas depreciate the latter, and think the former is pure academic study while the latter takes words too literally and interprets out of context. For example, the contribution of Lukacs, the founder of western Marxism, is certainly a discovery of doctrine, which, however, is based on textual interpretation; with respect to Althusser, who has opposite views with Lukacs, his basic judgments are also made from textual interpretation. Then, who is right between Lukacs and Althusser? Furthermore, it is unadvisable to run after western Marxism and too excessive to follow the leadership of western Marxology.

The positioning of Chinese Marxology does not lie in whether it is philosophy or science, but in whether it is philology or textology. If it is positioned as philology, it will face numerous difficulties, because Chinese scholars do not have basic conditions for literature research of originality within a certain period; if it is positioned as textology, it is not too different from existing research methods, and the only difference is that it specially stresses the importance of academic study based on text, focuses on material collection and the verification of publishing condition, and pays close attention to the combing of the writing process of classical texts and the exploration and analysis of textual structure.

In my opinion, it is necessary to attach importance to the working progress of foreign philology related to Marx and systematically sort out and introduce the research fruits of western Marxology, but is totally unnecessary to blindly follow and excessively believe in foreign philology related to Marx. We should be aware of the fact that the great influence of Marxist philosophy on the whole world is not because it is pure academism or it has pure academic value, but because it is the philosophy of transforming the world, and transforms the theoretical theme of philosophy from "how the world is possible" to "how human emancipation is possible". Thus, if Marxist philosophy is studied as a pure academic object, its tremendous times effect cannot be revealed.

I also do not appreciate "interpreting Marxism with the viewpoints in the original works of Marx and Engels". No matter whether to find out a sentence or some sentences from the text of Marxist philosophy and then "reconstruct" or "restructure" it or them according to one's own viewpoint or to preset a basic logic of Marxist philosophy and then use it to guide the interpretation of Marxian text, it is of no use in my eyes, and cannot fundamentally settling the issue of sticking to and developing Marxist philosophy.

In the history of thoughts, any "rereading", "reconstruction" or "restructuring" are at bottom activated by real practical activity. To insist on and develop Marxist philosophy, we should not only face the text of Marxist philosophy, but more importantly, the reality. The largest reality of contemporary China is the reform and opening-up and modernization. The most prominent feature and most significant meaning of such a social practice is that it concentrates three major social transformations, namely modernization, marketization and socialist reform, into the same era and space, constituting an extraordinarily special, complex, magnificent and great social transition. It will inevitably give rise to a series of significant and profound philosophical problems, and provide an extensive social space for our philosophical thinking. The contemporary Chinese researchers of Marxist philosophy cannot really understand Marx and Marxist philosophy unless they base themselves on this "text".

APPENDIX IV

A NEW UNDERSTANDING OF THE PHILOSOPHICAL TRANSFORMATION REALIZED BY MARXIST PHILOSOPHY*

The founding of Marxist philosophy is doubtlessly a revolutionary reform in the history of philosophy. In my opinion, the essence of this reform consists in the theme transformation of philosophy realized by it, from "how the world is possible" to "how human emancipation is possible". At the same time, the focus of philosophy is also turned from the noumenon of universe to the existence noumenon of man, from interpreting the world to changing the world.

Transforming from "how the world is possible" to "how human emancipation is possible"

A philosophy is the essence of the spirit of its own times. To really understand the theme transformation of philosophy from "how the world is possible" to "how human emancipation is possible" realized by the founding of Marxist philosophy, we should grasp the characteristics of the times which Marx faced and lived in.

The times which Marx faced and lived in was the times when capitalism was established and solidified in Western Europe and human history entered capitalism from feudalism, and meanwhile the times of transformation respectively from agricultural civilization to industrial civilization, from natural economy to commodity economy, and from "personal dependence" to "personal independence founded on objective dependence". The problem is that while winning great victory, the bourgeoisie also brought a huge social problem for themselves – the irreconcilable contradiction between production socialization and private ownership of the means of production, resulting in alienations of human labor, human social relations, and the human world. In other words, the living condition of men was alienated, and the world was made "a reversed world". To be specific, in capitalist society, "the devaluation of the world of men is in direct proportion to the increasing value of the world of things.", and the alienation of material and the self-alienation of man is the two sides of one process. According to Marx, under such an alienation condition, capital has individuality while individual does

*) Originally carried in Guangming Daily, May 19, 2009.

not – the individuality of man is dissolved; man becomes "isolated man", and state is nothing but "an illusory community".

It is thus clear that the western society in the mid-nineteenth century was a society in which the living condition of man was totally alienated by capital relations, and unmasking and eliminating that alienation was "the immediate task of philosophy, which is in the service of history"[7]. But traditional western philosophy, including classical German philosophy, was unable to fulfill that "immediate task". This is because traditional western philosophy, in general, is "metaphysics", i.e. a theory concerning the nature of transcendent being, which separates noumenon from human activity and from various urgent survival problems confronting human beings while "seeking the highest reason", thereby making being an abstract being, substance an "abstract substance", and noumenon an abstract thing-in-itself unrelated to real man and his activity. It is impossible to cognize real man and his reality by starting from such an abstract thing-in-itself. Traditional western philosophy existing in the form of "metaphysics" conceives "thing, reality and sensuousness", as well as truth, kindness and beauty, based on the "ultimate being" unrelated to real man and his activity, so what it shows to men is virtually abstract truth and kindness. Such "metaphysics" seems to give men a kind of hope, but it actually conceals the sufferings in reality and comforts the people oppressed, thus being incapable of eliminating the alienated living condition of man and saving real man out of the predicament.

Just because of that, Marx argued as natural sciences became independent and "marked out their independent fields", as the development of society made "real beings and earthly things the center of all interest", philosophy should fall from "Heaven" to "Earth", and pay attention to the elimination of the aliened living condition of man and to the emancipation of mankind. Marx had ever asserted, "(Metaphysics) It will be defeated forever by materialism, which has now been perfected by the work of speculation itself and coincides with humanism."[8] It is no other than Marx that erects a bridge between dialectics, humanism and materialism and makes the three "coincide". This "materialism, which has now been perfected by the work of speculation itself and coincides with humanism", is essentially Marxist philosophy.

---

7   *Selected Works of Karl Marx and Friedrich Engels.* 2nd Ed., Vol. 1, p. 2.
8   *Karl Marx and Friedrich Engels.* 1st Chinese Ed., Vol. 2, pp. 159 – 160.

We should see that Marxist philosophy is not general abstract human-ism which is concerned with the destiny of general abstract man. Marx finds that if the majority of the population, the oppressed people, such as workers and labors, are not offered with real interests and freedom, the emancipation of mankind is just an empty talk, and even a fraud. Therefore he puts forward the issue of "radical revolution, the general human emancipation", which transcends "political revolution", and be-lieves only the proletariat can assume the historical role of "emancipa-tor" and fulfill this historical mission. From Marx's point of view, the proletariat is a class needing to emancipate itself and showing "the com-plete loss of man"; meanwhile, the proletariat is a class which "can win itself only through the complete re-winning of man", and which cannot emancipate itself without emancipating the all mankind. In the process of human emancipation, philosophy finds its "material weapon" in the proletariat, so the proletariat finds its "spiritual weapon" in philosophy; if the proletariat is the "heart" of human emancipation, then philosophy is the "head" of this emancipation. An unclear "head" cannot establish the real goal of human emancipation, or understand the real connotation of this emancipation.

Hence, philosophically exploring the connotation, purpose and approach of human emancipation in combination with economic study and his-torical investigation becomes the primary work of Marx, and the fruit of this work is the establishment of the "philosophy in the service of history", namely Marxist philosophy. Theoretically, the essential feature of Marxist philosophy is that it takes the proletariat and human emancipa-tion as its theme, and answers "how human emancipation is possible".

Turning from the noumenon of universe to the existence noumenon of man, from interpreting the world to changing the world

To answer "how human emancipation is possible", Marx must probe into the mode of being or existence noumenon of man, and shifts the focus of philosophy from the noumenon of universe to the existence noumenon of man.

From the viewpoint of Marx, "the first premise" of human history is the existence of "living human individuals"; for existence, "living human individuals" need to do the activity of material production and produce material life itself first of all. The activity of material production is "the first premise" of human existence, "the first historical activity" of man.

Basically, man realizes his self-shaping, self-change and self-development during the activity of material production. Marx points out men "begin to distinguish themselves from animals as soon as they begin to produce their means of subsistence"[9]. What men are, "therefore, coincides with their production, both with what they produce and with how they produce."[10]

Man is not only a natural being but also a social being. In other words, man is the unity between natural being and social being. This unity is exactly accomplished during practical activity, and social relations immediately determining the essence of man are also generated during practical activity. Man creates his own social relations and social being through practice. To put it another way, man is a being in practice, and practice constitutes the mode of being of man, or to say, constitutes the existence noumenon of man.

Just because practice constitutes the mode of being or the existence noumenon of man, the living condition of man is not invariable, but is in continuous construction and change. The alienation of man's living condition and its sublation happen and finish in the process of practical activity, and "the medium through which estrangement takes place is itself practical"[11]. In capitalist society, labor, this alienation of man's life activity, renders the relationship between man and man shown as the relationship between materials; man is governed by objects instead of controlling them; man's own activity becomes an alien power opposed to him.

Through the critique on capitalist private ownership, Marx reveals the social attribute of man concealed by the natural attribute of object and the relationship between man and man concealed by that between materials, and pursues to eliminate the alienated living condition of man and "establish personalized individual" by means of "revolutionary practice". If we say the proletariat and human emancipation are the theoretical theme of Marxist philosophy, "establishing personalized individual" and realizing free and all-around development of man are the supreme proposition of it.

---

9   *Selected Works of Karl Marx and Friedrich Engels.* 2nd Ed., Vol. 1, p. 67.
10   ibid., p. 68.
11   *Karl Marx and Friedrich Engels.* 1st Chinese Ed., Vol. 42, p. 99.

To answer "how human emancipation is possible", Marx must probe into the existing world or the real world and its noumenon, and turns the focus of philosophy from interpreting the world to changing the world. In Marx's view, "man is the world of man", real man lives in the real world, and the existing world is composed of humanized nature and human society, social nature and natural society.

On the one hand, the existing world is generated in the practical activity of man, and nature and society in the existing world are integrated also in the practical activity of man. Practice plays the role as a converter, through which society infuses its objective into nature, making it the social nature, and meanwhile, nature enters society and converts into a constant factor in society, making society the natural society. Practice constitutes the foundation and base for the existence of existing world, and plays a guiding role in the movement of existing world; that is to say, men "set the mind for Heaven and Earth" by means of practice, and rebuild the world on the basis of material practice. "So much is this activity, this unceasing sensuous labor and creation, this production, the basis of the whole sensuous world as it now exists"[12]. Practice constitutes the noumenon of existing world.

On the other hand, after taking its shape, the existing world in turn restricts and even determines real man and his activity. How the state of real man will be coincides with how the condition of existing world is. In order to change the man in capitalist society and his alienation, capitalist society must be changed first; to change real man, the real world should be changed first. So Marx pays attention to "the real world of his times", and holds that "for the practical materialist, i.e. the communist, it is a question of revolutionizing the existing world, of practically attacking and changing existing things"[13]. In this sense, Marx thought philosophers were interpreting the world in different ways, but the problem was to change the world.

"The coincidence of the changing of circumstances with human activity or self-changing can be conceived and rationally understood only as revolutionary practice."[14] In the horizon of Marxist philosophy, practice is not only the existence noumenon of man but also the noumenon of existing world; it is the realistic approach to the change of existing

---

12   *Selected Works of Karl Marx and Friedrich Engels.* 2nd Ed., Vol. 1, p. 77.
13   *Selected Works of Karl Marx and Friedrich Engels.* 2nd Ed., Vol. 1, p. 75.
14   Ibid., p. 55.

world and the elimination of man's alienation, the real approach to "personalized individual", the ultimate state of the existence and development of man. Thus, Marxist philosophy realizes the unity between realistic concern and ultimate concern about man. This dual concern is the most exciting realistic concern about the existence and value of man in the whole history of philosophy.

Answering "how human emancipation is possible" from the perspective of world outlook

The issue of human emancipation is not a matter of science but a matter of "hominology". In fact, it is a world outlook of how to view and treat the relationships of man with nature and society, i.e. the relationship between man and world. Marxist philosophy grasps man in his dual relationship with nature and society, and answers "how human emancipation is possible" from the perspective of world outlook.

In Marx's opinion, a "living human individual" always exists in his dual relationship with nature and society. "The production of life, both of one's own in labor and of fresh life in procreation, now appears as a double relationship: on the one hand as a natural, on the other as a social relationship."[15] In the existing world, relationship between man and man is restricted by the relationship between man and nature, and vice versa.

"The object as being for man, as the objective being of man, is at the same time the existence of man for other men, his human relation to other men, and the social behavior of man to man."[16] That is to say, in the existing world, "objective" being is in effect the existence of man, and behind the relationship between "object" and "object" is the relationship between man and man, or we can say "object" does not only reflect the relationship between man and nature, but it also embodies the relationship between man and man. The epoch-making contribution of Marxist philosophy is that it discovers the existence of man behind "objective" being, as well as "the social behavior of man to man" and the relationship of man to nature behind the relationship between objects, and traces the significance of human practical activity from the dual relationship of man with society and nature.

---

15   Ibid., p. 80.
16   *Karl Marx and Friedrich Engels*. 1st Chinese Ed., Vol. 2, p. 52.

Practice, at bottom, is the process in which men cause, regulate and control the material exchange between man and nature through their own activity; for the purpose of the material exchange between man and nature, men must exchange their activities with each other and enter into definite social relations. The relationships of man to nature and other men are all generated during practical activity, and the practical activity of man always involve, and are embodied by, the relationships or contradictions respectively between man and nature and between man and man. As far as Marx is concerned, communism is "the genuine resolution of the conflict between man and nature and between man and man"[17].

Therefore, as "communist materialism", Marxist philosophy pays great attention to the practical activity of man and the relationships between man and nature and between man and man, namely the relationship between man and world, involved and embodied by it. Marxist philosophy is founded for practical activity that changes the existing world, and itself is a kind of theoretical reflection on contradictory relations in the practical activity of human beings. In this sense, Marxist philosophy is "the real positive science, the representation of the practical activity, of the practical process of development of men", and its basic content is from "the study of the actual life-process and the activity of the individuals of each epoch"[18]. Because it realizes that practical activity is the foundation for the relationships of man with nature and other men, Marxist philosophy strives to change the relationship between man and man by changing the appropriating relationship of man to material under private ownership, thereby realizing "reduction of the human world and relationships to man himself"[19] and the emancipation of the proletariat and mankind.

Realizing the emancipation of the proletariat and mankind and "establishing personalized individual" obsessed Marx and spiritually and directionally determined his theoretical activity throughout his lifetime. In *Economic and Philosophical Manuscripts of 1844*, Marx puts forward that communism is the positive transcendence of private property as human self-alienation, and therefore is the real appropriation of the human essence by and for man; man appropriates his "comprehensive essence" in a "comprehensive manner", that is to say, as a "whole man". In *The German Ideology*, Marx proposes to eliminate the phenomenon that "personal powers are transformed into material powers"

---

17   *Karl Marx and Friedrich Engels*. 1st Chinese Ed., Vol. 42, p. 120.
18   *Selected Works of Karl Marx and Friedrich Engels*. 2nd Ed., Vol. 1, pp. 73 and 74.
19   *Karl Marx and Friedrich Engels*. 1st Chinese Ed., Vol. 1, p. 443.

and man's own activity becomes an alien power opposed to him, so as to "establish personalized individual" and make "the individuals in a real community obtain their freedom in and through their association". In *The Communist Manifesto*, Marx also points out that communist society will be an "association", in which the free development of each is the condition for the free development of all. And in *Das Kapital*, he restates that communist society is to establish "the free individuality" of man and realize the free and all-around development of man.

So we can see that no matter whether he was in the so-called "immature" period or the "mature" period, Marx was concerned with the elimination of the alienated living condition of man and the realization of human emancipation all along. The proletariat and human emancipation constitute the theoretical theme of Marxist philosophy, and the in-depth and comprehensive investigation of this theme pioneers a path to conceiving the reality through ontology and sets up a new materialistic "critical view of the world"[20].

The value and significance of a thought or doctrine lies in the issues it brings forth, as well as the breadth and depth of the issues. "Marx went deep into the dimension of the essence of history while realizing alienation. That's why the viewpoint of Marxism on history is superior to those of other historical theories. However, Husserl failed to find out the essence of historical things from being, so did Sartre, in my opinion; therefore both phenomenology and existentialism do not arrive at such a dimension, but only in such a dimension can they be possibly qualified to talk with Marxism."[21] The evaluation of Heidegger is sincere, fair and reasonable. The issues brought forth by Marxist philosophy, that is, the elimination of the alienated condition of man and the realization of human emancipation, are indeed the essential subject of history, the issues concerning man himself, and the major issues coinciding with contemporary times. In contemporary times, the alienation of man has not been eliminated, but becomes even more violent and almost reaches the peak. In this connection, whether you agree with Marxist philosophy or not, you cannot evade or transcend the profoundness and fundamentality of the issues it puts forward – the elimination of the alienated condition of man and the realization of human emancipation. In my view, this is the essence and contemporary significance of the philosophical transformation realized by Marxist philosophy.

---

20   *Karl Marx and Friedrich Engels*. 1st Chinese Ed., Vol. 3, p. 261.
21   *Selected Works of Martin Heidegger*. Vol. I, p. 383.

APPENDIX V

SINICIZATION OF MARXISM: PROBLEMS AND ESSENCE*

The homeland of Marxism is Germany, but it does not merely belong to Germany and Western Europe and instead, it is a worldwide spiritual product generated based on the transformation of national history into world history. So it "has found representatives far beyond the boundaries of Germany and Europe and in all the literary languages of the world."[22] However, we should also know that Marxism largely reflected the traditional culture of Western Europe when it was founded, Marxist philosophy primarily reflected the traditions of classical German philosophy, Marxist economics mainly reflected the traditions of classical British economics, and socialist society more absorbed the traditions of French socialism. So if Marxism wants to take root, blossom, and yield fruits in "all the literary languages of the world", its nationalization will inevitably arise.

Engels realizes this soberly and clearly points out, "The ultimate platform of the American working class must and will be essentially the same as that now adopted by the whole militant working class of Europe, the same as that of the German-American Socialist Labor Party. In so far this party is called upon to play a very important part in the movement. But in order to do so they will have to doff every remnant of their foreign garb. They will have to become out and out American. They cannot expect the Americans to come to them; they, the minority and the immigrants, must go to the Americans, who are the vast majority and the natives."[23] That is to say, localization and nationalization of Marxism is the internal requirement of Marxism. Marxism cannot really bring its function of transforming the world into play unless it is combined with the specific reality of the corresponding state and the specific characteristics of the corresponding nation and translated into a part of the culture of this nation in a definite national form.

---

22 *Selected Works of Karl Marx and Friedrich Engels*. Beijing: People's Publishing House, 1995: 2nd Ed., Vol. 4, p. 212.
23 Ibid., p. 394.
*) Originally carried in Guangming Daily, Dec. 16, 2008.

For China, Marxism must be combined with the specific practice of Chinese revolution and construction. To this end, Marxism, this "immigrant" theory, must "have a national form" "so that its every manifestation has an indubitably Chinese character"[24], thereby "coming to" Chinese and becoming the thought weapon of Chinese people to cognize history and transform reality. Therefore the combination of Marxism with Chinese revolution and construction necessarily implies its combination with traditional Chinese culture. The process in which Marxism is combined with the specific practice of Chinese revolution and construction is the process when it is combined with traditional Chinese culture. Marxism must be combined with traditional Chinese culture; otherwise it will be hard to be Sinicizated. That's why Mao Zedong proposed that "we should sum up our history from Confucius to Sun Yat-sen and take over this valuable legacy"[25].

For a long time, we are accustomed to think the combination of Marxism with traditional Chinese culture is to explore positive thought resources from traditional Chinese culture and interpret them in a Marxist way. In current discussions, this opinion is reduced by some scholars to "transforming" traditional Chinese culture with Marxism, and they also correspondingly propose to "transform" Marxism with traditional Chinese culture. In my eyes, this is a silly unprincipled idea. The Sinicization of Marxism is never to adapt Marxism to traditional Chinese culture, because the adaptation in this way will only "hollow out" Marxism and change it into the so-called "Confucian Marxism"; the Sinicization of Marxism is also by no means to simply translate the categories, i.e. translating substance into Qi, contradiction into Yin and Yang, law into reason, communist society into "society of great harmony" … These are just language games. Fundamentally, the Sinicization of Marxism is to combine it with the actual problems confronting China, turn real problems into philosophical ones, answer them in a Marxist way, and enrich and develop Marxism with Chinese problems and their scientific answers in this process, and meanwhile to use Marxism to analyze and criticize traditional Chinese culture, absorb its essences, and creatively transform it so as to fuse it into the theoretical system of Marxism, thereby making Marxism "have a national form" and "an indubitably Chinese character". The implementation of Marxist Sinicization is inseparable from the masses of people and popularization. For this

---

24   *Selected Works of Mao Zedong.* 2nd Ed., Vol. 2, p. 534.
25   ibid., p. 534.

reason, Marxism needs to take on "the fresh, lively Chinese style and spirit which the common people of China love"[26].

From my point of view, this is a significance issue concerning the properties and characteristics of Chinese revolution and construction. The Chinese revolution and construction, having nothing to do with the minority cultural nobles and social elites, is a great social change through which the masses of people pursue national liberation and free individuality. "It would be a sheer illusion to try to build a socialist society on the ruins of the colonial, semi-colonial and semi-feudal order ... without the liberation and the development of the individuality of hundreds of millions of people"[27]. For this reason, Marxism is required to take on "the fresh, lively Chinese style and spirit which the common people of China love". During the Sinicization of Marxism, "Chinese character" and "Chinese style and spirit" are closely associated, or so to speak, integrated with Sinicization and popularization.

It is difficult to Sinicize Marxism without combining it with the essences of traditional Chinese culture, and also difficult to modernize Chinese culture if adhering stubbornly to traditional culture and using it to "transform" Marxism. The Sinicization of Marxism is meanwhile the modernization of Chinese culture, both of which are two sides of the same process. Marxism and traditional Chinese culture belong to two entirely different cultural systems in that the former is the product of modern industrial civilization whereas the latter is the result of ancient agricultural civilization. After the Opium War, the fundamental mission of Chinese society was to save the country, ensure survival, revitalize development, and seek for the transformation into modern society. Realizing modernization and reconstructing the existence mode and activity mode of Chinese nation had constituted the solemn theme of Chinese historical course since the Opium War, and embodied the thoughts, struggles, glories and dreams of several generations of Chinese. Marxism introduced into China during that period had played a tremendous times effect, just because it belongs to modern civilization. So far as we soberly realize that the Sinicization of Marxism is the modernization of Chinese culture, the opinion that the Sinicization of Marxism is to "transform" Marxism with traditional Chinese culture and establish the so-called "Confucian Marxism" will extremely ridiculous.

---

26   ibid., p. 534.
27   *Selected Works of Mao Zedong*. 2nd Ed., Vol. 3, p. 1060.

The core of traditional Chinese culture is the moral principle and ethical order with Confucianism being the main content and emphasis laid on adjustment of the relations between man and man. The traditional Chinese culture with Confucianism as its core is undoubtedly reasonable to a certain degree. Since ethical relations is a general kind of relation in human society, some rules of Confucianism are generally effective and coincident with some modern problems and have a certain modern value; besides, as Confucianism is farther and farther from the economic and political forms of feudal society that it tries hard to safeguard, the nature of its ideology becomes ever weaker, and the ideas with general meaning it implies become ever prominent. Spiritual production is different from species heredity, since race continuation based on gene as genetic material is congeneric, whereas theoretical thinking can lead to new theoretical and cultural forms through absorbing, digesting and recreating the fruits of different theories, cultures and even different disciplines. Ideal system has analyzability and reconfigurability, and ideal elements are both separable from and compatible with one another. Among the ideal elements contained in a theory or cultural form, some are inseparable from the original system, whilst some can be included into other theories or cultural forms after transformation. Thus, the **Sinicization** of Marxism should also involve the inheritance of traditional Chinese culture a nd Confucianism.

However, Confucianism is after all the official philosophy in feudal society. During the evolution from the pre-Qin period to the Western and Eastern Han Dynasties, and then to the Song and Ming Dynasties, it represented the mainstream ideology of feudal governors all along. It is antipathetic socialist market-oriented economy because it repudiates individual interest, individual independence, and personal individuality. Even the idea of "the unity of heaven and man" in traditional culture is also closely related to the ancient patriarchal ethics of China, and endows the "humanity" of patriarchal ethics with the holy halo of "the Law of Heaven". We must know that it was the victory of Chinese revolution rather than Confucianism and traditional culture that saved China and prevented Confucianism and traditional culture from declining along with the downfall of early modern Chinese society and nation; it is not Confucianism and traditional culture that lead the war-worn, poor and backward China to the world, but is the reform and opening-up of contemporary China and the great rejuvenation of Chinese nation that introduce Confucianism and traditional culture into the world and make it possible for traditional Chinese culture to revive. The Sinicization of Marxism is not to "transform" Marxism with traditional Chinese culture and construct the so-called "Confucian Marxism", let alone to honor Confucius and read scriptures. Instead, it essentially requires us to analyze and resolve the actual problems confronting China with Marxism, and during this process, to clean, transform and absorb factors with modern value in traditional Chinese culture, thereby making Marxism take on "Chinese character" and "Chinese style and spirit".

Every nation or state has its reality and special social problems in different times. We should not expect to graft a pastoral, peaceful, serene society with unsophisticated interpersonal relations onto the industrial civilization based on hi-tech, or rely upon traditional culture to resolve the problems of population, resource and environment, as well as the relationships between righteousness and interest and between individual and collective, arising during the reform and opening-up and modernization of contemporary China. We need Marxism to really settle these problems, and should not expect they can be solved by "returning to basis to open up a new road" and reinterpreting Confucianism and traditional culture. In the process of economic and political modernizations, we cannot still adhere to the traditional culture with Confucianism as core and take traditional Chinese culture as "essence" and Marxism as "function". The Sinicization of Marxism is not only the internal requirement of Marxism but also the actual need of Chinese revolution and construction, rather than a matter of being "essence" or "function". It is metaphysical to either regard traditional Chinese culture as "essence" and Marxism as "function" or traditional Chinese culture as "function" and Marxism as "essence". If "essence" and "function" are believed to be internally unrelated and optional, the result can only be the game of random assignment of the two.

In front of traditional culture, every generation faces the problem of what to inherit or what to reject, which does not only rest with traditional culture itself but with reality, with the needs of real practice. The Sinicization of Marxism must be based on reality rather than traditional Chinese culture. The largest reality of contemporary China is the reform and opening-up and modernization. The most prominent feature and most significant meaning of such a practical activity is that it concentrates three major social transformations, namely modernization, marketization and socialist reform, into the same era and space, constituting an extraordinarily special, complex, magnificent and great social transition. It will inevitably give rise to a series of significant and profound theoretical problems, and provide an extensive social space for our theoretical thinking. Only based on this reality can we really understand the modernity of Marxism, really know the modern value of traditional Chinese culture, and find out the coincidence between the modernity of Marxism and the modern value of traditional Chinese culture, thereby using Marxism to analyze and criticize traditional Chinese culture and creatively transform it, and meanwhile using traditional Chinese culture having been analyzed and criticized to creatively apprehend and interpret Marxism and make it assume "a national form", which are two sides of the same process, namely the process of the Sinicization of Marxism. What can represent the development direction of China in future is the the Sinicizated Marxism oriented to the 21st century.

APPENDIX VI

REFLECTING AND GUIDING REALITY BY MEANS OF PHILOSOPHY*

Philosophy should not merely become the "conversation" between philosophers or the "soliloquy" of an individual philosopher. A philosopher should not mutter awe-inspiring incantations that no one understands like a magician; a philosopher should not be like an "eminent monk in desert" who hides Buddhist allegorical words in his heart, speaks gatha, and prattles about wisdom; a philosopher also should not do as a spider does – spinning a web and then narcissistically appreciating the delicate web of speculation made by himself.

— Inscription

Dedicated to the Sixtieth Birthday of the People's Republic of China

In the history of China, it seems that the more ancient era is more glorious. The Song Dynasty, during which literature prevailed, the Yuan Dynasty, which focused on valiancy, the mighty Han Dynasty, the flourishing Tang Dynasty, Emperor Taizong of Tang, Emperor Taizu of Song, the First Emperor of Qin, Emperor Wu of Han, ... all of these constitute the glorious and resplendent ancient history of China. However, what goes up must come down. This is an old but ordinary truth. The development of history is always in a curve line rather than a straight one. The early modern history of China is too heavy and miserable to be opened and read – the grim and grave situation, the disaster of war, the pain of separation, the territory being ceded and indemnities being paid, the insult for a century ... "The night was long and dawn came slow to the Crimson Land; for a century demons and monsters whirled in a wild dance".

That page of history was turned finally. The victory of new democratic revolution helped Chinese people stand up and Chinese nation having experienced many vicissitudes revive. Those were days of passions,

*) Originally carried in China Education Newspaper, Sept. 24, 2009. The original title was "Philosophy: Deep into Reality and beyond Reality – Written on the Occasion of the Publication of The Rise of the Orient: A Philosophical Reflection on Chinese-type Modernization" is here in this book changed into the current one, and also the subheadings are deleted.

years of true and moving feelings … However, since 1957, the wrong theory and practice of "taking class struggle as the central task" gradually led the economy of China to the brink of collapse and the life of people into the condition of "general poverty", so that we had to "struggle again for necessities" after "the Cultural Revolution". That was a tragedy, an enormous historical tragedy.

The reform and opening-up takes China into a new age. These are the days when the wrongs are put to right, the years of solemn struggle … The Communist Party of China has led the Chinese People in writing a new splendid epic of Chinese nation's continuous self-improvement and tenacious endeavor with the spirit of undaunted perseverance and the spectacular innovative practice. The thirty years from 1978 to 2008 are just a "short span" in the human history, but in that period, earth-shaking changes had taken place on the old land of China, making a promising nation sail anew and China rise in the Orient of world.

I, from deep of my heart, understand very well that these achievements are hard-earned after the ups and downs, natural calamities and man-made misfortunes of the People's Republic of China. I love my country; I am genuinely concerned with the reform and opening-up and mod-ernization of contemporary China and deeply aware of the truth that only socialism can save China, and only reform and opening-up can develop socialism and China. "My motherland and I are like the sea and spoondrift; the sea talks to me through emotional pulse, and I share the sadness and joy of the sea". Just because of this, I dedicate *The Rise of the Orient: A Philosophical Reflection on Chinese-type Modernization* to the sixtieth birthday of the People's Republic of China.

Philosophy must make "conversation" with reality

I always hold that philosophy should not merely become the "conversation" between philosophers or the "soliloquy" of an individual philoso-pher. A philosopher should not mutter awe-inspiring incantations that no one understands like a magician; a philosopher should not be like an "eminent monk in desert" who hides Buddhist allegorical words in his heart, speaks gatha, and prattles about wisdom; a philosopher also should not do as a spider does – spinning a web and then narcissisti-cally appreciating the delicate web of speculation made by himself. The moon in water is the moon in the sky, and the person in your eyes is the person in front of you. It is indicated by the human history of philosophy that any successful philosophy, no matter whether seen from its cause or from the issues it puts forward and resolves, is very realistic, and has directly or indirectly resolved the subject of times more or less.

Philosophy seems to tower into the Heaven, but philosophers should not be otherworldly and isolated from the real society; they must conduct cognitive activity, put forward problems, and work out solutions to the problems under real conditions. The so-called advancement is nothing but the sufficient revelation of possibility. No matter how abstract and divine a philosophy is in form, it actually implies realistic problems. Philosophy should fall from "Heaven" to the Earth and focuses on real man and the reality of man; otherwise it will be neither credible nor lovable.

Philosophy should and must make "conversation" with reality, which is the foundation for the existence and development of philosophy; otherwise it will become the rootless duckweed. The most basic reality of contemporary China is the reform and opening-up and modernization. The fundamental mission of social development of contemporary China is to realize social modernization in the process of economic marketization; meanwhile, the social modernization and economic marketization are linked with socialist reform.

In other words, in contemporary China, the transformation of planned economic system into market-oriented economic system is not only the change in the mode of resource allocation but also the transformation in the mode of being of man, a significant social transformation. The most prominent feature and most significant meaning of the social transformation of contemporary China is that it concentrates three major social transformations, namely modernization, marketization and socialist reform, into the same era and space, constituting an unprecedentedly difficult, complex, magnificent and great social transition. It will inevitably give rise to a series of significant philosophical problems, and provide an extensive social space for our philosophical thinking. It is the conscience and mission that contemporary Chinese philosophers should assume to philosophically reflect the reality of the reform and opening-up and modernization of contemporary China and think and reconstruct the nation's modes of living, activity and thinking and values, and in turn to guide the movement of reality with philosophical concepts oriented to the 21st century.

There is a dual relationship between philosophy and reality: one the one side, philosophy cannot be separated from reality, and it must immediately face realistic issues when resolving the subject of times, otherwise it will become groundless; on the other side, philosophy has to enter the field of abstract conception, and reflects the movement of reality with conception movement, otherwise it can hardly be called philosophy. Philosophy must be linked with reality in a philosophical way. While being linked with reality, philosophy should not lose its independence, reflective character and criticalness, or degrade itself to the dependency of reality or just the interpreter of it. It is impossible for a philosophy that only adapts to a certain reality to look far ahead. Reality creates philosophy, and philosophy also influences reality; reality adjusts the development direction of philosophy, and philosophy also guides the movement of reality. Philosophy should not only go deep into but also surpass reality. It has been and is being proved that a political or social transformation tends to be guided by a philosophical one.

Philosophy implies politics in a unique manner

Here exists an unavoidable issue – the relationship between philosophy and politics. Philosophy is not politics, and philosophers are not politicians; some philosophers try every means to get away from and even divorce themselves from politics. However, philosophy is impossible to be separated from politics, and it always implies politics in its particular way. As Jaspers says, philosophy is inseparable from either politics or the consequences of politics. In fact, philosophy is both an intellectual system and an ideology, which pursues both truth and a certain faith; fundamentally, it reflects definite social relations and the interests, aspirations and requirements of a definite class or social group through an abstract conception system and definite cognition contents, so does straightforward and fiery French enlightenment philosophy, intricate and obscure classical German philosophy, or enigmatic deconstructivism. In the words of Derrida, the master of deconstructivism, deconstructivism challenges the established historical tradition and real political structure by deconstructing the established discourse structure. A philosophy always has its specific political background, implies politics more or less, and assumes this or that political effect.

Of course, the theoretical significance of a philosophical proposition is not equivalent to its political effect, but it is beyond doubt that philosophy has political effect anyway, and the same philosophical proposition will have different political effects under different historical conditions. Practice is the fundamental criterion for testing truth. This is a common-sense proposition of Marxist philosophy. However, in the social life of China in 1978, it turned into a strongly political proposition that gave a huge political effect and decisive influence on the social development of contemporary China. Philosophy cannot become the loud hailer or pleadings of any politics, because it is relatively independent; it also should not be far away from or even divorced from politics in that its unity with times is realized in the first place by its political effect. In my eyes, only with philosophical consciousness and keen political vision can a philosopher really understand, grasp and transcend reality and reflect the spirit of times.

True Description and Profound Reflection

The Rise of the Orient: A Philosophical Reflection on Chinese-type Modernization is divided into three parts: Part One, from Chapter I "Basic Principles of Scientific Socialism and its Practice in Contemporary China" to Chapter III "Inevitability of Socialist Revolution in Backward Countries and its Features", mainly theoretically elaborates the basic rules of socialist society, the inevitable replacement of capitalism by socialism and its historical process, and the inevitable formation of so-cialist revolution in economically backward countries and its features; Part Two, from Chapter IV "The Oriental Society and its Destiny in the World History" to Chapter XII "Deep Contradiction in the Social Development of Contemporary China: Tradition and Modernity", majorly expounds the generation of Chinese socialism and its inevi-tability, the exploration into the path of Chinese socialist moderniza-tion and its process, and the inner contradictions, fundamental impe-tus, historical role and great meaning of the reform and opening-up from the perspective of theory, history and practice; Part Three, from Chapter XIII "Deng Xiaoping Theory: Spiritual Pillar for Marxism and National Rejuvenation in Contemporary China" to Chapter XVIII "The Important Thought of 'Three Represents': Guiding China to the Twenty-first Century", mainly theoretically expounds the theoretical basis, especially philosophical basis, of socialism with Chinese char-acteristics, sets forth that Deng Xiaoping is the chief designer of the reform and opening-up and modernization of contemporary China and the founder of the theory of socialism with Chinese characteristics, and states the important thought of "Three Represents" guides China to the twenty-first century.

In this works, I strive to combine true description with profound reflection, and the penetrating power of philosophical thinking with the shocking power of philosophical critical spirit, in order to theoretically reproduce the inevitability of Chinese socialism as overwhelming as "the Yellow River from Heaven" and the arduousness of the exploration into the path of Chinese-style modernization, thereby showing the magnificent process of the reform and opening-up and modernization, the grand historical scene of how 1.3 billions of Chinese people solemnly rise in all directions, and how an ancient nation rises again in the Orient of World like a "splendid sunrise". Thus, it's not hard to understand why this book is named as *The Rise of the Orient: A Philosophical Reflection on Chinese-type Modernization*.

I had been thinking and preparing the writing of the book since 1989, and ultimately finished the writing, revision and final draft of it on the occasion that the sixtieth birthday of the People's Republic of China is coming. I cannot say that this book has great powers of conception, but it is by no means superficial. As my heart portrayal and honest record of my academic research, it condenses the fruits of my theoretical studies over 20 years, and embodies the dimension, depth and width of my philosophical thought. Of course, I know well my limitations in philosophical accomplishment, thinking mode and intellectual structure, as well as the defects of this book. What's more, the reform and opening-up and modernization of contemporary China are being ceaselessly expanded in terms of depth and width. Therefore I did not feel relaxed at all when I finished the book. I feel this is the beginning, rather than the end, of my theoretical studies. I expect to go deep into reality during new theoretical studies and climb to the commanding height of theory. I know very well, "High perching, far your voice would strew, to which the autumn wind aids nil."

ABOUT THE AUTHOR

Yang Geng is a native of Anhui Province born in 1956. He holds a Ph.D. in Philosophy. He is a Professor and Doctoral Supervisor. Yang graduated from the Department of Philosophy of Anhui University with a Bachelor's degree in Philosophy in 1982, and from the Department of Philosophy of Renmin University of China in 1991 with a Master's degree and a doctorate in Philosophy. From 1988 to 2003, Yang served as Professor and Doctoral Supervisor in the Department of Philosophy of Renmin University of China and as Editor-In-Chief of Teaching and Research and Editor-In-Chief of Renmin University of China Press.

He has worked for Beijing Normal University since 2003, as Vice Chairperson of the Dialectical Materialism Society of China and Vice Chairperson of the China Society for the History of Marxist Philosophy. Yang has been awarded Beijing Outstanding Teacher and listed among the Candidates of the Cross-century Training Program Supported by the Ministry of Education. Yang has published more than two hundred papers in journals, including China Social Science and Philosophy Research, and has published twelve books and monographs, monographs. He co-authored *Marxist Philosophy* with Chen Xianda in 2012, His major books include: *Defense for Marx: A New Interpretation of Marxist Philosophy*; *Reconstruction in Crisis: A Modern Interpretation of the Materialist Historical View*; *Orient Rising: A Philosophical Reflection on China-style Modernization*; *Introduction to Marxist Philosophy*, and *Collected Works of Yang Geng*.

He has also won several national awards, including the National Teaching Achievement Award.